2014

D0712773

LETTERS AND HOMILIES

for

JEWISH CHRISTIANS

Written by apollos 370

*A Socio-Rhetorical Commentary
on Hebrews, James and Jude*

Pretty Technical.

BEN WITHERINGTON III

IVP Academic

An imprint of InterVarsity Press
Downers Grove, Illinois

Apollos

Nottingham, England

InterVarsity Press, USA
P.O. Box 1400, Downers Grove, IL 60515-1426, USA
World Wide Web: www.ivpress.com
Email: email@ivpress.com

Inter-Varsity Press, England
Norton Street, Nottingham NG7 3HR, England
Website: www.ivpbooks.com
Email: ivp@ivp-editorial.co.uk

InterVarsity Press®, USA, is the book-publishing division of InterVarsity Christian Fellowship/USA®, a student movement active on campus at hundreds of universities, colleges and schools of nursing in the United States of America, and a member movement of the International Fellowship of Evangelical Students. For information about local and regional activities, write Public Relations Dept., InterVarsity Christian Fellowship/USA, 6400 Schroeder Rd., P.O. Box 7895, Madison, WI 53707-7895, or visit the IVCF website at <www.intervarsity.org>.

Inter-Varsity Press, England, is closely linked with the Universities and Colleges Christian Fellowship, a student movement connecting Christian Unions throughout Great Britain, and a member movement of the International Fellowship of Evangelical Students. Website: www.uccf.org.uk

Design: Cindy Kiple

Images: Cameraphoto Arte, Venice/Art Resource, NY

USA ISBN: 978-0-8308-2932-3

UK ISBN: 978-1-84474-198-4

Printed in the United States of America ∞

Library of Congress Cataloging-in-Publication Data

Witherington, Ben, 1951-
  Letters and homilies for Jewish Christians: a socio-rhetorical
  commentary on Hebrews, James and Jude/Ben Witherington III.
    p. cm.
  Includes bibliographical references and index.
  ISBN-13: 978-0-8308-2932-3 (cloth: alk. paper)
  1. Bible. N.T. Hebrews—Commentaries. 2. Bible. N.T.
  Hebrews—Socio-rhetorical criticism. 3. Bible. N.T.
  James—Commetnaries. 4. Bible. N.T. James—Socio-rhetorical
  criticism. 5 Bible. N.T. Jude—Commentaries. 6 Bible. N.T.
  Jude—Socio-rhetorical criticism. I. Title.
  BS2775.53.W58 2007
  227'.87077—dc22

                                                                2007031451

British Library Cataloguing in Publication Data
A catalogue record for this book is available from the British Library.

P	19	18	17	16	15	14	13	12	11	10	9	8	7	6	5	4	3	2	1
Y	21	20	19	18	17	16	15	14	13	12	11	10	09	08	07					

For **Mike Pasquarello**, a good colleague and friend who knows that rhetoric is a key to understanding the New Testament, especially its preaching.

And for **Ruth Anne Reese**, also a good colleague and friend who knows that rhetoric is a key to understanding the New Testament and whose work on Jude helped make this a better commentary.

Contents

PART 3: JUDE—ANOTHER BROTHER'S SERMON

Preface

The second volume of my three-volume set analyzes Hebrews, James and Jude. I have grouped these three documents together not because they have been previously studied together as units, such as the Pastoral Letters or the Johannine Letters, but because they seem to be written by and primarily for Jewish Christians. Naturally, issues of authorship and audience must be evaluated on a case-by-case basis as we study each document in turn. In some ways it may have been better to study Hebrews with the Pastoral Letters, for its author appears to have come from within the Pauline circle, and there are as many or more echoes of earlier Pauline Letters in Hebrews (particularly of Galatians, 1 Corinthians and Romans) as there are in the Pastoral Letters. There are particular affinities between James and Jude as we shall see, but in view of Hebrews, James and Jude all being homilies written to Jewish Christians they deserve to be studied together. It appears that no arrangement of the so-called Catholic Letters will be able to fully account for all the possible intertextual issues that these documents raise.

I will thus begin with Hebrews and then deal with James and Jude. What needs to be said in preparation for both this volume and volume two of *Letters and Homilies for Hellenized Christians* is that all these documents in various ways raise some of the same issues discussed at the beginning of *Letters and Homilies for Hellenized Christians*, volume 1, namely, whether they are letters at all and whether any of those that are letters are pseudonymous. In my view we are dealing with at least three or four encyclical documents (James, 1-2 Peter and Jude), one anonymous document (Hebrews), one composite document (2 Peter), and thus rhetoric and rhetorical analysis is germane to all of these documents, especially Hebrews.

It is also my view that several of these documents should definitely be seen as sermons or homilies, in particular Hebrews and James and perhaps Jude. Several of them submit more readily to epistolary analysis, particularly 1-2 Peter and Jude. The range and character of the Greek in these documents is also varied, with Hebrews perhaps exhibiting the best Greek in all of the New Testament, but 1 Peter is not lacking in excellent Greek at points, as my forthcoming study in this series will show.

All in all, these documents are fascinating windows into the early Christian movement in the second half of the first century, and since they tend to be overlooked in the rush to focus on the Gospels or the Pauline or Johannine literature, they will repay close scrutiny. We are about to learn that Jewish Christianity was more varied and widespread than has sometimes been thought and that the influence of James, Peter and Jude certainly reached beyond Jerusalem and the Holy Land, as did the influence of the anonymous author of Hebrews, who may well have been Apollos.

Finally, it will be useful here at the outset to explain exactly what I mean by a socio-rhetorical commentary. I am an historian, and so quite naturally I look at both rhetoric and the social sciences from a historical viewpoint. When I refer to "rhetoric" I am not talking about attempts to use modern rhetoric and rhetorical studies as windows into the New Testament text, however interesting. This is an ahistorical enterprise, not least because these methods did not exist in the first century. When I say "rhetorical commentary," I am limiting myself to the sort of rhetoric that existed and could have been used by the writers of the New Testament—early Jewish rhetoric and Greco-Roman rhetoric. The reason for this limitation is simple—it avoids most of the dangers of anachronism.

Likewise with social studies, for the most part I limit myself to material that can be derived from social historians of the relevant period. This involves using the work of Classics scholars who know the Greek and Roman social history and of social historians of early Judaism and early Christianity who can help us understand the very Jewish literature we are investigating in this volume. I make the occasional foray into the realm of social science (e.g., group-grid analysis) or cultural anthropology when it seems to work with the text of the New Testament as we have it, without trying to squeeze it into some sort of Procrustean bed.

One final reminder. In this series I have deliberately offered literal and sometimes polyvalent translations of the given texts. By the term *polyvalent* I mean I occasionally leave two translation options in the text when there are equally good options for a given word or phrase. I have deliberately not tried to smooth out all the infelicities, gaps and aporia in the text. I want my non-Greek-reading audience to realize where the text is rough and harder to translate and where it is smooth as butter. Overly idiomatic translations that offer seamless prose over-interpret the text in advance, rather than leaving it to the reader. I have chosen the other tack, quite deliberately. These texts are hard enough to understand without having various exegetical options foreclosed in advance.

Pentecost 2006

Abbreviations

Bible Books

Gen	Genesis	Nahum	Nahum
Ex	Exodus	Hab	Habakkuk
Lev	Leviticus	Zeph	Zephaniah
Num	Numbers	Hag	Haggai
Deut	Deuteronomy	Zech	Zechariah
Josh	Joshua	Mal	Malachi
Judg	Judges	Mt	Matthew
Ruth	Ruth	Mk	Mark
1 Sam	1 Samuel	Lk	Luke
2 Sam	2 Samuel	Jn	John
1 Kings	1 Kings	Acts	Acts
2 Kings	2 Kings	Rom	Romans
1 Chron	1 Chronicles	1 Cor	1 Corinthians
2 Chron	2 Chronicles	2 Cor	2 Corinthians
Ezra	Ezra	Gal	Galatians
Neh	Nehemiah	Eph	Ephesians
Esther	Esther	Phil	Philippians
Job	Job	Col	Colossians
Ps	Psalms	1 Thess	1 Thessalonians
Prov	Proverbs	2 Thess	2 Thessalonians
Eccles	Ecclesiastes	1 Tim	1 Timothy
Song	Song of Songs	2 Tim	2 Timothy
Is	Isaiah	Tit	Titus
Jer	Jeremiah	Philem	Philemon
Lam	Lamentations	Heb	Hebrews
Ezek	Ezekiel	Jas	James
Dan	Daniel	1 Pet	1 Peter
Hos	Hosea	2 Pet	2 Peter
Joel	Joel	1 Jn	1 John
Amos	Amos	2 Jn	2 John
Obad	Obadiah	3 Jn	3 John
Jon	Jonah	Jude	Jude
Mic	Micah	Rev	Revelation

Bibliographic

ANRW	*Aufstieg und Niedergang der römischen Welt*
CBQ	*Catholic Biblical Quarterly*
ET	*Expository Times*
EvQ	*Evangelical Quarterly*
JBL	*Journal of Biblical Literature*
JTS	*Journal of Theological Studies*
NovT	*Novum Testamentum*
NTS	*New Testament Studies*
PG	Patrologia graeca
PL	Patrologia latina
ZNW	*Zeitschrift für die neutestamentliche Wissenschaft*

Part One

THE SERMON TO
THE HEBREWS

Cf. James p400

see 369

on Paul

That the character of the diction of the epistle entitled "To the Hebrews" has not the apostle's [Paul's] rudeness in speech, who confessed himself rude in speech (2 Cor 11.6), that is in style, but the epistle is better Greek in the framing of its diction, will be admitted by everyone who is able to discern differences of style. But again, on the other hand, the thoughts of the epistle are admirable, and not inferior to the acknowledged writings of the apostle, to this also everyone will consent as true who has given attention to reading the apostle. . . . But as for myself, if I were to state my own opinion, I should say that the thoughts are the apostle's, but that the style and composition belong to one who called to mind the apostle's teachings and, as it were, made short notes of what his master said. . . . But who wrote the epistle, in truth God [alone] knows?—Origen, *Homilies on Hebrews* (quoted in Eusebius *Ecclesiastical History* 6.25.3-14)

Introduction to Hebrews

AUTHORSHIP, PROVENANCE AND DATE OF HEBREWS

In 1979 when Graham Hughes published his landmark study entitled *Hebrews and Hermeneutics*, he could complain that many, if not most, scholars had largely neglected the New Testament document whose Greek title is "to the Hebrews."[1] This complaint could hardly be made today with a plethora of excellent commentaries in English, French and German (though very few adequately deal with the rhetoric of Hebrews), numerous seminal monographs in print, and too many good articles to count. In the last twenty-five years, few New Testament books have received more scholarly attention. One of the fascinations of the book is that it has come to us, as more than one commentator puts it, like Melchizedek himself—without parentage or pedigree or descendents. It is a unique and truly one-of-a-kind document in various respects.[2] Yet as Fred Craddock says, for the ordinary reader of the New Testament, this remains a neglected book, and it is not difficult to explain why:

> In a New Testament of 251 pages, Hebrews begins on page 208. Justified or not, a position near the end is read as a value judgment. The reader of the New Testament moves through the Gospels, Acts, and Paul's writings as a traveler on a well-lighted street, not quite familiar but providing enough names and addresses so as to remove the sense of one's being a stranger. However, once past Paul, the traveler finds the road uncertain, the houses dimly lit, and no familiar landmarks. The temptation is to stop and turn back to the Gospels, Acts, and Paul. After all, for these areas there are excellent maps.

---

[1] Hughes, *Hebrews and Hermeneutics*, p. 1. Full bibliographical information on works cited in the notes can be found in the bibliographies.

[2] Johnson, *Writings of the New Testament*, p. 457.

[3] Craddock, *Hebrews*, p. 4. He is right to mention another reason for this document's neglect in the church today: "Especially for those who have luxuriated in a world of grace without ethical demand, who regard moral urgings as quaint echoes of a puritan past, Hebrews is not welcome reading" (p. 5).

The document we call Hebrews is both anonymous and written to a first-

mously said that "God only knows" who wrote this document (Eusebius, *Ecclesiastical History* 6.25.13).

The simple title "To the Hebrews" (without any authorial ascription) is first attested at the end of the second century by Pantaenus, Clement of Alexandria and Tertullian. Clement thought that this was a letter originally written in Hebrew by Paul and translated by Luke. This conjecture is made almost impossible because (1) it reflects elegant Hellenistic Greek, indeed it is the best Greek in the New Testament, and thus not awkward translation Greek, and (2) the author apparently used the Septuagint when he quoted the Old Testament, which someone writing in Hebrew would have been unlikely to do. It is apparently in the East first, in Alexandria, that the idea arises that this was a letter of Paul. Origen thinks it may have been a case of Pauline ideas written down by one of his disciples, but we have already seen the caveat he adds to this conjecture.

The letter was first accepted as Scripture (and as Pauline) in the whole Greek and Syrian churches in the third century and then finally in the Western part of the church in the second half of the fourth century, when probably most accepted it as the fourteenth Pauline letter. In 393 at the Synod of Hippo it was so accepted, and in 397 and 413 at the Third and Fourth Synods of Carthage the Western church reaffirmed its acceptance. Yet there continued to be serious doubts in the West about its Paulinicity. Ambrosiaster knows it but does not attribute it to Paul; likewise with Irenaeus and Hippolytus. Much later Calvin, Melanchthon and Beza all regarded it as non-Pauline, and Luther was not even sure it was canonical, much less Pauline. Hebrews has thus traveled a rather rocky road to get into the canon, and even once there doubts or neglect have plagued it. One reason there were doubts about this document was doctrinal: Hebrews 6:4-6, especially after the Decian persecutions of the third century, which led to some Christians recanting their faith, seemed to suggest that there could be no readmission of such a person into the Christian fold.

Internal clues to the provenance of the document are Hebrews 13:24, where we read that "those from Italy greet you," and Hebrews 13:23, which tells of the release of Timothy—surely the same one referred to in the Pastoral Letters—who is known to the audience of this document. Our author says in addition that he and Timothy will come to see the audience if possible. If we put these things together with the echoes of earlier Pauline Letters in this document, this document was likely written to Christians in Rome (hence the reason Clement knows and draws on this document already before the end of the first century) by someone who is part of the larger Pauline circle. In support of this conclusion the phrase *from Italy* in Acts 18:2 refers to those outside the Italian Peninsula, in this case Priscilla and Aquila, and the word *italias* means Rome in that same text, as the context makes clear.

The conjectures are endless as to why the document is anonymous and who in the larger Pauline circle could have written this document. Certain conjectures can be ruled out, including the notion that Paul wrote this document, although many in the early church assumed so. Not only does our author not identify himself as either Paul or an apostle anywhere in this lengthy sermon, but Hebrews 2:3 strongly suggests that the author was a second-generation Christian (the message of salvation was first spoken by the Lord and only later "confirmed to us by those who heard him"). Paul, of course, claimed to hear personally from Jesus, at least on Damascus road, and absolutely repudiated the notion that his gospel about Jesus came to him from others (Gal 1:11-12). The author of Hebrews has been in touch with eyewitnesses or, as he puts it here, "earwitnesses" of the Lord, but he was not among them.[7]

But why is this document anonymous? Is it because the author is neither an eyewitness nor an apostle? This hardly seems the likely cause, since other New Testament documents are attributed to noneyewitnesses and nonapostles, such as Luke's two volumes or the Revelation of the seer John of Patmos. Is it because the author is a woman? This is perhaps possible, but elsewhere women who played important ministry roles are named in Christian circles without any reservation. It is possible that the author is so well known to the audience that there was no need for identification here. There is, however, another primary reason for the anonymity of this document.

This document, like 1 John, is a homily;[8] and Daniel Harrington calls it "arguably the greatest Christian sermon ever written down."[9] It does not have the elements of a letter except at the very end of the document (Heb 13:22-25), and these epistolary features are added because this sermon had to be sent to the audience rather than delivered orally to them by the author. Hartwig Thyen, after studying all the evidence for early Jewish homilies, argues that Hebrews is the only completely preserved Jewish homily of the period, but this overlooks 1 John and James.[10]

Sermon manuscripts, ancient or modern, do not conform to the characteristics of a letter, with addressor or addressee expected at the outset. Neither do other rhetorical forms of speaking—and this document involves rhetoric of considerable skill. It is then, to use an oxymoron, an oral document—and a partic-

---

[7]See the discussion by Schenck, *Understanding the Book of Hebrews*, p. 89.
[8]Rightly Hagner, *Encountering the Book of Hebrews*, p. 29.
[9]Harrington, *What Are They Saying?*, p. 1.
[10]Thyen, *Der Stil der jüdisch-hellenistischen Homilie*, p. 106; Siegert, *Drei hellenistisch-jüdische Predigten*; Swetnam, "On the Literary Genre; and McCullough, "Some Recent Developments."

ular type of oral document: a homily in the form of a "word of exhortation," as
Hebrews 13:22 puts it. It is not an accident that this same phrase characterizes
Paul's sermon in Acts 13:15. Hebrews is not a haphazard discourse, but polished
rhetoric that is variously categorized as either epideictic rhetoric or deliberative
rhetoric or some combination of the two. The document's authority rests in its
contents, not in its author's claims to apostolic authority. To judge from the end
of Hebrews 13, it is assumed, but not argued for, that this author has some authority over this audience, who knows very well who he is and can anticipate
a visit from him and Timothy before long. The oral and homiletical character of
the document cannot be stressed enough. Here is how one professor of homiletics puts it:

> Hebrews, like all good sermons, is a dialogical event in a monological format. The
> Preacher does not hurl information and arguments at the readers as if they were
> targets. Rather, Hebrews is written to create a conversation, to evoke participation,
> to prod the faithful memories of the readers. Beginning with the first sentence, "us"
> and "we" language abounds. Also, the Preacher employs rhetorical questions to
> awaken the voice of the listener (see 1:5 and 1:14, for example); raps on the pulpit
> a bit when the going gets sluggish (5:11); occasionally restates the main point to
> insure that even the inattentive and drowsy are on board (see 8:1); doesn't bother
> to "footnote" the sources the hearers already know quite well (see the familiar
> preacher's phrase in 2:6: "Someone has said somewhere . . ."); and keeps making
> explicit verbal contact with the listeners (see 3:12 and 6:9, for example) to remind
> them that they are not only supposed to be listening to this sermon, they are also
> expected, by their active hearing, to be a part of creating it. As soon as we experi-
> ence the rise and fall of the opening words of Hebrews, the readers become aware
> that they are not simply watching a roller coaster hurtle along the rhetorical tracks;
> they are in the lead car. In Hebrews, the gospel is not merely an idea submitted for
> intellectual consideration; it is a life-embracing demand that summons to action.[11]

Who could the anonymous author from the Pauline circle be? Conjectures
include Barnabas (Tertullian *On Modesty* 20),[12] Clement of Rome or perhaps

---

[11] Long, *Hebrews*, p. 6.

[12] This conjecture has had a surprising amount of support, particularly in Germany in the early
part of the twentieth century. Attridge, *Hebrews*, p. 3, points out that the rift between Paul
and Barnabas came early on in Paul's missionary efforts (Gal 1—2) and that we have no evidence that this rift was ever healed to the point that Barnabas worked in Pauline communities later than the early 50s (Acts 15:36-41 records the final parting of the ways after the council in 50). Attridge is also right that some passages (e.g., Heb 7:11-19; 9:9-10; 13:9) suggest an
author who did not give the same credence to *kashruth* considerations that Barnabas showed
in Antioch. The author of Hebrews also knows Galatians, 1 Corinthians and Romans, which
suggests that he has remained within or in close contact with Pauline communities through
the late 50s at least.

Luke (Origen, in Eusebius, *Ecclesiastical History* 6.25, but with considerable hesitation), Priscilla (Adolf von Harnack, but the indirect indicators in the text of a male author, particularly in light of the masculine singular self-reference in Heb 11:32, suggest otherwise)[13] and Apollos (Luther), with perhaps most scholars thinking that the latter conjecture is the least unlikely.

In favor of Apollos are the following factors. First Corinthians 1—4 and Acts 18—19 suggest that Apollos circulated in Pauline communities and could well have been known to Timothy as well as to Paul, Aquila and Priscilla. And Acts 18:24-26 tells us that Apollos came from Alexandria and was learned in the Scriptures. Certainly the author of our document is learned in the Greek Old Testament (Septuagint), perhaps on a par with Paul's knowledge of the Old Testament. He does not, however, know the Hebrew Old Testament. From the content of this sermon it is highly likely that our author is also a Jew, but he is apparently a Diaspora Jew who seems to know something of Platonism, not unlike that other famous Jew from Alexandria, Philo. Again, the conjecture that Apollos is the preacher who authored this sermon best suits this set of data. But what was the focus of Apollos's ministry? To judge from Acts 18, he evangelized in synagogues; his focus was on Jews and Gentile synagogue adherents. This theory also helps explain little conundrums about Hebrews. For example, our author mentions instructions about "baptisms" (plural) at Hebrews 6:2. This often puzzles commentators, but it becomes more self-explanatory in the light of Acts 18:25, which tells us that Apollos knew only the baptism of John, even though he was a Christian, until he met Priscilla and Aquila in Ephesus. Quite naturally he would have included instructions about the differences between these two forms of baptism for his audiences, having learned the importance of distinguishing them sometime in the 50s. One more factor needs to be considered: our author is not merely a local church leader. He can distinguish himself from them and can call for support of them in Hebrews 13:7, 17, 24, but he can also

---

[13]For the original suggestion that Priscilla was the author of this document, see Harnack, "Probabilia." For a popular treatment of this thesis, see Hoppin's *Priscilla* and *Priscilla's Letter.* One of the problems with Hoppin's work is that she assumes that the name of the author is lost, whereas (since this is a homily and not a letter) one should assume that the author's name was well known to the audience and did not need to be mentioned. Hoppin does not consider the similarities with the case of 1 John, another homily. Additionally, if the document was by Priscilla we would expect Aquila to be involved, but clues in the text suggest a single author. I do not rule out this thesis entirely, but much stands against it, including the grammar of Heb 11:32. The author of this document is both very literate and well educated, which was a rarity for Jewish women of this era, who when they had education were not expected to do advanced studies in the Septuagint or rhetoric! Perhaps most tellingly, our author has some sort of authority over Jewish Christians in Rome. How many ancient Christian women fit this formidable profile in the mid-first century? Very few indeed.

assume authority over the entire audience, apparently including these leaders (Heb 13:17). He seems then to be an itinerant Pauline coworker with authority over local congregations and leaders.[14]

Acts 18:24-28 provides the following parallels to Hebrews:

1. Apollos was of the Jewish race, and so is the author of Hebrews.

2. Apollos was a native of Alexandria, where he certainly could have had contact with Philo and Alexandrian thinking. This suits our author as well.

3. Apollos was an eloquent man, meaning rhetorically adept. Our author was certainly that, for he writes the best Greek in the New Testament and he knows how to use the tools of a powerful preacher—rhythm, repetition, assonance, alliteration, colorful vocabulary, striking ideas and images that stick with the hearer.

4. Apollos was powerful in the Scriptures, and in his preaching he used those Scriptures in the synagogue in a christological way. This is certainly true of our author.

5. Apollos was able to teach accurately the things concerning Jesus. More than any other nongospel document, our author included material about the human nature and life of Jesus. There are references or allusions to his birth, baptism, temptations, Gethsemane, death.

6. Apollos was not afraid to speak boldly *(parrēsia)*. Is it accidental that our author uses this same word for boldness or free speech four times in Hebrews? While at times gentle, his approach is bold, for he suggests that Jews who are Christians are in danger of apostasy if they simply revert to Judaism.

7. Paul writes of Apollos as a missionary of note, familiar to the Corinthians, and one whom he would put in the same category as himself and Peter in work, if not also in authority (1 Cor 1:12; 3:22).

8. Apollos has a fervency of spirit about him. Hebrews has a very fervent and earnest appeal and exhortation.

9. Apollos would have had intimate knowledge of Roman Christians through Aquila and Priscilla, if not directly. Our author addresses these Christians in his homily.

10. Various Pauline influences in Hebrews suggest a person in the larger

---

[14]Craddock, *Hebrews*, pp. 6-7.

Pauline circle of associates—one who watered in the same turf where Paul had planted. In view of Hebrews 13 our author certainly has contact with the Pauline circle through Timothy, but perhaps also through those who are from Italy.

11. *First Clement*, which is addressed to the Corinthians, uses material from Hebrews in its argument. Corinth is the one place we know for sure from the Pauline Letters that Apollos had been—and had been of influence in the Christian community (in Acts 18 he is in Ephesus as well, but there he is in the synagogue and is endorsed to go on to Corinth [Acts 19:1]). It may well be that our document was written from Corinth, but we cannot be sure.

In the end, no one fits the bill so well as Apollos to be author of this document. Luke Timothy Johnson supports the argument that this letter was written by a Pauline coworker, most likely Apollos, during the period 50-70. He goes on to suggest, though not to insist, that the document might have been written to Corinth due to the echoes of 1 Corinthians in this document.[15] This conclusion about a Corinthian provenance, as Johnson himself freely admits, has its problems, not the least of which is that we have no evidence that the sorts of social distress and problems listed in Hebrews occurred also in Corinth, such as confiscation of property. Nor do we have reason to think there was such a large congregation of Jewish Christians in Corinth that they could be addressed separately from Paul's Gentile converts there. Furthermore, there are also echoes of Galatians in Hebrews, and this tells us more about our author's circulation within the Pauline orbit than it does about the location of the audience.

All of this comports well with the ascription placed on this document: "To the Hebrews," by which is meant "To the Jewish Christians" (2 Cor 11:22). This suggestion about the ethnic character of the audience should not be lightly dismissed as a pure conjecture by someone who later came to this conclusion from the document's contents but had no actual clue about the document's provenance. We do not have other early Christian documents with this sort of attribution from the first or early second century, so we can hardly conclude that it was a common generic label frequently used by Christians during that period. Especially in view of the increasingly Gentile character of the movement, it is hardly likely that this label would be picked out of thin air, even though it was not likely originally a part of this document. Furthermore, a synagogue in Rome was

---

[15]Johnson, *Hebrews*, pp. 38-44

specifically called a "synagogue of the Hebrews" in the latter half of the first century, and archeological evidence from Corinth, perhaps from the early second century, shows the same phrase.[16]

Since the term *Hebrews* is specifically used in such instances to distinguish Jews from Gentiles, we must assume that whoever put this label on the document was convinced that it was for Jewish Christians. In addition, as Raymond Brown points out, $\mathfrak{P}^{46}$—our oldest manuscript containing this work—already has this attribution for Hebrews, and this same label is in evidence already in 200 in Egypt and North Africa. The document's superscription "to the Hebrews" is known specifically in Alexandria by Clement of Alexandria prior to any manuscript attestation that we currently have of Hebrews (Eusebius *Ecclesiastical History* 6.14.4). To this we may add that no other rival destination or putative audience has every appeared in connection with this document.[17]

R. B. Hays argues that Hebrews is Jewish messianic covenantalism and not an attack on Judaism or Jewish leaders and that "supercessionist" is an anachronistic term;[18] nevertheless the phrase *God has made old the first covenant* (Heb 8:13) makes clear enough that this sermon contains an obsolescence argument. While Hays is right that Hebrews is not like *Barnabas*, which surprisingly suggests that non-Christian Israel never had a place among the elect, nevertheless to admit that the story of Israel has been typologically taken up into a new whole that consummates in the Christ event is to admit that our author has a completionist schema in mind. According to this sermon, one is not complete, perfect or saved to the uttermost without faith in Christ. Especially telling in this regard is Hebrews 13:10, where our author tells us that "we" Christians have an altar from which those who officiate in the tent have no right to eat! And Hebrews 13:15-16 says, "Through him [Christ] let us offer a sacrifice of praise to God." Clearly enough, our author distinguishes Christians and their sacrifices from those who still "minister in the tent."

Hays notes that this sermon never mentions Gentiles or their relationship with Jews. The sermon also does not suggest that the Jewish people have been replaced by a Gentile one, but it does suggest that failure to accept Christ and willingness to abandon Christ are both morally problematic moves. Hays's nuanced argument suggests that our author sees the new covenant as sustaining but transforming Israel's categories in the light of the Christ event. Even so, our author trusts that his audience will not be saved apart from pre-Christian Jews

---

[16]Witherington, *Conflict and Community in Corinth*, pp. 24-25.
[17]Brown, *Introduction to the New Testament*, p. 697.
[18]Hays, "Here We Have No Lasting City."

(Heb 11:40), and God is said to have prepared a city for them (Heb 11:16). Our author does not, however, comment on the fate of contemporary non-Christian Jews, though if he was influenced by Paul's argument in Romans he may well have been hopeful about them. What one cannot say is that our author thinks that anyone can be saved apart from the work of Christ or faith in him. Our author even speaks of Moses suffering for Christ (Heb 11:26), so committed is he to taking up the heritage of Israel into his christological and typological schema. We must conclude then that this discourse is in no way a polemic directly attacking Judaism but rather a completionist argument. It is an argument directed to Jewish Christians to make clear that going back to non-Christian Judaism is not an option for them any more than going forward into paganism is.

I cannot therefore agree with Markus Bockmuehl's way of putting things.[19] He wants to argue that what is most different in Hebrews is not who the people of God are or the nature of faith but rather the focus of worship. While I agree that the worship of Christ is what most distinguishes this text from early non-Christian Jewish texts, the object of worship is also the object of faith, namely Christ, and this in turn determines who is viewed as the proper people of God by implication at the point in time when this author is writing.

Bockmuehl fails to see that the hall of faith is meant to climax with the example of Jesus and that the audience is particularly exhorted to follow his example, not merely that of the previous examples. Loveday Alexander notes that the examples leading up to that of Christ are imperfect, as is more obvious in the case of someone like Samson or Rahab.[20] It is necessary to understand how the examples in Hebrews 11 lead up to the conclusion of this salvation-history kind of argument in Hebrews 12:1-2.[21]

There can be no doubt that the audience of this sermon is in some social distress and under some pressure to renege on their commitments to Christ and his community. Craig Koester chronicles three stages in the social life of this community: (1) proclamation and conversion, which is well in the past; (2) persecution and solidarity, which is in the more recent past and (3) friction and malaise, which is ongoing.[22] Particularly revealing is Hebrews 10:32-34, where the author stresses "remember those earlier days after you received the light,

---

[19]Bockmuehl, "Exemplars of Faith."

[20]Alexander, "Exemplars of Faith."

[21]Bockmuehl's argument depends on the contention that this document was written post-70, when both Jews and Jewish Christians were coming to grips with the loss of the Jewish sacrificial system. This conclusion in itself is problematic, as our author would have had very good reason to mention this demise if it had already happened. It would have cinched his argument.

[22]Koester, Hebrews, pp. 64-72.

when you stood your ground in a great contest in the face of suffering. Sometimes you were publicly exposed to insult and persecution, at other times you stood side by side with those who were so treated. You sympathized with those in prison and joyfully accepted confiscation of your property."

There were two periods of suffering for Jewish Christians in Rome in the middle of the first century. The first started at the hands of Claudius in 49 when Jews and Jewish Christians were expelled from Rome and lasted until the end of Claudius's reign in 54. This led to a fragmented and divided congregation of Christians in Rome, whom Paul wrote Romans to in 57 or 58 trying to get the Gentile majority of Christians to embrace the Jewish minority there, some of whom had only recently returned to Rome.[23] There had certainly been disenfranchisement of various Jewish Christians and confiscation of their property in 49, which was a regular concomitant act with the sending of someone into exile under Roman law and practice. But our author knows as well of some arrests and apparently some martyrdoms, which more probably places us in the later 60s.

A factor that must count against placing our document as late as the 70s is that it does not mention the demise of the temple. The usual rebuttal to this observation is that our author does not mention the temple at all but only the Old Testament institution of the tabernacle. This is not an adequate rejoinder, because it would have served our author's obsolescence argument enormously well if he could have said, "And further proof that the Old Testament system has been superceded by the sacrifice and priesthood of Christ can be seen from the recent demise of the temple in Jerusalem." This he does not do, even though our author is clearly a Jew who is passionate about the Old Testament and its institutions, and the greater benefit and glory now to be found in Christ's life, death and advocacy as the heavenly high priest. Barnabas Lindars puts it this way: "The repeated emphasis on the fact that the sacrificial system is obsolescent makes it almost inconceivable that Hebrews should not mention the destruction of the temple, if that had already taken place."[24] He rightly points out that once one concedes that Hebrews is written to a real and urgent social situation that the audience must cope with, this omission becomes all the more inexplicable if this document was written after 70. With a writer as rhetorically astute as this author, the deafening silences are very telling about the date of writing.

Accordingly this silence is likely a key indicator of the date of this document. *Barnabas* 16.4 contains a clear reference to the destruction of the Jerusalem temple in a similar sort of Jewish Christian argument. Raymond Brown points

---

[23]Witherington and Hyatt, *Romans.*
[24]Lindars, *Theology of the Letter to the Hebrews,* p. 20.

out, furthermore, that Hebrews 12:4 must count against the theory that this document was written during Domitian's reign, because that emperor's investigation and persecution of various Eastern religions, including Christianity, led to the deaths of some Jewish Christians in that era, including some in Rome (Cassius Dio *Roman History* 67.14.1-2).[25]

Our author speaks not only of confiscation of property but also of suffering and imprisonment, and he suggests that only "some" of their number suffered these ill effects, presumably the leaders of the group. Hebrews 13:7 probably alludes to the martyrdom of some of their leaders. No time frame better suits this entire description than sometime after the Neronian crackdown, when even Paul and Peter were arrested and executed along with others in various venues, including in the Circus Maximus in Rome for all to see.

Christians were subject to public ridicule, suffering, torture, confiscation of property and even execution for being part of a horrible superstition that was illegal and that led to accusations by Nero, in an attempt to find a scapegoat, that they had caused the fire in Rome. Under such conditions, and with Jewish Christians like Peter and Paul being especially singled out for these punishments, it is not at all surprising that other Jewish Christians were thinking of giving up their commitment to Christ and the Christian community, perhaps even going back to the Jewish synagogue community, which was protected as a recognized religion. This rhetorical exigence produces this remarkable discourse written to Jewish Christians in Rome and is meant to stave off further defections and the committing of apostasy and to make clear that, after all, the Old Testament institutions and rituals offer only the shadow of which Christ and his work are the substance and fulfillment.[26]

Written in the later 60s after the death of Peter and Paul, and even after the Pastoral Letters, which found Timothy in Ephesus, this document was probably produced at about the time the Gospel of Mark was written to the church in Rome, right at the end or just after the end of Nero's reign of terror. The mention of Timothy is important. He was the chief apostolic delegate of Paul in Ephesus, a community also frequented by Apollos, and had been under arrest for some time but just released (Heb 13:23). This would have had to have transpired after Paul wrote 2 Timothy,[27] which again points to a time not earlier than about 67-68. Affinities between 1 Peter and Hebrews also support this view. First Peter is written from Rome (1 Pet 5:13) to Jewish Christians outside of Rome before Peter's death in the late 60s. Yet our writer seems to know this document. Is it pos-

[25]Brown, *Introduction to the New Testament*, p. 699.
[26]Lane, *Hebrews*, 1.lvii-lxii.
[27]Witherington, *Letters and Homilies*, 1.184-86, 306.

sible that he could have been one of the recipients of this pastoral letter from Peter or part of a congregation that received it?

Weighing all the social factors cumulatively, we need a social situation where some local Christian leaders have lost their lives in the recent past but where the current audience being addressed has not yet suffered unto death. That no authorities are addressed or even mentioned by name in this document is perhaps a sign that the community had lost its greatest and most well-known leaders. No time better suits all these factors than the late 60s near the end of Nero's reign. The Neronian persecution apparently had several stages: (1) arrests and torture occurred when Christians were first suspected of the fire that broke out in 64; (2) the original charge of arson was dropped, and charges of "hatred of the human race" were made, resulting in many Christians being crucified and executed in the Roman arena as spectator sport by being set alight or sewn into animal skins and having lions and other wild animals turned on them and (3) some sympathy came for Christians and the persecution died down, however Christianity was now branded by official Roman jurisprudence as an attack on the Roman way of life, and so Christians were fair game—they could be brought to court simply on the charge of being a Christian, that is, one who disdained the Roman way of life and refused to worship the gods or the emperor. Hebrews does not suggest that we have yet reached the third stage. Rather it suggests that we are at or just after the second stage, which supports the suggestion made above about the date. Interestingly, considerably later, during Trajan's reign, Pliny is uncertain what to do with Christians brought to him for trial. This is perhaps because many of the policies of one emperor lapsed when the next one came to power. Thus the policies of Nero or Domitian toward Christians may have been known but not enforced without first checking with the current ruler.

Our author is not currently with Timothy, but says that if Timothy arrives soon they will both come to visit the audience of this discourse. This may suggest that our author is in another Pauline city where there was a Pauline congregation, for example, Corinth. In any case, our author knows that the lights are burning low and that the spirits are flagging among Roman Jewish Christians, who had apparently endured much during the reigns of the last two emperors.[28] That this document is written to them, apparently apart from the Gentile Chris-

---

[28]Heb 13:9 is no argument against the teachings (plural) being Jewish that our author's audience is being beguiled by. The term *xenos* can be used of any teaching that comes from a religion other than the one currently embraced. It has the sense of "foreign" or "alien" to the religion one currently adheres to, not something unfamiliar or unknown (*Shepherd* of Hermas, *Similitudes* 8.6.5; Josephus *Jewish War* 2.414). The plural "teachings" must count against the idea that our author is worried about the audience slipping back into some narrow sectarian form of Judaism.

tians in Rome, suggests that Paul's hoped-for rapprochement between Jewish
Christians and Gentile Christians in Rome may never have fully been realized.
There had been much suffering and further defections in Rome in the decade
between 57 and 67, climaxing with the loss of the two great apostles—Peter and
Paul. Between the writing of Romans and the writing of Hebrews much had
transpired in Rome, and very little of it was good for the struggling Christian
community in Rome.

Finally, Hebrews 13:17-19 suggests that the author has been one of the leaders of this group of Roman Jewish Christians because he asks for prayers that
he might be restored to them right after mentioning that they need to respect
and obey their leaders. What we know about Apollos, if he is the author of this
document, is that he was an itinerant evangelist and can be associated not only
with Alexandria and Ephesus but also with Corinth (Acts 18—19; 1 Cor 1—4;
16). Like Priscilla and Aquila, he may well have gone on, or gone back, to Rome
with the demise of Claudius in 54.

It ought to be one of the premises to sociological study of New Testament
documents that social theory can be fruitfully applied to the text so long as it
comports with the social history found in the text, in this case the social history
in Rome as described above. I can illustrate this point by considering briefly a
few recent studies.

Seeking to apply group-grid analysis and Mary Douglas's classification of societies to the book of Hebrews, R. W. Johnson suggests that the ideal society
our author is arguing for is a weak-group/weak-grid profile.[29] The word *group*
here refers to the experience of cohesion or bonding such that a "high group"
would be closely bonded with mostly closed boundaries, while the word *grid*
refers to the degree of social stratification based on rules that order the relationships (hierarchical or otherwise) of persons in the group. The problem with
Johnson's analysis is that he focuses on factors such as the importance of ethnicity and degree of welcoming of strangers and outsiders to the neglect of other
equally crucial factors.

The social situation addressed in this document suggests that the boundaries
of the community were not very porous, which is why hospitality had to be encouraged, and that members of the community were inclined to revert to Judaism suggests as well that ethnic identity was a factor affecting the situation. But
the strategy of our author to deal with this is not to set up a weak-group/weak-
grid structure that does not seek to build a strong group, but rather to urge commitment to a strong ideology, the belief that all persons of whatever gender, so-

---

[29]Johnson, *Going Outside the Camp*, and Salevao, *Legitimation in the Letter to the Hebrews.*

cial status or ethnicity can be united in Christ, in whom all one's religious and spiritual needs are met, including the need for cleansing of conscience. His exhortation about obedience to leaders makes clear not only that there are, but that there ought to be leaders, and so some stratification is seen to be desirable. Furthermore, the author expects his own instructions to be obeyed. He seems to be constructing a society with strong-group/mid-grid characteristics (hierarchical, but not rigidly so, and not a gender- or ethnic- or social-status-based hierarchy), which will be defined by their commitment to Christ and his sufficiency for all religious and spiritual needs.

More well grounded in the social history of the period is the detailed study of honor-and-shame conventions and their bearing on Hebrews by David deSilva.[30] DeSilva shows that our author tries to reconfigure honor-and-shame categories so that the audience can see the death of Jesus on the cross as both honorable and glorious in a higher sense, while it involves despising shame as defined culturally. Honor, by the same token, is redefined as one's estimation not in society's eyes but in the eyes of the God of the Bible, a very different view of honor. Our author is pursuing a strategy often used by minority sects: namely, while maintaining the large concepts of society such as honor and shame, they are redefined in terms of the core values of the sect. Faith in and faithfulness to the one true God, for example, are seen as the most honorable virtues, not *aretē* of a broader sort, for example. Daniel Harrington sums things up well:

> Their path to honor involves embracing the community of faith as a counterculture within Greco-Roman society and perseverance in faith, piety, and gratitude. Within the Christian minority culture, honor and shame serve to motivate the pursuit of [specifically] Christian virtues, to encourage the performance of deeds that demonstrate obedience to Christ, and to deter the wavering from falling away from their place in God's favor.[31]

It is often deduced that Hebrews inculcates a sort of martyr mentality and that the chief means of persuading the audience in this direction is by portraying Christ's death as a martyrdom. While I would not want to deny that these ideas are somewhat in play in Hebrews, Clayton Croy enlarges our understanding by showing that our author pictures suffering and perseverance as an athletic contest *(agōn)* and as a divine discipline that helps perfect the faithful.[32] Croy also denies that suffering is seen in Hebrews as punitive, though it is hard to deny

---

[30]DeSilva, *Despising Shame.*
[31]Harrington, *What Are They Saying?* p. 26.
[32]Croy, *Endurance in Suffering.*

that our author is warning about coming judgment if one should commit apostasy (Heb 12:25-29). Especially compelling is his presentation of Christ as the "agonistic" athlete who runs ahead of us blazing the trail and who finishes, reaching the goal before we do, modeling endurance and joy in the face of shame, hostility and persecution. Croy makes plain that Hebrews 12:2 is not about Christ perfecting our faith, but being the perfect model for believers' faithfulness. These sorts of studies grounded in first-century social history and cultural values reconfigured for a minority sect shed fresh light on Hebrews at many points.

Older discussions by Ceslas Spicq and others contend that there is considerable indebtedness of our author to Philo, indeed perhaps knowledge of some of his writings. While I would not rule out that our author knew some of Philo's work, the degree of indebtedness can be debated. The essentially negative conclusions of Ronald Williamson should be heeded:

> In the realm of vocabulary there is no proof that the choice of words displayed in the Epistle to the Hebrews has been influenced by Philo. . . . In the use of the O.T. made by the two writers striking and fundamental differences of outlook and exegetical method appear. . . . There is in the Epistle to the Hebrews no attempt to extract philosophical truths from the pages of the O.T. [unlike the case with Philo].

> But it is in the realm of ideas, of the thoughts which words and O.T. texts were used to express and support, that the most significant differences between Philo and the Writer of Hebrews emerge.[33]

For the writer to the Hebrews the Judeo-Christian tradition is essentially historical in character, and the Bible is not to be treated as a source of philosophical or esoteric wisdom, as is the case in Philo. Williamson also rightly concludes that Hebrews should not be seen as off the main track of New Testament theology, but rather in the mainstream of early Jewish Christian theology. He underlines the Jewish Christian character of the document, which certainly tells us something about the character of the author and perhaps also of his audience. To sum up, Hebrews is a situation-specific homily addressing Jewish Christians in Rome who have endured the traumas faced by such Christians in that city since 49. They have lost some of their leadership due to persecution, imprisonment and even martyrdom, and now they are facing further possible defections. Hebrews 13:7 probably indicates that most if not all the original leaders who "spoke" (past tense) the word of God are now gone, and Hebrews 5:12

---

[33]Williamson, *Philo and the Epistle to the Hebrews*, p. 576.

suggests that the community has existed for some considerable period of time. Some are apparently forsaking or showing signs of being about to forsake the house church meetings (Heb 10:25). Our author, a Jewish Christian of considerable skill in rhetoric and Greek who knows only the Septuagint, writes to them a "word of exhortation." Certainly the most probable conjecture of this person's identity is Apollos, not Paul—not only because of the differences in style between this document and Paul's undisputed letters, but also because our author's theology is distinct from Paul's, uniquely stressing the heavenly high priesthood of Christ and other non-Pauline concepts and reflecting some knowledge of the Jewish Alexandrian approach to combining ideas from Judaism and Platonism. His mode of argumentation also differs from Paul.

INTERTEXTUALITY, GREEK STYLE, RHETORIC AND LITERARY STRUCTURE OF HEBREWS

That Hebrews contains echoes or allusions to Pauline documents written at an earlier time is widely recognized by scholars. I elsewhere point out numerous echoes of Galatians, so here I allude to only a few in cursory fashion:[34]

- *Diathēkē* is used only twice in the New Testament in the sense of "testament" or "will" (Gal 3:15-17; Heb 9:15-17). The death of the testator was not required to ratify and put into effect a covenant in antiquity, but it was to put into effect a will or testament, and precisely that sort of death is referred to in Hebrews 9:16.

- In both Galatians 4:1-7 and Hebrews 5:12 *stoicheia* appears to refer to the elementary teachings to which the audience has no need to return.[35]

- The choice of Habakkuk 2:4 in Hebrews 10:38 seems to have been influenced by Galatians 3:11 and possibly Romans 1:17, which are the only two New Testament texts that cite this passage from Habakkuk.

- The seed of Abraham in relationship to believers is used comparably in Galatians 3:29 and Hebrews 2:16.

- Even closer is the use of the idea of being heirs of the promises of the Abrahamic covenant in Galatians 3:29; 4:28; Hebrews 6:17-18.

- The striking reference to the heavenly Jerusalem/Mount Zion in Hebrews 12:22 echoes the language of Paul in Galatians 4:26 and Romans 11:26.

- Our author operates with the same sort of salvation-history perspective as Paul enunciates about the law and its being made obsolescent by the coming

---

[34]Witherington, "Influence of Galatians on Hebrews."
[35]Witherington, *Grace in Galatia*, pp. 285-87.

of the Christ and the new covenant he inaugurated (Gal 3—4; Heb 8—10).

- The phrase *pistis christou* that crops up in Galatians, Romans and elsewhere referring to the faithfulness of Christ has its parallel in Hebrews 12:1-2, where we hear not about our faith, but about how Jesus is the trailblazer and finisher/consummator of faithfulness, the final and climactic example of faithfulness and perseverance unto death.

It is also possible to note close parallels with material in 1-2 Corinthians. The discussion of Israel's rebellion in 1 Corinthians 10:1-13 has a rather close parallel in its substance in Hebrews 3:12-14. The discussion in Hebrews 5:11-14 about the audience not being ready for solid food, but rather having to still be fed milk like infants, echoes what Paul says in 1 Corinthians 3:2. And the discussion in 2 Corinthians 3 about how the old covenant of Moses, while glorious, is obsolescent and is passing away is picked up and developed at length in Hebrews 8:6—10:14.

There are also echoes of Romans in Hebrews, and these are perhaps the most important since they tilt the probabilities in the direction of a Roman audience for Hebrews. Raymond Brown puts the matter thusly: "The parallels between themes in Paul's letter to the Romans ca. 58 and Heb[rews] could be explained if Heb[rews] were written to the same community a decade or two later."[36] Raymond Brown notes that the use of Jewish liturgical language is especially prevalent in Romans (e.g., sacrifice in Rom 3:25; 12:1; Paul's ministry as priestly in Rom 15:16) and also in Hebrews and more tellingly the language about the leaders of the community is the same: *proēgoumenoi* in Romans 12:10 and *hēgoumenoi* (leaders who are in charge of the care of souls) in Hebrews 13:7, 17. Perhaps equally telling on the other side of the equation chronologically is that in *1 Clement* the same language is used of the leadership in Rome (*1 Clement* 21.6 speaks of honoring leaders).[37]

With the author of the Pastorals, the author of Hebrews shares the perspective that Christ died for all, for the sins of everyone (Heb 2:9), not just for some

---

[36]Brown, *Introduction to the New Testament*, pp. 699.

[37]It is noteworthy that Ignatius of Antioch, who is especially concerned with monarchial bishops and the importance of this office and role in the church, mentions this functionary in six of his seven pastoral letters, but in his letter to the Romans (written ca. 110) there is no mention of bishops. Writing perhaps a little later, the *Shepherd* of Hermas also knows only elders in Rome (*Visions* 2.2.6; 2.4.3; 3.9.7). Perhaps there is a reason for this—perhaps the Roman church was never unified during this early period and did not have a unified episcopal structure or a "bishop/overseer" of Rome supervising everything. Perhaps the Jewish Christians still met separately. This clearly seems to be the case when Paul's letter to the Romans was written ca. 57-58, and it appears to continue to be the case when Hebrews was written.

elect group (1 Tim 2:3-6).[38] Self-conscious reflection on the living and authoritative and powerful character of the word of God in Hebrews 4:12-13 and 2 Timothy 3:16 emphasizes in both cases how the word convicts the conscience. The death of Jesus redeeming and purifying for him a people is seen in Titus 2:14 and Hebrews 9:14; 10:22.

The parallels between Hebrews and earlier Pauline Letters, including the Pastorals, are mostly at the level of ideas, for our author makes his material his own. Nevertheless, the parallels are sufficient to establish that our author is familiar with a variety of Pauline ideas and forms of expression and has been influenced by them. The parallels with Romans and the Pastorals are especially telling, for they suggest that Hebrews is later than these documents, and all of these parallels indicate that the author is in touch with or is a part of the wider Pauline circle, but focuses his ministry on Jewish Christians, hence the notable differences in theological and ethical approach to that in the Pauline Letters, particularly in his lengthy discussion about sacrifices and Christ as the heavenly high priest.

I would be remiss however if I did not discuss under the heading of intertextuality the sophisticated typological, christological, eschatological and thus thoroughly Jewish usage of the Septuagint in this document. And here is a clear clue that the audience is Jewish Christian. Fred Craddock puts it this way: "The author assumes an audience familiar enough with the Old Testament to make detailed exegesis of its texts convincing, word studies delightful, and swift allusions powerful."[39]

Depending on how one defines a quotation, there are about thirty or so quotations of the Old Testament in this discourse (not all of equal importance) and a further thirty-five to forty allusions to Greek Old Testament texts.[40] I use the term *Greek Old Testament* advisedly, because while our author sometimes clearly follows the Septuagint (e.g., Heb 10:5 quotes Ps 40:6 with the reading "body" instead of "ears"; or Heb 11:21 quotes Gen 47:31 with the reading "staff" instead of "bed"), sometimes he follows a text of the Greek Old Testament that does not conform to extant Septuagint readings.

Different recensions of the Septuagint may be seen in the two major codexes: A (Alexandrinus) and B (Vaticanus). Paul mainly follows the latter, but our author more often follows the former, yet not always. In particular, his quotations from Psalms seem to have used something other than manuscript A. Friedrich

---

[38]See the detailed discussion in Witherington, *Letters and Homilies*, 1.221-26.
[39]Craddock, *Hebrews*, p. 5.
[40]Lane, *Hebrews*, 1.cxv-cxvi.

Schröger's study details at least four quotations where our author cites a version no longer available (Heb 1:6; 10:30; 12:5; 13:5).[41] Many of the A/B variations in Hebrews are purely stylistic and not substantive. And our author appears to have modified the text either to avoid ambiguity or for the sake of emphasis; he does not simply play fast and loose with the text. It would be very surprising if he used a version exactly like any of today's extant copies. It may well be that his *Vorlage* goes back behind both A and B. In summary, there seems little doubt that our author cites the Septuagint from a manuscript he had ready to hand, a manuscript that is more like A in most places, though it is more like B say in the quotations from Psalms or Deuteronomy.

What we can say with some assurance, however, is that our author is not following the Hebrew text and simply translating it in these other cases (e.g., the citation of Jer 31:33-34 at Heb 8:10-12 and Heb 10:16-17). Sometimes our author may be paraphrasing or citing from memory (e.g., Ps 22:22 at Heb 2:12 or Ps 95:7-11 at Heb 3:9-10). His use of the Old Testament is complex and frequently christological and typological in character.[42] It is quite evident that our author is saturated in the Septuagint (perhaps especially the A text). His tendency to use the articular infinitive (e.g., with *en tō* at Heb 3:15 or *tou* at Heb 5:12; 11:5) can be cited as the influence of the Septuagint on the writer. One may also point to phrases such as *ep' eschatou* in Hebrews 1:2 (cf. Gen 49:1) or *heart full of unbelief* in Hebrews 3:12 or *throne of grace* in Hebrews 4:16.

In some twenty of the direct quotations of the Old Testament, God is the grammatical subject, such that God speaks directly to the audience of this discourse, for our author believes that the Old Testament is God's living word that still speaks authoritatively, even to an audience now under a new and different covenant. The phrases *God says, Christ says* and *the Holy Spirit says* (all present tense) introduce Old Testament quotations. But lest we think that our author is cavalier in his use of the Old Testament, Craddock rightly urges that "the writer of the epistle does not, in an act of interpretive tyranny, simply make irresponsible raids on the Old Testament to construct his own theological house, leaving among his scriptural sources not one stone upon another. Hebrews is not only the most extended treatment of the Old Testament in the New, but it is also, along with Luke, the most respectful of continuity. The Bible tells one story, not two, and it is the story of God's saving initiative toward humankind."[43]

Of equal interest is the hermeneutic our author applies with some skill in in-

---

[41]Schröger, *Der Verfasser des Hebräerbriefes.*
[42]See the discussion by Attridge, "Hebrews," p. 102.
[43]Craddock, *Hebrews*, p. 13.

terpreting the Old Testament. Careful examination of the way the Old Testament is interpreted shows that our author is not an allegorizer, unlike his contemporary Philo. Donald Hagner puts it this way:

> Unlike Philo, exegetically our author moves not so much between the real and the ideal, but rather, between the earlier and the later, the foreshadowing and the fulfillment. . . .
>
> If, however, we enter the author's world and share his presuppositions and perspective, we see that this kind of interpretation, found throughout the New Testament, is neither irresponsible nor indefensible. On the contrary, it is coherent, reasonable, and convincing. But this becomes apparent only if, with the author, we accept the sovereignty of God, the inspiration of the Scriptures (so that the recorded correspondences are not coincidental), the unity of God's saving purposes, and most importantly, Christ as the *telos*, or goal, of those purposes.[44]

Our author's worldview and that of his audience is far closer to the eschatological worldview of those at Qumran than to Philo of Alexandria's worldview.

Graham Hughes argues that our author "is the theologian who, more diligently and successfully than any other of the New Testament writers, has worked at what we now describe as hermeneutics. The question which has preoccupied him more deeply than any other . . . has been that of saying how we may conceive of the Word of God . . . as being subject to historical processes and yet remaining, recognisably, God's Word."[45]

The hermeneutical perspective of our author is intimated and in some respects even indicated in the first two verses of the prologue: "Partial and piecemeal in the past God spoke to our ancestors through the prophets, at the end of these days he spoke to us in the Son." Our author writes with an eschatological perspective, believing that God's climactic and perfect speaking and self-revelation has come in the Son, after partially revealing himself through the prophets in the past:

> There is certainly a conception of a longitudinal "revelation history," in which earlier and more fragmentary forms of God's Address have been overtaken and replaced by a perfected form of the same thing. There is thus established between the various moments of the revelation history a recognisable continuity which allows them, in spite of their discontinuity, to be construed as parts of a single process. . . . This means that it is the Speaking of God itself which contains the real continuity and which allows the historical (or empirical) forms which it takes to itself to be recognisably moments in an ongoing process.

---

[44]Hagner, *Encountering the Book of Hebrews*, pp. 34-35.
[45]Hughes, *Hebrews and Hermeneutics*, p. 3.

But there is also a strong *dis*continuity insofar as the perfected form of this Speaking stands over against the preliminary forms. As the goal, or the end term, of any process of development is recognisably something different from the process itself . . . so the Word in the Son stands over against the Word in the prophets. The process *has* reached its end term and has therefore achieved perfection because the Word in the Son is the eschatological form of what God has to say. . . . The Son, as bearer of the perfected form of God's Address, accordingly stands—as their fulfillment—over against the earlier, anticipatory forms mediated through the prophets.[46]

One of the things that follows from this historical and eschatological perspective is that Old Testament figures and institutions exist as antitypes and foreshadowings of Christ and various aspects of his life and work. The preliminary revelation is reinterpreted in light of its eschatological goal, rather than merely suggesting that the final revelation is just the completion of a long process, that the new covenant is just the final form of the old, that Jesus is Melchizedek redivivus, or that the events of the eschatological age are just fulfillments of Old Testament prophecy. All of this becomes especially clear when our author interprets a whole series of Old Testament passages in light of the Christ event, past and present, many of which were not messianic prophecies to begin with.

Promise/fulfillment is not all there is to our author's hermeneutic. That the Old Testament still has meaning and still speaks does not mean that the covenant it speaks mostly of, namely the Mosaic covenant, is still deemed valid or binding. The issue is not meaning or even truth or revelation. Our author believes that all the Old Testament still has meaning and truth and that it is a revelation from God. And the Old Testament takes on more meaning, not less, when interpreted through a christological lens. The hermeneutical issue is applicability, now that the Christ has come and the new covenant and the new age have been inaugurated. The former covenant is seen by our author as obsolete and therefore inapplicable even for Jewish Christians. They may and must learn from it. They are not obligated to keep it.

Since this homily is meant to be heard in the context of worship, we should evaluate it in that light. In worship we praise God for what he has done and is, and we draw near to him, as the letter exhorts us to do, but in worship we also hear and learn what we must go forth and do. Hebrews then is a vehicle for worship that leads to the right sort of service. The progression may be seen as follows: "Since we have [indicative] . . . let us draw near [imperative based on indicative] . . . so we may hold fast [possibility created by the first two steps]." What the believer has provides the basis for and enables his or her response.

---

[46]Ibid., p. 6 (emphasis original).

Believers are now better equipped to respond, since the final work of God through Christ has already come to pass. The work of God has effected what believers are and therefore has enabled them to do what they must do. Andrew Lincoln suggests that our author believes the Old Testament provides the following for the Christian: (1) aspirations that only Christ can fulfill; (2) a vision of our *telos* and perfection, that is, dominion over the cosmos, already obtained in Christ; (3) a dream of the day when we cease from our labors and enter into God's rest; (4) a desire to be free of sin's stain and a recognition that sin against God and fellow humans is the essential human problem; (5) a longing for free access into the divine presence; (6) picture language, or shadows and copies, to prepare for the coming of Christ and God's final word and (7) a partial anticipation in Melchizedek of the eternal priest and new covenant.[47] To this I add that it offers parenesis, which our author sees as often just as applicable to his own audience as to the Old Testament ones.

Detailed attention to the Greek style of Hebrews demonstrates that the author has a rather different style than that found in the undisputed Paulines and that this author knows how to use prose rhythm effectively as well as a whole host of rhetorical devices—alliteration, anaphora, assonance, asyndeton, hyperbole, rhetorical comparisons—to a greater degree than any other New Testament writer.[48] These points deserve to be illustrated each in turn.

Hebrews contains 4,942 words (1,038 different words), with some very elegant Greek sections, suggesting a rather well-educated author with a considerable vocabulary and facility with Greek and a considerable knowledge and understanding of the Old Testament. There are some 169 *hapax legomena* (words not found elsewhere in the New Testament), including various philosophical terms that speak to the educational background and sophistication of our writer.[49] Some 90 words are found in only one other New Testament document, and 10 words are not found in Greek literature before the time of Hebrews.[50] There is a general consensus that Hebrews contains the finest Greek in the New Testament; its Greek style goes beyond even the Pauline standard both in vocabulary and sentence building.[51] Our author is deeply indebted to the vivid vi-

---

[47] I was fortunate enough to have Andrew T. Lincoln as my seminary instructor in the exegesis of Hebrews, and at various junctures this commentary is indebted to his many insights, most of which have sadly never been published.

[48] Koester, *Hebrews*, pp. 92-96.

[49] The most expansive list of rhetorical and literary devices and features can be found in Spicq, *Hébreux*, 1.351-78.

[50] Johnson, *Hebrews*, p. 8.

[51] Turner, "Style of the Epistle to the Hebrews"; Westcott, *Hebrews*, pp. xliv-xlviii; and Spicq, *Hébreux*, 1.365-66.

sual imagery one finds in earlier Jewish sapiential and prophetic literature, so he speaks of a ship missing a harbor (Heb 2:1), a double-edged sword that penetrates to the innermost parts of a human being (Heb 4:12), fields watered by rain and producing either harvestable crops or weeds (Heb 6:7-8), an anchor gripping the sea bottom (Heb 6:19) or vivid Sinai theophany imagery (Heb 12) that brings his peroration to a conclusion. Since this document was meant to be heard, no one listening to this discourse would have thought that it was a letter, because the few epistolary elements we have do not come until the end of the document, much too late to signal what sort of document the audience was meant to think it was. Lincoln puts it this way: "Actually, once it is granted that the writer knows his addressees and is prevented by absence from delivering his homily in person, the epistolary conclusion makes good sense."[52] It was a necessary expedient since this discourse had to be written when the author was at a distance from the audience.

Making visual and vivid use of rhetoric was especially characteristic of epideictic rhetoric, so well known for its mesmerizing and grandiloquent amplification techniques. Despite the imagery often used, our author is addressing city dwellers who have to be reminded that they do not have a permanent earthly city to rely on (Heb 13:14) and that they are to practice hospitality with those who come their way, visit and identify with those in prison, avoid inappropriate social interaction of a sexual nature, not give way to greed and crass materialistic patterns of living (all in Heb 13). These sorts of reminders at the end of the discourse bear witness to the urban setting of the audience and, one might add, at least in some cases the social status and affluence of the audience. The poor do not need to be warned against hoarding wealth and crass materialism.[53] The educational sophistication of at least some of the audience is also presumed in light of the complexity of the rhetoric and its far-from-simple usage of the Old Testament: "They have an easy familiarity with the stories of the Bible, to which the writer can refer without elaboration (cf. Heb 12:17, 'for you know' with reference to the story of Esau, who was deprived of Isaac's blessing). The writer is confident that he can win a hearing for what he wished to say by employing vocabulary sanctioned by the Greek Scriptures."[54]

James Moffatt's careful study provides insights into the prose style and rhythm of the work[55] and supports the thesis that this document was intended

[52]Lincoln, *Hebrews*, p. 14.
[53]Lane, *Hebrews*, 1.liii.
[54]Ibid., p. liv.
[55]Moffatt, *Hebrews*, pp. lvi-lxiv.

to be read aloud, probably even performed as a sermon.

1. As was the case with the epideictic homily Ephesians,[56] Hebrews contains numerous long and carefully constructed sentences (Heb 1:1-4; 2:2-4, 14-15; 3:12-15; 4:12-13; 5:1-3, 7-10; 6:4-6, 16-20; 7:1-3; 8:4-6; 9:2-5, 6-10, 24-26; 10:11-13, 19-25; 11:24-26; 12:1-2, 18-24), yet there are also a good number of pithy and very effective short sentences (Heb 2:18; 4:3; 10:18) and even one example of diatribe style (Heb 3:16-18), which was appropriate in popular preaching.

2. Our author is a master at wordplays involving assonance (e.g., *parakaleite . . . kaleitai* in Heb 3:13; *emathen . . . epathen* in Heb 5:8; *kalou te kai kakou* in Heb 5:14; *menousan . . . mellousan* in Heb 13:14). "From first to last he is addicted to the gentle practice of alliteration,"[57] beginning with the very first words of the discourse: *polymerōs kai polytropōs palai . . . tois patrasin en tois prophētais.*

3. Care is taken with the cadences of prose rhythm, which reflects knowledge of the rhetorical rules about iambus, anapests and the like (Aristotle, *Rhetoric* 3.8.6-7).[58]

4. Like Paul (and perhaps a sign of indebtedness to Paul) our author has a fondness for compound verbs with the *syn-* prefix.

5. Our author is equally fond of rhetorical questions and other sorts of questions, even double and triple dramatic questions in a row (single questions in Heb 2:3-4; 7:11; 9:13-14; 10:29; 11:32; 12:9; double questions in Heb 1:5, 13-14; 12:5-7; and a triple question in Heb 3:16-18).

6. Our author is given to using explanatory asides, sometimes weighty ones (Heb 2:16; 3:7-11; 5:13-14; 7:12, 19; 8:5; 10:4; 11:13-16, 38; 13:14), and often these are used to explain an Old Testament phrase according to our author's hermeneutic (Heb 4:10; 6:13; 7:2, 7; 10:8). On the other hand, the author carefully avoids hiatus (i.e., the ending of one word with the vowel that begins the next word); and unlike Paul he also avoids anacoluthon (breaks in grammatical sequence). Anaphora (a series of lines beginning with the same word) is found in Hebrews 11, when eighteen sentences in a row begin with the word *pistei* ("by faith").

7. The author seems to reflect knowledge not only of Koine Greek but also of Classical Greek, for only this document contains Classical phrases such

[56]Witherington, *Philemon, Colossians and Ephesians*, ad loc.
[57]Moffatt, *Hebrews*, p. lx.
[58]Ibid., pp. lvi-lvii.

as *ei mēn* (Heb 6:14), *pou* (Heb 2:6; 4:4) or *pros ton theon* (Heb 2:17). Or-
atorical imperatives ("take heed" in Heb 3:12; "consider" in Heb 3:1; 7:4;
"call to remembrance" in Heb 10:32) reflect the oral character and rhetorical orientation of the author.

8. The author reflects knowledge of both Jewish wisdom literature and
   philosophical Hellenistic writings (e.g., his use of the term *will* in a manner like the Stoics, or *the final goal* in fashion like Epictetus).

Occasionally our author uses words and phrases in a way similar to Philo
(such as moral faculty, Demiurge, moderate one's feelings toward, bring to perfection, nemesis, model). Thus, our author not only has a considerable vocabulary, he also seems to have read rather widely (which is certainly possible if
he lived for a time near the greatest library in the then-known world in Alexandria). Moffatt concludes that our author knew not only the canonical Septuagint
books but Wisdom of Solomon, Sirach, the various Maccabean books and perhaps even Philo.[59] Moffatt ends by noting that our author has the style of a
trained orator: "He has an art of words, which is more than an unconscious
sense of rhythm," and he operates "as a preacher, whose first duty is to be faithful, but his second to be eloquent,"[60] David Aune is even more emphatic: "The
author obviously enjoyed the benefits of a Hellenistic rhetorical education
through the tertiary level."[61] This provides a natural segue to discussion of the
rhetoric of Hebrews.

We are now well served in regard to the rhetorical discussion of Hebrews,
and the consensus of opinion is not only that this document reflects macrorhetoric (the various divisions of a rhetorical speech) and microrhetoric, but that its
species is either deliberative or epideictic or some combination of the two. In
other words, there is agreement that it is definitely not judicial or forensic rhetoric[62] and that the recognition of individual rhetorical devices, which certainly
are plentiful in Hebrews, does not take the full measure of the way our author
uses rhetoric.

There are rather clear clues in the document itself as to what sort of rhetoric

---

[59]Ibid., p. lxi.

[60]Ibid., p. lxiv.

[61]Aune, *New Testament in Its Literary Environment*, p. 212.

[62]Ironically enough, the first major twentieth-century treatment of the rhetoric of this document
was in terms of forensic rhetoric; see von Soden, *Urchristliche Literaturgeschichte*, pp. 127-
28. More influential was his conclusion that Hebrews follows the pattern of a rhetorical
speech: exordium (Heb 1:1-4), proposition or thematic statement (Heb 1:5—4:16), statement
of the plausibility of the case (Heb 5:1—6:20), proof(s) (Heb 7:1—10:18) and peroration (Heb
10:19—13:25).

it is. Since parenesis or exhortation is found in both deliberative and epideictic rhetoric, we must consider what the author is trying to accomplish by this rhetorical masterpiece, as seen in the following statements in the discourse:

- "we must pay more careful attention therefore to what we have [already] heard, so that we do not drift away" (Heb 2:1)
- "therefore, holy brothers and sisters, who share in the heavenly calling, fix your thoughts on Jesus" (Heb 3:1)
- "see to it, brothers and sisters, that none of you . . . turns away from the living and true God" (Heb 3:12)
- "therefore, since the promise of entering his rest still stands, let us be careful that none of you be found to have fallen short of it" (Heb 4:1)
- "therefore . . . let us hold firmly to the faith we profess" (Heb 4:14)
- "therefore let us leave the elementary teachings about Christ and go on to maturity . . . we want each of you to show this same diligence to the end . . . we do not want you to become lazy but to imitate those who through faith and patience inherit what has been promised" (Heb 6:1, 11)
- "let us draw near to God with a sincere heart . . . let us hold unswervingly to the hope we profess . . . do not throw away your confidence" (Heb 10:22-23, 35)
- "we are not of those who shrink back and are destroyed" (Heb 10:39)
- "let us throw off everything that hinders . . . and let us run with perseverance the race marked out for us" (Heb 12:1)
- "let us make every effort to live in peace . . . see to it that no one misses the grace of God" (Heb 12:14-15)
- "keep on loving each other as brothers and sisters" (Heb 13:1)
- "the word of exhortation . . . I have written to you briefly" (Heb 13:22)

As George Guthrie rightly points out, alternating back and forth between exposition and exhortation, with the latter being the punch line, provides evidence that this discourse exists for the sake of the exhortation that directly addresses the issue of concern: "The expositional material serves the hortatory purpose of the whole work."[63]

If we look at all of this carefully it seems very clear that this discourse is not about urging a change in direction or a new policy, nor is the author correcting obvious new problems in belief or behavior. Further, the author is not trying to

---

[63]Guthrie, *Structure of Hebrews*, p. 143.

produce concord or reconciliation in the audience; he is rather trying to shore up their faith in the face of pressure, suffering and the temptation to defect. He is trying to confirm the audience in a faith and practice they already have, urging them to stand firm against the dangers of apostasy and wandering away and to stay the course with perseverance, continuing to run in the direction they are already going and have been going since they first believed, thus going on to perfection and exhibiting their faith and perseverance. This act of persuasion is surely epideictic in character, appealing to the values and virtues that the audience has already embraced in the past.[64]

The focus of the rhetoric in this document is, furthermore, clearly in the present. Our author focuses on what Christ is now doing as the heavenly high priest, what the audience is and ought to continue to be doing in the present, and there is appeal to continue to imitate the forebears in the faith and Christ himself. The appeal to imitation can be found in either deliberative or epideictic rhetoric; in the latter case it is an appeal to continue to imitate the models they already know and have looked to. When we couple all this with the doxological beginning of the discourse in Hebrews 1 and the worship climax in Hebrews 12:18-27, it seems clear that this discourse maintains an epideictic flavor throughout. Most rhetorically adept homilies in any case fell into the category of epideictic rhetoric.

Also comporting with this conclusion is the lack of formal arguments in this discourse; it is, rather, one long act of persuasion that involves comparison, enthymeme, repetition, amplification, catchwords and a toggling between exposition of texts (that provide the inartificial proofs or witnesses to the truths that the audience is being reminded of) and application or parenesis. Furthermore, after the exordium in Hebrews 1:1-4, it was not necessary to have a narratio or propositio, since there is only one long argument or act of persuasion in various parts throughout the discourse. The encomium of faith in Hebrews 11 does not stand out from its context, as if it were some sort of digression or different type of rhetoric or a rhetorical anomaly in the midst of a nonrhetorical document.[65] In addition, that this is epideictic rhetoric is supported by the enormous amount

---

[64]See the conclusion of Lane, *Hebrews*, 1.c: "The purpose of Hebrews is to strengthen, encourage, and exhort the tired and weary members of a house church to respond with courage and vitality to the prospect of renewed suffering in view of the gifts and resources God has lavished upon them. The writer's intention is to address the sagging faith of men and women within the group and to remind them of their responsibility to live actively in response to God's absolute claim upon their lives through the gospel." See also Koester, "Hebrews, Rhetoric."

[65]On Heb 11 as an encomium see Kennedy, *New Testament Interpretation*, p. 156. Cf. Cosby, *Rhetorical Composition and Function.*

of honor-and-shame language used in this discourse to make sure that the audience will continue to be faithful in their beliefs and behavior and life trajectory, not slipping back into pre-Christian forms of religion, in this case non-Christian Jewish ones.[66]

Most ancient commentators who were rhetorically attuned saw Hebrews as epideictic in character, and of modern commentators William Lane, Harold Attridge and Thomas Olbricht all see Hebrews as basically epideictic in character, with Olbricht concluding that it most resembles a funeral encomium.[67] Craig Koester and Lauri Thurén see the document as a mixture of deliberative and epideictic rhetoric, as do Luke Timothy Johnson and Andrew Lincoln, while Walter Übelacker argues that we have deliberative rhetoric here, a conclusion that Barnabas Lindars also reaches.[68] Lindars provides no justification for this conclusion at all, and Übelacker's analysis suffers, as Thurén points out, from his trying to find a narratio and a propositio where there is not one. Hebrews 1:5—2:18 is no narratio (a narration of relevant past facts) any more than it is an exordium— the latter is limited to Hebrews 1:1-4. Johnson and Lincoln are certainly right that the expositions lead to the exhortations and serve the latter, but exhortations are as common a feature of epideictic as deliberative rhetoric. It is the *nature* or *character* of the exhortation that decides the issue here, and careful analysis of all the parenesis in this document shows that it is aiming to help the audience maintain beliefs and behaviors they have already embraced. In other words, the exhortations are epideictic in character, as are the expositions.

That there is no propositio in this discourse should have been a dead give-away that we are dealing with epideictic rhetoric—the effusive, emotive and often hyperbolic rhetoric of praise and blame. The author is not trying to prove a thesis but rather to praise some important things—Christ and faith, for instance. To the contrary, at Hebrews 1:5 we dive right into the first part of the discourse itself, which entails an exposition of Scripture involving a negation that God ever spoke of or to the angels in the way he spoke of Christ. This is followed by the exhortation in Hebrews 2:1-4, which builds upon it. While Thurén is right that Hebrews 1:5-14 amplifies the exordium, it certainly ought not to be seen as simply part of the exordium.[69]

---

[66]See deSilva's detailed study in *Despising Shame*; and Johnson's *Hebrews*, who is much indebted to deSilva on this front.

[67]Especially Olbricht, "Hebrews as Amplification."

[68]Koester, *Hebrews*, p. 82; Thurén, "General New Testament Writings," pp. 589-92; Johnson, *Hebrews*, pp. 12-15; Lincoln, *Hebrews*, pp. 14-22; Übelacker, *Der Hebräerbrief als Appell*, pp. 185-92; and Lindars, "Rhetorical Structure of Hebrews."

[69]Vaganay, "Le plan de l'épître aux Hébreux," rightly argues that only Heb 1:1-4 should be seen as the exordium.

After seeing Hebrews 1:1—2:4 as the exordium, Koester suggests that Hebrews 2:5-9 is the propositio of the whole discourse,[70] but this simply does not work. Hebrews 2:5-9 is not a thesis statement that is then demonstrated in all the subsequent arguments. Far too much of what follows—especially from Hebrews 11:1 to the close of the discourse, but also much of Hebrews 4 and Hebrews 6 as well—is not about Christ's superior position, condition and nature. The issue is both Christology and parenesis/imitation of Christ and Christlikeness, as the author does not want the audience to commit either intellectual or moral apostasy. It comes down ultimately to whether they will continue to admire, emulate and worship Jesus. Koester is right, however, that the peroration begins in Hebrews 12, though not at Hebrews 12:28. It is best to see that in terms of macrorhetoric. All of this yields a simple structure:[71]

- exordium (Heb 1:1-4): the beginning of the discourse is linked to the exordium through using hook words, preparing for comparison with the angels introduced in Hebrews 1:4.[72]

- epideictic discourse composed of one long unfolding act of persuasion or sermon in many parts (Heb 1:5—12:17): this section can be profitably divided into subsections; Morna Hooker suggests a chiastic structure:[73]

imagery of pilgrimage, including first warning (Heb 4:14—11:40)

introduction of idea of Jesus as high priest (Heb 4:14—5:10)

first severe warning (Heb 5:11—6:12)

Jesus our high priest (Heb 6:13—10:18)

second severe warning (Heb 10:19-31)

importance of faith (Heb 10:32—11:40)

imagery of pilgrimage, including final warning (Heb 12:1-29)

On this showing the theme of Christ as the heavenly high priest is central to

---

[70]Koester, *Hebrews*, pp. 84-85.

[71]On the entire rhetorical structure I am in basic agreement with Lincoln, *Hebrews*, pp. 24-25. The argument that Heb 13 was not originally part of this document has no textual basis and has been refuted at length in terms of the issues of style and content by a variety of scholars; see Filson, *"Yesterday"*; and Lane, *Hebrews*, 1.lxviii. The Jewish homily in the Diaspora normally concluded with a final exhortation; see Witherington, *Letters and Homilies*, 1.38-46; Thyen, *Der Stil der jüdisch-hellenistischen Homilie*, pp. 87-96, 106-10; and Stegner, "Ancient Jewish Synagogue Homily."

[72]See Longenecker's *Rhetoric at the Boundaries* for detailed study on the rhetorical technique of using hook words to link sections of a discourse together.

[73]Hooker, "Jesus, the 'End' of the Cult."

the whole discourse. This makes excellent sense, and one could even talk about the imagery of visually placing Christ in the inner sanctum of the heavenly sanctuary just as he is placed at the center of the discourse verbally.

- peroration with concluding benediction (Heb 12:18-29): the emotional climax of the argument comes with the pilgrims assembled at the holy mountain and exhorted finally to worship God acceptably.[74]

- final parenesis (Heb 13:1-21), following the peroration (as is typical of all the expository sections) and summing up the major exhortations of the discourse: behave responsibly, persevere steadfastly, pray fervently, be prepared to "go outside the camp" as Jesus did.[75]

- concluding epistolary elements (Heb 13:22-25), which are a result of this sermon being written: explanation of the reason for writing, personalia, concluding greetings and a concluding grace wish.

The function of an exordium was to establish rapport with the audience and make them favorably disposed to hear what follows. One way to accomplish this is to use highly elevated and eloquent language at the outset, which will immediately get the audience's attention. We certainly have this in Hebrews 1:1-4, where our author unloads a variety of rhetorical devices, including a great deal of alliteration and impressive sounding phrases ("radiance of his glory"). It was important for the style to suit the subject matter. Thus Koester is right that "the elevated style of Hebrews' exordium suits the grandeur of its subject matter: the exalted Son of God."[76] We see the same sort of exalted style in Hebrews 11:1—12:3, where the other main thing that is praised in this discourse, faith, is discoursed on at length. Aristotle stresses that such elevated prose can impress and help gain the favor of the audience, appeal to their imaginations and make clear that an important subject is going to be dealt with (*Rhetoric* 3.6.1-7). It was a rhetorical must that weighty matters not be treated in an offhand matter, nor trifling things be invested with too much dignity (3.7.1-2). "When our audience finds [a speech] a pleasure to listen to, their attention and their readiness to believe what they hear are both increased" (Quintilian *Institutio oratoria* 8.3.5). In an oral culture, how something sounded had everything to do with whether it would be listened to, much less believed. It is hard to overestimate the impor-

---

[74]Rightly Lincoln, *Hebrews*, p. 17.
[75]Interestingly, the peroration is the emotional climax of the theological rhetoric, whereas Heb 13:1-21 is the emotive exhortation climaxing the ethical rhetoric. This is also found in Ephesians, another example of epideictic rhetoric, where the discourse does not stop at the peroration but offers up some concluding exhortations that sum up.
[76]Koester, *Hebrews*, p. 93.

tance of the oral dimensions of the text in helping to persuade the audience of the content of the discourse.

Thomas Olbricht points out that standard aspects of a person's life—noble birth, illustrious ancestors, education, fame, offices held, titles, wealth, physical virtues (e.g., strength), moral virtues and death—will be praised in a rhetorical encomium. Without question many of these topics surface in the praise of Jesus in this sermon.[77] And the comparisons (synkrisis)[78] in this discourse—for example, between Jesus and the angels, between Jesus and Melchizedek, between Jesus and Moses, between the believer's current life and what will be the case if they commit apostasy or go in a retrograde motion into a form of religion that will not save them—follow the conventions of epideictic rhetoric in regard to such comparisons. The function of such comparisons in an epideictic discourse is to demonstrate the superiority of the one person or thing that is being praised (Aristotle, *Rhetoric* 1.9.38-39; *Rhetoric to Alexander* 1441a27-28). Andrew Lincoln ably sums up how comparison functions in Hebrews:

> *Synkrisis* [is] a rhetorical form that compares representatives of a type in order to
> determine the superiority of one over another. It functions as a means of praise or
> blame by comparison and makes the comparison in terms of family, natural en-
> dowments, education, achievements and death. In Hebrews various earlier figures
> or types of Christ are seen as lesser by comparison with him, and family relations
> (Christ as divine Son), education (learning perfection through suffering), and death
> (the achievement of Christ's sacrificial death) all feature in the comparison. This
> sort of argument structures the discourse because, as in an encomium, a discourse
> in praise of someone, the *synkrisis* is used for the purpose of moral exhortation.
> So in Hebrews, the comparison of angels and the Son, of Moses and Christ, of
> Aaron and Christ, of the levitical priesthood and Christ, of the old covenant and the
> new covenant, is in each case followed by paraenesis.[79]

In this discourse Christ's superiority and the superiority of faith in Christ and following his example is being praised, and this is contrasted with falling away, defecting, avoiding shame or suffering. Christ is the model of despising shame and maintaining one's course in life faithfully to the end and of being "perfected" through death—sent directly into the realm of the perfect.[80] While the

---

[77]Olbricht, "Hebrews as Amplification," p. 278. One of the reasons we do not have both deliberative and epideictic in this discourse is that it does not have discreet arguments, but rather one long continuous one. There are, for instance, no deliberative digressions in this discourse; rather a series of topics are praised (e.g., Christ, faith) and negative behavior is "blamed" or warned against.

[78]On synkrisis as a rhetorical device, see Witherington, *Letters and Homilies*, 1.68-72.

[79]Lincoln, *Hebrews*, p. 19.

[80]DeSilva, *Perseverance in Gratitude*, pp. 34-35.

emphasis in this discourse is mainly on what is praiseworthy, our author does not hesitate to illustrate blameworthy behavior, for example, the unfaith and apostasy of the wilderness-wandering generation (Heb 3:7-19). Rhetorical comparison can be said to be the major structuring device for the whole discourse, right to its climax in the peroration at the end of Hebrews 12 as our author exalts the better mediator, the better sacrifice, the better covenant, the better example of faith, the better theophany—all by means of rhetorical synkrisis—not with something that is bad, but rather only with something that is less glorious or adequate or able to save people.[81]

Epideictic rhetoric characteristically uses a lot of picture language, visual rhetoric so that "you seem to see what you describe and bring it vividly before the eyes of your audience" and thus "attention is drawn from the reasoning to the enthralling effect of the imagination" (Longinus *On the Sublime* 15.1, 11). Epideictic rhetoric persuades by moving the audience with such images and so enthralling them, catching them up in love, wonder and praise. The appeal to the emotions is prominent in such rhetoric, stirred up by the visual images.

For example, the peroration contains a last harangue, a final appeal to the deeper emotions of these Diaspora Jewish Christians who have been pressured and persecuted and in many cases may have never had the joy of making the pilgrimage to Mount Zion: "But you have come to Mount Zion, to the heavenly Jerusalem, the city of the living God. You have come to thousands upon thousands of angels in joyful assembly, to the church of the firstborn, whose names are written in heaven. You have come to God . . . to Jesus the mediator" (Heb 12:22-24). These are Christians who, like the author, have likely never seen or heard Jesus in person. But now before their eyes is portrayed the climax of their faith pilgrimage, the same sort of climax that Jesus reached when he died, rose and then ascended into heaven. And the discourse ends with worshiping God with reverence and awe, a clearly epideictic topic meant to create pathos. Our author knows very well what he is doing in this epideictic discourse, and he does it eloquently and brilliantly from start to finish. He has made Jesus and true faith so attractive that it would be shameful to turn back now or defect and stirring to carry on with the beliefs and behaviors they have already embraced.

One of the consequences of recognizing and analyzing the rhetorical species of Hebrews is that it becomes impossible to see the exhortations or parenetic portions of the discourse as mere interruptions, digressions, afterthoughts or appendages to the christological discussion, which is seen as the essence of the discourse. To the contrary, the author chooses his Old Testament texts carefully,

---

[81]This is clearly demonstrated by Evans, *Theology of Rhetoric.*

gives his exposition, then offers his exhortations based on the exposition as part of an attempt to deal with the rhetorical exigence, namely the need to stand firm and not to fall back or backslide, the need to continue on the pilgrimage already begun toward perfection, the need to continue to believe and behave in ways that comport with such commitments.

But is there some rhetorical logic to the alternations between exposition and exhortation in this homily? T. W. Seid rightly answers yes. Pointing out that the expositions are part of a larger effort to draw comparisons principally between Christ and others, he sees the structure as follows:[82]

- comparison of Son and angels (Heb 1:1-14) and parenesis (Heb 2:1-18)

- comparison of Moses and Christ (Heb 3:1-6) and parenesis (Heb 3:7—4:16)

- comparison of Aaron and Christ (Heb 5:1-10) and parenesis (Heb 5:11—6:20)

- comparison of Melchizedek/Christ and the Levitical priesthood (Heb 7:1-25) and parenesis (Heb 7:26—8:3)

- comparison of the first covenant and new covenant (Heb 8:4—10:18) and parenesis (Heb 10:19—12:29)

- epistolary appendix (Heb 13:1-25)

This synkrisis/parenesis alternation encourages the audience to progress in moral conduct by remaining faithful to the greater revelation in Jesus Christ and by emulating the models of its Scripture, and it also warns the audience of the greater judgment to befall those unfaithful to the greater revelation.

What is praised and what is blamed in this discourse is not part of some abstruse exercise in exegesis for its own sake. It is part of a pastoral effort to deal with the struggles that Jewish Christians are having in Rome to remain true and faithful to the things they have already committed themselves to embrace. To this end, our author's rhetorical strategy in picking texts is not because of his intellectual curiosity about messianism or a christological reading of the Old Testament. Rather Psalm 8, Psalm 95, Psalm 110 (perhaps Ps 40), Jeremiah 31, Habakkuk 2 and Proverbs 3 are picked and dealt with because they help make the case that the inadequacy or ineffectiveness or "partial and piecemeal" character of previous revelation and covenants is self-attested in the Old Testament.[83] But that is only the negative side of the persuasion going on in this rhetorical masterpiece, with carefully selected inartificial proofs from the Old Testament. Other texts are brought in as well to support the positive side of the

---

[82]Seid, "Rhetorical Form of the Melchizedek/Christ Comparison."
[83]Caird, "Exegetical Method."

argument, which is that the good things that the Old Testament says are yet to come are now realized only in Christ and that faithfulness is required if these eschatological promises are to be also realized in the lives of those who follow Christ. Thus it can be said that in Hebrews "theology is the handmaiden of paraenesis in this 'word of exhortation,' as the author himself describes it." With these comments in mind, an expanded outline of the argument shows the relationship of the elements in the discourse.

- exordium (Heb 1:1-4): partial revelation in the past, full revelation in the Son
- probatio (Heb 1:5—12:17):

Section	Theme	Old Testament Text	Parenesis
Hebrews 1:5—2:4	Christ's superiority	catena (Heb 1:5-13)	Hebrews 2:1-4
Hebrews 2:5-18	"you crowned him"	Psalm 8 (Heb 2:6-8)	—
Hebrews 3:1—4:13	"today"	Psalm 95 (Heb 3:7-11)	Hebrews 3:12—4:13
Hebrews 4:14—7:28	"priest forever"	Psalm 110 (Heb 5:6)	Hebrews 4:14-16; 5:11—6:12
Hebrews 8:1—10:31	"new covenant"	Jeremiah 31 (Heb 8:8-12)	Hebrews 10:19-29
Hebrews 10:32—12:2	"by faith"	Habakkuk 2 (Heb 10:37-38)	Hebrews 10:32-36; 12:1-2
Hebrews 12:3-17	"do not lose heart"	Proverbs 3 (Heb 12:5-6)	Hebrews 12:3-16

- peroratio (Heb 12:18-29): pilgrim's end theophany at Sinai texts (Ex 19; Deut 4; 9; 31; Hag 2:6)
- final summary parenesis (Heb 13:1-21)
- epistolary closing (Heb 13:22-25)

Several concluding remarks are in order. All of these sections, with the exception of Hebrews 2:5-18, have parenesis, and in some cases the Old Testament citation has preceding and following parenesis in order to turn the exposition into exhortation or application. The parenesis is not relegated to the end of the discourse but is rather sprinkled liberally throughout the discourse. It takes up a good deal of the verbiage of the discourse and could hardly be called a series of appendages. The problem all along has been that many scholars find the expositions more interesting and challenging than the exhortations and therefore tend

---

I am indebted to Walters, "Rhetorical Arrangement of Hebrews," p. 66, for the basis for this outline, though strangely he does not count the first section based on the catena as one of the sections. Spicq, *Hébreux*, 1.38, also recognizes that Heb 1:1-4 should be seen as the exordium and Heb 12:18-39 as the peroration, with the major acts of persuasion in between.

to feature or privilege them in the ways they think about this discourse.

Second, the focus is clearly on the here and now and what is already true—hence the emphasis on "today," on the new covenant that is already extant and in force, on not losing heart but rather continuing to have faith and be faithful, on persevering in the present, and on what Christ has accomplished and is even now doing in heaven on behalf of the believer. The focus is on the here and now both theologically and ethically, which is appropriate in epideictic discourse.[85]

Third, our author sticks almost exclusively to texts from the Pentateuch, the Psalms and the Latter Prophets. There is nothing from the Historical Books, which is all the more striking since he is making a salvation-history kind of argument and since in Hebrews 11 he recounts some of the adventures and misadventures of the period chronicled in 1-2 Samuel, 1-2 Kings and 1-2 Chronicles.

Fourth, we will see in the commentary below that one part of this discourse leads naturally to the next as an unfolding message develops, involving both theology and ethics. Particularly striking is how the final section of the argument leads so smoothly into the peroration, with the imagery of running a race to a final destination introduced in Hebrews 12:1-3, and then the pilgrim arrives at the goal as described in the peroration, beginning at Hebrews 12:18. There is overlap, repetition, amplification, reinforcement in the argument, but this is precisely what one would expect in an epideictic discourse, as with 1 John.[86] One of the interesting differences between these two sermons is that 1 John is topically, not textually, driven, and so is less of an expository sermon in that sense, whereas Hebrews is certainly textually oriented and is far more expository in character. We begin to see the remarkable range of the Christian rhetoric of praise and blame in 1 John and Hebrews, and in both cases the sermons are directed in the main, if not almost exclusively, to Jewish Christians in two different major cities in the empire (Ephesus and Rome) that were seedbeds for the early Christian movement.

We need to keep steadily in view that the function of praise and blame of any topic was to motivate the audience to continue to remember and embrace their core values (involving both ideology and praxis) and avoid slipping into blameworthy beliefs and behaviors (Aristotle *Rhetoric* 1.9.36; Quintilian *Institutio oratoria* 3.7.28; *Rhetorica ad Herennium* 3.8.15). In other words, even when

---

[85]For a survey of the first twenty years of rhetorical analysis of Hebrews in the modern era, see Watson, "Rhetorical Criticism of Hebrews."

[86]Witherington, *Letters and Homilies*, 1.409-14.

using complex concepts and ideas, the ultimate aim of the rhetoric is practical and ethical in character.[87]

Other nonrhetorical analyses of the structure of Hebrews have been attempted with varying degrees of helpfulness. In his widely influential analysis, Albert Vanhoye finds a concentric or chiastic construction, with the introduction (Heb 1:1-4) and conclusion (Heb 13:20-21) pairing off. He identifies five large segments:[88]

- the name superior to the angels (eschatology) (Heb 1:5—2:18)

- Jesus faithful and compassionate (ecclesiology) (Heb 3:1—5:10)

- the central exposition (sacrifice) (Heb 5:11—10:39)

- faith and endurance (ecclesiological parenesis) (Heb 11:1—12:13)

- the peaceful fruit of justice (eschatology) (Heb 12:14—13:19)

- benediction about the superior shepherd (Heb 13:20-25)

The problems with such an analysis are multiple. In the first place this analysis does not take into account that this document was meant primarily to be heard, not to be read privately. It is written for oral delivery to a congregation or group of congregations. This why we have a conversational style and repeated reference to speaking and hearing rather than writing right until the very end of the document (e.g., Heb 2:5; 5:11; 6:9 ["even though we speak like this"]; 8:1; 9:5; 11:32 ["and what more shall I say?"]).

There is no way a listening congregation could detect this chiastic structure in a discourse that is so long. That would require reading and pouring over the document for hours, as Vanhoye has done. The nature of ancient oral culture and orality of this document have not been taken into account. Michael R. Cosby says: "There is an element of persuasiveness and understanding available only

---

[87] Here I part company with Koester, *Hebrews*, p. 82, and follow deSilva, *Despising Shame*, p. 35, and others who suggest that Hebrews functions as epideictic for those continuing to hold the core values but as deliberative for those tending to drift away. Epideictic rhetoric not only praises someone for standing and exhorts them to continue to do so, but also identifies blameworthy behavior and beliefs to be avoided. There is no evidence in Hebrews that the author assumes that any of his audience has already defected, or else, in light of his theology in Heb 6, exhortation would be pointless since they would have already passed the point of no return. Nor is he asking anyone to change direction or adopt a new course of action. He simply warns them against being tempted to do so under pressure, since they were already "running well" and do not need to change course. See Gray, *Godly Fear*.

[88] Vanhoye, *Structure and Message*.

through *listening* to the text in its original language."[89]

Since Hebrews is likely written to an audience in Rome, and while many Romans might neglect various of the liberal arts such as music or sculpting and in many cases even see training in athletics as optional, they considered training in speech and speaking persuasively essential. George Kennedy puts it this way: "The [Roman] world was a rhetorician's world, its ideal an orator; speech became an artistic product to be admired apart from its content and significance."[90] H. I. Marrou reminds us that "for the great majority of students, higher education meant taking lessons from the rhetor, learning the art of eloquence from him," which was not difficult since "rhetors were everywhere, in every self-respecting city."[91] If we do not keep the oral and rhetorical nature of the first-century world steadily before us, we quite naturally revert to treating these New Testament documents as if they were like modern texts, which in so many respects they are not.

Second, Vanhoye's exposition is largely based on the theology of the document, with only a little attention given to the parenesis, but the analysis above shows that the important parenesis throughout, indeed the theology, provides the foundation or backing for the pastoral thrust of this letter, which is found in the plentiful parenesis. To give but one example, the whole point of stressing the superiority of Christ and the obsolescence of previous covenants is so that the audience will not backslide or defect but rather will continue to maintain their previous faith commitments.

This brings us to another important point that is a consequence of recognizing epideictic rhetoric here. This is not some polemic against Judaism, nor is it part of a feud with one or more synagogues. There can be little doubt that Hebrews has been misused for such polemics, and part of this comes from not understanding rhetorical synkrisis or comparison. It also ignores that our author sees the Old Testament as still the living word of God and still valid.

That Jesus is said to be superior to angels, Moses, Joshua and other mediators does not mean that he in anyway denigrates these earlier mediators or sees them in a negative light. Typology by its nature and these examples of rhetorical comparison are part of the author's larger rhetorical strategy of using positive comparisons, such as "how much more so, then Christ (or Christian faith)." His is an eschatological argument that urges that the good has been

[89]Cosby, *Rhetorical Composition and Function*, p. 5.
[90]Kennedy, *Art of Persuasion in Greece*, p. 22.
[91]Marrou, *History of Education in Antiquity*, pp. 194, 197.

replaced in the last age of human history by the better or even the perfect. He uses the "superior" or "better" comparative language some twelve times throughout the discourse to make his point repeatedly. Much as in 2 Corinthians 3, the previous mediators and institutions are seen as glorious by our author, but as now made obsolete by the final form of God's saving revelation and activity.

Our author sees the first covenant as obsolete (Heb 8:13) and its institutions as inadequate to bring about a once-for-all-time atonement for sin and reconciliation between God and humankind (Heb 9:8-10). Those institutions and mediators are but foreshadowings of which Christ and the new covenant are seen as the reality and substance (Heb 10:1-4). A similar way of arguing may be observed in the Qumran documents, which are more directly negative about the Herodian temple and the ones called wicked priests. This is the rhetoric of an intramural squabble, and our author is using it to make sure his converts do not become "reverts" who annul the benefits they have already received in Christ (Heb 6:1-4).

Thus, while our author is telling the audience that they ought not to go back to what he sees as more elementary Jewish teaching, a more elementary covenant, and less than eternal or permanent mediators, this is not because of his seeing those things as in anyway bad things (unlike the critique at Qumran) and not of God. It is just that they have been eclipsed by the final form of God's revelation in Christ and the new covenant. The Johannine Letters show the danger of members of a largely Jewish group of Christians returning to their roots, and there as here the real sticking point was Christology, in particular an inadequate Christology on the part of those defecting or having already left the community. Hebrews seems to have been written to head off a schism, whereas the Johannine documents are written in response to one that has already transpired.[92] These documents make abundantly clear that early Christian communities had a variety of problems sustaining their existence in a cultural setting that was not congenial to their religious views. While all was not rotten in Rome and elsewhere for Christians, it was far from rosy. The impetus to defect from an illicit sect must have been considerable, especially after Nero's persecutions of Christians. One can still see the effects of the scars of that persecution in Revelation, written in the 90s.[93] It is thus very believable that in Rome in the late 60s our author might have to stave off defections of Jewish Christians, who were feeling the heat and thought it less problematic and safer to just be Jews—not

[92]Witherington, *Letters and Homilies*, 1.399-414.
[93]Witherington, *Revelation*.

Jewish Christians—since Judaism was a recognized ancient and licit religion, not a new superstition. Of course, being a Jew in the late 60s while Rome is fighting a war with Jews amounts to only a relatively safer status than being a Christian. But that was a long way from Rome and little affected the daily lives of those who lived in Rome. The other alternative of simply going forward into the pagan life of the Greco-Roman world was a bridge too far for most Jews.

Finally, something must be said about where our author could have acquired his considerable rhetorical prowess and skill, as it is sometimes doubted that Jews could have had such rhetorical skills or interests. There is no reason for such doubts, especially if we are talking about Jews educated in one of the major educational centers in the empire.

There were several major centers in the empire where one could obtain rhetorical training at a high level—Rome, Athens, Ephesus, Pergamon, Tarsus, Antioch, Jerusalem and Alexandria are on a short list, and it was possible to obtain elementary rhetorical training in many other places as well. In elementary education (*progymnasmata*) throughout the Greco-Roman world, one of the final and most important school exercises was the art of composing an encomium. Skill was acquired by copying, memorizing and imitating speeches from the great masters. The centers of learning that had great libraries to draw on were at a great advantage in this regard because they had access to more source documents. All other things being equal, those who studied elementary and advanced rhetoric in a city like Rome, Pergamon or Alexandria had a great advantage over those who studied elsewhere. If my hypothesis is correct that this document was likely written by Apollos from Alexandria, then it is important to examine this city in more detail.

Though the great library of Alexandria, which at its peak housed some seven

---

[94]While one could argue that the defection might be from a less to a more conservative Jewish Christian group (in which case our author is writing to only one particular house church), this hardly explains the thrust of the argument in Hebrews, which is not contrasting two different views of Jesus or of the church or of Christian faith. The lengthy arguments about the tabernacle, Moses and the like better suit the notion that the defection involves going back to some form of Judaism; see Lindars, *Theology of the Letter to the Hebrews*, pp. 4-21. That circumcision, sabbath observance and food laws are not really argued about (but Heb 13:9-10 reinforces that ceremonial food will not strengthen them in the faith) need imply no more than that the author and the audience of this document did not differ on these issues and so they were not up for debate. Almost all adult Jewish males will have long since been circumcised, and so that would be a moot point anyway, and various sorts of Jewish Christians continued to keep kosher and observe the sabbath (Acts 15; Gal 1—2). The issue in Galatians is about Gentiles choosing to get themselves circumcised and keep the law, a very different matter than what is being urged on Jewish Christians in this discourse. Nevertheless, Christianity would, for most Jewish Christians, have been seen as the only other legitimate religious option. In other words, there was nowhere else to hide.

hundred thousand papyrus scrolls, unfortunately burned in antiquity (possibly twice, if one counts the torching of Alexandria when Julius Caesar's troops took the city in the first century B.C.), we are fortunate that many literary papyrus fragments have been found, ranging in date from the third century B.C. to the fifth century A.D. These include a surprisingly large number of fragments of copies of famous rhetorical speeches made by Greek orators. There are some fifty fragments from the third century B.C. to first century A.D., including fragments of famous speeches made or written down by Aeschines, Anaximenes, Demosthenes (especially numerous), Homer, Hyperides, Isocrates, Lysias, Adespota and one particular Latin orator—Cicero. If we break down the evidence a bit further we discover that almost all of these fragments are examples of rhetorical speeches (Homer being the exception)—and famous ones at that—for example, Demosthenes' often imitated "De corona" speech or Hyperides' famous "Funeral Oration."[95] The concentration of the Greek tradition of rhetoric rather than the Latin tradition is not surprising, since Alexandria was still in the first century A.D.—and had been since its founding by Alexander—a Greek city that prided itself on its Hellenistic culture and the promotion and preservation of that culture.

One aspect of that culture that had been most fully developed was the art of rhetoric. Just how important this was to the citizens of that city can be seen from Papyrus Hibeh 26, found in a mummy cartonnage of the third century B.C. The papyrus is a portion of the important rhetorical treatise *Rhetorica ad Alexandrum* (*Rhetoric to Alexander*). In addition to this, the most important and earliest surviving textbook for young boys enrolled in elementary rhetorical schools originated in Alexandria, being written in the first century A.D. by one of its citizens, Aelius Theon. In an especially telling and interesting passage from his *Progymnasmata* (145), he complains about the children of Alexandria not being willing to do the heavy lifting of learning Greek philosophy but rather being so enamored of rhetoric that they raced right through the elementary education, skimming over the philosophical part of that training in order to get to "training in eloquence" (i.e., rhetoric), including especially the upper-level training in eloquence. He bemoans: "Nowadays most young men, far from taking up philosophy before they come to the study of eloquence, do not even touch the ordinary elementary branches [of learning], and, worst of all, they attempt to handle forensic and deliberative themes before they come through the necessary preliminary training."[96] Several things are important about this remark. For instance, this passage may be aptly compared to what our author says about elementary

---

[95]See the helpful charts in Smith, *Art of Rhetoric in Alexandria*, pp. 124-25.
[96]See the discussion in ibid., p. 134.

training, which his audience ought not to need a refresher course in (Heb 6:1-2) since they should be ready for the more advanced teaching that our author gives them in his sermon. Second, training in epideictic rhetoric (eulogies, encomiums of various sorts, rhetorical comparisons of a praise or blame nature) was a part of the final stages of elementary education, while training in deliberative and forensic rhetoric was part of the upper level of education. There were ten standard exercises in the *Progymnasmata*; the seventh is said by Theon to be "praise and blame" speeches, and the eighth is rhetorical synkrisis, which falls properly under the heading of encomiums. Theon stresses that the good student must daily practice writing out rhetorical pieces.

Alexandria was a rare city in many regards, not least because it had not only a great library but also a famous "museum" or lecture hall where the muses inspired philosophers, teachers, rhetoricians to speak or teach. In other words, Alexandria not only had elementary education and the gymnasium, like other great cities, but it also had a world-class lecture hall providing a sort of university education to its citizens. Even if our author did not have upper-level rhetorical training, he could have written this epideictic sermon based on what he learned on the elementary level in Alexandria (or the other cities previously mentioned) or by imitating what he heard in the public lectures in the museum. This brings us to a further point.

There were over one hundred thousand citizens in Alexandria in the first century A.D. So significant was the Jewish populace there that emperors like Caligula, no lover of Jews, received embassies from them on important matters (one of which involved Philo being an ambassador from Alexandria), and others like Claudius issued edicts trying to keep that community in check. Many of the Jewish citizens of Alexandria were well-to-do, well-educated Greek citizens of the city and received a considerable education in that city. One needs only to read the writings of Philo to see just how profoundly a devout Jew could be influenced not only by his own sacred traditions in Torah (the Septuagint was translated and found a home in this city) but also by Greek philosophy and rhetoric.[97] In Acts 18:24-25 Apollos is described as having skills in eloquence (i.e., rhetoric) and as a Jew learned in the Scriptures used in Diaspora synagogues. This description of Apollos and what we know about Alexandria and the scriptural and rhetorical phenomena found in Hebrews shows that absolutely no social locale in the whole Roman Empire is better suited than Alexandria as a place of social origin and education for our author.

Alexandria was the hometown of Apollos, the place where he was likely ed-

---

[97]Winter, *Philo and Paul amongst the Sophists.*

ucated and grew up and, if Acts 18 is to be believed, the place where he learned both the Septuagint and rhetoric. The more one probes the homily Hebrews, the more likely it becomes that Apollos is the author of this document. And perhaps we may learn one more thing from the Alexandrian background and the New Testament foreground in this regard. Acts 18—19 tells us two things about John the Baptist. The first is that Apollos knew only the baptism of John until he ran into Priscilla and Aquila in Ephesus. The second is that disciples of John were still wandering around the empire some twenty-five or thirty years after John's beheading. One must imagine that John's followers spread his message to various Jewish communities, perhaps especially to the places where there were large concentrations of Jews—places like Alexandria and Ephesus. It seems reasonable to conclude that Apollos would have learned of John's baptism while in Alexandria—and only later of Christian baptism. This may explain the reference to "baptisms" (plural) in Hebrews 6:2, and according to Acts 18 it was at Ephesus that Apollos himself received instructions on baptisms and the need to distinguish Christian baptism from John's. In short, Hebrews 6 bears the fingerprints of a man who had had to learn the difference between various sorts of water rites, particularly the difference between John's and Christian baptism. This small incidental detail—and its correspondence with Acts 18—provides clues about our author.[98]

THE HEAVENLY HIGH PRIEST: CHRISTOLOGY IN HEBREWS

The Christology of Hebrews is a perfect example of the dominant christological terminology used not necessarily being always the same as the most distinctive terminology used.[99] Without question, the major christological category or terminology in Hebrews and the term used to cover the scope of Christ's work is *Son.* In this regard the usage is very similar to that in the Pauline Letters, where the same term describes the preincarnate, earthly and postincarnate stages of Christ's career. Hebrew also contains the distinctive notion that Christ is the believer's *high priest*, the heavenly high priest still at work for the believer in the ultimate

---

[98] This may provide clues about other things as well. It tells us, for instance that people like Apollos, who presumably became Christians in Egypt, nevertheless did not learn about Christian baptism there. Were the oral tradition about Jesus' words and deeds what led them to faith in Jesus? Was teaching of the sort given to the Ethiopian eunuch from Old Testament texts such as Is 53 what led them to Christ (Acts 8)? Was it both? We cannot be sure, but Apollos's story suggests that news of Jesus' life and teachings spread more quickly than later Christian practices such as baptism. Jesus baptized no one, and one can readily see the need for early Christians to be able to distinguish the difference between being a disciple of John and of Jesus.
[99] A fuller form of this discussion can be found in Witherington, *Many Faces of the Christ.*

holy of holies—in heaven. In a third major motif in Hebrews, over and over again this author clothes Christ in the garb, with the attributes and in some cases with the tasks of *wisdom*—though he nowhere calls him God's wisdom. These three christological ideas are not developed discreetly in separate portions of the document but rather are neatly woven together in an impressive tapestry. Again, this document is a sermon or homily in excellent rhetorical form; it is not a theological treatise where the author intends to speculate on merely arcane or abstract notions. William Lane rightly says about its witness to Christ: "The key to that witness is the recognition that christology in Hebrews is pastoral response to crisis."[100] Like Paul our author writes as a pastor, and also like Paul he grounds his ethical exhortations in a high Christology at point after point.[101]

High Christology is evident immediately in the sermon's exordium in Hebrews 1:1-4, which is probably taken from an early Christian hymn. Here Christ is affirmed to be the eternal Son of God. Throughout this document there is a sustained christological focus, as our author wants to stress the superiority of Christ over angels and all other lesser beings who might garner human attention and worship. But his interest is not just in speaking of a hierarchy of being. He also wants to speak of a consummation of a plan for human history, and so he also uses the terminology and ideas that suggest that Christ eclipses all that has come before him: the revelation in the Son is full-fledged and completely fulfilling of God's plans and purposes, while the revelation that came before was partial and piecemeal.

More than many other New Testament documents, Hebrews seems to be built around at least seven biblical texts, and this demonstrates that our author is more concerned than some to explain how the Christ event is grounded in the Hebrew Scriptures, probably because his audience was made up largely of Jewish Christians for whom this was a crucial issue. It is also possible to divide the document thematically: (1) Hebrews 1:1—4:13 proclaims Jesus as the Son of God who is superior to angels; (2) Hebrews 4:14—10:31 focuses on Jesus as high priest and (3) Hebrews 10:32—12:2 stresses Christ as perfector of faith in order to appeal to the audience to persevere. On this showing, the christological perspective gives the document its structural unity. Yet we have already seen how the sermon uses the christological material to undergird the ethical exhortations. The larger structure of the sermon is mainly rhetorically not ideologically driven.

---

[100]Lane, *Hebrews*, 1.cxxxviii.

[101]The christological reflection is intertwined with the soteriological themes. The term *sōtēria* comes up more in this book than in any other New Testament book, and normally with a future sense, though as Marshall, "Soteriology in Hebrews," points out the discussion of present cleansing in Hebrews reveals the present dimension of salvation.

In Hebrews 1—2 our author is going to indicate both the full divinity and humanity of Christ in a variety of ways, but roughly speaking Hebrews 1 deals with Jesus as the eternal Son of God, and Hebrews 2 deals with him as a human being. At Hebrews 1:2 Jesus is said to be the heir of all things and also the agent through whom God made the universe. The author uses the language of wisdom to describe Christ's work, but he is not dealing merely with a preexisting idea or a personification of wisdom; he is talking about a preincarnate person, indeed an eternal one.[102] Hebrews 1:3 tells us that the Son manifests God's glory, bearing the very stamp or exact representation of his nature, something said of wisdom in Wisdom of Solomon 7.21-27. And Hebrews 1:3 also tells of Jesus' exaltation to the right hand of God. The main stress is on what Christ in heaven is now for the believer. This is a constant theme in this homily, though our author is also interested in the role of the Jesus in history as well.

The first major section of the homily, which continues up to Hebrews 2:4, endeavors to show the vast superiority of Jesus to angels, the other heavenly beings who have previously been messengers for God and mediators of a covenant with God's people. Jesus by contrast is not merely a messenger or a mediator, he was also involved in creating and now in sustaining all things by his powerful word. Jesus is seen as uniquely God's Son in a way that could not be said of either angels or human beings. Our author may be putting things as he does because some in early Judaism were given to angel veneration. In some ways the discussion here can be fruitfully compared to the argument in Colossians about "the worship of angels."[103] It can also be compared fruitfully with the Pastorals, where the deity of Christ is more often emphasized than in the earlier Paulines.

Hebrews 1:8 contains the important citation of Psalm 45:6-7, which appears rather clearly to call a duality of persons God. In all likelihood the traditional rendering of Psalm 45:6a—"your throne, O God, is forever and ever"—is the correct one. It would appear that Psalm 45:7 is the first of three places where the Father addresses the Son (Ps 45:7, 9, 12). In other words, the Son's role as the agent of creation and as God's coregent, which is spoken of in what follows, flows out of his essential divinity. This is not a surprising conclusion after we hear in Hebrews 1:3 that a person called the Son is the effulgence of God's glory and the visible and exact representation of God's being. Just as we will be told

---

[102]The efforts of Dunn in *Christology in the Making* to suggest that only the idea of Christ or Christ's role preexists are unconvincing. Only persons act in the way our author says the Son acted before and during the creation of the world. For a fuller discussion of the echoes of wisdom material in Heb 1, see Witherington, *Jesus the Sage*, pp. 275-82.

[103]Witherington, *Philemon, Colossians and Ephesians*, ad loc.

that the Son is set apart from sinful humans in that he was holy and without fault (Heb 7:26), so here we are told that he is set apart from the angels in that he is appropriately called *theos*.[104] In Hebrews 1:10, Psalm 102:25-27 addresses Jesus as Lord, which is a natural corollary to the address of him as God.[105]

In Hebrews 1:13 our author goes on to celebrate the exaltation of the Son to God's right hand, drawing on Psalm 110:1. This is by no means unique, being found elsewhere in other New Testament authors, but what is unique is that our author goes on to use Psalm 110:4: "You are a priest forever just like Melchizedek." William Lane says:

> No other Christian writer of this period draws attention to this passage, but in Hebrews there are more references to Ps 110:4 than to any other biblical text. In addition to three quotations of the passage (5:6; 7:17, 21), there are eight allusions to it in chaps. 5, 6, and 7, and each of the allusions is distinctive in form and function. The primary reason for the emphasis on Ps 110:4 in Hebrews is that it supplied a scriptural basis for the writer's priestly christology.[106]

The point of mentioning this here is that in Hebrews 1 our author has already established the divine credentials of the Son, which helps to prepare for the claim that he has a forever priesthood. The main emphasis in the crucial first chapter is to show that Jesus is Son, Creator, Lord, even God, and this makes possible the discussion of Christ as a unique sort of priest in what follows.

In Hebrews 2 we learn of Jesus as son of humanity. Our author uses Psalm 8 to bring out this theme and interprets this psalm christologically, such that he is the "Son of Man" who has been crowned with glory and honor and given dominion over the works of God's hand. Jesus was made a little lower than the angels for a little while during his time on earth and even went so far as to die, but now he is crowned with glory. It is characteristic of this homily that it moves from Jesus' death to his exaltation without discussing the resurrection.[107] Jesus' crowning happened because he suffered death—it was in a sense his reward for perfect obedience to God. The importance of certain key psalms, especially Psalm 8 and Psalm 110, to our author's christological reflections should not be underestimated, but it also becomes clear that our author knows the substance

---

[104] It is not impossible that Heb 1:9 is a second reference to the Son as God, but "your God" probably refers to the Father and should not be seen as a vocative—translated "O God" as in Heb 1:8.

[105] See the discussion in Brown, *Introduction to the New Testament*, pp. 683-704.

[106] Lane, *Hebrews*, 1.cxli-cxlii.

[107] This might be a clue to the earliness of this document, since this phenomenon is also found in the christological hymns. On the other hand, this document seems to reflect knowledge of various Pauline Letters or at least of their substance.

of some earlier christological hymns and apparently also the Pauline handling of a hymn such as Philippians 2.

At Hebrews 2:10, Christ is called the "*archēgos* of their [the believers'] salvation," who was made perfect through sufferings. The key Greek term, which recurs at Hebrews 12:2, means something like "pioneer/trailblazer," someone who does something first. In this case our author is suggesting that Jesus blazed a trail into heaven through many sufferings and so paved the way for believers to follow him. In what sense was he made perfect through sufferings? Knowledge of Platonism is probably necessary to understanding the author's logic here. In our author's view heaven is the perfect realm and the earth is the realm of incompleteness, transience, imperfection. By suffering, Christ is translated into the realm of perfection and eternality. Thus Christ's tasks were not complete, and so his work was not perfected until he reached heaven. The author is not commenting on the moral imperfection of Christ while on earth, as Hebrews 4:15 (cf. Heb 7:26) makes clear.

Hebrews 2:14 indicates that Jesus had real flesh and blood and that his death destroys the power of the one who had previously held sway over humans by death, namely, the devil. This motif is somewhat reminiscent of what is found in Pauline texts like Colossians 2:15 and Ephesians 4:8, where the powers and principalities are said to be disarmed by Christ's death. Our author wishes to stress that Jesus was made like humankind in every regard, except he was sinless, so that he could be the believer's brother and faithful helper, but most of all so that he could be the believer's faithful and holy high priest, making atonement for sins, with himself as the sacrifice.

Christ is seen as both priest and sacrifice, as both atoner and atonement. His humanity is such that he could and did suffer temptation, and so he is able to help others who suffer temptation. Obviously, the author is attempting to walk a fine line here. To be tempted is not the same as sinning, but to be tempted does imply a struggle and suffering. It implies the real possibility that one might be led to do what one ought not to do. There is no hint that this author thinks that Jesus' temptations were somehow unreal or that Jesus was merely play-acting but not really tempted.

The very reason our author sees Christ's life and death as meritorious (and rewarded) and his obedience as salutary and to be imitated is because Christ could have acted otherwise. That Jesus was sorely tried, tested or tempted implies that he actually considered the possibility of doing something other than God's will, especially in regard to going the route of the cross. Hebrews 5:7-10 may recount Jesus' agony in the Garden of Gethsemane or the way he responded to his trials in life in general. In either case, in the end he always submitted to God's will and his prayers were heard because of his reverent submission to God, even though the God who was able to rescue him from death did not do so.

At Hebrews 3:1 Jesus is called both the apostle and high priest of the Christian confession—in other words both God's sent one who represented God on earth and also the believer's representative in the heavenly sanctuary. The author pictures heaven as a great sanctuary and Jesus as the believer's priest there, offering himself as sacrifice to the Father for humanity's sake and offering up prayers for believers in God's very presence. Our author sees Christ continuing to fulfill the human tasks of the priest even after his death. It is not just as divine but also as human that he acts in heaven. For Jesus to be the believer's priest, he had to be fully human, and to be the believer's sacrifice he had to be truly alive in the flesh and so capable of being killed.

Jesus is seen as greater than Moses in all these matters. Moses was a servant in God's house, while Jesus is a Son over God's house (i.e., God's people). Salvation amounts to sharing in Christ (Heb 3:14), and so here we see the notion already present in the Pauline corpus of incorporation into Christ as a divine being. Jesus has gone up into heaven as the believer's great high priest, but also as the Son of God (Heb 4:14). The real thrust of Hebrews 4:15 seems to be that Jesus suffered the gamut of the sorts of trials and temptations humans suffer and yet did not sin. The pastoral thrust of these christological observations is clear: Christ understands and feels the tempted believer's difficulties and dilemmas and can relate to the trials these Jewish Christians are currently undergoing.

In Hebrews 5 we hear that the Son is a priest forever just like, or after the order of, Melchizedek. Why this order? There seem to have been two reasons in the mind of the author: (1) Jesus could not be a priest after the order of Aaron or Levi (or Zadok), for Jesus was of the line of Judah and (2) the author wishes to speak of a permanent or forever priesthood. He goes on to say that Jesus prayed for believers on earth and continues to do so in heaven. He offered himself as sacrifice on earth and continues to present this or offer this to God in heaven. In addition, he learned obedience from what he suffered, obedience to God's will.

The author returns to the Melchizedek argument at this juncture. He points out that this Melchizedek was without father or mother, without beginning or end of days, being a priest forever. This is a typical example of the early Jewish exegesis of the silences of the Old Testament, silences that are assumed to be pregnant. Because Melchizedek's origins and descendents are nowhere mentioned, because his birth and death are nowhere recorded in the text, this allows for the conclusion that he was a priest forever. Of course, our author's real interest is in saying these sorts of things about Christ, not about Melchizedek.

Jesus may be seen as the antitype of Melchizedek, with the latter only as the type. In typology the two figures are carefully compared but not identified, and here we see again the emphasis on Christ's superiority to all others he might be compared to—angels, Moses, Melchizedek. Christ is seen as the antitype in this case because the Son is seen as a preexistent being who is the one on whom Melchizedek is modeled, not the other way around, though in his role of high priest during and after his earthly ministry he is also "after the order of Melchizedek." In other words, our author's views on this are complex. In any event, Lane is surely right to stress that "the use that is made of Melchizedek in 7:1-10 is thoroughly christological. He has no independent significance; he is introduced only for the sake of clarifying the character of the Son. His function is prophetic. He is illustrative of those prophecies of the OT that pointed to the insufficiency of the old order and to the superiority and sufficiency of the new."[108]

Jesus lives forever and so has a forever priesthood. Jesus inaugurates a covenant that is permanent, not partial or temporary. Jesus has a greater nature and name than any angel. In short, Jesus is just what the believer needs—a priest and sacrifice who is truly holy, blameless, set apart from sinners, exalted above the heavens where nothing can prevent his fulfilling and completing his role for the believer (Heb 7:26-28). In the author's view, he always lives to intercede for the believer.

The portrait of Christ oscillates back and forth between the Son and priest images, and one aspect of the former is the suggestion that Jesus is a kingly figure who sits down at the right hand of the Father (Heb 8:1-2). This in turn is followed by a resurgence of the priestly images, such that in Hebrews 9:11-28 we hear of the efficacy of Christ's blood. His blood, offered in the heavenly sanctuary, obtains eternal redemption, and its effect is to cleanse human consciences. Jesus is both mediator of the covenant and the ransom price paid to reconcile the two parties. Christ's sacrifice is once for all time, for all people, for all sins—so it does not need to be repeated. Thus, the one-time act of dying on the cross was sufficient, and the presentation of it to the Father was effective for all the rest of human history. This emphasis on the universal scope of the atonement is reminiscent of that found in the Pastoral Letters.

As is noted by scholars, our author is drawing an analogy between Christ's sacrifice and the sacrifice offered in the temple in Jerusalem on Yom Kippur, the Day of Atonement, by the high priest. This sacrifice not only deals with the sins

---

[108]Lane, *Hebrews*, 1.cxlii.

of the past but is seen as a covenant-inaugurating act (Heb 9:15-22), fulfilling
the promises given through Jeremiah of a new covenant (Heb 8:7-13; 10:16-17).
It is precisely because this sacrifice inaugurates a new covenant that it has direct
implications for believers, not the least of which is that believers are called upon
to follow Christ's example of self-sacrifice through their own obedience unto
death (Heb 12:1-3).[109]

Hebrews 12:1-2 must be read in light of the hall-of-faith passage in Hebrews
11. When one undertakes such a reading, it becomes apparent that Christ is being portrayed as the ultimate example of faith/faithfulness and that the crucial
verse is to be translated "looking to Jesus the pioneer and perfector of faith/
faithfulness." Adding the English word *our* before *faith*, even though there is no
Greek textual support for this addition (no doubt it is done on the basis of the
assumed analogy with the earlier reference to the *archēgos*), misses the point.
Our author is writing pastorally and suggesting that, by being obedient even
unto death, Christ set the ultimate and only complete example of faithfulness.
He not only sets the example, he makes truly Christian faith possible by dying
and ascending to the right hand to add believers thereafter. This may also suggest that the perfect manifestation of faithfulness for the believer is to suffer for
and die in the faith. Christ endured the cross for the joy set before him, and his
followers can likewise endure suffering because they have "the assurance of
things hoped for" (Heb 11:1).

At Hebrews 13:8, Jesus is contrasted with all human leaders and priests as
mediators. They all died, and their deaths ended their service to other human
beings. By contrast Jesus' service and tasks go on—he is the same yesterday,
today and forever. Jesus then is finally seen as the permanent great shepherd of
the sheep—always looking after and interceding for believers. Believers can
count on the heavenly high priest never to change and never to change his mind
about his followers.

Here then in this homily we have seen a well-balanced presentation of Jesus
as both fully human and divine, as one who exercises his character and roles
both on earth and in heaven. In the author's mind Christ is both the believer's
heavenly high priest and also the preincarnate Son of God, who can be called
God by the Father. He is also the one who died on the cross, and because of
all the above he is greater than and superior to angels, prophets, priests including Melchizedek, and even Moses. None compares to the one who is both Son
of God and son of humankind. The narrative logic of our author's presentation
is evident. He must speak of the entire pilgrimage and ministry of the eternal

---

[109]So Attridge, "Hebrews," pp. 102-3.

Son, including his preincarnate, incarnate and postincarnate roles.[110] In this regard his approach is like that found in Paul's letters and in the christological hymns cited in the Pauline corpus. Underlying all of this is the hermeneutical move of assigning the status and roles of wisdom to God's Son. This is a common thread running from Jesus through the earliest Jewish Christians who compiled Q, through Paul, to the author of Hebrews. It is one of the things that binds New Testament Christology together.

Perhaps more than any other New Testament writer, the author of Hebrews shows how the divinity and humanity of Christ are interconnected and interdependent. Earl Richard states:

> By insisting that Jesus is the pre-existent Son and the exalted High Priest, the author sets the stage for the description of Jesus' soteriological role, since he is both an earthly and heavenly being who connects the heavenly and earthly realms. Employing traditional apocalyptic categories and applying current Platonic ideal categories, the author sees Jesus as the only real link between the world of shadows or copies (9:1-10) and the heavenly reality (8:5). His earthly existence (his sacrifice) established an eternal bond between earth and heaven and provided an entrance for all who would draw near.[111]

Finally we may ask—what assumed need does this Christology respond to? Fred Craddock says:

> At the heart of the crisis was a christology inadequate for their social context. Perhaps they had a christology that was long on divinity but short on humanity, providing no way to fit the flesh and blood, lower than angels, tempted, crying and praying, suffering and dying Jesus into the larger scheme of God's redemption. Or perhaps their christology ended with the exaltation and enthronement of the Son and offered no good news of his continuing ministry of intercession for the saints. At least in the writer's view, the crisis can best be met not with improved structures or social strategies but with a more complete christology.[112]

RECOGNITION AND CANONIZATION OF HEBREWS

There can be little debate that the author of *1 Clement* saw Hebrews as a valid and valuable early Christian document that had authority to teach his own audience on various subjects. In light of its teaching about postbaptismal sins, the *Shepherd* of Hermas (written probably between 110 and 140) knew and did not entirely agree with what Hebrews 6:1-6 seems to say to the Roman congregation

---

[110]Lane, *Hebrews*, 1.cxxxix: "The writer sees the eternal Son, the incarnate Son, the exalted Son."
[111]Richard, *Jesus: One and Many*, p. 374.
[112]Craddock, *Hebrews*, p. 10.

it is addressing (*Visions* 2.2.4-5). Both of these later texts know that Hebrews came from the Roman church. In addition Justin Martyr, Irenaeus and Hippolytus all know Hebrews, and the latter two at least recognize that it did not come from Paul's hand, yet they use it positively. The Muratorian Canon (end of second century) does not include Hebrews in its list (possibly because of Heb 6:1-6's insistence on a one-strike rule when it comes to apostasy), and our document was seldom quoted in the third century and first half of the fourth century in the Western part of the church. In part this is because the Western church did not agree with what it took to be the implications of Hebrews 6:1-6 about postbaptismal sin and the impossibility of repentance and restoration thereafter.[113] The book was, however, somewhat surprisingly recognized by the Western church and accepted as canonical in the latter part of the fourth century.

In the Eastern part of the church the path to recognition and canonization seems to have gone much more smoothly. Pantaeneus (about 180), Clement of Alexandria (about 200) and Origen (about 250) acknowledge Hebrews as included with a collection of Paul's letters, but also feel it necessary to justify that inclusion in one way or another. What they bear witness to is that by the end of the second century there seems to have been little debate in the East about this document, such that it could be included alongside Paul's letters and accepted as just as apostolic and authoritative.

Eusebius includes Hebrews within his list of the fourteen accepted Pauline documents (*Ecclesiastical History* 3.25.5; 6.20.3), and Athanasius (367) lists Hebrews in his collection of fourteen Pauline Letters (*Festal Letter* 39.5). Late in the fourth century a concordat between the Eastern and Western parts of the church accepted Hebrews as part of the Pauline corpus. While Hilary of Potiers (about 367) became the first Western church leader to explicitly accept Hebrews as Pauline and authoritative (*De trinitate* 4.11), it was the acceptance of the document by both Jerome (400) and Augustine (425) that settled the matter for the Western part of the church. It is interesting to see how much clout these two men had in this matter. William Lane points out that the 397 Council of Carthage accepted Hebrews but distinguished it from the thirteen letters of Paul, adding it as an appendix to that collection (a placement accepted and followed by manuscripts d, e, f and Latin Vulgate). Under the influence of those two luminaries, the 419 Council of Carthage described the "Pauline corpus" as including Hebrews.[114]

Today we may compare the situation with the Johannine literature. The only

---

[113]Lane, *Hebrews*, 1.clii.
[114]Ibid., p. cliv.

Johannine document with a named author is (Revelation), and it is surely by a different author, John of Patmos (who does not identify himself as an apostle much less as the Beloved Disciple), than the person or persons responsible for the Johannine Letters and/or the Fourth Gospel. Yet it was rightly judged to be a part of that corpus, coming from that circle of church communities. Similarly, while salient differences between Hebrews and the Pauline Letters were widely recognized, Hebrews was still judged to be a part of the Pauline literature despite its anonymity and despite the hesitations of various persons like Origen. When Jerome and Augustine entered the fray, concluding that it was a Pauline document, Hebrews was accepted in the East and West without further quibbles. That they were wrong that Paul wrote it does not affect its canonical status, which hinges on its revealed content, truthfulness, insight and intrinsic worth, not on later guesses about the authorship of an anonymous document.[115]

BIBLIOGRAPHY ON HEBREWS

Several useful guides introduce the study of Hebrews: Helmut Feld's *Hebräerbrief* and Daniel Harrington's *What Are They Saying About the Letter to the Hebrews?* Both of these slender guides are packed with helpful introductions to the study of Hebrews. A more extensive and masterful introductory survey of the book of Hebrews itself rather than the scholarly literature on it is Donald Hagner's excellent *Encountering the Book of Hebrews*. Tightly packed with excellent information is Andrew Lincoln's *Hebrews: A Guide*. One may also benefit by consulting Kenneth Schenck's slender *Understanding the Book of Hebrews*.

Commentaries

A nice synopsis of comments on Hebrews by the early church fathers may be found in Erik Heen and Philip Krey's *Hebrews* in the Ancient Christian Commentary series.

Attridge, Harold W. *The Epistle to the Hebrews*. Edited by Helmut Koester. Hermeneia. Philadelphia: Fortress, 1989. The standard critical commentary on Hebrews.

Bruce, F. F. *The Epistle to the Hebrews*. New International Commentary on the New Testament. Revised edition. Grand Rapids: Eerdmans, 1990. Still one of the most generally useful and best all-around moderately sized commentaries on Hebrews.

Buchanan, George Wesley. *To the Hebrews*. Anchor Bible 36. New York: Doubleday, 1972. Replaced in this series by Craig Koester's commentary.

---

[115]On the interesting history of the use, interpretation, influence and debates about Hebrews, see Koester, *Hebrews*, pp. 19-72.

Calvin, John. *Commentary on Hebrews.* Translated by William B. Johnston. Reprinted Grand Rapids: Eerdmans, 1949.

Craddock, Fred B. *The Letter to the Hebrews.* New Interpreter's Bible 12. Nashville: Abingdon, 1998.

Delitzsch, Franz. *Commentary on the Epistle to the Hebrews.* 1868-1870. Translated by Thomas L. Kingsbury. 2 vols. Reprinted Minneapolis: Klock & Klock, 1978. A classic that consistently repays close study.

deSilva, David A. *Perseverance in Gratitude: A Socio-Rhetorical Commentary on the Epistle "to the Hebrews."* Grand Rapids: Eerdmans, 2000. More specialized in its approach, with valuable insights drawn from social and cultural phenomena such as patron-client scripts, kinship language, honor discourse, purity codes and rituals.

Ellingworth, Paul. *The Epistle to the Hebrews.* New International Greek Testament Commentary. Grand Rapids: Eerdmans, 1993.

Fordon, R. P. *Hebrews.* Readings: A New Biblical Commentary. Sheffield: Sheffield Academic Press, 2000.

Guthrie, Donald. *The Letter to the Hebrews: An Introduction and Commentary.* Grand Rapids: Eerdmans, 1983.

Hagner, Donald A. *Hebrews.* Good News Commentary. San Francisco: Harper & Row, 1983.

———. *Hebrews.* New International Biblical Commentary. Peabody, Mass.: Hendrickson, 1990.

Heen, Erik M., and Philip D. W. Krey, eds. *Hebrews.* Ancient Christian Commentary on Scripture: New Testament 10. Downers Grove, Ill.: InterVarsity Press, 2005.

Héring, Jean. *The Epistle to the Hebrews.* Translated by A. W. Heathcote and P. J. Allcock. London: Epworth, 1970.

Hughes, Philip Edgcumbe. *Commentary on the Epistle to the Hebrews.* Grand Rapids: Eerdmans, 1977.

Johnson, Luke Timothy. *Hebrews.* New Testament Library. Louisville: Westminster John Knox, 2006. Of the medium-sized commentaries that largely eschew technical jargon, this is likely to become the standard for pastors and seminary students.

Koester, Craig R. *Hebrews.* Anchor Bible 36. New York: Doubleday, 2001. Deservedly one of the standard commentaries.

Lane, William L. *Hebrews.* 2 vols. Word Biblical Commentary 47A-B. Waco: Word, 1991. No commentary does a better job of dealing with the massive literature on Hebrews and the details of the text.

Long, Thomas G. *Hebrews.* Interpretation. Louisville: John Knox, 1997. One of the best homiletical commentaries on Hebrews.

Michel, Otto. *Der Brief an die Hebräer.* Kritisch-exegetischer Kommentar über das Neue Testament 13. Göttingen: Vandenhoeck & Ruprecht, 1966. The standard German commentary.

Moffatt, James. *A Critical and Exegetical Commentary on the Epistle to the Hebrews.* International Critical Commentary. Edinburgh: Clark, 1924.

Montefiore, Hugh W. *A Commentary on the Epistle to the Hebrews.* Black's New Testament Commentaries. London: Clark, 1964.

Nairne, Alexander. *The Epistle to the Hebrews.* Cambridge Greek Testament for Schools and Colleges. Cambridge: Cambridge University Press, 1922.

Pfitzner, Victor C. *Hebrews.* Abingdon New Testament Commentaries. Nashville: Abingdon, 1997.

Robinson, Theodore Henry. *The Epistle to the Hebrews.* Moffatt New Testament Commentary. London: Hodder & Stoughton, 1933.

Soden, Hermann von. *Hebräerbrief, Briefe des Petrus, Jakobus, Judas.* 3rd edition. Hand-Commentar zum Neuen Testament 3.2. Freiburg im Breisgau: Mohr, 1899 (rhetorical outline of Hebrews as forensic rhetoric on pp. 8-11).

Spicq, Ceslas. *L'épître aux Hébreux.* 2 vols. 2nd edition. Études bibliques. Paris: Lecoffre, 1952-53.

Westcott, Brooke Foss. *The Epistle to the Hebrews.* 1892. Reprinted, Grand Rapids: Eerdmans, 1952.

Monographs and Articles

Adams, Edward. "The Cosmology of Hebrews." Paper read at "Hebrews and Theology" Conference, St. Andrews, Scotland, July 2006.

Adams, J. C. "The Epistle to the Hebrews with Special Reference to the Problems of Apostasy in the Church to Which It Was Addressed." M.A. thesis, University of Leeds, 1964.

———. "Exegesis of Hebrews 6:1f." *NTS* 13 (1966-67): 378-85.

Alexander, Loveday. "Exemplars of Faith: Prophets and Martyrs." Paper read at "Hebrews and Theology" Conference, St. Andrews, Scotland, July 2006.

Allen, E. L. "Jesus and Moses in the New Testament." *ET* 67 (1955-56): 104-6.

Anderson, C. P. "Hebrews among the Letters of Paul." *Studies in Religion/Sciences religieuses* 5 (1975-76): 258-66.

Andriessen, Paul. "Angoisse de la mort dans l'épître aux Hébreux." *La nouvelle revue théologique* 96 (1974): 282-92.

———. "La communauté des 'Hébreux' était-elle tombée dans l^e relâchement?" *La nouvelle revue théologique* 96 (1974): 1054-66.

———. "Das grössere und vollkommenere Zeit (Hebr 9,11)." *Biblische Zeitschrift* 15 (1971): 76-92.

Attridge, Harold W. "The Christology of Hebrews," pp. 110-27 in *Who Do You Say I Am? Essays on Christology*. Edited by M. A. Powell and D. R. Bauer. Louisville: Westminster John Knox, 1999.

———. "God in Hebrews." Paper read at "Hebrews and Theology" Conference, St. Andrews, Scotland, July 2006.

———. "Heard because of His Reverence (Heb 5:7)." *JBL* 98 (1979): 90-93.

———. "Hebrews, Epistle to the." Vol. 3, pp. 97-105 in *The Anchor Bible Dictionary*. Edited by David Noel Freedman et al. New York: Doubleday, 1992.

———. "Let Us Strive and Enter That Rest: The Logic of Hebrews 4:1-11." *Harvard Theological Review* 73 (1980): 279-88.

———. "The Philosophical Critique of Religion under the Early Empire." *ANRW* 2.16.1 (1978): 45-78.

Auffert, P. "Notes sur la structure littéraire d'Héb 2,1-4." *NTS* 25 (1979): 166-79.

Aune, David E. "Heracles and Christ: Heracles Imagery in the Christology of Early Christianity," pp. 3-19 in *Greeks, Romans and Christians: Essays in Honor of Abraham J. Malherbe*. Edited by D. L. Balch et al. Minneapolis: Fortress, 1990.

———. *The New Testament in Its Literary Environment*. Philadelphia: Westminster Press, 1987.

Baaker, A. "Christ an Angel?" *ZNW* 32 (1933): 255-65.

Bacon, B. W. "Hebrews 1:10-12 and the Septuagint Rendering of Psalm 102:23." *ZNW* 3 (1902): 280-85.

Ballarini, T. "*Archēgos* (Acts 3,15; 5,31; Hebrews 2,10; 12,2): Autore o condottiero?" *Sacra doctrina* 16 (1971): 535-51.

Barrett, C. K. "The Eschatology of the Epistle to the Hebrews," pp. 363-93 in *The Background of the New Testament and Its Eschatology: In Honour of Charles Harold Dodd*. Edited by W. D. Davies and D. Daube. Cambridge: Cambridge University Press, 1956.

Barth, Markus. "The Old Testament in Hebrews: An Essay in Biblical Hermeneutics," pp. 53-78 in *Current Issues in New Testament Interpretation: Essays in Honor of Otto Piper*. Edited by William Klassen and Graydon F. Snyder London: Harper, 1962.

Bateman, H. W. *Early Jewish Hermeneutics and Hebrews 1:5-13*. New York: Lang, 1997.

Bauckham, Richard. "The Divinity of Jesus Christ." Paper read at "Hebrews and Theology" Conference, St. Andrews, Scotland, July 2006.

Beasley-Murray, G. R. "The Two Messiahs in the Testaments of the Twelve Patriarchs." *JTS* 48 (1947): 1-12.

Beavins, M. A. "The New Covenant and Judaism." *Bible Today* 22 (1984): 24-30.

Behm, Johannes. *Der Begriff διαθήκη im Neuem Testament.* Leipzig: Runge, 1912.

Bieder, W. "Pneumatologische Aspekte im Hebräerbrief," pp. 251-59 in *Neues Testament und Geschichte* (Oscar Cullmann Festschrift). Edited by Heinrich Baltensweiler and Bo Reicke. Tübingen: Mohr, 1972.

Black, David Alan. "A Note on the Structure of Hebrews 12.1-2." *Biblica* 68 (1987): 543-51.

———. "The Problem of the Literary Structure of Hebrews." *Grace Theological Journal* 7 (1986): 163-77.

Black, Matthew. "The Christological Use of the Old Testament in the New Testament." *NTS* 18 (1971-72): 1-14.

Blevins, J. L. "Preaching and Teaching Hebrews." *Review and Expositor* 82 (1985): 407-18.

Bligh, John. Review of Albert Vanhoye's *La structure littéraire de l'épître aux Hébreux. Heythrop Journal* 5 (1964): 170-77.

Bock, Darrell L. *Luke*, vol. 2: *9:51—24:53.* Baker Exegetical Commentary on the New Testament. Grand Rapids: Baker. 1996.

Bockmuehl, Markus. "The Church in Hebrews," pp. 133-51 in *A Vision for the Church: Studies in Early Christian Ecclesiology in Honour of J. P. M. Sweet.* Edited by Markus Bockmuehl and M. B. Thompson. Edinburgh: Clark, 1997.

———. "Exemplars of Faith: Abraham." Paper read at "Hebrews and Theology" Conference, St. Andrews, Scotland, July 2006.

Bomhauser, K. "Die Versuchungen Jesus nach dem Hebräerbrief," pp. 72-86 in *Theologische Studien: Martin Kahler.* Leipzig: Runge, 1905.

Bonsirven, J. *Saint Paul: Épître aux Hébreux.* Verbum salutis. Paris: Gabalda, 1943.

Borchert, G. L. "A Superior Book: Hebrews." *Review and Expositor* 82 (1985): 319-32.

Bornkamm, Günther. "Das Bekenntnis im Hebräerbrief." *Theologische Blätter* 21 (1942): 56-66.

Boyer, J. M. "Las variantes *mellonton y genomenon en Hebr 9,11.*" *Biblica* 32 (1951): 232-36.

Brandenburger, E. "Text und Vorlagen von Hebr 5,1-10." *NovT* 11 (1969): 190-224.

Braun, Herbert. "Die Gewinnung der Gewissheit in dem Hebräerbrief." *Theologische Literaturzeitung* 96 (1971): 321-30.

Bream, H. N. "More on Hebrews 12:1." *ET* 80 (1968-69): 150-51.

Brooks, W. E. "The Perpetuity of Christ's Sacrifice in the Epistle to the Hebrews." *JBL* 89 (1970): 204-14.

Brown, Raymond E. *An Introduction to the New Testament.* New York: Doubleday, 1997.

Brownlee, W. H. "Biblical Interpretation among the Sectaries of the Dead Sea Scrolls." *Biblical Archaeologist* 14 (1951): 54-76.

Bruce, F. F. "The Structure and Argument of Hebrews." *Southwest Journal of Theology* 28 (1985): 6-12.

———. "'To the Hebrews' or 'to the Essenes'?" *NTS* 9 (1962-63): 217-32.

Buchanan, George Wesley. "The Kerygma of Hebrews." *Interpretation* 23 (1969): 3-19.

———. "The Present State of Scholarship on Hebrews," pp. 299-330 in *Christianity, Judaism and other Graeco-Roman Cults.* Edited by Jacob Neusner. Leiden: Brill, 1975.

Buchel, C. "Der Hebräerbrief und das Alte Testament." *Theologische Studien und Kritiken* 79 (1906): 508-91.

Burns, L. "Hermeneutical Issues and Principles in Hebrews as Exemplified in the Second Chapter." *Journal of the Evangelical Theological Society* 39 (1996): 587-607.

Buschel, F. *Die Christologie des Hebräerbriefes.* Gutersloh: Bertlesmann, 1922.

Caird, G. B. "The Exegetical Method of the Epistle to the Hebrews." *Canadian Journal of Theology* 5 (1959): 44-51.

Calvert-Koyzis, Nancy. *Paul, Monotheism and the People of God: The Significance of Abraham Traditions for Early Judaism and Christianity.* Edinburgh: Clark, 2005.

Camachio, H. S. "The Altar of Incense in Hebrews 9:3-4." *Andrews University Seminary Studies* 24 (1986): 5-12.

———. "'To the Hebrews': A Document of Roman Christianity?" *ANRW* 2.25.4 (1987): 3496-3521.

Campbell, J. C. "In a Son: The Doctrine of the Incarnation in the Epistle to the Hebrews." *Interpretation* 10 (1956): 24-38.

Campbell, K. M. "Covenant or Testament? Heb 9:15, 17 Reconsidered." *EvQ* 44 (1972): 107-11.

Carlston, Charles E. "Eschatology and Repentance in the Epistle to the Hebrews." *JBL* 78 (1959): 296-302.

———. "The Vocabulary of Perfection in Philo and Hebrews," pp. 133-60 in *Unity and Diversity in New Testament Theology: Essays in Honor of George E. Ladd.* Edited by Robert A. Guelich. Grand Rapids: Eerdmans, 1978.

Chavasse, C. "Jesus: Christ and Moses." *Theology* 54 (1951): 244-50, 289-96.

Clarkson, E. "The Antecedents of the High-Priest Theme in Hebrews." *Australian Theological Review* 29 (1947): 92-93.

Clavier, H. "Ὁ λόγος τοῦ θεοῦ dans l'épître aux Hébreux," pp. 81-93 in *New Testament Essays: Studies in Memory of Thomas Walter Manson*. Edited by A. J. B. Higgins. Manchester: Manchester University Press, 1959.

Clements, Ronald E. "The Use of the OT in Hebrews." *Southwest Journal of Theology* 28 (1985): 36-42.

Cockerill, G. L. "Heb 1.1-14, 1 Clem. 36.1-6 and the High Priest Title." *JBL* 97 (1978): 437-40.

———. "The Melchizedek Christology in Heb 7:1-28." Diss., Union Theological Seminary (VA), 1976.

Cody, Aelred. *Heavenly Sanctuary and Liturgy in the Epistle to the Hebrews: The Achievement of Salvation in the Epistle's Perspectives*. St. Meinrad, Ind.: Grail, 1960.

Coppens, J. "Les affinités qumraniennes de l'épître aux Hébreux." *La nouvelle revue théologique* 84 (1961): 128-41, 257-82.

Coste, J. "Notion grecque et notion biblique de la 'souffrance éducatrice': A propos d'Héb. 5.7-8." *Recherches de science religieuse* 43 (1955): 481-523.

Cranfield, C. E. B. "Hebrews 13:20-21." *Scottish Journal of Theology* 20 (1967): 437-41.

Culley, R. C. "Structural Analysis: Is It Done with Mirrors?" *Interpretation* 28 (1974): 165-81.

Cullmann, Oscar. *The Christology of the New Testament*. Translated by Shirley C. Guthrie and Charles A. M. Hall. Revised edition. Philadelphia: Westminster, 1964.

Culpepper, R. A. "The High Priesthood and Sacrifice of Christ in the Epistle to the Hebrews." *Theological Educator* 32 (1985): 46-62.

———. "A Superior Faith: Hebrews 10:19—12:2." *Review and Expositor* 82 (1985): 375-90.

Dahms, J. V. "The First Readers of Hebrews." *Journal of the Evangelical Theological Society* 20 (1977): 365-75.

Daly, R. J. "The Soteriological Significance of the Sacrifice of Isaac." *CBQ* 39 (1977): 45-75.

D'Angelo, M. R. *Moses in the Letter to the Hebrews*. Missoula, Mont.: Scholars Press, 1979.

Daube, David. "Alexandrian Methods of Interpretation and the Rabbis," pp. 27-44 in *Festschrift Hans Lewald*. Basel: Helbing & Lichtenhahn, 1953.

Dautzenberg, G. "Der Glaube im Hebräerbrief." *Biblische Zeitschrift* n.s. 15 (1973): 161-77.

Davies, J. H. "The Heavenly Work of Christ in Hebrews." Vol. 4, pp. 384-89 in *Studia evangelica*. Edited by F. L. Cross. Texte und Untersuchungen 102. Berlin: de Gruyter, 1968.

Davies, W. D. "A Note on Josephus, Antiquities 15.136." *Harvard Theological Review* 47 (1954): 135-40.

Deasley, A. R. G. "The Idea of Perfection in the Qumran Texts." Ph.D. thesis, University of Manchester, 1972.

de Jonge, M., and A. S. van der Woude. "11QMelchizedek and the New Testament." *NTS* 12 (1965-66): 301-26.

Delling, Gerhard. "Ἀρχηγός." Vol. 1, pp. 487-88 in *Theological Dictionary of the New Testament*. Edited by Gerhard Kittel and Gerhard Friedrich. Translated by Geoffrey W. Bromiley. Grand Rapids: Eerdmans, 1967.

Delville, J. P. "L'épître aux Hébreux à la lumière du prosélytisme juif." *Revista catalana de teología* 10 (1985): 323-68.

Demarest, B. "Priest after the Order of Melchizedek: A History of Interpretation of Hebrews 7 from the Era of the Reformation to the Present." Ph.D. thesis, University of Manchester, 1973.

Dey, L. K. K. *The Intermediary World and Patterns of Perfection in Philo and Hebrews*. Society of Biblical Literature Dissertation Series 25. Missoula, Mont.: Scholars Press, 1975.

Dibelius, Martin. "Der himmlische Kultus nach dem Hebräerbrief." Vol. 2, pp. 160-76 in Dibelius's *Botschaft und Geschichte*. Tübingen: Mohr, 1956.

Doormann, F. "Deinen Namen will ich meinen Brüdern verkünden." *Bibel und Leben* 14 (1973): 245-52.

Dumbrell, W. J. "The Spirits of Just Men Made Perfect." *EvQ* 48 (1976): 154-59.

Dunkel, F. "Expiation et jours des expieations dans l'épître aux Hébreux." *Revue réformée* 33 (1982): 63-71.

Dunn, J. D. G. *Christology in the Making*. Philadelphia: Westminster Press, 1980.

Dunnill, John. *Covenant and Sacrifice in the Letter to the Hebrews*. Cambridge: Cambridge University Press, 1992.

du Plessis, P. J. *Teleios: The Idea of Perfection in the New Testament*. Kampen: Kok, 1959.

Eager, A. R. "The Authorship of the Epistle to the Hebrews." *Expositor* 10 (1904): 74-80, 110-23.

Eisenbaum, Pamela M. *The Jewish Heroes of Christian History: Hebrews 11 in Literary Context*. Atlanta: Scholars Press, 1997.

Ellingworth, Paul. "Hebrews and I Clement: Literary Dependence or Common Tradition." *Biblische Zeitschrift* 23 (1979): 262-69.

———. "Jesus and the Universe in Hebrews." *EvQ* 58 (1986): 337-50.

———. "Reading through Hebrews 1—7." *Epworth Review* 12 (1985): 80-88.

———. "The Unshakeable Priesthood: Hebrews 7:24." *Journal for the Study of the New Testament* 23 (1985): 125-26.

Elliott, J. K. "Is Post-baptismal Sin Forgivable?" *Bible Translator* 28 (1977): 330-32.

———. "When Jesus Was Apart from God: An Examination of Hebrews 2:9." *ET* 83 (1971-72): 339-41.

Farrar, Frederic W. *The Epistle of Paul the Apostle to the Hebrews.* Cambridge: Cambridge University Press, 1891.

Feld, Helmut. *Der Hebräerbrief.* Darmstadt: Wissenschaftliche Buchgesellschaft, 1985.

Feuillet, André. "Une triple préparation du sacerdoce du Christ dans l'ancien testament: Introduction à la doctrine sacerdotale de l'épître aux Hébreux." *Divinitas* 28 (1984): 103-36.

Filson, Floyd V. *"Yesterday": A Study of Hebrews in the Light of Chapter 13.* Naperville: Allenson, 1967.

Fitzmyer, Joseph A. "Further Light on Melchizedek from Qumran Cave 11." *JBL* 86 (1967): 25-41.

———. "Habakkuk 2:3-4 and the New Testament," pp. 236-46 in Fitzmyer's *To Advance the Gospel.* New York: Crossroad, 1981.

———. "'Now This Melchizedek . . .': Hebrews 7:1," pp. 221-43 in Fitzmyer's *Essays on the Semitic Background of the New Testament.* London: Chapman, 1971.

Flew, R. N. *The Idea of Perfection in Christian Theology.* Oxford: Oxford University Press, 1934.

Frankowski, J. "Early Christian Hymns Recorded in the N.T.: A Reconsideration of the Question of Heb 1:3." *Biblische Zeitschrift* 27 (1983): 183-94.

Galot, J. "Le sacrifice rédempteur du Christ selon l'épître aux Hébreux." *Esprit et vie* 89 (1979): 369-77.

Gheorghita, R. *The Role of the Septuagint in Hebrews.* Tübingen: Mohr, 2003.

Giles, Pauline. "Jesus the High Priest in the Epistle to the Hebrews and the Fourth Gospel." M.A. thesis, University of Manchester, 1973.

———. "The Son of Man in the Epistle to the Hebrews." *ET* 86 (1974-75): 328-32.

Glasson, T. F. "'Plurality of Divine Persons' and the Quotations in Hebrews 1:6ff." *NTS* 12 (1965-66): 270-72.

Glaze, R. E. "Introduction to Hebrews." *Theological Educator* 32 (1985): 20-37.

Glombitza, O. "Erwägungen zum kunstvollen Ansatz der Paraenese im Brief an die Hebräer x.19-25." *NovT* 9 (1967): 132-50.

Goppelt, L. *Typos.* Gutersloh: Bertelsmann, 1939.

Grässer, Erich. *Der Glaube im Hebräerbrief.* Marburg: Elwert, 1965.

———. "Hebräer 1,1-4: Ein exegetischer Versuch," pp. 55-91 in *Der Hebräerbrief.* Evangelisch-katholischer Kommentar zum Neuen Testament 3. Zurich/Neukirchen: Neukirchen Verlag, 1971.

————. "Der Hebräerbrief, 1938-63." *Theologische Rundschau* n.s. 30 (1964-65): 138-236.

————. "Das Heil als Wort: Exegetische Erwägungen zu Hebr 2,1-4," pp. 261-74 in *Neues Testament und Geschichte* (Oscar Cullmann Festschrift). Edited by Heinrich Baltensweiler and Bo Reicke. Tübingen: Mohr, 1972.

————. "Der historische Jesus im Hebräerbrief." *ZNW* 56 (1965): 63-91.

————. "Moses und Jesus: Zur Auslegung von Hebr 3,1-6." *ZNW* 75 (1984): 2-23.

————. "Rechtfertigung im Hebräerbrief," pp. 79-93 in *Rechtfertigung: Festschrift für Ernst Käsemann*. Edited by Johannes Friedrich, Wolfgang Pöhlmann and Peter Stuhlmacher. Tübingen: Mohr, 1976.

————. Review of George Wesley Buchanan's *To the Hebrews*. *Theologische Literaturzeitung* 100 (1975): 752-55.

————. "Das Wandernde Gottesvolk: Zum Basismotiv des Hebräerbriefes." *ZNW* 77 (1986): 160-79.

————. "Zur Christologie des Hebräerbriefes," pp. 195-206 in *Neues Testament und christliche Existenz: Festschrift für Herbert Braun*. Edited by Hans-Dieter Betz and Luise Schottroff. Tübingen: Mohr, 1973.

Gray, Patrick. *Godly Fear: The Epistle to the Hebrews and Greco-Roman Critiques of Superstition*. Academia biblica 16. Atlanta: Society of Biblical Literature, 2003.

Grayston, K. "Salvation Proclaimed: Hebrews 9:11-14." *ET* 93 (1982): 164-68.

Greenlee, J. Harold. "Hebrews 11.11: Sarah's Faith or Abraham's?" *Notes on Translation* 4 (1990): 37-42.

Greer, Rowan A. *The Captain of Our Salvation*. Beiträge zur Geschichte der biblischen Exegese 15. Tübingen: Mohr, 1973.

Grogan, G. W. "Christ and His People: An Exegetical and Theological Study of Hebrews 2:5-18." *Vox evangelica* 6 (1969): 54-71.

Gudorf, Michael E. "Through a Classical Lens: Hebrews 2:16." *JBL* 119 (2000): 105-8.

Guthrie, George H. *The Structure of Hebrews: A Text-Linguistic Analysis*. Grand Rapids: Baker, 1998.

Gyllenberg, R. "Die Christologie des Hebräerbriefes." *Zeitschrift für systematische Theologie* 11 (1934): 662-90.

————. "Die Komposition des Hebräerbriefes." *Svensk exegetisk årsbok* 22/23 (1957-58): 137-47.

Hagner, Donald A. *Encountering the Book of Hebrews*. Grand Rapids: Baker, 2002.

Hanson, R. P. C. *Allegory and Event*. London: Epworth, 1959.

Häring, T. "Über einige Grundgedanken des Hebräerbriefs." *Monatsschrift für Pastoraltheologie* 17 (1920-21): 260-76.

Harnack, Adolf von. "Probabilia über die Adresse und den Verfasser des Hebräerbriefs." *ZNW* 1 (1900): 16-41.

———. "Zwei alte dogmatische Korrekturen im Hebräerbrief," pp. 235-52 in Harnack's *Studien zur Geschichte des NT und der alten Kirche*. Berlin: de Gruyter, 1931.

Harrington, Daniel J. *What Are They Saying about the Letter to the Hebrews?* New York: Paulist Press, 2005.

Harris, Murray J. *Jesus as God: The New Testament Use of Theos in Reference to Jesus*. Grand Rapids: Baker, 1992.

———. "The Translation and Significance of ὁ θεός in Hebrews 1:8-9." *Tyndale Bulletin* 36 (1985): 129-62.

Hatch, Edwin. *The Organization of the Early Christian Churches*. Bampton Lectures 1880. Oxford/Cambridge: Rivingtons, 1881.

Hay, David M. *Glory at the Right Hand: Psalm 110 in Early Christianity*. Nashville: Abingdon, 1973.

Hays, R. B. *Echoes of Scripture in Paul*. New Haven: Yale University Press, 1993.

———. "'Here We Have No Lasting City': New Covenantalism in Hebrews." Paper read at "Hebrews and Theology" Conference, St. Andrews, Scotland, July 2006.

Helyer, L. R. "The *prōtotokos* Title in Hebrews." *Studia biblica et theologica* 6 (1976): 3-28.

Hengel, Martin. *Crucifixion in the Ancient World and the Folly of the Message of the Cross*. Translated by John Bowden. Philadelphia: Fortress, 1977.

———. *The Septuagint as Christian Scripture: Its Prehistory and the Problem of Its Canon*. Translated by Mark E. Biddle. Grand Rapids: Baker, 2002.

Higgins, A. J. B. "The Old Testament and Some Aspects of New Testament Christology," pp. 128-41 in *Promise and Fulfilment: Essays Presented to Professor S. H. Hooke*. Edited by F. F. Bruce. Edinburgh: Clark, 1963.

———. "The Priestly Messiah." *NTS* 13 (1966-67): 211-39.

Hoekema, A. A. "The Perfection of Christ in Hebrews." *Calvin Theological Journal* 9 (1974): 31-37.

Hofius, Otfried. "Das 'erste' und das 'zweite' Zeit: Ein Beitrag zur Auslegung von Hebr 9,1-10." *ZNW* 61 (1970): 271-77.

———. "Inkarnation und Opfertod Jesu nach Hebr 10,19f," pp. 132-41 in *Der Ruf Jesu und die Antwort der Gemeinde: Exegetische Untersuchungen Joachim Jeremias*. Edited by Eduard Lohse. Göttingen: Vandenhoeck & Ruprecht, 1970.

———. *Katapausis*. Tübingen: Mohr, 1970.

———. *Der Vorhang vor dem Thron Gottes*. Tübingen: Mohr, 1972.

Hollander, H. W. "Hebrews 7:11 and 8:6: A Suggestion for the Translation of *nenomothētai epi.*" *Bible Translator* 30 (1979): 244-47.

Hooker, Morna. "Jesus, the 'End' of the Cult." Paper read at "Hebrews and Theology" Conference, St. Andrews, Scotland, July 2006.

Hoppin, Ruth. *Priscilla: Author of the Epistle to the Hebrews.* New York: Exposition Press, 1969.

———. *Priscilla's Letter: Finding the Author of the Epistle to the Hebrews.* Fort Bragg, Calif.: Lost Coast Press, 1997.

Horbury, William. "The Aaronic Priesthood in the Epistle to the Hebrews." *Journal for the Study of the New Testament* 19 (1983): 43-71.

Horton, F. L. *The Melchizedek Tradition: A Critical Examination of the Sources to the Fifth Century AD and in the Epistle to the Hebrews.* Cambridge: Cambridge University Press, 1976.

Howard, G. "Hebrews and the OT Scriptures." *NovT* 10 (1968): 208-16.

Hughes, Graham. *Hebrews and Hermeneutics.* Society for New Testament Study Monograph 36. Cambridge: Cambridge University Press, 1979.

Hughes, J. J. "Hebrews ix.15ff. and Galatians iii.15ff.: A Study in Covenant Practice and Procedure." *NovT* 21 (1979): 27-96.

Hughes, Philip Edgcumbe. "Hebrews 6:4-6 and the Peril of Apostasy." *Westminster Theological Journal* 35 (1972-73): 137-55.

Hurst, L. D. "Apollos, Hebrews and Corinth." *Scottish Journal of Theology* 38 (1985): 505-13.

———. "The Christology of Hebrews 1 and 2," pp. 151-64 in *The Glory of Christ in the New Testament: Studies in Christology in Memory of George Bradford Caird.* Edited by L. D. Hurst and N. T. Wright. Oxford: Clarendon, 1987.

———. "How Platonic Are Heb viii.5 and ix.23f.?" *JTS* 34 (1983): 156-68.

Hutaff, M. D. "The Epistle to the Hebrews: An Early Christian Sermon." *Bible Today* 99 (1978): 1816-24.

Jeremias, Joachim. "Hebr 5,7-10." *ZNW* 44 (1952-53): 107-11.

———. "Hebräer 10,20: *tout' estin tēs sarkos autou.*" *ZNW* 62 (1971): 131.

———. "Μωυσῆς." Vol. 4, pp. 848-73 in *Theological Dictionary of the New Testament.* Edited by Gerhard Kittel and Gerhard Friedrich. Translated by Geoffrey W. Bromiley. Grand Rapids: Eerdmans, 1967.

Jewett, R. *Letter to Pilgrims.* New York: Pilgrim, 1981.

John, M. P. "Covenant-Testament-Will." *Bible Translator* 30 (1979): 448.

Johnson, Luke Timothy. *The Writings of the New Testament.* Minneapolis: Fortress, 1999.

Johnson, R. W. *Going outside the Camp: The Sociological Function of the Levitical*

Critique in the Epistle to the Hebrews. Sheffield: Sheffield Academic Press, 2001.

Johnsson, W. G. "The Pilgrimage Motif in the Book of Hebrews." *JBL* 97 (1978): 239-51.

Jones, P. R. "A Superior Life: Hebrews 12:3—13:25." *Review and Expositor* 82 (1985): 397-405.

Kaiser, Walter C. "The Old Promise and the New Covenant: Jeremiah 31:31-34." *Journal of the Evangelical Theological Society* 15 (1972): 11-23.

———. "The Promise Theme and the Theology of Rest." *Bibliotheca sacra* 130 (1973): 135-50.

Kamell, Mariam. "The Concept of 'Faith' in Hebrews and James." Paper read at "Hebrews and Theology" Conference, St. Andrews, Scotland, July 2006.

Käsemann, Ernst. *The Wandering People of God: An Investigation of the Letter to the Hebrews*. Translated by Roy A. Harrisville and Irving L. Sandberg. Minneapolis: Augsburg, 1984.

Kawamura, A. "'Αδύνατον in Heb 6:4." *Annual of the Japanese Biblical Institute* 10 (1984): 91-100.

Kiley, M. "A Note on Heb 5:14." *CBQ* 42 (1980): 501-3.

Kistemaker, Simon J. *The Psalm Citations in the Epistle to the Hebrews*. Amsterdam: Van Soest, 1961.

Klappert, B. *Die Eschatologie des Hebräerbriefes*. Munich: Kaiser, 1969.

Kline, Meredith. *By Oath Consigned*. Grand Rapids: Eerdmans, 1968.

Knauer, P. "Erbsunde als Todes Verfallenheit: Eine Deutung von Rom 5:12 aus dem Vergleich mit Hebr 2,14f." *Theologie und Glaube* 58 (1968): 153-58.

Knox, W. L. "The 'Divine Hero' Christology in the New Testament." *Harvard Theological Review* 41 (1948): 229-49.

Kobelski, Paul J. *Melchizedek and Melchireša'*. Catholic Biblical Quarterly Monograph Series 10. Washington, D.C.: Catholic Biblical Association of America, 1981.

Koester, Helmut. "Die Auslegung der Abraham-Verheissung in Hebräer 6," pp. 95-109 in *Studien zur Theologie der alttestamentlichen Überlieferungen* (Gerhard von Rad Festschrift). Edited by Rolf Rendtorf and Klaus Koch. Neukirchen: Neukirchen Verlag, 1969.

———. "'Outside the Camp': Hebrews 13:9-14." *Harvard Theological Review* 55 (1962): 299-315.

———. "The Purpose of . . . a Pauline Fragment." *NTS* 8 (1961-62): 317-32.

Kögel, Julius. "Der Begriff τελείων im Hebräerbrief," pp. 35-68 in *Theologische Studien: Martin Kähler*. Leipzig: Deichert, 1905.

Kosmala, H. *Hebräer-Essener-Christen*. Leiden: Brill, 1959.

Kuss, Otto. "Der theologische Grundgedanke des Hebräerbriefes: Zur Deutung des Todes Jesu im Neuen Testament." Vol. 1, pp. 281-32 in Kuss's *Auslegung und Verkündigung*. Regensburg: Pustet, 1963.

―――. "Der Verfasser des Hebräerbriefes als Seelsorger," pp. 329-58 in Kuss's *Auslegung und Verkündigung*. Regensburg: Pustet, 1963.

Lampe, Peter. *From Paul to Valentinus*. Minneapolis: Fortress, 2003.

Lane, William L. "Hebrews: A Sermon in Search of a Setting." *Southwest Journal of Theology* 28 (1985): 13-18.

―――. "Unexpected Light on Heb 13:1-6 from a 2nd Century Source." *Perspectives in Religious Studies* 9 (1982): 267-74.

LaRondell, H. K. *Perfection and Perfectionism: Dogmatic-Ethical Study of Biblical Perfection and Phenomenological Perfection*. Kampen: Kok, 1971.

Laub, F. "Verkündigung und Gemeindeamt: Die Authorität der ἡγούμενοι Hebr 13,7.17.24." *Studien zum Neuen Testament und seiner Umwelt* 6-7 (1981-82): 169-90.

Lehne, S. *The New Covenant in Hebrews*. Sheffield: JSOT Press, 1990.

Leonard, W. *The Authorship of the Epistle to the Hebrews*. London: Polyglot, 1939.

Lewis, C. S. *The Problem of Pain*. New York: Touchstone, 1996.

Lewis, Naphtali, and Meyer Reinhold, eds. *Roman Civilization: Selected Readings*, vol. 2: *The Empire*. 3rd edition. New York: Columbia University Press, 1990.

Lewis, T. W. "'And If He Shrinks Back' (Hebrews 10:38b)." *NTS* 22 (1975-76): 88-94.

Lightfoot, N. "The Saving of the Savior: Hebrews 5:7ff." *Restoration Quarterly* 16 (1973): 166-73.

Lincoln, Andrew T. *Hebrews: A Guide*. London: Clark, 2006.

―――. "Sabbath Rest and Eschatology in the New Testament," pp. 197-220 in *From Sabbath to Lord's Day*. Edited by D. A. Carson. Grand Rapids: Eerdmans, 1982.

Lindars, Barnabas. *The Theology of the Letter to the Hebrews*. Cambridge: Cambridge University Press, 1991.

Linss, W. C. "Logical Terminology in the Epistle to the Hebrews." *Concordia Theological Monthly* 37 (1966): 365-69.

Loader, W. R. G. "Christ at the Right Hand: Ps. cx.1 in the New Testament." *NTS* 27 (1978): 199-217.

―――. "Hughes on Hebrews and Hermeneutics." *Colloquium* 13 (1981): 50-60.

―――. *Sohn und Hoherpriester: Eine traditionsgeschichtliche Untersuchung zur Christologie des Hebräerbriefes*. Neukirchen: Neukirchener Verlag, 1981.

Loewenich, W. von. "Zum Verständnis des Opfergedankens im Hebräerbrief." *Theologische Blätter* 12 (1933): 167-72.

Lohmann, T. "Zur Heilsgeschichte des Hebräerbriefes." *Orientalische Literaturzeitung* 79 (1984): 117-25.

Lohmeyer, Ernst. *Diathēkē: Ein Beitrag zur Erklärung des neutestamentlichen Begriffs.* Untersuchungen zum Neuen Testament 2. Leipzig: Hinrichs, 1913.

Longenecker, Richard N. "The 'Faith of Abraham' Theme in Paul, James and Hebrews." *Journal of the Evangelical Theological Society* 20 (1977): 203-12.

————. "The Melchizedek Argument of Hebrews: A Study in the Development and Circumstantial Expression of New Testament Thought," pp. 161-85 in *Unity and Diversity in New Testament Theology: Essays in Honor of George E. Ladd.* Edited by Robert A. Guelich. Grand Rapids: Eerdmans, 1978.

Lorimer, W. "Hebrews 7:23f." *NTS* 13 (1966-67): 386-87.

Luck, Ulrich. "Himmlisches und irdisches Geschehen im Hebräerbrief." *NovT* 6 (1963): 192-215.

Lührmann, Dieter. "Der Hohepriester ausserhalb des Lagers Hebr 13,12." *ZNW* 69 (1978): 178-86.

Lyonnet, S., and Leopold Sabourin. *Sin, Redemption and Sacrifice: A Biblical and Patristic Study.* Analecta biblica 48. Rome: Pontifical Biblical Institute Press, 1970.

Manson, T. W. *The Epistle to the Hebrews: An Historical and Theological Reconsideration.* London: SCM, 1951.

————. "Martyrs and Martyrdom." *Bulletin of the John Rylands University Library* 39 (1956-57): 463-84.

————. *Ministry and Priesthood: Christ's and Ours.* London: SCM, 1958.

————. *Studies in the Gospels and Epistles.* Philadelphia: Fortress, 1962.

Marrou, H. I. *A History of Education in Antiquity.* London: Sheed & Ward, 1956.

Marrow, S. "*Parrēsia* in the New Testament." *CBQ* 44 (1982): 431-36.

Marshall, I. H. "Soteriology in Hebrews." Paper read at "Hebrews and Theology" Conference, St. Andrews, Scotland, July 2006.

Maurer, Christian. "'Erhort wegen der Gottesfurcht,' Hebr 5,7," pp. 275-84 in *Neues Testament und Geschichte* (Oscar Cullmann Festschrift). Edited by Heinrich Baltensweiler and Bo Reicke. Tübingen: Mohr, 1972.

————. "Σύνοιδα, συνείδησις." Vol. 7, pp. 899-919 in *Theological Dictionary of the New Testament.* Edited by Gerhard Kittel and Gerhard Friedrich. Translated by Geoffrey W. Bromiley. Grand Rapids: Eerdmans, 1971.

McCullough, J. C. "The Impossibility of a Second Repentance in Hebrews." *Biblical Theology Bulletin* 24 (1974): 1-7.

————. "Melchisedek's Varied Role in Early Exegetical Tradition." *Theological Review* 1.2 (1978): 52-66.

————. "The Old Testament Quotations in Hebrews." *NTS* 26 (1979-80): 363-79.

————. "Some Recent Developments in Research on the Epistle to the Hebrews." *Irish Biblical Studies* 2 (1980): 141-65; 3 (1981): 28-45.

McGrath, J. J. *"Through the Eternal Spirit": An Historical Study of the Exegesis of Hebrews 9:13-14.* Rome: Pontifical Biblical Institute Press, 1961.

McRae, George W. "Heavenly Temple and Eschatology in the Letter to the Hebrews." *Semeia* 12 (1978): 179-99.

————. "A Kingdom That Cannot Be Shaken: The Heavenly Jerusalem in the Letter to the Hebrews." *Tantur Yearbook* 1979-80: 27-40.

McRay, J. "Atonement and Apocalyptic in the Book of Hebrews." *Restoration Quarterly* 23 (1980): 1-9.

Mealand, D. L. "The Christology of the Epistle to the Hebrews." *Modern Churchman* 22 (1979): 18-87.

Meeks, Wayne A. *The Prophet-King.* Leiden: Brill, 1967.

Mees, M. "Die Hohepriester-Theologie des Hebräerbriefes im Vergleich mit dem Ersten Clemensbrief." *Biblische Zeitschrift* 22 (1978): 115-24.

Meier, John P. "Structure and Theology in Heb 1,1-14." *Biblica* 66 (1985): 168-89.

Metzger, Bruce M. *A Textual Commentary on the Greek New Testament.* London: United Bible Societies, 1971.

Michaud, Jean-Paul. "Parabole dans l'épître aux Hébreux et typologie." *Sémiotique et bible* 46 (1987): 19-34.

Michel, Otto. "Die Lehre von der christlichen Vollkommenheit nach der Anschauung des Hebräerfriefes." *Theologische Studien und Kritiken* 106 (1934-35): 333-55.

————. "Zur Auslegung des Hebräerbriefes." *NovT* 6 (1963): 189-91.

————. "Μελχισεδέκ." Vol. 4, pp. 568-71 in *Theological Dictionary of the New Testament.* Edited by Gerhard Kittel and Gerhard Friedrich. Translated by Geoffrey W. Bromiley. Grand Rapids: Eerdmans, 1967.

Miller, D. G. "Why God Became Man." *Interpretation* 23 (1969): 408-24.

Minear, Paul S. "An Early Christian Neopoetic." *Semeia* 12 (1978): 201-14.

Moberley, Walter. "Exemplars of Faith: Abel." Paper read at "Hebrews and Theology" Conference, St. Andrews, Scotland, July 2006.

Moe, O. "Der Gedanke des allgemeinen Priestertums im Hebräerbrief." *Theologische Literaturzeitung* 5 (1949): 161-9.

————. "Das Priestertum Christi im Neuen Testament ausserhalb des Hebräerbriefes." *Theologische Literaturzeitung* 72 (1947): 335-38.

Morrice, W. G. "Covenant." *ET* 86 (1974-75): 132-36.

Morris, Leon. "The Biblical Use of the Term 'Blood.'" *JTS* n.s. 3 (1952): 216-27.

Mosser, Carl. "Exemplars of Faith: Rahab." Paper read at "Hebrews and Theology" Conference, St. Andrews, Scotland, July 2006.

Motyer, S. "The Psalm Quotations of Hebrews 1: A Hermeneutic Free Zone?" *Tyndale Bulletin* 50 (1999): 3-22.

Moule, C. F. D. "From Defendant to Judge—and Deliverer." *Studiorum novi testamenti societas bulletin* 3 (1952): 40-53.

———. "Fulfilment Words in the New Testament: Use and Abuse." *NTS* 14 (1967-68): 293-320.

———. *An Idiom-Book of New Testament Greek.* 2nd edition. Cambridge: Cambridge University Press, 1959.

———. "Sanctuary and Sacrifice in the Church of the New Testament." *JTS* n.s. 1 (1950): 29-41.

Mugridge, A. "Warnings in the Epistle to the Hebrews: An Exegetical and Theological Study." *Reformed Theological Review* 46 (1987): 74-82.

Muir, Steven. "The Use of Images in the Roman Imperial Cult as a Context for Heb. 1.3." Paper read at "Hebrews and Theology" Conference, St. Andrews, Scotland, July 2006.

Muller, P. G. *Christos archēgos: Der religionsgeschichtliche und theologische Hintergund einer neutestamentlichen Christuspradikation.* Frankfurt: Lang, 1973.

Nairne, Alexander. *Epistle of Priesthood.* Edinburgh: Clark, 1913.

Nauck, Wolfgang. "Zum Aufbau des Hebräerbriefes," pp. 198-206 in *Judentum, Urchristentum, Kirche: Festschrift für Joachim Jeremias.* Edited by Walther Eltester. Berlin: de Gruyter, 1960.

Neeley, Linda L. "A Discourse Analysis of Hebrews." *Occasional Papers in Translation and Textlinguistics* 3-4 (1987): 1-146.

Nelson, R. D. *Raising up a Faithful Priest: Community and Priesthood in a Biblical Theology.* Louisville: Westminster/John Knox, 1993.

Neyrey, Jerome H. "'Without Beginning of Days or End of Life' (Hebrews 7:3): Topos for a True Deity." *CBQ* 53 (1991): 439-55.

Niebuhr, Richard R. "*Archēgos*: An Essay on the Relation between the Biblical Jesus and the Present-Day Reader," pp. 79-100 in *Christian History and Interpretation: Studies Presented to John Knox.* Edited by William R. Farmer, C. F. D. Moule and Richard R. Niebuhr. Cambridge: Cambridge University Press, 1967.

Nomoto, S. "Herkunft und Struktur der Hohenpriestervorstellung im Hebräerbrief." *NovT* 10 (1968): 10-25.

Oberholtzer, T. K. "The Kingdom Rest in Hebrews 3:1—4:13." *Bibliotheca sacra* 145 (1988): 185-96.

———. "The Thorn Infested Ground in Hebrews 6:4-12." *Bibliotheca sacra* 145 (1988): 319-28.

Olsen, S. N. "Pauline Expressions of Confidence in His Addresses." *CBQ* 47 (1985): 282-95.

Omanson, R. L. "A Superior Covenant: Hebrews 8:10—10:18." *Review and Expositor* 82 (1985): 361-73.

Omark, R. E. "The Saving of the Saviour: Exegesis and Christology in Hebrews 5:7-10." *Interpretation* 12 (1958): 39-51.

O'Neill, J. C. "Hebrews 2:9." *JTS* n.s. 17 (1966): 79-82.

Owen, H. P. "The 'Stages of Ascent' in Hebrews 5:11—6:3." *NTS* 3 (1956-57): 243-53.

Parker, Harold M., Jr. "Domitian and the Epistle to the Hebrews." *Iliff Review* 36 (1979): 31-44.

Peake, A. S. *The Epistle to the Hebrews.* Edinburgh: Clark, 1914.

Perkins, D. W. "Call to Pilgrimage: The Challenge of Hebrews." *Theological Educator* 32 (1985): 69-81.

Peterson, David G. *Hebrews and Perfection: An Examination of the Concept of Perfection in the "Epistle to the Hebrews."* Cambridge: Cambridge University Press, 1982.

———. "The Prophecy of the New Covenant in the Argument of Hebrews." *Reformed Theological Review* 38 (1979): 74-81.

———. "The Situation of the 'Hebrews' (5:11—6:12)." *Reformed Theological Review* 35 (1976): 14-21.

Pierce, C. A. *Conscience in the New Testament.* Chicago: Allenson, 1955.

Proulx, P., and Luis Alonso-Schökel. "Heb 6,4-6: *eis metanoian anastaurountas.*" *Biblica* 56 (1975): 193-209.

Pryor, J. W. "Hebrews and Incarnational Christology." *Reformed Theological Review* 40 (1981): 44-50.

Rapske, Brian. *The Book of Acts in Its First Century Settings*, vol. 3: *Paul in Roman Custody.* Grand Rapids: Eerdmans, 1994.

Renner, F. *An die Hebräer: Ein pseudepigraphischer Brief.* Munster: Schwarzach, 1970.

Rice, G. E. "Apostasy as a Motif and Its Effect on the Structure of Hebrews." *Andrews University Seminary Studies* 23 (1985): 29-53.

———. "Hebrews 6:19: Analysis of Some Assumptions concerning *katapetasma.*" *Andrews University Seminary Studies* 26 (1987): 65-71.

Richard, Earl. *Jesus: One and Many.* Wilmington: Glazier, 1988.

Rigaux, B. "Révélation des mystères et perfection à Qumran et dans le Nouveau Testament." *NTS* 4 (1957-58): 237-62.

Riggenbach, E. "Der Begriff der τελείωσις im Hebräerbrief: Ein Beitrag zur Frage nach der Einwirkung der Mysterienreligion auf Sprache und Gedankenwelt des

Neuen Testaments." *Neue kirchliche Zeitschrift* 34 (1923): 184-95.

Rissi, M. "Die Menschlichkeit Jesu nach Hebr 5,7-9." *Theologische Literaturzeitung* 9 (1955): 28-45.

Robb, J. D. "Hebrews 12:1." *ET* 79 (1967-68): 254.

Robinson, D. W. B. "The Literary Structure of Hebrews 1—4." *Australian Journal of Biblical Archaeology* 2 (1972): 178-86.

Robinson, W. *The Eschatology of the Epistle to the Hebrews*. Birmingham, U.K.: Overdale College Press, 1950.

Rooke, D. W. "Jesus as Royal Priest: Reflections on the Interpretation of the Melchizedek Tradition in Heb 7." *Biblica* 81 (2000): 81-94.

Sabourin, Leopold. "Crucifying Afresh for One's Repentance: Heb 6:4-6." *Biblical Theology Bulletin* 6 (1976): 264-71.

———. "'Liturge du sanctuaire et de la tente visible' (Heb 8,2)." *NTS* 18 (1971-72): 87-90.

———. *Priesthood: A Comparative Study*. Studies in the History of Religions 25. Leiden: Brill, 1973.

Sailer, W. S. "Hebrews Six: An Irony or a Continuing Embarrassment." *Evangelical Journal* 13 (1985): 79-88.

Salevao, Iutisone. *Legitimation in the Letter to the Hebrews: The Construction and Maintenance of a Symbolic Universe*. Sheffield: Sheffield University Press, 2002.

Sarvan, G. W. *Telling and Retelling: Quotation in Biblical Narrative*. Bloomington: Indiana University Press, 1988.

Schaeffer, J. R. "The Relationship between Priestly and Servant Messianism in the Epistle to the Hebrews." *CBQ* 30 (1968): 359-85.

Scheidweiler, F. "Καίπερ nebst einem Exkurs zum Hebräerbrief." *Hermes* 83 (1955): 220-30.

Schenck, Kenneth L. "A Celebration of the Enthroned Son: The Catena of Hebrews 1." *JBL* 120 (2001): 469-85.

———. *Understanding the Book of Hebrews*. Louisville: Westminster/John Knox, 2003.

Schenke, H.-M. "Erwägungen zum Rätsel des Hebräerbriefes," pp. 421-37 in *Neues Testament und christliche Existenz: Festschrift für Herbert Braun*. Edited by Hans-Dieter Betz and Luise Schottroff. Tübingen: Mohr, 1973.

Schierse, Franz Joseph. *Verheissung und Heilsvollendung: Zur theologischen Grundfrage des Hebräerbriefes*. Münchener theologische Studien 1.9. Munich: Zink, 1955.

Schille, G. "Erwägungen zur Hohepriesterlehre des Hebräerbriefes." *ZNW* 46 (1955): 81-109.

Scholer, J. M. *Proleptic Priests: Priesthood in the Epistle to the Hebrews.* Sheffield: Sheffield Academic Press, 1991.

Schröger, Friedrich. *Der Verfasser des Hebräerbriefes als Schriftausleger.* Regensburg: Pustet, 1968.

Schulz, Siegfried. "Σκιά." Vol. 7, pp. 394-400 in *Theological Dictionary of the New Testament.* Edited by Gerhard Kittel and Gerhard Friedrich. Translated by Geoffrey W. Bromiley. Grand Rapids: Eerdmans, 1971.

Scott, E. F. *The Epistle to the Hebrews: Its Doctrine and Significance.* Edinburgh: Clark, 1922.

Scott, J. J. "*Archēgos* in the Salutation History of the Epistle to the Hebrews." *Journal of the Evangelical Theological Society* 29 (1986): 47-54.

Selby, G. S. "The Meaning and Function of *synedeisis* in Hebrews 9 and 10." *Restoration Quarterly* 28 (1985-86): 145-54.

Sen, F. "Se recupera la verdadera lectura de un texto muy citado, cuyo sentido cambia substancialmente (Heb 10,1)." *Cultura biblica* 23 (1967): 165-68.

Sharp, J. R. "Philonism and the Eschatology of Hebrews: Another Look." *East Asia Journal of Theology* 2 (1984): 289-93.

Siegert, Folker. *Drei hellenistisch-jüdische Predigten.* Tübingen: Mohr, 1992.

Silva, Moisés. "Perfection and Eschatology in Hebrews." *Westminster Theological Journal* 39 (1976): 60-71.

Simpson, E. K. "The Vocabulary of the Epistle to the Hebrews." *EvQ* 18 (1946): 35-38, 187-90.

Smith, J. *A Priest Forever: A Study of Typology and Eschatology in Hebrews.* London: Sheed & Ward, 1969.

Soden, Hermann von. *Urchristliche Literaturgeschichte: Die Schriften des Neuen Testaments.* Berlin: Dunker, 1905.

Songer, H. S. "A Superior Priesthood: Hebrews 4:14—7:28." *Review and Expositor* 82 (1985): 345-59.

Sowers, S. G. *The Hermeneutics of Philo and Hebrews.* Richmond: John Knox, 1965.

Spicq, Ceslas. "L'épître aux Hébreux, Apollos, Jean-Baptiste, les Hellénistes et Qumran." *Revue de Qumran* 1 (1958-59): 365-90.

———. "L'origine johannique de la conception du Christ-prêtre dans l'épître aux Hébreux," pp. 258-69 in *Aux sources de la tradition chrétienne: Mélanges offerts à M. Maurice Goguel.* Paris: Delachaux & Niestlé, 1950.

———. "La panegyrie de Heb 12,22." *Studia theologica* 6 (1953): 30-38.

Sproule, J. A. "*Parapesontas* in Hebrews 6:6." *Grace Theological Journal* 2 (1981): 327-32.

Stanley, S. "Hebrews 9:6-10: The 'Parable' of the Tabernacle." *NovT* 37 (1995): 385-99.

Stegner, W. R. "The Ancient Jewish Synagogue Homily," pp. 51-69 in *Greco-Roman Literature and the New Testament*. Edited by David E. Aune. Atlanta: Scholars Press, 1988.

Stewart, R. A. "The Sinless High Priest." *NTS* 14 (1967-68): 126-35.

Still, Todd. "Christos as Pistos: The Faith(fulness) of Jesus in the Epistle to the Hebrews." Paper read at "Hebrews and Theology" Conference, St. Andrews, Scotland, July 2006.

Stott, W. "The Conception of 'Offering' in the Epistle to the Hebrews." *NTS* 9 (1962-63): 62-67.

Strobel, A. "Die Psalmengrondlage der Gethsemane-Parallel Hebr 5,7f." *ZNW* 45 (1954): 252-66.

Swete, H. B. *The Ascended Christ*. London: Hodder & Stoughton, 1910.

Swetnam, James. "Form and Content in Hebrews 1—6." *Biblica* 53 (1972): 368-85.

———. "Form and Content in Hebrews 7—13." *Biblica* 55 (1974): 333-48.

———. "'The Greater and More Perfect Tent': A Contribution to the Discussion of Hebrews 9:11." *Biblica* 47 (1966): 91-106.

———. *Jesus and Isaac*. Rome: Pontifical Biblical Institute Press, 1981.

———. "Jesus as Logos in Hebrews 4:12-13." *Biblica* 62 (1981): 214.

———. "On the Literary Genre of the 'Epistle' to the Hebrews." *NovT* 11 (1969): 261-69.

———. Review of F. Schrager's *Der Verfasser des Hebräerbriefes als Schriftausleger*. *CBQ* 31 (1968): 130-32.

———. "Sacrifice and Revelation in the Epistle to the Hebrews: Observations and Surmises on Heb 9:26." *CBQ* 30 (1968): 227-34.

———. "A Suggested Interpretation of Hebrews 9:15-18." *CBQ* 27 (1965): 373-90.

Tasker, R. V. G. *The Gospel in the Epistle to the Hebrews*. 2nd edition. London: Tyndale, 1956.

———. "The Integrity of the Epistle to the Hebrews." *ET* 47 (1935-36): 136-38.

Theissen, G. *Untersuchungen zum Hebräerbrief*. Gutersloh: Mohn, 1969.

Thiselton, A. C. "The Use of Philosophical Categories in New Testament Hermeneutics." *Churchman* 87 (1973): 87-100.

Thomas, K. J. "The Old Testament Citations in Hebrews." *NTS* 11 (1964-65): 303-25.

———. "The Use of the Septuagint in the Epistle to the Hebrews." PhD thesis, University of Manchester, 1959.

Thompson, J. W. *The Beginnings of Christian Philosophy: The Epistle to the Hebrews*. Washington, D.C.: Catholic Biblical Association, 1982.

———. "Hebrews 9 and Hellenistic Concepts of Sacrifice." *JBL* 98 (1979): 567-78.

———. "The Hermeneutics of the Epistle to the Hebrews." *Restoration Quarterly* 38 (1996): 229-37.

————. "Outside the Camp: A Study of Heb 13:9-14." *CBQ* 40 (1978): 53-63.

————. "'That Which Cannot Be Shaken': Some Metaphysical Assumptions in Heb 12:27." *JBL* 98 (1975): 580-87.

Thompson, M. B. "The Holy Internet: Communication between Churches in the First Christian Generation." Pp. 49-70 in *The Gospel for All Christians: Rethinking the Gospel Audiences.* Edited by Richard Bauckham. Grand Rapids: Eerdmans, 1998.

Thornton, T. C. G. "The Meaning of *haimatekchysia* in Heb 9:22." *JTS* n.s. 15 (1964): 63-65.

————. Review of Albert Vanhoye's *La structure littéraire de l'épître aux Hébreux. JTS* n.s. 15 (1964): 137-41.

Thurén, Jukka. *Das Lobopfer der Hebräer.* Åbo: Akademi, 1973.

Thurston, R. W. "Philo and the Epistle to the Hebrews." *EvQ* 58 (1986): 133-43.

Thusing, W. "Elementarkatechese und theologische Vertiefung in neutestamentlicher sicht." *Trierer theologische Zeitschrift* 76 (1967): 233-46, 261-80.

————. "'Lasst uns hinzutreten . . .' (Hebr 10,22): Zur Frage nach dem Sinn der Kulttheologie im Hebräerbrief." *Biblische Zeitschrift* 9 (1965): 1-17.

Thyen, Hartwig. *Der Stil der jüdisch-hellenistischen Homilie.* Göttingen: Vandenhoeck & Ruprecht, 1955.

Toussaint, Stanley D. "The Eschatology of the Warning Passages in the Book of Hebrews." *Grace Theological Journal* 3 (1982): 67-80.

Trudinger, L. P. "The Gospel Meaning of the Secular: Reflections on Hebrews 13:10-13." *EvQ* 54 (1982): 235-37.

Turner, Nigel. *Grammatical Insights into the New Testament.* Edinburgh: Clark, 1965.

————. "The Style of the Epistle to the Hebrews," pp. 106-13 in James Hope Moulton's *A Grammar of New Testament Greek,* vol. 4: *Style,* by Nigel Turner. Edinburgh: Clark, 1976.

Übelacker, Walter G. *Der Hebräerbrief als Appell.* Lund: Almqvist & Wiksell, 1989.

Ulrichsen, Jarl Henning. "*Diaphorōteron onoma* in Hebr 1,4: Christus als Träger des Gottesnamens." *Studia theologica* 38 (1984): 65-75.

van der Ploeg, J. "L'exegese de l'A.T. dans l'épître aux Hébreux." *Revue biblique* 54 (1947): 187-228.

Vanhoye, Albert. "De 'aspectu' oblationis Christi secundum epistulam ad Hebraeos." *Verbum domini* 37 (1959): 32-38.

————. "Discussions sur la structure de l'épître aux Hébreux." *Biblica* 55 (1974): 349-80.

————. "Esprit éternel et feu du sacrifice en Héb 9,18." *Biblica* 64 (1983): 263-74.

————. "Jesus fidelis ei qui fecit eum (Héb 3,2)." *Verbum domini* 45 (1967): 291-305.

————. "Litterarische Struktur und theologische Botshaft des Hebräerbriefes." *Studien zum Neuen Testament und seiner Umwelt* 4 (1979): 18-49, 119-47.

————. "'Par la tente plus grande et plus parfaite . . .' (Héb 9,11)." *Biblica* 46 (1965): 1-28.

————. "Sacredoce du Christ et culte chrétien en l'épître aux Hébreux." *Christus* 28 (1981): 216-30.

————. *Situation du Christ: Hébreux i et ii.* Lectio divina 58. Paris: Gabalda, 1958.

————. "Situation et signification de Hébreux 5,1-10." *NTS* 23 (1976-77): 445-56.

————. *Structure and Message of the Epistle to the Hebrews.* Subsidia biblica 12. Rome: Pontifical Biblical Institute Press, 1989.

————. "La structure centrale de l'épître aux Hébreux (Heb 8,1—9,28)." *Recherches de science religieuse* 47 (1959): 44-60.

————. *A Structured Translation of the Epistle to the Hebrews.* Translated by James Swetnam. Rome: Pontifical Biblical Institute Press, 1964.

Van Unnik, W. C. "The Christian's Freedom of Speech." *Bulletin of the John Rylands University Library* 44 (1961-62): 466-88.

Vawter, Bruce. "Levitical Messianism and the NT," pp. 83-89 in *The Bible in Current Catholic Thought.* Edited by John L. McKenzie. New York: Herder & Herder, 1964.

Venard, L. "L'utilisation des Psaumes dans l'épître aux Hébrews," pp. 253-64 in *Mélanges E. Podechard.* Edited by la Faculté de théologie de Lyon. Lyon: Facultés catholiques, 1945.

Vennum, E. "Is She or Isn't She? Sarah as a Hero of Faith." *Daughters of Sarah* 13 (1987): 4-7.

Verbrunge, V. D. "Towards a New Interpretation of Hebrews 6:4-6." *Calvin Theological Journal* 15 (1980): 61-73.

Viard, A. "Le salut par la foi dans l'épître aux Hébreux." *Angelicum* 58 (1981): 115-36.

Vorster, W. S. "The Meaning of *parrēsia* in the Epistle to the Hebrews." *Neotestamentica* 5 (1971): 51-59.

Vos, Geerhardus. "Hebrews: The Epistle of the *diathēkē*." *Princeton Theological Review* 13 (1915): 587-632; 14 (1916): 1-61.

————. "The Priesthood of Christ in the Epistle to the Hebrews." *Princeton Theological Review* 5 (1907): 423-47, 579-604.

————. *The Teaching of the Epistle to the Hebrews.* Grand Rapids: Eerdmans, 1956.

Weiss, H. "*Sabbatismos* in the Epistle to the Hebrews." *CBQ* 58 (1996): 674-89.

Welander, D. C. St. V. "Hebrews 1:1-3." *ET* 65 (1953-54): 315.

Wikgren, A. "Patterns of Perfection in the Epistle to the Hebrews." *NTS* 6 (1959-60): 159-67.

Williamson, Ronald. "The Eucharist and the Epistle to the Hebrews." *NTS* 21 (1974-75): 300-312.

————. "Hebrews 4:15 and the Sinlessness of Jesus." *ET* 86 (1974-75): 4-8.

————. "Hebrews and Doctrine." *ET* 81 (1969-70): 371-76.

————. "The Incarnation of the Logos." *ET* 95 (1983): 4-8.

————. *Philo and the Epistle to the Hebrews.* Leiden: Brill, 1970.

Witherington, Ben, III. *Conflict and Community in Corinth.* Grand Rapids: Eerdmans, 1994.

————. *Grace in Galatia.* Grand Rapids: Eerdmans, 1998.

————. "The Influence of Galatians on Hebrews." *NTS* 37 (1991): 146-52.

————. *Jesus the Sage: The Pilgrimage of Wisdom.* Minneapolis: Fortress, 1998.

————. *John's Wisdom.* Louisville: Westminster/John Knox, 1995.

————. *Letters and Homilies for Hellenized Christians, Volume 1: A Socio-Rhetorical Commentary on Titus, 1-2 Timothy and 1-3 John.* Downers Grove, Ill.: IVP Academic, 2006.

————. *The Many Faces of the Christ.* New York: Continuum, 1998.

————. *Philemon, Colossians and Ephesians.* Grand Rapids: Eerdmans, forthcoming.

————. *Revelation.* Cambridge: Cambridge University Press, 2003.

————. *What Have They Done with Jesus?* San Francisco: Harper, 2006.

————. *Women in the Earliest Churches.* Cambridge: Cambridge University Press, 1988.

Witherington, Ben, III, and Darlene Hyatt. *The Letter to the Romans.* Grand Rapids: Eerdmans, 2004.

Worley, D. R. "God's Faithfulness to Promise: The Hortatory Use of Commissive Language in Hebrews." Ph.D. diss., Yale University, 1981.

Wright, N. T. *The Resurrection of the Son of God.* Minneapolis: Fortress, 2003.

Yadin, Yigael. "The Dead Sea Scrolls and the Epistle to the Hebrews," pp. 36-55 in *Aspects of the Dead Sea Scrolls.* Edited by Chaim Rabin and Yigael Yadin. Scripta hierosolymitana 4. Jerusalem: Magnes, 1965.

————. "A Midrash on II Sam. 7 and Ps. 1-2 (4QFlorilegium)." *Israel Exploration Journal* 9 (1959): 95-98.

Yarnold, E. J. "*Metriopathein* apud Heb 5,2." *Verbum domini* 38 (1960): 149-55.

Young, Norman H. "The Gospel according to Hebrews 9." *NTS* 27 (1981): 198-210.

————. "*Haimatekchysia*: A Comment." *ET* 90 (1979): 180.

————. "Is Hebrews 6:1-8 Pastoral Nonsense?" *Colloquium* 15 (1982): 52-57.

————. "*Tout' estin tēs sarkos autou* (Hebrews 10:20): Apposition—Dependent or Explicative?" *NTS* 20 (1973-74): 100-104.

Zimmermann, F. *Die Hohepriester-Christologie des Hebräerbriefes*. Paderborn: Schoningh, 1964.

Studies Involving Rhetorical Criticism

Good surveys of the rhetorical criticism of Hebrews may be found in Lauri Thurén's "General New Testament Writings" and Duane Watson's "Rhetoric, Rhetorical Criticism" and "Rhetorical Criticism of Hebrews and the Catholic Epistles since 1978."

Achtemeier, P. J. "Newborn Babes and Living Stones: Literal and Figurative in 1 Peter," pp. 207-36 in *To Touch the Text: Biblical and Related Studies in Honor of Joseph A. Fitzmyer*. Edited by M. P. Horgan and P. J. Kobelski. New York: Crossroad, 1989.

Attridge, Harold W. "Paraenesis in a Homily (λόγος παρακλήσεως): The Possible Location of, and Socialization in, the 'Epistle to the Hebrews.'" *Semeia* 50 (1990): 211-26.

————. "The Uses of Antithesis in Hebrews 8—10." *Harvard Theological Review* 79 (1986): 1-9.

Black, David Alan. "Hebrews 1:1-4: A Study in Discourse Analysis." *Westminster Theological Journal* 49 (1987): 175-94.

————. "Literary Artistry in the Epistle to the Hebrews." *Filología neotestamentaria* 7 (1994): 43-51.

Bligh, John. *Chiastic Analysis of the Epistle to the Hebrews*. Oxford: Oxford University Press, 1966.

Blass, Friedrich. "Die rhythmische Komposition des Hebräerbriefes." *Theologische Studien und Kritiken* 75 (1902): 420-61.

————. "The Structure of Hebrews." *Heythrop Journal* 5 (1964): 170-77.

Bulley A. D. "Death and Rhetoric in the Hebrews 'Hymn to Faith.'" *Studies in Religion* 25 (1996): 409-23.

Cosby, Michael R. "Hebrews 11 and the Art of Effective Preaching." *Covenant Quarterly* 48.2 (1990): 29-33.

————. *The Rhetorical Composition and Function of Hebrews 11 in Light of Example Lists in Antiquity*. Macon, Ga.: Mercer University Press, 1988.

————. "The Rhetorical Composition of Hebrews 11." *JBL* 107 (1988): 257-73.

Croy, N. Clayton. *Endurance in Suffering: Hebrews 12:1-13 in Its Rhetorical, Religious and Philosophical Context*. Society for New Testament Study Monograph 98. Cambridge: Cambridge University Press, 1998.

———. "A Note on Hebrews 12:2." *JBL* 114 (1995): 117-19.

Daube, David. "Rabbinic Methods of Interpretation and Hellenistic Rhetoric." *Hebrew Union College Annual* 22 (1949): 239-64.

deSilva, David A. *Despising Shame: Honor Discourse and Community Maintenance in the Epistle to the Hebrews*. Society of Biblical Literature Dissertation 152. Atlanta: Scholars Press, 1995.

———. "Entering God's Rest: Eschatology and the Socio-Rhetorical Strategy of Hebrews." *Trinity Journal* 21 (2000): 25-43.

———. "Eschatology, Rest and the Rhetorical Strategy of Hebrews." *Trinity Journal* n.s. 21 (2000): 25-43.

———. "Exchanging Favor for Wrath: Apostasy in Hebrews and Patron-Client Relationships." *JBL* 115 (1996): 91-116.

———. "Hebrews 6:4-8: A Socio-Rhetorical Investigation." *Tyndale Bulletin* 50 (1999): 33-57, 225-36.

Ebert, D. J. "The Chiastic Structure of the Prologue to Hebrews." *Trinity Journal* n.s. 13 (1992): 163-79.

Evans, C. F. *The Theology of Rhetoric: The Epistle to the Hebrews*. London: Dr. Williams's Trust, 1988.

Forbes, C. "Paul and Rhetorical Comparison," pp. 134-71 in *Paul in the Greco-Roman World: A Handbook*. Edited by J. P. Sampley. Harrisburg, Penn.: Trinity, 2003.

Garuti, P. "Alcune strutture argomentative nella lettera agli Ebrei." *Divus Thomas* 98 (1995): 197-224.

———. *Alle origini dell'omiletica cristiana le lettera agli Ebrei: Note di analisi retorica*. Studium biblicum franciscanum 38. Jerusalem: Franciscan Printing Press, 1995.

———. "Ebrei 7,1-28: Un problema giuridico." *Divus Thomas* 97 (1994): 9-105.

Häring, T. "Gedankengang und Grundgedanken des Hebräerbriefs." *ZNW* 18 (1917-18): 145-64.

Heininger, B. "Sündenreinigung (Hebr 1,3): Christologische Anmerkungen zum Exordium des Hebräerbriefs." *Biblische Zeitschrift* 41 (1997): 54-68.

Horning, E. B. "Chiasmus, Creedal Structure and Christology in Hebrews 12:1-2." *Biblical Research* 23 (1978): 37-48.

Jennrich, W. A. "Rhetoric in the New Testament: The Diction in Romans and Hebrews." *Concordia Theological Monthly* 20 (1949): 518-31.

———. "Rhetorical Style in the New Testament: Romans and Hebrews." Ph.D. diss., Washington University, 1947.

Jobes, Karen H. "The Function of Paronomasia in Hebrews 10:5-7." *Trinity Journal* n.s. 13 (1992): 181-91.

————. "Rhetorical Achievement in the Hebrews 10 'Misquote' of Psalm 40." *Biblica* 72 (1991): 387-96.

Kennedy, George A. *The Art of Persuasion in Greece.* Princeton: Princeton University Press, 1963.

————. *New Testament Interpretation through Rhetorical Criticism.* Chapel Hill: University of North Carolina Press, 1984.

Koester, Craig R. "The Epistle to the Hebrews in Recent Study." *Currents in Research: Biblical Studies* 2 (1994): 123-45 (especially 125-28).

————. "Hebrews, Rhetoric and the Future of Humanity." *CBQ* 64 (2002): 103-23.

Koops, R. "Chains of Contrasts in Hebrews 1." *Bible Translator* 34 (1983): 221-25.

Lindars, Barnabas. "The Rhetorical Structure of Hebrews." *NTS* 35 (1989): 382-406.

Longenecker, Bruce. *Rhetoric at the Boundaries.* Waco: Baylor University Press, 2005.

McCall, M. H. *Ancient Rhetorical Theories of Similes and Comparison.* Cambridge: Harvard University Press, 1969.

Miller, M. R. "What Is the Literary Form of Hebrews 11?" *Journal of the Evangelical Theological Society* 29 (1986): 411-17.

Mitchell, A. C. "Holding on to Confidence: παρρησία in Hebrews," pp. 203-26 in *Friendship, Flattery and Frankness of Speech: Studies on Friendship in the New Testament World.* Edited by J. T. Fitzgerald. Novum Testamentum Supplement 82. Leiden: Brill, 1996.

————. "The Use of πρέπειν and Rhetorical Propriety in Hebrews 2:10." *CBQ* 54 (1992): 681-701.

Moore, B. R. "Rhetorical Questions in Second Corinthians and in Ephesians through Revelation." *Notes* 97 (1983): 3-33.

Nissilä, K. *Das Hohepriestermotiv im Hebräerbrief: Eine exegetische Untersuchung.* Schriften der finnischen exegetischen Gesellschaft 33. Helsinki: Oy Liiton Kirjapaino, 1979.

Olbricht, Thomas H. "Anticipating and Presenting the Case for Christ as High Priest in Hebrews," pp. 355-72 in *Rhetorical Argumentation in Biblical Texts: Essays from the Lund 2000 Conference.* Edited by Anders Eriksson, Thomas H. Olbricht and Walter Übelacker. Emory Studies in Early Christianity 8. Harrisburg, Pa.: Trinity, 2002.

————. "Hebrews as Amplification," pp. 375-87 in *Rhetoric and the New Testament: Essays from the 1992 Heidelberg Conference.* Edited by Stanley E. Porter and Thomas H. Olbricht. Journal for the Study of the New Testament Supplement 90. Sheffield: JSOT Press, 1993.

Pfitzner, Victor C. "The Rhetoric of Hebrews: Paradigm for Preaching." *Lutheran Theological Journal* 27 (1993): 3-12.

Rice, G. E. "The Chiastic Structure of the Central Section of the Epistle to the Hebrews." *Andrews University Seminary Studies* 19 (1981): 243-46.

Robbins, Charles J. "The Composition of Eph 1:3-14." *JBL* 105 (1986): 677-87.

Seid, T. W. "The Rhetorical Form of the Melchizedek/Christ Comparison in Hebrews 7." Ph.D. diss., Brown University, 1996.

————. "Synkrisis in Hebrews 7: The Rhetorical Structure and Strategy," pp. 322-47 in *The Rhetorical Interpretation of Scripture: Essays from the 1996 Malibu Conference.* Edited by Stanley E. Porter and D. L. Stamps. Journal for the Study of the New Testament Supplement 180. Sheffield: Sheffield Academic Press, 1999.

Smith, R. W. *The Art of Rhetoric in Alexandria: Its Theory and Practice in the Ancient World.* The Hague: Nijhoff, 1974.

Stanley, S. "The Structure of Hebrews from Three Perspectives." *Tyndale Bulletin* 45 (1994): 245-71.

Swetnam, James. "The Structure of Hebrews 1,1-3, 6." *Melita theologica* 43 (1992): 58-66.

Thurén, Lauri. "The General New Testament Writings," pp. 587-607 in *Handbook of Classical Rhetoric in the Hellenistic Period, 330 B.C.-A.D. 400.* Edited by Stanley E. Porter. Boston: Brill, 2001.

Übelacker, Walter G. "Hebr 7,1-10—dess struktur och function I författarens retoriska argumentation," pp. 215-32 in *Mellan tid och evighet: Festskrift till Bo Johanson.* Edited by S. Hidal, L. Haikol and S. Norin. Religio 42. Lund: Teologiska institution, 1994.

————. "Hebrews and the Implied Author's Rhetorical Ethos," pp. 316-34 in *Rhetoric, Ethic and Moral Persuasion in Biblical Discourse.* Edited by Thomas H. Olbricht and A. Eriksson. New York: Clark, 2005.

Vaganay, L. "Le plan de l'épître aux Hébreux," pp. 269-77 in *Mémorial [Marie Joseph] Lagrange.* Edited by L. H. Vincent. Paris: Gabalda, 1940.

Vanhoye, Albert. *La structure littéraire de l'épître aux Hébreux.* 2nd edition. Studia neotestamentica 1. Paris: Brouwer, 1976.

Vitti, A. M. "Le bellezze stilistiche della lettera agli Ebrei." *Biblica* 7 (1936): 137-66.

Walters, J. R. "The Rhetorical Arrangement of Hebrews." *Asbury Theological Journal* 51 (1996): 59-70.

Watson, Duane F. "Rhetoric, Rhetorical Criticism," pp. 1041-51 in *Dictionary of the Later New Testament and Its Developments.* Edited by Ralph P. Martin and Peter H. Davids. Downers Grove, Ill.: InterVarsity Press, 1997.

————. "Rhetorical Criticism of Hebrews and the Catholic Epistles since 1978." *Currents in Research: Biblical Studies* 5 (1997): 175-207.

Winter, Bruce W. *Philo and Paul amongst the Sophists.* Cambridge: Cambridge University Press, 1997.

Hebrews

EXORDIUM: THE RADIANCE OF THE SON (HEB 1:1-4)

> Do not be astonished if an emperor writes to us, for he is a man. Wonder rather
> that God wrote the law for human beings and has spoken to us through his Son.
> (Anthony, in Athanasius, *Life of Anthony* 81.)[116]

Hebrews opens with a poetic description of divine revelation as the speech act of
God (1:1). God is pictured not as a silent and distant force, impassively regulating
the universe, but as a talker, as One who has been speaking, arguing, pleading,
wooing, commanding, telling stories, conversing, and generally spinning words
across the lines between heaven and earth since the beginning of time.[117]

George Guthrie stresses that our author is saying that the revelation in the Son
is not only superior to all previous ones, being a fuller representation of God's
truth, but it is also the final and definitive such revelation, and—like in a good
whodunit—what happens at the end of the story is decisive for interpreting all that
has come before. It is not then just a case of fulfilling earlier promises, but also
going beyond any previous revelations. What follows tries to establish not merely
that Jesus fulfills previous hopes and promises but that he surpasses previous
forms of revelation. Only the Son is the exact representation of the being of God.[118]

The function of any exordium was to establish rapport with the audience and
to stir their emotions so they would be favorably disposed to receive the rest of
the discourse. In this particular case, since the main concern of our author is
about defection from the high Christology that the community in Rome had already embraced, he focuses on that, intending to hold up a vivid and visual, indeed a theophanic, portrait of Christ so that the audience could immediately see
what they would be giving up if they defected. The praise of Christ throughout

---

[116]Quoted from Heen and Krey, *Hebrews*, p. 4.
[117]Long, *Hebrews*, p. 7.
[118]Guthrie, *Structure of Hebrews*, pp. 116-19.

this discourse is at a very high level, and as exordiums were intended to do, this one provides a preview of coming attractions. Quintilian speaks about the character of epideictic rhetoric and its function during the empire: "The proper function however of panegyric is to amplify and embellish its themes" (*Institutio oratoria* 3.7.6). Quintilian stresses that this form of rhetoric is directed in the main to the praising of gods and human beings (3.7.6-7), such as that found here: "In praising the gods our first step will be to express our veneration of the majesty of their nature in general terms, next we shall proceed to praise the special power of the individual god and the activities by which he has benefited the human race. . . . Next we must record their exploits as handed down from antiquity. Even gods may derive honor from their descent" (3.7.7-8). This comment of Quintilian is almost a thumbnail sketch of that found in Hebrews 1:1-4! In general, humans are to be praised for their virtues and condemned for the vices, and the same applies to communities of humans as well. Jesus will be praised as a human being and for resisting temptation later in this discourse, and in Hebrews 11 many persons are praised for having the virtues of faith and faithfulness.

The function of an epideictic exordium such as that found in Hebrews 1:1-4 is to remind the audience of the common ground on which they stand—in this case christological common ground. The exordium also functions to make the listener sit up and take notice, be attentive and anticipate what will follow (*Rhetorica ad Herennium* 1.4.6; Quintilian *Institutio oratoria* 4.1.5), something our author accomplishes by both the exalted content and the elevated style and sound of Hebrews 1:1-4. And the audience could hardly object to God speaking directly to them through his Son. The chief object of praise in this discourse has been presented first.[119]

In his detailed rhetorical analysis of the structuring of periods within a long rhetorical sentence, Charles J. Robbins draws some important conclusions: (1) sentences like Hebrews 1:1-4 were not uncommon, especially in epideictic rhetoric, a classic example being found in Isocrates' *Orations* 4.47-49. As Cicero (*Orator* 207-8) points out: "In epideictic oratory . . . it is desirable to have everything done in the periodical style of Isocrates . . . so the language runs on as if enclosed in a circle until it comes to an end with each phrase complete and perfect." (2) Thus, it is not true that the colas and periods in this sentence are the way they are because of the content matter of the eulogy, for similar substance and similar structures are found in other parts of the New Testament that are not hymnic or prayers (e.g., the speeches in Acts). The form of this exordium is best explained on the basis of the rhetorical conventions the au-

---

[119]See the discussion in Koester, *Hebrews*, pp. 174-76.

thor is following (Aristotle *Rhetoric* 3.9). (3) What determines the length of the period within the extended sentence is the issue of how much one can say in one breath. According to Cicero: "It was failure or scantiness of breath that originated periodic structure and pauses between words; but now that this has once been discovered, it is so attractive that, even if a person were endowed with breath that never failed, we should still not wish him to deliver an unbroken flow of words; for our ears are only gratified by a style of delivery which is not merely endurable but also easy for the human lungs" (*De oratore* 3.46.181). Quintilian agrees (*Institutio oratoria* 9.4.125).[120] But if one was going to open with a sentence of this length, one needed to make sure it was pleasing to the ear. Thus our author serves up a liberal dose of alliteration, assonance, variation of word order and parallelism of sound and sense in Hebrews 1:1-4 so that the audience will be beguiled into listening to more of what the author wishes them to hear.[121]

We may compare the exordium in Hebrews 1:1-4 to the peroration in Hebrews 12:18-29, where we have even more vivid imagery of a theophany and where the deeper emotions of awe and even fear are inculcated to head off defection. The themes of God speaking through or in his Son the mediator and of his superiority to all other beings, which is announced in Hebrews 1:1-4, is picked up in Hebrews 12:24, where we hear of even his blood speaking more loudly than the blood of animals; and Hebrews 12:25 stresses, "See to it that you do not refuse him who speaks." It is not the priest or the sacrifice in Jerusalem, but the one in the heavenly Jerusalem to whom they should listen and to whom they should make pilgrimage. The angels referred to in Hebrews 1:4 are the worshiping angels in Hebrews 12:22, worshiping the Son. The themes announced in Hebrews 1:1-4 are echoed and amplified, bringing the discourse to a resounding conclusion. Having begun by citing a christological hymn fragment in Hebrews 1:1-4, the author finishes with a worship scene in Hebrews 12, which is exactly what one might expect in epideictic rhetoric that seeks to enthrall the audience and get them caught up in love, wonder and praise of the Christ once more.

> [1:1] *Partial and piecemeal/on many occasions and in many forms in the past God spoke to the ancestors through the prophets,* [2] *at the end of these days he spoke to us through his Son—*
>
> *Whom he appointed heir of all things,*
> *Through whom also he made the eons/universe;*
> [3] *Who being the radiance of glory*

---

[120]Robbins, "Composition of Eph 1:3-14."
[121]See Lane, *Hebrews*, 1.6, for a listing of the devices used here.

And the exact representation of his being,
Upholding all things by his powerful word;
Having made purification for sins,[122]
He sat down on the right hand of the Majesty on high,
[4]Having become as much better than the angels as he has,
(He) has inherited a more excellent name in comparison to them.

What a striking contrast this version of salvation history presents when we compare it to the similarly worded statement from a Jewish writer who witnessed the destruction of Jerusalem and its temple: "In former times, even in the generations of old, our fathers had helpers, righteous men and holy prophets. . . . But now the righteous have been gathered, and the prophets have fallen asleep. We also have gone forth from the land and Zion has been taken from us, and we have nothing now except the mighty one and his law" (*2 Baruch* 85.1, 3).

Hebrews 1:1 should not be seen as part of the christological hymn fragment, which does not begin until Hebrews 1:2. There is some debate as to how *polymerōs* and *polytropōs* should be translated. Some see here an emphasis on the myriads of times and ways God revealed himself to his people in previous ages, with the final and definitive revelation coming in the Son. These words are rather polyvalent, and *polytropōs* could be seen as just another way of saying "on many occasions" (Chrysostom *Patrologia graeca* 63.14).[123] Harold Attridge suggests that the basic sense of the first word is "fragmented or in multiple portions," whereas the latter term refers to "varied or multifaceted ways" (Wisdom of Solomon 7.22; Josephus *Jewish Antiquities* 10.142). Attridge also points out that the use of *poly-* was a common device in self-consciously rhetorical prologues (Demosthenes *Third Philippic* 110; cf. Lk 1:1; Sirach 1.1), and this sentence, sometimes said to be the most elegant prose in all the New Testament, is nothing if it is not an attempt to signal to the audience that the author is rhetorically adept and that his theme is a lofty one deserving the very highest forms of the art of persuasion.[124] Our author thinks of the whole of the Old Testament as prophetic in one sense or another and that God's revelation to his prophets was not continuous but intermittent.[125]

Very clearly our author operates with a concept of progressive revelation, but it is important that we understand what this means. Our author is not suggesting

---

[122]The phrase *di' autou* or *di' heautou* was a later addition meant to strength the force of the verb *made*, which is in the middle voice. The phrase is omitted in), A, B, 33, 81, though it is present 𝔓[46] and several others. See Metzger, *Textual Commentary*, p. 662.

[123]Koester, *Hebrews*, p. 177.

[124]Attridge, *Hebrews*, p. 37.

[125]Craddock, *Hebrews*, p. 22.

that what came before was bad. His comparison is between a good that was partial and piecemeal that came little by little and something better that came all at once in the Son. The comparison is between good and better, partial and definitive, ongoing and final, for our author, using the Septuagint phrase *the last days* to refer to the end times (Mic 4:1; Num 24:14), suggests that God has now offered his "last word"—the final revelation. The point he will be driving toward is that one dare not hand back God's final and definitive offer or neglect it. Now that one has received it, there can be no turning back. The phrase *in these last/final days* that begins **Hebrews 1:2** is eschatological to the core. It introduces passages that were read messianically in the author's era (Gen 49:1, 10; Num 24:14, 17; Hos 3:5) and are used in the Old Testament (Is 2:2; Mic 4:1; Hos 3:5; Dan 10:14), at Qumran (1QpHab [Habakkuk Commentary] 2.5; 1QSa [Rule of the Congregation] 1.1; 4QFlor [Florilegium] 1.12) and in the New Testament (Acts 2:17; 2 Tim 3:1) to talk about the eschatological age and more particularly about being in that age. 4QFlorilegium 1.15 begins an eschatological reading of Isaiah with "as it is written in the book of Isaiah the prophet concerning the latter days."

As in John 1, the hymn fragment found in the prologue of Hebrews is meant to make clear that God's revelation in his Son was full, final and definitive in a way that previous revelations were not and that no other beings, including angels, can compare to God's Son. This is conveyed in various ways, including the seven key phrases being predicated of the Son, and this is in turn followed by a catena of seven Old Testament texts indicating that Christ is the perfect one, the final fulfillment of things. The Son has more glory and a more excellent name and nature (being the exact representation of God), and he alone has made purification for sins, which is a major issue in this homily. This hymn fragment is part of one long Greek sentence in Hebrews 1:1-4 and involves alliteration and rhythm not evident in English translations.

While the author of Hebrews in the main calls Jesus the Son, in the hymn fragment he is called by no title; and it is striking that in none of the hymn fragments in the New Testament is Jesus called the Son (Jn 1; Phil 2:5-11; Col 1:15-20; 1 Tim 3:16). Sonship Christology seems to have arisen from some other source or quarter. One of the tip-offs that we are dealing with a quotation from a preexisting hymn fragment is that when the author alludes to Psalm 110:1 in Hebrews 1:3 he uses the genitival phrase *en dexia* (as in other allusions in Heb 8:1; 10:12; 12:2), but when he quotes Psalm 110:1 at Hebrews 1:13 we correctly have *ek dexiōn*, the dative form of the phrase. David Hay suggests that the allusions seem to be based on our author's memory of the liturgical confession or sung hymn.[126] Our author

---

[126]Hay, *Glory at the Right Hand*, pp. 35, 41.

has adopted and adapted the hymn text so that it has become a natural part of this larger sentence, which continues in Hebrews 1:4 beyond the echo of the hymn (which may be found only in Heb 1:2-3). The language of investiture and receiving not only a promise of inheritance but a new name may owe something to earlier investiture scenes, such as in Genesis 17:5, where Abraham receives both a new name and assurance that he has been appointed the father of many nations. By comparison, Jesus has been appointed heir of all creation.[127]

A variety of Old Testament texts are being drawn on to compose this hymn (e.g., Deut 32:43; Ps 2; 45:6-7; 104:4; 110:1), but the author is also steeped in later wisdom material such as that found in Wisdom of Solomon 7—9 (especially Wisdom of Solomon 7.25-26; 9.2, 9) and is saying of the Son and his glory what had been previously said of God's wisdom. In those texts wisdom is said to be "a breath of the power of God, . . . a pure emanation of the glory of the Almighty, . . . a reflection of eternal light, a spotless mirror of the working of God and an image of his goodness." The echoes of this Jewish sapiential tradition here were perfectly clear to Clement of Alexandria: "Christ is called Wisdom by all the prophets. This is he who is the teacher of all created beings, the fellow counselor of God who foreknew all things and he from above, from the first foundation of the world, 'in many and various ways' trains and perfects" (Stromateis 6.7).[128]

The hymn begins with the affirmation that God had a plan for the redeemer to be the inheritor of all things and furthermore to be the agent through whom God created the universe. Of course, there is a deliberate paradox in Hebrews 1:2 because ordinarily a son inherits when his father, who is the testator, dies. In this case the son inherits when the son dies![129] There is likely an echo here of Sirach 24.8, where it is said that wisdom receives an inheritance in Israel.

This verse features the theme of the Son as both aid in creation and inheritor of all things. He stands with God before all time and at the end of time as the creator, sustainer, redeemer and judge of all creation. He is involved in the creation of the eons (plural), which here likely means "worlds," not "ages" (but see Heb 6:5; 9:26), in light of Hebrews 11:3 and the indebtedness to the wisdom tradition (Wisdom of Solomon 13.9; 1 Cor 1:20; 2:6; 3:19). The similarity of motifs and concepts in all of these christological hymns shows that a core set of beliefs about Christ was widely shared in early Jewish Christianity and was propagated through the use of this hymnic material in various parts of the Di-

---

[127]Lane, Hebrews, 1.12; cf. Schenck, "Celebration of the Enthroned Son."
[128]See Witherington, Jesus the Sage, pp. 275-82, on drawing on wisdom literature to portray Christ here and elsewhere. Johnson, Hebrews, pp. 68-69, is quite right that the use of this material makes crystal clear that our author is asserting the divine status of the Son.
[129]Koester, Hebrews, p. 178.

aspora by Paul and others. Not only is the Christ involved in the beginning and end of all things, but he is the one upholding the universe by the word of his power. This is not dissimilar to the notion that in him all things cohere or hold together (Col 1:15-20). In other words, the author does not see the universe like a watch that God wound up and left to run on its own.

In terms of Christology, **Hebrews 1:3** is very important. "Both the form (participial style, [four] balanced clauses) and the content (the pattern of pre-existence, incarnation, and exaltation, the unique images of 'effulgence' and 'imprint') of this verse suggest that the author drew on an early Christian hymn, the vehicle through which such a high christology, based on the wisdom tradition, first emerged."[130] This verse contains two key terms: *apaugasma* and *charaktēr*. The former can be taken as active or passive, but in view of the background in Wisdom of Solomon 7.26 it is likely to be active and to mean "effulgence or radiance" rather than just reflection.[131] The connection between Hebrews 1:3 and Wisdom of Solomon 7.26 is rather secure since *apaugasma* is found in only these two texts in the whole of the Septuagint and New Testament! The difference between the two possible meanings of this Greek word is that a reflection is like a shadow, but not directly connected to the light source, whereas effulgence suggests a beam coming forth from that light source.

The normal referent of the second term, *charaktēr*, is to a stamp or impression a signet ring leaves on wax or that a stamping device would make on a coin; William Loader says that this term is being applied to the Son as the preexistent one who was involved in the creation of the universe.[132] The meaning would seem to be that the Son bears the exact likeness of God's nature. For example, in Philo the term refers to the impress left by a seal on wax or some other malleable substance (*On Drunkenness* 133). This material is remarkably close to Colossians 1:15-17, though with rearranged clauses.[133] In saying that the Son is the "impress of his being" or "bears the exact stamp/representation of his nature," the term *hypostasis* is brought into the discussion (see also Heb 3:14; 11:1), which, while it probably does not have its later technical or dogmatic sense of discrete entity/person within the Godhead, nonetheless the author is saying that the divine image and nature of God has been "stamped" onto the Son. Philo uses the term to refer to the substance of something that lies beneath the outward appearance (*On Dreams* 1.188). Clement of Rome was to find this passage

---

[130]Attridge, *Hebrews*, p. 41.
[131]Chrysostom, *Homilies on Hebrews* 2.2; Athanasius, *Four Discourses Against the Arians* 1.4.12.
[132]In other words, this is not a reference to Jesus being created in the image of God at the point of incarnation. See Loader, *Sohn und Hoherpriester*, p. 73.
[133]See the discussion in Witherington, *Philemon, Colossians and Ephesians*, ad loc.

sufficiently striking that he draws on it at length in *1 Clement* 36.

Steven Muir shows that the application of the terms in Hebrews 1:3 to Christ would have conjured up the use of the same terms of the emperor, particularly in regard to his image on coins. The implications for our study is that our author would be arguing that Christ is the reality, the true "image of God" in the flesh, of which the emperor is just the parody.[134] This discussion leads to the question of how our author views the relationship of the divine Son to God.

A CLOSER LOOK

God and the Son: The Question of Divine Identity

As Harold Attridge points out, on first blush, the author of Hebrews seems to treat God (as distinct from Christ) incidentally. Hebrews 6:1 suggests that faith in God need not be discussed at length with this audience of Jewish Christians.[135] Yet this initial impression turns out to be false. There is the mention right from the outset that God is the creator (Heb 1:1-4). There is also a stress, as Attridge notes, on God being the living God, the chief point of which is to make clear that God is a present and active judge of human conduct (Heb 3:12; 9:14; 10:31; 12:22). At Hebrews 12:29 God is famously called a consuming fire, echoing Deuteronomy 4:24. We may deduce, as Attridge suggests, that Hebrews 4:11 and its discussion of divine rest suggests that God is a Father who is intimately involved with and concerned about humankind. God is so involved and concerned about the fate of humankind that Hebrews 2:8-9 can speak about Christ tasting death for us "by the grace of God," which comports with Jesus' being perfected by God for his role as our heavenly high priest through suffering (Heb 2:10).

One of the most interesting of Attridge's observations is that while we hear of God speaking quite frequently to Jesus and of Jesus speaking to his followers, after Hebrews 10, God is not speaking to Jesus, and Jesus is quite silent. Thereafter God speaks only to the audience, for example, the citation of Habakkuk at Hebrews 10:37-38, the warning of catastrophe in Hebrews 12:26 or God's final word of promise ("I will never forsake you") in Hebrews 13:5. Before the end of Hebrews 10 the audience is allowed to listen in to the divine conversation between God and his Son and vice versa, and the impression left is that God's speech act is ongoing in the present. This comports with the author of Hebrews frequently using the present tense to introduce quotations from the Old Testament with phrases like "God says" or "the Spirit says" or

---

[134]Muir, "Use of Images in the Roman Imperial Cult."

[135]Here I am interacting with Attridge, "God in Hebrews"; and Bauckham, "Divinity of Jesus Christ."

"the Son says." Hebrews 1 depicts a pretemporal event in which the Father speaks to the Son, and in Hebrews 2:12-13 Jesus responds to God, proclaiming his trust in God, among other things.

God is also regularly depicted as one who swears (Heb 3:11), testifies (Heb 11:4), makes promises (Heb 6:13), calls (Heb 11:4), is not ashamed (Heb 11:16) and moves and shakes earthly things (Heb 12:26). In short, God is depicted as intimately involved in creation, redemption, final judgment, revelation, prophecy and its fulfillment. Attridge is right to conclude that the author of Hebrews speaks using many and diverse images of God, and one is left with the impression that God is always taking the initiative. Attridge concludes that our author's images of God are not distinctive from other New Testament witnesses in these regards. In light of all this, one may well wonder what our author's view of the Son might be in relationship to the Father.

Richard Bauckham suggests that like other New Testament witnesses, our author includes Jesus within the unique identity of God as understood in Second Temple Judaism. In other words, the defining characteristics predicated of God during that period are predicated of Jesus by our author. The Son is said to be the creator of all things, is said to be the ruler over all things, is known through his self-revelation in history and will achieve his eschatological goal and rule upon the earth. Furthermore, the Son is given the divine name, is said to be included in the audience's sole object of worship and is said to be eternal. Bauckham demonstrates at length how all these things that were predicated of the Father are also predicated of the Son in Hebrews. Bauckham's major thesis is that the main categories of identity for Jesus—Son, Lord, high priest—require that Jesus share both the divine identity and the human identity as well. Though Christ's priestly role highlights his humanity in various regards, it also stresses the everlasting nature of his sacrifice and other noncreaturely traits. In order to achieve his christological aims, our author is creative in the way he handles the Septuagint. For example, Bauckham points out that in the sixth quotation fragment in Hebrews 1:10 the author changed the order of the first three words from the Septuagint so it now reads "you in the beginning, Lord," thus making clear that Christ is being addressed in these terms and that Christ was there when the creation was made. Equally remarkable is Hebrews 7:3, where "true God" language is used, not merely of that shadowy figure Melchizedek, but more properly of the one who is after his order—Jesus, who turns out to be the model for Melchizedek, being without end of days. As Bauckham stresses, this language was used to distinguish true gods in Hellenistic literature from those who are merely semidivine. Jesus is seen to be on the divine side of the ledger. We should not then be surprised when we are told that Jesus sat down on God's throne when he entered heaven after having completed his sacrificial

work (Heb 10:12). As Bauckham stresses, the significance of this language is
that it indicates that Jesus participates in the unique sovereignty of God over
the entire world. The christological reformulation of what it means to affirm
that God is one is fully operational in Hebrews. But intriguingly, this does not
lead our author to affirm that the Son is the Father, nor should we simply amalgamate Son and Father. Only the Son dies on the cross and offers the sacrifice,
and, as Attridge shows, there is still a robust role for the Father to play in the
divine economy according to Hebrews. The Father is not eclipsed by the Son,
rather the divine identity is expressed on earth by the Son. Father and Son work
in tandem as part of the divine economy, the unique divine identity that expresses itself in more than one personal form. Few New Testament documents
provide more balance to the discussion of both the human and divine natures
of the Son, and perhaps Hebrews most clearly and emphatically affirms a high
or divine Christology among all the New Testament witnesses. Not surprisingly
then at the close of this great sermon our author emphatically tells us that Jesus
is the same yesterday, today and forever. His character is unchanging, unlike
all merely human beings.

While the author does not want to lead his audience to call the redeemer the
Father, he does want to make clear that the redeemer is divine and is God's final
self-expression and exact representation and is thus higher than any angel in
nature. The Son is not merely an act or power of God but a person who is the
spitting image of the Father and so is to be worshiped as no mere angel should
be. Chrysostom puts it this way: "For if he is Son only by grace, he not only is
not 'more excellent than the angels' but is even less than they" (*Homilies on Hebrews* 2.2). One of the ways that the Son's divine nature is made clear is by the
regular use of the term *doxa* to describe his character as well as his exalted existence in heaven, something that is especially emphasized at the outset of this
discourse (Heb 2:7, 9; 3:3; 13:21). In saying that the Son sustains all created
things, we should probably hear an echo of Wisdom of Solomon 7.27, where it
is said that because of wisdom's purity she pervades all things: "While remaining
in herself, she renews all things." Or we may compare Philo's remarks on the
logos as the instrument through which God sustains the world (*On the Migration
of Abraham* 6; *On Flight and Finding* 112).

It may be right, as many conclude, that this hymn is a rejoinder to those who
wished to see Christ as some sort of special angelic being, but it is also possible
that our author is stressing that the new covenant is superior to the one mediated by angels, namely the Mosaic covenant (Gal 3:19; Acts 7:53; *Jubilees* 1.29),
because this one is mediated by a divine being, not merely a supernatural one.

It is striking that the author withholds the human name of the redeemer until Hebrews 2:9, perhaps because he understood that the redeemer was, properly speaking, not Jesus until he took on a human nature.

Various scholars note the closeness between this hymn and the one in Philippians 2 on Christ's obedience. In Philippians, however, his obedience is discussed as an aspect of his relationship to the Father, while here it is discussed in relationship to the way it benefits the Christian community. The discussion of purification followed by the sitting down of the Son at God's right hand requires knowledge of sacrificial practices in antiquity. It entails seeing sin as something that defiles and that therefore one needs cleansing of, an idea expressed in similar terms in the Septuagint (Ex 29:37; 30:10; Lev 16:19). Job 7:21 is an interesting parallel, where Job laments to God: "Why do you not forget my offense and make cleansing for my sin *[epoiēso . . . katharismon tēs hamartias mou]*?" Our author's point is that the purification that the Son made was once for all time and so did not require repetition. Brooke Foss Westcott suggests that purification for sin, rather than purification of the effects of sin, is in view here, though the latter is spoken of in Hebrews 9:14.[136] He is likely right, for the verb *made* here is in the middle voice, suggesting that he made the purification in himself—that is, in his sacrifice and so not in something distinct from himself, for instance, not later in the believer. The use of the term *katharismos* is rare in the New Testament as a way of talking about Christ's atoning death, but we do find it also at 2 Peter 1:9. While other priests had to stand and repeatedly offer sacrifices, this priest did the job in such a definitive and final way that he could sit down thereafter (Heb 10:11-18). Here our author may be drawing on Sirach 24.10, where wisdom ministers before God in the earthly temple. What is hinted at here in these short, packed phrases will be expanded on in Hebrews 9—10. One of the functions of the exordium is to be a preview of coming attractions.

The author's own distinctive christological thrusts can be seen and are served here as well, for he wishes to say that Christ is the believers' heavenly high priest even now, and that he is a forever priest, since he is an eternal being. Our author combines various christological insights at the end of this hymn, in particular combining the preexistent-wisdom Christology with Christology of the enthronement of the Son at or after the resurrection.[137] Some see here the idea that Christ is presented as prophet, priest and king from the outset. The problematic part of that deduction here is the phrase *spoken in/through his Son*. The idea is probably not focusing on Christ's own prophetic speech (that would require

---

[136]Westcott, *Hebrews*, p. 15.
[137]Meier, "Structure and Theology."

"spoken *by* his Son"), but on Christ himself being the revelation on earth, the very speech of God, revealing what God has in mind. Jesus' priestly and royal aspect is the special focus, coupled with the notion that Jesus is the revelation or word of God come to earth.

The end of the hymn stresses God's endorsement of what the Son has done. Not only is he given the favored right-hand seat, the side of honor and power next to a ruler, but he is given a divine or throne name as well. This theme of receiving a name is also found in Philippians 2, though in Hebrews 1 we are not told explicitly what the name is, only that it is a higher name than angels could have. Here the emphasis is on *inheriting* a better name.

The Greek term *kreissōn/kreittōn* ("better") in **Hebrews 1:4** is a recurrent one in this work and characterizes one of the major things our author wants to say about any comparisons between what has come before and what is now the case in Christ. Not only is the Son said to be "better" (Heb 1:4) and to be a better Melchizedek (Heb 7:7), so are the salvation now on offer (Heb 6:9), the future hope (Heb 7:19; 11:16, 35, 40), the new covenant (Heb 7:22; 8:6), the promises (Heb 8:6) or present possession of them (Heb 10:34) and the sacrifice of Christ (Heb 9:23; 12:24) all proclaimed to be better. The Greek fathers stressed that this term indicates difference of kind and not just of degree (Athanasius *Orations Against the Arians* 1.59).[138]

From a rhetorical viewpoint, our author signals in Hebrews 1:4 that he will use in his discourse the comparative or a fortiori sort of rhetorical argument (Heb 2:2-3; 3:5-6; 7:20-23; 9:13-14; 10:25). These sorts of arguments where one chooses to persuade by showing how much better one thing is than another (without denying the goodness of the other thing) were common in both deliberative and epideictic rhetoric (Aristotle *Rhetoric* 2.23; Cicero *De oratore* 2.40.170).

The concept of a messianic figure not being called such until he has completed his work is found elsewhere in *Testament of Levi* 4.2-3 and *3 Enoch* 12. The influence of *1 Enoch* 42.1-2 (where wisdom takes her seat among, but as one superior to, the angels when she returns from earth to heaven) and Wisdom of Solomon 9.4 (where wisdom sits beside God's throne) is also possible at the end of this hymn. The reference to the seat at the right hand of God is clearly an allusion to Psalm 110:1, since nowhere else in the Old Testament do we hear about someone enthroned beside God, one of the most crucial texts for our author and for many New Testament authors in their attempt to grasp the full significance of the Christ event. It is too much to call all of Hebrews a "midrash"

---

[138]See the discussion in Westcott, *Hebrews*, p. 17.

(i.e., Jewish linguistic interpretation method) on Psalm 110 but "this scriptural text is of capital importance both for the literary structure and for the conceptuality of Hebrews."[139] The Jewish reverential circumlocution for God here—the Son sat down at the right hand of the Majesty (Heb 8:1; Jude 25; Ps 78:11; Deut 32:3; 1 Chron 29:11; *Testament of Levi* 3.9)—requires an in-depth look at the mostly christological use of the Psalms in the New Testament.

A CLOSER LOOK

The Psalms in Hebrews and Elsewhere in the New Testament
and Their Christological Use

The study of the use of the Old Testament in the New Testament continues to be a work in progress. The book of Psalms is quoted many times in the New Testament, and a few special verses from the Psalms come in for repeated use in both the New Testament in general and Hebrews in particular. For instance, Psalm 110:1 is referred to in the Synoptics, Acts, Romans, 1 Corinthians, Ephesians, Colossians and in abundance in Hebrews, as seen in the following list of Psalms quotations in the New Testament.[140] What sets the use in Hebrews apart is that our author goes on to the next step and applies Psalm 110:4 to Jesus, dubbing him a priest after the order of Melchizedek (Heb 7:1-22). The following list allows us to see that the author of Hebrews is not anomalous in his way of using the Psalms.

Psalms Reference	New Testament Reference	Notes
Psalm 2:1-2	Acts 4:25-26	royal psalm spoken by Holy Spirit through David, applied to Christ and his encounter with Pilate and Herod
Psalm 2:1-2	Revelation 11:17-18	God who brings wrath
Psalm 2:7 (with Is 55:3; Ps 16:10)	Acts 13:33	Christ as God's Son, who did not decay; cf. Psalm 45:6-7 below
Psalm 2:7	Hebrews 1:5; 5:5	Jesus as God's Son
Psalm 2:8-9	Revelation 2:26-27; 12:5; 19:15	applied to the saints who will be conquerors and rule (Rev 2) or to Jesus (Rev 12; 19)
Psalm 4:4	Ephesians 4:26	ethical exhortation to the Ephesians

---

[139]Attridge, *Hebrews*, p. 46.
[140]Loader, "Christ at the Right Hand"; and Hay, *Glory at the Right Hand*.

Psalms Reference	New Testament Reference	Notes
Psalm 5:9 (with Ps 14:1-3; 53:1-3; Eccles 7:20; Ps 140:3; 10:7; Is 59:7-8; 36:1)	Romans 3:13	condition of all of world's Jews and Gentiles and sinners is as the psalmist said ("as it is written"); seems to be a testimonia
Psalm 6:8	Matthew 7:23; Luke 13:27	Jesus using biblical language to describe his experience; in psalm of the psalmist
Psalm 8:2	Matthew 21:16	Jesus interprets infant's praise of himself; in psalm of God
Psalm 8:4-6	Hebrews 2:6-8	testified of Jesus; he is the "son of man"
Psalm 8:6	1 Corinthians 15:27; Ephesians 1:22	of Jesus in future
Psalm 10:7	Romans 3:14	see Psalm 5:9 above
Psalm 14:1-3	Romans 3:10-12	see Psalm 5:9 above
Psalm 16:8-11	Acts 2:25-28, 31	of Christ; in psalm of God
Psalm 16:10	Acts 13:35	see Psalm 2:7 above
Psalm 18:49 and 2 Samuel 22:50 (with Deut 32:43; Ps 117:1; Is 11:10)	Romans 15:9	testimonia about Gentiles; catchword *ethnē*
Psalm 19:4 (with Is 53:1; Deut 32:21; Is 65:1)	Romans 10:18	testimonia with theme: those who heard the message and who received it; Jews and Gentiles (possibly *laos/ethnē* as a catchword)
Psalm 19:9	Revelation 16:7; 19:2	Old Testament catchphrase expressing something always true of God's nature
Psalm 22:1	Matthew 27:46; Mark 15:34	Jesus from cross; in psalm of psalmist
Psalm 22:7-8	Matthew 27:39; Mark 15:29; Luke 23:35	two robbers die with Jesus
Psalm 22:8	Matthew 27:43	chief priest questions Jesus, who said, "I am Son"
Psalm 22:13	1 Peter 5:8	Satan as a lion roaring, looking for someone to devour; not a quotation
Psalm 22:15	John 19:28	"I am thirsty" (cf. Ps 69:21)
Psalm 22:18	Matthew 27:35; Mark 15:24	casting lots for clothes
Psalm 22:21	2 Timothy 4:17	Paul using scriptural language of himself: "I was delivered from lion's mouth"; not fulfillment

Psalms Reference	New Testament Reference	Notes
Psalm 22:22	Hebrews 2:12, 17	as if Jesus is speaking the psalm; declare name to brethren
Psalm 23:1-2	Revelation 7:17	Jesus as shepherd who leads by still waters
Psalm 24:1 (with Ps 50:12)	1 Corinthians 10:26	because earth is the Lord's, all food is acceptable to eat
Psalm 31:5	Luke 23:46	Jesus speaking David's words of himself commends himself into God's hands
Psalm 32:1-2	Romans 4:7-8	proof-text for justification by faith
Psalm 33:3	Revelation 5:9; 14:3	"new song"
Psalm 34:8	1 Peter 2:3	biblical language describing Christian experience
Psalm 34:12-16	1 Peter 3:10-12	ethical exhortation
Psalm 34:20	John 19:36	"not a one of his bones broken" in fulfillment of Scripture
Psalm 35:19	John 15:25	"they hated him without reason" in fulfillment of Scripture
Psalm 36:1	Romans 3:18	see Psalm 5:9 above
Psalm 37:11	Matthew 5:5	"meek will inherit land" in psalm
Psalm 40:6-8	Hebrews 10:5-11	as if the words of Christ
Psalm 41:9	John 13:18	"he who shared my bread lifted up his heel" in fulfillment of Scripture
Psalm 42:5, 11 (with Ps 43:5)	Matthew 26:38; Mark 14:34	"my soul is overwhelmed with sorrow"
Psalm 43:5	Matthew 26:38; Mark 14:34	see Psalm 42:5 above
Psalm 44:22	Romans 8:36	Jesus using scriptural language of his own experience of suffering
Psalm 45:6-7 (with Ps 2:7; 2 Sam 7:14; Deut 32:43; Ps 104:4; 102:25-27; 110:1)	Hebrews 1:8-9	testimonium about Christ—God speaks of "Son": "your throne, O God, will last forever"
Psalm 48:2	Matthew 5:35	earth as God's footstool; use of psalm to speak of a truth about God
Psalm 50:12	1 Corinthians 10:26	see Psalm 24:1 above
Psalm 50:14, 23	Matthew 5:33; Hebrews 13:15	Matthew is a quotation; Hebrews offers sacrifice of prayer
Psalm 51:4	Romans 3:4	"as it is written": God is true and right, as psalmist says
Psalm 53:1-3	Romans 3:10-12	see Psalm 5:9 above

Psalms Reference	New Testament Reference	Notes
Psalm 55:22	1 Peter 5:7	ethical exhortation: "cast all your anxiety"
Psalm 68:18	Ephesians 4:8	of Christ when he ascended
Psalm 69:4	John 15:25	royal psalm; cf. Psalm 35:19 above
Psalm 69:9	John 2:17; Romans 15:3	"it is written"; disciples remembered: "zeal for my house" of temple cleansing
Psalm 69:21	Matthew 27:34; Mark 15:36 and parallels	vinegar for thirst; fulfillment of Scripture (cf. Ps 22:15)
Psalm 69:22-23	Romans 11:9-10	used of apostate Israel due to their reaction to Christ; in psalm of enemies of the psalmist
Psalm 69:25 (with Ps 109:8)	Acts 1:20	of Judas's being replaced: "it is written in psalm"; example of midrash pesher?
Psalm 69:28	Revelation 3:5; 17:8; 20:12; 21:27	blotted out of book of life; in psalm of living enemies; in Revelation of book of eternal life (Lamb's book)
Psalm 75:8	Revelation 14:10	wine of wrath; those who worship the beast drink wine of wrath; in psalm all wicked drink it
Psalm 78:2	Matthew 13:35	"I will open my mouth in parables"; in Matthew fulfillment of what the "prophet" said (Psalms is considered written prophecy)
Psalm 78:24 (with Ps 105:40)	John 6:31	"as it is written"; "he gave them bread from heaven to eat"
Psalm 82:6	John 10:34	"it is written"; "I have said you are gods"
Psalm 86:8-10	Revelation 3:9; 15:4	Jesus' words; all nations will come and worship at *your* feet; *your* in psalm refers to God; *your* in Revelation refers to saints
Psalm 89:3-4	Acts 2:30	David as a prophet knew God would place a descendent on the throne; in Acts an allusion to the text speaking of Christ
Psalm 89:26-27 (with 2 Sam 7:14)	Hebrews 1:5	"I will be his Father"; in Hebrews spoken of Christ; in psalm of David
Psalm 89:27	Revelation 1:5	in Revelation Jesus as firstborn from the dead, ruler of earth's kings; in psalm David is the firstborn, most exalted of kings on earth
Psalm 90:4	2 Peter 3:8	"one thousand years as one day"; 2 Peter adds the converse
Psalm 91:11-12	Matthew 4:6; Luke 4:10-11	devil quotes Scripture; he commands angels to guard; in psalm used of any believer

Psalms Reference	New Testament Reference	Notes
Psalm 91:13	Luke 10:19	authority to trample on snakes and overcome enemy; Jesus to disciples; in psalm to believers in general
Psalm 94:11	1 Corinthians 3:20	"the Lord knows the thoughts of the wise'; in psalm used of "humankind"
Psalm 94:14	Romans 11:1-2	God will not reject; scriptural language to speak of Israel
Psalm 95:7-8	Hebrews 4:7	"through David he said . . ."
Psalm 95:7-11	Hebrews 3:7-11	simple quotation applied to the church rather than Israel: "today if you hear my voice"
Psalm 95:11	Hebrews 4:3	Hebrews speaks of believers who do not enter rest; psalm speaks of wilderness generation who did not
Psalm 97:7	Hebrews 1:6	Hebrews speaks of Christ worshiped by angels; psalm speaks of Yahweh
Psalm 102:25-27	Hebrews 1:10-12	see Psalm 45:6-7 above
Psalm 103:8 (cf. Ps 111:4)	James 5:11	God full of compassion and mercy; simple allusion
Psalm 104:4	Hebrews 1:7	see Psalm 45:6-7 above
Psalm 105:40	John 6:31	see Psalm 78:24 above
Psalm 106:20	Romans 1:23	exchanged glory for the image of a bull; alluded to in Romans
Psalm 109:8	Acts 1:20	see Psalm 69:25 above
Psalm 109:25	Matthew 27:39; Mark 15:29	taunting by adversaries of Christ described in language of taunters of psalmist
Psalm 110:1	Mark 12:36 and parallels; 14:62; 16:19; Acts 2:34-35; 1 Corinthians 15:25; Ephesians 1:20; Colossians 3:1; Hebrews 1:13; 8:1; 10:12-13; 12:2	most used single psalm verse for christological purposes and in all types of New Testament material; "sits at the right hand" presumably refers to king in the psalm, seen as prince regent, next to God, who is the real king; see Psalm 45:6-7 above
Psalm 110:4	Hebrews 5:6—7:17; 7:27	"you are a priest after the order of Melchizedek"; unique to Hebrews, applied to Christ
Psalm 111:4	James 5:11	see Psalm 103:8 above
Psalm 112:9	2 Corinthians 9:9	he has scattered abroad his gifts to poor; simple quotation; of Christians whom God takes care of

Psalms Reference	New Testament Reference	Notes
Psalm 115:4-7	Revelation 9:20	allusion, not quotation, to idols and their makeup (cf. Ps 135:15-17)
Psalm 115:13	Revelation 11:18; 19:5	saints who revere name, small and great; scriptural language
Psalm 116:10	2 Corinthians 4:13	different second half of quotation: "it is written"
Psalm 117:1	Romans 15:11	see Psalm 18:49 above
Psalm 118:6 (with Deut 31:6)	Hebrews 13:6	simple quotation; direct analogy
Psalm 118:22-23 (with Is 28:16; 8:14)	Mark 12:10 and parallels; Acts 4:17; 1 Peter 2:7	testimonia using catchword 'eben ("stone")
Psalm 118:25-26	Mark 11:9-10 and parallels; John 12:13	"blessed is he who comes in the name"
Psalm 118:26	Matthew 23:39; Luke 13:35; 19:38	Jesus of himself
Psalm 132:5	Acts 7:46	simple quotation about David wanting to build the temple
Psalm 132:11	Acts 2:30	simple allusion
Psalm 135:15-17	Revelation 9:20	see Psalm 115:4-7 above
Psalm 137:8	Revelation 18:6	allusion, but in reference to Rome
Psalm 137:9	Luke 19:44	Jesus refers to Jerusalem's children; originally of enemies' children
Psalm 140:3	Romans 3:13	see Psalm 5:9 above
Psalm 143:2	Romans 3:10; Galatians 2:16	scriptural language to speak of something else
Psalm 146:6	Acts 4:24; 14:15; Revelation 10:6	allusion to God making everything

Roughly speaking there seem to be seven or eight basic ways that New Testament writers used the Old Testament, and almost all of these uses serve the cause of making the point that Jesus is the Christ or that the church is the fulfillment of God's people and plan of salvation. In other words, the Old Testament is read through christocentric or ecclesiocentric glasses. The boldness of the hermeneutical move is much clearer when material from the Psalms or the Prophets is cited to make some point about Jesus' birth, life, death, resurrection or current roles in heaven or future roles at the eschaton.[141]

---

[141]See the still useful studies by Black, "Christological Use of the Old Testament"; and Mc-Cullough, "Some Recent Developments," pp. 28-35.

In my view the christological interpretation goes back to Jesus in various ways, but also more broadly back to early Jewish messianic readings of the Old Testament. The church simply followed the example of Jesus and other early Jews who were messianic minded. Luke 24 suggests that the risen Jesus taught his followers to interpret the Old Testament christologically, but it is believable that he did some of this even before his crucifixion, since he had a messianic self-understanding.

A second crucial point is that the events in the life of Jesus and the experiences of the risen Christ led Jewish Christians like the author of Hebrews to go scurrying back to the Old Testament to interpret these occurrences, many of which they had not anticipated. I do not agree with the view that portions of the gospel stories were created out of a pastiche of Old Testament texts, as if the gospel narrative was prophecy historicized. This hardly explains why the prophetic texts are used in such extraordinary and elastic ways to explain these gospel events. Of course, New Testament events are often couched in the language of Old Testament ones. There are deliberate echoes of older stories. And the Old Testament is used often to explain New Testament events. Neither of these hermeneutical moves, however, provides evidence that the story itself is generated out of Old Testament texts.

Our New Testament writers, including the author of Hebrews, were utterly convinced they lived in the eschatological age, that is, in the age of fulfillment of various promises, prophecies, Old Testament institutions.[142] In light of this, it was only natural for them to look for correspondences, sometimes even very tenuous ones, between the experiences of God's people as recorded in the Old Testament and the experiences of Jesus and his followers.

The use of the Old Testament in Hebrews and elsewhere in the New Testament can be categorized as follows:

1. moral or ethical use—especially imperatives, but also stories of Old Testament saints to make a parenetic point (as in Heb 11)

2. typological use

3. allegorical or allegorizing use

4. prophecy fulfillment use

5. testimonia use

6. midrash use—following the pattern of Jewish exegesis, especially involving catchword or keyword connections

---

[142]See the discussion by Barrett, "Eschatology of the Epistle to the Hebrews."

7. pesher use—"this is that," especially to elucidate how Christ fulfills various aspects of the Old Testament[143]

8. homiletical use[144]

David Hay points to Romans 15:4 as indicating some of the controlling assumptions behind these uses of the Old Testament, namely, that Christ is the key who unlocks the correct interpretation of the Old Testament and that all the Old Testament is fulfilled in him or in his people. In addition, the further belief that all Scripture was written especially for the instruction of God's people in the eschatological age when they would most need such instruction also controlled New Testament interpretation of the Old Testament.[145] Furthermore, a pneumatic component may be operative, which assumes that without the Holy Spirit one is not going to see these connections and fulfillments (2 Cor 3:14-16).

There seems as well to be the assumption that the Old Testament can be properly understood and handled only by those for whom it was written, namely, Christ's people. For example, 1 Peter 1:10-12 not only says that the prophets were told they were speaking to and about the messianic one yet to come and to the eschatological generation of believers, it also says that the prophets were serving the audience of 1 Peter, not themselves. The audience of 1 Peter is said to have had things revealed to them that even angels had longed to know about but had not been previously told of. In other words, the followers of Jesus are those for whom all these things were written, those who can understand them through listening to the gospel and following the guidance of the Spirit. This hermeneutical move can be called "completionist," if we believe that the church of Jew and Gentile in Christ is the continuation of the Old Testament people of God in the eschatological age, but non-Christian Jews, especially today, are bound to see this as supercessionist rhetoric.

This survey of the use of Psalms in the New Testament shows that sometimes the authors follow a grammatico-historical form of exegesis, but sometimes this is not the case, for example, our author's use of the Melchizedek typology or Paul's allegorizing of the story of Sarah and Hagar in Galatians 4.

---

[143]A christocentric or christological interpretation is possible with any or all of these approaches.

[144]While several of these hermeneutical moves could be placed in category 8, since the issue is not historical interpretation of "what it meant," I use the phrase *homiletical use* to refer to the simple use of scriptural language to describe one's own experience. For example, in Rom 15:21 Paul uses the Old Testament to describe his own experience, knowing perfectly well that that text was not written about him in the first place. He is convinced that such things repeatedly happen in the divine economy, and so this language could be applied to him as well as it its original referent. God—being the same God he always was—is free to recapitulate in Paul's experience what has happened before to others.

[145]Hay, *Glory at the Right Hand*.

One must keep steadily in view that, as was the case at Qumran, the New Testament interpretations of the Old Testament reflect an eschatologically aware group of interpreters, looking for explanations for their own experiences in light of the Old Testament. These interpreters are profoundly convinced that the Old Testament speaks to them directly and even that it was ultimately written for them and for their understanding.

The use of the Psalms in the New Testament is in some sense mostly christological in character, especially as an explanation of what has been true of Christ from the time of the Passion events onward. The author of Hebrews is especially concerned to use the Psalms to explain Christ's present roles in heaven, as heavenly high priest. But since a new view of Messiah also meant a new view of self, history, the future, it would be wrong to too radically distinguish between christological and ecclesiological uses of the Old Testament.

Interpreters like the author of Hebrews began with their experience of Christ and of his people and went back to the Old Testament to explain both. There is a certain circularity to the mode of argumentation. Scriptures show Jesus to be God's Son, but Christ is also used as the key to properly interpreting those Scriptures, and this latter move is the starting point for such interpreters. Christ is the irreplaceable and irreducible element; the Scriptures can be interpreted variously. Clearly enough, it did not trouble writers like the author of Hebrews or Luke in Luke-Acts that they were relying on the Septuagint, not the Hebrew Bible. The assumption is that the Septuagint was just as inspired and authoritative as the Hebrew version.

The complex matter of the Greek version used by New Testament authors is variously assessed.[146] Various Greek translations and revisions of the Old Testament existed from the fourth century B.C. to the fourth century A.D., and our surviving manuscripts are mixed texts (i.e., they were compiled or composed from several different translations). Moisés Silva presents a detailed study of one particular case involving Hebrews 11:21.[147] He concludes that the author presupposes a haggadah (a narrative expansion/exposition of the story) concerning Jacob's staff and so deliberately uses the Septuagint to make a theological point, because the Septuagint version incorporates a further Jewish interpretation of the Jacob story not found in the original Hebrew text. More is going on in Hebrews than simply looking up the Septuagint and citing it where appropriate; there is much we cannot understand until more manuscripts come to light and more study is done of the various Greek versions of the Old Testament.

---

[146]A good place to start the discussion is Hengel's *Septuagint as Christian Scripture.*
[147]Silva, "Perfection and Eschatology in Hebrews."

As we draw this discussion to a close, it will be well to highlight what a close study of the quotations and allusions to the Psalms in Hebrews and elsewhere can tell us. First, there is a heavy concentration of the royal psalms when talking about Jesus or his career, especially Psalm 110:1. Second, discussion of events that occurred during the last week of Jesus' life, especially his death, shows a heavy concentration of usage of the Psalms, in part because those events needed the most explanation, documentation, justification. For example, it is frequently said that a fulfillment of Scripture explains why this or that event happened (Jn 13:18; 15:25; 19:36); in other places the formula *it is written* (Jn 2:17; 6:31; 10:34) serves the same purpose. Third, allusions to the Psalms can carry as much weight—and do as much to shape what is said in a New Testament passage—as quotations.[148] This point is especially pertinent in Revelation, with its myriad of allusions but only a few direct citations. Revelation is an even more Scripture saturated book than Hebrews, but one would not know this just by consulting a list of Old Testament citations in the book.

A further key point is that the author of Hebrews is by no means alone in thinking that the Psalms should be seen in a prophetic light and that David, the putative author of the Psalms, should be seen as a prophet (Mt 13:35; Acts 2:30). The Psalms are often used to produce a christological catena or testimonia (Heb 1:5-14; Rom 10:18-21). It appears clear that New Testament authors saw the Psalms as more user-friendly for christological purposes than many other portions of the Old Testament. Typological use of the Psalms is not limited to the author of Hebrews, but it is typical of his use (e.g., Ps 8:4-6 in Heb 2:6-8, which refers to Jesus as the Son of Man; the same use of various Old Testament texts may be seen in 1 Cor 10). My point is that the author of Hebrews is not operating in a vacuum in the way he uses the Old Testament, but rather is part of a community of Christian interpreters, of which he is one of the most adept.

Finally, especially important for our author is the technique of transference—things said in the Old Testament of Yahweh are now said of Christ (Heb 1:6 quoting Ps 97:7)—but again this is also found elsewhere in the New Testament (e.g., Rev 7:17, where Jesus is said to be the Good Shepherd of Ps 23:1-3). Transference is the most frequent technique used in Hebrews—statements about David are now statements about Jesus, statements about God are now statements about Jesus, statements about humankind in general (e.g., Ps 8) are now applicable to Jesus, statements about Israel are now statements about Jesus' followers, perhaps especially the Jewish Christians among them. This suggests that pesher (the "this is that" technique) as much guides the author

---

[148]See, for example, Hays, *Echoes of Scripture in Paul.*

of Hebrews in his interpretation of the Old Testament as typology does.

As we conclude this discussion it will be useful to interact with two influential treatments of the use of the Old Testament in Hebrews that to some degree overlap and confirm what I have been saying. J. C. McCullough's extensive study of the use of the Old Testament in Hebrews concludes that our author treats the Old Testament as a sacred text. Our author has great respect for the Septuagint and alters it only to emphasize what he considers the text's more salient points or to fit a quotation more smoothly into a context in the homily. On other occasions he makes alterations for clarification—to avoid ambiguity in a passage: "These changes, however, did not involve, for the author, a change of meaning in the passage and he did not depend on them to justify his particular interpretation of any passage. . . . He showed a reverent and cautious attitude to his text which contrasts starkly with that found among many of his contemporaries. He avoided the pneumatic rewriting of passages which the sectaries of Qumran considered to be part of the work of an interpreter of Scripture."[149] Our author believes the Old Testament to be divine oracles relevant to the readers of his day, and thus they had to be interpreted and made understandable, not for arcane purpose or due to intellectual curiosity, but because they still had a message from God for the author's New Testament audience. J. W. Thompson also shows that our author tends to quote rather fully with few exegetical comments. He subtly reaudiences and recontextualizes these texts with just a word or line of introduction or even a question.[150]

I have no quibbles or qualms with these remarks, and they demonstrate not only the great reverence our author had for the Old Testament, but also that hermeneutically he was not as much of a radical or maverick as he is sometimes portrayed. There is reason, however, to object to some of Thompson's conclusions about the catena of Old Testament texts in Hebrews 1:5-14.

What is the point of these seven quotations of the Old Testament? Rather clearly as Thompson points out, their major function is to provide support for and further the argument that the Son is superior to angels. This argument does not seem to be necessary, however, until we reach the parenesis in Hebrews 2:1-4, where it is implied that the angels as mediators of the old revelation, in particular the Mosaic covenant, pale in comparison to the Son, who is both the mediator and the message of the new covenant.

The catena assumes the Son's exaltation, and Thompson may be correct that the controlling text, here as elsewhere in Hebrews, is Psalm 110:1.[151] Obviously our author had reflected deeply on this text, for it is also probably the

[149]McCullough, "Old Testament Quotations in Hebrews," pp. 378-79.
[150]Thompson, "Hermeneutics of the Epistle to the Hebrews."
[151]Also Thompson, *Beginnings of Christian Philosophy*.

partial source of his Melchizedek material (cf. Ps 110:4) and is alluded to in
Hebrews 1:3; 5:6, 10; 6:20; 7:3, 11, 15, 17, 21, 24, 28; 10:12-13; 12:2. But Thompson is wrong that it is strictly on the basis of the exaltation that the Son is
seen as superior to the angels, for in Hebrews 1:10-12 he is also spoken of as
a creator. There is throughout an implied contrast between the transitory nature of the created order and the Son who is part of the eternal order of things,
both from the beginning of things and due to his exaltation to heaven. The
created order passes away, wears out, changes, but the Son remains—and perhaps more importantly remains the same. Thus the point is not just his ongoing eternal existence but his unchanging character. In order to stress this point
at Hebrews 1:12 our author alters the Septuagint's future "will remain" to the
present "remain." Very clearly, everything found in Hebrews 1:5-14 serves as
the presupposition and foundation for the parenesis in Hebrews 2:1-4, which
begins "because of this" (i.e., because of what has just been argued). The
Scripture citation then can serve both theological and ethical purposes in the
hands of our author.

Something should be said about the comment in Hebrews 1:4 that the Son
has inherited a more excellent name. This theme of the name that Christ is given
at his exaltation is also found in Philippians 2:5-11 (cf. Eph 1:20; 1 Pet 3:22), and
the name in question is not "Jesus" but rather the divine name, *kyrios*, as may
be implied here but is made explicit in Philippians 2, though the title "Son"
could also be in view here. As Harold Attridge points out, our author does not
say "more excellent than the angels' names" but "more excellent than the angels."[152] This will set up the comparison of the revelation that came through angels—namely, the Mosaic revelation (Heb 2:2; cf. *Jubilees* 1.29; Acts 7:38-39, 53;
Gal 3:19; Josephus *Jewish Antiquities* 15.136)—and that which came through a
higher source—the Son. Christ is not merely a messenger of an interim revelation, but the message of the final revelation and the one who reveals that message (Heb 2:1-4).[153] In Jewish thought, names were in any case viewed not just
as labels; they were thought to connote something about the nature of the one
so named, so it is likely that the point here is that the Son is superior not just in
name but also in nature to the angels. The adjective *diaphoroteron* can mean
"different in kind" (Rom 12:6; Heb 9:10) or "different in quality" (hence "more
excellent"); in either case the comparison here is meant to establish the superiority of the Son to angels.

This whole way of speaking would make very good sense to a Roman audi-

---

[152]Attridge, *Hebrews*, p. 48.
[153]Spicq, *Hébreux*, 2.52-55.

ence, for in Roman practice someone adopted as a son inherited the full name of the father, as when Octavian received Caesar's name. One could even inherit a noble, patrician or royal name. There is another dimension to this as well, since the Greco-Roman world spoke of inheritance from someone's name (Papyrus Oxyrhynchus 247.30-31; 249.8-9). But, importantly, no Old Testament priests—save Melchizedek—were also kings. Since some Roman rulers claimed to be both priest and emperor, it is not difficult to hear a counterclaim here. The emperor was pontifex maximus (Greek *archiereus*), but here in Hebrews only the Son of God is the true high priest who intercedes from above and reigns from the throne room in heaven. Various Julian rulers claimed both offices. For example, Tiberius's coin has the titles "son of the divine Augustus" and "high priest," and he is depicted as a seated figure on a throne with an upright staff, symbol of a ruler. Nero was depicted as Apollo on statues with light beams emanating from his head. While Pliny the Younger was later to say that the emperor was "the man whose word or gesture of command could rule land and sea" (*Panegyricus* 4.4), here we are told that the Son sustains the universe by his powerful word.[154] Our author is slyly hinting that the Son is the reality of which emperors are parodies and Old Testament figures are mere foreshadowings.

Richard Bauckham introduces the implications that the Jewish discussion of an heir and a Son has for the nature of the Son, namely, that he shares in the divine identity.[155] Luke Timothy Johnson puts it somewhat differently: "In a patriarchal society, the notions of 'sonship' and 'inheritance' (*klēronomia*) are naturally linked. The extent and nature of one's inheritance depends on the wealth and power of one's father, and one's position among the offspring."[156] Both of these perspectives are helpful. Jesus is viewed as God's only Son and then appropriately the only heir, entitled to his parent's name and possessions. The Son then becomes the heir of all things and the possessor of the divine name. Of course, in the case of this Son this is all the more appropriate since the Son had a role in making all things in the first place. "Such statements about a historical human being who died a shameful death by crucifixion, not after centuries of reflection, but within two decades of his execution—ascribing to him a role in the shaping of the world!—are not to be attributed simply to a process of textual study, but above all to the impact of the resurrection experience, by which Jesus' followers experienced him after his death."[157]

---

[154]Here I am simply following the insights of Koester, *Hebrews*, p. 187.
[155]Bauckham, "Divinity of Jesus Christ."
[156]Johnson, *Hebrews*, p. 67.
[157]Ibid., p. 68.

Having already introduced the subject of Christ and angels, our author thereby introduced the subject of the first main section of his discourse (Heb 1:5—2:4), in which Christ will be praised to and in the heavens, and the angels, however bright they may be, will be placed in his shade. But thus far our author has used neither the personal name "Jesus" nor the titles "Christ" or "Lord" to describe the person in question. He must stress here Jesus' relationship to the Father as a Son and only later stress his relationship to human beings as their Messiah or Lord. The pattern of comparing Christ first to the Father, then to the angels and then to the ancient worthies such as Moses is a standard rhetorical pattern found especially in encomiums, a particular form of epideictic rhetoric. By comparison, the superiority of the favored subject will be demonstrated, not least in the hall-of-faith part of the argument in Hebrews 11:1—12:3, where Christ is the climactic example.

EXPOSITION AND EXHORTATION, ROUND ONE: THE SEVENFOLD WITNESS AND THE GREATER SALVATION (HEB 1:5—2:4)

Exposition (Heb 1:5-14)

Reading Heb 1 is something like looking at a mosaic that depicts the image of a person. The artist creates the mosaic by selecting various types of stones and arranging them in a way that conveys the subject's likeness. Those who look at the mosaic generally do not ask where the individual pieces came from or how each piece functioned elsewhere, but whether the arrangement of the stones conveys a genuine likeness of the person being portrayed. Similarly, to read Heb 1 on the author's own terms is to ask whether the mosaic of OT quotations is a faithful presentation of the exalted Christ.[158]

Do you see how we get dizzy over this subject and cannot advance to any point unless if be as far as this: that we know there are angels . . . ever circling in chorus around the First Cause, or how should we sing their praises? . . . They are ministers of God's will, . . . choristers of the majesty of the Godhead, eternally contemplating the eternal glory. (Gregory of Nazianzus, *On Theology: Theological Oration* 2([28].31)

It is an important principle of rhetoric to lead from strength, and our author follows it. He has already presented strong evidence in the exordium that the Son bears the very nature of God and so may even be called God in the pastiche of quotations that follow here ("your throne, O God"), and in this part of his act of persuasion he will show how much greater and better the Son is than the angels. Having established this, then he will be free to argue with greater ease

---

[158]Koester, *Hebrews*, p. 198.

that the Son is greater than all other human intermediaries (including Moses) or examples of faithful living and ministry. The claim is one long continuous argument, and the outcome is intended to lead to the praise and the emulation of the Son and also to the placing of lesser lights in his shade. In this way, our author staves off defection to lesser witnesses and more elementary practices (Heb 6:1-6). In some ways the chain of quotations found in Hebrews 1:5-14 leads to a climax with the citation of Psalm 110:1, which was clearly seen as crucial and compelling in early Christian circles.

Quintilian says that "the proper function . . . of panegyric is to amplify and embellish its themes" (*Institutio oratoria* 3.7.6). We must assume, then, that our author is going over ground already trod, texts already familiar, hymn tunes already sung (psalms are songs)—and sung to Christ. The best way to help the audience avoid apostasy is to get them caught up once more in love, wonder and praise of Christ and remind them of their previous commitments. Thus epideictic rhetoric can serve deliberative ends (Heb 2:1-4). But we are not dealing with polemics against angel worship or the like here. As David deSilva says, it is bad rhetorical form to correct the audience too quickly while still in the process of establishing rapport here. There is no denigration of angels here, but rather their positive importance is placed in the context of seeing the greater significance of the Son.[159]

We are dealing with epideictic rhetoric, whatever the other aims of the author were. Quintilian reminds us what is praised in such rhetoric and in what order: "In praising the gods our first step will be to express our veneration of the majesty of their nature in general terms, next we shall proceed to praise the special power of the individual god and the activities by which he has benefited the human race. . . . Next we must record their exploits as handed down from antiquity. Even gods may derive honor from their descent" (*Institutio oratoria* 3.7.7-8). The nature of the deity and its divine descent will be dealt with first, then its special power will be discoursed upon, then its activities or exploits will be handled. Broadly speaking, this is the arrangement of material in Hebrews 1:5—12:17. The divine nature of Christ is spoken of in Hebrews 1, and his human nature in Hebrews 2. This in turn is followed by a discussion of his powers and activities, as one example after another is trotted out, which shows that Christ is greater and due more honor than angels, Moses and a host of others. And lest we fear that the application be saved to the end, our author applies the material regularly throughout to the audience, toggling between exposition and exhortation, climaxing with making Jesus the pioneer of faithfulness even unto

---

[159]DeSilva, *Perseverance in Gratitude*, p. 95.

death, as the ultimate example to an audience that may be asked to pay the ultimate price for their faith in Jesus.[160]

One can also say that typology serves the larger purpose of comparison or rhetorical synkrisis, which in turn serves the larger agenda of showing the superiority of Christ and faithfulness to him. If he is the most honorable one, then the faith he has engendered is the highest form of faith and faithfulness, the most praiseworthy behavior. Throughout this discourse the audience is being asked to remember and recognize the beliefs and behaviors they have already embraced, not to decide to change their conduct. The peroratio in Hebrews 12 makes perfectly clear that the audience is being asked to stand firm and recognize that they have already arrived at their own Mount Sinai. They need not go hankering after another one. But, here at the outset the task is to create a sense of awe, wonder and gratitude for and adhesion to the Son in the hearts of the audience.

Another part of our author's rhetorical strategy seems to be to move from the more widely known and accepted to the less widely known and perhaps more controversial. Put another way, he puts the stronger arguments first, and those whose strength depended on being linked to the first arguments he puts later (Quintilian *Institutio oratoria* 5.12.14; *Rhetorica ad Herennium* 3.10.18). This in turn likely implies that however compelling or interesting one may find the arguments about Christ as sacrifice and heavenly high priest, our author does not assume that the audience will find this material automatically compelling or self-evident, and so he does not lead with such ideas, but rather works his way up to those concepts that are central to his case and argument.[161]

In a sense then the argument moves from the high ground of Psalm 110:1—the Son as royal and divine figure—to Psalm 110:4—the Son as heavenly high priest after the order of Melchizedek. There are brief allusions to the Son as priest at Hebrews 1:3 and then more fully at Hebrews 2:17, but the theme of Psalm 110:4 is not fully developed until this verse is quoted at Hebrews 5:6, and then in the following two chapters the author presents his main theme at the very center of his argument: "Such movement of ideas is not only artistic but is pedagogically and rhetorically sound."[162] Hermeneutically, a further strategy is also being pursued. S. Motyer argues that our author, since be believes that the revelation in the Old Testament was given intermittently and in various ways and was partial in character, sometimes looks for the tensions between Old Tes-

---

[160]See the discussion in Meier, "Structure and Theology."
[161]Rightly Koester, *Hebrews*, p. 199.
[162]Craddock, *Hebrews*, p. 26.

tament texts, which allows him to assert that Jesus is the fulfillment, the hermeneutical key, the answer to the puzzle, the one whose ministry and mission
make clear the deeper or eschatological meaning of these texts and how they
are part of a larger schema.[163]

> [1:5] *For to which of the angels had he ever said, "You are my Son, today I have begotten
> you"? And again, "I myself will be as a father to him, and he himself will be as a son
> to me"?* [6] *But when again he brought the firstborn into the inhabited world, he says,
> "And they worshiped him, all the angels of God."* [7] *And on the one hand, he says
> about the angels, "The one making his angels spirits and his ministers fiery flames";*
> [8] *but on the other hand concerning the Son, "Your throne, O God, unto the eons of
> eons, and the scepter of uprightness, scepter of your dominion.* [9] *You loved righteous-
> ness and hated iniquity/lawlessness. Because of this, God your God anointed you
> with the oil of exhilaration, rather than your associates."* [10] *And, "You in the begin-
> ning, Lord, laid the foundation of the earth and the works of your hands are the
> heavens.* [11] *These things will perish, but you remain; and all like a garment they will
> wear out,* [12] *and like a cloak you will roll them up." As a garment[164] "also they will
> change, but you are the same and your years will not come to an end."* [13] *But to
> which of his angels had he ever said, "Sit at my right hand, I will make your enemies
> a footstool of your feet"?* [14] *Are not all these ministering spirits unto service sent be-
> cause of those coming/destined to inherit salvation?*

The discourse proper begins with **Hebrews 1:5**, to which Hebrews 1:4 has
made a smooth segue by bringing up the topic of Christ and the angels. In a
sense this is a sort of "you are there" in God's heavenly throne room, overhear-
ing what God is saying to his Son at his enthronement scene.[165] This is not unimportant, as the author intends to take the audience from worship scene to
worship scene in this clearly epideictic rhetorical piece, as is especially clear
here at the outset and at the peroration in Hebrews 12:18-29. His desire is that
they get caught up in the worship and so forget about being discouraged, being
tempted to go back to their past religious life and the like.

Some of the audience may have flashed back to the sort of occasion that occurred in Rome from time to time when an emperor would designate a successor
by adopting him as son, as had happened with Julius Caesar and Octavian and
would happen again with Augustus and Tiberius and later with the adoption of

---

[163]Motyer, "Psalm Quotations of Hebrews 1," p. 21.
[164]Our author apparently inserted the phrase *as a garment* in his quotation of Ps 102:26 to demonstrate that the metaphor about the garment was continuing in the following quotation. The
phrase's inclusion here is well supported by $\mathfrak{P}^{46}$, $\aleph$, A, B, D* and other witnesses, and its
omission can be explained as the efforts of later scribes trying to conform our text to the
Septuagint. See Metzger, *Textual Commentary*, p. 663.
[165]Barth, "Old Testament in Hebrews."

Trajan. Pliny the Younger records this event, which transpired after our author wrote Hebrews: the emperor "stood before the gathered assembly of gods and men" and publicly declared that he chose Trajan as his royal son, which in turn was followed by public acclamation of loyalty on the part of the witnesses and even on the part of the subjects of the emperor in general throughout the empire (Pliny the Younger *Panegyricus* 8.3; 47.5; 94.5; Cassius Dio *Roman History* 59.24.3-4; 62.2). Epideictic rhetoric is intended to appeal to the visual imagination of the audience and to inspire and enthrall them, and that is what is happening here. Herein our author follows the topos of epideictic rhetoric on praising a virtuous ruler.

It is not an accident that this catena of Old Testament quotations involves exactly seven—the number of completion or perfection—Old Testament passages mostly culled from the Psalms:[166]

- Psalm 2:7 and 2 Samuel 7:14 in Hebrews 1:5

- Deuteronomy 32:43 in Hebrews 1:6

- Psalm 104:4 in Hebrews 1:7

- Psalm 45:6-7 in Hebrews 1:8-9

- Psalm 102:25-27 in Hebrews 1:10-12

- Psalm 110:1 in Hebrews 1:13

Especially important is Psalm 2:7 at the outset of these partial quotations, which is found not only at Hebrews 1:5 but also at Hebrews 5:5 (cf. Heb 7:28). Qumran also links Psalm 2 and 2 Samuel 7:11-14 in messianic discussions (4QFlor [Florilegium] 1.10-11, 18-19). These words were especially important to the writers of the Synoptic Gospels, who tell us that these words were spoken to Jesus in a heavenly vision at his baptism (Mt 3:17; Mk 1:11; Lk 3:22) and apparently also at another visionary experience on the Mount of Transfiguration (Mt 17:5; Mk 9:7; Lk 9:35). And this quotation is found yet again in a missionary sermon at Acts 13:33. Suffice it to say, this text was crucial to the early Christian witness about the divine character of Jesus as well as his anointing for ministry. Texts like Romans 1:4 make evident that in some cases the word *today* was understood to mean that at his resurrection Jesus was vindicated or demonstrated to be God's true Son. We should not then see remnants of some sort of adoptionist Christology here, as if Jesus became the Son at his exaltation. The issue is activity not ontology, and Jesus assumes the role of ruler at the right hand of God after his exaltation.[167] Our author has already affirmed in any case the Son's

---

[166]Motyer, "Psalm Quotations in Hebrews 1."

[167]Hagner, *Encountering the Book of Hebrews*, p. 47.

preexistence, and he will insist on it repeatedly in this discourse (Heb 2:8-13; 7:3; 10:5; 11:26).

What is immediately striking about this first section in Hebrews 1:5-14 is how our author lets the Scripture carry the argument or do the talking for him. Fred Craddock puts it this way: "Notice how minimal is the author's involvement in 1:5-14—only brief phrases join seven OT quotations. On the theological level, the implications of the author's rhetorical style are unmistakable: The OT is the very speech of God. The words of Scripture are not past speech being dragged into the present by means of hermeneutical maneuvers on the part of the writer; they are God's words to the present."[169] The author repeatedly introduces Old Testament quotations as the direct speech of God to the present: "God says" or a variant thereof is the formula preferred.[170] It does not appear that our author is trying to do polemics here against any worship or reverence of angels. If he were about that task, Craddock says, he certainly could have made fuller use of Psalm 2 to make clear that the Son has no real rivals.[171] The net effect of these citations is that they establish the subservient position and temporary roles of the angels in contrast to the superior sovereign and eternal position of the Son.[172]

The second quotation in Hebrews 1:5 is taken from 2 Samuel 7:14, perhaps the most important passage for the discussion of the Davidic monarchy and its ongoing claims to legitimacy. There God promises to be David's Father, and 2 Samuel 7:16 talks of a kingdom without end. Solomon is initially in view here, but what is apparently envisioned is an unending ruling line of Davidic descendents. When this chain was broken by exile, Jews (at Qumran, for example) began to think of this prophecy being fulfilled in Messiah, rather than in a series of kings who were linear descendents of David. Craig Koester puts it this way: "Israel's kings never attained the universal reign envisioned by Ps 2:7-8, so the text retained an ideal quality that lent itself to messianic interpretations

---

[168] Meier, "Structure and Theology," suggests that symmetry can be seen between Heb 1:1-4 and Heb 1:5-14, both involving seven items. This may be so, but it seems to be overpressing the exordium's clauses a bit. What is more convincing is Meier's argument that our author's theological logic starts with the ascension/exaltation, moves back to creation and then eternity, before moving forward to incarnation, death and entrance into the heavenly sanctuary—a sort of ring composition (p. 189). Koester, *Hebrews*, p. 197, says that there is a "general correspondence" between Heb 1:1-4 and Heb 1:5-14 "but one-to-one connections are not possible."

[169] Craddock, *Hebrews*, p. 25.

[170] On this inscripturated form of rhetorical argumentation see Sarvan, *Telling and Retelling*.

[171] Craddock, *Hebrews*, p. 29. I agree with his critique of Jewett's *Letter to Pilgrims*, who wrongly reads the exigence here as the same as that found in Col 2:8-19. But it is not clear in Colossians that anyone was worshiping angels; see Witherington, *Philemon, Colossians and Ephesians*, ad loc; and the critique of Attridge, *Hebrews*, p. 51.

[172] Helyer, "*Prōtotokos* Title in Hebrews."

(*Psalms of Solomon* 17:23; 4QFlor [Florilegium] 1.18-19; Acts 4:25-26; 13:33; Rev 12:5; 19:15). Hebrews assumes that messianic implications are familiar to the listeners."[173]

But our author has seen the point quite clearly—if one particular person is going to rule in this kingdom forever, that person must himself be eternal. This is why our author will go on to talk not merely about a forever king but also, on the basis of Psalm 110:4, a "priest forever." This will help distinguish the Son from other supernatural beings who are about to be characterized as more ephemeral—like wind or fire that can be extinguished. In the Old Testament angels are sometimes called sons of God (Gen 6:1-4; Ps 29:1; Job 1:6; 2:1; 38:7). It is then our author's task to make clear the distinction in honor and nature between the sons of God and the Son of God who is not merely one of them.[174]

In **Hebrews 1:6-7** the focus shifts to the angels, as first Deuteronomy 32:43 (clearly from the Septuagint) and then Psalm 104:4 is cited. The Septuagint version of Deuteronomy 32:43 is also found in a Qumran quotation of this verse, but the words "let all God's angels worship him" are not found in the Masoretic Text. In Hebrews "him" is the Son who is to be worshiped. The Son is also called *prōtotokos* ("firstborn") (applied to Christ in Rom 8:29; Col 1:15, 18). It is doubtful, however, that our author has in view the incarnation or the idea that Jesus was the first of all created beings, since he has already *said* in the exordium that the Son was on the side of the creator and was involved in the acts that produced creation (Heb 1:2). More likely the term is used in its metaphorical sense of "first over all creation/creatures," stressing his honor rating or primacy in rank.[175] Our author is particularly drawing on the idea from the Old Testament that the firstborn has certain prerogatives when it comes to the family inheritance (Deut 21:17; see Heb 12:16); in this case the Son is the heir of all things.[176]

The term *oikoumenē* may also have a special sense here. It commonly means "inhabited world," the human world all under one civilized roof with one language and culture, as the Hellenistic vision had it, and in due course the term came to refer to the Roman Empire. But in Hebrews 2:5 the term seems to refer eschatologically to "the world to come," not the present world, for which our author uses the term *kosmos* (Heb 4:3; 9:26; 10:5; 11:7, 38). Here then the term

[173]Koester, *Hebrews*, p. 191.
[174]In the Septuagint "sons of God" is sometimes rendered "angels of God" to make the referent clearer (Job 1:6; 2:1; 38:7; Dan 3:25; cf. Josephus *Jewish Antiquities* 1.73), since sometimes, as in Gen 6:1-4, "sons of God" are likely angels. The crucial point is that no individual angel is ever addressed or called God's son.
[175]Helyer, "*Prōtotokos* Title in Hebrews."
[176]Koester, *Hebrews*, p. 192.

can refer to Christ's entrance into the heavenly world, the perfect realm, the domain of the saints and God.[177] In the later Christian text *Ascension of Isaiah* 10.7-15; 11.23-32, the Son is not recognized by the angels when he becomes incarnate as a human being in the world, but when he returns to the right hand of God he manifests his glory and is worshiped by the angels.[178] The call for the worship of the Son accompanies the use of transference because in the Hebrew version of Deuteronomy 32:43 the "him" in question was Yahweh. It is the affirmation of the deity of the Son that then makes legitimate the call for the worship of the Son.

In Colossians 1:18 and Revelation 1:5 *prōtotokos* is applied to the risen and exalted Christ. In short, the term refers to his honor rating and preeminence as he assumes the role of regent on the throne at his ascension and exaltation; it does not refer to the incarnation or parousia. This "inhabited world to come" over which the Son rules is both now (in heaven) and not yet (on earth). But that is not all. Christ is the *prōtotokos* of many brethren (Heb 2:10-18), and his passage into glory presages theirs (Heb 12:18-29). It is no surprise then that we hear of the *ekklēsia* of the firstborn (again *prōtotokos*) enrolled in heaven (Heb 12:23). The pattern of Christ's life is recapitulated in the believer's life, for Christ is the pioneer trailblazing the path into glory for God's sons and daughters. We have then an echo of Romans 8:29 in Hebrews 12:23. In a sermon that intends not only to comfort and encourage the afflicted, but also to prepare them for the possibility of following Jesus on his path to glory by a martyrological death, these connections are pregnant, poignant and relevant.[179]

The second quotation, this time from Psalm 104:4, provides the description of the lesser supernatural beings, the angels. They are God's servants, not God's unique Son, and they are like wind or fire, not eternal like the Son. These points will be reinforced in Hebrews 1:12, 14 as this first segment of the discourse is brought to a close. The upshot is that nothing can compare to the Son. This point could never have been made with the Hebrew text, which says the reverse of the Septuagint—namely that God makes the wind and the fire to be his messengers or servants.

There is some question whether the word *again* in Hebrews 1:6 simply indicates another quotation or whether it goes with the verb *brings*, in which case we may see here a reference to the second coming of the Son, when every knee shall bow, including, in this case, the angels. The placement of *palin* may

[177]Ibid., p. 193.
[178]Helyer, "*Prōtotokos* Title in Hebrews," p. 11, following a suggestion of Albert Vanhoye.
[179]Ibid., pp. 18-22.

slightly favor the suggestion it has the same meaning as it did in Hebrews 1:5. Interestingly the quotation in Hebrews 1:6 is from Deuteronomy 32:43 and Psalm 97:7, but the former text is not found in many Hebrew manuscripts. It was known only in the Septuagint version until it was found in Hebrew in a Qumran manuscript. Importantly, in the original Yahweh is to be worshiped by the angels, but here it is the Son. This is because our author sees the Son as divine and so can quite naturally interchange the Son with God as the one addressed.

Hebrews 1:8-9 quotes Psalm 45:6-7, which was probably originally part of a wedding ode where the king in good epideictic fashion is praised hyperbolically as God's representative and so, in a sense, "God" on earth. But our author finds the ultimate meaning when applied to the Son. What is most surprising about Hebrews 1:8 is that God is depicted as addressing God! God said to God: "Your throne, O God, will last forever." Our author takes this as an Old Testament clue that there was always a plurality of persons in the Godhead (Justin Martyr *Dialogue with Trypho* 56.14; 63.3-5).[180] Here we see some of the rudiments of the developing doctrine of the Trinity, and our author wishes to affirm it in the face of possible denial by his Jewish Christian audience.

Who are the Son's associates or companions? Hebrews 2:14 may suggest fellow human beings or fellow kings, which is surely meant in the original Old Testament setting, but F. F. Bruce sees an allusion to the many sons of Hebrews 2:10. We cannot be sure.[181] The Son is God, but "his God" is the one who anointed him and set him above the rest of the heavenly host or royal entourage and also above all of his fellow human beings, which may be the primary meaning of "companions" here, rather than angels.[182] The anointing is said to be with the oil of exhilaration or great joy. There could be no greater joy or honor than to be picked by God to be the Messiah of God's people. Righteousness is an attribute of this royal figure, a theme to be developed at Hebrews 7:1, when another king of righteousness comes to the fore—Melchizedek. Righteousness is seen as the opposite of lawlessness and as a prerequisite for being a ruler (Wisdom of Solomon 1.1). Aristotle even says that it encompasses all the major virtues necessary for a civilized society (*Nichomachean Ethics* 5.3.1129b).

Hebrews 1:10-12 consists of one long quotation from Psalm 102:25-27,

---

[180]Glasson, "Plurality of Divine Persons."

[181]Bruce, *Hebrews*, pp. 60-61.

[182]Koester, *Hebrews*, p. 195.

which reiterates the point already made that the Son stands on the side of the creator, rather than the creature, as one who laid the foundations of the earth. The transference of this text from a discussion of Yahweh to the Son is facilitated by following the Septuagint version, which alone applies the word *kyrios* ("Lord") to God. This makes the application of the verse to the Son easier, more natural.[183] Unlike the creation, which will wear out and can be rolled up like a garment, God the Son is eternal and remains the same (in character), a theme that will be picked up again in the final exhortations in Hebrews 13:8. Many in the Greco-Roman world believed in the indestructible character of the world. This stands in contrast to the Christian and Old Testament view. Donald Hagner says that, while the dramatic contrast between the Son and the angels is made implicitly here, it is no less effective for that.[184] Setting up the theme of transitory versus permanent or temporal/temporary versus eternal prepares for discussion of the contrast between eternal heaven and temporal creation and also between temporary and eternal covenants.

It would be hard to exaggerate the importance of Psalm 110:1 for the christological reflections of the early church—perhaps most especially for our author. Hebrews contains at least seven quotations or allusions to this verse (Heb 1:3, 13; 4:14; 7:26; 8:1; 10:12-13; 12:2) and another ten citations or allusions to Psalm 110:4 (Heb 5:6, 10; 6:20; 7:3, 11, 15, 17, 21, 24, 28)—and this becomes all the more striking since only in Hebrews in the New Testament is this text used for christological purposes. We should see **Hebrews 1:13** then as something of an amplification of Hebrews 1:3. This collection of citations begins and ends with the rhetorical question, "To which angel did God ever say?" (Heb 1:5, 13), with Hebrews 1:14 adding a further rhetorical question that makes clear that the answer is "none." This form of rhetorical inclusio rounds off a rhetorical unit. To no angel did God every say what he has said to and about his Son. Angels are clearly shown to be subordinate creatures, because they worship the Son, they are ephemeral and they are ministering servants who serve the saints. The notion of making an enemy a footstool for a ruler is a vivid gesture of dominance, and it is often depicted in antiquity, with the ruler's foot placed firmly on the neck of the enemy (Josh 10:24; Baruch 4.25; Is 51:23).[185] The forced subjugation of enemies and forced submission to this public gesture is seen as a shaming device, whereas for the angels who voluntarily worship and submit to the su-

---

[183] On the application of the term *theos* to Jesus in the New Testament, see Harris, *Jesus as God*, pp. 205-27; and Hurst, "Christology of Hebrews 1 and 2."

[184] Hagner, *Encountering the Book of Hebrews*, p. 49.

[185] For Babylonian depictions, see pictures in Geoffrey W. Bromiley, ed., *The International Standard Bible Encyclopedia* (Grand Rapids: Eerdmans, 1982), 2.332, 453.

perior being, the Son, there is no shame, only honor in that act.[186]

Hebrews 1:14 is meant to round off this first expository section of the discourse and punctuate the point about the subordinate role of angels in the divine economy of salvation when compared to that of the Son. The Son is the bringer of salvation, the angels merely serve those who inherit salvation (Heb 1:7, quoting Ps 110:4). The term *leitourgos*, from which comes *leitourgikos*, is here translated "ministering," but it is also the basis for the term *liturgist*, one who does service in a sanctuary, and one could argue that angels are seen in some texts as the liturgists in the heavenly worship sphere (e.g., Rev 7:11-12). The direction of the ministry here however is toward humans rather than toward God, and so the translation "minister" is more appropriate.[187] Angels are not criticized here but rather seen as positive servants of God and helpers of humans. The concept of ministering angels who serve God's people is not uncommon (e.g., Philo *On the Virtues* 74 and *Jubilees* 2.2 [angels of fire, wind and natural phenomena in general]). The final clause here refers to salvation as something in the future yet to be inherited or taken full possession of. The verb *mellō* ("are [about] to, are coming to, are destined to") points to the future nature of this inheritance. That "destined" is probably not the best translation here is seen from the larger context, since our author will warn his audience that unless they persevere they will not inherit this salvation, and if they turn back or turn away there will definitely be no inheriting salvation. One must keep steadily in view that Hebrews 6:1-6 is directed at our author's entire audience as a warning.

Hebrews 1 then does not offer judicial or polemical rhetoric but the rhetoric of praise, in the service of giving highest praise to the Son, as Thomas Long shows:

> In the opening chapter [our author] sustains the sense of the glorious heights before he descends to the abyss. He knows that the gospel gains its power when the hearers are able to hold in their faithful imaginations the central paradox of the faith: the Jesus who was made "for a little while lower than the angels" was, is, and always will be the Son exalted above all things, "superior to the angels." The Jesus who suffered a humiliating death at the hand of evil is the same Son who is "the reflection of God's glory." The "heir of all things through whom God created the worlds" is the very one who, for our salvation, became one who had nowhere to lay his head and "endured the shame" of the cross.[188]

---

[186]DeSilva, *Perseverance in Gratitude*, p. 102.
[187]Attridge, *Hebrews*, p. 62.
[188]Long, *Hebrews*, p. 23.

This is a diatribe Sermon - 1 warning

Exhortation: Shall We Ignore So Great a Salvation? (Heb 2:1-4)

> And he took this form of speech . . . showing both the easiness of the fall and the *yes*
> grievousness of the ruin. That is, our disobedience is not without danger. And
> while by his mode of reasoning he shows that the chastisement is greater, yet again
> he leaves it in the form of a question and not as a conclusion. For indeed this is to
> make one's discourse inoffensive, when one . . . leaves it in the power of the hear-
> ers to draw their own conclusions and thus to be more greatly persuaded. (Chry- *good for*
> sostom *Homilies on Hebrews* 3.5) *Sermon*

Hebrews dares to suggest that getting clear about christology, as difficult and tangled as that doctrine is, actually leads to such virtues as steadfastness, hospitality,
and hope. . . . More surprising, perhaps, the writer of Hebrews appears also to be
persuaded that the reverse is true as well, that walking the pilgrim way obediently *x*
and with faithful endurance clarifies one's christology, deepens theological wisdom, and increases the knowledge of God. . . .

The relationship between theological knowledge and ethical practice . . . is interactive and reciprocal, each growing out of, leading into, and profoundly affecting the other. Sound doctrine leads to solid ethics, and, conversely, living the *yes*
Christian life leads to theological wisdom.[189]

The first full segment of the discourse is brought to some closure by the first
exhortation segment found in Hebrews 2:1-4, which is very clearly linked to its
immediately preceding context by *dia touto* ("because of this"). The issue here *me*
is drifting away from or ignoring what one has already heard, known, believed,
practiced. In other words, no change of direction or policy is being urged.
Rather the audience is urged to stand fast and adhere to what they have already
committed themselves to and what has been praised already in lavish terms. As
our author will say, there are consequences not only for what we do, but also
for what we neglect or drift away from.

Hebrews 1:1-4 and Hebrews 2:1-4 display symmetry: the latter is the introduction to the ethical enjoinders in this discourse, just as the former is for the
theological discussion. The former mentions the one who speaks, the latter
those who have and are listening to the revelatory speech.[190] Both of these brief
segments involve the aurally impressive use of alliteration using the percussive
p sound, driving home a point.

Rhetorical comparison can take many forms, and here it has a hortatory form.
Our author will suggest that if there was a penalty for violating or neglecting or
reneging on the former revelation that was given to Moses through angels, how

---

[189]Ibid., pp. 32, 31.
[190]Craddock, *Hebrews*, p. 33.

much more should we expect there to be a cost to neglecting so great a salvation. In the author's mind, turning back is virtually unthinkable after one has been offered or given so much in Christ. But in the end the author lets the audience make up their own mind, by leaving the matter in the form of a rhetorical question.

Our author uses a rhetorical strategy to include himself with his audience in the exhortation—not "you" but "we shall not escape if we neglect so great a salvation." In this way even the exhortations are not exercises in finger pointing by someone who sees himself as above the fray and fallibilities of the audience.[191] This is a good thing, because, as Harold Attridge notes, there is a crescendo of exhortation in this discourse, beginning with this short one and the brief one in Hebrews 4:14-16 and increasing in length and intensity to the point that the last two major exhortations (Heb 10:19-39; 13:1-19) are very lengthy.[192] This makes perfectly evident that exhortation is as important in this discourse as exposition and its amplification and explanation. One could say that the exposition exists in large measure for the sake of providing a basis for the exhortation, which is the real thrust and urgency of the discourse.

> [2:1]*Because of this, it is increasingly necessary to heed/hold fast to what we have heard, so as not to drift away/get carried away. [2]For if/since the word spoken through angels was valid and every transgression and disobedience deserved just retribution, [3]how shall we escape, ignoring so great a salvation? Such a salvation had been proclaimed by the Lord from the beginning and by those who heard him was confirmed to us, [4]the signs and also the wonders and various mighty deeds bearing joint witness of God and distributions of the Holy Spirit according to his will.*

Hebrews 2:1-4 should not be seen as an interruption of the discourse, but rather as an ethical application of the significance of what has been said in Hebrews 1. *Dia touto* not only links this segment with what precedes, but the allusion to the role of angels in giving the law also links this to the previous paragraph. The danger for the audience, as enunciated in **Hebrews 2:1**, is not willful error of whatever sort, but of "drifting away," a nautical term found nowhere else in the New Testament and only twice in the Septuagint (Prov 3:21; Is 44:4). The image of the Christian life that it conveys is of something in motion, something dynamic and not static—either a moving forward or a drifting away or, worse, a deliberate about-face. The audience is in danger of being careless, lax, losing their focus and so drifting away, without fully realizing what is happening it would seem. The verb *pararreō* can refer to the flow of a river (Hero-

---

[191]Koester, *Hebrews*, p. 208.
[192]Attridge, *Hebrews*, p. 63.

dotus 2.150; 6.20), to a ship slipping off course, to a guest slipping away from a table (Aelian *Varia historia* 3.30) or to a ring slipping off a finger (Plutarch *Amatorius* 9.12). It can have the passive sense of being carried away like a leaf in a strong current or the sense of simple drifting aimlessly in the wrong direction, which suggests a gradual process of falling away from the truth. Our author clearly believes that perseverance does not happen automatically but rather requires effort on our part, hearing and heeding warnings along the way.

The verb *prosechō* is found only here and at Hebrews 7:13 in this discourse, but in Matthew it is the verb of choice for "warning" or "watch out!" (Mt 6:1; 7:15; 10:17; 16:6).[193] This verb has the sense of holding fast to something or holding a ship on its course, which is very possibly the meaning here in view of the contrast with "drifting away."[194] Alliteration on the *p* sound throughout this verse once more brings the first segment of the discourse to a close. The verb "hold fast" will become a constant refrain in this discourse, delineating what must not be let go of (presuming they already have it in hand and need to grasp and cling to it). Thus, Hebrews 2:1 should be compared to holding fast to our boldness (Heb 3:6), holding fast to the assurance they had from the first (Heb 3:14) or holding fast to the confession without wavering (Heb 10:23).

Hebrews 2:2-4 is one long sentence loaded with assonance and alliteration *(terasin . . . dynamesin . . . thelēsin)*. This present, or real, conditional statement might well be translated "since" rather than "if." This is a clear example of our author's penchant (Heb 7:20-22; 9:13-15; 10:28-29) for using an a fortiori style of argument (from the lesser to the greater = the Jewish formula *qal wehomar*). One may wonder where the idea comes from that angels were involved in the giving of the law on Sinai, since the idea is not present in Exodus 20:1 (cf. Ps 68:17). But later texts reflect this notion (*Jubilees* 1.27-29; Acts 7:38, 53; Gal 3:19). In the Septuagint version of Deuteronomy 33:2 angels make a cameo appearance at the final blessing of Moses. Our author is not at all suggesting that these angels were anything but holy and good, and they delivered to Moses a holy and good revelation of God that was valid or binding (*bebaios* seems to mean "legally binding"; see Heb 9:17). But with his schema of salvation history, our author assumes that the law is now obsolescent, even for his Jewish Christian audience. This stands in contrast to Josephus (*Against Apion* 2.277) and Philo (*Questions and Answers on Exodus* 2.53), who both assume the law to be permanent. Our author agrees with Paul's assessment of the status of the Mosaic law (Gal 3:19-25; Heb 7:12-18; 9:10).

---

[193]Ibid., p. 64.
[194]Rightly Koester, *Hebrews*, p. 205.

It is characteristic of epideictic rhetoric to use two terms to refer to the same thing for the sake of amplification.[195] The first term, *parabasis* ("transgression"), means a willful overstepping of the bounds of a known law (Rom 2:23). The second term, *parakoē* ("disobedience"), means a refusal to listen, which is seen as a form of disobedience or transgression (i.e., a willful violation). Franz Delitzsch points out the participle *amelēsantes* carries the overtone of contempt or despising of the thing neglected.[196]

The language of escape here prompts the question—escape from what? But since our author wants the discourse, in good rhetorical form, to raise questions that will only gradually be answered for the audience, he does not tell us here. Here the task is to set the audience to thinking and wondering. He will tell them later that he has in mind eschatological judgment (Heb 6:8; 10:27, 31). The phrase sometimes translated "just punishment" is better rendered "fitting recompense" because the thought is that the punishment fits the violation. The noun *misthapodosia* is not inherently negative, as its positive use in Hebrews 10:35 and Hebrews 11:26 makes evident. Rejecting or violating Moses' law was one thing, and that was bad enough and came with penalties, but rejecting the word through the Son—the good news of salvation—is a far more serious offense, leading to a far more serious punishment (Heb 12:25). Our author clearly believes in a moral universe in which God, the righteous one, will in the end see that justice is done and that mercy and compassion happen. He does not think that the universe has some impersonal automatic moral mechanism, as if "what goes around, comes around." No, he believes that God responds directly to transgression or refusal to listen. Epideictic rhetoric relies a great deal on appealing to the deeper emotions, those that fall under the heading of pathos, such as fear. When such an emotion is evoked the idea is to leave "an impression of an imminent evil that causes destruction or pain" (Aristotle *Rhetoric* 2.5.1). As David deSilva notes, appeals to fear or the fearful consequences of defecting appear throughout this discourse (Heb 4:1-13; 6:4-8; 10:26-31; 12:25).[197]

What occurrence is our author thinking of when he speaks of the Lord speaking this message of warning and salvation? He seems to have in mind something akin to Mark 1:14-15 or Luke 4:16-21 or Acts 10:36-39.[198] Those who heard the Lord then told others, such as our author and those who converted his audience,

---

[195]On epideictic rhetoric in 1 John, see Witherington, *Letters and Homilies*, 1.431-36.
[196]Delitzsch, *Hebrews*, 1.97.
[197]DeSilva, *Perseverance in Gratitude*, p. 107.
[198]Craddock, *Hebrews*, p. 34.

Heb.

and so we are two steps removed from Jesus here, both in the case of the author and the audience. Our author does not claim to have seen Jesus, unlike Paul, but rather to have heard those who did.

Hebrews 2:4 presents a remarkable truth. Experience of miracles or gifts from the Holy Spirit is seen as the confirmation of the truth of the oral testimony. In other words, the oral testimony is seen as primary and is confirmed by miracles, mighty deeds and spiritual gifts—not the other way around. The primary thing in our author's mind is the revelatory word. Spiritual gifts and miracles are seen as God's own testimony to or corroboration of the truth of God's word.[199] The triad "signs, wonders, mighty deeds" is found several times in Paul (Rom 15:19; 2 Cor 12:12; 2 Thess 2:9; cf. Acts 2:22). The use of these three terms should not be seen as designating three radically different kinds of phenomena, especially since amplification is a normal feature of epideictic rhetoric. The one phrase that is different from these references to miracles is "distributions of the Spirit." These outpourings of the Spirit are seen as witnesses to the truth, not the transparent truth in themselves, since such gifts can come from various sources and miracles can be variously interpreted. But as witnesses of God to the truth, they are powerful. God then takes action to punctuate and bear witness through deed to the truthfulness of his own word. Fred Craddock says, "That they are acts of God does not mean that these acts are overwhelming and incontrovertible proof. God does not coerce faith but joins the rest of us in witnessing."[200] What is stressed is also found in 1 Corinthians 12, where spiritual blessings, miracles and gifts are distributed by the Spirit according to the divine will, not according to human preferences. Hebrews 2:4 should be compared with Hebrews 6:4. In both cases the Christian audience is the subject of discussion. They have received "distributions" from the Holy Spirit, but if they turn back or commit apostasy, they are in deep trouble. Our author then does not see having the work of the Holy Spirit within the life of the believer as some sort of ironclad sealant that prevents leakage, corruption, even turning back to a formerly unsaved condition. The phrase *various distributions of the Holy Spirit, according to his will* (reminiscent of 1 Cor 12:11) is crucial because, though our document places the emphasis on that which believers have yet to look forward to from God, the author is well aware that believers already have a foretaste of glory divine, in the Spirit and its manifestations, that was not true to the same degree of the Old Testament saints.

[199]*Synepimartyrō* has as its strong sense a legally binding testimony that clearly corroborates some truth. See Koester, *Hebrews*, p. 207.
[200]Craddock, *Hebrews*, pp. 34-35.

It is rightly said that Roman culture was a reciprocity culture, and this included the way Romans viewed their relationships with the gods. Thus, if it was believed that some great boon had been provided by a deity, it would be the height of ingratitude not to respond with sacrifices, professions of loyalty and behavior that honored that God. This would be all the more the case if it was believed by the Romans that they had been delivered or saved from some great calamity. Seneca puts it this way: "Who is so ungrateful as the person who has so completely excluded and cast from his mind the benefit that ought to have been kept uppermost in his thoughts, and always before him, to have lost all knowledge of it?" (*De beneficiis* 3.2.1). While our author is not accusing his audience of complete forgetfulness, nevertheless neglect or gradual drifting away was also seen as ingratitude, and our author is appealing to this well-known psychological dynamic in Roman culture. The connection between this and what precedes is clear—with a deity *that* is praiseworthy and beneficent, such "drifting away" is clearly very blameworthy.

EXPOSITION AND EXHORTATION, ROUND TWO: LOWER THAN THE ANGELS, GREATER THAN MOSES, GONE THROUGH THE HEAVENS, ENTERING HIS REST (HEB 2:5—3:19)

In Hebrews 2:5—3:19 exposition and exhortation are more interspersed than in the first section, though the net effect is the same. Basically a long block of exposition is followed by an equally long block of exhortation that includes some exposition (i.e., quotation with comments used as the tool of exhortation). The author's use of quotations for both exposition and exhortation is further evidence that a too rigid distinction of theology from ethics is artificial, especially when it comes to Hebrews.

Our author continues to attend to the rhetorical and aural dimensions of his exposition, as seen in the plentiful repetition of *hypotassō* and related forms in Hebrews 2:5-8. David deSilva notes that employing the same consonantal sounds and the same prepositional prefix underscores the completeness or totality of the subjection envisioned.[201] In addition, it is not an accident that our author has chosen a praise psalm to make his points about Jesus. Quotation of previous praises is what we would expect in an epideictic homily such as this one. But there is more. This is not just about the glorification of Jesus by quoting an Old Testament psalm, it is also about leading human beings to glory, unto a praiseworthy condition (Heb 2:10).

Craig Koester's attempt to find in Hebrews 2:5-9 a proposition for the entire

---

[201]DeSilva, *Perseverance in Gratitude*, p. 109.

discourse is forced.[202] In the first place, a proposition was not necessary in an epideictic discourse, though occasionally one finds one. In the second place, if this was the proposition it neglects and does not presage the enormous amount of hortatory material that follows in this discourse. Our author is not trying to prove a christological case polemically or otherwise, he is seeking to laud beliefs and virtues that the audience already has embraced. Many of those beliefs involve Christ, but they also involve other things. Finally, we would certainly have expected at least a mention of the high priestly Christology in these verses if it was a proposition for the discourse that follows, but that christological notion is nowhere to be found in Hebrews 2:5-9.

Koester is right, however, that our author in these verses does follow a normal rhetorical pattern of arguing: statement of key idea (Heb 2:8a-b), raising of potential objection (Heb 2:8c), answer to potential objection (Heb 2:9). The enthymematic form of arguing in this discourse is widely recognized and amply treated by Harold Attridge, Craig Koester, David deSilva and others. Basically, an enthymeme is an incomplete syllogism, or one that has an undisclosed member. In this case, the missing element would seem to be some kind of statement of assumed truth like "since Christ does not yet have all things under his feet, it follows that this must be going to happen in the future since God's word is true."[203]

Exposition (Heb 2:5-18)

For as a physician, though not needing to taste the food prepared for a sick person, tastes it first himself so that he may persuade the sick person to eat with confidence, so also, since all people are afraid of death, . . . he tastes it himself, though he did not need it himself. . . . So both the word "by grace" and "might taste death for everyone" establish this.[204]

The Preacher does not wish to argue that Jesus was just a tiny bit lower than the angels in the hierarchy of creation, that he came to the edge of human life and dipped his little toe into the pool of suffering. Rather, he wants to claim that, for a brief moment in time, the eternal and exalted Son purposefully and redemptively plummeted to the depths of human suffering and weakness. . . .

The Preacher's rhetorical skill is on vivid display here. He has slowed down the pace of the sermon and confided, to the sad assent of the congregation, that we do not yet see the victory of the Son. "What we *do* see . . . ," says the Preacher, and then he pauses to allow the tension to build. "What we do see . . . ," and the

[202]Koester, *Hebrews*, pp. 219-20.
[203]On enthymemes in general, see Witherington, *Letters and Homilies*, 1.70-71.
[204]Chrysostom *Homilies on Hebrews* 4.3

congregation, who saw pain and trouble at every hand, surely began to fill in the blanks with their sorrow. "What we do see . . . ," and now the Preacher swiftly raises the curtain on the stage of human history. "What we do see is . . . *Jesus*" (2:9). In Greek the suspenseful effect is even more dramatic since the name Jesus is positioned at the very end of the long sentence, a technique for creating emphasis that the Preacher employs on all eight occasions when he uses the name "Jesus" (the others are 3:1; 6:20; 7:22; 10:19; 12:2; 12:24; 13:20).[205]

²·⁵*For it is not to angels he subjected the world to come, concerning which we are speaking.* ⁶*But somewhere someone solemnly affirms, saying, "What is a human being that you remember him, the Son of Man that you visit him?* ⁷*You humbled him for a little while beneath the angels, you crowned him with glory and honor,*[206] ⁸*putting all things under his feet." In subjecting everything to (him), not a single thing was left not subjected to him. But now we do not yet see everything in subjection to him.* ⁹*But the one humbled for a short time beneath the angels we see, Jesus, through the suffering of death crowned with glory and honor, in order that by the grace of God*[207] *he might taste death for all.*

¹⁰*For it is fitting for him, for whom are all things and through whom are all things, the author/pioneer of their salvation brought many sons into glory through being made complete by suffering.* ¹¹*For the sanctifier and those being sanctified are all from one (family), because of which reason he is not ashamed to call them brothers,* ¹²*saying, "I will declare his name to my brothers, in the middle of the congregation I will praise you."* ¹³*And again, "I will be persuaded about him." And again, "Here I am and the children whom God gave me."*

¹⁴*Since then the children shared in blood and flesh, and he himself likewise partook of these, in order through his death to destroy the one having the power of death, that is the devil,* ¹⁵*and might free those who were subject to the slavery of fear*

---

[205]Long, *Hebrews*, pp. 36-37 (emphasis original).

[206]Some good witnesses add "and set him over the works of his hand" (א, A, C, D*, P and others), but the reading without this extension of the quotation from Ps 8:6 is well supported ($\mathfrak{P}^{46}$, B, K, L and others), and there is no good reason why it would be omitted if it was original. See Metzger, *Textual Commentary*, pp. 663-64.

[207]In an extraordinary alteration a large number of the fathers (Origen, Eusebius, Ambrose) and some Eastern and Western texts have the phrase *chōris theou* rather than *chariti theou* (0121b, 1739*). This seems to have been the result of a marginal gloss to explain that "everything" subjected to Christ in Heb 2:8 means everything "except God." But if so, why is the phrase introduced in Heb 2:9 rather than in Heb 2:8? See the discussion in Metzger, *Textual Commentary*, p. 664. There was no end of debate about this among the fathers, with Oecumenius insisting that the text read "by the grace of God" and that the variant was a Nestorian conspiracy, while Theodore of Mopsuestia and Origen favored the other reading as original (Heen and Krey, *Hebrews*, pp. 38-39). In light of the cry of dereliction from the cross ("my God, my God why have you forsaken me?"; Mk 15:34), one could make good sense of the text if "without God" is the reading in Heb 2:9, but Koester, *Hebrews*, p. 218, points out that Heb 2:10, the very next verse, makes evident that God is not envisioned as absent.

of death throughout all of life. [16]*For as you know it is not angels that he took respon-*
sibility for/took hold of, but the seed of Abraham that he took responsibility for/took
hold of. [17]*Hence he ought to become like his brothers in everything, in order that he*
might become our merciful and faithful high priest unto the making propitiation
unto God for the sins of the people, [18]*for in what he suffered he was tested to be able*
to help those being tested/tempted.

Hebrews 2:5-18 contains a remarkable example of christological exegesis of
the Psalms.[208] In its original context and sense, Psalm 8 had to do with human
beings in general and their being created but a little lower than *elohim*, which
means "God" in the Hebrew text but in the Septuagint is rendered "angels." This
is a statement about the nature of the hierarchy of the creation order.

Our author, in a tour de force argument, has turned this psalm into a text that
speaks of the preexistence, incarnation and exaltation of the Son of Man. It then
becomes a quandary for translators concerned about inclusive language
whether to render the phrase *huios anthrōpou* as "Son of Man" or "son of human
beings," in light of the use of the psalm in this context. What in its original context was a generic discussion about humankind is here a christological discussion about the Son of Man. This is all the more significant since there is little or
no evidence that Psalm 8 was ever read messianically before or during this period in early Judaism. On the other hand, we have clear evidence that Psalm 8:6
was linked with Psalm 110:1 in early Christianity to make comments about the
exalted Christ (1 Cor 15:25-27; Phil 3:21; Eph 1:22). This is in part because the
subject here is the "world to come" as opposed to "this world," but it is also
because our author wants to laud Christ, not the angels.

This way of reading Psalm 8 may be seen as an example of *Urzeit* becoming
Endzeit in Christian eschatology—"primeval time" becoming "prime (i.e., eschatological) time." Our author is clearly dependent on the Septuagint version of
the psalm, which has significant differences from the Hebrew; in particular,
where the Hebrew has "a little less than God," the Septuagint has "a little lower
than the angels" (plural *elohim* can refer to divine beings other than God in the
Old Testament; see Ps 82:1b). For the Hebrew phrase *a little*, the Greek has
brachy, a frequent designation of time ("for a little while"); seizing on this and
the reference to Son of Man, which in the original is simply another way of saying a human being and is parallel to the previous clause, our author uses this

---

[208]DeSilva, *Perseverance in Gratitude*, p. 108 n. 45, points to the recontextualization of Ps 8:6
in 1 Cor 15:23-28. In Hebrews, however, this psalm is applied to Christ's exaltation and to
the later subjection of all things under his feet. This is another small clue of our author's link
with and indebtedness to Paul and his christological reading of Old Testament texts.

psalm to say something about Jesus during and after his incarnation.

In the original psalm the tension was between humanity as ruler of creation and our seeming puniness and insignificance in comparison to the size and vastness of that creation. One look at the universe and it is very clear that we do not have control of it, indeed we are struggling just to stay alive in it. The confession of the psalmist is that, despite how things seem, God has given humans the status of rulers over creation. This might seem a hollow claim to the Jewish Christians who were under duress at this point. But our author has a trump card: one man does have sovereign control over creation—Jesus. Thus the psalm both describes the feeling of the audience and gives them hope since Jesus is in the position to make good or valid the claim of the psalm. In Hebrews 2:8 our author insists that nothing was left out of what is subject to the Son. But Hebrews 2:8b is also realistic—the problem is that we do not yet see the whole of creation in subjection to humanity, but we do see "Jesus." Here for the first time—and at this dramatic juncture—the author introduces the human name of the Son and stresses that through the incarnation we see one who is now reigning. Paradoxically, it was because of the act of dying, the surest sign of human vulnerability, that he was crowned with glory and honor. It was not just for his own benefit, but for humankind that he suffered death. He, by the grace of God, suffered death for everyone.

Scholars think it possible that the reason our author used this psalm to launch this discussion is because it has the phrase *Son of Man*, which is rare in the Old Testament but often found in the Gospels as a means of self-description on the lips of Jesus.[209] This may be so, but the remarkable things our author then does with the text place this in the category of creative homiletical use of a text, not exegesis. One of the ways this creativity shows itself is in the use of the phrase *brachy ti*, which, while it could have a qualitative sense ("a little lower"), is likely taken here in a temporal sense ("for a little while") speaking of the temporary duration of the incarnational presence of the Son on earth. Furthermore, our author takes the phrase *you crowned him with glory and honor* to refer not to the created status of human beings made in the divine image, but to the exaltation of the Son to the right hand of God. If this were not enough, the phrase *you put everything under his feet* refers not to the status of human beings as lords over all creation, but to the eschatological subjection of the world to come to this Son of Man—a still-future event. One can only call this handling of the psalm breathtaking, but what it suggests in a striking way is that the destiny of human beings is fulfilled in Jesus. Anthropological mandate receives christological fulfillment,

---

[209]For the full discussion see Attridge, *Hebrews*, pp. 73-75.

but this agenda is not yet completed ("until" in Ps 110:1). God in the end has not subjected the world to angels or mere mortals, but rather to his Son, the Son of Man.[210] But, as the author says, this consummation, however devoutly to be wished, "we do not yet see." What human beings have however seen is the incarnational presence: "We see Jesus." With this overview of what is going on here, we can consider some of the particulars verse by verse.

Hebrews 2:5 speaks about a subjection of the world to come by God, not by angels. Our author does not speak of the governing of the world by angels, though this was a common enough idea in early Judaism (Deut 32:8; Sirach 17.17; Dan 10:13, 20; *1 Enoch* 60.15-21; 89.70-76; *Jubilees* 35.17).[211]

Hebrews 2:6 begins with a phrase that makes it appear as if our author is having a "senior moment": "But someone says somewhere." This was, however, standard homiletical practice (it allows the audience to focus on the content, not the source of material),[212] and furthermore there were no chapter and verse divisions in the Old Testament in our author's day. As Craig Koester points out, the author also introduces his discussion of rest at Hebrews 4:3-4 in this fashion, and yet he clearly knows he is drawing on Genesis.[213] Philo uses this form of address when he clearly knows the identity of the speaker but chooses not to reveal it (*That God Is Unchangeable* 74; *On Planting* 90; *On Drunkenness* 61). Finally, a theology of revelation may also be in play that suggests that, since it is all the word of God, citing particular human authors or titles is superfluous.

In **Hebrews 2:7-8** our author operates with a theology that suggests that the sending of the preexistent Son to earth was a subjecting of him to a humble condition, but thereafter he was exalted to the right hand of God, and the world to come is in the process of being subjected to him. This is the trajectory of thought, or narrative flow, that our author has in mind. Donald Hagner says, "Our author was aware of the natural objection to his argument in chapter 1 concerning the superiority of the Son to the angels. By their nature, angels are superior to human beings. They are not subject to the weaknesses and limitations of the human body, nor are they mortal."[214] Our author thus emphasizes that it was only "for a little while" that the Son was humbled lower than the angels, but Psalm 8 goes on to suggest that he was then exalted above them once more.

According to **Hebrews 2:9** the exaltation and glorification of Jesus does not transpire simply because he submitted to the incarnation. Rather, it is specifi-

---

[210]Craddock, *Hebrews*, p. 37.

[211]Attridge, *Hebrews*, p. 70.

[212]Craddock, *Hebrews*, p. 37.

[213]Koester, *Hebrews*, pp. 213-14.

[214]Hagner, *Encountering the Book of Hebrews*, p. 56.

cally linked to his death. He is crowned with glory and honor because he submitted to that death, but not just any death. This was a substitutionary death, a death in which he "tasted death" for everyone else, on their behalf. And as a substitutionary death it is seen as perhaps the preeminent example or manifestation of God's grace. There can be little doubt that our author, like the author of the Pastorals, wants to stress that Jesus died "for everyone," not just for some elect group. While the Greek word *pantos* could be construed as neuter meaning "everything" rather than masculine meaning "everyone," there is no emphasis in Hebrews on cosmic Christology or the idea that Christ died for the whole of the created order. Harold Attridge points out that the immediately following verse, Hebrews 2:10, focuses on what Christ accomplished for human beings.[215] Even if *pantos* was neuter, it would mean that Jesus died for all human beings *and* all other sentient beings.

Our author will go on to use the word *hapax* to describe the character of Jesus' death (e.g., Heb 9:26, 28)—it was not only once for all time, making all subsequent sacrifices superfluous, but one person for all persons. Chrysostom puts it this way: "This occurred 'that by the grace of God he might taste death for everyone,' not for the faithful only, but even for the whole world, for he died for all. But what if all have not believed? He has fulfilled his own part" (*Homilies on Hebrews* 4.3).

The artfulness of the rhetoric here cannot really be conveyed in English. Attridge notes that our author, in good midrashic fashion, takes two key phrases from Psalm 8—"a little while lower than the angels" and "crowned with glory and honor"—and uses them to frame the name Jesus and the reference to his suffering death.[216] This in turn gives a narrative shape to the discussion of the psalm, charting now the pilgrimage of being subjected even unto death and then being exalted beyond death to a place and position of glory. Thus the name Jesus is especially applied to the crucified one.

The word *taste* in Hebrews 2:9 does not mean that Jesus took a small sampling of death, but did not drink the cup of death to the dregs. It simply is a creative and metaphorical way of saying he experienced death and did so for others. This use of this verb and its meaning becomes even more important in Hebrews 6:4, where the author is not suggesting that his readers can merely try a small sample of the heavenly gift, without really being saved (the next phrase there makes this evident: "who have shared in the Holy Spirit"). The church fathers were right to conclude that our author is going out of his way to stress that

---

[215]Attridge, *Hebrews*, p. 76.
[216]Ibid., p. 73.

the Son became a true human being. Theodore of Mopsuestia puts it aptly: "The man Jesus was like all humans and differed in no way from those whose nature he shares, save that to him a grace was given. The grace that was given does not change his nature" (Fragments from *Treatise on the Incarnation* 2). In an interesting reflection, Thomas Long points out that the audience of Hebrews knew the testimonies of the eyewitnesses about Jesus' life and death, but it is equally or more important that they were "earwitnesses" of the testimony about "what we have not seen," namely, the exaltation of Jesus to the right hand, his role in heaven at present and the future subjection of the world to come to him.[217] Faith in this book is not just based on believing a report about what has been seen, though it definitely includes that. It is also and equally about believing what one has heard about things not seen and yet to come: "the assurance of things hoped for, a conviction/certainty about things not seen" (Heb 11:1).

A CLOSER LOOK
The Rhetoric of Encomium: Heroic Trailblazer, Liberator and High Priest

In order to understand epideictic rhetoric in a Roman setting one needs to set aside the older Greek notions that panegyric was simply the rhetoric of display for its own sake and therefore not of practical use for persuasion about things of serious moment. Quintilian stresses that "Roman usage . . . has given it a place in the practical tasks of life" (*Institutio oratoria* 3.7.2). A Roman audience, such as is addressed in this homily, would be well aware of this. Interestingly, Quintilian gives the story of Romulus as Exhibit A of epideictic rhetoric and of how it fulfills its primary task of amplifying and embellishing its themes. Romulus was said to be the son of Mars, but raised by a she wolf under very humble circumstances; he nonetheless revealed his origins in Mars by winning many battles heroically, escaping harm on various occasions miraculously and in the end being translated to heaven to be part of the pantheon of gods (3.7.5). This narrative has the same V-shaped pattern our author uses to describe the career of the Son, with this important difference—the Son's trials, temptations and death must be explained as noble, self-sacrificial, honorable, whereas Romulus, one of the founders of Rome, escaped shameful death and was simply translated into heaven, à la Enoch or Elijah in the biblical tradition. What this shows is that a lot of rhetorical finesse would be required to tell Jesus' tale to a Roman audience as an honorable one worth praising even in his means of death.

---

[217]Long, *Hebrews*, p. 38.

Certainly one of the most common topics of epideictic rhetoric, especially in encomiums, is the praising of tests passed and sacrifices made, especially in the form of a noble death, of the hero who is being lauded. The remarkable rhetorical strategy of our author is to recast what would normally be seen as extremely shameful (death on a cross) or as a sign of weakness (undergoing many trials and temptations with many sighs and struggles) in a positive light so that these things are seen as praiseworthy, not least because they have been endured for others. They are even seen as exemplary, as they provide a pattern for the audience to follow as they trod the path toward glory. Quintilian tells us: "Weakness may contribute largely to our admiration, as when Homer says that Tydeus was small of stature but a good fighter . . . the glory of good deeds may be enhanced by the smallness of their resources" (*Institutio oratoria* 3.7.12-13). Quintilian stresses moreover that "what most pleases an audience is the celebration of deeds that our hero was the first or only man or at any rate one of very few to perform: and to these we may add any other achievements that surpassed hope or expectation, emphasizing what was done for the sake of others rather than what he performed on his own behalf" (3.7.16). Our author is well aware of what will most impress his audience, and it is no accident that he emphasizes the thing about Christ's tale that makes him unique, special, one of a kind and will make his deeds indispensable, irreplaceable, self-sacrificial, once for all time.

In regard to the noble and self-sacrificial death, rhetoricians were well aware that this subject was crucial in an encomium, especially because ancient peoples believed that how a person died was likely to most reveal his or her character. A noble death was seen as a thing of honor, crowning a life well lived, whereas a shameful death cast doubts on the goodness of the life lived before it. *Rhetorica ad Herennium* 3.7.14 is perfectly clear about the need to discuss the kind of death the hero endured and its consequences. The greater the sacrifice and the more persons it benefited, the more honorable the death and the more the deceased should be praised (Quintilian *Institutio oratoria* 3.7.16, 28; Aristotle *Rhetoric* 1.9.16-19). One virtue most regularly praised in encomiums was courage in the face of overwhelming odds or great trials and dangers. More particularly, Aristotle defines courage as the endurance of fearsome things, even death, for the sake of what is noble (*Nichomachean Ethics* 1115b12).[218] But there was much to overcome, because crucifixion was the most shameful way to die in the Roman world, and it was a way of memorializing a person with endless disgrace. Tacitus, for example, in his discussion of the notorious Christian superstition, stresses that the founder of this super-

---

[218]See the discussion in deSilva, *Perseverance in Gratitude*, pp. 111-12.

stition was crucified, which made perfectly clear that this religion was depraved and immoral (*Annals* 15.44).[219] Justin Martyr in his debates with Jews and pagans found objections from both to the notion of a crucified messiah who was proclaimed a divine Son of God. Pagans thought it madness "to put a crucified man in second place after the unchangeable and eternal God, the creator of the world" (*First Apology* 13.4), while Jews thought it blasphemy, for "this so-called Christ of yours was dishonorable and inglorious, so much that the last curse contained in the law of God fell on him, for he was crucified" (*Dialogue with Trypho* 32.1).

One of the things our author does to overcome this way of thinking about a crucified person was to portray Jesus as dying a noble death, which far from shaming Jesus actually "perfected" him or made him complete and fit for the role he now plays in heaven! Our author had much to overcome in this encomium to forestall his audience from believing the normal Roman rhetoric about crucified persons. How then does he overcome the obstacles and compel his audience to rethink things about Jesus and their relationship with him? Part of his strategy is not only to turn the normal logic about crucifixion upside down but also to turn the rhetoric of empire and emperor on its head, applying language to Jesus that was usually applied to the emperor.

In an honor-and-shame culture that was highly socially stratified, some persons obviously received a lion's share of the praise, and no one received more than the emperor, to whom dedications and laudatory descriptions could be found all over the empire. In addition, the emperor would also have his list of accomplishments and great deeds published all over the empire (the *Res gestae augusti*, for example), often accompanied by the erection of new statues. One of the more frequently erected statues showed the emperor as Pontifex Maximus, the great high priest, offering sacrifices to the gods. To praise the emperor in this role was in many ways to offer him the highest praise because he was modeling what Romans considered to be one of the highest virtues—*pietas/eusebeia*, that is, reverence for the gods and for the sacred traditions of one's Roman ancestors. It is then no surprise and no accident that, in order to properly laud Jesus to Roman Christians, our author chooses to laud him as the one-of-a-kind high priest, indeed as the heavenly high priest who is still serving in the heavenly sanctuary and who, in offering himself as a unique and totally propitiating sacrifice, made obsolete all other sacrificial systems. The rhetoric of praise of Christ as high priest, which begins to appear at this juncture in the discourse and dominates the central portion of this discourse, would have implications not merely for one's views of Jewish sacrificial sys-

---

[219]Ibid.

tems, but for Roman systems as well. Jesus, not the emperor, is the true Pontifex Maximus; only he has offered the perfect sacrifice, and only he has brought not only himself but also many others to true glory and everlasting salvation.

The prevalence of the discussion of Jesus' death and of his piety and role as a priest are precisely what we would expect in an encomium dedicated to reinforce the opinions of the audience about Jesus and persuade them to continue to embrace such opinions.[220] Then, too, the language about Jesus being a pioneer, a hero of sorts, is also precisely what we would expect in an epideictic piece such as Hebrews. Jesus is a greater hero and founder of a group of people than was Romulus, more pious than any other known priest, a more powerful liberator and benefactor than the emperor. Thomas Long puts it this way:

> The primary image, the one upon which the other two are overlaid, is the picture of Jesus as the mythic hero who descends into the world below, into the realm of death, to defeat the powers of death and to rescue those trapped in death's grip. . . . It is in this context of rescuer that Jesus is called the "pioneer" of salvation (2:10), a rendition of a multifaceted Greek word that has also been translated as hero, champion, founder, author, guide, leader, and scout, among others. . . .
>
> Bolted to this mythic chassis is a second constellation of images, all growing out of a military metaphor of Jesus as the liberator. . . .
>
> Finally, as a third metaphorical network juxtaposed onto the first two (and as something of a surprise), Jesus is described as a "merciful and faithful high priest" (2:17).[221]

What Long should have asked is: to what human being who lived in the first century A.D. were these three images also applied in a positive and honorific way? The answer is the emperor, the Pontifex Maximus, the one whose rhetoric claimed to bring Pax Romana and endless benefaction, the savior of the known world. Few emperors reveled more in such press clippings and reviews than Nero, the emperor who not long before this discourse was written had persecuted Christians in Rome, blaming them for the fire. In a sense then, our author could be said in this encomium to be fighting fire with fire, rhetoric of praise with inverted rhetoric of praise—except that our author believes that Jesus is the reality of which the emperor is only the parody and that prior figures in biblical history are only the foreshadowing.

The rhetoric of the emperor became especially pointed when an emperor

---

[220]Our author deals with departed saints—not current living saints—in his hall of faith in Heb 11, which is what we would expect in an epideictic encomium.

[221]Long, *Hebrews*, pp. 39-40.

like Caligula applied the story of Heracles to himself and even dressed like Heracles in order to suggest that he was a divine deliverer of humankind (Philo *On the Embassy to Gaius* 78-79, 90; Cassius Dio *Roman History* 62.20.5). This had ancient precedent, since Alexander the Great claimed to be a descendent of Heracles and portrayed himself this way, even on his coins (Arrian *Anabasis* 3.3.2; 4.10.6). For our purposes, it is important to point out that Nero had himself depicted as a Heracles figure (Suetonius *Nero* 53). Cassius Dio says that he was acclaimed in the following fashion: "Hail to Nero, our Heracles" (*Roman History* 62.20.5). The relevance of this to the discourse in Hebrews becomes clear when we recognize that Heracles was not only called "the pioneer" (Dio Chrysostom *Orations* 33.47), but it was said of him that "he was the best champion of human nature and guided all men toward the best" (40.14). Heracles was also said to have descended into the underworld, where he "cross[ed] the streams of Taratarus, subdued the gods of the underworld and return[ed]" (Seneca *Hercules furens* 889-90). Put another way, he "overcame the dark robed lord of the dead" (Euripides *Alcestis* 76, 843-44). The result of this act of bravery was that Heracles was deified and became the helper of those who feared or faced death. Belief in Heracles' death-defying act allows believers to lose their fear of death (Seneca *Hercules furens* 890 and *Letters* 24.4 [on Socrates]).[222] Once again, predicating these or similar sorts of ideas of Jesus is a way of diverting the rhetoric of emperors to enhance the presentation of Jesus. Whether one wants to call this "plundering the Egyptians" or simply "taking every thought captive for Christ" it amounts to a bold rhetorical strategy to keep Roman Christians in the fold and far from defecting to defective ideologies. In sum, it can be said that the rhetorical strategy of this epideictic discourse is to apply to Jesus the same dominant images already applied to the emperor, in order to suggest that there was only one God who walked upon the earth as a human being—Jesus.

Hebrews 2:10 begins the second salvo of this discourse with a bang. In daring language our author talks about what it was fitting or appropriate for God to do! Our author says that it was fitting for God to make the pioneer/trailblazer/author of human salvation complete through suffering, in the process of bringing many sons and daughters to glory. This verse is loaded with key terms that appear several times more in the discourse.

The term *archēgos* is rare in the New Testament outside of Hebrews (only Acts 3:15; 5:31), and there is some debate among scholars as to its precise meaning in Hebrews. This word is constructed from two Greek words: *archē* ("first"),

---

[222]See the discussion in Aune, "Heracles and Christ," pp. 13-19.

which could refer to primacy, and the verb *agō* ("to lead"). The term is used in the Septuagint to refer to those who led the tribes of Israel not only in the wilderness (Num 10:4; 13:2-3) but also in battle (Judg 5:15; 9:44; 1 Chron 5:24; 8:28). Craig Koester rightly notes that the term *archiereus* is also applied to Jesus in this section (Heb 2:17): Jesus is not only the believer's chief, he is also their chief priest.[223] In Acts 3:15 *archēgos* is applied to Jesus to indicate that he is the "author" or originator of life (similar to his being called the source of salvation in Heb 5:9). Both *archēgos* and *telos* are applied to Jesus in Hebrews 2:10 and Hebrews 12:2. The rendering "pioneer, completer, founder or finisher" of faith is seen in the image of trailblazers or lead runners completing the course first, which our author stresses in Hebrews 12:1-2. This too favors a particular translation of *telos* both here and in Hebrews 12:1-2. Here the trailblazer—the one who goes first—is made complete through suffering; there he is actively said to be the completer of faithfulness even unto death on the cross.

The *telos* language here clearly has nothing to do with suggesting that Jesus was somehow imperfect before he died. In particular the language is clearly not used in a moral sense because Jesus' sinlessness and blamelessness are clearly stressed in this discourse (Heb 4:15; 7:26; 9:14). What our author is getting at is that when Christ completed his earthly career by dying on the cross he became perfectly equipped and completely fit for a whole series of tasks, including that of being the believer's heavenly high priest, offering himself to God the Father as the perfect sacrifice for sins and interceding on their behalf in other ways with God in the heavenly holy of holies. He also was equipped to bring many along with him to glory and to identify with his brothers and sisters in their own trials, temptations and suffering. Furthermore, he was equipped to be their model and moral exemplar of how to live a life of faithfulness despite pressure, persecution and even execution. In Sophocles' *Electra* 1508-10, Orestes is "perfected" through a deed. Thus, through an event or the completion of a significant task one reaches one's intended goal, fulfills one's purpose, attains what one is aiming for. In such instances the occurrence has nothing to do with becoming morally perfect.

Hebrews 2:11 goes on to suggest that, since sacrifices are meant to atone for and cleanse from sin and so "sanctify" a person, putting them back in right relationship with God, Jesus' sacrificial death also equipped him to be the sanctifier of his brothers and sisters. Our author will unpack all of these ideas in due course. But here we may ask—is there a difference between being "made perfect" and "being sanctified"? This would surely seem to be the case, since the

---

[223] Koester, *Hebrews*, p. 228.

former language is applied to both Jesus and believers in Hebrews, while the latter language is applied only to believers.

A CLOSER LOOK
The Completion/Perfection of Jesus and His Brothers and Sisters

The various verbal, nominal and adjectival forms of the word *telos* and cognates show up some fourteen times in this discourse.[224] It is obviously a very important concept for our author. Donald Hagner notes that the author uses this terminology to point to the "completeness of God's purposes—as in 'bringing to perfection.' It is a particularly effective word for our author's argument, as he draws out the contrast between the preparatory character of the old covenant and the fulfillment of the new. What Christ has accomplished in his death brings us to what must be described as eschatological fulfillment, hence perfection."[225]

Some find here echoes of Platonic ideas of the eternal realm being the realm of the perfect, while the material universe is the realm of imperfect copies or replicas of the eternal, somewhat on a parallel to that found in Philo.[226] This conclusion perhaps has some small warrant, to judge from Hebrews 9:11, which speaks of heaven as the more perfect sanctuary; it fails, however, to take into account the eschatological character of most of the perfection language used in this discourse.

How very different the eschatological language in Hebrews is from Philo's appropriation of Stoic ideas when he argues that Moses was perfect in his lack of harmful emotions *(apatheia)* (*Allegorical Interpretation* 3.131) or that Isaac was perfect because he was the man of self-taught virtue (*Allegorical Interpretation* 1.94; *On Dreams* 1.162). Perfection in Philo can sometimes have the sense of the unmediated vision of God for those who love God (*Allegorical Interpretation* 3.74). This is the absolute opposite of the notion that someone is perfected through suffering or by experiencing profound emotions that draw one closer to God (Heb 5:7-10). Harold Attridge rightly concludes that "Philo's extensive use of perfection terminology derives from common educational theory and involves a complex notion of the human ideal."[227] It certainly does not derive from a sense of the eschatological moment or from Philo's Christology or even from his concept of salvation history in general.

---

[224]A helpful study of the perfection language can be found in deSilva, *Perseverance in Gratitude*, pp. 194-204. See also the major study by Peterson, *Hebrews and Perfection.*
[225]Hagner, *Encountering the Book of Hebrews*, p. 57.
[226]Carlston, "Vocabulary of Perfection in Philo and Hebrews."
[227]Attridge, *Hebrews*, p. 84.

If we are looking for precursors to the way perfection language is used in Hebrews, we should look to Wisdom of Solomon 4.13, where we hear of the righteous man who dies a tragic and untimely death through which his life has been "perfected" (*teleiōtheis*). Similarly in 4 Maccabees 7.15 we hear that Eleazar's life of faithfulness to God is climaxed and crowned by his martyrological death, which is said to have perfected his life.

For the most part the language is applied not to the material or heavenly realms but to either Jesus or believers being made perfect in some sense, with the usual thrust having to do with being made fit, complete, mature and so fully conformed to God's purposes for that individual (of Jesus in Heb 2:10; 5:9; 7:28; 12:2 ; of believers in the verbal form in Heb 9:9; 10:1; 11:40; 12:23; of believers in the adjectival or noun form referring to maturity or completion of what ought to be in Heb 5:14; 6:1).

What is especially striking is that our author distinguishes between holiness/sanctification and perfection/maturity when this terminology is applied to believers. For example, in Hebrews 10:14 we hear that Jesus through his death "has made perfect/complete perpetually those who are being made holy." The latter has to do with sanctification or moral condition, the former has to do with intended purpose. In Hebrews 12:23 our author speaks of the "spirits of the righteous made perfect." This surely refers to the saints being made complete or all they ought to be when they came into the presence of God, for they were already "the righteous." Hebrews 11:40 uses the same language to talk about all believers being made "complete/perfect" together. This clearly has to do with eschatological transformation (as at Heb 12:23). The Septuagint uses the verb *to perfect* to describe the consecration of the priest (Ex 29:9; Lev 16:32; Num 3:3), and our author may well have had this idea in mind when he uses this language about Jesus, since he goes on to stress the priestly role of Jesus. But our author does not suggest a sacerdotal role for believers, so this is not likely one of the overtones of the language when applied to Jesus' followers.

Our author believes that what is "up there" will one day be "out there" when Jesus returns and there is a corporate merger of heaven and earth or, better, when the current material realm is rolled up like an old coat and a new one is unveiled. Our author does not have a problem with the notion of eternal or permanent matter or material reality, unlike Plato.[228]

The essentially eschatological character of the language is made quite clear in a couple of texts. For example, Hebrews 7:11 speaks of how the Levitical

---

[228]On the eschatological character of the language in Hebrews, see Silva, "Perfection and Eschatology in Hebrews."

[handwritten annotation at top: Sd Paul, Heb. justifies X's death as / , perfect perfect atonement —, / both trying to explicitly Xst died / its purpose.]

system could not bring perfection, whereas Jesus' sacrifice could, which is also the thrust of Hebrews 9:9. Hebrews 7:19 again stresses that the law made nothing perfect, but that believers now have a better hope. All of this fits well with the salvation-history perspective of our author, who sees former things, such as the old covenant, as partial and inadequate, whereas the eschatological things accomplished by Jesus, including the inauguration of the new covenant, complete or perfect God's intended purposes for humankind.

[handwritten margin note: Heb's / new / covenant]

Attridge sums up well what we can learn from studying Hebrews in light of the wider corpus of literature:

> Hebrews's use of perfection language is complex and subtle and does not simply reproduce any of the various perfectionist ideals of the first century. Christ's perfection is certainly not a development of his moral capabilities, and he does not require, in a Stoic sense, to attain complete virtue, for he is presumed to have been sinless. Neither is Christ's perfection a cultic installation, although as a result of Christ's perfecting, he serves as a sanctifying High Priest. Christ's perfecting . . . may be understood as a vocational process by which he is made complete or fit for his office. This process involves, not a moral dimension, but an existential one. Through his suffering, Christ becomes the perfect model, who has learned obedience (5:8), and the perfect intercessor, merciful and faithful (2:17). . . . It is not through enlightenment or moral development, but through the sonship characterized by faithful endurance that Christ attains "perfection" and makes it possible for his "perfected" followers to take the same route.[229]

[handwritten margin note: Bk details]

One further idea is also present in Hebrews 2:10. While our author has already stated that Jesus died for everyone, here he states that he will bring or lead "many" to glory. This, coupled with other things said later in the discourse, reveals that our author is not a universalist in the sense of believing that all persons are automatically saved or all will ultimately be saved, even though Christ's death is sufficient to make that a possibility for all. As Hebrews 11 will make clear, grace, faith and faithfulness to the end will determine who will enter glory and who will not, who will receive eschatological salvation and who will not.

Hebrews 2:11 speaks of the sanctifier and the sanctified. In texts like Exodus 31:13; Leviticus 20:8; Ezekiel 20:12 God is the sanctifier, but here it is Jesus. In Hebrews 9:13; 10:10; 13:12 sanctification is said to come about by the shedding of blood, and in the case of believers Jesus' blood accomplishes this end. An extraordinary thing about Hebrews 2:11 is that it stresses that both the sanctifier and the sanctified are part of one human family, being children of God (Heb

---

[229]Attridge, *Hebrews*, pp. 86-87.

2:13). Our author will assert that believers have been sanctified (Heb 10:10, 29), are being sanctified (Heb 2:10; 10:14) and furthermore must diligently pursue sanctification (Heb 12:14) so as to share in God's holiness (Heb 12:10) and thus be prepared for the eschatological meeting with God at the holy mountain (Heb 12:18-29).[230]

Our author uses the language of shame here. Jesus is not ashamed to call us brothers and sisters for the very good reason that we belong to the same human family. In other words, this is not just the language of "fictive kinship," because Jesus really was a human being, he was truly one of us.[231] Here we may again have echoes of the wisdom tradition that sees Adam as the "one" from whom all humans derive (Wisdom of Solomon 7.1; 10.1; cf. Acts 17:26; Rom 5:12-21).

Thomas Long puts the connection between Jesus and humankind vividly:

The Preacher is saying that when the gaze of the eternal Son of God encompasses a criminal on death row, when the glorified Son sees a homeless woman crawling into a cardboard box to keep from freezing in the night, when the Lord of all sees a man robbed of dignity and purpose by schizophrenia, when the divine heir of all things sees a mother weeping over the death of her child or a man battling the last savage assault of cancer or the swollen body of a child slowly starving to death, he does not see a charity case, a pitiful victim, or a hopeless cause. He sees a brother, he sees a sister, and he is not ashamed to call us his "brothers and sisters" (2:11). The Son of God does not wag his head at misery and cluck, "There but for the grace of God go I." Instead he says, "There because the grace of God I am."[232]

In a bold move, in **Hebrews 2:12-13** our author has Christ speak to his audience as the voice of God in the Psalms. In other words, the Psalms in this case are treated as words of Jesus to his followers (the same rhetorical device is also found at Heb 10:5-10). According to Fred Craddock, "a pre-existent christology makes it possible to move across chronological and historical distinctions."[233] Our author makes one slight change to Psalm 22:22—"I shall tell of" is rendered "I shall proclaim"—to convey the notion of Jesus speaking about God directly

---

[230]DeSilva, *Perseverance in Gratitude*, p. 115.

[231]The reference to Jesus and the believers being from "the one" is probably not an allusion to the Stoic idea of all humanity being descendents of God (Seneca *De beneficiis* 3.28.1-2); see deSilva, *Perseverance in Gratitude*, p. 114. The point is the connection between Jesus and other believing human beings, not the connection of both to God. There may then be an allusion to origins in Adam, especially in light of the earlier use of Ps 8, even though our author does not develop an Adam Christology, unlike Paul (1 Cor 15; Rom 5).

[232]Long, *Hebrews*, p. 42.

[233]Craddock, *Hebrews*, p. 40.

to his brothers and sisters "in the assembly."[234] The word *ekklēsia* is used here since it is found in the Septuagint, but elsewhere our author uses this term of the final eschatological assembly (Heb 12:22-23), whereas he uses *episynagōgē* for the local Christian assembly in Rome (Heb 10:25). This may provide a clue about the audience, since Paul refers to the assembly of Gentile Christians meeting in the house of Priscilla and Aquila in Rome as *ekklēsia* (Rom 16:5). The use of *episynagōgē* in Hebrews 10:25 probably provides a further clue that our author is writing to Jewish Christians.

This first Old Testament citation is followed by two more, probably from Isaiah 8:17 and Isaiah 8:18. Harold Attridge suggests that their being cited separately suggests that two different points are being made.[235] This is the only place in the New Testament where Isaiah 8:17-18 is interpreted messianically, though we do find Isaiah 8:14 interpreted this way in Romans 9:33 and 1 Peter 2:8. The first of these two citations presents the theme of faithfulness (Jesus will put his trust in God), while the second stresses his solidarity with his brothers and sisters ("here I am and the children God has given me"). Believers are to be seen as children of God not in virtue of their humanity, but because they have become such through their faith in and relationship with Jesus: "As elsewhere in early Christianity [cf. Gal 3:26; 4:4-7; Rom 8:15-17, 19; Jn 3:3-5; 1 Jn 2:29; 3:9; 4:7], sonship is not a matter determined by nature, but by God's salvific act and the human response to it."[236] Jesus is conceived of as standing before God with those he has redeemed and also as standing with them.[237] We should maybe deduce that the reason Jesus is not ashamed to call them his brothers and sisters is precisely because he has sanctified them, not merely because they are his fellow human beings. It is important to recognize that while these quotations illuminate what has already been said, particularly in Hebrews 2:11, they are also prospective in nature, preparing for what will be said in Hebrews 2:14 and Hebrews 2:17, immediately following these citations. Our author's use of Scripture is deft and many-faceted and can hardly be said to fit one particular mold of preexisting interpretative or hermeneutical schemes from early Judaism or early Christianity.

Hebrews 2:14-15 is a single sentence. The intent is to make clear the soli-

---

[234]Scholars debate whether we are to envision Christ saying these things before, during or after his earthly ministry. All three could be envisioned as coming forth from the mouth of the earthly Jesus, though perhaps the last one is to be seen as spoken by the exalted Lord. The trust saying especially seems to reflect the *Sitz im Leben* of the earthly Jesus. See Koester, *Hebrews*, pp. 238-39.

[235]Attridge, *Hebrews*, p. 90.

[236]Ibid., p. 91.

[237]Hagner, *Encountering the Book of Hebrews*, p. 58.

darity between Jesus and human beings. The perfect-tense verb *share* here indicates an abiding or ongoing condition: "Since all human beings share blood (. . . perfect tense, indicating an abiding condition) and flesh, Jesus in every way participated (. . . aorist verb, indicating a completed act in the past) in the same things." "He was as we are, no pretensions, no appearances, no exemptions"—save sin.[238] The order "blood and flesh" is unusual but not unprecedented (Eph 6:12) and may reflect an emphasis on suffering associated with shedding blood.[239] What a difference two slightly different verbs can make: here human beings "share" in flesh and blood, while Jesus "partook" of blood and flesh, probably indicating a choice made to do so prior to being human.[240]

There is strong rhetoric here: through his death Jesus "destroyed" the devil, which surely means that he broke his power over humanity, for he can no longer hold death over their heads as a means of controlling or influencing them in their beliefs and behaviors. The same verb is used in 1 Corinthians 15:54 to refer to the victory that Jesus has over the powers and principalities, but the meaning is less than literal: "to subdue or strip" of power. The use of *katargeō* in Romans 3:31 and Ephesians 2:15 means "to deprive" something of power. It was not an uncommon notion in early Christian thinking that the devil controlled death (1 Cor 5:5; 10:10; Jn 8:44), and in early Judaism Satan was identified with the serpent in Eden's garden (Wisdom of Solomon 2.23-24; cf. Rev 12:9; Jn 8:44). It is possible that our author has in mind the story of hero figures like Heracles, who by dying set a group of people free from various things, including even a sentence of death (Seneca *Hercules furens* 858-92; cf. *2 Enoch* 22.8-10). Slavery of any kind was seen as something to be avoided, being the opposite of freedom. Dio Chrysostom puts it this way: "Freedom is the greatest of blessings, while slavery is the most shameful and wretched of conditions" (*Orations* 14.1).

The sentence about the devil attracted a good deal of attention from the church fathers. Chrysostom, for instance, points out "the wonder that, by that through which the devil prevailed, [he] himself was overcome. By the very thing that was [his] strong weapon against the world—death—Christ struck him. In this Christ exhibits the greatness of the conqueror's power. Do you see what great goodness death has wrought?" (*Homilies on Hebrews* 4.5). Our author subscribes to the theory that the chief purpose of the incarnation was that Jesus might come and die as a human being for all human beings, thus reversing the

---

[238]Craddock, *Hebrews*, p. 40.
[239]Attridge, *Hebrews*, p. 92.
[240]Westcott, *Hebrews*, p. 52.

three great powers that enslaved human beings since the Fall—sin, death and the devil.[241] The particular focus here is on death, but later our author will say a good deal about sin. Our author applies the notion here that a person is enslaved to whatever he or she fears—in this case death. Plutarch writes of the fear of death: "Who can be a slave if he gives no heed to death?" (*Moralia* 34B). In pagan thought, however, death was often seen as a welcome release from suffering (Euripides *Orestes* 1522) and so is not seen as something evil or a result of sin. Our author does not agree: Christ's own death is seen as a means of liberating human beings from living on the basis of that fear. Craig Koester sums things up well:

> Unlike others, Jesus did not encounter death as a slave, but as an assailant; he intruded into death's domain in order to overcome it. By dying and being raised, Jesus showed that death's power is not absolute, but is subject to the power of God. . . . After this point in his speech, the author will no longer speak of the devil, but will address listeners as people who have been freed by Christ. The author recognizes that sin and death continue to threaten people, but he insists that Jesus' death and resurrection free people from the fear that would hold them captive to evil. Therefore, as free people, the listeners are accountable to God and called to manifest boldness in their confession (cf. Heb 3:6).[242]

Our author continues in **Hebrews 2:16** with his conversational style by asking yet another rhetorical question: "Surely it is not angels he takes hold of?" There is some question as to how we should translate the verb *epilambanomai* (lit., "to take hold of"). Some commentators take this to mean that the author is denying that the Son took on an angelic nature, but Harold Attridge says the verb "does not mean 'assume the nature of.'"[243] Furthermore, such a translation ignores the final clause in this verse: "but rather the seed of Abraham." Had our author wanted to say that the Son took on a Hebrew nature instead of saying that he took on an angelic nature, there were certainly more obvious ways to do it. In Hebrews 8:9 this verb occurs in a quotation of Jeremiah 31:31-34 to describe the helping action of God on behalf of the exodus generation.[244] And in Sirach 4.11 wisdom "lays hold of those seeking her" in the sense of helping or rescuing or protecting them.[245] Our author does not say a human nature here: the contrast is between angels and the descendants of Abraham. It is thus more probable that the verb should be translated "to lay hold of," which gives force

---

[241]Hagner, *Encountering the Book of Hebrews*, p. 59.
[242]Koester, *Hebrews*, pp. 239-40.
[243]Attridge, *Hebrews*, p. 94.
[244]Gudorf, "Through a Classical Lens."
[245]See the discussion in deSilva, *Perseverance in Gratitude*, p. 120.

to the phrase *seed of Abraham* because he is addressing Jewish Christians. Jesus in the first instance certainly came to rescue Jews.[246] Attridge suggests that the image of Christ the pioneer taking hold of his children by the hand and leading them on to glory makes perfectly good sense.[247] William Lane helpfully points out that our author may be engaging in a recontextualization of Isaiah 41:8-10: "Seed of Abraham whom I loved, of whom I took hold . . . I am your God who helped you."[248] Fred Craddock adds that the

> drama of salvation, which hinges on incarnation, suffering, and death, is not an angel story. While angels are in divine service for the benefit of those who inherit salvation (1:14), they are neither the agents nor the beneficiaries of that salvation. With this sentence angels leave the stage of Hebrews, but they leave honorably. They have their place in God's work (2:2), but it is not the central place. They enjoy God's presence, but they do not sit at God's right hand. Nor are they portrayed as competitors or enemies of Christ.[249]

Nor did Jesus become human and die for them, as he did for the "seed of Abraham."

Thus **Hebrews 2:17** affirms: "Hence he ought to become like his brothers in everything, in order that he might become a merciful and faithful high priest in the things concerning God unto the making of propitiation for the sins of the people." Again, our author is not affirming only that it was necessary for Jesus to be a human to accomplish this for Abraham's seed; it was necessary for him to be a Jew to be like the seed of Abraham (thus fulfilling the promise to Abraham in Gen 12) in all respects and the high priest of the Jewish God, though his priesthood would be after the order of Melchizedek, rather than Aaron or Levi or even Zadok. A priest is a representative of the people to God, so his work is chiefly directed toward God, for example, in the offering of sacrifices and the making of propitiation. This is why our author says that the priest deals with things in a Godward direction *(ta pros ton theon)*; he provides ministerial service in the things that should be directed to God—chiefly prayers and sacrifices.

William Lane notes that the image of someone who bests the devil is combined with the image of someone who is high priest in *Testament of Levi* 18.2, 10, 12: "Then shall the Lord raise up a new priest. . . . And he shall execute a

---

[246] While our author may include Gentiles within the seed of Abraham, there is certainly no indication that he is doing so here. Here is another small clue that the audience is Jewish, in this case Jewish Christians.

[247] Attridge, *Hebrews*, p. 94.

[248] Lane, *Hebrews*, 1.63-64.

[249] Craddock, *Hebrews*, p. 41.

righteous judgment upon the earth. . . . And he shall open the gates of paradise and shall remove the threatening sword against Adam. . . . And Beliar shall be bound by him, and he shall give power to his children to tread upon evil spirits."[250] The introduction of the high priest title for Jesus here is important, and one could argue that Hebrews 3:1—4:13 unpacks the notion that he is faithful, while Hebrews 4:14—5:10 unpacks the idea that he is merciful.[251]

This verse gives the chief reason for the incarnation—so that Jesus could become the sacrificial lamb and make atonement for sins. The word *hamartia* ("sin") is found more often in Hebrews than in any other New Testament book except Romans. Jesus is both a merciful and a faithful high priest—mercy is directed toward the people by making atonement or propitiation for their sins,[252] but faithfulness is directed toward God, as he knows that God requires that sins be atoned for: "The two adjectives wonderfully capture two central characteristics of Jesus Christ: his faithfulness to the will of God that took him to the cross (see 3:2, 6), and the mercy displayed to sinners by his death on that cross."[253] Here for the first time we have the direct introduction of the theme of Jesus being the high priest, a theme that will dominate the christological segments of the discourse to follow (especially Heb 4:14—5:10 and Heb 6:20—7:28). That propitiation is necessary is shown, for example, by our author thinking that wrath threatens his audience just as it threatened the wilderness-wandering generation (Heb 3:7—4:13; 10:26-31; 12:29).

In the history of Israel, the high priest became the central figure in Israel during the late Ptolemaic period leading up to 200 B.C., as the poetry of Ben Sira (Sirach 45.6-26; 50.1-21) and the Maccabean literature (1 Maccabees 10.15-21; 13.42; 14.4-47) make evident. Qumran literature reflects the crucial nature of the priestly role as well, even to the point of speaking of a priestly messianic figure (1QS [Manual of Discipline] 9.11) and the heavenly Melchizedek figure (11QMelch [*Melchizedek*]). Similarly exalted ideas are also found in *Testament of Levi* 18, most tellingly in the remark that this priest in his eternal priesthood will cause sin to cease, provide rest for the righteous and defeat the devil (*Testament of Levi* 18.9-12).

Thus our author, in addressing Jewish Christians, is not speaking out of or into a vacuum of ideas. Harold Attridge is right to stress that "neither of the two major characteristics of Jesus as High Priest, his heavenly intercessory function

---

[250]Lane, *Hebrews*, 1.65.
[251]Craddock, *Hebrews*, p. 41.
[252]*Hilaskomai* can certainly mean "propitiate," but it also has the connotation of "expiate." Both meanings can be found in the Septuagint (Lev 4:20, 26, 31; 5:10; 16:16, 33-34; Sirach 3.3, 30).
[253]Hagner, *Encountering the Book of Hebrews*, p. 61.

and his self-sacrifice, are found in connection with these eschatological priests. Neither are the judgmental or revelatory functions of the messianic priests characteristic of Jesus in Hebrews. Hence, the immediate sources of Hebrews' christology are not to be found here."[254]

The figures in both 11QMelch and *Testament of Levi* 18 are likely angelic figures, not ordinary human beings, which contrasts on both ends of the divine-human spectrum with our author's presentation of Jesus. In *Testament of Levi* 3.4-6 the priestly angels are described as offering propitiatory sacrifices in the heavenly temple for sinners.[255] Our author would flatly deny an angelomorphic Christology. If our author borrowed some of these ideas and applied them to Jesus, he has "deangelized" and demythologized them by focusing on the death of Jesus in space and time as the point and place where atonement was made. In the end, one must allow that our author was a creative handler of whatever traditions he used and is not slavishly following any earlier models. Even the Old Testament models of priesthood are inadequate because they apply to ordinary mortals, not a preexistent being. This is why Craig Koester rightly stresses that "unlike priests, who first had to be set apart from other people in order to minister (Exod 29; Lev 8; Sir 45:6), the Son who had been with God at the beginning of time (Heb 1:2) first had to become *like* people in order to minister on their behalf (2:17)."[256]

Hebrews 2:18 concludes this subsection on a practical note, which our author is frequently driving toward throughout this discourse. This verse introduces Hebrews 3, in which an imperative about fixing one's attention on the example of Jesus is supported by discourse and quotations and even exhortation (via quotation) in Hebrews 3:7-11. In Hebrews 2:18, however, the focus is on a particular way in which Jesus can be empathetic with his fellow human beings. The verb *peirazō* can mean either "tempt" or "test." Because he himself suffered being tested/tempted, he is able to give help to those undergoing being tested/tempted.[257] It is quite likely that our author is not thinking here of temptations in general, but more specifically of the trial of being pressured,

---

[254]Attridge, *Hebrews*, p. 99.

[255]Even more remote are some of the parallels found in Philo's *On Flight and Finding* 90-118. Philo so allegorizes his use of the imagery (e.g., the high priest can symbolize the human soul or mind, or the divine Logos can symbolize the divine creative principle) that it is stretching things to find much indebtedness of our author to the Philonic discussion. See Attridge, *Hebrews*, p. 100.

[256]Koester, *Hebrews*, p. 241 (emphasis original).

[257]Chrysostom is emphatic that the discussion here is about suffering and temptation/trials, not "suffering temptation" as if that merely meant undergoing temptation in some general sense: "Now he is not ignorant of our sufferings, not only because as God he knows them, but also because as man he knows them through the trial with which he was tested. Since he suffered many things, he knows how to sympathize with suffering" (*Homilies on Hebrews* 5.2).

persecuted, suffering for one's faith. When our author reiterates and amplifies this idea at Hebrews 4:15, it appears that he has something more specific in mind than general temptations. He is addressing Christians who are under fire because of their faith and are tempted to defect or return to their previous religious orientation, as Hebrews 10:32-34 makes perfectly clear. It is thus appropriate to render Hebrews 2:18 "because he himself was tested/tempted by what he suffered."[258] Suffering is a trial that, like the fear of death, can tempt a person to become unfaithful to what one believes, to that which one has previously committed one's life. Jesus demonstrated that one can endure and prevail over such trials, and furthermore he does not leave the believer to do so on his own: "The one who has led the way can now lend a hand. . . . Christ 'is able' . . . to give aid because, as a fellow sufferer, he is merciful and sympathetic, but also because, by his suffering, he has been brought to that position of honor and glory whence true help comes."[259]

Interestingly, our author will draw analogies between his audience and the wilderness-wandering generation. While they have been liberated from the slave driver (in this case Satan), they are not out of the woods, nor have they yet entered the promised rest in the promised land. The arc of their narrative ranges from redemption through trials and suffering to glory. But now they are in *medias res*—in the middle of things, tempted to turn back rather than go forward because the going has gotten rough. Fortunately they have someone greater than angels or Moses on their side leading them by the hand on to glory. It is not an accident that the climax of this discourse in Hebrews 12:18-29 ends at the new Jerusalem, a place at which they have not yet arrived but can "see" from where they are, by faith. The narratological logic of the discourse must be such that the current situation of the audience fits the analogies and the point in the story that the author says they are now inhabiting.[260]

THE ONE GREATER THAN MOSES REQUIRES A BETTER RESPONSE AND PROVIDES A BETTER RESULT (HEB 3:1-19)

He said "today" that they might never be without hope. "Exhort one another daily," he says. That is, even if persons have sinned as long as it is "today," they have hope; let them not then despair so long as they live. Above all things, indeed, he says, "Let there not be an evil unbelieving heart." But even if there should be, let no one despair, but let that one recover; for as long as we are in the world, the "today" is in season. (Chrysostom *Homilies on Hebrews* 6.8)

---

[258]Long, *Hebrews*, p. 45.

[259]Attridge, *Hebrews*, p. 96.

[260]Koester, *Hebrews*, p. 240.

As long as things go well, of course, remaining faithful is little challenge, but when trouble starts, when the storms of sorrow begin to rage, when the weeds of failure grow in the garden, when the valley of the shadow of death closes in, when the mouth goes dry in the spiritual desert, when all hell breaks loose, then we are tempted to ad-lib the ending, to trade God's story for one that is happier, easier, more upbeat, safer, less demanding, or at least one we can touch and see and hold in our own hands. . . .

What it means to be faithful is to harmonize all of one's actions to God's essential plot. On the seventh day, God the playwright rested, and the basic outlines of the plot were finished, complete, and perfect. We actors are told the plot and know where the play is surely going in God's providence, but we have been given the freedom to work our way to this denouement.

The problem however, is that the play is so long, the plot so complicated, so full of twists and unexpected turns, so ironic, so rich and tragic and painful moments, that it is easy to get lost, to get so caught up in one of the scenes that the outcome of the whole play is forgotten. . . . Some, losing track of the plot, become disheartened and abandon the play in the middle. Others, despairing of finding meaning in the play, begin to drift away from the plot. The cast is restless, sometimes in disarray, and the only way to keep us faithful, of course, is to keep reminding us of the basic plot. That is precisely what the Preacher in Hebrews is doing in his sermon-within-a-sermon.[261]

Hebrews 3:1-19 is often seen as a further section of exposition and commentary on key texts. This, however, overlooks that each of its three main subsections are introduced with imperatives. Hebrews 3:1 is clearly a conclusion drawn on the basis of the previous discussion in Hebrews 2, particularly Hebrews 2:10-18, and this conclusion entails an exhortation or imperative to very carefully consider *(katanoēsate)* Jesus. In Hebrews 3:7-8 the Holy Spirit addresses the audience directly, using Scripture and exhorting them not to harden their hearts if they hear the voice of God today. And in Hebrews 3:12 our author, building on the Scripture citation in Hebrews 3:7-11, exhorts the audience directly to "see to it" or "take care" that they not have an unbelieving heart (unlike the wilderness-wandering generation), but to the contrary that they encourage each other. The exhortation then ends with a string of rhetorical questions and a concluding word in Hebrews 3:19. Thus, Hebrews 3 must be seen as a hortatory part of the discourse that grows out of and depends upon what has been said in Hebrews 2 and is built around the three major exhortations that introduce each subsection of the chapter.

There is no polemic here at all against Moses, but those who were rebellious

---

[261]Long, *Hebrews*, pp. 56-58.

come in for some heavy weather. As with the comparison with angels, our author is following the normal rules about a rhetorical synkrisis when the point of comparison is between two good persons or things. The basic concept of this comparative technique is to show how one person is worthy of greater praise than the other, for good reasons that must be enumerated. The first point to stress is that "comparison . . . was primarily a set of techniques for the 'amplification' of good and bad qualities in speeches involving praise and blame [i.e., epideictic speeches]."[262] Aristotle is quite emphatic that this rhetorical technique is most appropriate in epideictic oratory (*Rhetoric* 1.9.38). Quintilian tells us what the proper use of this technique involves: "The first words of alternate phrases are frequently repeated to produce correspondence" (*Institutio oratoria* 9.3.32). We certainly see this in our discourse when our author compares Jesus and Moses; for example, in Hebrews 3:5-6 a *men . . . de* construction is used to compare the two men while predicating the same virtue, *pistos*, of both of them. Aristotle stresses that the proper way to amplify the praise of a good person is to "compare him with illustrious persons, for this affords grounds for amplification, and is noble, if he can be proved better than men of worth" (*Rhetoric* 1.9.38). Certainly we see this when our author stresses that while Moses served well *within* the "house," Jesus was greater still in his service as Son *over* the entire house. The point of praising such virtues is the attempt to inculcate a desire to emulate them in the audience. It is then no accident that the virtue touted here is the "faithfulness" of Moses and Jesus, the very thing our author wants out of his audience, as both Hebrews 3 and Hebrews 11 make abundantly clear.

There is a subtlety to our author's rhetoric in this respect. A good orator knew whom to safely and overtly compare his subject with and whom to avoid speaking of directly. Thus our author has no hesitation in comparing Jesus to angels, Moses, Melchizedek, Isaac and others, but he could not directly compare Jesus with the emperor for the very good reason that it would be subversive and seen as seditious and would have brought only more suffering to his audience.

Yet it was precisely emperors who most often in our author's age received the sort and quality and magnitude of comparisons found in this discourse. For example, Menander Rhetor stresses that in royal panegyrics no degree of amplification was too grand. One should compare and contrast the emperor with lesser royal figures or previous emperors by comparing nature with nature, upbringing with upbringing, education with education, reign with reign, exploits with exploits, triumphs with triumphs, until the one currently being praised outshines the other in every department (2.372.20-22; 2.376.31-377.9).

---

[262]Forbes, "Paul and Rhetorical Comparison," p. 134.

Synkrisis was a technique found most often and deemed most appropriate in epideictic rhetoric, and its being featured in various places in Hebrews speaks volumes about the character of the rhetoric in this discourse. Aristotle stresses that comparison of a person with another of high repute is called amplification, "which is one of the forms of praise" (*Rhetoric* 1.9.39). Our author is wise enough to praise Jesus in a way that demonstrates that he outshines everyone else on the planet, even the emperor, but he does so by comparisons with positive supernal and mortal examples to which his audience would readily assent. And he does all this without getting himself or the audience in trouble by mentioning Exhibit A, which generated epideictic rhetoric all over the empire. Jesus is of a higher nature than angels. He is more faithful and has more authority than Moses. These sorts of comparisons could only raise the question: Who then can he be?

Hebrews 3:1-6 seems to have a carefully constructed chiastic pattern that gives it a certain logic:

A   identity of the congregation: brothers and sisters, holy partners (Heb 3:1a)

B   Jesus and Moses: both faithful (Heb 3:1b-2)

C   Jesus worthier, because through him God built the house (Heb 3:3-4)

B'   Jesus and Moses: Moses is a servant in the house, Jesus a son over the house (Heb 3:5-6a)

A'   identity of the congregation: God's house (Heb 3:6b)[263]

The center of this part of the argument is obviously the synkrisis of Moses and Jesus. The surprise ending is the observation that the audience can be said to be a "house"; put another way, Christians are under construction. Not just the universe or even the people of God in all generations are the house, but this specific congregation being addressed in Rome is God's house. We might have expected the author to say that the audience was servants in the house like Moses, but no, they are now the house that is being built. This gives the sense that what God has been building all along has culminated in the building up of the audience of Hebrews! No wonder he will add at Hebrews 3:6: "Go ahead and crow, hold firm to the free speech and the boast of your hope."

Quintilian reminds us that the quickest method of securing assent to some course of action (or in this case refraining from a course of action—namely defecting) was to point the audience to historical parallels from which they could

---

[263]Long, *Hebrews*, p. 51.

draw valid inferences (*Institutio oratoria* 3.8.36). Since our author is not suggesting a change in direction, but rather the avoidance of such a change, this
comports nicely with epideictic rather than deliberative aims. No new policy or
course of action is urged here. Aristotle reminds us that the appeal to historical
examples often persuades because it was assumed that the future, when it
comes to causality, will be like the past (*Rhetoric* 1.4.9; 2.20.8). David deSilva
rightly stresses that the orator can convincingly predict future outcomes because, as Aristotle says, "it is by examination of the past that we divine and judge
the future" (*Rhetoric* 1.9.40).[264] Our author, however, focuses on "today," not on
the future, in his use of Psalm 95, and thus his focus is on avoiding in the
present a future that was like Israel's past.

The house or household was a major source of identity for ancient peoples.
Different houses had differing honor ratings, and the one with the highest
honor rating was the house of Augustus, which ruled the empire from Jesus'
day right through the time when Hebrews was written (Philo *Against Flaccus*
104), with a vast network of slaves and others who worked in and for Caesar's
household (Phil 4:22). On the surface, this seems to contrast drastically with
a small group of Jewish Christians meeting in a villa or in some apartment
complex in Rome for worship and fellowship. "Nevertheless, the author insists
that their relationship to Christ gives them reason to be proud (3:6), since they
belong to the household of God, who is worthy of the highest honor (3:3-
4)."[265] This being the case, joining any lesser household would involve a de-
cline in the degree of honor. Our author seeks to forestall such a mistake by
any in his audience.

[3:1] *Hence holy brothers, sharers of the heavenly calling, consider closely the apostle
and high priest of our confession, Jesus, [2] being faithful to the one appointing him,
just as also Moses was in (the whole of)[266] his house. [3] For this one is considered of
greater glory than Moses just as inasmuch as the builder of a house has greater
honor than the house itself. [4] For every house is built by someone, but the builder of
everything is God. [5] And Moses, on the one hand, was faithful in the whole of his
house as an assistant unto the testimony of what was to be said, [6] but Christ on the
other hand was (faithful) as a Son over his house, whose house we ourselves are, if*

---

[264]DeSilva, *Perseverance in Gratitude*, p. 141.
[265]Koester, *Hebrews*, p. 253.
[266]Most manuscripts include the word *whole*, but 𝔓[13], B and some church fathers (e.g., Ambrose, Cyril) omit the word here. On the one hand, the word *whole* is found at Heb 3:5 and
is well grounded in Num 12:7. But it is hard to understand any reason why later scribes
would omit the word if it was original in Heb 3:2. Metzger, *Textual Commentary*, p. 664,
suggests that it was omitted for stylistic reasons—to enhance the parallelism between the example of Jesus and Moses.

we have held firm to/preserved the free speech/confidence and boast of the hope.[267]

[7] *Therefore, just as the Holy Spirit says,*

"Today, if you hear his voice, [8] *do not let your heart be hardened, as in the provocation/rebellion, according to the days of testing in the wilderness* [9] *when your fathers were putting me to the test in examination and saw my work* [10] *for forty years. Therefore, I was angry with that generation and said, "Always they are gone astray of heart, but they do not know my ways,"* [11] *as I swore in my anger, "(See) if they will ever enter into my rest!"*

[12] *Watch out/take care, brothers, lest any of you have an evil, unbelieving heart falling away/defecting from the living God,* [13] *but beseech each other every day as long as it is called "today," in order that some from you not be hardened by the deceit of sin.* [14] *For we have been partners/sharers of Christ, if, that is, we hold fast the source of assurance firmly to the end.* [15] *As it has been said:*

"Today if you hear his voice, do not harden your heart as in the provocation/rebellion."

[16] *For who was it that, hearing, rebelled? But did not all those leaving from Egypt do so through Moses?* [17] *With whom was he angry for forty years? Was it not those who sinned, as the corpses fell in the desert?* [18] *But who was it that he swore that they would not enter into his rest, if not those who disobeyed?* [19] *And we see that they were not able to enter because of unbelief.*

Hebrews 3 begins with in-group language and with rhetorically attractive alliteration: *adelphoi, hagioi, apostolon, archierea.*[268] It is not very helpful to call the use of family language here an example of "fictive kinship" language because our author, like Paul, believes that Christians are spiritually united with one another, having a real spiritual kinship through Christ. The term *spiritual kinship*, an actual relationship created by the Spirit, would be more apt. The audience is addressed in **Hebrews 3:1** not only as "holy brothers" but also as sharers or partners in a heavenly calling. Harold Attridge points out the difference between being called from or to heaven and a guarantee of entrance into heaven.[269] Our

---

[267]After the word *hope* the Textus Receptus (with ℵ, A, C, D, K, P and other manuscripts) adds *mechri telous bebaian* ("firm to the end"). This is probably an interpolation based on Heb 3:14—and a grammatically incorrect one at that, because we would have expected *bebaion* to qualify the substantive "the boast." See Metzger, *Textual Commentary*, p. 665; Attridge, *Hebrews*, p. 104.

[268]This section is quite clearly a continuation and a drawing of conclusions based on what has been previously said, as *hothen* ("because") makes clear. Koester, *Hebrews*, p. 242, points out that this term consistently shows up in the middle of an argument or segment of an argument, not at the outset (Heb 2:17; 7:25; 8:3; 9:18; 11:19). But Hebrews is one long, running discourse with a series of points being made, so we need to be cautious about making too much of artificial divisions in the discourse that stretches from Heb 1:5 to near the end of Heb 13.

[269]Attridge, *Hebrews*, p. 102.

author likes using the word *epouranios* ("heavenly"), and it is understandable that many of the church fathers, especially in the Middle Ages, understood the author to be speaking about "being called to go to heaven."

Our author is, however, talking about the influence of heaven right here on earth. The calling is for those still on earth, and the heavenly gift referred to in Hebrews 6:4 is something already offered in space and time (salvation). Even when our author speaks of a heavenly sanctuary (Heb 8:5), heavenly things (Heb 9:23), heavenly country (Heb 11:16) or heavenly Jerusalem (Heb 12:22), he is talking not just about heavenly realities, but otherworldly realities that are coming to earth—in other words, eschatological realities. Our author believes that what is currently "up there" will one day be "out there" in the future when Jesus returns. This is why Donald Hagner is right to say "rather than reflecting a strictly vertical dualism, the word 'heavenly,' like the word 'perfect,' is used to point to the fulfillment of eschatological realities, the historical foreshadowings of which pale by comparison."[270] Our author's dualism has more to do with the traditional Jewish idea of "this world" and "the world to come" than it has to do with Platonic dualism. Craig Koester rightly points out that three major Old Testament images or sequences of events are drawn on and appealed to in Hebrews: wandering in the wilderness (= wandering away from God), entering the sanctuary (= entering the promised land) and journeying up to Zion within the land (= going up to eschatological Zion).[271] This sequence is both logical and chronological, and it is not an accident that our author introduces these three motifs precisely in the order that he does—with Hebrews 12 being the climactic pilgrimage recounted in the peroration. A story or narrative logic drives the discourse toward its conclusion, though the story keeps appearing and disappearing, being referred to, then alluded to, as the discourse progresses.

But it is not just the church to which special language is applied. This is also true of Jesus in Hebrews 3:1. Here Jesus is called, for the only time in the New Testament and in all early Christian literature, the apostle (and high priest) of our confession.[272] The term *apostolos* has its most basic sense of a "sent one"— God's sent one: "God had many messengers and intermediaries, but Jesus alone is apostle and high priest of 'our confession.'"[273] The terms *apostle* and *high*

---

[270]Hagner, *Encountering the Book of Hebrews*, p. 65.

[271]Koester, *Hebrews*, p. 262.

[272]The idea however of Jesus being the sent one or agent of God is certainly present in the Gospel of John (Jn 14—17). See Witherington, *John's Wisdom*.

[273]Craddock, *Hebrews*, p. 45. Both of the two major rhetorical comparisons in the first four chapters of Hebrews—comparisons with angels and with Moses—are with someone who is an intermediary between God and human beings and, further, one who is sent by God. Our author is suggesting that Jesus eclipses all such intermediaries.

priest span the gamut of Jesus' earthly career: he came to earth as God's sent one, and he returned to heaven to be our heavenly high priest after completing his earthly mission.

The Christian confession then spans the entire trajectory or arc of Jesus' career. It does not involve confessing things that were true about only the preexistent Son or only the incarnate one or only the exalted high priest. It involves confessing who he was, who he is, what he was sent to do, what he did, what he continues to do. The name Jesus is applied to the one who is both apostle and high priest. Our author does not have an adoptionist Christology, that is clear. The word *our* is important here. This in-group language—"our" confession—makes clear that this community has a distinct identity and a distinct sense of its identity. It confesses to the world and to God things that other religious communities would not confess.

The aorist imperative verb *katanoēsate,* also used at Hebrews 10:24, refers to reflecting or ruminating on or giving close attention to Jesus—who he is and what he has done and does (*Letter of Aristeas* 3; Lk 12:24, 27; Acts 7:31-32; Rom 4:19; *1 Clement* 37.2). Jesus is the one professed and confessed (Heb 4:14; 10:23; 11:13; 13:15). To defect from the faith does not mean to just leave behind a set of ideas or ideals. It means to turn one's back on the living Christ and one's relationship with him. Our author sees belief as important as behavior. The Christian faith was not just about orthopraxy, though that was clearly a crucial part of it. One thing that distinguished early Christianity from early Judaism was the stronger stress on maintaining the good confession, what would later be called orthodoxy.

When one reflects on Jesus and what he has done, the term *pistos* in **Hebrews 3:2** immediately comes to mind. He was faithful to the one who appointed him, as was already stated in Hebrews 2:17. The question is whether the audience will remain faithful to their heavenly calling as well. Fred Craddock points out that *pistos* and its cognates dominate the terminology of Hebrews 3:1—4:13, and so not surprisingly we also have more exhortations in this section to faithfulness in various forms.[274] The opposite of this is unfaith or, better, distrust or untrustworthiness, as David deSilva suggests (Dio Chrysostom *Orations* 73-74).[275] And even when our author quotes the Old Testament (with Ps 95 coming in for repeated citation in this and the next chapter), the quotations serve a parenetic purpose, as the author intends "to bring all of the authority of God and his word to bear on his readers problems."[276] In

---

[274]Craddock, *Hebrews,* p. 45.
[275]DeSilva, *Perseverance in Gratitude,* p. 144.
[276]Burns, "Hermeneutical Issues and Principles," p. 597.

our author's view the Old Testament is still the living voice of God speaking directly to the audience about matters theological and ethical, including the issue of being faithful. There may even be some echoes of 1 Samuel 2:35 here, which speaks of God's promise to Eli to raise up a faithful priest for whom he will build a house.

Moses is introduced into the discussion of **Hebrews 3:3-5** on the basis of Numbers 12:7, which explains the use of the rare word *therapōn* ("servant").[277] What is especially telling about the introduction of Moses into the discussion at this juncture is that Numbers 12:7-8 sets up a comparison between Moses and prophets. Prophets are said to receive God's word in visions and dreams, but "not so with my servant Moses; he is entrusted with all my house [a metaphorical reference to God's people]. With him I speak face to face—clearly and not in riddles; and he beholds the form of the Lord." For those who knew this text the point would be obvious: Moses was the most special and favored intermediary between God and human beings in the entire Old Testament period. If the Son was greater than Moses, he was greater than all Old Testament figures. This can be even better illustrated by considering what is said of Moses in Sirach 45.1-3 in light of what has already been said of Jesus in Hebrews 1—3: "From his descendants the Lord brought forth a man of mercy, who found favor in the sight of all flesh and was beloved by God and humanity, Moses, whose memory is blessed. He made him equal in glory to the holy ones . . . , and made him great in the fears of his enemies. By his words he caused signs to cease; the Lord glorified him in the presence of kings. He gave him commands for his people, and showed him part of his glory."[278]

Our author wants to make clear that those contemplating going back to the safer confines of Judaism are turning their backs on God's ultimate intermediary. Jesus not only has more glory than Moses, but Jesus is the Son of the builder[279] of the house called "God's people"—not merely a servant within the house. If one leaves the Son of the builder to return to the servant, one has left the house

---

[277]Our author does not treat the subject of Moses as a priest, though that is a minor theme in the Old Testament (Ex 2:1; Ps 99:6) that is developed further in later Jewish sources (Sirach 45.4-5; *1 Enoch* 89.36-38 [Moses transformed into an angel]; Philo, *On the Life of Moses* 1.158; 2.166-86). Numbers 12:7 is the jumping off point for Philo to talk about Moses as a priest, yet our author makes nothing of this here. Here is one more example that our author will go his own way from his Jewish heritage, not being a slavish imitator of earlier discussions. Comparisons with Philo show that our author and Philo share a universe of discourse, but they often use it very differently.
[278]Here I follow deSilva's translation in *Perseverance in Gratitude*, p. 135.
[279]The more closely one looks at the vocabulary of Hebrews the clearer it seems that our author knew Wisdom of Solomon. The verb *kataskeuazō* is used of God's creative activity in both Wisdom of Solomon 9.2; 13.4; and here to speak of God's fashioning of things.

as well (Heb 6:1-4).[280] The assumed continuity between God's Old Testament people and the church is made explicit in **Hebrews 3:6**: "we are his house." There is precedent for using house language for a particular Jewish sect (e.g., the Qumran community is called "the holy house" in 1QS [Manual of Discipline] 8.5-9; 9.6), and this language is common elsewhere in the New Testament (1 Cor 3:9-17; Eph 2:22; 1 Tim 3:15; 1 Pet 2:5; 4:17). Moses (and the other Old Testament saints) are "in the house" as well. Our author is not a supercessionist, as if God's New Testament people replaced God's Old Testament people. Rather he sees those who are in Christ as the continuation of God's Old Testament people, much the same as Paul did. While there is covenantal discontinuity between the old and new eras, there is also ecclesiological continuity.

There is no polemic here against Moses, nor is this Moses Christology; it is simply an assumption of the progression of salvation history, that Moses was part of an era that has been eclipsed with the coming of God's Son.[291] Harold Attridge rightly stresses: "The comparison between Christ and Moses serves rhetorical, not polemical, purposes. As in encomia generally, the comparison serves not so much to denigrate the comparable figure as to exalt the subject of the discourse."[282] Thomas Long puts it this way: "Like a doorman whose job it is to announce who is about to enter the ballroom, Moses' job was 'to testify to the things that would be spoken later' (3:5). This clear reference to Hebrews 1:1-2 puts Moses in the prophet's role, anticipating and pointing to the Son who was to come."[283] Our author will say more about Moses as one of those in the hall of faithfulness (Heb 11:23-28). Craig Koester writes: "Identifying Moses as a 'witness' allowed Christians to affirm the importance of Moses and the Law without making them the basis for faith and life."[284]

Christians in the meantime are urged to hang on to "the boast of hope," language that has parallels with Romans 5:2 and 2 Corinthians 3:12. Attridge con-

---

[280]Our author is playing on various senses of house, including the literal one in Heb 3:3b-4. In Heb 3:4 it even refers to the universe that God built! But the main focus is on house as God's people.

[291]For a full discussion of the Moses material in Hebrews see D'Angelo, *Moses in the Letter to the Hebrews*, pp. 65-199. Long, *Hebrews*, p. 49, catches the force of the rhetoric here quite well: "The intent is not to cast a shadow on Moses but to shine a light on Jesus. It was a stock topic in early Christian preaching to describe Jesus' superiority to key Old Testament figures, such as Abraham (see John 8:53), Jacob (see John 4:12), Solomon (see Matt. 12:42), David (see Matt. 22:45) and Moses (see 2 Cor. 3:7-18). The point was never to tarnish the luster of these giants but to build on their greatness by conveying the truth that something greater even than Abraham or David or Moses is here."

[282]Attridge, *Hebrews*, p. 105.

[283]Long, *Hebrews*, pp. 50-51.

[284]Koester, *Hebrews*, p. 246.

cludes: "'We' are God's house only if we maintain our boldness and hopeful
boast."[285] The language of boasting is unsurprising and quite appropriate in epideictic rhetoric dedicated to praising things of recognized value (Rom 5:2; 2 Cor
3:12; Jas 1:9; 4:16). The term *parrēsia* here, while sometimes translated "confidence," has in rhetorical contexts the meaning of free or bold speech, which is
likely the sense here.[286] But confidence or self-assurance results in boldness or
freeness of speaking, even in a context where the speech or confession would
be controversial. David deSilva stresses that our author will urge the audience
to take advantage of the direct access they have to God through Jesus and so
be bold and speak freely with God in their travail (Heb 4:16; 10:19-25).[287]

Hebrews 3:7-11 quotes what is for our author a crucial psalm, Psalm 95:7-
11, introduced as the living voice of the Holy Spirit speaking directly to our author's Jewish Christians in Rome "today." The word *today* that introduces the
quotation makes it easy to contemporize the text and apply directly to the audience, but the reference to the Holy Spirit has the same contemporizing effect.
Our author has previously introduced such quotations as the voice of God (Heb
1:5 9, 13) or of Christ (Heb 2:12-13) speaking directly to the audience. There
can be little doubt that he sees all three as personal expressions of the one God
he worships, and so we must recognize the implicit trinitarianism here: "The effect of such attribution is to allow no discontinuity between past and present
people of God."[288] This hermeneutical move is made easier because it was
David himself, in 2 Samuel 23:2, who claimed that the Spirit of the Lord spoke
through him, and as Hebrews 4:7 will make evident, David is assumed to be the
author of Psalm 95.[289] There is also little doubt that our author believes that he
and his audience are living in the age called "today."

The psalm quotation sets off a chain of linked comments: the opening words
of the quotation are reiterated at Hebrews 3:15 and Hebrews 4:7, with the final
part recurring in Hebrews 4:3 and Hebrews 4:5. Clearly the discourse is ongoing, and we should not set a hard division at the end of Hebrews 3. The psalmist
is alluding to the experience of Israel as recorded in Exodus 17:1-7 and Numbers
14:20-35. Using the story indirectly through the psalm—rather than directly from
the Pentateuch—puts our author in good company, for he is doing for his own

[285]Attridge, *Hebrews*, p. 111.
[286]Rightly Van Unnik, "Christian's Freedom of Speech"; Vorster, "Meaning of *Parrēsia*"; and Marrow, "*Parrēsia* in the New Testament."
[287]DeSilva, *Perseverance in Gratitude*, p. 139.
[288]Craddock, *Hebrews*, p. 47.
[289]Koester, *Hebrews*, p. 254, also discusses the rather minor differences between Ps 95 and Heb
3.

audience what the psalmist did for his: he is contemporizing, or what the French call *relecteur* ("making a past word a present word").[290] In addition, the quotation is incomplete: Hebrews 3:11 reads "if they enter my rest . . ."—offering the protasis but not the apodosis of a conditional statement. This incompleteness is reflected in the Hebrew text, the Septuagint and the quotation in Hebrews and is probably done deliberately. A curse would normally follow in the second half of the statement (see, e.g., Ps 7:4-5; 137:5-6), but neither the psalmist in his homily nor our author is comfortable leaving the audience with a curse sanction, perhaps in the case of our author because Jesus said "no oaths."[291]

Hebrews 3:12 and Hebrews 3:19 form a rhetorical inclusio with key terms like "see to it" and "unbelief" *(apistia)*—found only here in Hebrews—being repeated. The rhetorical force of the words in Hebrews 3:12 is emphasized by assonance and repetition of similar sounds *(apistias, apostēnai)*. The exhortation becomes more strident when we see that the imperatives in Hebrews 3:12 ("see to it") and Hebrews 3:1 ("closely consider") are both qualified by the word *brothers*, making clear this is an in-house matter. There is an urgency to the exhortation in Hebrews 3:12. Harold Attridge writes: "The object clause with the indicative suggests that the threat is real and urgent. The author asks that the danger not affect any individual . . . in the community. He then specifies the danger as one of a 'wicked, faithless heart.' . . . Faithlessness involves not simply passive disbelief, but active resistance to the will of God."[292]

Scholars often compare the use of the Old Testament here to Paul's use of the story of the wilderness-wandering generation in 1 Corinthians 10:1-11. The most obvious similarity is the typological use of the Old Testament, but Paul's reading of the Old Testament text is more overtly christological, whereas our author, writing to Jewish Christians, does not merely say—"it happened to *them* so it could happen to *you*"—as Paul does for his largely Gentile audience. Rather, our author is more direct: the Holy Spirit *says*, "Do not harden your hearts as *you* did in the rebellion." There is an ethnic and religious continuity between this audience in Rome and the rebellious Jews of long ago. Our author sees their story as the continuation of the story of Israel, not merely analogous to it. And our author's concern is that the audience might act like their ancestors—giving way to unbelief and turning away, hardened by sin and going astray.

Thus at **Hebrews 3:13** our author picks back up the first verse of the psalm

[290]Craddock, *Hebrews*, p. 48.
[291]Koester, *Hebrews*, p. 257.
[292]Attridge, *Hebrews*, p. 116.

even harsrully

and urges them to "exhort [*or* keep exhorting] one another every day, as long as it is called 'today.'" Every day is a test, and every day the call to faithfulness needs to ring out and be positively responded to. Fred Craddock is right that the word *sin* here refers to apostasy and unfaithfulness, not moral aberrations such as sexual sin.[293] The verb *apisteō* is the root of the terms *unbelief* and *disobedience* in Hebrews 3:18-19.

Our author is very adept at the Jewish technique of handling Scripture known as midrash pesher. The word *pesher* means "interpret," a procedure already seen in our author's handling of Psalm 8 in Hebrews 2:6-9. A pesher proceeds by taking up certain keywords from the cited text and incorporating them in an address or argument to one's audience. It also involves molding the quotation to fit the situation being addressed to make it more apropos. This use of Scripture is well known to us now from Qumran and elsewhere in early Jewish literature, and it is puzzling only if one assumes that the author is citing the text as a proof-text for an argument that is coherent without the citation. The argument is often not coherent apart from the citation and the way the citation is woven into the discussion. It also frequently presupposes an understanding of the setting and significance of the original text, something a Jewish Christian audience would be more likely to have than a Gentile one.

As already noted, the textual base cited in our case is Psalm 95, which is first cited extensively and then piecemeal no less than five times in Hebrews 3:7—4:16. This psalm has two major parts: Psalm 95:1-7a is a call to worship, while Psalm 95:7b-11 is a warning against disobeying God, reinforced by a reminder of what happened to Israel in the wilderness. Our author uses only the second half of the psalm. Like the psalmist, he is concerned with the events the psalm alludes to (recorded in Ex 17:1-7 and Num 14:20-35), which are important to understanding the argument here. Our author draws an analogy between the situation of the wilderness-wandering generation and the fate that befell them in not entering the resting place (i.e., Canaan) and the situation of his audience, who were in danger of not entering a more ultimate form of God's promised rest. In due course (Heb 4:7), he will also bring into the argument the story from Genesis 2:2 about God resting from his creation labors.

These Scriptures plus intertestamental ideas about rest provide the grist for our author's mill. The key assumption of our author is that the situations of the wilderness-wandering and his audience are analogous in some ways. The trials are seen as the same (Heb 3:12, 19; 4:1-2, 6), and Hebrews 4:1 suggests that the same promise of rest is extended to both groups of God's peo-

---

[293]Craddock, *Hebrews*, p. 49.

ple. Both cases involve the pilgrim people of God, and here in this subsection our author introduces this theme, which becomes increasingly major in the homily and climaxes in Hebrews 12.

Our author's argument proceeds as follows. (1) Psalm 95 makes clear that the wilderness-wandering generation did not enter God's promised rest, that is, the resting place of Canaan. (2) Furthermore, since the psalmist is still extending the promise in his own time by using the phrase *today if you hear this promise*, the promise is still outstanding, that one can still enter the rest, even though David lived so much later than the time of Moses and Joshua. (3) Further, Genesis 2:2 indicates that the rest to be entered is God's own. This means it has existence—since God ceased creating—and is continuing even now (this is based in part on Gen 2:2 not mentioning evening and morning, and thus in early Jewish exegesis it was assumed that God's rest was still ongoing since it was not said to end, that is, he is still in his seventh day so far as rest is concerned).

There is a major debate among scholars as to whether our author believes that Christians can and do enter the rest prior to death, or whether like the Old Testament saints they simply have the promise that they shall enter it later. In part this issue is determined by whether "rest" in Hebrews means "resting place" or an eschatological condition that believers may participate in here and now. It appears that our author sees the concept of rest as something that exists in heaven now, but will one day exist on earth at the eschaton. If this is correct, then believers now have the assurance of this state that is hoped for, but not the condition itself just yet. Donald Hagner points out that our author stands in a long line of expositors, including Christian expositors (1 Cor 10), who use the exodus/Sinai typology to enforce a vital exhortation on their present audiences.[294] At Hebrews 3:7 the reference to the Holy Spirit speaking in the Old Testament means that the Spirit is seen as not merely the one who inspires it but as the one who speaks in these words. This is important, for our author believes that this is a living word of God for his audience, not least because the same Holy Spirit that believers have in their lives speaks throughout the Scriptures.

It is sometimes argued by scholars that our author would never accuse those lapsing back into Judaism of falling away from the living God, but that depends, as F. F. Bruce says, on whether our author thought a response to Christ was ultimately essential to salvation and entering that eschatological rest.[295] If he did, then for him to turn back to a shadow when we have the substance that revelation foretold is a sin against the light, a form of apostasy. This, it seems to me,

[294]Hagner, *Encountering the Book of Hebrews*, pp. 65-69.
[295]Bruce, *Hebrews*, pp. 96-99.

is clearly our author's view—Christ is essential in the "today" age to having a relationship with the living God, he is the mediator of that relationship—the old has passed away, the new has come in this regard.

One interesting aspect of using the Septuagint instead of the Hebrew text of Psalm 95 is that the place names in the Masoretic Text become human experiences in the Septuagint when the names Meribah and Massah are translated: "rebellion" and "testing." But the place names may have come from the experiences of God's people in those places in the first instance. In any event, our author is highlighting the potential parallels between the wilderness-wandering generation and his own audience. Another interesting aspect of our author's choice of citing the psalm instead of the original story in the Pentateuch is that it tips his hands—it shows his epideictic homiletical purposes. Fred Craddock puts it this way: "By using the psalmist's account and not that of the historical books themselves, the author has appropriated a piece of liturgy for a homily that is liturgical in nature. Psalm 95 is a call to enter God's presence with praise, and in that setting it urges the people to fidelity, avoiding Israel's ancient failure."[296]

A phrase in **Hebrews 3:14** could be read "partners in Christ" (as in Rom 12:5; 2 Cor 5:17; Eph 4:15-16) or "partners with Christ" (as in Rom 8:17). Either way, the Pauline influence seems present.[297] It is debated how the phrase *tēn archēn tēs hypostaseōs* should be rendered. It is something the audience is to hold firm to, and if we take *archēn* in its primal sense then it has to do with something that they took hold of at the beginning of their faith journey—something like their initial resolve, their initial grasp on the substance of the gospel.[298]

At **Hebrews 3:15-17** our author deals with the terrible irony and tragedy that the very ones whom Moses led out of Egypt were those who rebelled in the wilderness. They had every evidence of God's love and grace and had been miraculously rescued from Egypt, and yet they still committed apostasy. This is a sobering story, a sort of wake-up call, to tell to an audience under pressure and thinking of defecting.

Just because one is part of God's chosen people does not mean that a particular individual will be saved—particularly not if he or she is unfaithful. Unbelief and disobedience are virtually synonymous for our author.[299] "There seems to be a shift from exhortation to exposition through v. 19, but this only appears to be the case. Both the quotation and the comments that follow are

---

[296]Craddock, *Hebrews*, p. 48.

[297]Koester, *Hebrews*, p. 260. The issue is whether this is an objective or subjective genitive, since our text literally reads "partners of Christ."

[298]Attridge, *Hebrews*, p. 119.

[299]Rightly noted by Hagner, *Encountering the Book of Hebrews*, p. 67.

clearly hortatory; the move is simply from direct to indirect. The writer is speaking *about* Israel but in so doing is speaking *to* the readers. Rhetoricians understood that relief from confrontational style was often more effective than continuous confrontation."[300] The rhetorical technique our author is following in miniature here is called *insinuatio*—an indirect way of exhorting an audience by telling someone else's story and letting the parallels come gradually into view with the audience's situation.

Near the end of this section, in **Hebrews 3:18** our author introduces what will be a major theme of his ongoing discourse—the theme of rest, which is a multivalent term for our author, with a range of meanings: the rest God that experienced when he ceased creating, arriving in the promised land and resting from traveling, taking control of the promised land and putting an end to hostilities during the reign of David in that land, the rest one has from harm in the sanctuary or tabernacle when one grasps the horns of the altar, entering into the *shabbat shalom* here and now, entering into eternal rest in heaven or at the eschaton. **Hebrews 3:19** concludes the section on the note that disbelief and disobedience—or mistrust and misbehavior—work hand and hand. By the same token, so do real trust and real obedience to God.

The "Rest" of the Story (Heb 4:1-13)

> Sharper than any earthly two-edged sword, the speech of God knifes through the curtain between heaven and earth. . . . This sword is so sharp that it can separate even "the soul from the spirit," dividing between what really matters and what seems to matter. No one can hide from this speech act of God; the word of God unveils every human life, laid bare before the eyes of God. The word of God takes an ordinary day and makes it "today," takes an ordinary moment and makes it the time of crisis and decision, takes an ordinary event and makes it the theater of the glory of God, takes a routine life and calls it to holiness.[301]

Rhetoric is the art of persuasion, and that primary purpose undoubtedly fuels all that is being done here. The interplay of exposition and exhortation; alliteration; repetition of words and sounds; perfectly rounded inclusios; the rhythm of direct and indirect discourse; anticipation and restraint—these and other techniques are in the service of persuasion. But rhetoric is an art, and like all art it gives pleasure to the reader or hearer. The skillful writer or speaker, no matter how weighty the issue, how noble the cause, gives pleasure, and that pleasure is not for the purpose of sedating or seducing, or simply to curry the favor of an audience. Pleasure is a fundamental force in human history. Biological continuity, cultural continuity, in-

---

[300]Craddock, *Hebrews*, p. 50.
[301]Long, *Hebrews*, p. 61.

Seems.

(tellectual continuity—all are indebted more to pleasure than to logic. The ancient Greeks understood that.[302]

In Hebrews 4 we reach the conclusion of the discourse based on the interpretation of Psalm 95, which began as early as Hebrews 3:7. Probably we should see an inclusio, with the two exhortations "let us be afraid/careful" (Heb 4:1) and "let us be eager" (Heb 4:11) framing the section. This in turn means we should see Hebrews 4:12-13 as a transitional piece that takes us into the next segment of the discourse, beginning at Hebrews 4:14.[303] This is clearly one of the more complex portions of our author's discourse, as he continues to unpack the meaning of Psalm 95 for his audience and deals with the concept of God's rest and how believers can and should enter into it. He is not arguing that they have already entered into it and should beware of losing it. His concept is clearly eschatological: there is something incomplete, at present, about the salvation and final rest of believers. Our author believes that the Israelites already had a proleptic form of the good news preached to them about God's rest (Heb 4:6). There is continuity of message as well as continuity of people of God in our author's way of thinking about salvation history: "Despite differences due to the progress of revelation in history, a basic continuity exists between what the Old Testament saints experienced in their time frame and what is now experienced in the church."[304] Our author's eschatology has an already-and-not-yet dimension to it: the audience is "entering" (present continual tense) the rest, but they must eagerly strive to enter it as well.

In order to instill in an audience the need to do as they are exhorted to do, there must at some juncture be an appeal to the deeper emotions, such as fear. Sometimes this is withheld until the peroration, but in an epideictic discourse deeper emotions tend to be appealed to throughout the discourse. In Hebrews 4:1 we have a strong appeal to fear—the fear of failing to "enter his rest." David deSilva stresses that this fear is appealed to repeatedly in this whole section by repetition of the theme of "entering his rest," hammering home the importance of keeping going in the direction they had been heading in since conversion (Heb 3:18-19; 4:1, 3, 5, 6, 10, 11).[305]

[4:1] *We ought to fear then, lest, since the promise remains to enter into his rest, some from among you think to come too late, [2]for also we have had the gospel preached just as others also, but the word that was heard did not benefit them because they*

[302]Craddock, *Hebrews*, p. 56.
[303]Ibid., p. 51.
[304]Hagner, *Encountering the Book of Hebrews*, p. 73.
[305]DeSilva, *Perseverance in Gratitude*, p. 153.

were not associated/blended with/united in[306] faith with those who heard.

[3] For we enter into the rest, we who have believed just as it says, "As I swore in my anger, if they enter into my rest," and yet his work has been completed from the foundation of the cosmos. [4] For he says somewhere concerning the seventh day: "And God rested on the seventh day from all his work." [5] And in this context, "They shall never enter into my rest." [6] Since then it remains for some to enter into it, and those being preached to before did not enter because of unbelief. [7] Again he defines a certain day "today," saying a long time later through David just as he said before, "Today if you hear his voice, do not harden your hearts." [8] For if Jesus/Joshua had given them rest, he would not have spoken through others concerning another day. [9] Therefore there remains a sabbath observance of the people of God, [10] for those entering into his rest and themselves rest from their own works just as God did from the same.

[11] Be eager then to enter into that rest, in order not (to follow) in the example of some who fell due to unbelief. [12] For living is the word of God and active and sharper than any two-edged sword and penetrating as far as the separation of life breath and spirit, joint and marrow, and discerning reflections and thoughts of the heart, [13] and there is not a creature invisible before him but all are naked and laid bare to his eyes, to whom we (must speak) the word.

Our author's concept of rest is complicated. For a start, it refers to God ceasing from his creating activities and then by extension to his enjoying the ongoing rest he has had ever since that time. "Rest" in this more extended sense refers to a positive state of being, not just the absence of creative activity. Since God's rest is continuing, it continues to be a possibility that believers may enter it, especially since many in the past who were offered the chance to enter it failed to do so due to unbelief. Thus the opportunity still exists in part due to the disobedience and disbelief of some of God's people in the past. Unlike that found in the later Gospel of Thomas, our author is not primarily talking about rest/peace entering the believer, but rather the believer entering rest, an eschatological rather than psychological view of things. Our writer does not evaporate "Israel's history in some grand allegory of the pilgrimage of the soul. History remains history; neither past nor present is consumed by the other."[307] Herein lies an essential difference between the way our author treats the Old Testament and the way Philo does (*On the Embassy to Gaius* 51-52, 60).

---

[306] The nominative singular form is supported by א, 57 and a few minuscules, and the accusative reading is supported by the Alexandrian and Western text types and preserves the more difficult reading. It is hard to imagine the more difficult reading being later than the nominative singular, so it is probably original. See Metzger, *Textual Commentary*, p. 665; Attridge, *Hebrews*, p. 122.

[307] Craddock, *Hebrews*, p. 55.

Our author is not an allegorizer, but is he a spiritualizer—turning physical rest in a land into eternal rest in heaven (*Joseph and Aseneth* 8.9; 22.13)? One must be careful in suggesting such a view. While our author does believe that dying and going to be with the Lord is a blessing and a rest from trials, ultimately he sees the consummate rest as not in heaven but rather on earth at the eschaton. In this he is like Paul, though our author places more stress on what is true now in heaven, for the very good reason that the time focus of epideictic rhetoric is "today," speaking about what is true in the present. History is moving toward a goal of sabbatical, but our author also thinks that "there is rest in movement and movement in rest."[308]

There is nothing static or stultifying or stilted about our author's view of rest. If we must be precise, our author is saying that "today" we must embrace the promise of rest and continue to move faithfully forward to it. He is not suggesting that believers enter that rest in any full sense in the present, as the exhortations in Hebrews 4:1, 11 stress, unless one counts the sabbath observance as a foretaste. The parallels with the wilderness-wandering generation are persuasive and apt only if the present audience is still *in medias res* and on the way to the rest, but in danger of missing it.[309] This means that the present-tense verb *enter* should be seen here as a futuristic present tense, as in Matthew 17:11; John 14:3; 1 Corinthians 16:5. Striving to enter and already entering are two different things. We would have expected a perfect tense here if entering has already been completed.[310] Rather, believers are in the process of crossing the threshold and so of entering, but it is only after one finishes entering that one has complete rest. It is still possible to hesitate or waver or fall back from the threshold. To stand at the entryway to the promised land and be in the process of filing in is not the same as having entered. Our author draws the analogy between (a) the wilderness-wandering generation "treading the verge of Jordan" and being in the process of crossing over with Joshua as the pioneer going before them into the promised land and (b) the Jewish Christian audience following their own Joshua into the rest. The pioneer—not those who must still strive to follow his example—has fully crossed the threshold into his rest (Heb 12:1-2).

---

[308]Ibid., p. 56.

[309]Despite the protestations of Lane, *Hebrews*, 1.99; and Lincoln, "Sabbath Rest and Eschatology," p. 212. I agree with deSilva's critique of their view in *Perseverance in Gratitude*, pp. 153-54. The problem is partly a failure to pick up the epideictic rhetorical signals here. "Today" must be the topical focus, embracing and endorsing the promise of rest today. The rest is entered later.

[310]Rightly deSilva, *Perseverance in Gratitude*, pp. 154-55.

A CLOSER LOOK

Sabbath Rest for Jewish Christians?

What should we make of Hebrews 4:3 and its present-tense verb: "For we who have believed enter into rest"? F. F. Bruce wants to see this as a generalizing present "entry into that rest is for us who have believed."[311] On this showing, the rest is purely future and presumable to be identified with the heavenly resting place, which in due course will also descend to earth. But what does our author mean by rest?

The psalm quotations make clear that this is God's rest first and foremost; it is something that God has been enjoying since the end of his work of creation—when he sat back and savored the goodness of a job well done, indeed perfectly done. The term *katapausis* used in Psalm 95 is found in Hebrews 3:11, 18; 4:1, 3 (twice), 5, 10, 11, with the intransitive verbal cognate in Hebrews 4:4, 10 and the transitive verbal cognate in Hebrews 4:8. Since our author does not specifically define what he means by this term, we must assume that it was understandable to his audience.

The more usual term for rest in the Septuagint and New Testament (outside of Hebrews) is *anapausis*, which shows our author to be drawing on the Septuagint terminology of Psalm 95 and Genesis 2:2 (which has the verbal form *katapauō*). In the Septuagint *katapausis* means either "state of rest" (four times) or "resting place" (six times). In Psalm 95:11 it could refer to either. What might favor resting place in Psalm 95 is that the worshiper is invited to enter the temple (i.e., the earthly resting place or sanctuary of God). Again, the warning example of the wilderness-wandering generation entering the promised land—a resting place—is in view. Both the land and the temple as the resting place could be described by *katapausis*.

The primary reference must be to a place, for in Psalm 95 the alternative to entering into his rest is falling dead in the desert, and in Deuteronomy 12:9 we also hear of the land as a resting place. But we must go beyond the Old Testament. In Jewish intertestamental exposition, Psalm 95 was linked to an eschatological resting place, so much so that some rabbis called the new Jerusalem God's resting place. Intertestamental literature used Psalm 95:11 to refer to the eschatological resting place of the elect, a heavenly place entered at death (*Joseph and Aseneth* 7—9). Our writer is certainly familiar with this idea and probably is referring to an eschatological resting place, also associated with a heavenly land (Heb 11:14-16) or heavenly city (Heb 11:10) or heavenly sanctuary (Heb 6:19-20). This idea is probably confirmed later in this homily

---

[311]Bruce, *Hebrews*, pp. 106-8.

when our author stresses that the heavenly sanctuary is where God is now resting, where some of the saints now are and where Christ is the high priest.

But this rest is something God entered at creation. The land of Canaan is a mere type of the true rest of God, as is the temple. By juxtaposing Psalm 95 and Genesis 2:2 the whole purpose of creation and redemption is juxtaposed. On this showing God's rest—not the creation of humanity—is the climax of the creation story. More important is the word our author uses at Hebrews 4:9: *sabbatismos*. The verb *sabbatizō* in the Septuagint means "to keep the sabbath," and thus the noun literally means "sabbath keeping." Thus, when our author refers to a sabbath that remains (Heb 4:9), he presumably means that "there remains a celebration of the sabbath for God people."

The idea of a day of rest is then seen as yet another type on earth of God's ultimate rest—which means not so much an absence of activity, though that is a component, but the presence of joy, a sense of fulfillment, and completion (we may compare the idea of perfection at this point). It is also clear from Hebrews 4:11 that our author sees this rest as in the main a future condition/ event even for Christians, for they are to strive to enter that rest still, and disbelief *(apistia)* and disobedience *(apeitheia)* can disqualify them. But even this rest is only fully in heaven now, for our author will say elsewhere that we have already come to the heavenly Jerusalem (Heb 12:22) and that faith is defined as a present assurance about or grasp on the future truth (Heb 11:1)—a truth that, while it exists in heaven now, will one day appear more fully on earth. Thus it is quite possible, in the age of "today" that our author means to convey the idea that the audience has a foretaste of the rest, just as they have in part realized the benefits of salvation, for they are already partakers in Christ. It is possible that the rest also is already/not yet. At Hebrews 4:8 we are reminded that Joshua, even though he entered the land, did not give the people rest, for the promise is renewed later in Psalm 95.

In lectures on Hebrews delivered at Gordon-Conwell Theological Seminary, Andrew Lincoln suggests that we emulate God by ceasing from our (dead) works and by exercising faith in the promises (Heb 6:1; 9:14). Dead works are those that do not but might be thought to contribute to our salvation. Our author does not talk about works righteousness, as does Paul, and justification by faith is not a big issue in our homily. Our author is concerned with pointless works, not works righteousness. It may be that the Jewish Christian audience assumed that by some particular Jewish form of sabbath observance they might enhance their chance to enter the rest of God. Our author would seem to deny this. As far as we can tell, the church very early on assumed the practice of observing a new special day for Christ—the Lord's Day, celebrating the resurrection (Rev 1:10). Thus it is unlikely that our author is saying that even Jewish Christians have now a rest by keeping the sabbath. More likely what he means is that the audience has a rest here and now by living by faith in Christ and ceasing from dead works. Like God, they are to cease from works that no longer need to be undertaken. They are to appreciate the rest they have in Christ—the shalom they have in him. By redemption they have entered a foretaste of the final rest of God—a rest from sin, the fear of death and so on. They have this foretaste of rest in part now, to the extent that salvation is already present. But it will be consummated only later—either when they enter the heavenly city at death or at the eschaton. The rest affirmed here for the Jewish Christian audience is not different than the rest available to Gentile believers as well.

This interpretation of "rest" is confirmed by **Hebrews 4:2,** where we hear about "the promise of entering his rest" that still stands. The warning against "falling short of it" makes clear that they have not yet obtained it or arrived at the goal that can be called "rest."

Hebrews 4:2 speaks of the Israelites being "evangelized" by the message of redemption and rest. This clever paronomasia relates *euangelion* ("good news") to *epangelias* ("promise").[312] It was not, however, as though the message came to each one, individual by individual; rather, redemption and the message of further redemption and rest was given to the group and experienced by the group.[313] Fred Craddock puts it this way: "The writer clearly understands that the desert journey was a group experience, the behavior of some affecting the behavior of all. There was no subjective captivity of the good news of God's promise; they heard it together (4:2). Likewise, the message of this letter-sermon is addressed to the whole congregation."[314]

At **Hebrews 4:3-6** our author will underscore his point that faith and perseverance are necessary to entering the rest by giving a scriptural example, in this case Ps 95:7-8, that not all the Israelites entered the rest after wandering in the wilderness; indeed most did not. God has been resting ever since the end of creation, but he swore an oath that some would never enter that rest—namely, those who disobeyed and so were not allowed to enter the land of rest. Again the reference to "somewhere he has spoken" is not a memory lapse by the author, but reflects the lack of enumeration in the Old Testament text.

The reference in **Hebrews 4:7** to David who spoke "a long time after" makes

---

[312]Attridge, *Hebrews*, p. 125.
[313]The phrase *the word of hearing*, meaning the word heard, is reminiscent of 1 Thess 2:13 and is perhaps another small clue that our author knows some of Paul's earlier letters.
[314]Craddock, *Hebrews*, p. 55.

the point that had the previous generations experienced this rest, it would not still be on offer by a prophetic figure these many years later. Ergo, the rest in question cannot have had to do with Joshua entering the promise land.

Hebrews 4:8 uses a double entendre with the name *Iēsous*, which is the Greek rendering of both Jesus and Joshua. Interestingly, our author does not here develop the typological potential of this fact.[315] Here the primary reference is to Joshua and the rest theme, a theme that Joshua himself speaks to in Joshua 22:4 (cf. Josh 21:43-45), though there the subject is the more mundane matter of gaining relief from hostilities. Joshua did enter the land and lead others in (Heb 4:8); he was one of only two people to depart Egypt and enter the promised land (the other was Caleb). In later Jewish texts (Sirach 46.1; Philo *On the Change of Names* 121) Joshua is seen as the savior of Israel from its enemies. It is no surprise under these circumstances that our author would think of many from the wilderness-wandering generation who did not enter God's rest.

According to **Hebrews 4:9** the subject of this exhortation is not just any kind of rest but God's own sabbath rest. Occurring here for the first time in Greek literature (Plutarch *Moralia* 166A), the somewhat rare word *sabbatismos* should be translated "sabbath observance."[316] Sabbath observance has to do with rest from certain kinds of activities, as seen in **Hebrews 4:10**, though clearly not from worshiping and praising God.[317] **Hebrews 4:11** presents the somewhat humorous paradox of actively and vigorously seeking and pursuing rest![318]

Hebrews 4:12-13 is closely linked to what has come before, not merely by *gar* ("for"), but also in the sense of providing the ground or basis for the exhortation given in Hebrews 4:11. These verses fittingly bring to a close our author's reflection on the theme of the divine speech.[319] Our author here is speaking about the living and active voice of God speaking his own words, not a written text, much less the Johannine concept of the Logos (i.e., Christ), though we have already seen that our author believes that God speaks in and through the written text of the Old Testament and also through and in his Son. One could profitably compare the theology of the living word here to what is said in Psalm 139. Fred Craddock notes that the word is seen as the eyes of God, searching the human being's innermost thoughts and feelings.[320]

The interesting distinction here between *psychē* and *pneuma* has led to end-

---

[315]Attridge, *Hebrews*, p. 130.

[316]Ibid., p. 131.

[317]See the discussion in Weiss, "*Sabbatismos* in the Epistle to the Hebrews."

[318]Hagner, *Encountering the Book of Hebrews*, p. 75.

[319]Attridge, *Hebrews*, p. 133.

[320]Craddock, *Hebrews*, p. 54.

less speculation about our author's anthropology.[321] As Donald Hagner says, however, the author is not trying to teach anthropology but is merely saying that God scrutinizes the deepest recesses of our inner being and personality.[322] Our author can use these terms interchangeably for the inner self of a person or personality: thus in Hebrews 10:39 we hear about the salvation of the *psychē*, but in Hebrews 12:23 we hear about the completion of one's *pneuma* in the new Jerusalem. Nothing is hidden from God, or as Seneca puts it: "Nothing is shut off from the sight of God. He is witness of our souls and he comes into the midst of our thoughts" (*Letters* 83.1-2). Nevertheless, we have to assign some semantic sense to these two distinguished terms, and so *psychē* probably refers to the animating principle, the life breath that keeps a physical body alive, whereas *pneuma* refers to the human spirit conceived of as the nonmaterial internal part of a human being.

The rhetorical device of personification is used to give God's word human or divine qualities of being alive, active, discerning and also the properties of a sword, such as being penetrating, sharp, cutting and the like. "The image is crafted to arouse the emotion of fear by creating an impression of imminent harm (Aristotle *Rhetoric* 2.5.1-2) about to befall those unprepared to give an acceptable account."[323] Since we have seen other echoes of the Wisdom of Solomon in this work (e.g., in Heb 1:1-4), it is entirely believable that our author knows and is influenced by Wisdom of Solomon 18.14-16, where the word of God is personified as a warrior who bears a sharp sword of God's decrees of judgment. We may also rightly compare Revelation 19:15, where the two-edged sword comes out of Jesus' mouth to slay the enemies; Ephesians 6:17, where the Christian puts on the sword that is God's word; but especially Isaiah 55:10-11 (cf. Is 49:2), where we hear about how God's word accomplishes God's will. It is doubtful, however, that our author is developing a Logos Christology here.[324]

The difficult word *tetrachēlismena* has as its most rudimentary sense "breaking one's neck," "laying bear one's throat" or even "being gripped by the neck" (Diogenes Laertius *Lives of Eminent Philosophers* 6.61). Chrysostom has a helpful explanation: "The metaphor comes from the skins that are drawn off from the prey.

---

[321]See the discussion in Attridge, *Hebrews*, p. 135. It is not at all clear that we should compare this phrase to Philo's comparison of spirit and mind, or to Aristotle's theoretical distinction between soul and mind for the very good reason that our author does not affirm the Greek notion of the immortality of the soul. He believes in salvation through conversion (also Heb 12:23—where the spirits of the righteous need to be made eschatologically complete or perfect).

[322]Hagner, *Encountering the Book of Hebrews*, p. 76.

[323]DeSilva *Perseverance in Gratitude*, p. 170.

[324]Rightly Koester, *Hebrews*, p. 273.

. . . When one has killed them and draws aside the skin from the flesh, he lays open all the inward parts and makes them manifest to our eyes; so also do all things lie open before God" (*Homilies on Hebrews* 7.2). But it could equally be said to come from the context of human judgment when a person's throat is laid on the chopping block or laid bare for slitting or when an animal's neck is exposed to the knife (Theophrastus *Characters* 27.5).[325] We may rightly contrast the strong word of warning about the all-seeing eye of God with the following discussion of the merciful high priest who also sees and is in heaven.[326]

The section concludes with a reminder that the believer must render account to God for his or her life. Here a different sense of *logos* comes into play, showing our author's rhetorical skill and his ability to use different nuances in meaning of the same word.[327] "Through subtle shifts in meaning, the author suggests that God's word *(logos)* demands a human account *(logos)*."[328] In this passage it can be said that our author wields Psalm 95:7-11 as a two edged sword to support his exhortation to strive to enter God's rest.[329]

A CLOSER LOOK
The End and Aims of Eschatology in Hebrews

There has been no little debate about the eschatology (or lack there of) in Hebrews, and all too often the rhetorical character of the discourse, and how that might affect the eschatological language, is not taken into account at all. We will start then with this factor and explore it a bit.

In epideictic rhetoric the focus is necessarily on the present, on "today." This is not because the author is fixated on the present or because he is not much interested in the future; rather it is a rhetorical convention used because the author believes this is the most persuasive way to address his current audience—in this case an audience who is Christian but who is being tested and is in danger of wavering, defecting, committing apostasy. A second rhetorical factor that affects the way eschatological language is used is that epideictic rhetoric is the rhetoric of praise and blame, the rhetoric of encomiums and eulogies, the rhetoric of hyperbole and the ongoing appeal to the deeper, more visceral emotions like love and hate, fear and faith/trustworthiness. The failure to take into account the temporal focus of epideictic rhetoric leads to the as-

---

[325]DeSilva, *Perseverance in Gratitude*, p. 171.
[326]Attridge, *Hebrews*, p. 134.
[327]Ibid., p. 136.
[328]Koester, *Hebrews*, p. 275.
[329]Ibid.

sumption that our author's eschatology or afterlife theology is almost exclusively otherworldly and ethereal, rather like Philo's. This is an enormous mistake and ignores too much of the evidence from the climactic section of the discourse in Hebrews 9—12.

Hebrews 9 could hardly be a more otherworldly chapter, speaking as it does of Christ's high priestly role being performed in heaven for believers on earth. The otherworldly nature of the discussion is clear, but at the end of the chapter we hear: "And just as it is destined that each person dies only once and after that comes the judgment, so also Christ died only once for all as a sacrifice to take away the sins of the many. He will come a second time, but not to deal with our sins again. This time he will bring salvation to all those who are eagerly waiting for him." Even though salvation as a work in progress is clear enough, our author is equally clear about the return of Christ to bring salvation in the future to those who are awaiting his second coming. But nothing is said about judgment coming at death, it is simply said to come *after* death.

In Hebrews 10:12-13 we are told that Christ is enthroned in heaven awaiting the time when all his enemies are put under his feet. While this may be a process that has already begun on earth, our author does not see it as completed. Then in Hebrews 10:25 we hear that "the day draws near" in the context of the discussion of receiving the full benefits of one's salvation. This is contrasted very clearly with looking forward to "the terrible expectation of God's judgment and the raging fire that will consume his enemies." This is about as clear as one could want, and one may compare the apocalyptic rhetoric of 2 Thessalonians 2, which is of a similar ilk. Both final judgment and final salvation and rest await the return of Christ. Our author says that, for those who have rejected Christ (Heb 10:29), "it is a fearsome thing to fall into the hands of the living God" (Heb 10:31). What is coming is said in Hebrews 10:34 to be a "superior means of existence and a lasting one," and Hebrews 10:35 speaks of the "greater" reward. What is not said is that it is an otherworldly one.

Hebrews 11:13-16 is an important text for the discussion as well. Hebrews 11:16 speaks of aspiring to a better country, one that is "of heaven"—not "in heaven" but rather the genitive "of heavenly" and thus heavenly in source and quality. Many translations seem to miss the nuance that use of the word *epouranios* (rather than *ouranos*) gives: "heavenly" in character, not "heaven" as a destination or location. In Hebrews 11:35 saints who were tortured and martyred are said to have placed their hope and faith in "a better resurrection," a term that has a clear bodily sense in early Judaism.[330] Again our author is not

---

[330]See the definitive study by Wright, *Resurrection of the Son of God.*

talking about life in heaven as the terminus or final stop on the Christian pilgrimage. Hebrews 11 climaxes with the announcement that the saints mentioned in the hall of faith had not received what was promised, and one of the reasons why was "so that only together with us would they be made perfect/complete." This is probably a reference to the resurrection of all the saints when Christ returns.

In Hebrews 11—12 our author is not talking about entering the Holy Land as it exists today (or even some peaceful version thereof). He says as plainly as he can in Hebrews 11 that Abraham himself, even while in the Promised Land, had not yet received the promised rest and lived as a stranger or foreigner in the land. Our author was not an early advocate of some dispensational schema of the return of the Jews to their homeland. Instead, in a grand rhetorical comparison (synkrisis) he contrasts the theophany at Mount Sinai with "having come to Mount Zion, to the city of the living God, to the Jerusalem that is heavenly." For this comparison and contrast to work, since the focus in each case is on a theophany—an event of God coming "down" from heaven onto a mountain to meet his people—our author must be talking about an event at the end of human history that will put all previous theophanies in its shade. The worship at Sinai will pale in comparison to the worship when the heavenly Jerusalem comes down and believers are incorporated into it. The believer stands on the threshold of the great rest, awaiting the return of Christ, and with him shall come the heavenly Jerusalem.

This amazing event involves the replacement of the temporary shakable order of created things with a permanent dwelling place in the presence of God (Heb 12:27). The big "shake-up" is said to involve both the heaven and the earth, not just the earth. Greek *ton ouranon* does not speak only of "heavens" plural, as if the sky were meant. The previously created portion of heaven and earth, that part that can be shaken, will be removed. What remains is the everlasting part, not the created parts. Our author is not talking about replacing the material realm with an immaterial one, any more than that is the case in 1 Corinthians 15 or Revelation 20—21. He is talking about replacing the temporary with the everlasting.

The saints on earth are the church expectant, and as Hebrews 13:14 puts it, "Here we do not have an enduring city, but we are looking for the city that is to come." Our author does not say, "We are looking to go to a heavenly city." To the contrary he envisions the city coming to the believers on earth and incorporating them in some fashion. In this whole discourse our author says precious little about "dying and going to heaven." The passing reference in Hebrews 12:23 to "the church of the firstborn" and "the spirits of the righteous made complete/perfect" presumably means that they will come with

Jesus when he returns. One reason our author says little about saints in heaven is precisely because he believes that Christ may come soon and that his audience may live until the parousia, or if they do die they will spend very little time in heaven before Christ comes again.

Thus while this epideictic discourse focuses on the preparation, perseverance, faith and faithfulness required *in the present* to meet one's maker when he comes to earth again, the climax of this discourse is full of future eschatology. The climax of the earthly pilgrimage is when the final theophany of God/Christ, the saints, the angels and the heavenly Jerusalem come to earth from heaven, just as God came down to Moses and the Israelites at Sinai.

Our author does not pause to distinguish between a millennial period after Christ returns to earth, followed by a new heaven and new earth (as in Rev 20—21). His is a more compact and compelling climax, as he cuts straight to the chase of the final state in the new Jerusalem on earth. The point is, however, that our author—like John of Patmos—does not view this heavenly Jerusalem as merely the old one refurbished or reclaimed. No, that is lost in the final "shake-up" of the material order. Rather, he sees it as a much larger, all-encompassing entity that replaces the previous one. This new entity has substance to it, has everlasting substance, but is not made of the previously created stuff.

This view of the climax of Hebrews makes much better sense than the argument that our author views the future either in purely otherworldly terms or as some sort of temporary millennial kingdom. For example, the attempt of Walter Kaiser, Stanley Toussaint and T. K Oberholtzer to identify the future promise with Palestine comes up short when one considers that Hebrews 11:13-16 makes perfectly clear that even Abraham did not find a home in Canaan but was looking for a more permanent dwelling place, a country of heavenly origins and quality.[33] The rest that our author has in mind involves much more than the respite that Israel received upon entering the land of Canaan or some such future respite in the same piece of real estate (Heb 4:8). If Joshua was unable to deliver the rest, neither can modern Zionism; nor is there a concern that all Old Testament prophecies must be fulfilled for Israel and apart from the church. Hebrews 11:10 is perfectly clear about what our

---

[33]Kaiser, "Promise Theme and the Theology of Rest"; and Toussaint, "Eschatology of the Warning Passages." Even more problematic is Oberholtzer's "Kingdom Rest in Hebrews 3:1—4:13" and "Thorn Infested Ground in Hebrews 6:4-12," who not only wants to see this material as referring to a millennial kingdom in Palestine, but also wants to bracket out any suggestion that the author really suggests that Christians might be able to commit apostasy. As Barrett, "Eschatology of the Epistle to the Hebrews," p. 372, says, "the 'rest' is and remains a promise, which some of the readers of the Epistle may fail through disobedience to achieve (iv.1) and all are exhorted to strive to enter."

author has in mind—a city whose architect is God and whose foundations are permanent. David deSilva is perfectly right to point to this passage to refute these views.[332]

DeSilva goes astray, however, in assuming that the alternative to this is that our author is equating "entering the divine rest" with "entering the divine realm" (i.e., heaven).[333] Our author does, of course, affirm that this happened in the case of Christ. But that is not the end of the story, for our author just as clearly envisions Christ coming down from heaven to meet with the saints, who are the church expectant. Our author believes that the rest, the realm, the ruler that is now "up there" in heaven will one day be "out there" on earth when the kingdoms of this world become the kingdoms of our God and of his Christ. In other words, our author's story line has a down-to-earth conclusion, not an otherworldly one. Instead, he envisions a corporate takeover—what is up there will come down and replace what is down here, so there will be an everlasting city, an everlasting fellowship, an everlasting life in resurrection bodies in the new Jerusalem. In other words, our author's view differs little from Isaiah 66:22 or Revelation 21:1 or 1 Corinthians 15. He affirms a well-known form of early Jewish eschatology (e.g., *2 Baruch* 4), as these other writers did as well, which speaks of an intersection of the heavenly and earthly involving a heavenly Jerusalem coming down to earth, which replaces what is temporal and temporary with what is permanent and glorious without replacing the material world with an immaterial realm. The rest, which is a heavenly reality, in due course will be an earthly blessing for believers.[334]

Our author's line of thinking is not far from the way it is put in the apocalyptic treatise *Life of Adam and Eve* 51.2-3: "Rest on the seventh day is a symbol of the resurrection of the age to come, and on the seventh day the Lord rested from all his works." Perhaps more importantly rest was associated with the return to Eden and the new Jerusalem on earth not in heaven: "The saints shall rest in Eden; the righteous shall rejoice in the new Jerusalem" (*Testament of Dan* 5.12). The same motif, speaking as in Hebrews of a city being built and of a rest being furnished by God, is found in 2 Esdras (4 Ezra) 8.52 (see also *Joseph and Aseneth* 8.9; 22.13; Rev 14:1, 13). The heavenly and permanent quality of the city does not indicate that the city is either immaterial or in heaven. One might ask what it could possible mean to say God was the architect and builder of a city "in heaven."

---

[332]DeSilva's discussion in *Perseverance in Gratitude*, pp. 157-64, repays close reading.

[333]DeSilva, "Entering God's Rest," follows Attridge, *Hebrews*, p. 128.

[334]Attridge, *Hebrews*, p. 123, is right that God's rest is not a earthly realm (i.e., Canaan) in the first place. It is what God entered after the acts of creation, and so it is a state of being or a condition.

The evidence of future eschatology that crops up toward the climax of the discourse in Hebrews must be given its full weight. Our author at the end of the day is not a spiritualizer of the promises about rest and the new Jerusalem to God's chosen people; however he also does not envision their fulfillment in some temporary and temporal kingdom either. He has in mind the final permanent "heaven on earth" state of affairs, as is made perfectly clear when he speaks of the second coming to earth of Jesus and the resurrection of the saints. Even Craig Koester, who favors the believer's-rest-equals-entering-heaven view, finally admits that "the author does not say whether Christians enter rest immediately upon their own deaths (12:23)."[335] Indeed not—and neither did Jesus enter rest immediately upon death; he entered it only after he was raised from the dead in a body and then ascended to the right hand of God.

Resurrection, which constitutes the completion and perfection of the saint, must precede full rest, which comes only when a person is all that God intended them to be and is immune to disease, decay and death. Our author did not sell his resurrection birthright for a spiritualized bowl of lentil soup. Nor did he trade it in for a Platonic "now" or eternal "today" in heaven. Hebrews 3:13 makes clear that "today" is the time of repentance that lasts only until the day of judgment at Christ's return (compare Heb 10:25 with Acts 17:31). As the author of Mishnah, tractate *Tamid* 7.4 said, resurrection will bring "the day that shall be all sabbath and rest in life everlasting." None of this line of thinking is a surprise when we realize how much not only early Jewish ideas in general but the Psalms in particular have influenced our author's reasoning and his rhetoric. He knows perfectly well that Psalm 132:13-14 says that God had chosen earthly Jerusalem as his place of rest: the Lord "has chosen Zion; he has desired it for his habitation," saying "this is my resting place forever."

Finally, the detailed study of Edward Adams demonstrates that the Platonic reading of Hebrews by James Thompson and others does not work,[336] not least because our author is not affirming some sort of eternal dualism between the world of shadows and a substantive heaven. Equally certainly Plato did not affirm the notion of the end or replacement of the earthly realm with a subsequent, more permanent material one, as does our author. Adams stresses that our author is thoroughly Jewish in being "procreational," by which is meant a strong understanding of God as creator and the goodness of his creation of a material world. The final salvation that our author envisions fully embraces a material existence following the return of Christ and the resurrection.[337]

---

[335]Koester, *Hebrews*, p. 270.
[336]Adams, "Cosmology of Hebrews"; Thompson, *Beginnings of Christian Philosophy*.
[337]Lincoln, *Hebrews*, p. 100.

Exposition and Exhortation, Round Three: The Well-Tested High Priest (Heb 4:14—5:10)

Lowliness is taken on by majesty, weakness by power, mortality by eternity, and the nature which cannot be harmed is united to the nature which suffers, in order that the debt which our condition involves may be discharged. In this way, as our salvation requires one and the same mediator between God and human beings, the human being who is Jesus Christ can at one and the same time die in virtue of the one nature and in virtue of the other be incapable of death. That is why true God was born in the integral and complete nature of a true human being, entire in what belongs to him and entire in what belongs to us. . . . Each nature retained its characteristic without defect. (Leo the Great, *Letter to Emperor Flavian*)[338]

How is it that we should "approach boldly"? Because now it is a throne of grace, not a throne of judgment. Therefore boldly, "that we may obtain mercy," even such as we are seeking. For the affair is one of munificence, a royal largess. (Chrysostom, *Homilies on Hebrews* 7.6)

Indeed, the Preacher's main purpose in this section is to encourage the congregation toward daring, even audacious prayer, to "approach the throne of grace with boldness" (4:16). The Preacher wants them to move past fearful prayers, tidy prayers, formal and distant prayers toward a way of praying that storms the gates of heaven with honest and heartfelt cries of human need. He does not want them to pray like bureaucrats seeking a permit but like children who cry in the night with their fears, trusting that they will be heard and comforted.[339]

We now come to the heart of the discourse in terms of having arrived at the major distinctive theme that our author wants to introduce into the discussion. Our author has already introduced the theme of Christ as the believer's high priest (Heb 2:17; 3:1), but now it becomes the central focus of discussion in the central section of the discourse (Heb 4:14—10:18), a very long segment of the discourse with several subsections, the first of which is Hebrews 4:14—5:10. Thomas Long calls the discussion of the high priest theme here a "preview of coming attractions," perhaps because Hebrews 5:11—6:12 from this perspective looks like a detour (a digressio, in rhetorical terms).[340] This view is wrong. The theme of Christ as high priest is not merely previewed here, it is introduced, and then—as before—our author goes right into exhortation mode at Hebrews 5:11 to apply the lesson he is preaching. Hebrews 5:11—6:12 is thus

---

[338] This letter was written for the Council of Chalcedon in 450; see Heen and Krey, *Hebrews*, p. 66.
[339] Long, *Hebrews*, p. 63.
[340] Ibid., p. 62.

not a digression, but an exhortation that grows out of the exposition in Hebrews 4:14—5:10. More helpful and accurate is David deSilva's argument that Hebrews 4:14-16 and Hebrews 10:19-23 form a rhetorical *inclusio*—the beginning and the end of the discussion of Jesus as high priest—as seen in the themes common to these sections:[341]

Hebrews 4:14-16	Hebrews 10:19-23
having therefore a great high priest	having therefore . . . a great priest
Jesus	through the blood of Jesus
the Son of God	the house of God
let us hold onto the confession	let us hold onto the confession
let us draw near	let us draw near
with boldness	since we have boldness

Equally on target are the remarks of Graham Hughes, who shows how the introduction of the theme of Jesus as high priest here and in the next chapter presages what will be said when the subject is taken up fully in Hebrews 7. The ending of the subsection in Hebrews 4:14—7:28 sums up what has come before:[342]

1. Jesus' exaltation through the heavens (Heb 4:14; 7:28)
2. conflation of Psalm 2:7 and Psalm 110:4—Son forever (Heb 7:28)
3. Jesus' perfection (Heb 5:9-10; 7:28)
4. Jesus' sinlessness (Heb 4:15; 7:26)
5. Levitical priesthood (Heb 5:1-3; 7:27-28)
6. the verb *proserchomai* (Heb 4:16; 7:25)

From a rhetorical viewpoint, beginning at Hebrews 5:1 our author enumerates the advantages, honorable titles, claims to fame that Jesus has when it comes to the priesthood. Clearly enough these epideictic topics are part and parcel of eulogies in general and of the rhetoric of praise and blame more specifically. From a Jewish viewpoint, and despite the corruption of the high priestly office by the family of Caiaphas in living memory, the office itself was still highly regarded. Josephus says that the title of high priest is "the most honored of revered names" (*Jewish War* 4.164; cf. 4.149; Philo *On the Special Laws* 1.142). By ascribing this office to Jesus, our author is thus attributing the highest

[341]DeSilva, *Perseverance in Gratitude*, pp. 179-80. See also Guthrie, *Structure of Hebrews*, pp. 79-80.
[342]Hughes, *Hebrews and Hermeneutics*, pp. 12-14.

honor to Jesus.[343] We need to keep steadily in view that it would take some powerful rhetoric to convince ancient persons that one particular sacrifice and one particular priest could be sufficient for all times and all persons and all purposes. There had never been a "forever" priest before. Neither pagans nor Jews believed in this sort of thing, prior to the time of Jesus.[344] It is no surprise then that this central argument here is offered at length and in detail, pulling out all the emotional and logical stops and using the full array of rhetorical devices to convince the audience that when they received the good news they had not been sold a bill of goods or an elixir that fell short of its claims to save to the uttermost. Another regular topic of encomiums—the education of the hero figure—is broached here when the discussion turns to what Jesus learned through suffering—namely obedience. Finally, throughout this section the rhetorical device known as amplification is in play. It is a form of praising a person by showing the superiority of this person to other similar noble and exalted persons (Aristotle *Rhetoric* 1.9.39). The goal is not to denigrate the lesser high priests, but to show how much worthier of praise is the Christian's high priest. Our author strengthens his argument by drawing analogies from practical life, for example, by citing the principle that one learns things through suffering (*Rhetorica ad Herennium* 4.17, 25). But in our case the author will go further to make the point that not only does suffering not negate one's salvation, in fact suffering in Christ's case became the means of human salvation.[345] Hebrews 5:10, which concludes the section, is intended to be something of a teaser, arousing curiosity about Jesus' connection to the obscure figure Melchizedek (see *Rhetorica ad Herennium* 3.22 on the rhetorical effectiveness of this tactic in stimulating the audience to pay closer attention in the middle of a complex discourse).

> [4:14]*Having then a great high priest who passed through the heavens, Jesus the Son of God, we hold fast to the confession.* [15]*For we do not have a high priest who is not able to sympathize with our weaknesses, but tested/tempted in all respects just as likewise we are, but without sin.* [16]*We come then with free and bold speech/confidence to the throne of grace in order that we might receive mercy and might find grace for timely help.*
>
> [5:1]*For every high priest taken from humankind is appointed by human beings for the things of God, in order to offer gifts and sacrifices for sins,* [2]*being able to moderate his feelings toward the ignorant and erring, for he also was beset by weakness,* [3]*and for himself he ought, just as concerning the people so also for himself, to offer gifts for sins,* [4]*and not for himself does anyone take/receive this honor, but being called by God, just as also Aaron.*

---

[343]DeSilva, *Perseverance in Gratitude*, p. 186.
[344]See the discussion in Nelson, *Raising up a Faithful Priest*, pp. 30-88.
[345]Koester, *Hebrews*, p. 299.

[5]Thus also the Christ did not glorify himself to become high priest, but the one said to him: "My son you are, I today have begotten you," [6]just as in another place he says, "You are a priest for eternity according to the order of Melchizedek," [7]who in the days of his flesh prayed and entreated to the one who was able to save him from death with strong cries and tears offered, and he was heard because of his reverence, [8]although being a Son he learned obedience from what he suffered, [9]and being made complete/perfect, for all who obey him, [10]he became a source of eternal salvation, proclaimed by God high priest according to the order of Melchizedek.

Hebrews 4:14-16 expands on some of the things that have been said before about Christ and his humanity. First of all, in Hebrews 4:14 we hear about his journey to heaven, which is described as a "passing through the heavens," perhaps echoing the idea of the high priest passing through the curtains into the holy of holies. More pertinently, early Jewish listeners would perhaps think of the earlier experiences of Enoch (Gen 5:24; *1 Enoch* 14—19, 70—71) or Elijah (2 Kings 2:11) or the post–Old Testament traditions about the ascension of Isaiah (*Martyrdom and Ascension of Isaiah* 6—7). In addition, early Jews thought of several levels of heaven, and in some cases the sky or earth's atmosphere was seen as the lowest level through which one must pass to get to the higher levels of heaven, where God and the saints were. Along the way, one would pass through the realm where angels and the devil dwelt (this concept matches the devil being called the "prince of the power of the air"). Unlike later medieval cosmologies, demons and the devil were not conceived as being or coming from below but rather from above. Job 1—2 mentions Satan in the heavenly council, and Revelation records the threefold fall of Satan from heaven to earth, from earth to the pit and from the pit to the lake of fire. That Jesus successfully passed through the heavens into heaven would be called a good outcome. "Heavens" (plural) consistently refers to a part of the material universe (Heb 1:10; 4:14; 7:26; 8:1; 9:23; 12:23), whereas "heaven" (singular) refers to the invisible divine realm (Heb 11:12; 12:26).[346]

The phrase *great high priest* is not unprecedented (1 Maccabees 13.42, of Simon), and the high priest is often called a great priest in the Septuagint (Lev 21:10; Num 35:25-28; Zech 6:11). But our author means something special by the appellation—he means one of a whole different ilk and priestly line. The audience is urged to "hold fast" to their confession already given about this great high priest.[347] Though his methodology is more subtle, our author's argument is not different in thrust than Paul's—namely, one already has in Christ all that one

---

[346]DeSilva, *Perseverance in Gratitude*, p. 181.
[347]The verb here is in the present subjunctive and is hortatory in character.

might look or long for from Old Testament religion.

Our author makes clearer here that "Christ's full humanness and his sinlessness are not contradictory. Being sinful is not intrinsic or necessary to being fully human, nor, to state the opposite, is being sinless an obstacle to full humanness."[348] It is a modern notion that sinning makes one more human or approachable, a notion not shared by our author or other early Jews. Early Judaism had the notion of a righteous messiah who would come (*Psalms of Solomon* 17.36). The phrase *tested in every respect/way* probably does not mean that Jesus endured every basic temptation that humans undergo, but rather that he underwent the full gamut of types of temptation we experience. He is thus able to sympathize with his fellow human beings' struggles and weaknesses.

Thomas Long is right to add: "To say that Jesus is 'without sin' is not to say that he was 99% human—human in every way except for the fact that he was without sin—but rather to affirm that Jesus experienced the full ambiguity and uncertainty, the weakness and the vulnerability, the temptations and the sufferings of life without compromising his humanity, without straying from his calling to be a human being."[349] The phrase *kath' homoiotēta*, as suggested in the translation, could mean tested "according to the likeness" of our temptations or "according to his likeness" to us. The point in either case is that Christ experienced all the sorts of temptations we have, and being like us he thus understands what we go through. The final clause in Hebrews 4:15 means literally "without sin." Traditionally this has been taken to mean that Christ went through the same sort of temptations as we do but came out unscathed. This is challenged by Ronald Williamson, whose view is that Jesus struggled and overcame sin in the end, but that he was not perpetually sinless.[350] The reason for this argument is the presumption that one cannot be truly human unless one has partaken of sin, but this modern assumption is not shared by biblical writers such as our author. In view of Hebrews 7:26 this assertion of sinlessness applies to Jesus not only in heaven and as a result of his death, but before his death, when he offered a pure and unblemished sacrifice. He was not only a high priest without sin, but a sacrifice without sin as well, so that he did not have to die for himself, but could offer the perfect and full sacrifice that brings about final atonement.

This line of reasoning is integral to our author's argument, and so Williamson's suggestion must be rejected. This is not to say that Jesus in his human nature

---

[348]Hagner, *Encountering the Book of Hebrews*, p. 78.
[349]Long, *Hebrews*, p. 64.
[350]Williamson, "Hebrews 4:15 and the Sinlessness of Christ."

could not have sinned. Were that the case the temptation would not have been truly tempting, since it would have been impossible to give in to it. It does not make much sense for our author to say that Jesus could sympathize with us if he could not have known the full allurement of temptation. James Moffatt points out that some sins arise out of the commitment of previous sins (for instance, a lie that perpetuates other lies). Jesus would not have been susceptible to this kind of temptation (i.e., a temptation to go on sinning).[351] The point here is that Jesus knew all kinds of temptation, not every single possible sort of temptation.

Fred Craddock reminds us that the church fathers said that Christ "was as we are, and therefore he will help; he was not [in other ways] as we are, and therefore he can [help]." The double negative in Hebrews 4:15 has rhetorical forcefulness: "We do not have a high priest who is not able."[352] The implication is that other high priests are unable to help in some respects. All of this should give the audience boldness to approach God in prayer, in the same fashion that Jesus did.

In regard to the exhortations in these verses—"holding on firmly" to the confession and "drawing near" to the throne of grace—the second verb *proserchōmetha* (also in Heb 7:25; 10:22; 11:6; 12:18-22) is almost a technical term in the Septuagint for the liturgical work of the priest drawing near to the altar or worshipers drawing near to God (Lev 9:7; 21:17, 21; 22:3; Num 18:3). It is a mirror opposite of the warning against "shrinking back" or "turning away" (Heb 3:12; 6:6; 10:38-39). David deSilva reminds us that "the author's choice of words here reveals his ideological strategy at work. Joining the Christian movement has not pushed believers out to the margins but rather has brought them closer to the divine center of the universe."[353] This is typical sectarian language where the normal perceptions are inverted. While the audience may feel alienated from the macroculture at the moment or even from the Jewish subculture, our author stresses that they are right where they need to be, in the center of God's will, having already arrived at the doorstep of Zion and are in the process of entering God's blessed rest and eternal salvation. Now is no time to look back with longing or to shrink back from the finish line.

Then at Hebrews 5:1 our author begins to unpack what the role of the priest, particularly the high priest, was, but first he explains what the prerequisites were to playing this role. Harold Attridge shows that the carefully laid out rhetorical structure of Hebrews 5:1-10 is chiastic in nature:[354]

---

[351]Moffatt, *Hebrews*, pp. 59-60.
[352]Craddock, *Hebrews*, p. 58.
[353]DeSilva, *Perseverance in Gratitude*, p. 185.
[354]Attridge, *Hebrews*, p. 138.

A   the function of the high priest (Heb 5:1)

B   the person of the high priest (Heb 5:2-3)

C   the appointment of the high priest (Heb 5:4)

C'   the appointment of Jesus as great high priest (Heb 5:5-6)

B'   the person of Jesus as great high priest (Heb 5:7-8)

A'   the function of Jesus as great high priest (Heb 5:9-10)

Fred Craddock points out that it would not be at all obvious to the audience that Jesus was a high priest. Jewish Christians would query such an assertion on the basis of Jesus' genealogy, the geographical locale and character of his ministry, not to mention the little incident in the temple in Jerusalem when Jesus overturned the tables of the money changers.[355] Jesus went through none of the events normally accompanying investiture with the office of high priest: purification bath, donning sacred vestments, being anointed with oil, offering sacrifices and especially going into the holy of holies on the Day of Atonement (Ex 28:41; 29; Lev 8). Rhetorically speaking, our author must exercise no little amount of persuasion (off and on in the entire section, Heb 4:14—10:39) to make a convincing case that Jesus was a priest at all, much less a high priest. One could say he does so by a tour de force argument where he in essence argues that Jesus was a high priest on a whole different level—in heaven, not on earth. Although Jesus offers himself as the sacrifice while on earth, he assumes the mantle of full-fledged priest in heaven.

We do not know where our author got the ideas he shares here, though perhaps there are some parallels with the Qumranite concept of a priest/king or priest/messiah. For the Hasmoneans and later the Sadducees, Melchizedek was the prototype of their priestly/kingly view of rulers. For the Pharisees he was identified with Shem and demoted for his irreverence from any continuing priestly succession; for Philo he was mainly the manifestation of the eternal Logos; for Josephus he was a Canaanite chieftain who became God's priest at Jerusalem due to his piety; and most importantly for Qumran he was a heavenly and eschatological figure, perhaps even an archangel redeemer who exercised certain priestly characteristics in atoning for sin (11QMelch *[Melchizedek]*).[356] In view of the Qumran finds, Joseph Fitzmyer notes that it is easy to see how our author might be able to argue for the superiority of Christ over the Levitical priesthood, on the basis of a connec-

---

[355]Craddock, *Hebrews*, p. 58.
[356]This summary is courtesy of Longenecker, "Melchizedek Argument of Hebrews," p. 171.

tion to the order of Melchizedek, since some Jews viewed him as a heavenly redeemer figure.[357]

But one need look no further than the Old Testament example of the king-priest Melchizedek, which is probably the source of our author's train of thought. Jesus will be presented here as both royal Son and priest, after the order and fashion of Melchizedek but greater. Whatever the source of the ideas, our author has made them his own and turned them into a unique and specific commentary on Jesus, with elements such as self-sacrifice, that could have come only from his knowledge of Jesus' own story.[358]

Obviously the most fundamental requirement for Christ to be a priest is that he had to be a human being. Angels may play the role of messengers or even warriors, but they are not mediators, because they do not partake of a human nature. Priests are a different sort of intermediary than angels, not least because they primarily represent human beings to God, whereas angels do the reverse. The priest's most basic role was offering "gifts and sacrifices" to God (a stock phrase and so we should not differentiate between the two terms; see 1 Kings 8:64; cf. Heb 8:3),[359] and in due course we will hear about the special form that takes with the high priest (Heb 9:7, 25).

Only in **Hebrews 5:2** in the New Testament do we have the verb *metriopatheō*, which literally means "to moderate the pathos" or "to control one's deeper emotions." The issue here is not sympathy, but the ability to control one's anger with ignorant or spiritually wayward people. This term was a buzzword with Peripatetic philosophers, who insisted that one must learn to control one's emotions, especially anger (Diogenes Laertius *Lives of Eminent Philosophers* 5.31; Plutarch *Consolatio ad Apollonium* 3)—unlike the Stoics, who said that one must eliminate emotion. While the ordinary priest controls his anger, Jesus is said to actively sympathize with his fellow humans.[360]

It is not expected that a priest be perfect and without sin, though it is expected that he be cleansed, forgiven, shriven of sin when he takes up his holy tasks. One of those tasks is offering sacrifices for himself and his own sins, as well as for the sins of others, as **Hebrews 5:3** makes clear. On the one hand it is a good thing that the priest is weak and knows his own shortcomings, as he is better able to identify and empathize with other weak mortals, but at the same

---

[357]Fitzmyer, "Further Light on Melchizedek," p. 41.
[358]Craddock, *Hebrews*, p. 60.
[359]Attridge, *Hebrews*, p. 143.
[360]Ibid., p. 144.

time his weakness is not a strength in another respect, namely that he must sacrifice for his own sins.

Old Testament sacrifices for sin were efficacious if they were offered for sins of ignorance or for sins that were unwitting or unintentional in nature (Lev 4:13; Ezek 45:20). These sins are viewed differently than sins committed intentionally or willfully or, as the Old Testament puts it, "with a high hand" (Num 15:30-31). Acts 13:39 states clearly that through Christ's death atonement is now possible for intentional sins that were not covered under Old Testament law. This is one of the reasons our author will emphasize that Christian believers have a very merciful high priest. He will also stress, in making clear the mercy of Christ, that in the Old Testament deliberate sin was viewed less mercifully.[361] Thus when our author speaks of how gently Jesus deals with his audience, there is an implicit contrast with other priests and earlier sacrificial systems. Just how merciful is further demonstrated by his being not a sinner, unlike all other priests. At Hebrews 7:27 our author will make much of Jesus being unlike other high priests in respect to not needing to sacrifice for his own sins. Jesus was the one person for whom Jesus did not have to die to atone for their sins.

At **Hebrews 5:4** our author will make the further point that priesthood is not an office and an honor earned but rather granted by God who "calls" priests.[362] Aaron is singled out as the example of this process of divine selection (Ex 28:1), and our author totally ignores that in Herod's temple a whole series of high priests were not divinely chosen, to say the least, but rather were appointed by human rulers, involving a political process. The controlling of who became high priest was one of the most vital and volatile political issues that a procurator had to supervise without appearing to interfere or control.

According to **Hebrews 5:5** Jesus met the essential requirement of being selected by God, not being self-selected, to be priest. Here again Psalm 2:7 comes to the fore, as it did in Hebrews 1:5, only this time the issue is God selecting the Son to be a priest, rather than for a different royal role. Our author moves on to consider another psalm, Psalm 110:4, and he reads this psalm in light of Psalm 110:1, which links our author's reading of Psalm 2:7 to that of Psalm 110:4.[363] The logic of Hebrews 5:5 and **Hebrews 5:6**, which involve the quoting of phrases from Psalm 2:7 and Psalm 110:4, is that, because the Son has been exalted to rule from God's right hand, he is in the place and condition where he

---

[361] Attridge (ibid.) points out that this attitude about deliberate sin carries over into the new covenant in this respect—there is no atonement or forgiveness for apostasy (Heb 6:4-8; 10:26-31; 12:17).

[362] For a detailed treatment of this subject as it bears on Hebrews, see Scholer, *Proleptic Priests*.

[363] Hagner, *Encountering the Book of Hebrews*, p. 83.

can be the perfect heavenly high priest, a forever high priest always in the inner sanctum, right in the presence of God forever. His exalted sonship role allows him to play the role of heavenly high priest.

Perhaps surprisingly and suddenly our author seems to turn in **Hebrews 5:7** to the Gethsemane scene, with Christ struggling to obey what God's will is for him. The description is full of pathos and meant to evoke the deeper emotions of the audience. Presumably part of what is going on here is demonstrating how Christ can identify with the audience in their own struggles and in their own pressure-packed situations, which may lead to their suffering and death. This shows another dimension of the priestly portrait of Jesus, for prayers were something the priest was supposed to offer to God, for himself and for others.

While *eulabeia* can mean "piety" or "devotion" in a general sense both here and at Hebrews 12:28 (its only other occurrence in the New Testament), it is used in the context of talking about Christ's priestly service. Thus it suggests "the attitude or behavior appropriate to that [priestly] service: bowing in reverence."[364] *Eulabeia* carries the connotation of a pious attitude, such as godly fear; elsewhere our author uses the ordinary term for fear, *phobos* (fear of death in Heb 2:15). It is thus far-fetched to think that this verse refers to Jesus' fear of death.

There is great debate—beginning with the church fathers and continuing to today—about what "he was *heard* because of his reverence" means.[365] When had he been pleading that he be spared from death?[366] Donald Hagner suggests that this part of the prayer was heard when Jesus said "nevertheless your will be done."[367] This may be correct, but our author would then be assuming that his audience knows the fuller Gethsemane story beyond his dramatic characterization of it here, including the "nevertheless" remark.

This sermon was likely composed before any gospel account of the Gethsemane episode was written down, and so this phrase may be compared to Matthew 26:36-46 or Luke 22:43-44: "And being in anguish he prayed more earnestly, and his sweat was like drops of blood falling to the ground." This Western reading of Luke 22 is possibly drawing on some traditions also known to our author. Many important early manuscripts do not have Luke 22:43-44 ($\mathfrak{P}^{69}$, $\mathfrak{P}^{75}$, ℵ, B, T, W, Clement, Origen), and others mark them with an obelisk,

---

[364]Craddock, *Hebrews*, p. 62.

[365]Some even translate here "he was heard and delivered from fear of death," but this labors under the difficulty that words with the *eulab-* root indicate reverence, not abject fear, such as a fear of death. See Koester, *Hebrews*, pp. 289-90, on the translation options here.

[366]Attridge, "Heard because of His Reverence"; and Lightfoot, "Saving of the Savior."

[367]Hagner, *Encountering the Book of Hebrews*, p. 84.

indicating doubt (D, P, 1079, 1195 et al.). In family 13 and several lectionaries, these verses are transferred to follow Matthew 26:39, which suggests that they are not composed by Luke and are looking for a home. Yet just as clearly these verses are ancient and are cited in the second century by Justin, Irenaeus and Hippolytus.[368] On balance it appears that they are an early addition to the Lukan text, probably from the Western textual tradition (D et al.).[369] They could reflect an early authentic tradition known to our author but not originally part of any canonical gospel.

If one draws this conclusion, what do these verses add to our understanding of the Gethsemane story? (1) Jesus' humanity and his great distress in the garden are emphasized; an angel appears to him and strengthens him so he can survive the test (Mk 1:13). (2) Jesus is a man of prayer dependent on the Father for help. (3) Jesus' sweating was like (i.e., presumably the size of) blood droplets. (4) Jesus was in anguish, which is compatible with the picture of Jesus praying for the cup to be taken from him.[370] In other words, rhetorically speaking, this Lukan text serves much the same purpose as does the brief telling of the Gethsemane moment of testing in Hebrews. Here we have Exhibit A of how Jesus was tempted to bail out but passed the test. This brief vignette from the life of the historical Jesus serves to illustrate our author's point about Jesus' being tempted/ tested in every respect like us, save without sin, and his ability to identify with human struggles to remain faithful and obedient to God. I am unpersuaded by the suggestion that our author is thinking of the cry of dereliction from the cross (Mk 15:34, quoting Ps 22:1). The scenario envisioned here involves multiple prayers, not merely a cry of anguish. If we ask why our author refers to this episode from the life of Jesus, the answer is likely to be because it provides a paradigm for the audience to follow in their own trials, suffering and possible martyrological death. Here is simply another way that Jesus is seen as their pioneer or trailblazer.[371]

In the Maccabean literature, earnest prayer is described as involving loud cries and tears (2 Maccabees 11.6; 3 Maccabees 1.16; 5.7, 25), but this material simply reflects the way early Jews entreated God when they were in a crisis situation. It need not suggest any literary dependence between this material

---

[368]Metzger, *Textual Commentary*, p. 177.

[369]Luke tends to delete Mark's reference to Jesus' emotions, but here he is adding to this, if this account were Lukan. See Bock, *Luke*, pp. 1763-64.

[370]Nothing here stands against the notion of the divinity of Christ. Rather it simply further highlights his true and full humanity. It is thus unlikely to have been deleted from Luke later because it compromises the notion of his divinity.

[371]Attridge may be right that we should read the key phrase to mean "he was saved out of death" (i.e., by resurrection beyond death); *Hebrews*, p. 150.

and Hebrews, though I would not rule out that our author knew the Maccabean literature.

Hebrews 5:8 says that Jesus learned obedience through his suffering[372] (with a neat aural wordplay: *emathen* ["learned"] and *epathen* ["suffered"]) and that he was made complete—that is, fully equipped and enabled to play the role of heavenly high priest and thus be a source of salvation, having himself been the perfect sacrifice that makes atonement for sin and on this basis interceding with the Father in heaven. Hebrews 2:10 also speaks of perfection, and here we are talking about a sort of completion of ministerial training, his preparation to be high priest in heaven. Instead of a "trial sermon" he had a trial sacrifice—of himself! In Leviticus 4:5; 8:33; 16:32; 21:10; and Numbers 3:3 the appropriate translation of the perfection terminology used of priests in the Septuagint is "consecrated" or "ordained." Jesus was thus "consecrated" to the ministry of being heavenly high priest by his suffering and death. In this sense he was made holy, set apart, complete, perfect through suffering. It is not a statement about his moral condition.

Hebrews 5:9 contains a proviso: Jesus is the source of salvation for all who obey him. Our author is not satisfied to say only that Jesus is our high priest; he also wants to make clear that Jesus eclipses all previous ones. One of the ways he accomplishes this is to make clear that, unlike ordinary high priests, Jesus is the source of salvation and that the salvation he offers is eternal (only here in the New Testament do we have the phrase *eternal salvation*), not the temporary expedient of short-term atonement by one sacrifice after another. The "how much more" or "can you top this" motif we have seen before in the comparison with Moses is carried out here as well, not only in the two ways just mentioned but also by means of stressing that Jesus was of a greater priestly order than Aaron—namely the Melchizedekian one, a theme to which our author will not return until Hebrews 7. Here our author is content to say that Jesus exceeds the high priestly job description and surpasses all rivals and comparisons. Through his death he became fully qualified to be appointed a priest, and God assigned him a forever priesthood according to Hebrews 5:10. And nobody before or since has been assigned a job quite like that. From a rhetorical viewpoint, our author has built up the suspense and sense of anticipation to hear more about

---

[372]The phrase about learning obedience through suffering is especially close to Aeschylus's *Agamemnon* 176-77 (cf. Sophocles *Trachiniae* 143; Herodotus 1.207), which speaks of the path of wisdom Zeus set for mortals (i.e., it comes through suffering). Our author then is borrowing a commonplace and using it to his own advantage. The word *learned* here may mean "experienced" a form of obedience or an extent of obedience he had not experienced before and thus is not a comment on Jesus' cognitive omniscience or lack thereof. The stress is that, even though he was God's Son, he learned this hard truth or lesson. It does not imply prior disobedience.

Jesus as high priest, but he will defer the discussion until Hebrews 7, for first he must exhort his wavering audience once more.[373]

EXHORTATION: AVOID APOSTASY, IMITATE THOSE PERSEVERING (HEB 5:11—6:12)

> Just as we say that it is possible to have faith without being literate, so we assert that it is not possible to understand the statements contained in the faith without study. To assimilate the right affirmations and reject the rest is not the product of simple faith but of faith engaged in learning. . . . We admit that it is easier and quicker to track down virtue if we have a preliminary education. It can be hunted down without these aids, although even then those with learning "with their faculties trained by practice" have an advantage. (Clement of Alexandria *Stromateis* 1.6.35)

We have by now become accustomed to toggling back and forth between exposition and exhortation, and normally the exhortation is built upon and flows out of the previous exposition. This is also the case here, but this exhortation is also prospective, setting up the audience for the discussion that follows about Christ the high priest.[374] This section is not a digression but rather another exhortation.[375] Rhetorically speaking, an orator must be able to keep the attention of the audience, especially if the discourse is going to be long, and by now it has become apparent that it is going to be long (it would have taken well over an hour to deliver orally). This being the case, and since "attention slackens everywhere else rather than at the beginning [of a speech]" (*Rhetorica ad Herennium* 3.14.9), the wise rhetor will pull out the emotional stops, use more colorful language, engage in rhetorical hyperbole, up the volume on "amplification," make the sound of the discourse even more pleasing, exhort the audience directly to pay attention, and thus, in short, do whatever it takes, within reason, to keep the audience engaged and paying attention.

Hebrews 6:4-12 is filled with pathos; the author first appeals to fear and then to confidence and faithfulness to produce the desired response. Again, it was characteristic of epideictic rhetoric to engage the emotions all through the discourse, not just at the beginning and the end, and in a praise-and-blame discourse we may rightly expect a lot of shaming to go on, as conduct that is seen as dishonorable is thus stigmatized. Aristotle says that shame is a pain in regard to misdeeds that tend to bring dishonor (*Rhetoric* 2.6.2). One of the clear rhetorical signals that Hebrews 5:11—6:12 is a unit (and that we should not carry

---

[373]Craddock, *Hebrews*, p. 63.
[374]Ibid., p. 66.
[375]Against Koester, *Hebrews*, p. 306.

it over to Heb 6:20) is the theme of sluggish ears in the end verse, which frames the discussion and forms an inclusio.

Our author is clearly a master teacher, and so it is no surprise that he pulls out of his rhetorical arsenal a standard device used in pedagogy—that of shaming students into pursuing a higher level of understanding by calling them children. Philosophers and rhetors used the contrasts between children and adults and between partaking of baby's milk and meat to talk about the need to get beyond elementary education. Epictetus, for example, says: "Are you not willing, at this late date, like children, to be weaned and partake of more solid food?" (*Discourses* 2.16.39). At a rhetorical level, we are dealing with the device of "distribution"—the putting of people in categories according to roles, abilities, qualities, maturity. Thus the author of *Rhetorica ad Herennium* 4.35.47 speaks of the infants and the mature as two key categories. The rhetorical discussion of such matters is a closer match with that found here in Hebrews than is the philosophical discussion.[376]

One of the issues that many commentators misunderstand, because of failure to read the rhetorical signals, is that our author to some degree is being ironic here and engaging in a preemptive strike. That is, we should not read this text as a literal description of the present spiritual condition of the audience. If most of the audience were dullards or sluggards or laggards, then our author had no business going on to give them the "meat" in Hebrews 7—10. That would have been exceedingly inept.

And if various members of the audience had already committed apostasy, then on his own showing, this exhortation about apostasy would be a day late and a dollar short. No, our author is simply trying to shame an audience that is shook up into getting beyond the elementary and embracing the mature faith and its substance rather than considering defecting under pressure. He is trying to keep any of them from committing apostasy. The most one can say is that this audience is teetering on the brink of disaster, is weary and considering other options rather than growing and going forward in their Christian faith. Our author's tactic will be to unveil a more appealing spiritual path to follow, which will both intellectually stimulate and help them to maturity, while painting the course of action he sees as defection in as black as terms as possible—it would be apostasy, not merely a return to an earlier and simpler form of religion. Harold Attridge points out that Hebrews 5:11-14 is an ironic *captatio benevolentiae*, for the alternation between the shaming remarks and the more positive re-

---

[376]See the discussion of deSilva, *Perseverance in Gratitude*, pp. 211-12; and Attridge, *Hebrews*, pp. 158-61.

en defection

marks is meant to prod the audience to respond: "No, we are not really infants and dullards, we are ready for the more advanced teaching you have to offer."[377]

We have arrived here at perhaps the most controverted part of the whole discourse, especially in the medieval debate about postbaptismal sin and whether one could be restored after abandoning the Christian faith. This text is about apostasy, a very specific grave sin, not about sins in general that might be committed after baptism. One of the key factors in analyzing this section is to realize that our author is trying to put the "fear of God" into his audience by using rhetoric to prevent defections, and so one is not sure how far to press the specifics here, since it is possible to argue that some of this involves dramatic hyperbole. More clearly, our author sees his audience as Christians who need to be moving on to more mature Christian teaching and reflection and living. Instead, they had become stagnant or sluggish in their progress toward full maturity, and so to some extent the rhetoric serves as an intended stimulus so they will persevere and press on to the goal, and our author gives a passing reference to his beliefs and hopes for better things from them than apostasy. A good deal of this section is meant as a kind of honor challenge, meant to force the audience to wake up and be prepared to grapple with harder concepts about Jesus' priesthood, but it is also a moral wake-up call as well, reminding the audience that those who are not busily moving forward are instead treading water at best and falling back or defecting altogether at worst. The Christian life is not a static thing, not least because it is based in faith that is either increasing or in a process of diminution.

This section uses the term *hagioi* in a technical sense, namely Jewish Christians, a usage found from time to time in Paul.[378] If this is correct, then we have a further clue about the insular nature of this Jewish Christian community in Rome, serving only other Jewish Christians, but serving them commendably. It is also possible that the term refers to those who have been suffering and in some cases have even been martyred (Heb 10.32-34).

Our author's rhetorical strategy here can be called stick and carrot, heavy and light, shock and reassurance, for confrontation is followed by encouragement in Hebrews 5:11-14 and Hebrews 6:1-3 and in Hebrews 6:4-8 and Hebrews 6:9-12 (cf. Heb 10:26-31 and Heb 10:32-39).[379] Plutarch says that reproofs should be followed by more reassuring comments, as a physician uses ointment to soothe the incision he has just made (*Moralia* 74DE).

[377]Attridge, *Hebrews*, p. 157.
[378]Witherington and Hyatt, *Romans*, on Rom 15—16.
[379]Craddock, *Hebrews*, p. 69.

$^{5:11}$*Concerning which the word has much for us, and it is difficult to explain, since your ears have become sluggish.* ^{12}*And though you ought to be teachers by this time, again you have need of being taught some of the elementary principles of the beginning of the word of God, and you have become (persons) having need of milk, not solid food.* ^{13}*For all the partakers of milk without experience of the word of righteousness are infants.* ^{14}*But for the mature there is solid food, and through the training by practice of their faculties, they have ability to distinguish good and evil.*

$^{6:1}$*So then, leaving behind the word about the beginning/origin of Christ, let us move along to completion/maturity/perfection, not laying again the foundation of repentance from dead works and faith in God,* ^{2}*teaching about baptisms, the imposition of hands, resurrection of the dead and eternal judgment.* ^{3}*And this we will do,*[380]*if, that is, God permits.* ^{4}*For it is impossible (the once enlightened, those who have tasted of the heavenly gift, and being sharers/partakers of the Holy Spirit,* ^{5}*and having tasted the good word of God, the powers of the coming age,* ^{6}*and having gone astray) to renew again to repentance those crucifying again the Son of God to themselves and exposing him to ridicule.* ^{7}*For the earth that drinks in the rain falling upon it many times, and bearing useful plants, for those by which it is cultivated, shares the blessing from God.* ^{8}*But (land) producing thorns and thistles is useless and nearly cursed, the end of which is incineration.*

^{9}*But we have been persuaded concerning you, beloved, of better things relating to salvation, even though we speak thusly.* ^{10}*For God is not unjust to forget your works and the love that you showed for his name serving the saints according to righteousness.* ^{11}*But we long for each of you to show the same eagerness for the full assurance of the hope unto the goal/end,* ^{12}*in order that you not become sluggish, but be imitators through faithfulness and patience, inheriting the promises.*

At the outset of the exhortation in **Hebrews 5:11** our author accuses the audience of being sluggish or dull in their hearing (we might say "hard of hearing"). The teaching in this setting has both an oral and aural character, much as when Jesus repeatedly exhorted his audience: "Let those with two good ears hear." Our author nevertheless plows ahead and gives them more advancing teaching about Christ the heavenly high priest, beginning in the latter part of Hebrews 6. Here he starts with a reminder that the "word" has much to say to his audience, but that does not mean it is easy to either explain or understand, especially if one is spiritually deaf or if there are obstacles to hearing clearly and grasping the implications of what has been heard. We have heard all along that our audience had such hearing deficiencies (Heb 2:1; 3:7-8, 15; 4:2, 7). The clar-

---

[380]Orthographic confusion of omicron and omega—which could sound identical if a scribe was copying from oral dictation—results in two readings: imperative ("let us do it"), supported by A, C, D, P and some minuscules, or future, which better suits the context, especially the clause *if God permits*. See Metzger, *Textual Commentary*, pp. 666-67.

ity of the word is one thing, the acuteness of the hearer quite another. The word *nōthros,* found only here and at Hebrews 6:12 in the whole New Testament, is the notion that sets off this unit from what follows. Our author may be thinking of the striking passage in Isaiah 50:4-5, which literally says "the Lord God dug out my ear" (we might say "cleaned the wax out of my ear"). When this term is not used of a physical attribute, it refers to being dull-witted, timid, negligent (Polybius *Histories* 3.63.7; 4.8.5; 4.60.2). For example, Epictetus rebukes the sluggish who refuse to discipline themselves by using their reason (*Discourses* 1.7.30). To be sluggish in this case is to be slow to hear; it does not quite connote the idea of hardness of heart, though the author fears that they may be headed in that direction, perhaps due to outside pressure.

Hebrews 5:12 makes the interesting remark that by now the audience members ought themselves to be teachers rather than needing to be taught. Seneca complains in a similar way: "How long will you be a learner? From now on be a teacher as well" (*Letters* 33.8-9). This suggests a situation where people have been Christians for a considerable period of time, hence the exasperation of the author with his audience. It is time for them to grow up and get on with it. The phrase *stoicheia tēs archēs* has caused a good deal of debate. The word *stoicheia* means "rudiments or parts" and can refer to a part of a word (a letter or syllable, hence the alphabet) or a part of the universe (i.e., an element or an original component). This second nuance is its meaning in Wisdom of Solomon 7.17; 19.18. There is much debate as to what *stoicheia tou kosmou* means in Galatians 4:3, 9 and Colossians 2:8, 20, but probably it means "elementary teaching."[381] This last meaning especially seems to suit Colossians 2:8. In any case *stocheia* linked with *archēs* surely means "first principles" or "elementary rudiments" of teaching that they had already heard from the beginning of their Christian pilgrimage. Classical parallels show clearly enough that the phrase refers to the elementary teaching or principles, not to some elemental spirits or beings (Xenophon *Memorabilia* 4.1.1). Of even more relevance is the beginning of Quintilian's famous study on rhetoric:

> I would therefore have a father conceive the highest hopes of his son from the moment of his birth. If he does so he will be more careful about the foundation/groundwork of his education. For there is absolutely no foundation for the complaint that but few men have the power to take in the knowledge that is imparted to them, and that the majority are so slow of understanding, that education is a

---

[381]Witherington, *Philemon, Colossians and Ephesians*, ad loc. On the debate about the *stoicheia tou kosmou* in Galatians, see Witherington, *Grace in Galatia*, on Gal 4:3. The meaning "elementary spirits" is not attested before or during the New Testament era.

waste of time and labor. On the contrary you will find that most are quick to reason and ready to learn. (*Institutio oratoria* 1.1.1)

In this context the *stocheia* are the beginnings of instruction in the art of persuasion, presumably some of the elements of the *progymnasmata* program. Our author is clearly trying to shame his audience into learning more, since "milk" was for infants and his audience was adults; put another way, elementary education was for those between seven and fourteen. It was never flattering to suggest that adults were acting like the age of children.

What is the "word/teaching about righteousness" mentioned in **Hebrews 5:13**? One may presume that it has to do with the subject of apostasy, which our author will dole out a significant dose of in a moment. However, in Greco-Roman settings instruction in righteousness meant being trained to discern the difference between good and evil (Xenophon *Cyropaedia* 1.630-31). In rhetorical contexts, this language referred to reaching a "state" in which they could be rhetors (Quintilian *Institutio oratoria* 10.1.1; 10.5.1). **Hebrews 5:14** identifies Christian maturity with the capacity to distinguish moral good from moral evil, which in turn means being able to continue to pursue the course of righteous action and avoid apostasy.

Hebrews 6:1 uses the interesting verb *pherōmetha*, which can be translated "move along" or "be carried along." Both actions are part of the process of maturing in Christ, of moving toward the goal of moral and intellectual excellence. Our author does not want his audience to forget what they learned at the earlier stages, for example, forgetting to repent when necessary; these things are foundational.[382] Rather, he wants them to move along to more advanced subjects, building on top of the original elementary learning.[383] Unlike the English gloss "maturity," which is sometimes used to translate it, the term *teleiotēs* has the connotation of arriving at a goal or completing something that one was striving toward, which is why it is sometimes translated "perfection/completion." In this case, the author has in mind an intended eschatological goal and state (see also Heb 3:14; 6:11). "The mature Christian is expected not only to 'ingest' the solid food but also to follow Christ on that path to final perfection, whatever the cost."[384]

There is debate about the phrase translated "the word about the beginning of Christ" or "the beginning of the word of Christ." This could refer to what our author was talking about in Hebrews 1:1-4, but it can be questioned whether this suits this context. It could also refer to the basic moral teaching of Christ,

---

[382]Attridge, *Hebrews*, p. 162.
[383]Koester, *Hebrews*, p. 303.
[384]Attridge, *Hebrews*, p. 163.

which according to the summary in Mark 1:15 was "repent and believe the good news." That comports rather nicely with the content of the rest of Hebrews 6:1. Our author has assumed before now in the discourse knowledge of the historical Jesus' life on the part of the audience (Heb 5:7-8), and presumably this would include some knowledge about his teachings. But is this "beginning" material to be seen as synonymous with "the elementary principles/teachings of the oracles of God" referred to in Hebrews 5:12? I suspect that in his summary in Hebrews 6:1-2 our author is referring to both the doctrinal and ethical foundational teachings, in which case "the word about the beginnings of Christ" probably does allude to Hebrews 1:1-4.

A textual problem in **Hebrews 6:2** involves the word *didachēs*: some important manuscripts ($\mathfrak{P}^{46}$, B) have the accusative *didachēn*. The accusative is probably a stylistic improvement, however, since there are so many genitives in this section, but F. F. Bruce argues the opposite way.[385] If the accusative is accepted, the term is in apposition to the word *foundation*, explaining it. In any case all the terms that follow *didachēs* are likely seen as the content of this teaching. Once again our author must stress that becoming a Christian back then not only involved activities, but also involved believing certain things. Early catechisms talked about such matters, and we know that early on there was a probationary period for catechists. There appears to be nothing particularly Christian about these matters: while any good Pharisee could have made up this list, Christianity—though it taught about many of the same subjects as the Pharisees—did not take the same view about them. For instance, for the Christian, faith in God meant faith in God through Christ. Resurrection meant not just at the end of history, but already in Christ. Imposition of hands in early Judaism usually was for blessing or ordination of rabbis; in Christianity it was connected with receiving the Spirit and/or taking on a work of ministry.

Most commentators assume that the list in Hebrews 6:1-2 refers to the subject matter of elementary Christian teaching, and there can be little doubt that this is correct since our author stresses that his audience has heard such teaching before and needs to move on to the more advanced teaching. However, something should be said for the generic character of this list of paired opposites, which could well have been said to be the substance of Jesus' own teaching:

repentance from past dead works	faith toward God
instructions about baptisms	laying on of hands
resurrection of the dead	eternal judgment

---

[385]Bruce, *Hebrews*, pp. 137-42.

There is nothing here that Jesus could not have commented on, especially if baptisms (plural) refers either to ritual ablutions or more likely to John's baptism as opposed to that practiced by Jesus' own disciples (Jn 3:22; 4:2). The observation that all these topics could have arisen in synagogue teaching is accurate, and some of the audience may have heard of these things in that context first and even have been tending in a retrograde motion to focus on such things as they sought to move back under the umbrella of early Judaism. Craig Koester insightfully points out the progression in this list from repentance at the beginning of the Christian life to final judgment at the end and after the resurrection of the dead.[386]

This is all the more reason to suggest that Jesus commented on and taught about these topics. He engaged in laying on hands (a practice having to do with blessing, healing or setting apart for some service or task), and he certainly spoke about coming judgment and the coming resurrection of the dead. This could then be a shorthand version of the elementary teaching of Jesus taken over into the elementary teaching of the church and called "the beginning of the word/teaching of Jesus." While scholars puzzle over the reference to plural baptisms in Hebrews 6:2, this conundrum is solved if the suggestion just made is accepted, especially if the author of this document is Apollos, who had to be instructed about the difference between Christian baptism and John's baptism (Acts 18:24-26), a lesson that he then applied in his own teaching thereafter, passing on his own "elementary education." One could object that another form of the word *baptismōn* would have been used if Christian baptism was in view (i.e., *baptisma*), but this overlooks not only the plural but also ignores that the Jewish Christian audience being addressed would know different types of ritual ablutions (see Heb 9:10 and Mk 7:4). In contrast, in Hebrews 10:22 it is not the water ritual that cleanses the conscience, but rather the internal application of grace by the Spirit resulting from the shed blood of Christ. Whether we see this elementary teaching as essentially Jewish or essentially Christian or both, it is something our author wants the audience to move beyond as they grow toward maturity. Luke Timothy Johnson sums up helpfully:

> The term *baptisma* was used for John's baptism for repentance (Mark 1:4; Matt 3:7; Luke 3:3; Acts 19:3) and also for the ritual of initiation practiced by Jesus' followers (Rom 6:4; Eph 4:5; Col 2:12; 1 Pet 3:21). But Hebrews here uses the noun *baptismos*, which is used for ritual Jewish washings (Mark 7:4) and for John's baptism (see Josephus, *Antiquities* 18.117). In 9:10 Hebrews speaks of "diverse washings" *(diaphorois baptismois)* together with Jewish practices of eating and drinking (see also Philo,

---

[386]Koester, *Hebrews*, p. 311.

Special Laws 1.261; 1QS [Manual of Discipline] 3:4-9; 5:13-14). The usage in the present passage suggests the ritual initiation of baptism, but the plural is puzzling. We must remember, however, that a single person could conceivably have undergone, in sequence, a proselyte baptism, circumcision, John's baptism, and baptism into the Jesus movement. An instruction concerning baptisms, therefore, could well involve the distinctions between other washings and baptism into Christ.[387]

Hebrews 6:3 reveals something of the piety of the author. He intends in this discourse to go on beyond the elementary teachings, but he knows he is not the master of his own time or life, so he adds "if God permits."

To make sense of Hebrews 6:4-8 we must realize from the start that if our author believed that any of the immediate audience had already committed irrevocable apostasy and was irretrievable, there would be no point in this warning, at least for those particular listeners. In addition, Hebrews 6:9 makes clear that he is not responding to already extant and known cases of apostasy in the audience, he is just warning against it.[388] That said, we must take absolutely seriously the word that stands at the outset of **Hebrews 6:4** like a sentinel at the door: *adynaton*, which can mean "impossible, completely unable, without power to accomplish the end in view." *Shepherd* of Hermas, *Similitude* 9.26.6, perhaps dependent on this usage, seems to take the word to mean "impossible," not just incapable. From other places where the author uses this (or related) Greek words, it quickly becomes apparent that *adynaton* does not mean merely "improbable":

- "impossible that God would prove false" (Heb 6:18)
- "impossible for gifts and sacrifices to perfect the conscience" (Heb 9:9; cf. Heb 10:1)
- "impossible for the blood of bulls and goats to take away sins" (Heb 10:4)
- "impossible for the same sacrifices offered again . . . to take away sin" (Heb 10.11)
- "impossible to please God without faith" (Heb 11:6)

From a rhetorical viewpoint the theme of the impossible was a standing topic in all three genres of rhetoric (Aristotle *Rhetoric* 2.19.1-27), and so this does not tip the author's hand in regard to the species of rhetoric found in Hebrews. Commentators debate where the impossibility lies. Does the author mean it becomes psychologically impossible for an apostate to repent? William Lane suggests that a person who has rejected the saving death of Jesus has repudiated

---

[387]Johnson, *Hebrews*, p. 159.
[388]Craddock, *Hebrews*, p. 73.

the only basis upon which repentance can be extended.[389] The problem with this view is that the author does not say it is impossible to repent, but that it is impossible to restore a person who commits apostasy. That leaves one to consider whether what is meant is human efforts or divine efforts to restore them. Craig Koester suggests the latter, not meaning that God does not have the power, but that God would refuse to do so if someone "crucified Christ afresh."[390] This may be correct, but our author is deliberately engaging in dramatic rhetorical statements for the purpose of waking up the audience. The function is not to comment on something that is impossible for God (some commentators draw attention to Jesus' remark in Mk 10:27 that what is humanly impossible is not impossible for God, for all things are possible with God).

The description of the person who is impossible to restore is said to be one who once (hapax)[391] (1) has been enlightened, (2) has tasted of the heavenly gift, (3) has become a sharer of the Holy Spirit, and (4) has tasted the goodness of God's word and the powers of the age to come. A more fulsome description of a Christian would be hard to find in the New Testament. In the first place the term enlightened is regularly used in the New Testament for those who have come out of darkness into the light and so have gone through the necessary conversion of the imagination and intellect (Jn 1:9; 2 Cor 4:4-6; Eph 1:18; 2 Tim 1:10; 1 Pet 2:9). In the second place, the verb taste means to genuinely experience, as we have already seen in Hebrews 2:9, which speaks of Christ experiencing death. In the third place, the term metochous has already been used in this discourse in relationship to the heavenly calling of Christians (Heb 3:1) and to Christians being sharers or partners with Christ. Having "shared in" the Holy Spirit is the hallmark of being a Christian, as Hebrews 2:4 stresses, along with numerous other New Testament witnesses, particularly Paul (1 Cor 12) and Luke (Acts 2; 10). Koester says that the phrase means to have taken the Spirit into one's own being.[392] If it were not perfectly clear that this is someone with the divine presence and power of God in their life, our author goes on to add that this person has experienced the goodness of God's word and also the eschatological power of the age to come. Paul called such experiences the foretaste of glory divine that only Christians experienced (2 Cor 1:22; Eph 1:14). "In this and the three preceding participles, the writer withholds nothing in reminding the addressees of the abundance of God's investment in them. Upon them God has

---

[389]Lane, *Hebrews*, 1.141.
[390]Koester, *Hebrews*, p. 313.
[391]*Hapax* normally carried the connotation of something that occurs only once and so is unique.
[392]Koester, *Hebrews*, p. 314.

poured out more than they could ever have asked or imagined."[393]

There is some debate as to whether we ought to match up what our author says in Hebrews 6:4-8 about some of the initial things experienced in Christ with the elementary elements mentioned a few verses before. For example, enlightenment could refer to baptism; partaking of the Holy Spirit could correlate with the laying on of hands; tasting the goodness of God's word and the power of the age to come could correlate with the teaching about resurrection of the dead, which in this case would have to mean something like spiritual resurrection at the new birth, which is unlikely; and renew unto repentance could correlate with the initial repentance of faith. There may be some force in this argument, but it should not be overpressed.

David deSilva tries to cut the Gordian knot of this problematic text by stressing that for the author of Hebrews salvation is a (purely) future and eschatological matter.[394] This is not quite correct, however. While the clear emphasis in Hebrews is on final or eschatological salvation (Heb 1:14; 9:28) and while deSilva is right to criticize those who read into the discussion Ephesians 2:5, 8 (which speaks of initial salvation through faith, not eternal security),[395] it is false to say that the author of Hebrews thinks of salvation only as something future. At the very least one must give the last clause of **Hebrews 6:5** its due, which speaks retroactively of those who have already tasted the powers of "the age to come." In other words, future salvation and its benefits have broken into the present, and one can presently begin to experience its benefits—in the form of enlightenment, life in the Spirit, empowerment with the power of the eschatological age and so forth. This is surely a description of a person who is saved and converted in the initial sense of the term *saved*. It is then a distinction without a difference to argue that our author is speaking about Christians who have every advantage presently available through God's grace and have every characteristic of Christians, but then to insist our author does not prefer to say they are saved. They have partaken of the heavenly gift—this is surely the same thing as saying they are saved, at least in the sense that they have been genuinely converted and are Christians at present.[396]

And then our author says in **Hebrews 6:6** what seems almost unthinkable—

---

[393]Craddock, *Hebrews*, p. 75.

[394]DeSilva, *Perseverance in Gratitude*, pp. 221-22; idem, "Heb 6:4-8: A Socio-Rhetorical Investigation"; and idem, "Exchanging Favor for Wrath."

[395]Witherington, *Philemon, Colossians and Ephesians*, ad loc.

[396]Attridge, *Hebrews*, p. 170, says: "The 'heavenly gift' . . . is best understood as a general image for the gracious bestowal of salvation, with all that entails—the spirit, forgiveness, and sanctification." For an attempt to deny that the text says what it says about the apostasy of saved persons, see Hughes, "Hebrews 6:4-6 and the Peril of Apostasy."

he uses the verb *parapiptō* (found nowhere else in the New Testament) to speak of falling away, not in the sense of accidentally or carelessly falling down, but in the sense of deliberately stepping into a black hole. In the Septuagint this verb describes acting faithlessly or treacherously, especially in regard to the covenant (Ezek 14:13; 20:27; Wisdom of Solomon 6.9; 12.2). "The act of falling away is not so much against a dogma as against a person, at 3:12 against God, at 6:6 against the Son of God. The remainder of v. 6, crucifying again the Son of God and holding him up to ridicule, makes this abundantly clear. Apostasy . . . is the sin of abandoning God, Christ, and the fellowship of believers (cf. 10:25)."[397] It is possible that "crucifying the Son to themselves" means that they have cut themselves off from the Son or have killed off his presence in their lives. They have thereby ended their relationship with Christ. He is dead to them.[398] The two clauses are related, because "to make a public spectacle/paradigm" of someone was one of the functions of public crucifixion on public roads (Quintilian *Declamations* 274). Our author is suggesting that to commit apostasy is to publicly shame Jesus as well as snuff out one's personal relationship with him. Hebrews 10:26-29 suggests that we should not try to alleviate the severity of the judgment spoken of here in regard to the apostate, for such a person there no longer remains a sacrifice for their sins, but rather a terrifying prospect of judgment. Koester suggests that we read the stern remarks here in the light of equally stern ones in the Old Testament, which served as a warning against apostasy and tried to prevent it rather than being definitive statements about perdition (so Philo *On Rewards and Punishments* 163). In other words, these words were intended to have a specific emotional effect, not comment in the abstract about what is impossible.[399] The wilderness-wandering generation and their fate lie in the background here (Heb 3:7-19), and Luke Timothy Johnson points out how the argument here is very similar to 1 Corinthians 10:1-4, where the fate of the wilderness-wandering generation warns Corinthian Christians against assuming that apostasy was impossible for them since they have been converted and had various divine benefits and rituals.[400] Johnson stresses, however, that our author says that they are in danger of falling away not just from rituals but from actual Christian experience itself: "The enormity of apostasy is measured by the greatness of the experience of God it abandons." That is why it is impossible to 'renew to repentance' people who have proven capable of

---

[397]Craddock, *Hebrews*, p. 76.
[398]Koester, *Hebrews*, p. 315.
[399]Ibid., p. 320.
[400]Johnson, *Hebrews*, pp. 161-62.

turning away from their own most powerful and transforming experience."[401]
Hebrews 12:17 will use Esau as the model of the apostate who sold his birthright
for a single meal and "even though he sought it with tears, he was rejected, for
he found no opportunity to repent."

Our author chooses then to describe apostasy in horrific terms—to abandon
one's loyalty to Christ is the same as crucifying him all over again or standing
and ridiculing and deriding him as he dies on the cross. In an honor-and-shame
culture this is intended to be shocking language about the most shameful behavior imaginable for one who has been so richly blessed by God in Christ. Similar language about defection crops up throughout the discourse: "turn away"
(Heb 2:1), "shrinking back" (Heb 10:38-39), "falling short of God's gift" (Heb
12:15), "selling one's birthright" (Heb 12:16). We should take very seriously the
word *impossible* in this text, without suggesting that anything is totally impossible for a sovereign God. Our author seems to believe that one can go too far,
past the point of no return and no restoration. This text then cuts both ways,
against either a facile notion that forgiveness is always possible no matter how
severe the sin in question is, but it equally must count against the "eternal security" sort of argument as well. Our author clearly emphasizes the future and
eschatological dimension of the pilgrimage to being fully and completely saved,
and short of that climax one is not viewed as eternally secure, for one is not yet
securely in eternity.

A CLOSER LOOK

The Exegetical Arm-Wrestling of Protestants over
Hebrews 6:1-6: A "Taste" of the Debate

It will be worthwhile to lay out the traditional interpretations of this text by
Calvinists and Arminians to show the different assumptions brought to the task
of interpretation in each case. Theological systems, while not bad in themselves, can often lead to very strained interpretations of biblical texts, especially when the system is the primary intellectual grid through which the text
is being read. This can easily be illustrated from a close reading of Protestant
commentaries on Hebrews 6:1-6 since the Reformation. Differences of interpretation are usually based on whether a Calvinist or an Arminian is reading
this text.

For example, interpreting the key notion of being "once enlightened" depends on both the word *once* and the aorist tense of this participle. It surely

---

[401]Ibid., p. 163.

must refer to a definitive experience, a one-time experience in the past. The question is—is the author talking only in objective or also in subjective terms? That is, could "once enlightened" merely be a code phrase for having been baptized, or does it refer to some sort of subjective enlightenment? Naturally the Calvinist tends to favor the former idea, and the Arminian the latter.

The phrase "having tasted of the heavenly gift" may be understood as merely partaking of the Lord's Supper on the one hand or actually partaking subjectively of God's gift of salvation. "Having become [aorist participle] *metochous* of the Holy Spirit" is said to mean having been given some spiritual power or gift, and F. F. Bruce and others compare the case of either Simon Magus or those mentioned in Matthew 7:22-23. On the other hand, Arminians insist that what is meant is an actual sharing in the Holy Spirit, with no reference being made to spiritual gifts here.

"Having tasted [aorist participle] of the goodness of God's word" in Hebrews 6:5 may simply mean instructed, perhaps with some understanding (the analogy to the parable of the sower is often brought up), whereas others argue that this is a subjective experience of goodness, not merely a hearing of the word.

Those of the Reformed persuasion (one should read Philip Edgcumbe Hughes and I. Howard Marshall to get the real flavor of the debate) tend to say the following things about this passage: (1) we must define who is a Christian by whoever perseveres to the end; if one does not persevere to the end then one never was a Christian; and (2) the covenant community received the blessings mentioned in Hebrews 6:4-8 but not necessarily each and every individual in that community; thus one should be in the context or environment where one can benefit from such blessings, at least indirectly. There are many problems with this approach, and most recognize that this text is the most difficult to reconcile with a doctrine of eternal security. Several factors are key:

1. These words are addressed to the whole community, not just "some among you," and when the author says he is persuaded of better things, he calls them all "beloved" (Heb 6:9). There is no hint that our author thinks of some invisible elect group within a larger mixed multitude. One must also ask what would be the urgency of warning reprobates if there was no possibility of their turning back anyway. One could perhaps argue that maybe God would use the word of exhortation to keep the elect straight, but if it had been decreed from before the foundation of the earth that they were going to be saved, such an exhortation would hardly be absolutely necessary one way or another it would seem.

2. There is a serious problem in reading second- and third-century interpretations of this passage back into the New Testament, for though the

word *enlightened* did come to have the objective meaning of baptism and though *heavenly food* was later a term for the eucharist, it is very difficult to argue that here.[402] Apostasy is by definition a falling away or rebellion against something one has had a part in and partaken of—namely the faith. One cannot fall away from something one never stood for. More importantly, the word *tasted* very strongly suggests subjective experience, not merely objective giving, and it also suggests a real sampling, not merely a taste-testing, as is very clear from Hebrews 2:9, where Christ is said to have tasted death, which means fully experienced subjectively, not merely had a light taste of (contra John Owen).

3. The parallel passage in Hebrews 10:26-32 strongly supports the contention that Hebrews 6:1-6 is directed to those who are considered Christians. There the author says, "If *we* deliberately keep on sinning after receiving knowledge of the truth, no sacrifice for sins is left but only a fearful prospect of judgment. . . . Remember the earlier days after you received the light" (using *phōtisthentes,* just as in Heb 6:4, though the case differs). This must strongly suggest that our author is talking about having received and believed the gospel in Hebrews 6.

4. The phrase *became sharers of the Holy Spirit* says nothing of the charismatic gifts, and the term *metochous,* already encountered at Hebrews 3:1, 14, refers to those who share in Christ and the heavenly call, that is, Christians. The analogy with Simon Magus fails, for we are never told that he received the Spirit; we are not even told *what* he believed (Acts 8:13), and in view of what follows, where he tries to "buy the Holy Spirit" and the power that goes with (Acts 8:18), we must assume that he did not have it or share in it. The analogy with the unknown exorcists in Matthew 7 also fails, since that was before Pentecost; and besides, our author says nothing about only receiving the Spirit's charismatic gifts—he says "partakers of the Holy Spirit."

5. C. F. D. Moule points out that the accusative means that the phrase should be translated "tasted *that* the word of God is good."[403]

I thus conclude that the Reformed argument does not make sense of this particular text. Our author is concerned lest Christians apostatize. In the New Testament a Christian is not defined as one who perseveres to the end, though that is urged and indeed necessary if one is to make it to heaven; but rather a Christian is defined as one who has received Christ as Lord and Savior and received the Spirit here and now. On this showing, our author is talking about

---

[402]See, for example, the interpretations from the fathers in Heen and Krey, *Hebrews,* pp. 84-86.
[403]Moule, *Idiom-Book of New Testament Greek,* p. 36.

dangers confronting Christians, perhaps especially Christians under persecution. And perhaps we should not even have such a theological debate without
fully taking into account the rhetorical nature of this source material. Andrew
Lincoln's remarks should give us pause when it comes to how we read the
first portion of Hebrews 6:

> Overstatement for effect was another frequent feature of powerful rhet-
> oric. The assertion that certain people are crucifying again the Son of God
> (6.6) is clearly not a literal possibility but achieves maximum rhetorical im-
> pact in suggesting how unthinkable the rejection of Christ and his benefits
> should be. . . . Is the statement in 6.4 that it is impossible to repent after fall-
> ing away an exaggeration designed to put the perils that face the readers in
> the strongest possible terms? Or is the assertion that follows in 6.9, designed
> to gain the goodwill of the addressees—"we are confident of better things
> in your case"—also hyperbole? If the writer really were confident, would he
> be writing to issue such a warning in the first place?[404]

> In my judgment, these are the right kinds of questions to ask about an epi-
> deictic discourse clearly given to hyperbole at points. Two things result from
> taking such rhetorical factors into account: (1) our author really does think that
> at least some of the audience is in danger of apostasy and warns against it and
> (2) we may suspect that the "no restoration" remark functions as a device to
> make clear how horrible committing apostasy really is. It is another way of
> pleading "please don't go there." The consequences of apostasy are thereby
> shown to be grim by the use of hyperbolic language.

It is sometimes questioned what the illustration in **Hebrews 6:7-8** is meant
to prove. Our author is talking about two possibilities that *one* piece of ground
may produce (the word *land* is used only once in these verses); he is not talking
about an elect versus a reprobate piece of land (i.e., two different pieces of
land). He speaks of land that has drunk deeply and many times of God's blessed
rain. If it produces good plants under cultivation (which is needed and is what
our author is trying to do—cultivate more mature Christians), then it shares in
God's blessings; but if it produces thorns and thistles, it is useless and about to
be cursed, heading for an end of being burned up.

There is, however, some hope in the illustration, as Chrysostom points out:
"Worthless . . . and near to being cursed. Oh, how great consolation in this
word! For he said 'near to being cursed' not 'cursed.' . . . And not only by this
did he encourage them, but also by what follows. For he did not say 'which shall
be burned' but what? 'Its end is to be burned.' If he continues in this way to the

---

[404]Lincoln, *Hebrews*, p. 21.

end" (*Homilies on Hebrews* 10.3). The illustration points out that ground that has received such a blessing from God as good rain and then produces thorns and thistles rather than good fruit is ground fit for and tending toward being burned off, a graphic image of final judgment. The text also seems to imply that the rain bestowed on each piece of ground is the same. The illustration does not suggest that God chose to favor one piece of ground over the other with special blessings of salvation. It is then entirely the ground's fault, and its refusal to produce good fruit leads to its judgment. In this regard the illustration is like the saying of Jesus of how God makes his rain to fall on the just and the unjust (Mt 5:45).[405] This illustration is meant to reinforce the points just made in Hebrews 6:4-6. Therefore the emphasis falls on the thorny ground and its failure to produce the appropriate response after all it has received.

In **Hebrews 6:9** we swing back to the positive side of the equation once more, and for the only time in this discourse the audience is called "beloved"—perhaps because our author has just given his sternest warning, and like a parent he does not want the listener to think he no longer cares for and about them. The stick has been traded in for a cookie rather than a carrot. Called palliation, this approach follows the advice of earlier rhetors: "If frank speech of this sort seems too pungent, there will be many means of palliation, for one may immediately thereafter add something of this sort: 'I appeal here to your virtue, I call on your wisdom, I speak of your old habit,' so that praise may quiet the feelings aroused by frankness. As a result, the praise frees the hearer from wrath and annoyance, and the frankness deters him from error" (*Rhetorica ad Herennium* 4.37.49; cf. 1.4.9). Expressions of confidence were a conventional rhetorical way to establish rapport with the audience (1 Thess 2:19-20; Rom 15:14; 2 Cor 7:4, 16; Gal 5:10; 2 Tim 1:5).[406] Here again we see our author carefully following the rhetorical conventions. The function of returning to encouragement and praise in Hebrews 6:9-12 is to restore the rapport between the author and audience so they will be receptive to what follows. "Praise of an audience's past [and present] choices serves as a means of maintaining their goodwill."[407]

Our author skillfully changes his tone of voice. The audience is "you" throughout Hebrews 6:9-12, and in Hebrews 6:11-12 even more personally it is "each of you." He speaks directly and personally to them when he has something

---

[405]See the discussion in Koester, *Hebrews*, p. 323.
[406]On the function of this motif, see Olsen, "Pauline Expressions of Confidence." In a rhetorical context, the appropriate translation of this verb is not "I am confident that . . ." but rather "I am persuaded that . . ." (e.g., Gal 5:10). Our author is seeking to persuade his audience about important things in part by saying that he is persuaded of good things about them.
[407]DeSilva, *Perseverance in Gratitude*, pp. 245-46.

positive to say. He uses the same sort of rhetorical affirmation found in Paul: "But we are confident/persuaded that . . ." (Rom 15:14; Gal 5:10; Philem 21).

Hebrews 6:10 indicates that two different factors have persuaded our author of better things about the audience.[408] The first factor is that our author believes God has by no means given up on the audience. God is faithful and continues to work in their midst (Heb 2:4; 6:4-5). As a secondary reason, our author adds that he knows the fruit of their faith both in the past and in the present in their service to the saints, an activity that continues to go on despite their difficult circumstances. This is a clear token that their faith is genuine and is still being adhered to. It is this persistent and continued faithfulness despite opposition or difficulties that the author says he deeply desires from them, using a verb *(epithymoumen)* that reflects both his own emotional commitment to the audience and his willingness to make an emotional appeal to them.

Hebrews 6:11 says that they must strive for the full assurance/conviction of hope, or perhaps the fulfillment *(plerophoria)* of hope. In Hebrews 10:22 the word seems to have the sense of assurance or conviction. Here the author is not suggesting that this assurance comes automatically with the territory, once one becomes a Christian. This is a conviction or attitude that a believer must strive to have until the end.

Hebrews 6:12 speaks of the matter of imitating the faithfulness of those who through faith and patience inherit the promises. This could be a reference to the Old Testament saints, especially in light of the immediately following discussion about Abraham. Since, however, what is said about the saints of the past is that they did not inherit the promises (Heb 11:39), the reference here is more likely to Christians who have died of late while remaining faithful to the end, Christians whom this audience may have served when they were imprisoned, on trial, about to be executed (Heb 10:32-34). The call for imitation can be a sign that we are dealing with deliberative rhetoric, but since we are being told that the audience is already imitating the good example of previous saints by their service to the saints, this is an epideictic motif—reminding of values and virtues already embraced and practiced.

TRANSITUS: THE FOREFATHER AND THE FORESHADOWED PRIEST (HEB 6:13-20)

As the anchor, dropped from the vessel, does not allow it to be carried about even

---

[408]"Better things" is a much reiterated phrase in this discourse (Heb 1:4; 7:7, 19, 22; 8:6; 9:23; 10:34; 11:16), and for good reason. When one's most fundamental rhetorical device is comparison (or synkrisis), then one must reiterate how one's favored person, course of action, outcome is "better," more to be praised than the alternatives.

if ten thousand winds agitate it but, being depended upon, makes it steady, so also does hope. Note what a fitting image he has chosen. He did not speak of a foundation that would not be suitable, but of an anchor. For that which is on the tossing sea and seems not to be very firmly fixed stands on the water as upon land and is shaken yet not moved. For in regard to those who are very firm and who love the truth, Christ with good reason spoke of one who "has built his house on a rock." But in respect of those who are giving way and who ought to be carried through by hope Paul [sic] has more suitably set down this metaphor. For the surge and the great storm toss the boat, but hope does not permit it to be carried back and forth, although winds innumerable agitate it, so that, unless we had this hope we should long ago have been sunk. (Chrysostom *Homilies on Hebrews* 11.3)

Hebrews 6:13-20 serves as a bridge passage before the major exposition of the "difficult subject" in Hebrews 7:1—10:18, before the author turns once more to exhortation in Hebrews 10:19-39. It is connected to what has come immediately before by key terms like *blessing, promises, faith* and *endurance* (Heb 6:7, 12). Fred Craddock suggests that this passage be seen as an expansion of the theme in Hebrews 6:10, namely that God is not unjust.[409] But more is accomplished in this little section. Not just a rounding off of what precedes, it introduces several aspects of the coming discussion in Hebrews 7—10. For example, we hear in this section about a promise that is confirmed by an oath (Heb 7:20-25), and it also reminds of Christ's exalted status, again bringing into play Psalm 110:4 and thereby announcing the theme of what follows in Hebrews 7—10.[410]

This transitional segment is about Abraham, and one of the more astounding rhetorical moves made in this segment is that father Abraham serves as the dramatis persona who introduces us to Melchizedek. In other words, father Abraham plays second fiddle here, a rather astounding rhetorical move considering the way Abraham was viewed in early Judaism.[411] Abraham is introduced here so that he may be given prominence later in the hall-of-faith chapter (Heb 11.8-12, 17-19). This section shows how very much our author's way of thinking is grounded in a salvation-history perspective. He is not interested in simply discoursing in the abstract about concepts like faith, priesthood or atonement. To understand Melchizedek one must understand the story of Abraham, and to understand Jesus and his tale, one must understand the story of Melchizedek. Thus, in an effective rhetorical move our author approaches the less familiar subject of Melchizedek by way of the much more familiar and widely embraced story of Abraham. Another dimension to his strategy to per-

---

[409]Craddock, *Hebrews*, p. 79.
[410]Attridge, *Hebrews*, p. 178.
[411]Calvert-Koyzis, *Monotheism and the People of God.*

suade is that our author mixes Old Testament images with images familiar to the audience from everyday life (e.g., human oaths, anchors).[412] As one rhetorician puts it, people can better understand and are more likely to be persuaded by images and ideas they are familiar with, which they can apply directly to their own situation, than those that are foreign or unfamiliar (*Rhetorica ad Herennium* 4.17).

What makes this section work logically is the Jewish theology of oaths. God, in this case, has sworn an oath to keep a promise to Abraham. How much more then (another lesser-to-greater argument) will God keep his promises and remain faithful to our author's audience, especially since he already kept his promise to raise up the priest of the order of Melchizedek. But the real question is, will the audience respond to the promise and to God's oath the way that faithful Abraham did?

> [6:13] *For God promised to Abraham, since there was no one greater he can swear by, "swore by himself,"* [14] *saying, "Surely, blessing I shall bless you and multiplying multiply you."* [15] *And this one, waiting patiently, attained the promise.* [16] *For human beings swear by someone greater and all contradiction of them ends, the oath (serving) as a confirmation.* [17] *And so even more willing is God to demonstrate to the inheritor the immutability of the promise, he mediated/guaranteed an oath of his purpose,* [18] *in order that through two immutable deeds, about which it is impossible for God to lie,* [19] *we have strong encouragement, those having fled hold fast the hope that lies before us, since we have as an anchor of the spirit, safe and firm and entering into the inside of the curtain* [20] *where the forerunner for us entered in, Jesus, became a high priest according to the order of Melchizedek forever.*

Oath-taking was a serious matter in antiquity, and in oral cultures oaths that were orally sworn by a deity were considered very serious. Philo, for example, says that "an oath is an appeal to God as a witness on some disputed matter" (*On the Sacrifices of Cain and Abel* 91—94). The normal function of an oath was to provide a surety for the truthfulness of something that is being claimed or said. It was a way of invoking God as a witness, on pain of God's judgment. This is why a curse is pronounced on those swearing falsely (Zech 5:3-4). The Old Testament does not (unlike Jesus) prohibit oaths, but says they must be in the true God's name, not some alien deity (Deut 6:13). Of course, when one is dealing with God swearing an oath, there is no other name above God's by which God might swear, so God swears by himself in **Hebrews 6:13**, an extraordinary thing for God to do since divine veracity is presumably not in doubt. Philo says: "God alone therefore is the strongest security first for himself, and in

---

[412]Koester, *Hebrews*, p. 332.

the next place for his deeds also, so that he naturally swore by himself when giving assurance regarding himself, a thing impossible for anyone else" (*Allegorical Interpretation* 3.205-6). Rabbi Eleazar is credited with saying: "Lord of all the world, if you had sworn to them by heaven and earth, I would say that even as heaven and earth pass away, so shall your oath pass away. But now you have sworn to them by your great name, and just as your great name endures forever and ever, so shall your oath endure forever and ever" (Babylonian Talmud, tractate *Berakhot* 32a).

Eventually two divine oaths will be in play (a later one in Heb 7:21 is based on Ps 110:4 about Melchizedek), but in **Hebrews 6:14-15** the oath has to do with the paraphrased Genesis 22:17, and the context there may be significant. The first oath has to do with promise of offspring to Abraham, a promise reiterated three times (Gen 12:2; 15:5; 22:17). The promise with an oath, however, comes directly after Abraham's faith has been tested in the near sacrifice of Isaac. Fred Craddock helpfully suggests that our author wants his audience to look to the example of Abraham if they think their trials have been hard and that they have suffered much (which they have; see Heb 10). The logic is that if God is faithful to his promise to Abraham and Abraham could be faithful and endure trials, so can the audience.[413]

In order to understand this and subsequent sections it is necessary to understand ancient treaties. In ancient Near Eastern practice there were various sorts of treaties or covenants (parity treaties between equals that had some mutual interests) and lord-vassal treaties (as in Hittite literature). One of the major features of an ancient treaty was the oath that went along with it, in particular the oath curse ("may I be struck down by the gods if I do not fulfill this oath").[414] This was a way of indicating one's seriousness of intention to fulfill the treaty. Obviously, a treaty between God and his people is not a parity treaty but a lord-vassal treaty in which the lord dictates the terms—both the stipulations and benefits (promises). The nature of ancient treaties is dependent on who swears the oath: if the vassal swears then it is a law covenant, which was the case at Sinai with the Mosaic covenant; but if God swears then it is a promise covenant, as in the case of the Abrahamic covenant and the new covenant (our author refers to swearing of God only in regard to these two covenants; see Heb 6:13; 7:20-22). In the latter, God swore an oath promise to Jesus the mediator of the better

---

[413]Craddock, *Hebrews*, pp. 81, 83. Craddock goes on to say, however, that there is neither comfort nor effective exhortation in telling suffering people that others have suffered more. This is not quite true, because often they will be inspired to endure as others have before, saying to themselves "if so-and-so can do it, so too can I."

[414]Still helpful and relevant to this entire discussion is Kline's classic *By Oath Consigned*.

covenant. Keeping this in mind allows a good deal of what follows in Hebrews 9—10 to make a lot better sense.

Our author first speaks in **Hebrews 6:16** of human oath-taking, which is done literally "against one who is greater." This may seem strange language to us, but it is well explained by David deSilva, who says that this phrase shows "the adversarial quality of an oath. In effect, the oath invites the hostility and reprisal of the deity in whose name an oath is sworn should the oath be deceitful or violated, since the name and honor of that deity was taken as a surety. As one might take out a loan 'against' some collateral . . . , so an oath was a 'loan' of reliability taken out 'against' the honor and reliability of a god."[415] Papyrus Oxyrhynchus 240.3-9 provides an excellent example of oath-taking, which doubtless went on throughout the empire with regularity: "I swear by Tiberius Caesar Novus Augustus Imperator, son of the deified Jupiter Liberator Augustus, that I know of no one in the village aforementioned from which extortions have been made by the soldier . . . or by his agents. If I swear truly, may it be well with me, but if falsely, the reverse." Some oaths could be reneged on without penalty (e.g., if one decided to change one's will), but some oaths were viewed as irrevocable, especially in Jewish contexts (3 Maccabees 5.42).

Our author affirms in **Hebrews 6:17** that, not only did God promise something, but he backed up the promise by swearing an oath—a double witness to the certainty that the promise is valid and will be honored by God. The term *mesiteuō* may be a deliberate double entendre here since it can mean either "mediate" or "guarantee" and often refers to a person who mediates.[416] Our author speaks of two immutable testimonies—the promise and the oath. Clearly this promise is not seen as conditional. In addition, our author affirms that the reliability of the promise rests both on God by nature not being able to lie and even more importantly on his will being "immutable." God's will is not something that is ever in danger of changing, and he is as good as his word—truthful.

Our author is possibly familiar with early Jewish exegesis of Genesis 22.16, which reflected on the notion of God swearing by his own name and what that might mean.[417] Our author presumes a lot of knowledge of the Old Testament on the part of at least some of the audience, which supports my thesis that he is writing to Jewish Christians. In any case, he will return later to the theme of

---

[415]DeSilva, *Perseverance in Gratitude*, p. 249 n. 93.
[416]Koester, *Hebrews*, p. 328; Attridge, *Hebrews*, p. 181.
[417]Lane, *Hebrews*, 1.149; and Attridge, *Hebrews*, p. 179.

God's oath in Hebrews 7:21-28. Throughout Hebrews our author stresses the resident-alien status of the author and audience. In **Hebrews 6:18** they are called refugees (*katapheugō* [literally "to flee persecution"]; Acts 14:6). At Hebrews 11:9, 13 we will hear about being resident aliens, foreigners and even transients upon the earth. This is the rhetoric of disengagement from placing too much value on Roman or other sorts of earthly citizenship.

As Thomas Long says, in **Hebrews 6:19-20** it becomes apparent why our author is expending all this energy supporting the trustworthiness of God's promise to Abraham: it was a promise to Christians as well, and Christian hope is anchored in the promises made to Abraham. God has made a commitment, not a conditional promise or a bargain.[418] The hope spoken of here is likened to an anchor, but the hope is not merely personified, it becomes a person—Jesus—who has passed through the veil into the very presence of God. Based on Jesus' exaltation, this hope is what the believers must grasp with both hands. The hope offered is the salvation-history trajectory of the Son, who began and finished his arc of triumph in the presence of God. The "anchor" is said to be both firm and secure/steadfast (*bebaios* in Heb 2:2; 3:14; 9:17). Virgil speaks of "the firm grip of the anchor's teeth holding the ship fast" (*Aeneid* 6.3-5), thinking no doubt of an iron anchor with two wings, rather than an ancient stone anchor.[419] There is a deliberate wordplay here, as Harold Attridge notes: "Hope is firm (βεβαία) because it has received the confirmation (βεβαίωσις, vs 16) of God's oath."[420]

Even more telling is that our author is drawing on a familiar metaphor. Heliodorus says that "every hope is an anchor" (*Aetheopica* 8.6.9), but Epictetus warns that "we ought neither to fasten our ship to one small anchor nor our life to a single hope" (*Fragment* 30). Our author would disagree, if the hope is as large as God's exalted Son. This is the text from which later Christians would get the idea to associate Christ and the cross with the image of the anchor.

Hebrews 6:20 makes three affirmations about Jesus that will be unpacked shortly: (1) he entered the inner sanctum behind the veil; (2) he is the forerunner and (3) he entered on behalf of believers. The veil in question is the one that separated the holy of holies from the holy place (Lev 16:2-15; Ex 26:31-35). *Prodromos* ("forerunner"), a New Testament *hapax legomenon* (like numerous words in Hebrews 6—9), is a racing term and refers quite literally to the runner

---

[418]Long, *Hebrews*, p. 78.
[419]Koester, *Hebrews*, p. 329.
[420]Attridge, *Hebrews*, p. 183.

who is out in front, the frontrunner. In the Septuagint and other Greek literature it refers to the herald who goes before a dignitary, an advance scout who goes before the army or the firstfruits that foreshadowed or presaged the full crop. The term is frequently used for a person sent ahead by Caesar to set up camp and prepare a spot for encampment. The sense is not just someone who arrives in advance to announce that others will follow, but it is someone who does something once he arrives to help accommodate or prepare for those following.[421] Jesus went ahead "for us," not as only a forerunner but as one who had by his death and exaltation become a high priest forever after the order of Melchizedek. Thus in Hebrews 6:20 the subject of Melchizedek is finally broached again, after an interval since Hebrews 5:10.

While Christ entered the holy of holies alone like the high priest did, he did so on behalf of others. In the ritual of the earthly tabernacle, the priest did this alone and was followed by no one. The analogy thus breaks down, because our author is not concerned to speak about Christ going to prepare a place so his audience may follow him.[422] He says little or nothing in this discourse about believers following Jesus to heaven. Instead he speaks about the eschatological future for the believer as in the end involving something else.

One must beware then in reading too much into the term *prodromos*. The believer's hope lies behind the veil because that is where Jesus is, but the final goal or completion of the hope comes at resurrection, not in a disembodied state in heaven. It is a mistake to view our author's afterlife theology as singularly otherworldly when it comes to the *telos* or end of all things. The believer's hope is now in the heavenly sanctuary, but when Jesus returns he will be bringing heaven with him to earth in the form of the heavenly city, the new Jerusalem.

Epideictic rhetoric needs to emphasize what the deceased hero (even if he achieved apotheosis) has uniquely done or has been the first to do (Aristotle *Rhetoric* 1.9.38; Quintilian *Institutio oratoria* 3.7.16). Our author is not trying here to emphasize that Jesus died and went to heaven and so paved the way for his followers to do so. He is emphasizing that Christ, the believer's only high priest, is the only one who has access in the inner sanctum to the Father and can intercede with God on the basis of the sacrifice he alone has offered. This benefits the audience in that God's eschatological promises to Abraham of progeny and land will be realized, albeit not in the fashion Abraham expected, when Jesus returns and the dead are raised.

---

[421]Simpson, "Vocabulary of the Epistle to the Hebrews," p. 187.
[422]Koester, *Hebrews*, pp. 334-35.

A CLOSER LOOK

Let Us Praise Our High Priest

The one truly unique concept in this document that makes it stand out from all other New Testament documents is our author's vision of Christ as the heavenly high priest. If one has an understanding of this major issue most of the rest of the homily falls into place rather readily. It is difficult to say what sparked our author to write about Christ in this way. It may have been his penetrating study of the Old Testament and its institutions. He may have been looking for a way to say that Christ fulfilled their intention and eclipsed and replaced them. But it is also possible that he was familiar with the varieties of messianic speculation in early Judaism, which at Qumran and perhaps elsewhere included the idea of a priestly Messiah.[423]

Whatever his state of knowledge of the speculation about a priestly messiah, our author certainly goes beyond what we know of these concepts from these other sources, for he insists not only that Messiah died, but that he was both perfect high priest and unblemished sacrifice offered by the priest. Speculation about Melchizedek existed before the time of Jesus, as the Qumran documents show clearly enough. And there was certainly Jewish speculation about Messiah being a priest before our author wrote.

When our author wishes to describe Jesus as high priest he uses as his basis the messianic interpretation of Genesis 14 and Psalm 110. The whole idea of priesthood in the Old Testament is dependent on the idea of covenant. The shape that a priesthood takes depends on the shape and stipulations of the covenant or treaty that God's people are called upon to live by. Our author demonstrates that the Levitical priesthood is obsolescent by showing (1) that there was a higher and prior priesthood in the case of Melchizedek and that Jesus is connected to an eternal priesthood, (2) that the Levitical priesthood is linked to heredity and thus is dependent on death and descendents to determine who will next be priest and (3) that Abraham, the forebear of Levi, was blessed by and tithed to Melchizedek. In all of this our author, like Jesus before him, operates with the idea that the earlier idea or institution has precedence and thus has higher claim to authority. Texts like Hebrews 7:27 or Hebrews 9:28 make clear that our author is no slave to previous concepts, for he goes on to talk of Jesus voluntarily offering himself up as sacrifice. Hebrews 9:28 seems to refer to Isaiah 53:12, and perhaps more than any other New Testa-

---

[423]Not surprisingly the literature on this subject is vast, most of it focusing on Heb 7. See, e.g., Culpepper, "High Priesthood and Sacrifice of Christ"; Horton, *Melchizedek Tradition*; Neyrey, "Without Beginning of Days or End of Life"; and Rooke, "Jesus as Royal Priest."

ment writer (except the author of 1 Peter) our author is affected by reflection on Isaiah 53.

Texts like 4 Maccabees 6.29 show that a Maccabean martyr could offer an atoning sacrifice, and in the case of Eleazar he was a priest. Yet there is a difference here, for death as atonement is not quite the same as a deliberate sacrifice of atonement, and more to the point the Maccabean concept is tied up with the idea of the suffering of the righteous, which does not seem to be in the foreground here. Our author operates out of the concept of cultic sacrifice, not martyrdom for a cause, per se.

One of the essential elements in understanding the high priestly concept in Hebrews is that the Son of God had to be a human being to be a priest. In other words, all of this reflection on Christ as high priest tells us a lot about his perfect humanity and his human roles, but very little if anything about his divinity. The latter ideas are bound up with our author's presentation of Jesus as also God's unique and preexistent Son and word. Jesus is the perfect human being and thus is the perfect candidate to be a perfect sacrifice. But he is also a perfect high priest and thus is the perfect one to freely offer such a sacrifice, and when he does so he is perfected in his intended vocation. It is not that his going to heaven perfects him in any moral sense, but what is meant is that he completes his vocation to perfection. The language of perfection in application to Christ is sometimes thought to be cultic (i.e., in terms of consecration rather than moral sanctification), but I am not at all convinced on this score. Yet it is also true that in this homily we learn of Jesus' moral perfection as well, for he was tempted like all humans in every regard save without sin. This resistance to sin is conceived of as part of the way he fulfilled his vocation and so could be both perfect high priest and sacrifice.

But there is more to this than one might imagine, for Christ is able to forgive sins and be the perfector/completer of faithfulness for believers, leading them on to maturity/completion in their vocation because he was in a position both to have compassion (because he knows their temptations) and to judge sin and offer forgiveness (because he successfully passed such tests), which he himself did not need to receive.

The claim that Jesus was sinless is not very meaningful unless it means he voluntarily and willingly resisted temptation, that is, that it was possible for him to have done otherwise. By definition, temptation is not tempting unless one is actually inclined and could attempt to do what one is tempted to do. Thus we must take seriously statements like Hebrews 2:17 or Hebrews 4:15 and assume that Jesus was subject to all the common temptations, including sexual ones, that we are, yet he had the victory over them.

We are also told at Hebrews 5:8 that Jesus learned obedience. This means that he learned through experience, and it may be that he knew it prior to that conceptually, but Jesus as a human learned things through experience just as we do. His life manifested a normal development and progressive consciousness. What is the connection between learning obedience through death and being made perfect through suffering? Simply this: Jesus fulfilled God's will for his life that he die on Golgotha, and so he completed the task that would not have been made perfect and complete without that death.

Our author is able to talk of Jesus as a human being having faith (Heb 12:2), as our pioneer or model for faith and faithfulness. One of the key things that sets apart Jesus' work as high priest and all previous such attempts is the unique character of his sacrifice: it was once for all time, unlike the previous repeated sacrifices (which shows that at most they had only temporary and limited efficacy; our author would probably dispute that they had even that value). There is a great deal in Hebrews that could lead to the conclusion that our author was antiritual and or that he has spiritualized the very material promises in the Old Testament about rest, land and other things. Against this conclusion it must be argued that our author maintains that only one sacrifice is and was truly cultic—the sacrifice of the human will of Jesus—and by extension he calls for believers to make that same sort of sacrifice through the praise of their lips and lives (Heb 13). It is not the abolition of ritual but its perfection in human form that our author is about, for God ultimately wants the obedience and self-giving of humans, the highest form of his creation, the only form of it that can be in personal relation with its maker, the only form of it that could have Psalm 8 spoken about it. Furthermore, our author does not simply spiritualize the Old Testament, as does Philo in the service of his higher philosophy. Quite the contrary, our author believes that God's promises are now fulfilled in heaven, but that that reality will one day come to earth as well and transform earth. Nor is our author's perspective simply that the Old Testament merely has to do with externals and imperfection. Our author says nothing of the Old Testament being imperfect; he does say that it is partial, piecemeal, shadow and inadequate finally to deal with human sin. For him the essential spiritual promises of God are found in the Old Testament, and Melchizedek is more than a mere shadow, he is a likeness of Christ.

Our author's complaint is not with the Old Testament per se or with ritual per se, but with a particular ritual system—the inadequate Levitical system. He never says that it was bad or incorrect in its intent, just inadequate to meet human needs. Our author's terminology when he discusses old and new is comparative, not merely positive: the old is a shadow in comparison to the new reality in Christ. But the conceptual discontinuity, the once-for-all aspect (Heb 9:12), means that Jesus not only fulfills all the Old Testament priesthood but goes beyond it and overcomes its inadequacy.

What is striking about all this high priest language is that our author in this one concept has a way to bridge both the earthly and heavenly work of Christ, for Christ offers the sacrifice on earth, then takes the blood into the heavenly sanctuary and intercedes for us on an ongoing basis and proclaims sins forgiven. Herein we see the picture of the Old Testament priest sacrificing the animal outside the temple, then taking the blood and pouring it on the altar, going into the holy of holies on Yom Kippur, and then coming back out and pronouncing forgiveness of sins and reconciliation between God and his people.

It is the genius of our author's conceptualizing of things that he is able to bridge the past and the ongoing work of Jesus for believers, as a human being. Our author seems to operate with the well-known ancient concept of the earth as the vestibule of the heavenly sanctuary. One enters the heavenly sanctuary by passing through the earthly one, and he envisions the sacrifice of Christ as offered in that earthly portico of the heavenly sanctuary, after which he enters into the sanctuary with the blood to sprinkle.

The analogy with Old Testament practice should not be pressed too far. Does our author really think Jesus took a bowl of his blood with him to heaven? Is there really an altar or curtain in heaven where he sprinkled it? Probably not, but Jesus effected on earth and in heaven what these ritual acts symbolized—atonement for sin, placation of God's wrath, cleansing of the sinner, reconciliation with God. He conveys these profound concepts by using the Old Testament picture language. In contrast to earthly priests Jesus is a priest forever, thus forestalling anyone else ever being or needing to be a priest in this sense (this has implications for one's view of the pastoral ministry). Christ is a priest forever because he lives forever, and as Hebrews 7:25 says he always lives to make intercession for believers. Oscar Cullmann sums up his masterful investigation of Christ as high priest in Hebrews: "The High Priest concept offers a full Christology in every respect. It includes all three fundamental aspects of Jesus' work: his once-for-all earthly work, his present work as the exalted Lord, and his future work as the one coming again. Yesterday, today and forever."[424]

In closing one might wish to ask how the second coming fits into this schema. The answer intimated by our author is that the high priest had to come forth again from the temple to proclaim to the people the results of his work and the benefits. So also Christ will come again from the heavenly sanctuary. Thus we see the single most comprehensive christological concept in the New Testament, which exalts the perfect human work of Christ the believer's high priest.

---

[424]Cullmann, *Christology of the New Testament*, pp. 103-4.

CENTRAL EXPOSITION, PART ONE: ABRAHAM, MELCHIZEDEK AND JESUS (HEB 7:1—8:6)

> The old has passed away,
> Behold all things have been made anew.
> The letter withdraws, the Spirit advances.
> The shadows flee, the truth breaks in.
> Melchizedek is summed up, the motherless
> Becomes fatherless.
> The first without a mother,
> The second without a father,
> The laws of nature are abrogated
> That the cosmos above be brought to perfection.
> (Gregory of Nazianzus, *Oration* 38.2 ["On the Birth of Christ"])

Between Hebrews 7:1 and Hebrews 10:18 there is nothing but exposition of our author's central theme, for exhortation is eschewed until Hebrews 10:19-39. Hebrews 7:1—10:39 should be seen as the great central section of the discourse, however we may divide its subunits. Probably we should see Hebrews 7:1—8:6 (or perhaps Heb 7:1—8:13) as the first major subunit, with Hebrews 8:7—10:18 being the second.[425]

From a rhetorical viewpoint our author has been following an approach that can be called *insinuatio*—saving for later in the discourse a new or controversial subject that might not receive immediate praise or consent from the audience. The subject has been foreshadowed and alluded to in various ways before Hebrews 7—10, but it has not been properly discussed, and in view of this image of Christ being both the most central and crucial one for our author—the one our author most wants the audience to embrace—it is somewhat surprising that it is expounded upon only in the climactic exposition of the homily. One must assume that our author has been, in all the preliminary parts of his argument, laying the foundations and groundwork so this part of the act of persuasion will be well received. The high priestly image and role helps us make sense of other images, such as Christ as the trailblazer or initiator, which will also come to the fore in Hebrews 7—10. We must assume that our audience had previously embraced the notion of Jesus as an atoning sacrifice and perhaps even the notion that Jesus was a priest of some sort, but surely some of the material in these climactic chapters must fall under the heading of new information meant to evoke fresh praise of Jesus.

But the rhetorical device used most frequently in this section to move the dis-

---

[425]DeSilva, *Persevering in Gratitude*, p. 261.

course forward is synkrisis—the comparison and contrast of the old priesthood with the new, the old covenant with the new, the old sacrifices with the sacrifice of Christ. Jesus' merits will be exalted and his roles praised in an attempt to adequately honor Christ and so inculcate a like-minded attitude in the audience, thereby heading off defection.[426] Theon, a second-century A.D. rhetorician, says of the rhetorical device synkrisis: "We will compare their actions by choosing those that are more noble and the reasons for the numerous and greater blessings, those actions that are more reliable, those that are more enduring, those that were done at the proper time . . . those which few have done rather than those that many have done, . . . those . . . done with effort rather than easily" (*Progymnasmata* 10.8-24). This very aptly sums up what is going on when our author embarks on his central exposition of the "difficult" or more advanced subject, and it makes quite apparent that we are dealing with epideictic rhetoric here, since Theon is listing the topics that are appropriate for an encomium (see also Quintilian *Institutio oratoria* 3.7.19; Aristotle *Rhetoric* 1.9.38).[427]

Our author chooses to talk about the heavenly high priesthood of Christ by way of discussing one of the more interesting figures in Genesis—Melchizedek. As we have already seen, he introduces this figure by beginning to talk about Abraham, who had a notable encounter with Melchizedek in Genesis 14. The discussion in the transitus in Hebrews 6:13-20 is also linked to the later discussion in Hebrews 7 by God's promise to Abraham being confirmed by oath, as is God's promise to his Son (Heb 7:20-25). "Encomia . . . regularly included comparisons between the subject of the speech and other persons of renown. The sole purpose of this comparison was to amplify the honor and achievement of the subject of the encomium" (Aristotle *Rhetoric* 1.9.38-39; *Rhetoric to Alexander* 1441a27-28).[428] In other words, while our author is not really engaging in polemics against the old covenant, the way and the degree to which he praises Christ and the new covenant by going back and forth, contrasting it with the old, serve the purpose of strengthening the wavering and preventing their taking retrograde steps in their spiritual pilgrimage.

Thomas Long notices this toggling back and forth between old and new, good and better, shadow and full substance:[429]

---

[426]Ibid., p. 262.

[427]Ibid., p. 292. It seems to me, however, that deSilva underestimates our author's skill in using persuasion to achieve dissuasion as well as shore up conviction about things already believed. Yes, our author does not want his audience to revert to Judaism, to defect, to commit apostasy, but he also wants them instead to continue to embrace what they have long embraced—the all-sufficient Christ and his work.

[428]DeSilva, *Persevering in Gratitude*, p. 263.

[429]Long, *Hebrews*, p. 82.

A   the identity of Melchizedek, who resembles the Son of God (Heb 7:1-3)

B   the greatness of Melchizedek, who was superior even to Abraham (Heb 7:4-10)

C   the imperfection of the old priesthood (Heb 7:11)

D   a new law (Heb 7:12)

A' the identity of Jesus, who resembles Melchizedek (Heb 7:13-17)

B'   the greatness of Jesus as high priest, mediator of a better covenant
          (Heb 7:18—8:6)

C'   the imperfection of the first covenant and need for the new (Heb 8:7-12)

D'   a new covenant (Heb 8:13)

Only the first three of these items works as a contrast, as the last one involves two "new" items, which in turn suggests that we should insist on these items. The principle, however, of weaving together these contrasts and moving back and forth between commentary on the old and the new is beyond cavil.

There is considerable debate as to whether the controlling text that we should focus on is Genesis 14 or the text we have heard mentioned before: Psalm 110:4. If it is agreed that the importance of the Melchizedek figure for our author is primarily in the apparent permanence of his priesthood and that the forebear of the Levitical priesthood acknowledged Melchizedek as a superior, it will become apparent that both Genesis 14 and Psalm 110:4 are important to our author's discussion, and while Psalm 110 was more important earlier in the discussion, in these verses Genesis 14 and also Genesis 22 come to the fore.

Otto Michel provides an interesting structure to Hebrews 7:[430]

- what the Bible says about Melchizedek (keyword *Melchizedek*) (Heb 7:1-3)
- the giving of the tithe to Melchizedek (keyword *tithe*) (Heb 7:4-10)
- the overthrow of the old priesthood (keyword *order*) (Heb 7:11-14)
- the abolition of the law (keyword *law*) (Heb 7:15-19)
- the confirmation by oath (keyword *oath*) (Heb 7:20-22)
- the eternity of the heavenly high priest (keyword *forever*) (Heb 7:23-25)
- the superiority of the heavenly high priest (keyword *high priest*) (Heb 7:26-28)

There was considerable and varied discussion in early Judaism about Melchizedek. In 11QMelch *(Melchizedek)*, Melchizedek is an agent of eschatological judgment on the wicked and vindicator of the righteous, rather like the

---

[430]Michel, *Der Brief an der Hebräer,* p. 259.

role that the archangel Michael is said to play in other texts. This vindication is associated with the final year of Jubilee, and in the same text Melchizedek is given a crucial role on the Day of Atonement as well. Josephus calls Melchizedek a priest of God, the true God (*Jewish Antiquities* 1.179-82; cf. *Jubilees* 13.25; 1QapGen [Genesis Apocryphon] 22.12-25). Philo says he is worthy of God's own priesthood (*Allegorical Interpretation* 3.79-82) but goes on to turn the man into an allegorical figure when he interprets Melchizedek as "the right word or principle" in all human beings. Just as interesting is Babylonian Talmud, tractate *Sukkah* 52b, which links Melchizedek with the eschatological Elijah. Perhaps in the same stream of thinking is *2 Enoch* 71—72, which speaks of Melchizedek being taken by Michael into the heavenly paradise, where he remains forever, a not surprising conclusion in light of Psalm 110:4. Later rabbinic tradition combined Genesis 14:17-20 with Psalm 110:4 and concluded that Melchizedek transferred his priesthood to Abraham and that Psalm 110:4 was thus spoken of Abraham (Babylonian Talmud, tractate *Nedarim* 32b; *Leviticus Rabbah* 25.6).[431] Our author is hardly the first or last to handle this material creatively. In later Gnostic speculation about Melchizedek, he is rather clearly identified with Jesus himself. Even beyond this is the polemic of Epiphanius of Salamis against a group of sectarians he calls the Melchizedekians, who claimed that Melchizedek was greater than Christ:

> Based, if you please, on the literal wording of "you are a priest forever after the order of Melchizedek," they believe that Christ has merely come and been given the order of Melchizedek. Christ is thus younger than Melchizedek, they say. For if his place were not somehow second in line, he would have no need of Melchizedek's rank. . . . But we find that Paul says at once "resembling the son of God, Melchizedek continues a priest forever." Now if he *resembles* the Son of God, he is not *equal* to the Son of God. . . . "Without father or mother" is not said because he had no father or mother but because his father and mother are not explicitly named in the sacred Scripture. (*Panarion* 4 ["Against Melchizedekians" 1.1—3.8])[432]

For our purposes the primary story we need to keep in mind is the one from Genesis 14:17-20, which tells the odd tale of Abraham having just returned from a military victory and his running into the King of Sodom. Before anything can transpire between them, the king of Salem, who is also called a priest, appears out of nowhere and interrupts the encounter. He produces bread and wine and gives Abraham a blessing in the name of "the God most high," and following

---

[431]Horton, *Melchizedek Tradition*, pp. 114-30.
[432]On all of this in relationship to interpreting Heb 7, see Cockerill, "Melchizedek Christology."

the usual reciprocity conventions Abraham offers him one tenth "of everything" (whatever that might entail). Melchizedek's later cameo appearance in Psalm 110:4 rounds out the references to this enigmatic figure in the Old Testament. In the creative hands of our author, this brief enigmatic tale becomes a typological foreshadowing of Jesus and his role as high priest—not an example of seeing Jesus as Melchizedek, but of seeing Melchizedek as a foreshadowing of "our great high priest." Perhaps our author is the first to make such a connection, but wherever it comes from it is certainly a stroke of genius, for it suggests that all along the journey of God's people through history God had been leaving clues and hints of the climax and consummation that was yet to come and "devoutly to be wished." Our author also knew that novelty was striking and more rhetorically effective because it was more likely to be remembered: "When we see in everyday life things that are petty, ordinary, and banal, we generally fail to remember them, because the mind is not being stirred by anything novel or marvelous. But if we see or hear something extraordinary, great, unbelievable or laughable, that we are likely to remember for a long time" (*Rhetorica ad Herennium* 3.22.35). Our author's central argument here certainly could be said to meet this rhetorical criteria for effectiveness.

> [7:1]*For this Melchizedek, king of Salem, priest of God most high, is the one who went to meet Abraham returning from the slaughter of the kings and he blessed him.* [2]*To whom also Abraham divided a tenth of everything, (to the one) first translated king of righteousness and then also king of Salem, which is king of peace—* [3]*without father, without mother, without genealogy, having neither beginning of days nor end of life, having been made like unto the Son of God, he remains a priest continuously.*
>
> [4]*Contemplate how great this one is to whom Abraham gave a tenth from the first-fruits/booty—the Patriarch (no less!).* [5]*And those on the one hand from the sons of Levi receiving priesthood have a commandment to exact a tithe from the people/ their brothers according to the law, although having come from the loins of Abraham.* [6]*But on the other hand, Abraham tithed to the one not descending from them, and he blessed the one having the promises.* [7]*But without any contradiction, the lesser is blessed by the greater!* [8]*And in this case on the one hand mortals who die receive the tithe, but in the other case it is attested that he lives.* [9]*And so to speak through Abraham and Levi the tenth receiver exacted a tithe,* [10]*for when they were in the loins of the father was when Melchizedek met him.*
>
> [11]*If then perfection was to be had through the Levitical priesthood, for the people on the basis of it/in relationship with it were given a law, why then was the need mentioned for another priesthood according to the order of Melchizedek to arise and not according to the order of Aaron?*
>
> [12]*For when the priesthood is changed of necessity there is also a change of law.* [13]*For about him it says this one shared another tribe from which no one has devoted*

themselves to the altar. ¹⁴For it is clear that our Lord sprang from Judah, about which tribe Moses spoke nothing concerning the priesthood. ¹⁵And it is still more obvious if according to the likeness of Melchizedek another priest has been raised up, ¹⁶who became (a priest) not according to the law of physical/fleshly commandments but according to the power of an indestructible life, ¹⁷for he has a witness borne that "you are a priest forever according to the order of Melchizedek."

¹⁸For on the one hand annulment/setting aside is effected for the previous commandment/regulation because of its weakness and uselessness, ¹⁹for the law perfected/completed nothing, but on the other hand there has been brought in besides a better hope through which we draw near to God. ²⁰And to the degree that nothing happens without swearing, ²¹(there are) those on the one hand who have become priests without swearing, but on the other hand there is one (who became a priest) with swearing through the one who said to him, "The Lord swore and will not change his mind, 'You are a priest forever.'" ²²According to the same degree Jesus became surety/guarantor of a better covenant. ²³And on the one hand numerous were those who have become priests who were prevented from remaining such because of death. ²⁴But on the other hand the one who remains forever has an endless priesthood, ²⁵and so he is able to save completely those coming through him to God, always living to intercede for them.

²⁶For just such a one was fitting to also be our high priest—devout, guileless, undefiled, separated from sinners and having become high in the heavens, ²⁷who does not have the everyday necessity like the former high priests to offer sacrifice for his own sins and then subsequently for the people. For this one made it once for all, having offered himself. ²⁸For the law appoints as high priests human beings having weakness, but the word of the swearing that was after the law (appoints) a Son having been perfected forever.

^{8:1}But the main point/essence of what has been said is we have such a high priest who is seated at the right hand of the throne of the Majesty in the heavens, ²minister of the sanctuary/holy place and the true/real tabernacle that the Lord erected, not human beings. ³For all high priests are appointed to offer gifts and sacrifices, hence this one too had something to offer. ⁴If then he was on earth, he would not be a priest, since there are (already) those offering gifts according to the law, ⁵who serve/worship (that which is) figure and shadow of the heavenly, just as Moses warned that he was to erect the tent/tabernacle. For "see," he says, "that you make everything according to the pattern shown to you at the mountain." ⁶But now he has obtained a ministry that is as much superior (to theirs) as is the covenant of which he is mediator, which has been drawn up upon superior promises.

Melchizedek's credentials are established immediately in **Hebrews 7:1**, where he is called both king of Salem and priest of the most high God—a rendering of El Elyon, who was at the top of the Canaanite pantheon, and a phrase later applied to Yahweh. Melchizedek is the very first priest mentioned in the

Old Testament, and even more remarkably his priesthood is seen as valid, though it is not of any Israelite priestly line (similarly Ex 2:16). In Genesis 14:17-20, the basis for our author's exposition, one point in the Hebrew is not certain; who gives a tithe to whom? Our author is very sure that Abraham gives the tithe to Melchizedek, and his argument hinges on that conclusion, but the point was strongly disputed in early Jewish exegesis.

To understand the rhetorical power of this argument one must recognize the following logical chain of thinking: (1) Levi is the grandson of Abraham; (2) if Abraham pays a tithe to Melchizedek, then Levi (seminally present in Abraham) is paying the tithe to Melchizedek, which is ironic since later tithes were paid to Levi; (3) this in turn implies that the Melchizedekian priesthood is greater than the Levitical and that Melchizedek is greater than either Abraham or Levi; (4) this in turn implies that the ultimate Melchizedekian priest, Jesus, is greater than all the above; (5) the icing on the cake proving the logic of all this is that Abraham was blessed by Melchizedek, and as Hebrews 7:7 says the superior person blesses the inferior. While this may not seem like perfect logic to us, in our author's world this certainly passed muster:[433] "While the argument seems to be from Melchizedek to the Son of God, it is from the Son of God to Melchizedek. The conviction that Christ is our eternal high priest finds its support in Psalm 110, which then becomes the key for interpreting Genesis 14."[434]

In **Hebrews 7:2-3** our author follows a widespread practice of drawing significance from the etymology of a person's name. The name Melchizedek means "king of righteousness,"[435] and as king he is king of Salem, king of shalom (presumably Yeru Salem).[436] "Salem" is the Septuagint transliteration of the Hebrew place name "Shalem," identified as Jerusalem by 1QapGen (Genesis Apocryphon) 22.13 and Josephus (*Jewish War* 6.438; *Jewish Antiquities* 1.180). There was in Jewish tradition the expectation that a messianic figure would bring both vindication/justice and shalom/peace when he came (Is 9:6-7; 11:1-9; 32:16-18; 2 Esdras [4 Ezra] 13.37-39; *Testament of Levi* 18.2-4; *Psalms of Solomon* 17.21-32 [the righteousness of the messianic one]). Our author may be indebted here to Philo, who first interprets Salem as meaning peace (*Allegorical Interpretation* 3.79-82), but since that practice was widespread both authors could easily have come up with this separately. Philo sees Melchizedek as a personification of rea-

---

[433]Hagner, *Encountering the Book of Hebrews*, p. 100.

[434]Craddock, *Hebrews*, p. 86.

[435]Attridge, *Hebrews*, p. 189, suggests the rendering "my king is Zedek" (i.e., the Canaanite deity).

[436]Koester, *Hebrews*, p. 341, points out that the tip-off to most commentators that Jerusalem was meant is the reference to the King's Valley in Gen 14:17, which was in Jerusalem (2 Sam 18:18; Josephus *Jewish Antiquities* 7.243).

son, unlike our author, who treats him as a crucial historical figure. The typology he is about to engage in requires a historical antitype of Christ, and there is no question that our author sees Melchizedek as a real historical figure. He also follows the Jewish practice of reading a lot out of the silence of the Old Testament, in this case Melchizedek's ancestors and descendents are nowhere mentioned.[437] This may simply be an ad hoc ploy, using a standard form of Jewish arguing, but it is also possible that our author really saw Melchizedek as an eternal figure of some sort. Clearly this was the case at Qumran, where he is a heavenly redeemer and avenger for Israel (11QMelch [Melchizedek]).

In Hebrews 7:3 the word *telos* simply means the end of life. Hebrews 7:3 makes clear that Christ is the type and Melchizedek merely the antitype, for Melchizedek has been made like the Son, in that he remains a priest forever. F. F. Bruce argues that the word *forever* means "continuously" in the biblical narrative, that is, so far as he is discussed at all in the Bible.[438] Our author may have meant it only literarily, or he may have meant more, in view of the Qumran use of the tradition. What is clear from Hebrews 7:3 is that he does *not* identify Melchizedek with the Son: they are comparable in only some ways; they are not identical. Melchizedek has been made "like Christ"; he is not viewed in our author's mind as Christ in another guise before the incarnation. Our author uses a different word for Melchizedek remaining a priest "continuously": *diēnekes* instead of *aiōna* (as in Heb 6:20), but we do not know if this is different from "eternally" (see Heb 10:1, 12, 14). In any case, he means that Christ is eternally such a priest, and that is his real point.

That he is not interested in Melchizedek as a preincarnate Christ figure is clear from Melchizedek dropping out of the argument halfway through this chapter! What our author is interested in the most is the qualities he sees in both Melchizedek and Christ—righteousness, peace, timelessness and the priestly role.[439] While at the mundane level being without father, mother or genealogy would be a considerable liability, perhaps suggesting that one was an orphan, it would disqualify someone from the hereditary Levitical priesthood. Our author does not view this mundanely, but rather as a sign that Melchizedek is part of a more transcendent and special priesthood, like Jesus.[440] The direction of the comparison—Melchizedek is like the Son rather than the reverse—con-

---

[437]In part the Jewish principle was that whatever was not in Scripture was not in the world, and so they were apt to think that even the silences of the Scripture must be pregnant since God surely must be addressing every pertinent subject. See Long, *Hebrews*, p. 85. In this case, since Melchizedek's parents are not mentioned in Scripture the assumption is that they were not in the world.

[438]Bruce, *Hebrews*, pp. 159-60.

[439]Long, *Hebrews*, p. 85.

[440]Koester, *Hebrews*, pp. 342-43.

trols the text, and Psalm 110:4 guides our author's reading of Genesis 14. He does not mention Melchizedek giving Abraham bread and wine, something that later church fathers were to make much of (Cyprian *Letter* 62.4). Scholars sometimes consider the assonance, alliteration and other rhetorical devices found in this verse (e.g., *apatōr, amētōr, agenealogētos*) as signs that our author is drawing on a poetic hymn fragment, but this conclusion is not necessary. This is an oral document, and our author is using the sort of rhetorical devices one would expect in a sermon to make the audience listen, learn and remember.[441]

Hebrews 7:4 then asks the readers to contemplate what a great person Melchizedek must be if even "the patriarch" (emphatic position last in the sentence) tithed to him. This way of approaching the subject is typical of epideictic rhetoric, as our author suggests: "Let us now praise great persons." We should not, however, overread the argument, for, as Quintilian says, the more extraordinary the subject, the more one should signal this by using dramatic hyperbole (*Institutio oratoria* 8.6.67, 73, 75). **Hebrews 7:5** then begins a series of *men . . . de* antitheses: "On the one hand this is true, but on the other/in the other case this. . . ." This verse mentions that some of Levi's sons "received a priesthood." Not all the Levites do so, but only some of them, and thus even in their case it is not simply a matter of heredity. Heredity is just a prerequisite; the law and its commandments stipulate what will happen in the case of the Levitical priesthood, and our author must establish this fact. Here is the first place he mentions this Mosaic law, about which he will say a lot more in Hebrews 9—10. The Levites as a whole received a tithe from the people, and a tenth of this was given to the Levitical priests (Num 18:21, 26-29). Our author is concerned only with the former matter. At the end of Hebrews 7:5 he stresses that the Levites are those who have come from the loins of Abraham, as do all Israelites. This will become very significant in Hebrews 7:10.

Hebrews 7:6 introduces the first antithesis. Abraham who had received the promises tithed to someone who was not descended from the Levites and who was blessed by him. Hebrews 7:6 stresses that the lesser is always blessed by the greater one, which is a bit of a rhetorical hyperbole since we could cite examples to the contrary (2 Sam 14:22; 1 Kings 1:47), but perhaps we are not catching the nuances in the discussion.[442] The lesser may perhaps honor the greater, but only the greater can truly bless the lesser, in the sense of "bless" that our author has in mind in **Hebrews 7:7**—unconditional favor bestowed by a higher power or person. **Hebrews 7:8** then stresses the impermanence and lesser na-

---

[441]Attridge, *Hebrews*, p. 189.
[442]DeSilva, *Perseverance in Gratitude*, p. 267.

ture of the Levitical priesthood in comparison to Melchizedek. All the Levites who received the tithe were men who died, but the Old Testament suggest that Melchizedek still lives. Then **Hebrews 7:9-10** brings the "seminally present" idea back to the fore, again with a bit of rhetorical hyperbole: the Levites seminally present in Abraham tithed to Melchizedek. They met him in Abraham. One needs to avoid dismissing this as exegetical sleight of hand.[443] Our author introduced this part of the argument with "one might say," which signals a rhetorical move involving a stretching of categories (Philo *On the Creation of the World* 107; *On the Cherubim* 112; Josephus *Jewish Antiquities* 15.387).[444] Fred Craddock says that ancient peoples believed in the solidarity of a race or kin group over all generations of its existence, and so this argument has force in such a setting.[445] They had a sense of collective or corporate personality extending over generations that we in our individualistic age have difficulty grasping.

Our author has now established two key points for his case: (1) the Melchizedekian priesthood must be greater because Melchizedek blessed Abraham and in him the Levites, and the greater blesses the lesser and (2) the Melchizedekian priesthood must be greater because Melchizedek who was tithed to by Abraham lives on, but those Levites who received the tithe from Israel are all dead, and even more importantly heredity does not settle the priesthood since only some of them became priests. Thus in Melchizedek the person and the priesthood permanently coalesce (as is also true in Christ, who is the one new high priest), unlike the case with the Levitical priesthood. Our author has now established that what might have been considered the strength of the Levitical priesthood, its connections of heredity, is actually a sign of its impermanence and weakness! In the case of Melchizedek and Christ it is their personal condition and dignity that establishes their priesthood. For Christ it is the power of an indestructible life, but for the Levites this was never so. Their very multiplicity shows it to have been a priesthood affected by obsolescence and death and therefore impermanence. The transitory/permanent contrast that has already been seen in the comparison of Christ and angels and of Christ and Moses is here taken up a notch higher when Christ is contrasted with the whole Levitical system, which is seen as impermanent, transitory, bound to earthly conditions such as death. Our author is not the only one who noticed the difficulties with having one's priests die and needing replacement. *Testament of Levi*

---

[443]Attridge, *Hebrews*, p. 197.

[444]The phrase indicates going beyond the evidence in order to state something that is in some sense true. See Koester, *Hebrews*, p. 345.

[445]Craddock, *Hebrews*, p. 88.

18.8 wistfully looks forward to the day when there will be a good and just high priest who will have no successor "forever"!

At **Hebrews 7:11** the argument of our author shifts a bit, and the Melchizedek speculation is essentially left behind, which suggests that our author is not interested in Melchizedek himself, but in what he represents as a antitype of Christ.[446] What comes to the fore is Christ, and his priesthood is set forth in comparison to the Levitical priesthood. There is, however, overlap of several key themes in Hebrews 7:1-10: (1) the interrelationship of law and priesthood is further developed; (2) the transience/permanence contrast is carried over and (3) the priest-forever argument is seen again in Hebrews 7:17. "The Preacher basically argues that the only reason the psalmist would talk about a priesthood of the 'order of Melchizedek' is if there were something lacking in the regular order of priests, the Levitical priests, the priesthood of the 'order of Aaron.' In other words, you don't switch horses in midstream unless the first one is broken down, and you don't get a new priestly order unless there is something wrong with the old one."[447]

Even more to the point, the people were given a law on the basis of a particular priesthood. The law was dependent on the cultus, such that if the priesthood changed, it followed a fortiori that the law had to change. Our author views the law through a priestly lens, and thus it is not surprising that he views the law through a covenantal lens, since priests are menders of things for the covenant breakers through offering of prayers, tithes, sacrifices.[448] His discussion differs from Paul's, which focuses not on priestly connections but on the character of grace and works and merit. The use of the word *heteros* instead of *allos* means that our author is not talking about just "another" priesthood here, but clearly one of a "different" sort. Our author clearly does not agree with the author of *Jubilees* 13.26, who indicates that the laws about the Old Testament priesthood were eternally valid. He also does not agree with the Greco-Roman notion of pluralism—that multiple priesthoods (like multiple deities) are just fine, even to the degree that anytime a new temple or sanctuary was established, and especially if a new god was being worshiped, a new priesthood likewise needed to be established.[449]

Our author also introduces a new matter that is going to become prominent: *diathēkē* ("covenant, testament, dispensation, agreement, contract"). This topic will become very important in Hebrews 10.

---

[446]Attridge, *Hebrews*, p. 191, but see his detailed discussion on pp. 192-95.
[447]Long, *Hebrews*, p. 86.
[448]Craddock, *Hebrews*, p. 89.
[449]Koester, *Hebrews*, p. 359. Rome had some seven priesthoods, including four major colleges of priests. Clearly our author stands in the Jewish tradition on this matter.

A CLOSER LOOK

Covenant or Testament?

The word *diathēkē* is in the Septuagint the translation of the Hebrew word *bĕrit.* We are accustomed to translating it "covenant" or "testament" (as in "Old Testament"), but both words have a wider range of meaning than that.[450] Ancient treaties in the Bible are like lord-vassal treaties, and thus their stipulations are essentially unilateral, with the lord dictating terms to the vassal. They are not the result of a mutual agreement between two parties. This likely explains why *bĕrit* is always translated by *diathēkē*, rather than *synthēkē*, for the latter conveys the idea of a mutual agreement between two equal parties. The biblical covenants are a declaration of the divine will for God's people, and therefore the terms in question mean something more like "decree," except that the people bind themselves to actively obey and keep it, hence the word *covenant/treaty.*

The unique relationship of God and his people likely dictates how this word should be translated, for we do not find in the Bible the late Classical meaning "compact" or "contract," with rare exception. And, with two possible exceptions, the meaning "testament" (as in "last will and testament," which requires the dispensation of property upon the death of the testator) is not found in the New Testament. But these two exceptions are important. As we shall see, the meaning "will" or "testament" is probably found in Hebrews 9:16-17 and Galatians 3:15-17 since the death of the testator is referred to.

Unlike a will, it is not characteristic of a normal covenant that the testator must die for it to be in force; quite the opposite is true. When a lord makes a treaty with a vassal, it is understood to be in force as long as the lord lives, and sometimes until the time of his descendents. In this regard, we may think of a marriage covenant. This is particularly important since our author uses the term *diathēkē* seventeen times in the material we are about to examine, but it is found only sixteen times elsewhere in all the New Testament (nine in Paul), which is perhaps surprising, for one might have expected more to be said about the "new covenant."

One interesting factor is that the testator—the one who draws up the covenant—can abrogate it if he so chooses. This was as true of ancient lord-vassal treaties as it was of contracts and wills in the first century A.D. For example, Papyrus Oxyrhynchus 492.9 includes the warning of the will-maker: "So long as I live I am to have power over my own property, to make any further pro-

---

[450]Campbell, "Covenant or Testament?"

visions or new dispositions I choose and to abrogate this will, and any such provisions shall be valid." *Athetēsis* ("abrogation") is technical legal language, and our author uses it at Hebrews 7:18 to make clear where things stand with the "first" or old covenant.[451] In this case, only God can annul a covenant he has made with his people, and Hebrews 7:12 says that God was prepared to do that (so also Heb 7:18). This goes flatly against the dominant strain of Jewish thinking that the law does not pass away or perish, nor is it abrogated but rather survives in all its glory (2 Esdras [4 Ezra] 9.36-37; 2 Baruch 77.15; Philo, *On the Life of Moses* 2.14-15; Josephus, *Against Apion* 2.272). This, in turn, was based on a particular understanding of texts such as Psalm 19:7, which says that the law was perfect, reviving the inner self (as in Ps 119). Here as elsewhere in his discussion of covenants, our author resorts to using technical and legal language (e.g., *aparabaton* in Heb 7:24, which means "inviolate" and so remaining valid).

A promise is distinguished from a law covenant because it functions like a dispensation or a disposition, which is closer to the root meaning of *diathēkē*. Perhaps the essential characteristic of a *běrît* /*diathēkē* is the absolute confirmation of the agreement (by strong oath, even an enactment of a maledictory oath by, for example, circumcision) and its binding character. A good deal of technical or juridical language goes along with the idea of a *diathēkē*, such as when the treaty or disposition is ratified, sworn to, annulled, confirmed, valid, legal, enacted as law (Heb 8:6). This language is used in the upcoming discussion, mixed in with a good deal of cultic language (draw near to God, cleansing of sins, etc.). Two other key terms dealing with this matter are *engyos* ("surety, guarantor") and *mesitēs* ("mediator"), the latter of which can mean a mediator between two hostile parties, a person with whom warring parties deposit an object of dispute, a witness in a lawsuit or a person who guarantees the accomplishment of an agreement or promise—that is, a guarantor. To help determine which of these meanings is in play in Hebrews, Don Hagner presents our author's contrast between the first covenant and the new/eternal covenant:[452]

First Covenant	New Covenant
called "first" (Heb 8:7; 9:1, 15, 18)	called "new" (Heb 8:8, 13; 9:15; 12:24)
good but weak (Heb 8:7-13)	better (Heb 7:22; 8:6)
temporary and now obsolete (Heb 8:6, 7, 13)	eternal (Heb 13:20)

---

[451]Rightly Attridge, *Hebrews*, p. 203n71, and examples cited there.
[452]Hagner, *Encountering the Book of Hebrews*, p. 104.

Not surprisingly, the same contrast between the first covenant and the new covenant in regard to obsolescence and permanence is also applied to the priesthoods enunciated or mandated in each of those covenants. Again, the author is not saying that the first covenant was a bad thing; to the contrary, he sees it as a good thing foreshadowing a better thing. And he believes that, since the better covenant has come, the first has been eclipsed and made obsolete. He thinks that the old covenant had a built-in obsolescence because it could not "perfect" anything, it could only point to such perfection, and one of the chief reasons it was "weak and ineffectual" was that it provided rules for fallen human beings. In other words, the problem lay not only in the lack of power in the law but in the lack of capacity in the covenant keepers.

Aristotle stresses that when two contracts or covenants or laws exist on the same topic, one must determine whether the former nullifies the latter or vice versa (*Rhetoric* 1.15.25). He also stresses that the reliability of the covenant depends on the reliability of the guarantor (1.15.21). In Roman law, which presumably our audience was familiar with, there was no question but that the later edict or treaty superceded the earlier one. For example, Claudius's banishment of Jewish Christians from Rome in 49 was annulled by the coming of the new emperor, which set all such arrangements in the obsolete category. Thus, our author could assume on the basis of both scriptural and cultural logic that the audience would likely find his argument here persuasive. Chrysostom, as usual, aptly sums things up:

> In calling it new, Paul [*sic*] says, "he treats the first as obsolete, and what is becoming obsolete and growing old is ready to vanish away." . . . Paul here uses a familiar [rhetorical] figure of speech, as if one should say the house is not faultless; that is, it has some defect, it is decayed. The garment is not faultless, that is, it is coming to pieces. He does not, therefore, here speak of the old covenant as evil, but only as having some fault and deficiency. (*Homilies on Hebrews* 14.6-7)

This section is characterized by a series of *men . . . de* constructions, and it seems we have made a definite turn in the argument since we have virtually left Melchizedek behind. Hebrews 7:11 has the one and only use of the noun *teleiōsis* ("perfection") in this homily. The sense here is of completion or the ability to deliver all we need or all God intends for us. There is considerable debate about the phrase *ep' autēs:* does it mean "on the basis of" or "with relation to"? If the former, it might seem to contradict what has been said before (i.e., on the basis of it people were given a law, which would seem to contradict the idea that the priesthood came on the basis of the law). But it means, first, that though the priesthood is dependent on the law for its very existence, the law is dependent on the priesthood for its "implementation," and so a law is enacted only for or given to the people in this matter when the priesthood is operating. Only as the law is implemented by the priests does it effectively become the law of the land. Second, *ep' autēs* means "in relationship with"; thus law and priesthood come together and are interdependent. In what follows, our author is quite convinced about the ineffectiveness of the old priestly system to bring real atonement for sins or cleansing of conscience.

Hebrews 10:1 says that the sacrifices of the law are quite incapable of making anyone perfect, because it affects only the physical side of things, the outward side of cleansing. Our author may believe that though the old sacrifices might change the believers' outward position with God, the law did not change their inward condition as the new covenant sacrifice does. As the argument develops, we will see whether our author only thinks the old system does not get to the heart of the matter—our inner condition—or whether he thinks it is totally ineffective. I tend to think the former is in view. The point in any event is that if the Levitical system had been able to perfect or make completely holy and acceptable in God's sight, there would certainly be no need for another priesthood like the Melchizedekian one to arise.

Hebrews 7:12 shows the interdependency of the law and the priesthood. An inadequate priesthood renders the law not fully effective or operative—it renders it unfulfillable. A change in the priesthood necessarily entails and implies a change in the juridical basis of that priesthood. This in turn implies that the Mosaic law is no longer in force as it was when the Levitical order was the priesthood for the people of God. And this is not because of the events of A.D. 70, which are never mentioned, but because our author believes that Christ has come and has been exalted to his high priestly role. Had our author known about the destruction of the temple, here is surely a place it would have added punch to his argument to mention it. The obsolescence of the law, then, is argued for on the basis of several considerations. (1) Moses says nothing about a Judahite priesthood, thus Jesus' priesthood must be on the basis of another covenant or law; the task of the priest in **Hebrews 7:13** is to devote himself to the altar, that is, the service performed on the altar—offerings and sacrifices. (2) The audience apparently accepts as given that Jesus was not from the tribe of Levi, but rather from the tribe of Judah in **Hebrews 7:14**, though our author makes little or nothing of this (Rom 1:3; 2 Tim 2:8; Mt 1:1).[453] (3) His priesthood is of the order of Melchizedek in **Hebrews 7:15**, and thus it is not according to the Mosaic law, which is called in Hebrews 7:16 a collection of *sarkinēs* commandments or regulations (Heb 9:9-10,

---

[453]Attridge, *Hebrews*, p. 201.

13). This term here does not likely have the sense that *sarx* sometimes has in Paul, implying something morally bad or corrupt. Rather it has its more literal sense here "of physical, of the flesh," that is, mortal.[454]

In what sense is the commandment fleshly? Not presumably because it is material or written on material substance, but either because it is a commandment that affects only the outer physical nature of human beings or, more likely, because it is a commandment that is about and dependent upon human mortals and conditioned by mortality, that is, death (and thus it is about and dependent on human descent for its implementation). In view of the contrast with the "power of an indestructible life," it seems to mean here not "made of flesh" but "belonging to the realm of the mortal, of the flesh." Mosaic law and priesthood are about and are constituted by mortals and belong to their realm, as is shown by its ancestry rules. Hebrews 9:9-10 says it is fleshly in the sense that it cleanses only the outside, provides only physical purity, regulating the body not the conscience. Only the new order gets through to the conscience and heart. Our author thus goes on to say that Christ both fulfills perfectly the function of law and priesthood and meets the needs that the priesthood serves—atonement. Geerhardus Vos points out that our author is interested in describing the purpose of atonement (cleansing, etc.), whereas Paul focuses more on the process of the atonement.[455]

The interesting phrase *the power of an indestructible life* in **Hebrews 7:16** contrasts Jesus with a Levitical priest in several ways: (1) he has real power to change humans, over against Levitical weakness and inadequacy; (2) his priesthood is dependent on his personhood, not his descent; and (3) because he has an indestructible life he can be a priest forever, unlike any Levite.[456] The phrase does not suggest that Jesus never died, but only that death—far from ending his priesthood—made it so that it could be fully activated forever. Again, it is not just that Jesus' life lasted longer but that his character differs from the Levites, as Hebrews 7:26 will make abundantly clear by saying that he is devout, guileless, undefiled, separated from sinners like the Levites and exalted into the highest heaven.[457] He is right where God is and has free access. The power of an indestructible life is self-

---

[454]Ibid., p. 202.

[455]Vos, *Teaching of the Epistle to the Hebrews*.

[456]The rare word *akatalytos* occurs only here in the New Testament. In Dionysius of Halicarnassus's *Antiquitates romanae* 10.31.5 it refers to indestructible power, in this case the indestructible power of a stable policy.

[457]In Heb 7:14 our author freely admits that Jesus is of the Judahite not Levitical line, and yet he insists he is a priest, even though priests did not come from that line. He is able to turn a negative into a positive by saying that he was of "another" line of priests—the Melchizedekian one. The relationship of Jesus to Melchizedek is not one of heredity, but rather of similarity of character, hence the word *resembling* in Heb 7:15.

authenticating and is the basis of Jesus' heavenly high priestly work.

Hebrews 7:17 indicates that Jesus was such a Melchizedekian priest (Ps 110:4 again). **Hebrews 7:18** is direct and to the point: as a result of Jesus' exaltation and full assumption of his priestly intercession in the very presence of God, the previous commandment is annulled/set aside, not because it was bad but because it was replaced by something better. It was, however, weak and ineffective: it could not make us good or make good the claim to make perfect atonement and so change us inwardly. The law is said in **Hebrews 7:19** to have perfected nothing *(ouden)* and, Hebrews 10:1, adds "no one." This is why a better hope was brought forth by God, so that we might draw near to him, having free access ("draw near" is cultic language). One of the proofs of the inferiority of the Levitical priesthood is that it is not confirmed by an oath, whereas the Melchizedekian priesthood is confirmed by God's own oath according to **Hebrews 7:20-21**, indicating a covenant of promise. When a priest was sworn into a Roman priesthood, he was admitted into that college of priests only after the emperor himself had sworn an oath that he was worthy of such an office (Suetonius *Claudius* 22). This is of special relevance and force if our author is writing to Christians in Rome who knew about such practices. If God has sworn an oath about Jesus as the believer's high priest, woe betide those who turn back to lesser priests and lesser sacrifices who were not vouchsafed by such a divine oath.

This is no mere paper agreement—it has a guarantor, one who will make sure that these promises come into effect—Jesus! Thus on these grounds it is a better covenant (Heb 9:15; 12:24) based on better promises with a guarantor. The word *engyos* in **Hebrews 7:22** is a *hapax legomenon* in the New Testament and refers to a surety or guarantee; it suggests that Jesus is the guarantor of the better covenant and its efficacy. Sirach 29.15 reads: "Do not forget the kindness of your guarantor, for he has given his life for you." Those who made surety (or posted bond) for another realized that this was a very serious matter, which could even lead to the guarantor suffering the same penalties that would have been applied to the person in question, should they default (Sirach 29.18-19). Such a person guarantees the work or commitments of another, sometimes at the risk of life. In essence we are learning that Christ is the guarantor of God's oath and promise, as is witnessed by his sacrifice.[458] The logic here is that God would swear an oath only about something that has lasting or eternal significance, and the absence of such an oath with previous covenants speaks volumes about their temporary character (Heb 3:11—4:3; 6:13-18).

Hebrews 7:23 says the obvious: Levites could not go on being priests be-

---

[458]Craddock, *Hebrews*, p. 92.

cause of death, but paradoxically Jesus could fully become our priest only after death. The word *aparabaton* ("permanent, unchangeable") describes Jesus' priesthood because he himself remains forever—having the power of an indestructible life. If the latter were not true the former would not be either. Thomas Long puts it this way: "We do not have a priest who gets sick or dies, or who goes on vacation, or falls down on the job, or grows tired of our need, or compromises his office, or takes advantage of us for his own gain; we have a faithful and steadfast great high priest who can be trusted."[459] Josephus calculated that there were eighty-three high priests from Aaron to Phanasus, the last high priest (*Jewish Antiquities* 20.227). Our author does not seem to know the end of the Levitical system, as it would certainly have well suited his argument here to mention its demise in 70 as a demonstration of its obsolescence. Harold Attridge points out that our author in **Hebrews 7:24** does not say that Christ remains a priest forever, but he simply says that he "remains" in some profound sense. This is linked to his priesthood being *aparabaton*—inviolable or absolute and not revocable.[460] In other words, our author has fixed in his audience's mind that Christ is, even as they hear the words of this discourse, operating as a priest in heaven on their behalf and will continue to do so until he returns. He will have no successors in this role, either in heaven or on earth.

In **Hebrews 7:25** Jesus is able to save *eis to panteles* those coming to God through him, not least because it is his current function to always intercede for us and plead our case. In a sense, that is what he always lives for now. The key phrase can mean "completely/totally" or, as in the papyri, "forever/for all time." The former meaning suggests that the old system did save partially; in favor of the translation "completely" is the earlier use of the language of perfection and the complaint that perfection (i.e., complete restoration of the right human condition) could not be had by the Levitical system. The same phrase in Luke 13:11 does not have a temporal sense but means "fully/completely": "She could not completely straighten up." The ancient Armenian translation of the New Testament understands Hebrews 7:25 to mean "completely/totally," and so do various modern commentators. But the use of *pantote* suggests the translation "forever," as does the use of forever language in Hebrews 7:24. This view comports with our author's already-and-not-yet view of salvation, with cleansing coming in the present, but final salvation coming only later.[461]

In regard to Jesus' intercession for believers, an idea also found in Paul (Rom

---

[459] Long, *Hebrews*, p. 88.
[460] Attridge, *Hebrews*, p. 210.
[461] Marshall, "Soteriology in Hebrews."

8:34), we are not to envision someone pleading and begging a reluctant Father. Jesus is an enthroned priest-king, and God always hears his pleas instantly. His once-for-all-time offering was and is always effective, and whatever is asked on the basis of it will be, indeed must be, granted. Fred Craddock stresses that this is an answer to how the blessings of Christ's death and resurrection overcome the constraints of space and time and have a timeless quality, continually benefiting the believer.[462] Again the social context enhances the force of this argument, because requests brought to the emperor by someone close to the throne were most likely to be favorably received (Pliny the Younger *Letters* 10.5-6, 104-6; Sophocles *Oedipus tyrannus* 771-74). How much more would this logic apply when the one interceding is the Son of the ruler. The character of the intercession here surely entails interceding on behalf of sinners for their forgiveness or for deliverance from divine judgment (Gen 18:22-33; 1 Sam 7:5-9; 2 Maccabees 7.37-38; 4 Maccabees 6.27-29; *1 Clement* 56.1; Rom 8:34).[463]

Hebrews 7:26-28 must be seen as a summing up of what has been said before in this chapter, and not surprisingly our author accomplishes this with some rhetorical flourish meant to appeal to the ear and be memorable—thus he omits conjunctions and juxtaposes words that have the same sounding Greek ending or beginning.[464] This "sharp staccato speech" is seen as a way of grabbing the attention of an audience whose interest might be flagging in a long discourse (*Rhetorica ad Herennium* 4.19.26).[465] Hebrews 7:26 makes clear once again the perfect character of Jesus, perfect both to be priest and sacrifice, which will be mentioned shortly. The phrase *separated from sinners* should probably not be seen as simply another way of saying what the following clause says about Jesus being in heaven.[466] Jesus' separation in view of the previous adjectives is in terms of his sinless condition, not merely his heavenly position, and he must have been sinless in order to have been a perfect sacrifice for others. Otherwise he would have needed a sacrifice for himself, as our author specifically denies. Jesus did not have that everyday necessity of sacrificing twice, first for his own sins and then for believers.[467] The three adjectives used to describe Jesus here

---

[462]Craddock, *Hebrews*, p. 93.

[463]Koester, *Hebrews*, p. 366.

[464]Attridge, *Hebrews*, p. 212 and nn. 81-83.

[465]See the discussion in deSilva, *Perseverance in Gratitude*, p. 274.

[466]Long, *Hebrews*, pp. 89-90, humorously points out that saints are "figures out of the Christian past whose lives have been insufficiently researched."

[467]As is often noted, our author conflates the role of a normal priest and the high priest here, for the ordinary priest offered daily sacrifices, morning and evening (Ex 29:38-42; Num 28:3-8; Sirach 45.14). Our author is not referring to Christ offering literal sacrifices in the heavenly sanctuary. See Attridge, *Hebrews*, p. 213.

(*hosios* ["holy"], *akakos* ["blameless"], *amiantos* ["undefiled"]) are not common in either the Septuagint or the New Testament. The author is striving to suggest the special or unique character of Christ, with an echo or rhetorical amplification of Hebrews 4:15. From a rhetorical viewpoint, our author is following the rules for an encomium quite well here by describing and lauding the "excellences," in this case the personal characteristics of the hero figure (*Rhetorica ad Herennium* 3.7.13). Quintilian stresses that what should prompt such praise is not the mere having of such excellent qualities but their being exercised or used honorably on behalf of others (*Institutio oratoria* 3.7.13).[468]

Hebrews 7:27b tells us for the first time that Jesus offered himself as a sacrifice and that his sacrifice was made *ephapax* ("once for all"), which might mean "once for everyone" or "once for all time" or both. *Ephapax* (also in Heb 9:12; 10:10) is a strengthened or emphatic form of *hapax* (Heb 6:4; 9:7, 26, 27, 28; 10:2; 12:26, 27). It conveys the sufficiency and finality of Jesus' sacrifice, which needs no repeating or even any representing since Christ is in heaven interceding for believers. We henceforth need no human priests offering sacrifices or even reminding God about Christ's. The best encomiums demonstrate how the subject is unique or the only one to accomplish something and therefore worthy of praise above all others because of this (Aristotle *Rhetoric* 1.9.38; Quintilian *Institutio oratoria* 3.7.16), and certainly we see that here as our author praises Christ.[469]

Hebrews 7:28 is crucial for the thesis that our homily has all along been comparing God's word in his Son with the previous forms of his revelation. Here we learn that the revelation in the Son who has been perfected forever is to be contrasted with the previous form of revelation, which is manifestly weak, for it entailed appointing human priests who were sinners. The old covenant delivered by angels, mediated by Moses and implemented by Levitical priests pales in comparison to the new covenant, of which Christ, God's final word for and to us, is the surety or guarantor—the enactor and implementer of its promises. In the contrast between the law and the word in this verse, our author understands the new covenant not merely to be a renewal and completion of the old Mosaic one, but a replacement of it, though it entails a fulfillment of the promises to Abraham. Our author is sensitive to the charge that God could be accused of changing his mind if he made the old covenant obsolete, and so he stresses that God can be trusted with this new covenant not least both because he has

---

[468]See the discussion in deSilva, *Perseverance in Gratitude*, p. 271.

[469]I would stress, in contradistinction to deSilva, *Perseverance in Gratitude*, p. 279 and n. 33, that the aims here are clearly epideictic not deliberative. Our author is not trying to change the audience's behavior but to strengthen their adherence to values already embraced and affirmed.

sworn an oath and because Jesus stands surety or guarantor of God's word about this new covenant arrangement.[470]

Hebrews 8:1-6 can be seen as transitional, going with what precedes or with what follows or more logically with both, since it is transitional. Craig Koester takes it with what follows and produces the following helpful analysis, which notes how our author goes back and forth between matters Levitical and the new covenant, whether the subject is priests or sacrifices:[471]

part 1 (Heb 8:1-13)

Jesus' ministry and Levitical ministry (Heb 8:1-6)

the promise of the new covenant (Heb 8:7-13)

part 2 (Heb 9:1-28)

Jesus' ministry and Levitical ministry (Heb 9:1-14)

the making of the new covenant (Heb 9:15-28)

part 3 (Heb 10:1-18)

Jesus' sacrifice and Levitical sacrifices (Heb 10:1-10)

Jesus' sacrifice and the new covenant (Heb 10:11-18)

This helpful outline makes clear where the break comes in the argument with the shift to the hortatory section, which begins at Hebrews 10:19 and continues to the end of that chapter. But Koester fails to note that in this to-ing and fro-ing our author is following the conventions of how to do a rhetorical comparison and contrast for the intent of getting the audience to continue to affirm and embrace the new covenant with its benefits. He also mistakes the hortatory application in Hebrews 10:19-39 for a digression.

Hebrews 8:1 begins with the word *kephalaion,* which may mean "main point" or the "pith/sum" of things (Acts 22:28). The word is used in the former sense by Philo and in Classical Greek. If, however, it means "summary," Hebrews 8:1 provides not a short synopsis of all the previous main points, but the one main point that our author is driving at—that we "have now a high priest seated next to the Father in heaven who is a minister *[leitourgos]*[472] in that holy place,"[473] which may be said to be the true/real tent or tabernacle, one not made with human hands. It is likely then that our author is using the word in its rhe-

---

[470]Koester, *Hebrews,* pp. 370-71.

[471]Ibid., p. 336.

[472]In Heb 1:7 *leitourgos* is used of heavenly attendants, though there are places in the Septuagint where it refers to priests on earth (Is 61:6; Neh 10:39; cf. Sirach 50.19; Rom 15:16; *Testament of Levi* 2.10; 4.2; Philo, *Allegorical Interpretation* 3.135).

[473]This is not likely a reference to Christ being a minister to the saints. Elsewhere in Hebrews *tōn hagiōn* refers to the holy place, not the holy ones (Heb 9:2-25; 10:19; 13:11).

torical sense of "head/main" argument or idea (Quintilian, *Institutio oratoria* 3.11.27).[474] The word *alēthinēs* in **Hebrews 8:2** can mean either "true" (as opposed to false) or "real/authentic" (as opposed to phony; Heb 9:24). Even if the meaning "true" is meant here, it might not be opposed to false, but opposed to that which is but a copy or shadow. Since part of the job description for high priests is to offer something (i.e., gifts and sacrifices), we are told in **Hebrews 8:3** that Jesus also has something to offer in heaven, but we are not told at this juncture what that something is.

Hebrews 8:4 goes on to make the point that Jesus would not be a priest at all on earth since he was no Levite and since they were already properly offering gifts according to the law. This again suggests that Jesus was not a priest prior to his death, but only in and after it. It also suggests that our author does not simply dismiss the Mosaic covenant as an example of a false faith, but views it as only an inadequate and partial form of God's revelation.

We might have expected our author to say that the old system was a figure and shadow of what has now come on earth, but in **Hebrews 8:5-6** he says it is a shadow and figure (*hypodeigma*) of what now exists in heaven.[475] This involves a form of metaphysical dualism combined with our author's eschatological dualism. In other words, our author believes that what is currently the case "up there" will one day be the case "out there" when the kingdoms of this world become the kingdom of Christ. Our author, like the author of Revelation, envisions the permanent and eternal new Jerusalem and its ruler descending from above and replacing the obsolete on earth. Debates whether our author has a temporal or metaphysical dualism and whether he is more like John of Patmos or Philo are misplaced. He is something like both, and he has found a way to affirm both notions. The things of earth here and now only foreshadow the things that are currently extant in heaven but will one day transform earth. This goes beyond Plato and Philo in an eschatological direction without simply ignoring or dismissing metaphysical dualism.[476]

---

[474] Thus, our author means a bit more than "this is the point I am stressing in this part of the discourse." Other points are made in this discourse, but this main one is flagged by the use of term *kephalaion*. See Koester, *Hebrews*, p. 375.

[475] *Hypodeigma* can mean "example" (Heb 4:11; Sirach 44.16; 2 Maccabees 6.28) or the perceptible "shape/form" of the temple (Ezek 42:15) or creatures (Deut 4:17; Ezek 8:10). When coupled with the word *skia* ("shadow"), one would expect it to refer to the form or representation of something.

[476] Rightly Craddock, *Hebrews*, pp. 98-99; Williamson, *Philo and the Epistle to the Hebrews*; and Hurst, "How 'Platonic' Are Heb viii.5 and ix.23f.?" Craddock stresses rightly that we must not reduce the both/and approach of our author's spatial and temporal dualism to a mere either-or. But clearly more stress needs to be placed on the eschatological tension than is sometimes done in the discussion of Hebrews.

What follows is perhaps a bit confusing since what is now in heaven with Christ has been so only since Christ was exalted. But then in Hebrews 8:5-6 our author points out that Moses himself says that the tabernacle was set up according to a pattern shown to God's people on Mount Sinai. We are told no less than five times in the Pentateuch that Moses was given a "type" or pattern or blueprint (Ex 25:9, 40; 26:30; 27:8; Num 8:4). The point in those texts is that the tabernacle was not of Mosaic or earthly origins but was God's design and plan— but according to our author it was God's design pro tempore. The word *typos* ("type") occurs only here in Hebrews, but *antitypos* ("antitype, copy") appears at Hebrews 9:24. This shows the temporary and temporal nature of the old tabernacle: it was not the perfect or ideal sanctuary but only a copy or figure of the ideal one in heaven; it was not ultimate reality but only a picture or reflection of it. Paul states these things more clearly at Colossians 2:17 (and Gal 4:25-26). It was not at all uncommon in early Judaism to think of the earthly tabernacle or temple as having a heavenly counterpart (*1 Enoch* 14.10-20; *2 Baruch* 4; Wisdom of Solomon 9.8). Our author then is not pulling rabbits out of a hat in a fashion that would be a total surprise to the audience.[477]

Our author apparently thinks that Moses and the Israelites were not shown the heavenly sanctuary itself, but a model or pattern. Thus our author does not distort his historical argument after all. He then goes on to add that the better covenant is better not least because it has a better mediator who is also guarantor and also because it is enacted on better promises. Thus Jesus has a better ministry than that of Moses. The word *better* characterizes the new covenant in comparison to the old. It is not a straight contrast between good and bad; rather, the question is one of fulfillment, completion, adequacy. The final word of Hebrews 8:6 means "has been legally enacted" or "drawn up." This covenant is not merely proposed, it is in effect already, and thus the old is annulled, no longer in effect. The gist of the argument here and its real force is quite similar to Galatians 3—4, where Paul also argues that the Mosaic covenant and its requirements has had its day and ceased to be.

Finally, our author does not contrast an old order of earthly priests with a new and improved order of the same. He contrasts the old order of earthly priests with the one permanent and eternal heavenly high priest. In other words, he affirms only the heavenly high priest as the priest for the new order of things. While the community of the new covenant on earth is said to have earthly leaders (Heb 13:7, 17), they are neither called priests nor expected to function as priests because Christ has made that unnecessary by both his sacrifice and his ongoing

---

[477]Attridge, *Hebrews*, pp. 222-24.

priestly service. It remained for other New Testament writers to talk about a priesthood of all believers on earth (1 Pet 2:9; Rev 1:6), but even they do not suggest that there should be a special class of ministers on earth called priests or functioning as priests.[478] This is likely because other than offering oneself as a sacrifice or offering up sacrifices of praises—both clearly metaphorical ways of using sacrificial language—the New Testament writers see no reason for an ongoing offering of material sacrifices of any kind upon the earth, which was the chief task of priests. If Christ's sacrifice was once for all time and persons as our author says, then it is both unrepeatable and no one should attempt to repeat it, as the act would be otiose at best. Furthermore, as Craig Koester says, for the author of Hebrews "the heavenly tent does not provide legitimation for, but an alternative to the earthly sanctuary. . . . Since Christ serves as 'a priest forever' (Ps 110:4), he requires a sanctuary that will endure forever, and the only sanctuary that is eternal is the tent that God set up in heaven (cf. Exod 25:9, 40)."[479] Our author says that if Christ were still on earth *even he* would not be a priest!

CENTRAL EXPOSITION, PART TWO: CHRIST, THE SACRIFICE OF THE NEW COVENANT (HEB 8:7—10:18)

All Scripture is divided into two testaments. What preceded the advent and passion of Christ—that is the law and the prophets—is called the Old; but what was written after his resurrection is named the New Testament. The Jews make use of the Old, we of the New. Yet they are not dissonant. The New Testament is the fulfilling of the Old, and in both there is the same testator, even Christ who suffered death for us and made us heirs of his everlasting kingdom. . . . When, therefore, we who in times past were blind, and as it were shut up in the prison of folly, were sitting in darkness, ignorant of God and of the truth, we have been enlightened by him, who adopted us by his testament; and having freed us from our cruel chains and brought us out to the light of wisdom, he admitted us to the inheritance of his heavenly kingdom. (Lactantius *Divine Institutes* 4.20)

We indeed who are of the church rightly receive Moses and read his writings, believing that he is a prophet who wrote down the future mysteries that God revealed to him in symbols, figures and allegorical forms, which we teach were fulfilled in their own time. . . . Therefore, the law and all things that are in the law are, according to the opinion of the apostle, "imposed until the time of the reformation." . . . Those whose craft is to make tokens from copper and to pour statues, before

---

[478]It could be argued that Hebrews implies a priesthood of all believers when Heb 13 talks about believers offering sacrifices. This is a fair enough observation, but our author does not make the point explicit, and he certainly does not direct such remarks only to the leaders in the Roman church.

[479]Koester, *Hebrews*, p. 382.

they produce a true work of copper or of silver or of gold, must first form figures from clay to the likeness of the figure image. The model is necessary only until the work that is principal is completed, for when that work for which that image was made of clay is completed, its use is no longer sought. . . . For the artist and creator of all himself came and transformed "the law that has but a shadow of the good things to come" to "the true form of these realities." (Origen *Homilies on Leviticus* 10.1.1-4)

For as in a painting, so long as one only draws the outlines, it is a sort of "shadow," but when one has added the bright paints and laid in the colors, then it becomes "an image." Something of this kind also was the law. (Chrysostom *Homilies on Hebrews* 17.5)

The section we are about to examine contains the longest single quotation from the Old Testament found in the New Testament—the quotation is from Jeremiah 31:31-34, which is the only prophecy in the Old Testament where a "new covenant" is specifically mentioned, though it may be alluded to in remarks by Isaiah and Ezekiel.[480] A portion of this same Old Testament prophecy will also be found again at Hebrews 10:15-18. It is thus of fundamental importance to our author in order to establish his arguments about the obsolescence of the old covenant and the necessity and efficacy of the new covenant, and ironically he must do it by quoting from the very source that he says speaks of an obsolescent covenant. Rhetorically, this is tricky business, and so he must carefully choose the portions of the Old Testament that are self-critical or suggest moving on from the Mosaic covenant. One of the key rhetorical markers that we should see Hebrews 8:7—10:18 as a unit is that it begins and ends with a quotation of Jeremiah 31, the longer one coming at the outset of the section. It is no accident that this is the longest Old Testament quotation in this or any other New Testament book. Our author is trying to convince Jewish Christians that the first covenant is outmoded, and so he must do it using the very source of religious authority they most revere—the Old Testament. The length of the quotation here reflects our author's need to make his point about the new covenant with Jewish Christians in Rome in an emphatic and decisive manner. He alters the text very little, lest the audience complain that the idea comes from his handling of the text rather than from the text itself. The central or core thesis of this discourse must be established on the basis of the best authorities and arguments one can muster, those most likely to persuade Jewish Christians who are seriously con-

---

[480]Hagner, *Encountering the Book of Hebrews*, p. 113, says that it is stunning that Jer 31 is not cited elsewhere in the New Testament, though there are allusions to it at Rom 9:5; 11:27; Jn 6:45.

sidering fading back into the woodwork of the Jewish community in Rome.

Our author keeps in balance two fundamental perspectives throughout Hebrews 8:7—10:18—the vertical and the horizontal—but historical consciousness is the controlling factor. The vertical comparison of the earthly and heavenly sanctuary is found in Hebrews 8:1-5; 9:1-14; 9:23—10:14, but these are intermingled with and seen in light of the discussion of the two covenants at Hebrews 8:6-13; 9:15-22; 10:15-18 (both themes occur in Heb 10:15-18 as the section is being wrapped up). The proof that our author's fundamental perspective is ultimately horizontal, looking to the future, is not found only in Hebrews 11, but comes from the very fact that he believes that what is now true in heaven will one day come down and be true on earth. Thus, current heavenly realities represent and anticipate horizontal things to come. The priesthood will be dealt with on the heavenly side of things, due no doubt to Christ being the believer's high priest in heaven, and covenant is dealt with on the historical level, on the earthly side of things. The vertical highlights what is going on in the horizontal—thus Aaron's priesthood works in terms of the old covenant (and it becomes clear that when our author speaks of the first covenant he always means the Mosaic one, as opposed to the new covenant), even though his service was vertical—lifting up offerings to fix the relationship between God in heaven and his people on earth. Likewise Christ, though he is now in heaven, has put into operation the new covenant and continues to do so from heaven, with its effects on earth. Of course, the association of new covenant with Christ in heaven lends to it the eternality and finality and perfection of heaven itself. It is thus impossible to interpret these chapters from a purely Platonic or Philonic perspective. As Hebrews 8:13 will make clear, the main point is historical—we now have the fulfillment of the promises and institutions of the old order; thus the new covenant annuls and makes obsolescent the old covenant.

It comes as something of a surprise that besides Jeremiah 31 being seldom cited in the New Testament (nor are other relevant prophetic texts about a coming everlasting covenant; see Ezekiel 11:19-20; 16:60-63; 36:26-29; 37:26-28), there is in general only a little discussion about a "new covenant/testament" in the New Testament! Texts like Luke 22:20 or 1 Corinthians 11:25 or 2 Corinthians 3:6 or Galatians 4:24 do refer to this idea, but it is our author who most explains and discourses on this subject, though it often seems to be just below the surface elsewhere. My explanation for this is that these other texts are addressed to largely Gentile audiences, which hardly needed much convincing to talk about a new agreement between God and humankind. Our discourse, however, is directed to Jewish Christians considering going back to Judaism, hence the stress here.

Besides the usual use of microrhetoric, this section includes things like paronomasia to make the text sound more convincing and coherent,[481] a brilliant christological use of Psalm 40 to speak of the preexistent one being given a body[482] and the rhetorical device known as parable. Our author's use of the term *parable* in Hebrews 9:9 as a rhetorical figure entails the entire discussion of the tabernacle and its comparison and contrast with the heavenly sanctuary.

The term *parabolē* was used for a comparison or comparative illustration from at least the time of Aristotle.[483] If, as is quite likely with a Roman audience, our author was dealing with a rhetorically informed audience, one would expect them to read his parables with a recognition of the way the term was used in Greco-Roman rhetoric. Aristotle treats parables as a subclass of comparative proofs, which he calls paradigms *(paradeigma) (Rhetoric* 2.20.1-4). These artificial inductive proofs make their points by means of comparison or through illustration. Parables can be distinguished from fables (called *logoi*) in that they are shorter comparisons that draw on actual historical examples. Rhetorically their function is to prove or support the veracity of the general proposition being advanced, in this case that the heavenly sanctuary, new covenant, new high priest are better. Quintilian agrees with Aristotle that a *parabolē* is rightly seen as a subcategory of paradigms drawn from common experience and used as an auxiliary to inductive proofs. His view is that they are most effective when they have as little metaphorical qualities as possible, but rather speak in plain language where their referents are immediately apparent *(Institutio oratoria* 5.1.30-35). He obviously would not have been enamored with modern theories about parables as giant metaphors.

There is also the possibility in rhetoric that a parable would be used as a figure of thought. But if one reads *Rhetorica ad Herennium* closely, it becomes clear that, even as a figure, a parable is not some sort of enigmatic metaphor but an analogy, linked very closely to the historical illustration or the example (4.48.61). As a figure, however, a parable has as its function not clinching a proof but clarifying or making a point more vividly. Quintilian likewise disassociates parables from metaphors and links them closely with historical analogies *(Institutio oratoria* 4.1.70; 6.3.61-62).

In general, the length of a parable or its specific form (is it more like a straight analogy or more like a brief narrative?) does not make a parable a parable from a rhetorical viewpoint. Rather, the content is determinative: it must involve a

---

[481]Jobes, "Function of Paronomasia."
[482]Jobes, "Rhetorical Achievement."
[483]McCall, *Ancient Rhetorical Theories*, pp. 1-23.

comparison from everyday life or history, whether elaborated at length, whether involving a story element and so a plot. Rhetoricians like Quintilian also specified that in general a parable should more often than not be about things or concepts rather than about persons. Equally striking, ancient rhetors urge that good parables were not characterized by multiple layers of dark meaning and so were not oblique but rather were the contrary—clearer illustrations of the principle or proof being argued for on other grounds as well. Quintilian is emphatic at this point: the metaphoric quality of the parable must be kept to a minimum (*Institutio oratoria* 5.11.22).

Our author uses a straightforward historical analogy in Hebrews 9—10, focusing on an institution and its functions rather than on a person and comparing it to a heavenly reality. No plot is involved, nor is the usage enigmatic or mysterious, as it involves no apocalyptic figures or symbolic numbers or the like. In other words, his use of the term *parabolē* suits well the rhetorical descriptions of what that ought to look like and how it could be used to achieve certain rhetorical goals—in this case the praise of "our great high priest," his sacrifice, the new covenant and the great sanctuary, compared and contrasted with the glorious but obsolete tabernacle and its rituals. His use of *parabolē* in Hebrews 11:19 clearly means "figure" or "figuratively speaking." The author of Hebrews is the only New Testament writer to use this word other than the gospel writers, and it is no surprise that his use differs from theirs, in that he is the most rhetorically adept and attuned of the New Testament authors. Craig Koester stresses the point: "In rhetoric, a *parabolē* was a comparison of things where the resemblance was not obvious (Quintilian *Institutio oratoria* 5.11.23)."[484] In this case, what was not obvious was that Christ was a priest at all, much less that he was the most important high priest of all time.

One addition rhetorical point is important. If one is going to introduce an idea that is difficult to accept, one needs an unimpeachable witness. Thus our author quotes at length from Jeremiah 31 at the beginning and end of this section to prove his point that a new covenant makes the previous covenant obsolete. "Rhetorically, the persuasiveness of a speech depends not only on its logic but also on the listeners' conviction that the one speaking is reliable (Quintilian *Institutio oratoria* 4.1.7)."[485] Thus, especially with his central argument our author puts forth his star witness, God, who vouches for the truth of what our author is saying by means of these Scripture quotations, nicely edited to make his point crystal clear. The new covenant has a better warranty, a lifetime guarantee,

---

[484]Koester, *Hebrews*, p. 398.
[485]Ibid., p. 389.

This scenario didn't happen — our 2400 yrs — dat tile your [illegible]

[handwritten marginalia at top]

and it is backed up by a better guarantor, not Moses but the Messiah and God himself.

^{8:7}*For if that first (covenant) was faultless, there would not have been a place for a second.* ⁸*For finding fault with them he says, "Behold, days are coming, says the Lord, when I will bring to an end/accomplish upon the house of Israel and upon the house of Judah a new covenant.* ⁹*Not according to the covenant that I made with their fathers in the day I took hold of their hands to lead them out from Egypt, because they did not remain in my covenant and I overlooked them," says the Lord.* ¹⁰*"This is the covenant that I will make with the house of Israel after those days," says the Lord. "I will put my law in their mind/understanding, and upon their hearts I will write it.*[486] *And I will be to them for a God, and they will be unto me for a people.* ¹¹*And no more will they teach each his fellow citizen*[487] *and each his brother, saying, 'Know the Lord,' because all will know me from the least unto the greatest of them* ¹²*because I will be merciful to their wrongdoing and I will remember their sins no more forever."* ¹³*In saying "new" he treats as old the first, but being worn out and growing old it is near to disappearing.*[488]

^{9:1}*Now on the one hand the first (covenant)*[489] *had a regulation of worship for the earthly holy place/sanctuary.* ²*For the first tent was constructed a tent in which was a lampstand and a table and the laying of the bread of the Presence; this was called the holy place.* ³*But behind the second curtain on the other hand, a tent called the holy of holies,* ⁴*having a gold censer/incense altar and the ark of the covenant that was covered all over with gold,*[490] *in which there is a gold jar having the manna and the rod of Aaron that sprouted and the tablets of the covenant,* ⁵*but above which were cherubim of glory overshadowing the place of propitiation/mercy seat, concerning which it is not now (time) to speak in detail.*

⁶*But when this was constructed thusly, into the first tent continually the priests are going, performing acts of worship,* ⁷*but into the second (tent) only once a year the high priest goes, not without blood, who offers for himself and the people for sins of ignorance.* ⁸*Showing this the Holy Spirit had not yet revealed the way of the holy/*

---

[486]These two clauses are likely parallel, saying the same thing in two different ways. Since the heart is also the center of cognition in Hebrew anthropology, God will not only make them understand but he will change them so they will receive and live by his word.

[487]Some manuscripts have the word *plēsion* ("neighbor") rather than *politēn* ("citizen"). The latter reading is strongly supported by 𝔓[46], ℵ, A, B and should be kept.

[488]Our author uses the midrashic technique of taking up a keyword in the following argument.

[489]While a few scribes (81, 104, 376) took the word *first* to refer to the "first tent," in Heb 8:13 it clearly refers to the covenant, and so we should see the feminine form of "first" to have the same referent here. See Koester, *Hebrews*, p. 393.

[490]Several witnesses (B and some Coptic manuscripts) obviously had problems with what is said concerning the location of the golden altar of incense in the tabernacle, and so some small omissions or alterations are made to preserve the author's form, which was seen as an error. See Metzger, *Textual Commentary*, p. 667.

way into the holy place, ⁹while the first tent is standing that is a parable for the present time in conformity with which gifts and sacrifices being offered are not able to make perfect the conscience of the worshiper. ¹⁰Only upon food and drink and different washings having imposed fleshly regulations until the reformation/putting right/new order.

¹¹But Christ appeared, the high priest[491] of the good things that came with him,[492] through the better and more perfect tent that is not handmade, this is not a part of creation, ¹²nor through the blood of goats and calves but through his own blood he entered once for all into the holy place and found by himself eternal redemption. ¹³For if the blood of goats and bulls and the ashes of the red heifer when sprinkling the common/impure consecrate (them) so that they have the purity of the flesh, ¹⁴how much more will the blood of Christ, who through eternal spirit offered himself unblemished to God, purify our consciences from dead works unto the worship of the living God.

¹⁵And for this reason he is mediator of the new covenant in order that death having happened for the redemption of the transgressors on the basis of the first covenant, that those called might receive the promise of the eternal inheritance. ¹⁶For where a testament is involved it is necessary that the death of the testator be involved, ¹⁷for a testament is operative upon death since it is never valid while the testator lives. ¹⁸Hence, not even the first (covenant) has been inaugurated without blood. ¹⁹For when he proclaimed each commandment according to the law of Moses to all the people, taking the blood of calves (and of goats)[493] with water and crimson wool and hyssop and sprinkled the book itself and all the people, ²⁰saying, "This is the blood of the covenant that God enjoined for you."²¹But also the tent and all the vessels of worship were likewise sprinkled with blood. ²²And nearly everything is cleansed in/by blood according to the law, and without shedding of blood there is no forgiveness.

²³It is necessary then for the figure/emblem of that which is in heaven to be cleansed by this means, but the heavenly (sanctuary/things) by better sacrifices than these. ²⁴For Christ did not enter into a handmade holy place, the antitype/representation of the true holy place but into heaven itself now revealed to the face of God for us. ²⁵Not in order to offer himself frequently, like the high priest entering into the holy place yearly in the blood of another, ²⁶since it would have been necessary for

---

[491]Various manuscripts have "high priest" instead of "priest." This is likely a later correction in light of Heb 5:1 or Heb 8:3.

[492]Some manuscripts have "of the good things to come" rather than "of the good things that came with him." Both readings are well attested, but the latter probably has the edge due to the geographical spread of the manuscripts and the tendency to conform this text to Heb 10:1.

[493]Some manuscripts add "and of goats." The omission is supported by good witnesses but it is hard to say whether the phrase was added here due to Heb 9:12 or omitted by oversight. See Metzger, *Textual Commentary*, p. 668.

him to suffer often from the foundation of creation. But now once for all at the consummation of the ages he is revealed for the annulment/destruction of sins through his sacrifice. [27] And just as it is in store for human beings to die once, and after that judgment, [28] thus also Christ has been offered once for many to bear upon himself sin, a second time without sin he will appear to those who await eagerly for salvation.

[10:1] For the law was a shadow of the good things to come, not the image of the thing itself.[494] Yearly its sacrifices, which are offered continually, are never able[495] to perfect those drawing near. [2] For would they not have stopped offering them, seeing that those worshiping, once cleansed no longer have consciousness of sins? [3] But by them/the sacrifices remembrance of sins happens yearly, [4] for it is impossible for the blood of bulls and goats to take away sins.

[5] So it is that he says entering into the cosmos, "Sacrifice and offering you did not wish, but a body you prepared for me. [6] Burnt offering and sin offering you did not approve." [7] Then he said, "Behold, I have come, in the scroll of the book it is written concerning me, to do, God, your will." [8] Earlier it was saying that "sacrifice and offering" and "burnt offering and sin offering you did not wish nor approve of" such as those offered according to the law. [9] Then he said, "Behold, I have come to do your will." He does away with/abolishes the first in order to establish/confirm the second. [10] By which will we have been made holy through the offering of the body of Jesus Christ once for all.

[11] And on the one hand every priest stands daily offering worship and offering the same sacrifice often, such as are never able to remove sins. [12] But on the other hand when this one offered one sacrifice for sins continually/forever, he sat down at the right hand of God, [13] henceforth waiting until his enemies are made a footstool for his feet. [14] For one offering perfected continually those being sanctified.

[15] But the Holy Spirit also testifies to us for after saying, [16] "This is the covenant that was drawn up for them after those days," says the Lord, "I will put my law in their hearts and in their minds I will write it [17] and their sins and wickedness I will remember no more forever." [18] But where there is forgiveness of these, there is no longer an offering for sin.

In this lengthy passage our author follows the Septuagint very closely, which in turn follows the Hebrew very closely. The only significant change our author makes is in Hebrews 8:8, where he uses the verb *synteleō* ("to accomplish, ful-

---

[494] Our earliest manuscript, $\mathfrak{P}^{46}$, has "shadow and image" rather than "shadow not the image." The latter reading is probably correct since (a) it is so widely supported; (b) *eikon* normally means more than a mere copy: it is an exact representation and (c) the wording of the sentence leads us to expect a contrast, for our author goes on and speaks of contrast using *men . . . de* (Attridge, "Uses of Antithesis").

[495] Some very good manuscripts ($\aleph$, A, C, P) have the plural "they are not able," which may well be original, but the singular is also well supported ($\mathfrak{P}^{46}$, H, K and others) and is perhaps preferable.

fill") instead of the verb *diathēsomai* ("to establish") found in the Septuagint. This change may have been suggested to our author by Jeremiah 34:8, 15, where the phrase *syntelein diathēkēn* is found in reference to a covenant made under Zedekiah. But the change is significant in terms of our author's hermeneutics. It is only with the new covenant that God's purposes are completely fulfilled or accomplished by God himself through Christ. Only in it are things brought to completion and perfection. And it is, after all, God who fulfills his own prophecy not merely to establish a new covenant, but through Christ to fulfill both its obligations and promises. The Septuagint changes the Hebrew twice: it omits from Jeremiah 31:32 the phrase *although I was like a husband to them*, and in Jeremiah 31:33 "within them" becomes "in their minds" in the Septuagint. In neither this quotation nor the exposition on the tabernacle that follows in Hebrews 9 does our author give way to allegorizing. He understands these matters fundamentally from a historical perspective. He does not try to alter the original meaning of this text insofar as its fundamental substance is concerned. He still sees it as being addressed to the house of Judah and Israel, not to the church, but that includes Jewish Christians. Although this message was offered to Israel by Jesus and his immediate successors, by and large they rejected the idea of its fulfillment through Christ, and hence it takes on a wider audience. Of all the early Jewish sects and their offshoots, only Christians saw Jeremiah 31:31-34 as a crucial text that indicated a real supplanting of the old covenant. The only other group to give significant attention to this text, the Qumran community, took it to mean the perfecting of the old covenant: by means of following the Teacher of Righteousness's reading of Torah the Qumranites would be able to perfectly observe the law.[496]

I will not give a detailed exposition of the lengthy quotation in **Hebrews 8:7-13** from Jeremiah, but a few points are worth stressing. The stress is on the *new* covenant, which will accomplish three new things: (1) God will put his "torah" into their very minds/consciences/hearts, which stresses the inwardness or inward effect of this new sort of instruction;[497] (2) "all shall know me" in an intimate and free way unknown previously and (3) the comprehensive statement—"their sins I will remember no more"—emphasizes that forgiveness will extend not only to sins committed out of ignorance but even deliberate sins, which was not true under the Mosaic covenant.[498] In Hebrews 8:8 what is blameworthy is

---

[496]Lehne, *New Covenant in Hebrews*, pp. 32-61.
[497]Long, *Hebrews*, p. 92.
[498]In Ex 34 forgiveness of deliberate sins could come only from a new, direct divine fiat. This is clearly how Paul is depicted as understanding the situation in the synagogue sermon in Acts 13.

not "it" but "them": the fault primarily lies with the people, only secondarily with the first covenant.[499] Hebrews 8:9 laments that "they did not remain faithful to my covenant."[500] Finally, Hebrews 8:13 is important as it provides our author's concluding remark on the Jeremiah quotation. Donald Hagner is on the right track: "The words 'will soon disappear' may well be an allusion to Jesus' prophecy concerning the destruction of the temple, known to the author and readers from oral tradition underlying the Synoptic Gospels (see Mk 13:1-2 and parallels). The word 'soon' clearly seems to indicate that Hebrews was written before the destruction of the temple in A.D. 70. Was the Roman invasion of Jerusalem already on the horizon?"[501] This provides one more small clue that this letter was likely written in the mid- to late 60s to Jewish Christians in Rome who would be worried about the turmoil in the Holy Land. David deSilva helpfully translates the key phrase in Hebrews 8:13: "God 'rendered it out-of-date.' . . .\The old covenant is likened to a law that is outdated and practically out of use. All that remains is to erase it from the books."[502] This was not the view that other Jews held of the Mosaic covenant, which was seen as eternal (Sirach 17.12; 2 Esdras [4 Ezra] 9.36-37; *2 Baruch* 77.15; Josephus *Against Apion* 2.272).

G. B. Caird argues that, within the larger argument of this homily, Jeremiah 31 is the last of four key Old Testament texts (Ps 8; 95; 110; Jer 31) that control the drift of the argument, all other allusions being ancillary: "His argument falls into four sections, each having as its core an OT passage which declares the ineffectiveness and symbolic or provisional nature of the OT religious institutions."[503] There is however more to it than that. Our author has been moving progressively through several comparisons: Christ versus angels, Christ versus Moses, Christ as high priest versus Aaronic/Levitical priesthood, heavenly versus earthly sanctuary—all in the service of indicating what was clearly stated in Hebrews 8:13: "In saying new, he makes old the first [covenant]; being worn out and growing old, it is near disappearing." This is the essence of our author's case—the old covenant has had its day and is now ceasing to be.

The first ten verses of Hebrews 9 are divided into two parts, describing first the physical setting and furniture of the Old Testament tabernacle (Heb 9:1-5) and then the sacrificial ritual associated with it (Heb 9:6-10). Hebrews 9:5 shows

---

[499]Hagner, *Encountering the Book of Hebrews*, p. 113.

[500]There is a good body of literature on this subject: see Peterson, "Prophecy of the New Covenant"; Kaiser, "Old Promise and the New Covenant"; Lehne, *New Covenant in Hebrews*; and Omanson, "Superior Covenant."

[501]Hagner, *Encountering the Book of Hebrews*, pp. 114-15.

[502]DeSilva, *Perseverance in Gratitude*, p. 287.

[503]Caird, "Exegetical Method," pp. 45-46.

that our author is not interested in describing the tabernacle in detail for its own sake, lest he invoke too much admiration in the audience for what was a thing of the past. There is a good deal of confusion, however, over some elements in the description. For instance, it seems rather clear from Hebrews 9:4 that our author is suggesting that the altar of incense was in the holy of holies, something that is at variance with what Leviticus 16:18 (and probably Ex 30:6) suggests when Aaron goes out of the holy of holies, and beyond the curtain is this altar. But in the Septuagint *thymiatērion* never means "incense altar," but rather "censer." The root meaning is simply a place where the incense is put or possibly a vessel for burning incense. Both Josephus and Philo, however, use it to refer to the incense altar. The Greek participle *echousa* ("having") applies to both this item and the ark of the covenant, so that whatever it means for one it surely means for the other as well. Literally, it simply says that the holy of holies has a *thymiatērion* and the ark. There is a special connection between the incense altar and the holy of holies—its incense was supposed to penetrate the curtain and so rise up to God—and so this altar was placed right in front of the second curtain leading into the holy of holies. Furthermore, *2 Baruch* 6.7 says that this altar was in the holy of holies in Solomon's temple, and this is also true of the temple excavated in Hazor. The word *have* here may mean only belonging to in function, or perhaps our author is following his knowledge of other temple arrangements, or he may be mistaken, which seems unlikely in view of his detailed and exact knowledge already shown of the Old Testament and especially the institutions mentioned in the Pentateuch.[504] Whatever the case, our author is trying to give a general description for rhetorical effect, and it is generally in accordance with Exodus 25—31, with the exception that the author of Hebrews places the manna jar and Aaron's rod within the ark[505] (other Jewish traditions suggest that many things were also placed in the ark).[506]

The second major difficulty with this section is that it is difficult to figure out what is going on at Hebrews 9:8. First, does "holy place" means earthly sanctuary (as in Heb 8:2; 9:2) or heavenly sanctuary (as in Heb 9:12)? Furthermore, does "the holy (places)" means the whole sanctuary (as in Heb 8:2), only the outer part (as in Heb 9:2) or only the inner part (so most translations)? And does "first tent" refer to the outer part of the earthly sanctuary (as in Heb 9:2, 6) or the earthly sanctuary as a whole contrasted with the greater tent (as in Heb 9:11)—that is, first in place or first in time? How we answer these questions de-

---

[504]See the discussion in Attridge, *Hebrews*, pp. 236-38.
[505]Craddock, *Hebrews*, p. 104.
[506]Koester, *Hebrews*, p. 395, though these seem to be later traditions.

termines what the parable in Hebrews 9:9 is referring to.

In **Hebrews 9:1** the word *first* surely means the first covenant, looking back on Hebrews 8:13. The interesting phrase *to hagion kosmikon* refers to the earthly holy place, that is, the tabernacle about to be discussed. William Barclay aptly translates "a this-worldly one [i.e., sanctuary]."[507] The definite article is important, as our author has a specific place in view—the Old Testament tabernacle of the wilderness period. In **Hebrews 9:2** the word *first* refers to the tent, not the covenant, but **Hebrews 9:3**—which speaks of a second (implied) tent—shows that these two verses must be taken together. The first is called the holy place and includes the lampstand, table and twelve loaves of bread (often called "bread of the Presence" or "shewbread," to use the King James Version term). This tabernacle had two linen curtains, behind the second of which was the holy of holies. **Hebrews 9:4** appears to show our author also arguing that the manna and the rod and the covenant tablets were also in the same gold jar.[508] The reason for calling each of the two parts of the tabernacle a tent is surely because the outer court had been called the tent of meeting. This means that the term *first tent* does not refer to the whole tabernacle, contrary to the suggestion of F. F. Bruce,[509] but only to the outer court, which is part of the larger holy place or holy zone.

In **Hebrews 9:5** the cherubim of glory refers to the Shekinah glory of God: his very presence was supposed to reside over the *hilastērion*. The function of the cherubim was to support the invisible presence of God. The Greek word *hilastērion* renders Hebrew *kappōret* and means "place of propitiation" or more broadly "place of atonement" (Ex 25:17, 21). As a result, since God's wrath is assuaged at this place, it becomes a place from which his mercy can flow; hence it is translated "mercy seat." The noun occurs in the New Testament only here and in Romans 3:25, but the cognate verb occurred earlier at Hebrews 2:17 (compare Lk 18:13). Our author says that this is not the place to speak in detail about these things, which shows that his description serves as a foil for Christ's work.[510] Rhetorically, passing by something without detailed comment was

---

[507] Attridge, *Hebrews*, p. 232, points out that the word is not a synonym for the similar sounding *kosmion* ("well ordered") and has a pejorative thrust. According to Attridge, the worldliness or earthiness of the temple is seen as part of its weakness and limitations.

[508] Koester, *Hebrews*, p. 403. Clearly, our author has a tendency to see three items within the holy of holies (the manna and its jar, Aaron's rod and the incense altar), whereas other schemas see the incense altar in the holy place and the other two items in the holy of holies but not in the ark.

[509] Bruce, *Hebrews*, pp. 220-21.

[510] Contrast this to Philo, *On the Life of Moses* 2.97-100, who gives an item-by-item detailed account of the furniture in the tabernacle. Our author is not interested in these things in themselves.

called *paraleipsis* (*Rhetorica ad Herennium* 4.27.37). By identifying some aspects of a large topic while refusing to make detailed comment, the speaker alludes to his familiarity with the subject matter, while relativizing its importance."[511]

Hebrews 9:6 speaks of the continual activity of the priests, and this surely refers to their activity in the outer court. By contrast, the second tent is entered only once a year, only by the high priest, only with blood to make propitiation for his and others sins on the Day of Atonement, and then apparently only for sins of ignorance (i.e., sins not committed deliberately or knowingly). The author's point is to indicate that access to God was limited under the old regime and thus atonement was limited as well. Thomas Long says that our author is playing tour guide on a very limited basis here: he "causes a gasp by pulling back this curtain, too, and beckoning us to look into its mysterious and forbidden depths. Immediately our eyes are dazzled by gold: the golden incense altar, the ark of the covenant covered with gold. In the ark are the golden jar of manna (Ex. 16:33-34), Aaron's rod (see Num. 17:1-11), and the two tablets of the Decalogue (1 Kings 8:9). On top of the ark is the golden mercy seat with its two pure gold cherubim hovering above (Ex. 25:17-21). In short, gold is everywhere, along with the staggering monuments of the covenant."[512] This facilitates a comparison in which our author will make clear that there is a far greater sanctuary with far more precious things inside, and so in a sense these verses are a tease suggesting that our author's readers have not seen anything yet.

In **Hebrews 9:7** our author continues his fondness (Heb 4:15; 6:10; 7:20; 9:18, 22) for the emphatic double negative: it is "not without blood" that the high priest enters the holy of holies once a year. Our author's presentation of the high priest's role is guided by what our author has said and wants to say about the high priestly ministry of Christ.[513] Even what the ancient high priest did was of help only for inadvertent sins (Heb 10:26; Num 15:22, 30), although some early Jewish traditions read Leviticus 16:5, 9, 16 to mean that voluntary sins were also atoned for on the Day of Atonement (Philo *On the Special Laws* 2.196). Later traditions held that if someone said, "'I will sin and the Day of Atonement will effect atonement' then the Day of Atonement affects no atonement" (Mishnah, tractate *Yoma* 8.9; cf. *Jubilees* 5.17-19). Our author likes the *men . . . de* construction, and he uses it liberally, including twice in this chapter to contrast the old and new regimes (Heb 9:1-3 and Heb 9:6-7).

---

[511]Koester, *Hebrews*, p. 404.
[512]Long, *Hebrews*, p. 93.
[513]Young, "Gospel according to Hebrews 9," p. 209.

In **Hebrews 9:8** we see that the Holy Spirit speaks in these Old Testament matters. The way of the holy was not yet revealed while the first tent was standing. Here the word *first* could mean the whole tabernacle, but the point seems to be that a system requiring two tents means that access into God's holy presence has not yet been revealed. I agree with Donald Hagner's interpretation of this verse.[514] The question then becomes—in **Hebrews 9:9**—is the outer court a parable indicating limited access to God under the tabernacle system?[515] What then does "unto the time here present" mean? Surely this refers to the time of the author and readers. If so, the point then would be that the readers should now deduce that this system is one of limited access and limited atonement for God's people. Our author goes on to say that that system imposed only human or fleshly regulations on matters of food and drink (presumably a reference to kosher food laws) and various sorts of ceremonial cleansings. Again, this follows the theme that what is accomplished by that system affects only external things, material things that make food or human bodies clean, but that system is not able to make perfect the conscience of the worshiper. Here "make perfect" must surely mean something like make completely clean or in a right condition, to make holy in the full sense of the term, not just externally but internally. In short, it refers to sanctification of the inner person. Our author thinks that his listeners "had already experienced 'the powers of the age to come' (6:5), but had not yet received their inheritance in the world to come (1:14; 2:5). The new covenant had been inaugurated, but the old had not yet vanished (8:13).[516] In short they lived when the ages overlapped. It is a mistake to ignore the fundamentally eschatological way our author thinks about these matters.[517]

The noun *syneidēsis* is an important one in Hebrews, as it refers to the inner thoughts or consciousness of the person in question, sometimes called the heart (Heb 9:14; 10:2, 22; 13:18). It does not simply have the narrow sense of the modern idea of conscience, though that is included (as in the Septuagint: Job 27:6; Eccles 10:20; Wisdom of Solomon 17.10; Sirach 42.18). What sets the new covenant apart is its ability to deal with the root of the human problem—the inner core of the human being. "To be perfected in conscience is to be both cleansed of and freed from any hindrance preventing one's entering into God's pres-

---

[514]Hagner, *Encountering the Book of Hebrews*, pp. 115-16.
[515]Stanley, "Hebrews 9:6-10," who does not recognize that the term *parable* is here used in its rhetorical sense.
[516]Koester, *Hebrews*, p. 398.
[517]Rightly noted by Attridge, *Hebrews*, p. 241, who stresses that our author thinks that "now" is the "time of correction."

ence."[518] God's own word is written in and on the heart of the believer in the new covenant era, though this should not be seen as a substitute for the external word of God, as is perfectly clear in this discourse for our author constantly cites and relies on it.

Our author then observes in **Hebrews 9:10** that such food and drink regulations are "only until the time of reform/putting right," which he most certainly believes has already broken into the present era of history through Jesus Christ. Only since Jesus' death have believers been truly and totally—both inwardly and outwardly—put right with God. The implication is that humans were not truly or fully put right with God or truly cleansed inwardly by the old order of atonement. The coming of Christ is the actual time of reformation, the real putting right of fallen human beings. Our author is not just talking about reshaping or reformulating the structure of Israelite religion; he is concerned with putting right human beings themselves, though the former is true as well.[519] There are some foreshadowings in early Judaism of a final priest who decisively changes the situation. *Testament of Levi* 18.9 reflects on the final messianic priest: "On the basis of his priesthood, sin will cease."

Our author now states his argument about the nature of Christ's work in various ways in Hebrews 9:11—10:18. Several key *dia* clauses help explain what the author is intending, and an understanding of them is crucial to the argument. In general, these clauses have to do with the instrumentality "through" which Christ accomplished his mission (through eternal spirit, through his own blood, etc.). He is the high priest of the good things that have come.[520] **Hebrews 9:11** tells us that Christ went through the better and more perfect tent—the one not made with human hands, which implies that the Mosaic one had some greatness and perfection to it.[521] The word *cheiropoiētos* occurs here and Hebrews 9:24 in this section. It may reflect our author's knowledge of some saying of Jesus about such a temple (compare Mk 14:58 to Acts 7:48; 17:24, which may reflect later knowledge of the Jesus saying). While acknowledging the goodness of the old tabernacle, our author wants to stress that we now have a better and more perfect one that does not suffer from the flaws of a human-made one. Hebrews 9:11 says Jesus "arrived as high priest," making clear that Jesus did not seize priestly prerogatives, even though he was not of a priestly line.

Hebrews 9:11 makes clear that our author is not talking about a tabernacle

---

[518]Craddock, *Hebrews*, p. 105.

[519]Against Bruce, *Hebrews*, p. 121.

[520]He is not the high priest of the good things "about to come." The oldest and best manuscripts here say "have come." See Hagner, *Encountering the Book of Hebrews*, p. 121.

[521]Koester, *Hebrews*, p. 413.

that is part of the material creation. The proper understanding of **Hebrews 9:12** is important, for here we have one of the crucial *dia* clauses. Jesus did not enter into the heavenly sanctuary through the blood of bulls and goats but through his own blood, and when he entered it was once for all time. The point of this is that (1) shed blood is the means or the necessary prerequisite for Jesus to be able to enter the most holy place, as was also true for the high priest on earth; (2) his own blood, not the blood of others, qualified him to enter this heavenly holy place and (3) such was the efficacy of his shed blood that he could enter once for all time, having made final and effective atonement. By this death and this entering he found or obtained eternal redemption all by himself.[522] The word *lytrōsis* ("ransom") derives from *lytron* (Mk 10:45) and was often used of buying back slaves (Ex 21:30; Lev 25:48) or deliverance from oppressive powers (Lk 1:68; 2:38; *Testament of Joseph* 8.1). While its basic connotation is thus redemption, as in buying back slaves, it could also speak of liberation from prison or from sin.[523] This is the only place the noun is found in Hebrews, but its cognate *apolytrōsis* ("redemption") is found at Hebrews 9:15 and Hebrews 11:35 (also Rom 3:24; Eph 1:7; Col 1:14; cf. the verb *lytroomai* ["to ransom"] in Tit 2:14; 1 Pet 1:18), often connoting release from prison or slavery (*Letter of Aristeas* 12, 33; Josephus *Jewish Antiquities* 12.27). The redemption is eternal not only because of its eternal effect but also because of the nature of the one who procured it and how he did so.[524] It is qualitatively and not just quantitatively different from the redemption that came by means of the earthly tabernacle system. Our author will go on to allow in this passage that that system did provide ritual or material or cultic cleansing for uncleanness and sins of ignorance, and so in a sense the criticism here is less severe than the criticism from Qumran of the Herodian temple (1QpHab [Habakkuk Commentary] 12.8-9; *Testament of Moses* 6.1; cf. *Sibylline Oracles* 4.8.27).

Hebrews 9:13-14 contains one of those a fortiori, or how much more, arguments that our author is fond of. If the blood of bulls and goats and the ashes of the red heifer (which when mixed with water was used to make ritually pure the unclean or common; see Num 19, where it is specifically stated to be a ritual for ceremonial impurity) is able to make possible the purity of the flesh, how

---

[522]Brooks's argument in "Perpetuity of Christ's Sacrifice" that the atoning work was accomplished upon Christ's entrance into God's presence and not on the cross is unconvincing. He forgets our author's emphasis that atonement is accomplished by the shedding of blood, and Brook's argument involves the overpressing of the analogy with the tabernacle.

[523]Craddock, *Hebrews*, p. 107.

[524]On the Jewish use of the phrase *eternal redemption* see 1QM (War Scroll) 1.12; 15.1; 18.11; Dan 9:24.

much more the blood of Christ, which will purify even our consciences from dead works and for the worship of the living God? The author does not dispute that the former ritual is effective in the outer and material sphere for ceremonial cleansing. This is not a polemic against the Old Testament institutions, however obsolescent they may be.[525] The phrase *from dead works* when attached to *our conscience* surely rules out the idea that our author means "meaningless outward Jewish rituals." Rather it means here what it meant in Hebrews 6:1—sinful acts that are death dealing, not life giving.[526] This is why these works are associated in Hebrews 6:1 with repentance and here with conscience. They must by definition amount to something that is not merely useless but something that defiles the conscience and requires repentance. Thus our author does not use the term *dead works* to refer to the same thing as Paul does when he speaks of works of the law. Christ's sacrifice is accepted not least because it is perfect or, as it says here, unblemished. Our author is not the only one concerned about heart piety in early Judaism; one could equally well refer to Philo's remark that "genuine worship is that of the soul bringing simple reality as its only sacrifice; all that is mere display, fed by lavish expenditure on externals, is counterfeit" (*That the Worse Attacks the Better* 21). Our author is more concerned about the effect of Christ's work on the inner self of the believer rather than the sincerity of the worship itself.

There is a good deal of debate as to what to make of the phrase *dia pneumatos aiōniou*? Is it a reference to the Holy Spirit? If so why did not the author use the word *holy* to make that clear? Prior to Hebrews 9:14 all references to "spirit" in the singular (except Heb 4:12) have been to the Holy Spirit, which makes it likely that this is the subject here as well.[527] If not, is it a reference to Christ's divine nature, his eternal spirit that made the offer of his death to God in heaven? The problem with this last idea is that Jesus did not simply go to heaven as a divine spirit—he went as a risen God-man. If, however, the idea behind this *dia* clause is agency, the point may be that God's eternal spirit, that is, the Holy Spirit, was the means by which the human Jesus' blood was offered to God. A few manuscripts read "Holy Spirit" here, but that clearly was not the original reading. Two additional considerations favor seeing a reference to the Holy Spirit here: (1) it should not be objected that our author would have had to use the definite article since with the adjectival modifier the noun becomes definite

---

[525]Attridge, *Hebrews*, p. 248, points to Ps 50:13 and Is 1:11 as similarly minimalizing remarks on what the old sacrificial system could accomplish.

[526]Koester, *Hebrews*, p. 415.

[527]Ibid., p. 410.

anyway and (2) had our author wanted to talk about Christ's divine spirit, we would have expected the modifier "his." Finally, when Jesus says he is conveying his spirit into God's hands it probably means his human spirit or life or human personality, not his eternal nature. It would hardly have made sense to say that he was offering back to God his divine spirit, which by definition was always one with the Father and never unconnected from him since there is only one God.[528]

The phrase *through his blood* does not likely mean "with his blood," as though he actually carried his blood to heaven and finished the work of atonement there. The word *once for all time* indicates an act of atonement in time that is unique, final and definitive, not continued in heaven. Thus F. F. Bruce stresses that there is no warrant here for the idea of the atonement happening in two acts (the analogy with the human practice in the tabernacle is not perfect but rather selective) or of Christ continually re-presenting his blood to the Father and so in this fashion pleading for us or that we as priests are called to continually offer up Christ in such fashion.[529] Donald Hagner shows the comparisons the author is making:[530]

New Covenant/Order	Old Covenant/Order
the good things already here (Heb 9:11, 23-24)	shadows, copies (Heb 8:5; 9:23; 10:1)
greater and more perfect tent (Heb 9:11, 24)	human-made tent (Heb 9:1, 11, 24)
Christ entered holy place once for all (Heb 9:12, 25-28; 10:1-3, 10-14)	priests entered every day or year (Heb 7:27; 9:7; 10:1)
through Christ's own blood (Heb 9:12; 10:4-10)	through the blood of goats and bulls (Heb 9:12, 18-22)
Obtained eternal redemption and purifies conscience (Heb 9:12-15)	obtained ritual/outward cleansing (Heb 9:9-13; 10:2, 11)
the consummation of the ages (Heb 9:26)	until the time of reformation (Heb 9:10)

Beginning with **Hebrews 9:15** we again have technical language about covenanting and treaties. Christ is the mediator and the testator of the new *diathēkē*, which, as earlier, can mean either "covenant" or "testament."[531] In the next verse

[528]Craddock *Hebrews*, p. 108.
[529]Bruce, *Hebrews*, pp. 225-26.
[530]Hagner, *Encountering the Book of Hebrews*, p. 122.
[531]Attridge, *Hebrews*, p. 255, suggests that the rhetorical device of reflexio (Quintilian *Instttutio oratoria* 9.3.68) is in play here, where two meanings of a single word are used, alternating back and forth.

our author uses *diathēkē* in the later sense (cf. Gal 3:15-17).[532] Hebrews 9:15 speaks of something quite striking: Christ's death atones for transgressions (which by definition are violations of a code of law, in this case the Mosaic code) that happened under the first covenant. This means that his death is efficacious for those under the law (i.e., the Jewish forebears) so those among them who are called might receive both redemption from those transgressions and the promised eternal inheritance. Quite clearly our author is no anti-Semite. It is just that the solution to the problems of the old system is found under the new order through Christ's death. This statement would be important if the author's audience was of Jewish extraction, and since he does not qualify whether the transgressions he has in mind are the deliberate ones or the unwitting ones, one may presume an all-encompassing idea here (i.e., Christ covers that for which the old system could never atone, as well as for any other kind of transgression).

The term *mesitēs*, which outside of Hebrews is found in the New Testament only at Galatians 3:19 and 1 Timothy 2:5, refers to a "mediator," a person who has credibility with two different groups and can bridge their differences. This is different from an emissary or ambassador, who generally represents only one side of the mediatorial efforts, speaking for one part rather than the other, though he may take the reply of the other party back to the one(s) who sent him.

At **Hebrews 9:16** our author appeals to the practice involved when someone dies and has a will. The will has a testator *(diathemenos)*, the one who draws up its stipulations but who must die for it to go into effect. This verse very clearly speaks of the death of the testator; there is no mention of the covenant practice where animals are sacrificed to show earnestness of purpose. While this practice was certainly known in covenanting, it did not amount to a representative death in place of the treaty makers. The reason this is suggested by Brooke Foss Westcott and others is the desire for our author to use *diathēkē* in only one sense—that is, as "covenant"—throughout this passage and the homily in general.[533] But this is quite unnecessary, for our author is rhetorically skillful and perfectly capable of playing with several different nuances and meanings of a single term (e.g., *aiōniou* means "eternal" in Heb 9:14 and "ages" in Heb 9:26). Wordplay was one of the chief devices used by ancient rhetoricians (*Rhetorica ad Herennium* 4.14.20-21).[534] William Lane points out that a covenant-ratification cere-

---

[532]Here is another example where our author seems to know Paul's way of handling a key term in Galatians. See Hughes, "Hebrews ix 15ff. and Galatians iii.15ff."

[533]Westcott, *Hebrews*, p. 265.

[534]Craddock, *Hebrews*, p. 109.

mony involved "dead bodies" (which is what the text literally says here), with the animal sacrifice being the means by which fealty to the covenant is pledged and by which the covenant takes effect (Gen 15:6-21; Jer 34:18).[535] Death, then, was necessary for either a covenant or a will to take effect—and either could be in view here. **Hebrews 9:17** simply restates the matter—a *diathēkē* is not valid until the testator dies. Then, in **Hebrews 9:18** our author turns back to his main comparison of old and new covenants. He knows that the analogy is not perfect, since he admits at Hebrews 9:22 that some things are cleansed without blood according to the Old Testament (Lev 5:11-13). There is some question whether the verb in Hebrews 9:18 means "restored" or "inaugurated" or "dedicated." Probably, the latter two definitions are in mind.

The author proceeds in **Hebrews 9:19** to speak of what Moses did after he proclaimed the whole law to the people. Apparently combining several texts (Ex 12:22; 24:3-8; Lev 8:15-19; 14:4; Num 19:18-19), our author mentions the blood of calves, red wool and hyssop and sprinkling the book and all the vessels of the tabernacle. Since Exodus 24 and Leviticus 19 were associated in the synagogue liturgy, there may be a reason for this combination here. In any case the real point is made when Exodus 24:8 is quoted in **Hebrews 9:20**—God enjoined the blood of the covenant for you. The blood of the covenant is what ratified it and also bound the people to obey it lest they suffer the curses of the covenant. **Hebrews 9:21** expands this to the sprinkling of all the vessels used in worship. And **Hebrews 9:22** then states what may have become a proverb: "Without shedding of blood there is no forgiveness." This is the only place in Hebrews that the word *forgiveness* appears without qualification. It is based on the statement in Leviticus 17:11 ("for the life of the creature is in the blood . . . it is the blood that makes atonement for one's life"), but our author believes that it applies in the new order of things (cf. Babylonian Talmud, tractate *Zevahim* 6a). Why should God insist on such a principle? Because blood represents life, and God requires that we give him our very lives. Failure to do so is a breaking of the covenant bond. God is a righteous God who is also loving and desires relationship with us. But that is possible only if we realize that what violates or prevents such a relationship—transgressions—must be dealt with, indeed must be atoned for, because a holy God can have no relationship with an unholy people. God cannot change his character, so he either must provide for the changing of ours so we may be his holy people or go without a people. God has chosen the former. Forgiveness then is possible only with atonement or payment for sins—for both God's justice and mercy must be maintained, his whole char-

---

[535]Lane, *Hebrews*, 2.242-43.

acter must be manifested and served. The only exceptions to the rule that everything is cleansed by blood are the poor, who were allowed to offer flour or incense since they could not afford the cost of an animal sacrifice, and a few things purified by water or fire (Lev 15:10, 13; 16:26, 28; 22:6; Num 19:7-8; 31:22-23).[536] Blood sacrifices were common in antiquity and believed in by Greeks and Romans as well as by Jews (Plutarch *Moralia* 290D; Aeschylus *Eumenides* 280-83). It was not just the shedding of blood, but the priestly applying of the blood in the right places that made it efficacious, for it was believed that blood shed and sprinkled did have cleansing power that in turn led to forgiveness, however much we may find this idea troubling. Forgiveness from God came at a cost in all these ancient cultures.

Hebrews 9:23 shows how far our author is willing to push the analogy between the earthly and heavenly sanctuary. The earthly tabernacle, which is a figure and antitype of the true tabernacle, must be cleansed by blood, but the heavenly sanctuary has better sacrifices than these. He does not specifically say that the heavenly must be cleansed, but the analogy has led him to speak of sacrifices plural. The new order has a better sacrifice that cleanses even internally. Thus the idea of the heavenly things being cleansed need not be pressed unless he is thinking of the heavens as a part of the material creation. In **Hebrews 9:24** our author uses the word *antitype* in the sense that *type* is used in Hebrews 8:5. Clearly the language is flexible, and epideictic rhetoric always involves saying the same thing in various different ways. Hebrews 9:24 also makes clear that our author does not conceive of heaven as a static place where nothing changes or happens; it has some sense of temporal development. Rather, it is now the place where Christ has been revealed to the very face of God—a phrase indicating his intimacy and closeness to the Father. He has his ear indeed. And this revelation was for the believer's benefit. In some Jewish contexts the outer court of the temple was seen as representing earth, while the inner courts or chamber represented heaven (Josephus *Jewish Antiquities* 3.123, 181).

Hebrews 9:25 simply reiterates that Christ did not need to offer himself over and over again, which would mean he would have had to die over and over, indeed ever since the foundation of the creation, since there has always been sin since Adam and Eve. The earthly high priest went into the holy of holies only once a year and then in the blood of another, that is, on the basis of the shedding of the blood of another. But at the consummation or end of the ages (1 Pet 1:20 has the same idea) things are different. Our author shares with many

---

[536]Hagner, *Encountering the Book of Hebrews*, p. 124. Our author is well aware of these exceptions, and so he says "almost" *(schedon)*.

other New Testament writers the conviction that Christ's coming inaugurates the end times (Mt 13:39-50; 24:3; 28:20; 1 Cor 10:11; Gal 4:4). Christ has been revealed (on earth) for the annulment or destruction of sin. Nothing less than that was his purpose. But he needed to do it only once *(hapax)* for all time. It was through *(dia)* his sacrifice that this destruction of sin was accomplished. This means the nullification of the power or effects of sin; since sin is an act or an attitude that is punctiliar, it is not precisely sin that is destroyed but rather its effects or power over us. We are dealing with an act of persuasion that involves a *reductio ad absurdum*: "By transferring the idea of repetition from the sphere of animal sacrifice, where it is assumed, to the sphere of Christ's death, where it is absurd, the author indicates that Christ's sacrifice is superior to all others (cf. 10.1-18)."[537]

Hebrews 9:26 speaks of Christ appearing at the consummation of the ages: "It is not that Christ happened to come at the time of fulfillment but that his coming made that time the time of fulfillment.[538]

Hebrews 9:27 develops a further analogy: just as it is destined for each one of us to die one time and then face the judgment (our author does not state whether this happens immediately)—and where we might have expected him to say, "so Christ died once and then will come as judge,"[539] he instead draws on Isaiah 53 and says—so Christ himself bore the sins of many by offering himself once to die. Perhaps it does not need to be repeated since our author has already stated that Christ died for everyone (Heb 2:9). If there is a contrast here it is between the one who dies and the many (i.e., everyone else) who potentially benefit from the death; the contrast is not between a death intended to benefit some and a death for all (compare Rom 5:15-19, which speaks of both a death for all and for the many). If we press the matter, we discover that the reason the death of Christ benefits only many rather than all depends on the response to the event. In any case, Craig Koester points out that the emphasis in Hebrews, as in 2 Esdras (4 Ezra) 14.34-35, is on judgment falling at the end of time rather than immediately upon death.[540]

Hebrews 9:28 mentions a second coming of Christ, the only time this idea is specified by that name in the New Testament. This time Jesus will come with-

---

[537]Koester, *Hebrews*, p. 428.

[538]Bruce, *Hebrews*, p. 231.

[539]Our author seems to be quoting a familiar maxim that Jews or Gentiles could have accepted, but in view of the reference to Christ's second coming, deSilva, *Perseverance in Gratitude*, p. 315, is surely right in rejecting Attridge's suggestion in *Hebrews*, p. 265, that a postmortem judgment is meant (à la Greek mythology) rather than an eschatological one.

[540]Koester, *Hebrews*, p. 423.

out and not for sins, but rather to complete the program of the redemption of those who eagerly await him.[541] It is not clear whether he will appear only to the saved and only for their salvation, but that seems to be the gist of it. Thus the second coming, like the first, will be about good news for those who eagerly await him. Here, as elsewhere in Hebrews, salvation is seen to be consummated in the future not in the past, and the second coming here, as in Philippians 3:20 and 2 Timothy 4:8, is seen as something that believers eagerly await. Fred Craddock may be right that there is an echo of the idea of the high priest coming forth from the holy of holies after having made atonement for sin, with the people eagerly awaiting and looking for his return when he emerges from the inner sanctum of the temple.[542]

What is the difference between a shadow and an image, both referred to in **Hebrews 10:1**? The question is worth asking since in Platonic thought, which our author is not really trying to adhere to, these two terms—*skia* and *eikōn* were synonyms (Plato *Republic* 509E-510E). Here the former is seen as a bare outline, the latter a full representation (Col 2:17). Our author is saying that that is the relationship of the Old Testament sacrifices and Christ's sacrifices—the former is a bare sketch and preview of coming attractions, the latter is the masterpiece itself. Perhaps we could imagine a person coming toward you with a light behind them so that their shadow is cast in your direction and arrives before them. The shadow is in the same general shape or outline as the substance casting the shadow, but it is not substantial like the reality that casts the shadow.

The phrase *good things to come* is used because the author is thinking historically from the perspective of the Old Testament period. Our author is not just comparing earthly and heavenly, but earlier and later earthly realities. The reference to the yearly sacrifice is to the Day of Atonement sacrifice in particular. It is offered, says our writer, continually. This may well suggest that he is writing while the temple is still in operation. But the problem is that these sacrifices, of whatever sort and however good, never perfect those offering them. They are simply inadequate to that end. Our author does not come to this conclusion out of the blue. He knows full well the self-critical character of some Old Testament texts about sacrifices and their efficacy (Ps 40:6; 51:16; Is 1:11; Hos 6:6; Amos 5:21-22; Mic 6:6-8). Donald Hagner says that the function of these texts is not to

---

[541]It is a mistake to assume that our author, when he speaks of the "things to come," is doing so only from the vantage point of Old Testament religion or the time of the tabernacle. True, he sometimes views things from this vantage point, but he also speaks of events that are in the Jewish Christian audience's future. This becomes apparent, for example, when we hear about the second coming of Jesus.

[542]Craddock, *Hebrews*, p. 113.

suggest that God did not like sacrifices, which God himself had commanded after all.[543] What God did not like was sacrifices in lieu of (i.e., unaccompanied by) living a life that accords with God's revealed will. It is thus incorrect to suggest that our author is simply extending the Old Testament critique of hypocrisy when it comes to sacrifices. He is saying that they are inadequate, however sincere their offerers may be, and he says this on the basis of his convictions of the adequacy, once and for all of Christ's sacrifice.

The rhetorical question in **Hebrews 10:2** is pointed—would they not have stopped such sacrifices if they had ever been finally effective, if the worshiper was once and for all finally cleansed? Quintilian says that rhetorical questions are very effective tools of persuasion, as they require the audience to pass judgment on the matter and not be noncommittal (*Institutio oratoria* 9.2.7). The structure of the argument is as follows: if the worshiper has once been completely purified, then people are no longer conscious of sin and so sacrifices would stop. In this rhetorical question our author is talking about an unreal condition, which again implies that they were still sacrificing when he wrote. If he was writing after 70, he could easily have added, "As in fact they have stopped because Christ has effected such a sacrifice." The noun *syneidēsis* here has its broader sense of "consciousness," which is the prerequisite context out of which conscience can arise.[544] At **Hebrews 10:3** our author turns the whole idea of the Day of Atonement on its head: is it not a day for remembering that we continue to sin and that there still is no effective permanent way of dealing with sin? Yom Kippur would normally be seen as a day of removal of sin, of God's remembering these sins no more. But our author in a neat turn of phrase uses the word *remember* in just the opposite sense—it reminds us that we still have this problem that has not been permanently solved.[545] In the Old Testament the "remembrance" of sin by God mainly means retribution (1 Kings 17:18; Ps 25:7; compare Rev 16:19, where "remember" means no longer remembering and judging their sins). We may sense a contrast between the old covenant, where one is constantly reminded of one's sin, and the new, where God will remember our sin no more (Heb 10:15-18).[546]

At **Hebrews 10:4** our author flatly states that the blood of bulls and goats

---

[543]Hagner, *Encountering the Book of Hebrews*, p. 129.
[544]Selby, "Meaning and Function of *Syneidēsis*." For the use of this term in the New Testament, see Pierce, *Conscience in the New Testament*. Craddock, *Hebrews*, p. 117, is right that we must avoid the etymological fallacy (i.e., assuming we know the meaning of a word on the basis of understanding where it came from). Craddock calls this the mistake of thinking the meaning of something is explained when it is only surrounded.
[545]DeSilva, *Perseverance in Gratitude*, p. 319.
[546]Koester, *Hebrews*, p. 436.

cannot take away sin. This seems to mean defilement of conscience and willful sins, though he could mean all sorts of sin except ritual impurity in light of the previous discussion. It is quite clear from **Hebrews 10:5-6** that our author believes in the preexistence of the Son, for here as he enters the stage of the material universe Psalm 40:6-8 is placed on his lips as being addressed to the Father. This is very apt, not least because the Septuagint refers to the "body" prepared by God for him (the Hebrew speaks only of ears being dug out, but the translators of the Septuagint doubtless took the part for the whole and spoke of a whole body being prepared).[547] The only significant way our writer has changed the wording of the psalm itself is by changing the verb "you have not asked" to "you do not approve/are not pleased," perhaps in contrast with his good pleasure already mentioned. This psalm is said to be Davidic, but it is possible to take it as messianic since we know that David did offer sacrifices, and so presumably then it would be about one of his descendants. Thus the *relecteur* or reaudiencing here is not such a stretching of the original focus.

Hebrews 10:7 uses the quotation to indicate that the very purpose of Christ's coming is to do God's will—to offer the final and perfect sacrifice.[548] Our author is one among many whose perspective is that the purpose of the incarnation is the atonement. The references in Hebrews 10:5-6 to four sacrifices—peace offering, meal offering, burnt offering and sin offering—are meant to be comprehensive or representative of the whole gamut of Old Testament sacrifices and offerings. The Old Testament itself critiques the Levitical system (Ps 51:16; 1 Sam 15:22; Is 1:11; Hos 6:6; Amos 5:21-22; Mic 6:6-8), as does Jesus (Mt 9:13; Mk 12:33).[549] Interestingly, Donald Hagner points out that after 70 these sort of texts were also used by Pharisaic Judaism, which survived the disaster, to speak of the availability of forgiveness without animal sacrifice.[550] The phrase *scroll of the book* literally refers to the knob on the top of papyrus roll/scroll. But what book is in view? From our author's viewpoint, this is the written Torah, not some heavenly record. The commentary on the text that follows in **Hebrews 10:8** is midrashic in character, giving running commentary with interspaced quoted words and phrases.

Hebrews 10:9 is very important and emphatic and reinforces the ideas of

[547] Jobes, "Rhetorical Achievement," thinks that the reading "body" originated with Hebrews but was transferred to the Septuagint. Koester, *Hebrews*, pp. 432-33, says this is unlikely in light of the manuscript evidence.

[548] See deSilva's detailed discussion in *Perseverance in Gratitude*, p. 322, of the modifications by the author to make this psalm especially user friendly for his argument.

[549] Our author relies primarily on this scriptural critique rather than those made in the wider culture; see Attridge, "Philosophical Critique of Religion."

[550] Hagner, *Encountering the Book of Hebrews*, p. 129.

Hebrews 7:12-19 and Hebrews 8:7, 13. The strong verb *anairei* ("to abolish, destroy") is contrasted with *stēsē* ("to confirm, establish"). "First" refers to the sacrifices of the Levitical system, while "second" applies to Christ. Here we have a definite theology of discontinuity and replacement—the one replaces the other. Our author could not have said it much more emphatically. But how has Christ done this? By the once-for-all *(ephapax)* offering of the body of Jesus Christ. In **Hebrews 10:10** he uses the perfect "having been sanctified" to refer to the believer's actual condition, because he is thinking of the ultimate effect of the finished work of Christ, but in Hebrews 10:14 he uses a continual present participle: "those being sanctified." But whatever the term *perfected* means in Hebrews 10:14, it does not mean "entirely sanctified." If it has a moral sense at all, the phrase *perfected continually* refers in all likelihood to the continual cleansing of our conscience, but perhaps as David Peterson suggests it means to continually be in right relationship or perfect relationship of intimacy with God, having free access to his presence and continual forgiveness.[551] It would seem to mean that in Christ believers are no longer alienated from God and so no longer need to be repeatedly reconciled to him. This means more than just the idea of being forever set apart for him or "consecrated," as the term *teteleiōken* is sometimes wrongly translated. Believers are not merely reserved or made fit for a relationship with God; they now have an eternal and direct relationship with God and already receive some of the benefits of that—Spirit, power, forgiveness. This is a good deal more than just being set apart. Thus, in terms of the believers' moral condition they are being sanctified, having had their consciences cleansed from guilt by the sacrifice of Christ (unless they sin again, at which point they may ask and receive a new application of forgiveness without a new sacrifice).

Our author is no docetist. He knows that salvation has come only by Christ's historical coming and in particular his sacrifice on the cross. In **Hebrews 10:11-14** we see a contrast by now already familiar. In the old order the priest continually stands to offer sacrifice because his work is never finished. As soon as one sin is dealt with, another comes along, but the problem is that those sacrifices never remove sin; they never remove the uncleanness and guilt and alienation caused by sin. This is just the opposite of Christ, who offers a sacrifice once and then sits down at the right hand of God (again an allusion to Ps 110:1). The former posture suggests continued activity and the necessity of the activity; the latter posture suggests finality—once for all time. This can only be called a rhetorically brilliant use of visual contrast to reinforce the theological point. "In

---

[551]Peterson, *Hebrews and Perfection*, pp. 151-52.

terms of epideictic topics, the author is again underscoring Jesus' honor and the nobility of his achievement, since he performed it first, alone, and completely (see Aristotle *Rhetoric* 1.9.25)."[552]

There is considerable controversy as to whether the phrase *eis to diēnekes* in Hebrews 10:12 goes with what precedes or with what follows. If it goes with what precedes, then the translation must not be rendered so the meaning is self-contradictory. Christ cannot offer (aorist, in the past, punctiliar action) a sacrifice both once in the past and also do so continually. If one takes the phrase with what precedes, then it would be better to translate the word as "forever": he offered it once forever, indicating that once his work was finished he sat down continually in the seat of honor beside the Father. The translation "continually" seems to conflict with what follows, which says that he is seated and waiting only until all his enemies are made a footstool for him. Hebrews 10:13 contains the first mention of the footstool, even though our author has quoted the earlier part of Psalm 110:1 previously. F. F. Bruce suggests that it is mentioned here because our author is concerned to get back to the parenesis and help out the audience, who is experiencing some enemies just now.[553] On the whole it looks like *eis to diēnekes* goes with what precedes it and means "forever." The section concludes in **Hebrews 10:15** once more with the Holy Spirit's witness about this new order, drawn from Jeremiah 31:33-34. The quotation in **Hebrews 10:16-17** varies slightly: (1) it is shortened; (2) the terms *mind* and *heart* are swapped in the closing clauses; (3) "for/with them" is substituted for the longer version in the actual text and (4) the clause "and their wickedness" is added, perhaps to enhance the effect. Whereas before our author quoted this passage to establish the obsolescence of the old covenant, here he quotes it to round off his argument by demonstrating the permanence of the new, as what follows in **Hebrews 10:18** makes clear that where there is forgiveness of these sins there is no longer offering for sin. In short, Christians cannot go back to the old way of doing things, for it is in Jesus' community that these things—and this complete forgiveness—are now in effect.

We can sum up the differences between Christ's sacrifice and animal sacrifices, following a 1976 lecture course by Andrew Lincoln on Hebrews: (1) Christ's sacrifice is not that of a dumb beast but rather a conscious act of a human being; (2) Christ's sacrifice was a voluntary act, whereas animal sacrifice is involuntary on the part of the sacrifice; (3) Christ's sacrifice was an equal substitution of one human for the sins of humans; it was more than equal, for it was

---

[552]DeSilva, *Perseverance in Gratitude*, pp. 323-24.
[553]Bruce, *Hebrews*, pp. 233-34.

one truly perfect human for various flawed, weak and sinful ones; and (4) the
Yom Kippur sacrifice could bring only one person, the high priest, directly into
the presence of God, whereas Christ's sacrifice opened the door so all might go
in to the inner sanctum. Our author wants us to understand that Christ's death
has transformed the whole method of approaching God. In both the Gentile and
Jewish world one could not approach God without continual sacrifice, but now
it is done in light of the full and final and eternally effective sacrifice of Christ.
Worship has fundamentally changed therefore. Those who talk about Christ
eternally offering his blood in heaven have mistaken the idea of an offering that
must be ceaselessly offered for an offering that is eternal in its efficacy.

It is perfectly clear that our author believes that believers must be not
merely forgiven, they must be perfected, sanctified, completed like their high
priest to enter into God's presence. Their consciences and very inner beings
must be cleansed. It is not just a matter of a change of their objective status
before God or even a change of God's attitude about them. "Hebrews warns
about hard and evil hearts that lead people astray (Heb 3:8, 10, 12), and the
new covenant is instituted in order that hearts might be true rather than evil,
and faithful rather than faithless (10:22)."[554] Completeness of obedience as
well as internalization of God's word and sanctifying power is the issue. This
in turn means that our author believes that being saved not only has to do
with one's condition but also with one's position as a forgiven sinner. He believes that salvation has a volitional and ultimately an eschatological dimension—the believer must look forward to the future for full and final salvation
and in the meantime he or she must *keep the faith*. Until then, the believer is
a work in progress, a pilgrim on a path who can go forward or turn back. No
wonder our author eagerly awaits the return of Christ when salvation will fully
dawn on and in believers' life.

EXHORTATION: HOLDING ON UNSWERVINGLY AS THE DAY APPROACHES (HEB 10:19-39)

> [Apostasy is] the clear, firm, informed, and deliberate rejection of the gospel by those
> who have already lived its joy, who have felt its purifying power, and who know in
> the marrow of their souls the promise of God and the grace God offers (10:29). . .
> Apostasy is to know in the depths of one's soul that "death has been swallowed
> up in victory" (1 Cor. 15:54) but to choose nonetheless to pitch one's tent in a death
> camp. Apostasy is to know full well where the next earthquake will be and to leave
> "a kingdom that cannot be shaken" (12:28) to build one's life on the fault line.

---

[554]Koester, *Hebrews*, p. 387.

Apostasy is to have been a child in heavenly Jerusalem's palace but to choose to leave home in order to be a slave in Sodom. Apostasy is to have been drawn by a strong cord into the lifeboat and then to jump back into the raging sea.[555]

In any sort of rhetorical discourse the appeal to the deeper emotions of love and fear and anger and grief and the like was supposed to be made near the end of the discourse, to reinforce the points made and to insure that the audience will hear and heed the message urged upon them. Our author knows these conventions well, and so it is no surprise as he heads toward the finish line that in his exhortations he becomes somewhat more strident in tone: in this section he holds before his audience's eyes the prospect of judgment and of missing out on the blessed hope; he is not afraid to conjure up a fearful prospect. The rhetoricians spoke of the need to make terrible and terrifying the picture of what would happen if the audience veers from the proper course being urged in the discourse. In this case, our author is urging the audience to remember their past conduct and to continue to embrace the good confession and good works they have previously adhered to. He urges nothing new on them. But he makes them well aware of the consequences of swerving from such a course. There is irony in what he says, because on the one hand he is urging the audience to enter into the presence of the living God, and on the other hand he is telling them that it is a fearsome thing to fall into the hands of the living God (in an inappropriate condition).

Craig Koester stresses that Hebrews 10:19-25 contains a sort of peroration for this particular cycle of arguments (Quintilian *Institutio oratoria* 6.1.1, 54-55): "Stylistically, 10:19-25 is a single complex sentence or period that summarizes the ideas of the section (*Rhetorica ad Herennium* 4.19.27)."[556] It was the function of an epideictic exhortation using emotive terms to make sure that, while some elements of the argument may have not made much impact, the cumulative effect of what had been said and argued would be felt and acted on (Quintilian *Institutio oratoria* 6.1.1).

Fred Craddock notices the deliberate symmetry between this exhortation in Hebrews 10:19-39 and the previous one in Hebrews 5:11—6:20: they both follow the same pattern of (1) admonition (Heb 5:11—6:3; 10:19-25), (2) stern warning (Heb 6:4-8; 10:26-31) and (3) encouragement based on the audience's past behavior (Heb 6:9-20; 10:32-39).[557] Many other scholars notice how Hebrews 10:19-25 echoes various themes from the exhortation in Hebrews 4:14-

---

[555]Long, *Hebrews*, pp. 109-10.
[556]Koester, *Hebrews*, p. 447.
[557]Craddock, *Hebrews*, p. 119.

16, while Hebrews 10:26-39 transitions into the next major argument on faith.[558] This reminds us once more that this document is not haphazardly thrown together. Care has been taken in its composition, both structurally in a general sense and more specifically in a rhetorical sense.

Equally unsurprising is that in an epideictic discourse such as this one our author holds up images of worship, images praising the ultimate being, as he draws the discourse to a close. The images of two judgments here (one from Moses' day, one eschatological) may be contrasted with the images of two theophanies (one on Sinai, one when Christ returns) in Hebrews 12 at the climax of the discourse. In both cases our author has in mind what will happen when the Lord returns at the climax of the eschaton, as is perfectly clear from the end of Hebrews 10:19-39. Thomas Long puts it this way: "Christian worship is an eschatological event; it is a participation here and now in the eternal praises of God. . . . Now the knees that bend and the tongues that confess are serving as midwives of the future of God, always with an eye on 'the Day approaching' (10:25). As the words of the familiar hymn state, 'O that with yonder sacred throng, we at his feet may fall! We'll join the everlasting song, and crown him Lord of all!'"[559]

But before the rhapsody of the theophany, before arriving at the gate of the new Jerusalem, there is this deep crevasse that the audience is bid look down into and warned not to fall into. The visual journey that this discourse is leading the audience on will end in love, wonder and praise—but nonetheless must cover some dangerous terrain before the goal is reached. This section warns of that dangerous terrain, warns about deliberately swerving off path and free falling into outer darkness. In other words, our author conjures up an image of the consequences of apostasy. In a discourse about "truth or consequences" here in this exhortation, our author bids the audience to look carefully at the consequences of so momentous and horrible a thing as "trampling the Son of God underfoot."

Even in a hortatory section like this one, there is some variety, as we go from exhortation (Heb 10:19-25) to sanction for the exhortation (Heb 10:26-31) to a concluding exhortation to continue to pursue the Christian virtues and conduct they had already embraced and exhibited (Heb 10:32-39) in earlier times (Heb 6:9-10), with a specific focus on faith and faithfulness rising to the forefront of the discussion as the author transitions to the encomium in Hebrews 11—12.[560]

---

[558]DeSilva, *Perseverance in Gratitude*, pp. 333-34.
[559]Long, *Hebrews*, p. 107.
[560]DeSilva, *Perseverance in Gratitude*, p. 334.

We should not expect, and we do not find here, a proposal of new policy but rather a recapitulation of previous exhortations somewhat amplified. The author of *Rhetoric to Alexander* reminds us that "recapitulation is a brief reminder. It should be employed both at the end of a division of a speech [as here] and at the end of the whole [which is the function of most of Heb 13]. In summing up we shall recapitulate either in the form of a calculation or of a proposal of policy or of a question of an enumeration" (1433b29-34). It seems clear that we have the first of these here, which involves drawing ethical conclusions based on the previous arguments and recapitulating some of the previous exhortative material in the discourse.[561]

10:19 *Having then confidence unto the entering of the holy place in the blood of Jesus,* [20] *which recent and living way was inaugurated for us through the curtain that is his flesh,* [21] *and a great priest of the house of God,* [22] *let us draw near with true hearts in assurance of faith. Our hearts having been sprinkled clean from an evil conscience and the body having been washed with pure water,* [23] *hold fast the confession of our hope unwaveringly, for the promise is faithful.* [24] *Take notice of one another unto the incitement of love and good works,* [25] *not abandoning the gathering of ourselves together, just as is the custom/ethos, but encourage one another, and all the more so as you see the day draw near.*

[26] *For if we deliberately sin after receiving the knowledge of the truth, there is no sacrifice left for sin,* [27] *but rather a terrifying expectation of judgment and to be consumed by raging fire ready for adversaries.* [28] *But anyone who flouts the law of Moses without pity upon the testimony of two or three witnesses dies.* [29] *How much worse punishment do you think you will be considered worthy of for those who trample the Son of God underfoot, and the blood of the covenant regard as profane, and the spirit of grace insult?* [30] *For we know the saying, "Vindication is mine, I will repay." And again, "The Lord judges his people."* [31] *It is terrifying to fall into the hands of the living God.*

[32] *But recall the earlier days in which, being enlightened, with much wrestling you endured suffering,* [33] *on the one hand being publicly exposed by this abuse and persecution,* [34] *but on the other hand showing a sharing in common with the living that this was happening to, and with the prisoners[562] sharing suffering and the theft of your possessions, you welcomed with joy, knowing you have a superior means of existence and a lasting one.* [35] *Do not throw away then your confidence, for which*

---

[561] I disagree with deSilva, *Perseverance in Gratitude*, p. 335, about the deliberative function of this material. This material is a reminder of things already said by the author and embraced by the audience. It is a reconfirmation of extant values and virtues and codes.
[562] The preferred reading is *desmiois*, referring to prison or being in chains, which best explains the variants and is well supported by Western and Alexandrian text types. See Metzger, *Textual Commentary*, p. 670.

there is a great reward. [36]*For you have need of endurance, in order that doing the will of God you may receive the promise.* [37]*For "yet a little while the one coming will be here, and he will not delay.* [38]*But my righteous one from faithfulness shall live."* [39]*And "if we shrink back my inner being will not take pleasure in him." But we, we are not of those shrinking back unto destruction, but faithful unto the securing of life.*

This is by no means the first hortatory section in this discourse, nor will it be the last, and it has echoes of previous ones (especially Heb 4:14-16). Donald Hagner points out that Hebrews 10:19-25 centers on three crucial verbs: "let us draw near" (Heb 10:22), "let us hold fast" (Heb 10:23), "let us consider" (Heb 10:24); strikingly enough, each of these three verbs is linked with one of three cardinal Christian virtues—faith, hope and love, in that order.[564] Again we have reason to suspect that our author had spent time listening to or reading Pauline material (1 Cor 13:13). The author includes himself within the exhortations ("let us . . .") and attempts to establish rapport at the outset by using the term *brothers*. In **Hebrews 10:19** the audience is now said to "have" the quality they were earlier urged to keep having—confidence/boldness/free speaking (Heb 3:6; 4:16). *Parrēsia* has both subjective (confidence) and objective (verbal boldness or free speech) dimensions.[565] This reassuring affirmation is a good rhetorical tactic as one draws a discourse to a close and its final peroration. Aristotle reminds us that confidence is the opposite of fear, and so our author will play the one off against the other in the appeal to the emotions in this section. Aristotle says that confidence/hope in what is good is often accompanied with the impression that it is near at hand, while the things to be feared are either far off or nonexistent (*Rhetoric* 2.5.16). The appeal to draw near and have confidence, then, is a natural combination from a rhetorical viewpoint, and it is here contrasted with shrinking back, committing apostasy and having good reasons to fear.

This exhortation begins with the stunning parallel between Christ's flesh and the curtain of the temple. The believer enters the holy place "in the blood" of Jesus and through his flesh. Hagner may be right that our author is thinking of a parallel between the rending of the veil in the temple (Mk 15:38; Lk 23:45)

---

[563]Later scribes, undoubtedly influenced by the absence of the word *my* in the quotation of Hab 2:4 in Rom 1:17 and Gal 3:11, delete it here, but it should be retained, as it is well supported by 𝔓[46], ℵ, A and many other manuscripts (though there is some question as to whether it belongs after "righteous one" or "faithfulness"). See Metzger, *Textual Commentary*, pp. 670-71.

[564]Hagner, *Encountering the Book of Hebrews*, p. 134.

[565]Attridge, *Hebrews*, p. 284.

and the rending of the flesh of Jesus that opened up a "recent"[566] and living way" (quite literally through Jesus!) into the presence of God.[567] Craig Koester notes that our author is suggesting that unprecedented access to God for every believer is available through Christ.[568] The language here again portrays Christ as a sort of trailblazer (Heb 2:10; 6:20), and we may think of the inscriptions along roadsides that speak of emperors paving a new road (e.g., "Trajan, son of the deified Nerva, high priest, . . . paved a new road from the border of Syria to the Red Sea").[569] Even more telling is the story of consul Decius Mus who "while acting upon a warning from heaven, with veiled head devoted himself to the infernal gods in front of the whole army, in order that by hurling himself where the enemy's weapons were thickest, he might open up a new path to victory along the track of his own lifeblood" (Lucius Annaeus Florus *Epitome* 1.14.3).

The verb *inaugurated* in **Hebrews 10:20** suggests the beginning of something important, like a covenant by an important person (Heb 9:18).[570] But Jesus did not enter the inner sanctum simply as blood upon the believer or the means through which they entered, he entered before them as their great priest who is over God's whole house—a noteworthy epideictic theme that should lead to the praising of Jesus (Heb 3:1-6; 4:14-16). Here the author is simply echoing and building on earlier treatments of the subject. The exposition provides the foundation and basis for the exhortation, as is the case in Paul's letters as well.

The believer is not asked to go first or alone into the presence of God. Jesus has both paved the way and is there waiting, which is a stark contrast to what is said in Hebrews 9:8 about the way being closed before, with a no trespassing sign. And unlike in other ancient religions, the worshiper is not asked to stay outside while the priest as his or her representative goes within to effect the rapprochement. In the Christian faith all worshipers are beckoned to draw near to the divine presence, a stark contrast to Numbers 4:20 or Numbers 17:13, which say that the ordinary worshiper is subject to death if he or she enters the inner chamber. Christian believers have good reason to draw near with true hearts and in full assurance that they will be accepted. They have been cleansed both inwardly in their conscience and outwardly in their bodies (possibly an allusion

---

[566]This is the only use of the word *prosphatos* in the New Testament. Since the normal meaning of this word is "recent," it may reflect our author's perspective that the Christ event had happened within his lifetime or at least within living memory, thus providing another small indirect clue to the dating of this document. Though rare in the New Testament (the adverbial form occurs at Acts 18:2), the adjective is common in Greek literature.

[567]Hagner, *Encountering the Book of Hebrews*, p. 135.

[568]Koester, *Hebrews*, p. 443.

[569]Lewis and Reinhold, *Roman Civilization*, 2.72-75.

[570]Craddock, *Hebrews*, p. 120.

to baptism; see 1 Pet 3:21). Some find an echo of Ezekiel 36:25-26 here, talking about the effects of Christ's work and the new covenant on the believer, which comports better with the cultic context where the ritual ablution was necessary for the priest before he entered the holy zone.[571]

By reference to the "body" of the believer in **Hebrews 10:21-22** our author is not envisioning the disembodied spirit of the believer drawing near to God in the heavenly sanctuary, but rather on earth. For one thing, the author is exhorting a *living* audience to draw near. Drawing near happens in the present and in the flesh. Our author is not urging the audience to have a death wish so they can enter heaven more quickly, following literally in Jesus' path, even if they are "dying to meet Jesus." Nor by saying "draw near" is our author urging the audience to be prepared to die and go to heaven, where they will have unfettered access with God. They already have that access, and they are to draw near now while living. The end of this exhortation in Hebrews 12 describes theophanies of God drawing near to the believers while they are still on earth. The focus of this exhortation then is not otherworldly, but rather primarily eschatological, as the reference to "the day" makes evident here.

Our author is preparing to talk about the final drawing near to God when Jesus returns, and that drawing near also involves an embodied state, in this case the resurrection state. This becomes especially clear in **Hebrews 10:23**, where we hear about holding fast to the confession of our "hope." True confession in the early church not only involved affirming certain things about the past (of Christ or salvific events); it also involved affirming things about the future, things that a faithful God (or Christ in Heb 2:17; 3:2) made promises about but have not yet transpired (1 Cor 1:9; 10:13; 2 Cor 1:18; 1 Thess 5:24; 2 Tim 2:13). Our author clearly thinks that "keeping the faith" is more likely to happen if the faithful continue to congregate together.

Our author also reminds us in **Hebrews 10:24** to "provoke" one another to love and good deeds and not to "abandon" (see Mt 27:46; 2 Tim 4:10, 16) the congregational meetings. While the word *paroxysmos* can have a negative sense ("pester"), it can also be used in a positive sense to motivate the apathetic or fearful to do something (Josephus *Jewish Antiquities* 16.125; Xenophon *Memorabilia* 3.3.13).[572] An eschatological sanction is put in play in **Hebrews 10:25** with the reference to the "day" approaching, clearly a reference to the parousia and the judgment day associated with that event. There is no attempt to identify which day the writer has in mind. The audience is assumed to know this escha-

---

[571]Koester, *Hebrews*, p. 444.
[572]Craddock, *Hebrews*, p. 121.

tological code language. This passage is also revealing in regard to the social situation being addressed in this discourse. Clearly there is distress and danger of apostasy and abandonment of the community on the part of some. Some seem to be looking for a way out or the path of least resistance.

The term used for the congregational meeting here, *episynagōgē*, is probably significant, especially since the similar *synagōgē* was often used for Jewish gatherings, Jewish Christian gatherings (Jas 2:2) and Christian gatherings (Ignatius *To Polycarp* 4.2; *Shepherd* of Hermas, *Mandates* 11.9-14). The etymology of the term seems to refer to a local meeting—a meeting "at" a certain place, in view of the prefix *epi*. The nominal and verbal forms of this word are used elsewhere of the ingathering of Israel (2 Maccabees 2.7; 2 Thess 2:1; Mt 23:27; 24:31; Mk 13:27; Lk 13:34).[573] In all, the use of this term suggests strongly that the audience is Jewish Christian, which comports with what we have deduced earlier in this study.

In Hebrews 10:26-31 our author returns to themes already dealt with in Hebrews 6:1-8, particularly apostasy and its dangers and irrevocable character, here however couched in cultic language.[574] Repeating the theme in a theme-variation-theme pattern is a standard form of rhetorical amplification. The first word in **Hebrews 10:26**, *hekousiōs* ("willfully, deliberately"), is in the emphatic position, but the present/continual-tense verb ("persist in/keep on sinning") echoes Numbers 15:22-31 and its discussion about intentional sin. Our author says that if someone rejects and refuses the one recourse from sinning—the one means by which one can be saved—then one has committed apostasy. "By definition, apostates have cut themselves off from the single source of grace."[575]

The horrific nature of this is made plain by the use of the vivid language. It entails trampling[576] the Son of God underfoot, profaning[577] the blood of the covenant, outraging[578] the Spirit of grace. These are no small sins, and clearly they are sins that our author envisions some Christians in Rome in danger of committing.[579] This language, which makes the sins in question seem as horrific as one can imagine, involves the rhetorical technique called deinosis, which "gives

---

[573]Koester, *Hebrews*, p. 446.

[574]On the parallels see Lane, *Hebrews*, 2.296-97.

[575]Hagner, *Encountering the Book of Hebrews*, p. 137.

[576]Trampling is a strong metaphor for showing utter contempt (Mic 7:10; Is 26:6), not unlike the ritual of placing an enemy's neck under a conqueror's foot.

[577]The word *koinos* ("common") refers to making profane something that is holy or sacred—an act of degradation. Ignatius, *To the Smyrnaeans* 7, reads this anachronistically to refer to later disputes about the nature of the Lord's Supper, as did other later church fathers.

[578]*Enybrizō* is a verbal form of hubris and refers to an arrogant and outrageous act.

[579]Craddock, *Hebrews*, p. 122, rightly points out that the warnings in Heb 10:26-31 are all in the first person plural, so the author is including himself within the warning.

additional force to things unjust, cruel, hateful" (Quintilian *Institutio oratoria* 6.2.24)—in this case to ward off apostasy.

Conversion is spoken of as "having received knowledge of the truth" (Heb 6:4; Jn 8:32; 17:3; 1 Tim 2:4; 4:3). The ideational component of the conversion, that it involves a certain amount of knowledge, is important—it is not just about experience or relationship. "The writer's logic moves forward without wavering: If this sequence held for those who violated the old covenant, those who reject life under the new can expect even more severity. Greater blessings imply greater judgment; the measure of height is the measure of depth."[580]

Hebrews 10:27 indicates that what awaits a person who does this is a fiery judgment (possibly alluding to Is 26:11; cf. Zeph 1:18) or a living God who is a consuming fire to the wicked (Heb 12:29). They have become enemies of God and are treated as such. Our author forces the audience to participate in the judgment of such persons by a rhetorical question: What do you think these perpetrators deserve? Concluding a sentence about judgment with a rhetorical question that urges the audience to render judgment on the apostates closely parallels that found in Philo, who also refers to "great . . . judgment" on apostates (*On Flight and Finding* 84; *On the Special Laws* 2.255)—which perhaps suggests that our author knew Philo's similar discussions.

There is irony to **Hebrews 10:28**. Our author speaks of the judgment that fell on those who annulled or rejected the law of Moses. However, our author could be said to be doing the same thing! The rhetorical logic of the discussion comes to the surface again in **Hebrews 10:29**, where a "how much more so" (a fortiori) argument uses an example from Old Testament times to suggest that the judgment will be even more severe for apostates under the new covenant.[581]

To reinforce the vivid images, our author quotes Deuteronomy 32:35-36 in **Hebrews 10:30** and suggests that if a horrific judgment awaited those who committed apostasy under Moses (Num 16:35), how much more will that be the case for those who commit apostasy under the new covenant. The form of the citation of Deuteronomy 32:35 does not correspond to either the Masoretic Text or the Septuagint, but it does match that found in Romans 12:19, another reason to believe that our author knew some of Paul's writings.[582] One could argue that this text is

---

[580]Ibid., p. 123.

[581]Attridge, *Hebrews*, p. 294.

[582]We also find this form in the Aramaic targums (particularly Targum Onkelos), which our author and Paul may know. Since in general our author does not reflect knowledge of Aramaic, I am skeptical of his reliance on a targumic reading at this juncture. With Paul the case is otherwise, since we have clear evidence that he knew some Aramaic. See Attridge, *Hebrews*, p. 295.

Here Heb. clearly refutes Paul

a conflation of the Masoretic Text and the Septuagint.[583] The attempt to create pathos here is so clear with the appeal to fear (Heb 10:27, 31) and the reference to an angry living God in **Hebrews 10:31**. Aristotle defines fear as an inward pain caused by the sense of imminent harm or imminent evil (*Rhetoric* 2.5.1-5). "The passage concludes with a reaffirmation of what the addressees truly need to be fearing—not falling into the hands of their neighbors, but falling into the hands of the living God in God's capacity as judge and avenger (10:30-31)."[584]

What has just been said is contrasted with **Hebrews 10:32-37** by the connective word *but* at the beginning of Hebrews 10:32. In the last paragraph of this exhortation (Heb 10:32-39), our author reminds the audience that they have already managed to persevere in good faith through a lot. They had undergone public verbal abuse (being made a spectacle of; cf. 1 Cor 4:9; Philo *On the Embassy to Gaius* 359, 368),[585] physical abuse leading to suffering, tribulations of various sorts and the confiscation of their property. But all the while this was happening they were not merely enduring it, they were ministering to even less fortunate and more abused believers who were in chains or in jail, something that Hebrews 13:3 will encourage them to continue to do. One could argue that our author has already begun the encomium of faith here by praising the audience's past conduct (*Rhetorica ad Herennium* 1.4.9). In a sectarian way, our author redefines what is honorable conduct and what is dishonorable conduct. Repudiating a crucified Jew would not be seen as dishonorable conduct by the society at large, and aiding and abetting his followers would not be seen as honorable conduct. Thus the core values of the community referred to here are countercultural in their referents, even though they are clothed in the usual rhetoric of the culture about faithfulness and honorable conduct. Such countercultural behavior and belief is seen here as "the will of God" and its implementation.

Our author is probably thinking back to the events of 49 during the purging of Jewish Christians from Rome by Claudius. Violence against Jews, including Jewish Christians, was not uncommon in the first century, especially in major

---

[583]DeSilva, *Perseverance in Gratitude*, p. 352.

[584]Ibid., p. 355.

[585]Persecuting Christians made ("good theater" (the English word *theater* comes from *theatrizō*). Attridge, *Hebrews*, p. 298, makes the point that this text could be an allusion to the persecutions of Nero (Tacitus *Annals* 15.44), but backs off this suggestion in light of Heb 12:4 and suggests perhaps that the audience came to Rome after the persecution of Nero. This is unnecessary. Obviously, Hebrews is written to the living! Thus Heb 12:4 refers to many if not most of the rank and file Jewish Christians who escaped the harshest treatment of the pogrom. While they are not leaderless, their leaders are not named (perhaps in part to protect them; see Heb 13), and perhaps this is another reason the author remains anonymous, if he was also one of this beleaguered church's leaders.

cities with a large number of Jews (Philo *Against Flaccus* 56; Acts 18:1-2). In any case, these verses suggest that the Jewish Christian community in Rome had existed for some considerable period of time and had gone through a lot. It is equally telling that neither Paul, writing in the later 50s, nor our author, writing in the mid- to late 60s, ever mention Peter or any other major apostolic figure as being present and guiding the Jewish Christian community in Rome. This is less telling in the case of Paul, since he is mainly addressing Gentiles in his Romans letter, but that is not the case in Hebrews.

Hebrews 10:38 is important, not least because it gives us another chance to evaluate the creative way our author handles the Old Testament. The partial quotation of Habakkuk 2:4 occurs in three places in the New Testament: Galatians 3:11; Romans 1:17; Hebrews 10:38.[586] The most notable difference in the citations is that the word *righteous* has no modifier in the two Pauline quotations, but in Hebrews the word *my* modifies the noun. In order to understand this we need to keep in mind that the Hebrew text reads "the righteous will live by his [God's] faithfulness," but in the Septuagint the word *my* modifies "faith/faithfulness" in some manuscripts and "the righteous one" in others. Further, the thrust in the Pauline usage of the text involves taking *pistis* to mean "faith" rather than "faithfulness," whereas in Hebrews and the Septuagint it seems more likely that "faithfulness" is meant. In Hebrews the exhortation is to those who already have faith, to live faithfully. Harold Attridge says that the citation of the text in Hebrews is not part of some apologetical program urging salvation or right standing with God by grace through faith, though our author certainly believes in this notion.[587] Rather, our author is trying to head off apostasy. If we ask who is more closely following the Septuagint—our author or Paul—the answer is our author. Our author connects living faithfully as a Christian in the present with the coming one (Heb 9:28), who will rectify matters and vindicate the "righteous ones."[588]

Hebrews 10:38 and **Hebrews 10:39** should be seen as transitional, for the theme of the faith/faithfulness of true believers has been introduced, as has the note that faithfulness entails not shrinking back but rather going forward in faith. Faith has not been mentioned in Hebrews 7:1—10:18, but now we are about to engage in a real faith fest. The Habakkuk quotation is inverted so that "my soul takes no pleasure in anyone who shrinks back" can thereby help provide the transition to the hall-of-faith chapter that follows and also make clear that "my righteous one" is the believer who must not shrink back in the quotation. "The

[586]Fitzmyer, "Habakkuk 2:3-4 and the New Testament."
[587]Attridge, *Hebrews*, p. 304.
[588]See the detailed discussion in Gheorghita, *Role of the Septuagint in Hebrews*.

coming one" (noting the addition of the definite article before *erchomenos*) is
seen as clearly referring to Jesus.

The Rough Ride to the Kingdom (Heb 11:1—12:17)

> Faith needs a generous and vigorous soul, one rising above all things of sense and
> passing beyond the weakness of human reasonings. For it is not possible to be-
> come a believer otherwise than by raising oneself above the customs of the world.
> . . . For when a soul finds one that shares its same sufferings, it is refreshed and
> recovers it breath. This we may see both in the case of faith and in the case of af-
> fliction, "that we may be mutually encouraged by each other's faith." (Chrysostom
> *Homilies on Hebrews* 22.1-2)

Faith, as a biblical theological concept is large, round, and complex, and the
Preacher's description encompasses but a few degrees of its circumference. But the
Preacher is not writing a dogmatics. He is preaching a sermon, and he crafts a
working definition of faith that will serve his immediate sermonic goals. Instead of
providing a comprehensive definition, the Preacher simply names those aspects of
faith he hopes to encourage. He does not need a three-masted doctrinal schooner
with all the sails and rigging; he needs a landing craft to get his congregation onto
the beachhead that lies on the far horizon.[589]

In any given situation, the cross is the heaviest piece of furniture to move, and
Christians are charged with the considerable task of picking it up and carrying it
every single day.[590]

Thus far our author has been discoursing on the substance of things hoped for,
believed and for the most part not seen. In particular he has been discoursing on
Christ and his role in heaven as the heavenly high priest. But in Hebrews 10:19-
39 he turned once more to exhortation, which led quite naturally into this powerful soliloquy in praise of faith. More than just wanting to strengthen his audience's need to behave, he wants to strengthen their resolve to believe, to trust
God and to continue their spiritual journey toward the new Jerusalem. The expositions and exhortations up to Hebrews 11 were all about the substance of what
they already believe and know they ought to do, but the resolve, trust and faith
to do it is another matter. Thus our author offers up one of the great encomiums
in all of ancient literature on faith, on a par with that other great epideictic piece
on love in 1 Corinthians 13. The connection between what comes before Hebrews
11 and what we see in the climax of the discourse in this unit is clear enough:
having described the substance and object of their faith both in terms of ortho-

---

[589]Long, *Hebrews*, p. 113.
[590]Ibid., p. 131.

doxy and orthopraxy, our author now turns to the faith response itself—the act of trusting, believing, being reassured and convinced, which leads to conviction and resolve. Whereas before this chapter we see exposition and exhortation in alternating sections, from now on in this discourse they will be intertwined, with the hortatory tone of the remainder of the discourse quite evident. Luke Timothy Johnson reminds us that the faith that our author is referring to is "not simply belief, or even trust or obedience; it was all these extended through trial by endurance. Jesus, the pioneer and perfecter of faith, 'endured the cross' (12:2-3) and they are to endure for the sake of the same 'education' in perfection."[591]

In many ways we are not well served by the chapter divisions in various biblical books. There is most definitely a connection between the material at the end of Hebrews 10 and the material in Hebrews 11 as our author proceeds to give numerous examples of those who lived by faith and faithfulness and thus showed that they were God's righteous ones. I quite agree with Barnabas Lindars that the real climax of the argument of this word of exhortation comes not in Hebrews 7:1—10:18 but in Hebrews 10:19—12:17.[592] The urgent issue is a matter of orthopraxy, of living by faith, which is also linked with orthodoxy. But it is wrong to treat the parenetic sections as interruptions in the main argument, which is seen to be theological. The theological argument is given to support and bolster the ethical appeal, not the other way around.

Beginning in Hebrews 11 we see in earnest the story of "pilgrim's progress" and how we are the wandering people of God and have been from the time of Abraham and even before. Here in Hebrews 11 our author stresses the continuity of all believers—both the Jewish patriarchs before Christ and current Christians. Thus, when he discusses faith here he is not talking about what Christians might call "the faith" (i.e., what Christians believe about Christ and other uniquely Christian doctrines). He is talking about that most basic form of trust in God—the faithful living and obedience of believers that should grow out of that trust.

This chapter is a rhetorical masterpiece, as Michael R. Cosby shows.[593] Eighteen times our author uses anaphora (repetition of the same word in successive sentences), even beginning each sentence with the same term: *pistei* ("by faith").[594] This would have significant impact in a setting where this document would be read aloud. Momentum would be building up, and the intention and effect is to suggest to the reader that the author could give an infinite number

[591]Johnson, *Hebrews*, p. 272.
[592]Lindars, *Theology of the Letter to the Hebrews.*
[593]Cosby, "Rhetorical Composition of Hebrews 11"; idem, *Rhetorical Composition and Function*; and Miller, "What Is the Literary Form of Hebrews 11?"
[594]On anaphora as a rhetorical device see *Rhetorica ad Herennium* 4.19-20.

of examples. But unlike other similar lists in Greek rhetorical settings, our author deliberately sets his in a salvation-history order to give a sense of progression from past into the present, and in this regard his "hall of faith" or catalogue is much more like some Jewish examples (e.g., Sirach 44.1—50.21; 1 Maccabees 2.51-60; 2 Esdras [4 Ezra] 7.106-11).

Furthermore, our author is not trying to illustrate some native human virtue, but to give examples of trust that results in assurance and conviction, which ultimately is a gift from God that is then used and exhibited by his people. His interest is not in some eternal or timeless principle for all people, but historical precedents of the faithful for his audience to follow in the footsteps of. God's people have "*always* lived by faith, believing that they would one day receive God's promises which they could not see except through the eyes of faith."[595] The implicit undercurrent throughout is that God is not asking something impossible of the audience—such faithfulness and perseverance and trust has been exhibited in historical reality innumerable times before. These examples were chosen with some care; by and large they are examples of people who rejected earthly success and security and demonstrated faith in an otherworldly and this-worldly reality, about which God had given them promises, but at best they saw only part of the fulfillment of those promises.[596]

The chapter first defines faith and then illustrates what is meant countless times (Heb 11:3-38), thus attempting to overwhelm the sluggishness, fears or doubts of the audience about the ability to pursue such a course of faith. Our author wants this list to be seen as representative, not just the odd exception to the rule, but part of a great cloud of witnesses.

The terms *faith* and *faithfulness* are used throughout Hebrews. In the first place we must not confuse *pistis* ("faith") with *pistos* ("faithful, faithfulness"). The term *pistos* occurs some sixty-seven times in the New Testament, but it is not found in abundance in Hebrews.[597] In Hebrews 2:17 we hear of Christ becoming a merciful and faithful high priest (cf. 1 Sam 2:35). This theme of Christ being faithful is continued in Hebrews 3:1-2, and his faithfulness is compared to that of Moses, faithful in God's house (Heb 11:6). Does Hebrews 12:1-2 then refer to "the faith" or "the faithfulness"? Or is this making too fine a distinction between *pistos* and *pistis* in a phrase that literally reads "looking to, the of the faith pioneer and perfector, Jesus"? Here the correct translation is surely "faith" rather than "faithful" (compare Heb 10:22-23, which speaks of drawing near with a true heart

---

[595]Cosby, "Rhetorical Composition of Hebrews 11," p. 261 (emphasis original).
[596]Eisenbaum, *Jewish Heroes of Christian History.*
[597]Still, "Christos as Pistos."

in fullness of faith *[pisteōs]*. But in Hebrews 11:13 or Hebrews 11:39 the term *pistis* carries a nuance of faithfulness to the end as well as trust/faith, as is especially clear when we note the parallels between what is said of faith and what is said of endurance (Heb 11:40; 12:2). Linking hope to faith is also telling and suggests qualities that help one persevere. Mariam Kamell suggests that for the authors of both Hebrews and James there is no true faith but faithful faith, and Jesus is clearly the prime exemplar of such faithfulness and trust, such faith.[598] This active and lived-out faith is what our author means by "the faith."

> [11:1] *But faith is the assurance/substance of things hoped for, the conviction/proof of things not seen.* [2] *For this the elders were testified to.* [3] *By faith we understand the word of God formed the eons, so that not from visible things were the things we see created.* [4] *By faith Abel offered a greater sacrifice than Cain to God,*[599] *through which he was attested to be righteous, approved by God for his offering, and through this (faith) though dead he still speaks.* [5] *By faith Enoch was removed, who did not see death and "was not found because God removed/translated him." For before the removal it was witnessed "he had been pleasing to God."* [6] *For without faith it is impossible to please, because for those coming to God it is necessary to believe that he is and that he is one who rewards those seeking him out.* [7] *By faith Noah was instructed concerning things he was not yet seeing, taking heed he constructed an ark unto the salvation of his household, through which (faith) he condemned/judged the world, and he became inheritor of the righteousness according to faith.*
>
> [8] *By faith Abraham being called, obeyed to go out unto a place that he was to receive as an inheritance, and he went, not knowing where he was going.* [9] *By faith he came unto the land of the promised as (if it was) another's he made his home in a tent with Isaac and Jacob as fellow heirs of the same promise.* [10] *For he was looking forward/expecting the city that has foundations, the builder and creator of which is God.* [11] *By faith even barren Sarah herself (along with Abraham) received power unto the deposit of seed even beyond the time of life, since he/she counted faithful the one who promised.*[600] [12] *Therefore also from this one was born, and he having*

---

[598]Kamell, "Faith in Hebrews and James."

[599]$\mathfrak{P}^{13}$ omits "to God," which should likely be included.

[600]The difficulties are legion in Heb 11:11. The least of the difficulties is that some manuscripts do not include the word *barren*, which should probably be included. The main difficulty lies in what to make of the clause *even Sarah herself barren*, in view of the word *katabolē* universally meaning "deposit," not "reception" of seed, which would surely thus refer to a male—not Sarah—as its subject. The text literally reads "received power unto the deposit of seed." This might mean "received power to make such a deposit," but could not it also mean "received power concerning the deposit of seed"? The difficulty then lies in what follows, because in the Genesis story Sarah was the one who laughed and—at least initially—did not trust in the one who promised. Perhaps the best way out of the dilemma is not to emend the text but to take *autē sarra* (1) not as a nominative but as a dative (which requires a change

become dead/lifeless,[601] *just as the stars of the heavens are a multitude and as the grains of sand along the edge of the sea are countless.* ₂\ꞩ ꞇ .

[13] *By faith all these died, not receiving the promise, but seeing it from afar off and greeting it, and they confessed that they were strangers/foreigners and settlers upon the earth/land.* [14] *For saying such things they show plainly that they were in search of the fatherland.* [15] *And if they had had in mind that land from which they set out, then they would have returned.* [16] *But now they aspired to a better one, that is the heavenly one. Therefore, God is not ashamed to be called their God, for he has made ready a city for them.*

[17] *By faith Abraham,*[602] *being put to the test, offered Isaac, the only begotten on the point of being offered by the one who accepted the promise.* [18] *To whom it had been said that "In Isaac shall there be promised seed for you."* [19] *Reckoning that God was also able to raise the dead; hence also he in a parable/figure received him back.* [20] *By faith also Isaac blessed Jacob and Esau concerning the future.* [21] *By faith Jacob when he was dying blessed the sons of Joseph and "prostrated/leaned himself on the top of his staff."* [22] *By faith Joseph coming to the end (of life) had in mind the exodus of the sons of Israel and gave instructions concerning his bones.*

[23] *By faith Moses, when he was born, was hid for three months by his parents because they saw the child was beautiful, and they were not afraid of the king's edict.* [24] *By faith Moses when he became great, refused to be called son of Pharaoh's daugh-) ter,* [25] *choosing to endure hardship of the people of God rather than have the short-lived pleasure of sin,* [26] *he considered greater wealth the disgrace/insult of Christ than the treasure of Egypt, for he looked unto the reward.*

[27] *By faith he left Egypt not fearing the anger of the king, for the unseen, as if he saw (it), he remained steadfast.* [28] *By faith he kept the Passover and the pouring out of blood in order that the destroyer might not touch his firstborn.* [29] *By faith he crossed the Red Sea as through dry land, but when the Egyptians tried it they were swallowed up.* [30] *By faith the walls of Jericho fell when they had been encircled for seven days.* [31] *By faith Rahab the prostitute did not perish with the unbelievers, having welcomed the spies with peace.*

[32] *And what more shall I say? For time will fail me if I tell about Gideon, Barak, Samson, Jephthah, David and also Samuel and the prophets,* [33] *who through faith conquered kingdoms, practiced justice, attained promises, shut the mouths of lions,*

---

of the originally nonexistent diacritical marks, not of the letters) and thus the text would read "by faith he, also with Sarah herself barren, received power"; or (2) as a Hebrew circumstantial clause, yielding "even though Sarah was barren." Either way, emending the text becomes unnecessary. See Bruce, *Hebrews*, pp. 260-61.

[601]The Greek does not say "as good as dead"; it says "one who had become dead/lifeless" and so impotent; deSilva, *Perseverance in Gratitude*, p. 398.

[602]The name Abraham is in various positions—some manuscripts have it after testing, some after offering and some omit it. The variety of positions may suggest that the name is a secondary insertion.

[34]*quenched the power of fire, escaped the edge of the sword, were made strong out of weakness, became powerful in war, broke the army camps of others;* [35]*women received their dead out of resurrection, but others were tortured, not accepting the release in order to attain a better resurrection.* [36]*But others received the trial of jeering and lashes, while (others received) bonds and prison.* [37]*They were stoned, they were sawed in two,*[603]*in murder they were killed by the sword, they went about in sheep's skin, in goat's skin, being in want, oppressed, ill treated,* [38]*the world was not worthy of them, wandering in the desert and the mountains and caves and the crevices of the earth.* [39]*And these all bore witness through their faith they had not received the promises,* [40]*God provided/foresaw something better concerning us in order that they might not be perfected without us.*

[12:1]*Consequently also we, having been surrounded by so great a cloud/host of witnesses, putting off every burden and easily besetting* [604]*sin, we should run with perseverance the race that lies before us,* [2]*fixing our eyes only upon the trailblazer and finisher of the faith, Jesus, who for the joy set before him endured the cross, thinking nothing of the shame, is seated at the right hand of the throne of God.* [3]*For consider the one who endured such opposition/hostility from the sinners against himself*[605] *in order that your life would not be worn out growing faint.* [4]*You have not yet resisted to the point of blood in your struggling against sin,* [5]*and you have forgotten completely the exhortation that was addressed to you as sons: "My son, do not make light of the discipline of the Lord, do not give up when he reprimands you;* [6]*for whom the Lord loves he disciplines, but he scourges everyone whom he receives as a son."* [7]*Endure it as discipline. God brings it to you as sons. For is there any son whom a father does not discipline?* [8]*But if you are without discipline that all sharers have,*

---

[603]Heb 11:37 contains the most complex textual problem in this section. Should the rather innocuous *epeirasthēsan* ("they were tempted") appear in the midst of descriptions of violent death, or should it be omitted? The early manuscript 𝔓[46] and a few other manuscripts omit the word. Rather than omission, many conjecture that this word is a corruption of some other original word, such as *epyristhēsan* ("they were burned"), *eparthēsan* ("they were pierced") or even *etaricheuthēsan* ("they were pickled"). This one is a toss-up, but since *epeirasthēsan* is found in various places in the manuscripts, perhaps it was not original here, nor are the various conjectures based on that reading.

[604]𝔓[46] and 1739 read *euperispaston* ("easily distracting"). In view of the earliness of the reading some think it original. But this modification was probably made early on because the word is so rare. It is not found in any known Greek document prior to Hebrews. By derivation, however, the sense is rather clear—entrammeling or besetting, which fits the context nicely of running a race—and is witnessed by the vast majority of manuscripts.

[605]External evidence strongly favors "against themselves" in one form or another, while A, P and others have "against himself." The difficulty in the former reading is making sense of it in context. Did the sinners have hostility against themselves? Or does it mean that by opposing Jesus the sinners were really fighting against themselves, i.e., were at cross-purposes with themselves since Jesus is the supreme human being who came for sinners? I would not rule this out, though opposition "against himself" is perhaps more natural here.

then you are bastards and not sons. [9] Then again we have had those who on the one hand are our physical fathers who have disciplined/trained us and we respected them, but on the other hand should we not all the more submit to the Father of our spirits and live. [10] For the former on the one hand are short of days (and) discipline according as it seems good to them, but the latter on the other hand (does it) for our benefit in order that we might share in his holiness. [11] But all discipline at the present time on the one hand does not seem to be a joy, but rather a grief, but later on, on the other hand, being exercised/trained through it, it yields the peaceful fruit of righteousness.

[12] Therefore brace up drooping hands and weak knees [13] and make straight the paths of your feet, lest your limbs be put out of joint rather than being healed. [14] Pursue peace with everyone and holiness, without which no one will see the Lord, [15] watching lest someone misses the grace of God so that no root of bitterness grow up, cause trouble, and through it many are defiled, [16] (watch that) no one is immoral or godless as Esau, who in exchange for one dish of food, sold his birthright as eldest son. [17] For you see that also later on wishing to inherit the blessing he was rejected, for a place to change his mind/repent was not found, although he sought it with tears.

Hebrews 11:1 gives an apparent definition of faith. Quintilian says that a definition is a statement in appropriate and concise language of a fact called into question (*Institutio oratoria* 7.3.2; cf. *Rhetorica ad Herennium* 4.25.35). How we understand our definition hinges on the interpretation of two key terms: *hypostasis,* which we have met twice before (Heb 1:3; 3:14), and *elenchos,* which is a New Testament *hapax legomenon.* The debate about these words is that they may be taken in either an objective or subjective sense. *Hypostasis* has the objective sense of "substance" in Hebrews 1:3, but in Hebrews 3:14 it has the sense of "assurance." *Elenchos* can certainly have the objective sense of "evidence" or even "proof," but subjectively it seems to have the sense of the effect of firm evidence on one's belief—namely, internal "conviction." The meaning here can be determined only by context. The question can be put this way: does faith give substance to our hope, or is it that substance itself? Andrew Lincoln rightly objects to this view, for the realities our author is hoping for are already extant before we believe in them.[606] Our author does not think that faith makes God's promises real, and the text says nothing about giving substance to something; rather, it is telling us what faith *is.* Craig Koester puts it this way: "The author does not assume that things exist simply because people believe they exist. Human faith does not create divine reality, but divine reality creates human faith. The unseen realities of God give proof of their existence by their power to

---

[606] Lincoln, *Hebrews,* pp. 102-3.

evoke faith where otherwise there would only be unbelief."[607]

Here then I part company with Donald Hagner, who thinks that the objective rendering of both terms is the natural one here. He argues that faith gives substance to what is not seen by making appear in deeds that which is hoped for.[608] This could hardly be more wrong. Our author is not advocating a self-actualization program through faith. Faith does not make eschatological realities that already exist above in heaven and will eventually exist on earth "real." Nor is faith the substance of such eschatological realities, as if our author had trivialized eschatological realities by reducing them to the capacity to trust.[609] It cannot give them any substance or reality whatsoever. These realities already exist in heaven. Nor do Christian deeds manifest the resurrection or final epiphany of God that is yet to come. Further, our author does not say that faith expresses the reality of what it hopes for (whatever that might mean); he says that faith *is* the *hypostasis* and *elenchos*. True enough, faith involves both belief and behavior, but neither of these provides substance to eschatological realities. Rather, faith trusts in these realities and acts on the assurance that they are real and will come to pass. Luke Timothy Johnson plausibly suggests that *hypostasis* has the sense of "pledge" here, as it has in some papyri (Papyrus Elephantine 15.3; Papyrus Tebtunis 61[b].184). But a pledge is not the same as a down payment or first installment, as Johnson tries to suggest.[610]

In view of the examples that follow of faithful living based on confidence in God's word, it is surely more likely that *hypostasis* means something like subjective "assurance."[611] Faith provides the assurance about things to come that is necessary in order for one to go on living faithfully in the light of those hopes. Faith is something that assures us that God will be true to his word. While *hypostasis* can be translated in secular papyri as "guarantee" or "title deed" when the subject is real estate, if this is our author's meaning here, then he would be saying something similar to what Paul says about the Spirit being God's down payment or earnest of things to come (Rom 8:23; 2 Cor 1:22). I would not rule this

---

[607]Koester, *Hebrews*, p. 480.

[608]Hagner, *Encountering the Book of Hebrews*, p. 143.

[609]But see deSilva, *Perseverance in Gratitude*, p. 383. I do not agree with him that those who believe already have in hand "the essence" of what they seek. More promising is the idea that they have the "title deed" for what they seek (in light of the property discussion in Heb 10:34, *hypostasis* may have this meaning here). See Worley, "God's Faithfulness to Promise," pp. 87-92.

[610]Johnson, *Hebrews*, pp. 277-78.

[611]While in the Septuagint (Ruth 1:12; Ps 39:7; Ezek 19:5) *hypostasis* translates the Hebrew term for hope, our author is surely not merely talking about "the hope of things hoped for," which would be redundant. Craddock, *Hebrews*, p. 131, is right, however, that faith is seen as joining the subjective inner commitment of the trusting one with the object of faith and trust.

out, especially in view of evidence of Pauline influence elsewhere in Hebrews, but our author knows persons who have made shipwreck of their faith, of those who will not receive the guaranteed things, and so on the whole the idea of assurance or confidence is more probable.

Elenchos too can have an objective sense and be translated "proof" or "evidence," particularly in a rhetorical context (Demosthenes *Oration* 4.15; in *Rhetoric to Alexander* 1431a7-10 it refers to an irrefutable fact), but in the New Testament its cognates can mean "conviction" in either an objective or subjective sense—conviction of error (2 Tim 3:16) or of wrongdoing (Jn 8:46; Jas 2:9) is the objective sense, while conviction about something is the subjective sense.[612] One must again ask: is faith proof of the object that one believes in? Certainly not, for many have believed wrongly in false gods, but faith can amount to having a conviction about the unseen realities, and this is likely its meaning here. It is natural to take both words in tandem as two ways of speaking of the same thing and so to take them both either objectively or subjectively. Most translators agree, and I prefer the subjective rendering in view of what follows. There is one difference between the two parts of the definition: one speaks of the future things hoped for and so represents the horizontal eschatology, the other speaks of things not seen and so speaks in spatial rather than temporal terms of what is above but will one day come down. It is certain that our author believes that Christians and the Old Testament saints shall fully enter into the future inheritance now above only when Christ returns and they are raised, so the horizontal and temporal focus names the tune here. In the end, I agree with Michael R. Cosby's conclusion that we do not have a strict parallel construction here. Assurance and conviction are not two ways of speaking about exactly the same thing. Rather we have the rhetorical technique of amplification, not duplication. Faith involves assurance about the future, but it also involves conviction, deep belief about and in things not yet seen.[613] Our author is following the rhetorical advice about starting with definitions that are pithy and to the point, such that "it sets forth the full meaning and character [of the term in question] . . . so lucidly and briefly that to express it in more words seems superfluous, and to express it in fewer is considered impossible" (*Rhetorica ad Herennium* 4.25.35).

Offering up definitions of virtues is an essential part of epideictic rhetoric that

---

[612] Koester, *Hebrews*, p. 473, points out that the evidence for the rendering "conviction" in the subjective sense is slender, but since there is plenty of evidence for the objective sense of convicting someone else of something, it is a small further extension to speak about being convicted oneself. In addition, this is quite clearly how Clement of Alexandria understood the term in *Stromateis* 2.2.8-9.

[613] Cosby, *Rhetorical Composition and Function*, pp. 25-37.

seeks to present praiseworthy traits to the audience that they need to continue to embrace, and none is more crucial for an audience considering defecting than faith and faithfulness. The somewhat similar extolling of wisdom in Wisdom of Solomon 10.1—11.1 arranges its examples in a basic chronological order, and the praise of famous persons in Sirach 44.1—50.21 shows how this epideictic rhetoric works in a Jewish context where praise of humans has its limits (and so it is not surprising that here the praise starts with God as the ultimate exemplum of faithfulness and ends in Heb 12 with Christ as the same). The praise of humility in *1 Clement* 17—19 is most like our text, but the topic is different, and it may well be that *1 Clement* knows our text.[614] In any case, "this verse does not by any means exhaust what can be said of faith, even within Hebrews, but it does provide, in a highly focused and hence somewhat paradoxical way, the essential characteristics that inform our author's understanding."[615]

Hebrews 11:2 says that for/by this faith our ancestors were testified to, using the passive verb *emartyrēthēsan*. Our author does not, however, have in mind human testimony to the faith of the saints, but God's attestation to their faith in Scripture itself.[616] These attested ones become the "witnesses" of Hebrews 12:1.[617] This theme of being witnessed about or attested to appears again in Hebrews 11:39, and in both texts the verb is sometimes rendered "commended," but here the connection between faith and bearing witness even unto death must dictate the translation. It carries the overtone of being praised for something.[618] The honorific use of the term *hoi presbyteroi* shows that the ancient worthies, "the elders" in the faith, will provide example and flesh out what is meant by faith here.

It is striking that our author begins his faith list in **Hebrews 11:3** not with a human example but an example from God's creative work. The doctrine of *creatio ex nihilo* was not one the Greeks and many others accepted, but it was found in early Judaism (2 Maccabees 7.28; Wisdom of Solomon 11.17; Philo *On the Life of Moses* 2.267).[619] Most believed in the eternality of matter in some form. Our author here indicates that we understand and accept this idea of God's word creating something out of nothing only by faith, since we were not there

---

[614]I see this as one more small piece of evidence that Hebrews is not from the last decade or two of the first century, but does have Rome as its provenance.

[615]Attridge, *Hebrews*, pp. 307-8.

[616]Koester, *Hebrews*, p. 473.

[617]Lane, *Hebrews*, 2.328.

[618]DeSilva, *Perseverance in Gratitude*, p. 385.

[619]Lane, *Hebrews*, 2.332, is quite right that our author is following neither Plato nor Philo here, both of which speak of creation as a fashioning of preexistent stuff. He quite clearly says "not out of anything observable."

to see, though the Son was there and a part of it. This faith is in focus at various points in this passage, for what our author wants us to have faith in is not something that will inevitably happen due to the historical process, but something that will come down from above, as Ernst Käsemann points out.[620] Here, though, our author is thinking of God's faithfulness as exhibited from Genesis 1 to Joshua 6.[621] The seen universe was created from the invisible spoken word of God, but one can understand this only "by faith."[622] This first example of "by faith" is more generic, applied to both the author and his audience as a whole, whereas what follows gives specific examples of individuals who exercised faith.[623]

A CLOSER LOOK
The Use of Examples in Epideictic Rhetoric

Though it was more of a commonplace in deliberative rhetoric, examples would be trotted out for praise or blame also in epideictic rhetoric, even to the extent of providing lists of examples of praiseworthy or blameworthy behavior. Such examples in epideictic rhetoric served the function of reinforcing values or virtues already embraced by the audience in the past, though perhaps more tenuously in the present. Aristotle reminds us that "all orators produce belief by employing as proofs either examples or enthymemes and nothing else" (*Rhetoric* 1.2.8). This statement is especially apropos for epideictic rhetoric, which does not require that a case be laid out in full to make some point, with detailed syllogistic or logical argument. Rather, by example and enthymeme, both of which are found aplenty in Hebrews 11, the audience is persuaded to continue to embrace core values already affirmed.

Examples fall under the heading of argument or proof by similitude: "The adducing of some past action real or assumed that may serve to persuade the audience of the truth of the point that we are trying to make" (*Institutio oratoria* 5.11.6). Quintilian says that before using examples, one must consider whether the parallel is partial or complete, and if it is partial then naturally one will want to refer to the part that helps inculcate or promote the continuance of the desired behavior. Arguing from "the like" is deemed more effective when one is dealing with virtues, and arguing from "the unlike" when one is trying to help the audience to avoid some sort of behavior by way of exhor-

[620]Käsemann, *Wandering People of God.*
[621]Craddock, *Hebrews*, p. 129.
[622]Koester, *Hebrews*, p. 474.
[623]Hagner, *Encountering the Book of Hebrews*, p. 144.

tation (5.11.10). This rhetorical way of dividing examples is said to be the same in deliberative rhetoric or in panegyric (5.11.8).

Quintilian goes on to stress that examples may be used to serve a "from the lesser to the greater argument" or vice versa. So, for example, here the net effect of saying that all of these persons were able to act on faith and be faithful is that if even lesser Old Testament saints can manage this without Christian advantages such as the Holy Spirit, so too can the audience of Hebrews. Aristotle advises the use of lists of examples, and the more illustrious the list, the better (*Rhetoric* 2.23.1). Michael R. Cosby notes that there was no set literary form for an example list of famous persons, nevertheless providing examples (plural) of virtues or vices was common enough as a tool of persuasion to begin or continue certain kinds of conduct.[624]

In the Jewish tradition, what is being praised in general is not so much the person in himself/herself or as a whole, but some commendable spiritual quality or behavior that needs to be emulated. For example, in 2 Esdras (4 Ezra) 7.106-11 Abraham, Moses, Joshua, Samuel and David provide an example of prayer. Our list is like this, as our author is not interested in creating a cult of personality, but rather in encouraging the continued exercise of faith like these previous examples. Cosby points out that one of the cleverer parts of the rhetoric here is that our author creates the impression at the end, simply by mentioning names, that he could go on and on listing examples: "And what more shall I say? I do not have time to tell about Gideon, Barak, . . ." (Heb 11:32).[625] Craig Koester says: "Rapidly listing examples impresses upon listeners the breadth of material that supports the author's point. Showing how person after person manifests faith gives the impression that many more examples could be added. . . . The author assumes that listeners are familiar with the OT figures, so that citing only a few details will call a story to mind and focus attention on the relevant point."[626]

This technique works only if the audience is not only already familiar with these examples, but finds them admirable. In other words, this passage tells us a lot about the Jewish Christian audience and how the rhetoric of praising famous persons of Jewish faith works. Our author is not asking the audience to do anything other than emulate what they already find admirable. The call to faith is not a call to some new or foreign course of conduct, and the exempli of faith cited are familiar ones that do not require extensive rhetorical window dressing for the audience to embrace them and their virtues. Examples, then, in the encomium of faith can be short and pithy and to the point, hoping to

---

[624]Cosby, *Rhetorical Composition and Function*, pp. 18-21.
[625]Ibid.
[626]Koester, *Hebrews*, p. 470.

overwhelm the audience with the great cloud of witnesses. In one sense this passage functions indirectly like the encouragement of Paul to the Corinthians when, after using other Old Testament negative examples, he adds in 1 Corinthians 10 that no temptation has overcome them that is not common to humanity, so that they can persevere and escape misbehavior. In both 1 Corinthians 10 and Hebrews 11, it is the common behavior, the behavior that all believers can exhibit when called upon, that is lauded, not some behavior that only the exceptional can manifest. Faith and faithfulness is such common behavior with a multitude of examples.

In the end, what is most striking about the use of the Old Testament examples in Hebrews 11 is that, while the term *faith* is applied to two dozen people, not all of them are singled out in the Old Testament itself as examples of faith/faithfulness (Abraham was singled out in this regard in Genesis). Our author brings this perspective to the Old Testament text in order to make his point. In keeping with the principles of epideictic rhetoric, so that all of the audience could be included in the implied exhortation, our author has in mind here the most generic sort of faith—true biblical faith, not specifically Christian faith, a sort of faith and faithfulness that Jesus himself is made the preeminent example of at the end of the hall of faith.

Beginning in **Hebrews 11:4** our author turns to particular historical examples. "The names cluster into four groups of ancestors; each of the first three groups foreshadows one of the faithful virtues that comes to perfection in Jesus. Like Jesus, these forebears in the faith were (1) righteous; (2) journeyed obediently in faith; (3) were tested by suffering. The fourth group, a rapid-fire listing of events and names, is a mixture of the three virtues."[627] It becomes evident that the examples are chosen not due to any biographical interest but because these persons model certain Christlike virtues, which rhetorically speaking is the right reason to mention them in an encomium on faith and faithfulness.

Since he could not use Adam and Eve as examples of faith, our author begins with the first figure in Genesis that could be said to be such an example—Abel. Abel offered a greater sacrifice than Cain. Genesis 4:2-10 does not say that his sacrifice was greater, nor does it mention his faith. How then are we to understand "greater"—greater in quantity or simply better? Some conjecture that more was meant, some that a more adequate sacrifice was offered because it was a blood sacrifice (Philo *On the Sacrifices of Cain and Abel* 88;

---

[627]Long, *Hebrews*, p. 115.

Josephus *Jewish Antiquities* 1.54), but F. F. Bruce says that this sacrifice was more adequate because of the faith and righteousness involved, not due to quantity or type of sacrifice.[628] God's pleasure in the gift shows that it was offered in the right spirit; the acceptance of the sacrifice attested that he was a righteous one. David deSilva suggests that the virtue behind the sacrifice, the trust in God, makes it acceptable and makes Abel a model of such virtue in our author's eyes.[629] Even though Abel is dead, his example still speaks to us.[630] This may be an echo of the Genesis story, which says that Abel's blood cried out from the ground to God (Gen 4:10; Heb 12:24), but here it is his example of faith and righteousness that continues to speak after his death. In Matthew 23:35 and 1 John 3:12 Abel is referred to as righteous, as the first example of a righteous martyr. But while there is a foreshadowing of Jesus here, Thomas Long notes that Hebrews 12:24 reminds us that Jesus offered a better word than the blood of Abel: "Abel's blood cries out for revenge, but Jesus' blood brings an end to vengeance and grants forgiveness (9:22; 10:10)."[631] Walter Moberly suggests that Abel's blood, if he is seen as a prototype of Christ here, cries out for mercy on his brother Cain, a mercy that God shows Cain, just as Christ's blood pleads for mercy on us all.[632] In what sense does Abel's blood still speak today? The most reasonable suggestion is that Christ's blood speaks a "better word" in the sense of a more comprehensive and effective plea for mercy. Throughout the discourse, our author has been comparing what is good with what is better (e.g., angels and Christ, Moses and Christ), and this comparison may well be in play between Abel's and Christ's blood. That our author says "Abel speaks" may suggest that he, like Philo, views Abel as still alive (the righteous like Abel "live an incorporeal life"; *Questions and Answers on Genesis* 1.70).

Next in line for comment in **Hebrews 11:5** is Enoch, whom the Bible says walked with God (i.e., obeyed him, followed his ways) and was taken up from earth without experiencing death (*1 Enoch* 12.3; 15.1; *2 Enoch* 22.8; 71.14; *Ju-*

---

[628]Bruce, *Hebrews*, pp. 285-86.

[629]DeSilva, *Perseverance in Gratitude*, p. 388.

[630]Koester, *Hebrews*, p. 476, points out that our author assumes Abel is still dead, even though he is an exemplar of faith. This speaks volumes about our author's theology of the afterlife, which does not primarily consist in the concept of "dying and going to heaven." Enoch is seen as exceptional under this schema of afterlife thinking. DeSilva *Perseverance in Gratitude*, p. 389, is mistaken in seeing Abel as an example like Enoch of one who lives on in heaven. The text literally reads, "Through it [i.e., faith], having died, yet he speaks." See Lane, *Hebrews*, 2.335.

[631]Long, *Hebrews*, p. 116.

[632]Moberly, "Exemplars of Faith."

bilees 4.23; 10.17; 19.24-27; Josephus *Jewish Antiquities* 1.85).[633] Our author seems to know not only Genesis 5:24, which he partially quotes, but perhaps also the various traditions about Enoch found in Sirach 44.16; *1 Enoch* 70; Wisdom of Solomon 4.10; and elsewhere, though he shows far more restrain in what he does with this tradition than does *1-2 Enoch* (also *1 Clement* 9.2-3).[634] Our author says that Enoch was pleasing to God, as is obviously shown by his "translation" to heaven.[635] The Septuagint speaks of Enoch's being pleasing, which in turn is the basis of assuming that Enoch must have had faith, since without faith one cannot please God.

Hebrews 11:6 states a principle that is true for all the examples: without faith it is impossible to please God. The reference to the impossible is familiar by now (Heb 6:4, 18; 10:4), as is the form of this inferential argument (Heb 6:16; 7:12; 9:22), which is enthymematic in character. Since it is impossible to please God without faith, therefore Enoch must have had faith, even though the text of Genesis does not mention it directly. Here faith is defined as believing that God exists and that he rewards those who seek him out.[636] Again, a generic definition of faith could apply to the Old Testament saints as well as to the New Testament saints. By implication, our author believes that once Christ comes, it is impossible to please God fully without belief in him. Donald Hagner stresses that the reality of the unseen and the coming of the hope are major themes throughout this chapter, as the author uses different means to talk about the same reality—a city to come, a heavenly country, events yet unseen, a heavenly reward.[637] All of this indicates that faith has an inherently prospective aspect, whereas especially in Paul the main emphasis when faith is discussed is faith in the completed or partially present work of Christ. So does our author believe that heaven is a reward, or only that there are rewards in heaven for the faithful? It is probably the latter. Less likely is the suggestion that our author is referring to rewards here and now for those who seek God.[638]

According to **Hebrews 11:7** Noah was instructed concerning the coming

---

[633]Attridge, *Hebrews*, pp. 317-18.

[634]Craddock, *Hebrews*, p. 133.

[635]The emphasis on being "taken up" (the root form of the word appears three times in Heb 11:5) is not surprising since Enoch is a prototype of Christ whose "translation" is also stressed in Hebrews.

[636]*Misthapodotēs* ("rewarder") is found only here in the Bible. It is, however, a cognate form of *misthapodosia* ("recompense, payback"), which occurs at Heb 2:2; 10:35; 11:26. For the concept of rewarding the holy for their efforts, see Wisdom of Solomon 10.17.

[637]Hagner, *Encountering the Book of Hebrews*, p. 146.

[638]Johnson, *Hebrews*, p. 284.

judgment, and so he built an ark that saved his family. *Sōtēria* has the sense of rescue or keep safe; it does not refer to eternal salvation here.[639] This comports with the notion in Hebrews that salvation brings rest. Also, *eulabētheis* here suggests that Noah reacted to God's word to him about judgment with reverence or religious awe—with the fear of the Lord that prompts godly and obedient action.[640] But Noah's "folly" turned out to be a symbol of God's judgment on the rest of the world.[641] This is very similar to the argument in 1 Peter 3:19-22, which refers to those who were by faith righteous and so are inheritors. Noah is not, however, portrayed here as a preacher of repentance (as in 2 Pet 2:5 and *1 Clement* 7.6). Here the seed idea found in Habakkuk 2:4 is reused again in a fashion somewhat similar to Paul's usage. Only here is the "unseen" something threatening, namely judgment, rather than something that is promising. But there is analogy with the situation of the audience of Hebrews, for our author has warned them that they live in the shadow of the coming day of judgment (Heb 10:25, 36-37).[642] This analogy reminds us once more that our author is primarily holding out for his audience an eschatological prospect of recompense or judgment, not otherworldly compensation. "Like Noah, the addressees are to use their time and resources in this life to prepare for salvation at the day of judgment, at the return of Christ."[643] The phrase at the end of the verse—"he became an inheritor of the righteousness that comes by faith"—certainly sounds Pauline, and while *kata pistin* is used here instead of the Pauline *ek pisteōs* we still probably have another hint that our author is familiar with Galatians and/ or Romans.[644] This becomes all the more likely when we consider the next example chosen—Abraham. Here "righteousness" probably refers to the right standing one obtains on the last day—in other words, final justification or righteousness.

Our author then proceeds in Hebrews 11:8-19 to use the example of Old Testament faith par excellence—Abraham, choosing three episodes from his life.

---

[639] DeSilva, *Perseverance in Gratitude*, p. 391. On the mostly future sense of the term *sōtēria* in Hebrews, see Marshall, "Soteriology in Hebrews."

[640] Attridge, *Hebrews*, p. 319.

[641] On Noah's righteousness see Gen 6:9; 7:1; Ezek 14:14, 20; Sirach 44.17; Wisdom of Solomon 10.4. Here it would appear that his faith in God is the judgment on the world.

[642] DeSilva, *Perseverance in Gratitude*, p. 391.

[643] Ibid.

[644] The term *dikaiosynē* has here the sense of "right standing" that it has in Paul at various points in Galatians and Romans (e.g., Rom 3:21-26), rather than the more sapiential use of the term found in James. Alternatively, this phrase may mean that Noah's faith enabled him to live righteously and obediently to God. But if that was meant, we would hardly expect the term *inherit* here, which suggests a future obtaining of something or some condition or status.

This is not the first time he has used Abraham as an example (Heb 6:13-15).[645] More space is given to Abraham than to anyone else, including Jesus, in this hall of faith. The phrase *by faith* is applied to Abraham four times (Heb 11:8, 9, 11, 17). But our author also pauses to generalize the lesson about the virtues and example of Abraham in Hebrews 11:13-16, where he reflects on the life of faith as the life of an alien or sojourner on earth.[646] Our author stands in a long Jewish tradition that sets forth Abraham as an ideal or paradigm (Gen 12—22; Sirach 44.19-21; Wisdom of Solomon 10.5; 1 Maccabees 2.52; Philo's two treatises on Abraham: *On the Migration of Abraham* and *On the Life of Abraham*; Gal 3:6-9; Rom 4; Acts 7:2-8; *1 Clement* 10). Our author stands in the sapiential stream of this tradition, for he uses this story to inculcate virtues and good behavior; but equally, he also stands on the Christian side of the interpretation of these stories, for like Paul he stresses Abraham's trust or faith as leading to his acceptability to God, whereas in some Jewish treatments Abraham's obedience is what lead to his right standing with God.[647]

Abraham's faith is demonstrated in his obedience to what God commanded him to do, as well as in his trust in God's promise. Our author takes his trip to the promised land and his nomadic existence there as a sign that Abraham knew there was a greater reality, a city with real foundations above. In **Hebrews 11:8** our author deliberately uses the term *place* rather than *land* to speak of what was promised to Abraham, a term that had already been used in this sermon with positive effect.[648] Our author is not alone in interpreting the promises to Abraham as involving a city. Philo, for example, says that Abraham's motivation for what he did involved "a city good and large and prosperous" (*Allegorical Interpretation* 3.83). Later tradition speaks of a city prepared by God before the beginning of time and shown to Adam, Abraham and Moses (*2 Baruch* 4). Our author stands in the same line of thinking as found in 2 Esdras (4 Ezra) 7.26; 8.52; 10.27; 13.36; Galatians 4:26; Revelation 21:2-19, which refers to a heavenly city that will come down to earth (Ps 87:1-2; 48:8 speaks of the earthly Jerusalem whose foundations are said to be laid forever).

Hebrews 11:9 calls the Holy Land the "land of promise," an interesting phrase found only here in Scripture. It may be worded this way because our author sees the Holy Land not merely as a place where some divine promises come true, but also as the land that figures forth a greater place in which God

[645]Longenecker, "Faith of Abraham."
[646]Craddock, *Hebrews*, p. 135.
[647]See the discussion in Witherington, *Grace in Galatia*, on Gal 3—4.
[648]Craddock, *Hebrews*, p. 136.

intends for his people to dwell. This interpretation is confirmed in **Hebrews 11:10**, where we are told flatly that the promise to Abraham was not completely fulfilled by take possession of a piece of dirt (cf. Ps 105:11). No, a city designed and built by God would be the ultimate fulfillment of the promise. Using a poignant contrast between the temporary tent home of Abraham and the permanent city he was looking forward to,[649] our author's perspective is especially clear from the use of the term *paroikeō* ("to reside as an alien"): Abraham resided as an alien in the promised land, clear proof that he "still had not found what he was looking for."[650] Abraham immigrated to a land of promise, but lived in it as if he had still not reached his destination, as if the land belonged to another. Typical epideictic praise rhetoric for cities involved praising their founders and fortification (Quintilian *Institutio oratoria* 3.7.26-27), just as here.

Our author sees Isaac and Jacob as fellow heirs of this promise and as fellow resident aliens (Heb 11:9, 20-21), and he also believes that obedience is an essential component of faith or at least the proper way to act out one's faith and show one's faithfulness. God alone is the creator of that city; Abraham did not go to Israel to build it. The terms *technitēs* ("designer") and *dēmiourgos* ("builder") are applied to God only here in Scripture, but this terminology builds on Psalm 87:1; Isaiah 33:20; 54:11. This is the same sort of language used in early Judaism of God in his creation of the world or material realm (Josephus *Jewish Antiquities* 1.155; Philo *On the Creation of the World* 18-20, 146).[651] The language clearly implies that God was dealing with material stuff. In other words, the language is not suggesting that God has built or is building a city made out of some sort of nonmaterial or heavenly substance, to coin an oxymoron. This city is heavenly in origin, but it will become part of the material realm at the eschaton. This is why at Hebrews 13:14 it is called the city that is to come, and people are said to enter it through the resurrection of the dead, not merely by dying. And Hebrews 11:19 intimates that Isaac's deliverance from death foreshadows the resurrection of the faithful.

---

[649] Buchanan, *Hebrews*, pp. 188-89, suggests that the author of Hebrews is envisioning repossessing the land of Israel and rebuilding earthly Jerusalem. Our author, however, gives no hint that the city is at present destroyed. Buchanan is right in one sense: while our author does not envision the rebuilding of the city, he does envision a heavenly city coming down to earth, presumably centered in the Holy Land. He is not envisioning the promise to Abraham being fulfilled "in heaven."

[650] Koester, *Hebrews*, p. 483.

[651] Attridge, *Hebrews*, p. 324.

A CLOSER LOOK
Resident Aliens in Their Own City

This whole way of discussing the matter is especially appropriate for an urban audience, and doubly so for those who lived in the so-called eternal city—Rome.[652] But there is perhaps another nuance as well here. Jewish residents in Rome, especially those who were not Roman citizens, would have viewed their status as being like that of resident aliens in the capital, no matter how long they had lived there, and this is the way others would likely have viewed them as well. Seneca says of such persons: "The majority of them are aliens . . . most of them you will find have left home and come to Rome, the greatest and loveliest city in the world—but not theirs" (*Ad Helviam* 6.2-3).

In Hebrews 10:32-34 we learn that many in our author's audience had suffered public insult, persecution, jailing and confiscation of property. This treatment was far more likely to happen to resident aliens than to citizens of a major metropolis in the Roman Empire.[653] But we must factor in one more thing—the audience of this homily is Jews. Even those who had citizenship could suddenly find it rescinded, and Philo reports that this very thing happened a couple of decades before in Alexandria, where there were even more, and more prominent, Jews than in Rome:

> When his attack against our laws, by seizing the meeting houses without even leaving them their name, appeared to be successful, he proceeded to another scheme, namely the dismantling of our citizenship so that when our ancestral customs and our participation in political rights, the sole mooring on which our life was secured, had been cut away, we might undergo the worst misfortunes with no rope to cling to for safety. For a few days afterward he issued a proclamation in which he denounced us as foreigners and aliens [*xenous kai epelydas*] and gave us no right of pleading our case but condemned us unjudged. . . . And then to the first two wrongs he added a third by permitting those who wished to pillage the Jews as if at a sacking of a city. (*Against Flaccus* 53-55)

This clearly portrays the tenuous situation that Jews could find themselves in when considerable resentment had built up against them in a major city. Even citizenship would not protect them from such abuse in various cases. It is altogether likely that our author's rhetoric here should be seen as pointed and on the mark, making clear how his audience's condition was not unlike that of many of these listed in the hall of faith, who found themselves resident

---

[652]Koester, *Hebrews*, pp. 494-95.
[653]See the helpful discussion in deSilva, *Perseverance in Gratitude*, pp. 394-95.

aliens even in places given or promised to them. This could be doubly the case for Jewish Christians in Rome, since they were both part of the Christian superstition and ethnically Jewish. The rulings of Claudius, Nero's predecessor, in 42 and 49 had led to Jews being abused and marginalized and to Jewish Christians being expelled in 49 from Rome.

The Greco-Roman world was a highly stratified social world in which clear distinctions were made between relatives, citizens, enemies and foreigners, with the latter category only slightly less tenuous than that of enemies (Philo *On the Special Laws* 4.70). Just how tenuous foreigner status was, especially if they were expelled from a country as a foreigner—as some Jewish Christians in Rome had been in 49—is readily seen in a man threatened with being expelled as a foreigner pleading with an official not to "make me a man without a country, do not cut me off from such a host of relatives, and bring me to utter ruin. Rather than abandon them . . . I will kill myself, that at least I may be buried by them in my homeland" (Demosthenes *Against Eubulides* 70). This man was apparently not a foreigner, but his fear of being treated like one is palpable. To be sure, resident aliens were treated somewhat differently than transient foreigners, but the social boundary between these two categories, even in Rome, was not great, and in a time of crisis both categories were treated alike. This flew in the face of the rhetoric of Roman emperors and the empire, which promoted the notion that Rome was "the single homeland of all the races" (Pliny the Elder *Natural History* 3.5.49; cf. Josephus *Jewish Antiquities* 20.11). We will have occasion to discuss the issue of Jewish resident aliens in more detail in the discussion of 1 Peter in *Letters and Homilies for Hellenized Christians, Volume 2*.

The language that our author uses to describe Abraham, and the prominent attention he is given in this hall of faith, provides a reminder that the audience is not only Jewish but also part of a tiny minority sect of Jews in Rome that had already had much misfortune befall them in the recent past and anticipated more such treatment—hence the need for urging them to remain faithful and not commit apostasy. The rhetorical strategy of our author is then twofold: (1) to ground them in their own heritage and show how many examples of faithfulness had preceded their own opportunity to "go and do likewise" (the implicit message is that if all these witnesses could do it, so could our author's audience) and (2) to remind them not to place their hopes in earthly things like land and Roman citizenship, but rather to look forward to the promised eschatological city that was to come when Jesus came back and the dead were raised. Heritage and eschatology then are praised and given as a basis for current virtue and future faithfulness for this audience. We must assume that this rhetorical strategy worked to some degree, or this document, especially in view of its anonymity, would hardly have been preserved as it was in the Roman community. Yet we should not underestimate the pressure on these converts to revert to their previous lifestyle and life. David deSilva writes that "apostasy would provide the surest route back to favor within the unbelieving society."[654] Yet apparently most of the audience resisted this temptation. Once Nero designated Christians as responsible for the fire in 64, though being a non-Christian Jew would be only relatively better than being a Christian one, it certainly would be safer than remaining a Christian, especially if one was of relatively high social status and had property, family and business investments at risk.

The second episode from Abraham's life that is an example of faith is the trust that both Abraham and Sarah had to have in order to conceive a child by normal means, despite their great age and Sarah's barrenness. The word translated "as good as dead" is also applied to Abraham in Romans 4:19, another hint that both writers shared a common tradition or, more likely, that our author, as already suggested, had read or knew some of Paul's letters, specifically Galatians, 1 Corinthians and Romans. There is debate about how to render **Hebrews 11:11**, and translations vary between ascribing faith to Sarah (e.g., "by faith Sarah was enabled to conceive") and suggesting that she is mentioned only in passing (e.g., "by faith Abraham received power of procreation even though he was as good as dead, and Sarah herself was barren").[655] Several factors lead to a decision on this matter:

1. Hebrews 11:11 literally reads "received power for the laying down of seed," which under any normal circumstances refers to the male act of procreation (*Greek Apocalypse of Ezra* 5.12).

2. In Genesis 18 Sarah is hardly portrayed as an example of faith.

3. There is uncertainty as to whether the noun *Sarah* is in the nominative or dative case, the difference being only a subscript iota, which would not have been present in the original manuscript since it was written in all capital letters and had no such markings. If it is a dative of accompaniment, then it can be rendered "together with barren Sarah, he received power to procreate."

4. Sarah is mentioned first after *pistei*, so on first blush it appears that she is at least included in the statement "by faith," but Abraham is equally clearly the subject of Hebrews 11:12, as the gender of the term *one* there demonstrates.[656]

---

[654]DeSilva, *Despising Shame*, p. 186.
[655]For all the scribal emendations and conjectures, see Swetnam, *Jesus and Isaac*, pp. 98-101.
[656]Greenlee, "Hebrews 11:11."

One must conclude then that while the focus is on Abraham's faith, Sarah is included in the statement about being empowered to have a child.[657]

Hebrews 11:12 paraphrases Genesis 22:17, which is also used in Romans 4:16-18 to include Gentiles. Our author does not mention Gentiles, focusing entirely on Jews in this hall of faith. He simply amplifies by two analogies the nature of the promise of descendants: they will be as numerous as the stars in the sky or the grains of sand on the beach. By implication, our author is referring to those who like Abraham exhibit faith and faithfulness.

There is a sense in which Abraham by receiving Isaac received a foretaste of the promise, or a first installment. In **Hebrews 11:13** our author says not only that these patriarchs died in faith but that they had not, properly speaking, received the promise, but had only seen it and saluted it from afar, thereby indicating that they were strangers/foreigners and settlers/Bedouins upon the earth (Gen 23:4; 24:37; 1 Chron 29:15; Ps 39:12; 1 Pet 2:11).[658] They were still seeking the true homeland in **Hebrews 11:14** and will not inherit except when all do at the eschaton (Heb 11:40). Thomas Long tells how French travelers journeying over the Pyrenees in the Middle Ages on pilgrimage for the Cathedral of St. James in Spain vied for the front position in the group so that whoever got the first glimpse of the great cathedral could shout "my joy."[659] This same cry of joy by the pilgrim glimpsing his or her destination can already be seen in Virgil's *Aeneid* 3.524. Something similar is in view in Hebrews 11:13. Fred Craddock is right that our author takes a salvation-history perspective and does not allegorize the Old Testament stories, unlike Philo.[660] But the promises made to Abraham and the other patriarchs *are* relativized and are not considered to be the full meaning of what God had in mind for them; apparently we are meant to think that Abraham realized this when he chose to live in the promised land, as though it were just the land of future promises.

Hebrews 11:15 contains a hypothetical condition: if the patriarchs had Mesopotamia in mind they would have simply returned to their earthly home, but they

---

[657]Johnson, *Hebrews*, pp. 291-92, makes the strongest case yet for Sarah being the subject here.
[658]The concept of Christians being resident aliens upon the earth continued to develop well after New Testament times as a way of helping Christians live with a sense of detachment from the dominant cultural value system and at the same time a sense of anticipation of longing for something better that was yet to be seen on earth. The postapostolic-era document *Letter of Diognetus* 5.5 says that Christians "inhabit their own lands, but as resident aliens; they take part in all things as citizens, but they endure all things as aliens. Every foreign land is a fatherland, and every fatherland is a foreign land." See the discussion in deSilva, *Perseverance in Gratitude*, p. 402.
[659]Long, *Hebrews*, p. 119.
[660]Craddock, *Hebrews*, p. 137.

were looking for a greater place. This counterfactual argument helps establish the point in **Hebrews 11:16** that the patriarchs considered themselves to be aliens not because they longed to return to their homeland but because they aspired to or yearned for[661] a better heavenly city, where God would not be ashamed to be called their God.[662] This whole concept of God being proud or ashamed of his people tells us something significant about our author's worldview, where honor and shame were far more important categories than life and death. Better to die prematurely in the good graces of God than to live a long life of which God was ashamed. In this case God is not ashamed of the patriarchs, because they did not settle for an ordinary inheritance but in faith looked forward to a better one.[663]

Hebrews 11:17 contains the third episode from Abraham's life that shows faith: the willingness to sacrifice Isaac, his only son, begotten by Sarah. The verb *prosenēnochen* may be an inceptive imperfect: "he began to offer." Jewish traditions about the Aqedah or binding of Isaac do not appear to be reflected here (Wisdom of Solomon 10.5; Sirach 44.20; *Jubilees* 17.15-18; 18.16;[664] Judith 8.25-26; 4 Maccabees 13.12; 16.20; Philo *On the Life of Abraham* 167-207; Mishnah, tractate *Avot* 3.5), for our author says nothing about this offering being some kind of atoning work. The use of "only son" in Hebrews rather than "beloved son" as in Genesis 22:2 emphasizes that the promise could be fulfilled only through Isaac, the only legitimate son. This was a severe test, as **Hebrews 11:18** makes clear, because it seemed to go flatly against the divine promise made about Isaac in Genesis 21:12 (compare the handling of this story in Jas 2:21-23).[665] God put Abraham to this test. Why then did Abraham go through with it, if it was so contrary to God's previous promise (here Gen 21:12 is partially cited)? Because, says our author, Abraham reckoned that God could raise Isaac again from the dead. This conclusion is based on Abraham telling his servants that he *and Isaac* would return from the mountain. This may amount to allegorizing, or our author may have seen a portent of Christ's death and resurrection in this act, in which case his handling of the story does become an allusion to the Aqedah.[666] In Romans 4:17-21 Paul also refers to the birth of Isaac as life

---

[661]*Oregomai* refers to a deep longing or yearning and is found elsewhere in the New Testament only at 1 Tim 3:1; 6:10.

[662]Attridge, *Hebrews*, p. 331.

[663]Koester, *Hebrews*, p. 490.

[664]In *Jubilees* it is not God who tested Abraham but rather an evil figure; see Koester, *Hebrews*, p. 491.

[665]Hagner, *Encountering the Book of Hebrews*, p. 150. On the Aqedah tradition, see Daly, "Soteriological Significance of the Sacrifice of Isaac."

[666]Bockmuehl, "Exemplars of Faith," calls this the clearest reference to the Aqedah in the New Testament. If so, these ideas are not much in play in the New Testament.

from the dead.[667] The word *parable* in **Hebrews 11:19** has its rhetorical sense and means "figuratively speaking," but Abraham really—and not merely figuratively—received Isaac back. Abraham received him back from the dead in that the ram became the substitute for the required sacrifice and was sacrificed. Alternately, our author may mean that this act prefigured the coming great resurrection of Christ.[669] In any case, the testing was severe: "By leaving his father's house, Abraham gave up his past; by sacrificing Isaac, Abraham would give up his future."[670]

Hebrews 11:20-22 concludes this paragraph with reference to Isaac's blessing of his two sons, Jacob's blessing of his two grandchildren[671] when at the end of his life and leaning on his staff[672] (partially citing Gen 48:15-16),[673] and Joseph's foreseeing the exodus from Egypt and asking that his bones be carried back to the promised land when that happened (Ex 13:19; Josh 24:32; Acts 7:16). The key link between these three examples is that blessing requires faith that there will be a future, as does giving orders about one's future bones.[674] Thomas Long says that Joseph "staring into the grave . . . saw grace."[675] "From these aspects of the patriarch's life, the addressees are to learn that God's promise is more certain than death, and that the person of faith need not flinch before any hardship."[676] It is in every way appropriate in epideictic rhetoric that the author should hold up examples of faith and hope in the face of death and discourse on the relationship of the one to the other.

Beginning with **Hebrews 11:23** our author offers a new section of his catalogue that summarizes further examples and finally binds all the examples together with Christians to participate in the realization of God's promises. The pattern for both Abraham and Moses is four episodes directly connected with the primary figure, followed by three episodes about subordinates or descendants of the chief figure. In Abraham's case those three are Isaac, Jacob and Joseph, while in Moses' case it involves the Israelites (Heb 11:29), the

---

[667]Craddock, *Hebrews*, p. 138.
[668]Chrysostom recognizes that "parable" means "rhetorical figure"; *Homilies on Hebrews* 25.3.
[669]Lane, *Hebrews*, 2.362-63; and Attridge, *Hebrews*, p. 335.
[670]Koester, *Hebrews*, p. 499.
[671]Hagner, *Encountering the Book of Hebrews*, p. 151, points out that blessing his grandchildren rather than his sons shows Jacob once more playing favorites.
[672]This bowing could be seen as a gesture of worship; see Koester, *Hebrews*, p. 493.
[673]The issue is what pointing the Masoretic Text takes: the same consonants (*mth*) can produce the word *bed* or *staff*. The Septuagint version of Gen 47:31 follows the latter reading.
[674]DeSilva, *Perseverance in Gratitude*, p. 404, rightly notes how closely our author follows the Septuagint version of Gen 50:26, even in his choice of words to speak of Joseph's "dying."
[675]Long, *Hebrews*, p. 121.
[676]DeSilva, *Perseverance in Gratitude*, p. 405.

walls of Jericho (Heb 11:30) and Rahab (Heb 11:31).[677]

In Hebrews 11:23-28 the example of Moses is held up at some length, and it is quite clear that our author is following the Septuagint version of the exodus story because Exodus 2 in the Septuagint mentions parents (the Masoretic Text says "mother") and the beauty of the child. Moses and Abraham are clearly the two major figures held up as examples of faith, and each case uses the formula "by faith" four times and mentions four specific acts of faith.[678]

Hebrews 11:23 is not about Moses' faith but about that of his parents.[679] The question is what to make of the word *asteion,* found only here and in Acts 7:20. In the Septuagint it is part of a phrase *beautiful before God,* which suggests not simply physical beauty but being well pleasing to God, as Acts 7:20 may also suggest. We are perhaps meant to think that Moses' folks saw something special in him and so hid him, defying the edict of Pharaoh. Chrysostom assumes that physical beauty is meant and adds: "The very sight of him drew them on to faith. Thus from the beginning—yes from the very swaddling clothes—great was the grace that was poured out on that righteous man, this not being the work of nature. For observe, the child immediately on its birth appears fair and not disagreeable to the sight. Whose work was this? Not that of nature but of the grace of God" (*Homilies on Hebrews* 26.3). Moses has already been held up as a paradigm of faithfulness at Hebrews 3:2-5, which is in line with the fourfold reiteration of the phrase *by faith* in this subsection.[680]

Hebrews 11:24 indicates a deduction on the basis of Moses being identified with the oppressed Israelites and taking up the cause of one who was beaten, even though he had become a son of Pharaoh's daughter and so a royal heir (Ex 2:10). The direct refusal of a title is not mentioned in the Old Testament. In **Hebrews 11:25** Moses is a figure who refuses short-term gains or short-lived pleasure of sin, but rather chooses hardship with his people. The term *synkakoucheisthai* is a *hapax legomenon* perhaps coined by our author to refer to mal-

---

[677]Attridge, *Hebrews,* p. 339. Clearly this material has been carefully schematized and laid out.

[678]Craddock, *Hebrews,* p. 140.

[679]DeSilva, *Perseverance in Gratitude,* p. 406, is right that our author does not even mention the Mosaic covenant or Moses' giving of the law, which would have suited his supercessionist views. Rather he uses Moses as a positive example rather than as a foil for Christ the greater one.

[680]A few later Greek manuscripts insert between Heb 11:23 and Heb 11:24 the following: "By faith Moses, when he was grown up, killed the Egyptian, because he observed the humiliation of his people." While our author likely knows various postbiblical stories about Moses (cf. Josephus, *Jewish Antiquities* 2; Philo, *On the Life of Moses* 1), this addition is not likely original and seeks to make the connection between Heb 11:23 and Heb 11:24 clearer. See Craddock, *Hebrews,* p. 141. Attridge, *Hebrews,* p. 338 says that this incident is hardly a good example of the faithful endurance being inculcated in this paragraph.

treatment with others (the simple form of the verb is used at Heb 11:37; 13:3).[681] The word *sin* here refers to turning one's back on the plight of one's own people and choosing instead to live in luxury, whereas faith/faithfulness is living in solidarity with God's suffering people. The relevance of this as part of the implied exhortation to the Jewish Christians in Rome is obvious.[682]

Hebrews 11:26 is clearly anachronistic. Nothing suggests that Moses considered the disgrace of Christ as the cause of his identifying with his people's plight and refusing the wealth of Egypt. This verse is apparently echoing Psalm 89:50-51, which includes the keywords *reproach, anointed one* and *reward.* These echoes do not suggest that our author is seeing Moses as some sort of anointed one, but perhaps he is viewed as a visionary who foresaw the anointed one and his coming suffering, for the next verse says that he saw the invisible God.[683] The point our author is trying to make is that Moses "by faith", identified with the greater purposes of God, "looking to the reward" and considering it greater to suffer, as in time even Christ would, in the service of a just and godly cause than to receive the earthly rewards he would have gotten from remaining in the Egyptian court. In principle, as Donald Hagner says, suffering disgrace for God was like suffering for Christ or like the suffering of Christ.[684] "Hebrews says that one's relationship with Christ is its own reward, even when it entails suffering."[685]

It is most unlikely that our author is saying that Moses suffered as God's anointed, since it was Aaron and not Moses who was anointed. Rather, Moses suffered disgrace like the anointed/Christ. Moses suffered such disgrace because, says our author, he looked forward to a greater reward. The point is his trust in God and forward-looking faith in God's promises. This material has been shaped so that it will be a word on target for the Christians under fire in Rome, who themselves will be called upon to suffer like Christ (Heb 11:25; 13:3, 13). Thomas Long puts it this way: "The Preacher's assessment of Moses' choice is actually his verdict on the congregation's option: Moses faithfully and wisely chose 'rather to share ill-treatment with the people of God than to enjoy the fleeting pleasures of sin' (11:25)."[686]

It is not certain which of Moses' leavings is in view in **Hebrews 11:27**. Some see here a reference to his flight into Midian, but the Old Testament says that

---

[681]Attridge, *Hebrews*, p. 340.
[682]DeSilva, *Perseverance in Gratitude*, pp. 408-9.
[683]Attridge, *Hebrews*, pp. 341-42.
[684]Hagner, *Encountering the Book of Hebrews*, p. 152.
[685]Koester, *Hebrews*, p. 503.
[686]Long, *Hebrews*, p. 122.

he fled out of fear on this occasion (Ex 2:11-15). More likely our author has in mind the exodus itself, though he then backtracks to talk about the Passover (since our author does not preserve strict chronology in Heb 11:32 or Heb 11:8-19, he need not do so here). It is also not to the point to say that Pharaoh was not angry when Moses left, since he ordered him to leave after the last plague. Pharaoh's pursuit of Moses shows that he was angry. The reference to Moses' remaining constant/steadfast because he saw the unseen may be the burning bush, but it could as easily be the pillar of smoke and fire that lead out of Egypt. The point stresses his faith in the invisible God: so great was his faith that it was as if he saw God. The reference to God as the invisible one is not found in the Septuagint but it becomes a commonplace in early Christian texts, in particular some Pauline ones that our author may have known (Rom 1:20; Col 1:15; 1 Tim 1:17).[687]

Hebrews 11:28 refers to the first Passover and the pouring of the blood on the door mantle to avoid the destroyer or angel of death (Ex 12:1-28). Thomas Long says: "If in the first Passover the blood of the lamb kept God from touching the flesh of the faithful, in the new Passover God through the Son became human flesh so we might not fear his touch, so that we might not dread destruction but 'may receive mercy and find grace in time of need' (4.16)."[688] Our author does not make these connections explicit,[689] but it is possible that he expected his audience to already know such correspondences, as Paul does when he speaks of "Christ our Passover who has been sacrificed for us" without elaboration (1 Cor 5:7-8). The concern of our author is to reveal the character of Moses as something worth emulating. Aristotle says that "character is that which reveals moral choice" and is revealed by what "a person chooses or avoids in circumstances where the choice is not obvious" (*Poetics* 1450B). What this subject has made clear is that in almost every case the more difficult choice is the faithful and better one.

Hebrews 11:29 contrasts Moses and the people crossing the Red Sea by faith and what happened to those who tried to do so without such faith. In **Hebrews 11:30-31** we hear of the fall of the walls of Jericho. Surely this procedure was an act of faith, for who would normally expect walls to fall down just because one blew some horns and marched around a city? Though various traditions later tried to alleviate the difficulty that Rahab was a harlot, our author mentions the matter very straightforwardly. She is said to welcome with

---

[687]Craddock, *Hebrews*, p. 142.
[688]Long, *Hebrews*, p. 123.
[689]Koester, *Hebrews*, pp. 504-5.

peace (shalom?) the spies. James 2:25 also mentions this story in a similar vein, but in Babylonian Talmud, tractate *Megillah* 14b she becomes the wife of Joshua(!), and in *1 Clement* 12.7 she is made into a prophetess. Most remarkably, in Matthew 1:5 she is the mother of Boaz who marries another non-Jewess, Ruth. Carl Mosser suggests that Rahab is the climax of the hall of faith, but this fails to deal with either Hebrews 11:32-38 or the final example of Christ himself (Heb 12:1-2). Mosser points out that our author's failure to name Joshua (he simply says that "by faith" the walls came down) seems strange since he then mentions Rahab by name—especially since Josephus emphasizes the role of Joshua throughout his discussion (*Jewish Antiquities* 5.1-120). Probably, however, our author does not name Joshua in order to save the name "Jesus" for last in the list (he has already implicitly compared the two Joshuas earlier in the discourse; Heb 4:8). Mosser is very likely right that the text alluded to in Hebrews 11:30-31 is not Joshua 2 but Joshua 6:20-25,[690] which speaks both of the walls collapsing and of Rahab. Nothing, however, is made here in Hebrews 11 of Rahab coming "out of the city" or "camp." What can be said, as Luke Timothy Johnson suggests, is that Rahab is depicted in advance as behaving the way our author wants his audience to behave, namely pursing peace with all people (Heb 12:14).[691]

Michael R. Cosby demonstrates the care of our author in constructing the material in this section to maximize its rhetorical effect. For instance, in Hebrews 11:32-34 our author gives a list of names without deeds, followed by a list of deeds without names, the former without conjunctions to add force to the piling up of examples. In Hebrews 11:37 we again see paronomasia—rhyming ends of words—though the anaphora has been left behind. Again, after showing examples of triumph over and through tragedy and death, our author then shatters any illusions that all the saints had smooth sailing on earth, by giving a list of grisly endings of some saints in Hebrews 11:35b-38. Our audience is thus shown that either prospect is possible for them and that faith can and has been maintained in both sets of circumstances innumerable times before, which is the major point of this catalogue. Living by faith in unseen realities is made to seem the only reasonable response to whatever circumstances one faces in view of so great a cloud of witnesses who have successfully done it before.[692]

[690]Mosser, "Exemplars of Faith."
[691]Johnson, *Hebrews*, p. 304.
[692]Cosby, *Rhetorical Composition and Function*, pp. 57-73.

A CLOSER LOOK
A Guide for Those Perplexed by Hebrews 11:32-38

There were many hero lists in antiquity, and they were common enough in Jewish and Greco-Roman literature.[693] What makes Hebrews 11:32-38 especially interesting—and to some extent odd—is that our author, until he gets to Jesus in Hebrews 12, has been listing only Jewish examples of faith, not Christian ones, and this continues to be the case in Hebrews 11:32-38, where we have very compact summaries of certain names and actions. Loveday Alexander reminds us that, as Hebrews 11 rolls along, "faith" becomes progressively more costly and the accomplishments are proportionally depicted as greater, until we get to the very greatest and most costly example, that of Christ.[694] Donald Hagner provides a helpful chart summarizing these verses, which I adapt here:[695]

Examples of faith by name (Heb 11:32)

- Gideon (Judg 6:11—8:32)
- Barak (Judg 4:6—5:31)
- Samson (Judg 13:2—16:31)
- Jephthah (Judg 11:1—12:7)
- David (1 Sam 16—2 Sam 24)
- Samuel (1 Sam 1—12)
- various other later prophets

Examples of faith by action (Heb 11:33-38)

- conquered kingdoms (Joshua, David)
- administered justice (David, Solomon)
- obtained promises (David?, Solomon?)
- shut the mouths of lions (Samson in Judg 14:6; David in 1 Sam 17:34-36; Daniel in Dan 6:22)
- quenched an inferno (Shadrach, Meshach, Abednego in Dan 3:13-30)
- escaped the edge of the sword (Elijah in 1 Kings 19:1-8; Jeremiah in Jer 26:23-24)
- won strength out of weakness
- became mighty in war

---

[693]Eisenbaum, *Jewish Heroes of Christian History.*
[694]Alexander, "Exemplars of Faith."
[695]Hagner, *Encountering the Book of Hebrews,* p. 153.

- put foreign armies to flight (David?, Solomon?)
- women received back their dead by resurrection (1 Kings 17:17-24; 2 Kings 4:25-37)
- suffered mocking and flogging (Jeremiah)
- were stoned to death (Zechariah in 2 Chron 24:20-22)
- were sawed in two (Isaiah in *Martyrdom and Ascension of Isaiah* 5.11-14)
- were put to death by the sword (prophets in 1 Kings 19:10)
- went about in sheepskins and goatskins (Judas Maccabeus and others in 2 Maccabees 5.27)
- wandering in deserts, hiding in caves and holes (Jews under Antiochus in 2 Maccabees 6.11; 10.6)

This list is in general chronological order, and our author is as happy to use examples from after Old Testament times and before the time of Jesus as he is to use Old Testament examples of faith. Martyrdoms are set alongside miracles and victories as examples of things that happen to the faithful, turning them into examples or even hero figures. The comprehensiveness of types of suffering and death endured suggests to the audience that nothing they face had not been faced before in faith and faithfully to the end. The implied message is that if these examples can do it, so can the audience of Hebrews. Chrysostom writes in the same spirit of our author when he comments on the latter part of Hebrews 11:

> So great a good is faith. When we fall into perplexity, then we are delivered, even though we come to death itself, even though our condition is desperate. For what else was left to them? They were unarmed, surrounded by the Egyptians and the sea. They must either be drowned if they fled, or fall into the hands of the Egyptians. But nevertheless God saved them by impossibilities. That which was spread under the one as land overwhelmed the other as sea. In the former case it forgot nature; in the latter case it actually armed itself against them. . . . Do you see that in all cases it is not by natural sequence, nor yet by any law of nature, that it was changed, but all is done contrary to expectations? (*Homilies on Hebrews* 27.2-3)

Still, there are some oddities in the list. We would have expected Deborah to be mentioned with Barak (especially since our author cites Rahab!), and the mention of Jephthah without his daughters is odd as well.[696] Samson is hardly much of an example of biblical faith and morality in the normal sense of those terms. Our author is not, however, drawing on just the Old Testament here but

---

[696]So Alexander, "Exemplars of Faith."

on early Jewish and Christian use of such stories (e.g., 2 Maccabees 6—7 and *Martyrdom and Ascension of Isaiah* 2.7-8). It is certainly worth comparing this list to other encomiastic lists, such as Sirach 44—50, which is much longer than our list.

The examples in Hebrews 11:33-35a are all of triumph over or through weakness and tragedy. At **Hebrews 11:32** our author uses a typical rhetorical device meant to indicate that the list could become endless if he were to mention all the heroes of the faith: "What more can I say?[697] Time would fail me to speak of . . ." (cf. Josephus *Jewish Antiquities* 20.257). This device was regularly used to signal that the peroration was not far off (Isocrates *Orations* 11; 8.56). As we move toward the end of the hall of faith, our author stops using "by faith," though we do find "through faith" (Heb 11:33, 39).[698] The "time would fail me to speak of" remark, which leads to going on and doing it anyway, though in telegraphic fashion, is a rhetorical device called paraleipsis (Isocrates *Orations* 1.11; 6.81; 8.56). Our author is acting like a preacher running out of time who uses an appropriate rhetorical device to signal that the argument is drawing to a close.[699] Our author then goes on to mention various others in summary fashion in Hebrews 11:32-38. He does not present them in chronological order, which would have been Barak, Gideon, Jephthah, Samson, Samuel and David. It is understandable why he moved Samuel to link him with the other prophets who were models of faith. It is somewhat surprising that he includes Barak rather than Deborah. Gideon, Jephthah and Samson are all said to have had God's *rûaḥ* ("spirit") rest on them (Judg 6:34; 11:29; 13:25). It is possible to think of examples to fit most of the phrases in **Hebrews 11:33** (see Hagner's list above). The phrase *eirgasanto dikaiosynēn* means something like "practiced justice/righteousness," perhaps referring to David's actions (2 Sam 8:15). **Hebrews 11:34** refers to being given power out of weakness to overcome Israel's enemies, which could allude to the story of Jael and Siserah (Judg 5:24-27) or of Judith (Judith 13.7).

Hebrews 11:35 speaks of women who received their dead back out of resurrection. This is likely a reference to the miracles of Elijah and Elisha, but our author does not see these acts as what we call resurrection, for he goes on in the same verse to talk about those who died in order to obtain a "better" resur-

---

[697]This is one of only four places in the homily where our author speaks in the first person singular (Heb 13:19-23). This too signals that he is drawing to a close by using more personal language.
[698]Craddock, *Hebrews*, p. 143.
[699]Hagner, *Encountering the Book of Hebrews*, p. 153.

rection—that is, it is not just a matter of restoration. Nevertheless, this verse shows once more the essentially eschatological rather than otherworldly emphasis of the author. The word *tympanizō* ("tortured"; literally "beat like a drum") might be referring to Eleazar Maccabeus (2 Maccabees 6.19-20), for the word indicates "stretched on the rack or *tympanon* and beaten to death."[700] The word *kreittonos* ("better") characterizes this whole homily's description of how the covenants differ—the new covenant offers better promises, better sacrifice, better resurrection and so on—but what it does not promise is the absence of suffering or martyrdom, thus these pre-Christian examples become pointed here. Christians triumph through and over suffering and death. This is hardly like modern forms of triumphalism.

In **Hebrews 11:36** our author may be thinking of the experience of Christ, reminding the audience of some of the things they went through earlier, or thinking of the Maccabean martyrs, which were popular examples in the early church (2 Maccabees 6.18—7.42; 4 Maccabees 5—18).[701] Though not found in the Old Testament, the tradition about Isaiah being sawed in half was widely known (*Martyrdom and Ascension of Isaiah* 5.11-14; Babylonian Talmud, tractates *Yevamot* 49b and *Sanhedrin* 103b; Justin *Dialogue with Trypho* 120). In **Hebrews 11:37-38** we have the rhetorical device of asyndeton, leaving us with short clipped words or phrases fired off in staccato fashion: "stoned, sawed in two, gutted by a sword."[702] In an interesting reversal of normal perspective, our author says that, though these saints were treated like outcasts and unworthy of society, the world was not worthy of them.[703] Jewish lists of heroes tended to paint the figures as ideal, whereas figures in Greco-Roman lists often had checkered histories, like Jephthah or Samson, for example.[704] Our author chooses examples that his flawed audience could identify with, because, in spite of their flaws, those chosen for this list still exhibited faith/faithfulness at some crucial juncture or in general. Rhetorically, this was wise since he is writing to an audience that is under severe social pressure.[705] The lesson from all these examples is, as Chrysostom says, that faith both accomplishes and suffers great things (*Homilies on Hebrews* 27.5). To a real extent our author is arguing from the greater endurance to the lesser, because, as he will go on to suggest in Hebrews 12:4, the audience by and large had not suffered as greatly as some of these

---

[700]Aristotle, *Rhetoric* 2.5.14; Attridge, *Hebrews*, p. 349.

[701]DeSilva, *Perseverance in Gratitude*, pp. 419-20.

[702]On the aural effect of isocolon, see Cosby, *Rhetorical Composition and Function*, pp. 61-65.

[703]Koester, *Hebrews*, p. 515.

[704]Eisenbaum, *Jewish Heroes of Christian History*, p. 77.

[705]Koester, *Hebrews*, p. 517.

examples. The severity of these various examples builds an effective greater-to-lesser argument (Quintilian *Institutio oratoria* 5.11.9).

Hebrews 11:39-40 brings this lengthy discussion to a close. Our author says that they bore witness through their faith in what was to come, that they had not yet received the promises. The reason is now revealed—so that they would not receive the completion of their salvation without us. God had something better in mind for us, and so these Old Testament saints did not receive what they longed for. Our author is clearly convinced that he lives in the eschatological age, when it is finally possible to talk about the completion of God's salvation plan for all his people. Throughout this chapter one gains the impression that we stand in one long list of believers in both Testaments (though our author mentions no New Testament believers here) who will finally receive what God promised in full. Our author sees the church as the group who can and should claim that it is in a direct line of faith with these Old Testament saints and may learn from their examples. We have heard about the better resurrection, and now our author has spoken about all the faithful ones still awaiting the consummation. The author does not pause to explain how Old Testament saints will inherit what is promised when they did not have faith in Christ, but clearly he believes they will inherit what was promised. The receiving of something "better" had to await not only the coming of Jesus, but also the "better" resurrection. Only at the resurrection would both Jewish and Christian saints be "made perfect together." The language of Hebrews 11:40 speaks of eschatological consummation in conjunction with a better resurrection, not merely entering the better realm called heaven. Thomas Long points out the staggering claim that the Old Testament saints needed "us" before they could receive the complete fulfillment of the promises, or at least apart from "us" they would not receive it.[706] Chrysostom puts it this way: "Do you also consider what a thing it is, and how great, that Abraham should be sitting and the apostle Paul waiting till you have been perfected, so that they may then be able to receive their reward? For the Savior has told them before that, unless we also are present, he will not give it to them. . . . In order that they might not seem to have the advantage over us of being crowned before us, God appointed one time of crowning for all. . . . God did not wrong them, he honored us" (*Homilies on Hebrews* 28.2). Whatever else one may say, Hebrews 11:40 means that our author does *not* think that believers are made perfect at death or upon entry into heaven. The analogy with Christ's case then should not be pressed to suggest this. Our author

---

[706]Long, *Hebrews*, p. 126.

believes that all this "perfecting of believers" awaits "the better resurrection," which will involve all the faithful at once, as Hebrews 12:22-24 will make even clearer. Here at the end of this section our author returns again to direct address ("us") for the first time since Hebrews 10:39.[707] He is pressing home his point and about to give a penultimate exhortation based on the truths set forth in Hebrews 11.[708]

Hebrews 12:1 returns to the more direct form of parenesis, based on what has just been set forth as examples in Hebrews 11. It was typical of encomiums to conclude with exhortations to imitate the person who was the subject of the encomium (e.g., Dio Chrysostom's eulogy for the deceased boxer Melancomas in *Orations* 29.21).[709] The use of *toigaroun* ("consequently") in Hebrews 12:1 shows that what follows is based on what has come before in Hebrews 11 and that these verses should never have been separated by a chapter division. Though our author has mentioned numerous examples of faith in Hebrews 11, he has purposely left till last the most important of all—Jesus the trailblazer/pioneer and completer/perfector of faith, a subject that he introduced us to at Hebrews 2:10. Jesus himself suffered greatly, as much or more than any of the previous examples, for the sake of the joy he saw beyond the suffering. Like the patriarchs then, he lived in forward motion and looking forward to the fulfillment of the promises later, which is here called the joy set before him.[710] Thus, Jesus will finally be set forth as the ultimate and final example of faith in this argument. Here Christology and parenesis are truly wed in the closing argument of the homily, and athletic imagery unites the entire subsection of Hebrews 12:1-13 (especially Heb 12:1-3, 12-13).[711] But the metaphors shift here, the marathon pilgrimage has entered the stadium for the finish of the ordeal, and now the faithful are asked to sprint, following the example of Jesus and in the pres-

---

[707]Craddock, *Hebrews*, p. 145.

[708]Many mistakenly assume that our author is saying that Old Testament saints cannot be perfected without Christ and his sacrificial death and then assume that this transpires upon entry into the heavenly sanctuary (Lane, *Hebrews*, 2.393-94; Attridge, *Hebrews*, p. 352). Perfecting is possible only because of Christ and his death, but this is not at all the point our author is making here. He is saying here that Old Testament saints will not experience perfection "without us"—without Christians also experiencing it. But when does this happen? Not in the full sense until the "better resurrection," which transpires when Christ returns. It happens as a collective experience ("with us") of the whole body of believers, not one by one as they enter heaven. Spicq, *Hébreux*, 2.368, is clearly on the right track to associate this perfecting with the better resurrection.

[709]DeSilva, *Perseverance in Gratitude*, p. 425 and n. 110.

[710]Hagner, *Encountering the Book of Hebrews*, p. 158.

[711]Attridge, *Hebrews*, p. 354.

ence of the "witnesses" who have run before them and are now in the stands, presumably cheering them on.[712]

The word *martys* ("witness") has an interesting history. It originally had the sense of someone who saw something (e.g., a spectator at a game) or who bore witness to something they saw. But in the course of time it came to have a more technical and specifically religious meaning of one who died for their faith and thereby witnessed to its validity.[713] This Greek word is the source of the English word *martyr*. The real question is where we stand in the development of the word when our author uses it. In view of Hebrews 12:1 being retrospective and our author having just given us a long list of those who have died for their faith—and will give us one more in the case of Jesus—it is not impossible that the word *martys* here already has the more specialized meaning of those who have died for their faith. T. W. Manson thinks that the idea of suffering had been associated with the idea of witnessing as early as Nehemiah 9:26 (cf. Jer 23:18, 22).[714] This is not impossible, but in view of the running metaphor in our context, our author may be thinking of a crowd of spectators watching the race. On the other hand, who are these spectators? They are those who have passed on, being faithful witnesses to God. Our author says there is a great cloud of these witnesses. David deSilva stresses that our author wants his audience to see themselves as surrounded by friendly and encouraging witnesses from the hall of faith, not hostile and violent neighbors wishing them ill.[715] *Nephos* here may well have the sense of "host/crowd" rather than "cloud," which is the way this word is often used in secular Greek.[716] The idea is that of being surrounded by a multitude, much like a fog or cloud engulfs everything that goes into it. Found only here in the Bible, *euperistatos* means something that clings to something else and so surrounds or besets it, but it apparently can also have the sense of something that distracts.[717] Here sin is seen as a hindrance to the successful running of the race of faith.[718]

The running metaphor begins and ends this section (Heb 12:1-2, 12-13). We picture the runner casting off all weights and excess clothing (in antiquity, especially in the Greek games, contestants ran naked), but this is a metaphor for spiritual endurance until one reaches the goal and the burdens are put off, especially sin that so easily tempts and besets the believer. The believer is to con-

---

[712]Long, *Hebrews*, p. 128.
[713]See Witherington, *Revelation*, pp. 67-68, for a detailed word study.
[714]Manson, "Martyrs and Martyrdom."
[715]DeSilva, *Perseverance in Gratitude*, p. 429.
[716]Lane, *Hebrews*, 2.408; Herodotus 8.109; Virgil *Aeneid* 7.793.
[717]Koester, *Hebrews*, p. 522, says that the notion of distraction is not well attested for this word.
[718]Craddock, *Hebrews*, p. 148.

centrate on the task at hand and run the course that lies before him or her with perseverance *(hypomonēs)*, which refers to endurance in the face of opposition or competition. When combined with *eis,* the verb *aphorōntes* in **Hebrews 12:2** means a definite looking away from other things and a fixing of one's eyes on only the goal or only one particular object. The image is familiar: if a runner looks over the shoulder or is distracted, he or she may well lose the race. One must fix the gaze on the finish line and ignore all distractions, however interesting. Here believers are to fix their eyes on the one who has already run this race of faith from start to finish successfully, persevering to the very finish line, namely Jesus. Our author uses here the human name of God's Son and refers to his human activities. He is seen here as the first faithful one to actually achieve faith's goal, and hence he is the paradigm.[719] Craig Koester says that it was common for a Greek runner to fix his gaze on the one sitting in the seat of honor, which would be halfway down the track in a special box near to the field.[720] This comports with the earlier imagery of Jesus seated in the seat of honor on the right hand of God the Father.

I have already discussed the meaning of Jesus the originator/trailblazer and finisher or completer of faith. The word *our* is nowhere to be found in this text. Rather, Jesus is seen as the primal and primary example of faith and how to run the race of faith and ignore the shame and taunting heaped on the runner (Heb 13:13), and Esau becomes the counterexample of how not to go forward (Heb 12:16-17).[721] Jesus fought the good fight and finished the course and so kept faith with the Father's plan for his life—obedient even to death. Only here, in dramatic fashion, does our author use the word *cross* in this discourse to refer to Jesus' suffering and death. As such he is being held up to his audience as the great example of persevering faith. Thus he is called the originator/trailblazer and finisher/perfector of faith. Here alone in Scripture do we have the noun *teleiōtēs* ("perfector/completer").[722] Jesus is the first and last word on the subject, he is the primary and final example of it. "When we see the disciplined, loving, strong, merciful, and faithful way that Jesus ran the race, we are motivated to lace up our running shoes, to grasp the baton, and to sprint for the finish line."[723] What is being brought to perfection in Jesus here is "faith," not believers or even Jesus himself. He is the perfector of faith just as he is its pioneer, boldly going to the finish line

---

[719]Attridge, *Hebrews,* p. 356.
[720]Koester, *Hebrews,* p. 523.
[721]DeSilva, *Perseverance in Gratitude,* p. 431.
[722]Dionysius of Halicarnassus, *Dinarchus* 1, uses the term to refer to a rhetorician who was said to be neither the inventor nor the perfector of rhetorical styles invented by others.
[723]Long, *Hebrews,* p. 129.

that no one before him had yet reached.[724] "The predicates express the conviction that from first to last Jesus exercised faith in an essential sense and brought it to its triumphant conclusion."[725]

Thus our author in Hebrews 12:2 shows that Jesus was a good runner, who regardless of the obstacles and opposition endured to the end, even endured the cross, thinking nothing of the shame. "Despising shame" is much the same as despising public opinion of one's actions.[726] Our author may be thinking of what was shameful from a Jewish perspective—namely, being naked in public, which not coincidentally was the normal condition of both runners and those hanging on crosses. Cicero calls the cross "the tree of shame" (*Defense of Rabirius* 4.13). It is a major reversal of opinion and a rhetorical coup if one could turn negative opinions about crucifixion into seeing it as a noble death.[727] "A shameful death was the most feared of evils among many ancients [Epictetus *Discourses* 2.1.13] since it left one with no opportunity to regain one's honor. The last word on one's life was a judgment of worthlessness."[728]

There is considerable debate over how to take *anti* in Hebrews 12:2. On the one hand, Jesus gave up various normal joys in order to die on the cross;[729] "instead" is a perfectly possible meaning here. But the word can also mean "for the sake of" (as in Heb 12:16), and in view of the analogy with the saints in Hebrews 11 who are specifically said to have endured things for the sake of the heavenly reward or the promise yet to be fulfilled, this view is likely to be correct here.[730]

There was a reward for Christ's perseverance to the end. He would have the joy of becoming the author of our salvation, and he would regain his rightful seat beside the Father. These were prizes worth looking forward to, working for, even dying for, and so Jesus did. At the end of Hebrews 12:2 this later joy of exaltation is specifically mentioned.

In **Hebrews 12:3** we are told that Jesus endured the hostility of sinners so that we would not grow faint in faith or be worn out by life's trials. He did it so

---

[724]Lane, *Hebrews*, 2.411, points out that there is but one definite article before "pioneer and perfector of faith," suggesting that these two concepts must be considered together, one having to do with first things and the other to do with last things. They are a sort of dyadic pair. If we are puzzled by the notion that Christ is the first to the finish line, we must remember our author's eschatological bent—Jesus is the first to experience the eschatological resurrection, and this means that he is the first to reach the end state or condition intended for humankind.

[725]Ibid.

[726]DeSilva, *Perseverance in Gratitude*, pp. 433-34.

[727]Hengel, *Crucifixion in the Ancient World*.

[728]DeSilva, *Perseverance in Gratitude*, p. 432.

[729]Turner, *Grammatical Insights into the New Testament*, pp. 172-73.

[730]Craddock, *Hebrews*, p. 149; and Lane, *Hebrews*, 2.413-14.

believers might make it as well, so that believers might persevere as well. It is not just that he has set us an example, it is that he has enabled us to follow such an example by giving us the Spirit and power to persevere. Chrysostom indicates the way that Christ's example is used here: "If then he who was under no necessity of being crucified, was crucified for our sake, how much more is it right that we should endure all things nobly! . . . But what is 'despising the shame'? He chose, he means, that ignominious death. For suppose that he died, some wonder why he should die so ignominiously? For no other reason than to teach us to make no account of glory from the human sphere" (*Homilies on Hebrews* 28.4).

In his helpful study of Hebrews 12:1-13, Clayton Croy makes clear in great detail that our author uses the language of the athletic contest not only to describe in a general way the faith journey of believers, but also more specifically to suggest that the suffering endured by believers along the way is not punitive, but is like the discipline that an athlete undergoes on the path to achieving his or her goals:

> The view of suffering as an athletic contest that requires endurance contains no hint of culpability for hardships endured. Indeed, such hardships are willingly assumed for the sake of participation in and completion of the agon [contest]. . . .
>
> The social context of the readers . . . was primarily one of persecution rather than moral failure. The need of the community was for endurance, confidence, and faith. . . .
>
> The paradigm of Jesus . . . also fits this pattern. . . . What is of importance to the author in 12.1-3 is Jesus as the model of endurance in extreme suffering. Jesus was not punished by God; he did not suffer for his own sins (4.15; 7.26-28). . . . In suffering not condign punishment, but hostility at the hands of sinners (12.3; cf. 2.10; 5.7-8), Jesus learned obedience, was perfected, and became "the pioneer and perfecter" of faith for the readers of this epistle who similarly faced hostility.[731]

Our author reminds his audience in **Hebrews 12:4** that they had not yet endured to the point of blood, which may mean that they had not yet physically been persecuted, but in view of just talking about Christ's death on the cross and Hebrews 10:33-34, it is far more likely to mean that they had not yet poured out their life blood as martyrs. Fred Craddock says that martyrdom is hardly a means of discipline, and so what follows in the discussion about disciplinary suffering applies to an audience that has not yet suffered to the point of death.[732] They are said to be struggling against sin, and the sin of apostasy is likely in

---

[731]Croy, *Endurance in Suffering*, pp. 213-14.
[732]Craddock, *Hebrews*, p. 151.

view as that which might beset them if they do not keep persevering.

Our author asks in **Hebrews 12:5** if his audience had completely forgotten what Scripture says about discipline, and then he quotes Proverbs 3:11-12, the advice of father to son (in our text "Lord" means more than human parent or master). He follows the Septuagint (except for the addition of the word *my*), which in turn follows the Masoretic Text quite closely. **Hebrews 12:6-7** draws a connection between scourging (*paideuō* literally means flogging; Lk 23:16, 22) and discipline. Here the term *discipline* has its ancient sense of corporal punishment of one sort or another. Our author is inviting his audience to see their suffering as a form of discipline from God himself, perhaps not in origin, but as a means of helping them to walk the straight path to the heavenly reward. God brings it to believers as sons. The function of such *paideia* is correction, it is not punitive in character.[733] This becomes especially clear in **Hebrews 12:8**: when our author says that all God's children have shared in God's *paideia*, he surely does not mean that all the challenges they faced were punishments.[734] The outcome of this discipline is not repentance but rather a larger capacity for endurance.[735]

The point of the contrasts that follow are twofold: (1) God is treating believers as his sons, for he disciplines his genuine sons; and (2) if believers have not endured discipline then it is obvious that God does not really think of them as sons, but as children he would not bother with—as illegitimate children. Philo uses this same passage from Proverbs to speak of the positive and disciplinary role of suffering in a believer's life (*On the Preliminary Studies* 175-77). Our author is following the wisdom tradition in general, which saw God as a disciplining parent (Wisdom of Solomon 11.10; 12.20-22; Sirach 23.1-2; 4 Maccabees 1.17; 5.24; 10.10; 13.22), even though the original discipliner in Proverbs was not said to be God.

Beginning in **Hebrews 12:9** we get a series of three *men* . . . *de* contrasts between earthly and heavenly fathers, as part of an a fortiori argument. If our earthly fathers disciplined us and we still respected them, even though they were human just like us (i.e., temporally limited) and disciplined us according to what seemed good to their judgment, how much more should believers submit to the discipline of their Father, who is complete in his knowledge of what

---

[733]Croy, *Endurance in Suffering*, pp. 83-159, makes abundantly clear that early Jewish sources did not all universally see suffering as a sign of divine punishment, any more than all Greco-Roman sources saw suffering as disciplinary, educational or corrective. There were a variety of views, and our author clearly sees the suffering from persecution as in no way punitive or deserved due to sin.

[734]Koester, *Hebrews*, p. 526.

[735]These same ideas about divine discipline were present in Stoic sources; see Seneca *On Providence* 1.6; 4.7.

The explanation of suffering doesn't complete (except Jesus' Temptation = proof of His being genuine)

is best for them. *Paideutas* may have the more extended sense of self-discipline of the body, that is, training, but the word can simply mean correctors rather than trainers, and this is probably its meaning here. God is called the "Father of our spirits," which stands in contrast to the "fathers of our flesh *[sarkos]*" mentioned earlier in the verse. Our author is not trying to give a dissertation about anthropology, and he probably means that God is the Father of spirits in the same sense that a human father is the father of our flesh—our spirit or spiritual life comes from God, he is our spiritual father, and so we should take advice about or discipline for our spirits from him (Num 16:22; 27:16). If we submit to that sort of discipline, the end result will not be death but life, indeed eternal life (2 Cor 4:17; 1 Pet 1:6-7; 4:12-14).[736]

Hebrews 12:10 says that the final benefit is that we shall share in "his holiness"—the perfection and sanctification of his nature. The word *hagiotētos* occurs only here (and possibly 2 Cor 1:12) in the New Testament. These permanent character-improving benefits of God's discipline, unlike the temporary benefits of the discipline of a human father, are described in **Hebrews 12:11** as the peaceful fruit of righteousness (which sounds similar to Jas 3:18). To be sure, discipline when it is being endured seems to be a grief, not a joy, but our author says, "No pain no gain." Suffering is a possible agent of sanctification if the believer allows it to drive himself or herself to God; it can make the believer better; it can draw the believer closer to God and to the narrow path. C. S. Lewis puts it this way in *The Problem of Pain:* God whispers in our pleasures, speaks in our conscience, but shouts in our pain. It is his megaphone to a deaf world. Our author again uses athletic language here: suffering is seen as part of a Christian's "training" *(gymnazō)*. "We need to remind ourselves that the Preacher is addressing a pastoral problem, not writing a theodicy. Taken as an absolute principle, the idea that all human suffering is actually the hand of a loving God teaching us good lessons is untenable. . . . But the Preacher is not trying to account for all suffering; the Preacher is trying to make sense of his congregation's struggle to be faithful and not to fall away from the faith" due to persecution or social pressure and ostracism.[737] In short he is dealing with suffering for and on account of one's faith: "He is not speaking of disease or illness, domestic abuse, poverty, or subjection to an oppressive regime. He is speaking particularly of the censure, insult, abuse, and deprivations suffered by the believers as a result of their association with Jesus and the people of God. . . . The deprivations faced on account of their commitment to Christ and to one another are actually

---

[736]See the discussion in Hagner, *Encountering the Book of Hebrews*, pp. 159-60.
[737]Long, *Hebrews*, p. 134.

core courses in God's curriculum . . . shaping them for their citizenship in the New Jerusalem."[738]

Hebrews 12:12 is introduced by "therefore" *(dio)*, indicating that our author will now draw a practical conclusion or exhortation based on what he has just said. In light of God's using suffering to discipline and better fit believers for the kingdom, they must support those who are drooping in hand and need braces on their knees. Our author is doubtless drawing on a potent image first found in Isaiah 35:3. It may tell us how he views at least some of his audience's spiritual condition, namely that they are spiritual cripples in need of such supports and helps (in Heb 6:1-4 he calls them infants, who likewise need such braces and supports to walk straight). Philo also uses this athletic metaphor, saying that some "faint before the struggle has begun, and lose heart altogether . . . and like weary athletes drop their hands in weakness" (*On the Preliminary Studies* 164).

Hebrews 12:13 draws upon Proverbs 4:26 and speaks of clearing the path as one would for an inexperienced or young or feeble walker. If the rocks are not removed one might trip and put some of those weak limbs out of joint, rather than helping them be healed by straight walking, which builds up one's muscles and in the end helps one reach the destination. *Ektrapē* normally means "turned aside," but with this image it means something like "dislocation, put out of joint." Our author has thus begun by talking of running, but in the end he speaks of just helping some to walk a straight path unencumbered. Obviously, some among his audience are spiritually crippled or immature and in need of such help, are not mature enough to see suffering as an honor or opportunity for growth or witness, but only as a burden or plague. Our author began this section by talking about elite runners following the trail blazed by Jesus, but here, as Thomas Long puts it, we are at the back end of the marathon, where runners are struggling just to put one foot in front of the other and will require assistance to make it to the finish line: "God's race is not the Olympics; it is the Special Olympics, and runners who are . . . encumbered in so many ways, are encouraged to get out on the track and to 'make straight paths for your feet.'"[739]

Beginning at **Hebrews 12:14** our author winds up his final exhortations in this argument and returns once more to the themes of sanctification, apostasy and the better revelation that believers have when compared to the Sinai revelation. This brief subsection is connective tissue that both concludes the final main argument and links it to the following peroration, which begins at He-

---
DeSilva, *Perseverance in Gratitude*, p. 450.
[739]Long, *Hebrews*, p. 135.

brews 12:18. These verses are transitional then and not part of the peroration.[740]

Our author begins by insisting that believers must pursue peace and holiness (or, if *shalom* is in mind here, wholeness and holiness, well being and purity or sanctification of being. This is quite possibly an echo of Romans 12:18. These things are portrayed as being out in front of these "runners" and needing to be pursued, and the peace envisioned is between community members.[741] Perhaps a balance is intended here, because pursuing peace with one another can sometimes be at the expense of maintaining one's moral standards, and so the author says that holiness or sanctification is equally to be pursued. The "all" that one is to pursue peace with certainly includes the community of faith, but the author may mean even one's non-Christian neighbors as well.[742]

Only here do we have the word for sanctification in Hebrews, *hagiasmos,* and it is quite clear from what follows that our author means a subjective condition that is expressed by good deeds and negatively affected by evil deeds. Without these, the audience shall not see God, a clear reference to the final eschatological theophany to be discussed in the peroration. These are the prerequisites for final salvation at the eschaton. Possibly our author is thinking of two of Jesus' beatitudes here (Mt 5:8-9).[743] If so, "seeing God" in the beatitude happens on earth at the eschaton, not in heaven (contrast 2 Esdras [4 Ezra] 7.87-98).[744] Perhaps because he has mentioned seeing God and holiness, the author's mind reflects back once again to the premiere Old Testament theophany—the one at Sinai. He is fearful that some might miss the big event. The verb *episkopountes* in **Hebrews 12:15** simply means "watching over/out for something/someone" and is applied to all the audience, who are to watch out for each other on the final and eternal expression of God's grace, even though they have already experienced some of it (Heb 10:24-25). As usual Chrysostom puts it eloquently: "As if they were traveling together on some long journey, in a large company, he says 'Take heed that no one be left behind: I do not seek this only, that you should arrive yourselves, but also that you should look diligently after the others.' 'That no one fails to obtain the grace of God.' . . . Do not tell me, 'It is only one that perishes.' Even for one Christ died. Have you no care for him; for whom Christ died?" (*Homilies on Hebrews* 31.1). Whatever else one can say, our author believes that it is not God's wish that anyone miss out on the final saving grace of God. Chrysostom saw this clearly.

---

[740]Craddock, *Hebrews,* p. 153.
[741]Ibid.
[742]DeSilva, *Perseverance in Gratitude,* p. 459.
[743]Hagner, *Encountering the Book of Hebrews,* p. 161.
[744]Attridge, *Hebrews,* p. 367.

By harboring a root or bitterness, which grows up and causes trouble not only in oneself but also in the community (1 Maccabees 1.10), one can become an agent spiritually defiling many and thereby miss out on the goal. Here "defiled" is seen as the opposite of "sanctified." The allusion is to Deuteronomy 29:18-19, and once again our author presumes that his audience is not only is familiar with the portion of text he cites but also what follows it, which he does not cite: "Make sure that there is no one here today who hears these solemn demands and yet convinces himself that all will be well with him, even if he stubbornly goes his own way. That would destroy all of you good and evil alike." The "bitter root" then is the false thinking and practice that has caused some to at least contemplate falling back into some form of sectarian Judaism that is less than fully Christian and thus less than fully acceptable to God. The problem is that if one does it others are enticed. Our author obviously believes that a house, and especially one experiencing difficulty, divided against itself cannot stand. Christians must watch out for each other lest someone apostatize. Chrysostom says: "Nothing so especially makes persons easily vanquished and subdued in temptations as isolation" (*Homilies on Hebrews* 30.2). Working out the salvation given to the community of Christ and avoiding apostasy turns out to be a team effort, as Paul also makes clear (Phil 2:12). While salvation is a personal matter, it is not a private one.

At **Hebrews 12:16** the negative example of Esau (Gen 25:33-34) is called "immoral" *(pornos)*,[745] which could have its Old Testament meaning of idolatrous, as F. F. Bruce suggests (Judg 2:17).[746] Extrabiblical traditions (*Jubilees* 25.1, 7-8; Philo *On the Virtues* 208) about Esau call him immoral, largely expanding on his polygamous marriage to the two daughters of Heth. He is also called godless, largely based on his selling his birthright for a single meal. He becomes the ultimate negative epideictic paradigm of one who embraces the wrong values—short-term gain in exchange for everlasting blessings. The extreme example chosen of bad choices is typical of epideictic rhetoric's approach to warding off defection of some sort.

Hebrews 12:16 uses *anti* in the sense of "in exchange for, for the sake of," just as we saw in Hebrews 12:2. The phrase "when he thought better of it and had changed *[metanoia]* his mind" in **Hebrews 12:17** could also be rendered "when he repented of his hasty decision and wanted to inherit the blessing"

---

[745] Possibly, as Long, *Hebrews*, p. 135, says, our author decided on closing this exhortation with this example because he had just been thinking of runners with a limp, which reminded him of the story of Jacob and his limp (Gen 32:22-32), and this brought to mind Esau.

[746] Bruce, *Hebrews*, pp. 366-67.

handwritten marginalia at top of page

(Gen 27:30-40). Here our author is clearly drawing on what he has already said in Hebrews 6:4-6 and Hebrews 10:26 about no recovery after apostasy.[747] The idiom "found no place of repentance" means that he had no opportunity or possibility of repentance (Wisdom of Solomon 12.10; *1 Clement* 7.5) despite his tears (Gen 27:34-38; *Jubilees* 26.32). The point is this: one's commitment to Christ and his better covenant must be irrevocable if one wishes to inherit the eternal blessings. Craig Koester is right that our author would not sternly warn the audience about apostasy if they had already committed it, for in his theology there would be no point to such a futile warning.[748] And Donald Hagner says that Esau is the perfect antithesis to the heroes of faith in Hebrews 11, for he trades off what is unseen and what lies in the future for immediate material gratification in the present.[749] It is this same contrast between the seen and the unseen benefit that initiates the comparison between Mount Sinai and Mount Zion and the two covenants and words of God that each represents.

PERORATION: THEOPHANIES BEHIND AND BEFORE THEM (HEB 12:18-29)

The Preacher's congregation . . . have come to a place where two roads diverge, and like the traveler in Frost's poem, the one they choose to take will make "all the difference."

The signpost that points down one fork reads "To Mount Sinai," and the sign pointing down the other fork reads "To Mount Zion." . . . The Preacher has been laboring throughout the whole sermon to get us to go to Mount Zion. . . .

In order to urge his congregation to choose the high road, to travel to Mount Zion, the Preacher uses a classic travel agent's strategy: get them to imagine that they are already there. Think of a video travelogue that opens with the scene of a harried man driving in rush hour traffic. Suddenly the scene dissolves to a shot of a lovely lagoon, a picture-perfect sailboat bobbing gently at anchor. A narrator's voice is saying, "Forget the traffic and the tension, forget the phones and the faxes. You aren't at the office any more; you have come to the magical island of St. Lucia." The fact is you *aren't* on the magical island of St. Lucia; you are in your den watching this on TV. But in your imagination you are already taking a dip in the warm Caribbean waters, and this whets your appetite all the more to go.

So the Preacher begins his travelogue with a word even more dramatic than,

---

[747]Attridge, *Hebrews*, p. 369, suggests that, since the text says that Esau is giving up his rights as firstborn, we should hear an echo of Heb 1:6 and a foreshadowing of Heb 12:23, where Jesus is called the firstborn and his community is the community of the firstborn. The implication is clear—apostasy is an abandonment of Jesus and his community and thereby a giving up of the promised inheritance.
[748]Koester, *Hebrews*, p. 542.
[749]Hagner, *Encountering the Book of Hebrews*, p. 161.

"You aren't at the office any more." He begins, "You have not come to something that can be touched, a blazing fire, and darkness, and gloom, and a tempest. . . . You have come to Mount Zion and to the city of the living God."[750]

As would be expected in the peroration of epideictic rhetoric, our author chooses to finish quite literally in a blaze of divine glory, using highly emotive rhetoric to bring his argument home and indelibly imprint it in the audience's mind. In any oral discourse like Hebrews, the final salvo needs to be memorable, as it is probably what the audience will most remember about the speech or proclamation. From a rhetorical viewpoint the final exhortation is in the emphatic position, and one may conclude that this is what our author has been working toward all along as a climax to his discourse.

The peroratio in epideictic rhetoric should emphasize behavior in the present, which will reflect the values and virtues of the community addressed and help them to live out those values. It is no accident that this peroratio emphasizes "standing before the mountain," having already arrived at the spot, rather than advancing or retreating, which would involve a change in behavior.

Our author is well aware of the conventions that applied to peroratios, which is the place where one should give free rein to the torrent of one's emotions and eloquence (Quintilian *Institutio oratoria* 4.1.28; 6.1.51; cf. 6.1.9-10). "While the chief task of the peroration consists of amplification, we may legitimately make free use of words and reflections that are magnificent and ornate. It is at the close of our drama that we must really stir the theater" (6.1.52). "For it is in its power over the emotions that the life and soul of oratory is to be found" (6.2.7).

The two major functions of the peroratio were to offer something of a recapitulation of major themes and to exhibit pathos, appealing to the deeper emotions of the audience, particularly anger, fear, pity (Quintilian *Institutio oratoria* 6.2.20; Aristotle *Rhetoric* 3.19.1-6; *Rhetorica ad Herennium* 2.30.47). On this latter matter, it is especially important to have a rhetorically informed view of what our author is doing here, or else one may take the *Sturm und Drang* of the emotive rhetoric to signal that the author is teaching the audience something new. To the contrary, our author is following the proper rhetorical conventions here, seeking to refresh the memory as well as arouse the deeper emotions, with a stirring call to arms (Aristotle *Rhetoric* 3.19.1-6; Quintilian *Institutio oratoria* 6.1.1). There need not have been specific issues with this audience for our author to have spoken this way, since the worldview enunciated here was widely

---

[750]Long, *Hebrews*, pp. 136-37.

shared by early Christians. Christians are called here to preserve and hold on to their core values against the attacks of the outsiders. They are to stand on that which they have petitioned God about and praised him for in the beginning of the discourse.

This peroration also does a fine job of meeting the requirements of appealing to authority as a form of amplification and making the discourse's conclusion more compelling. Thus, for example, our author draws on a number of passages from the Septuagint version of the Old Testament to enforce his conclusions about the need to hold one's ground and not fall afoul of the living God, who is a consuming fire (Cicero *De inventione rhetorica* 1.53.101; *Rhetorica ad Herennium* 2.30.48).

Cicero says that amplification should above all include metaphors or dramatic imagery to conclude and cinch an act of persuasion (*Partitiones oratoriae* 15.53). Quintilian urges a use of a variety of figures of speech in a recapitulation, even though he adds that "this final recapitulation must be as brief as possible. . . . On the other hand the points selected for enumeration must be treated with weight and dignity, enlivened by apt reflections and diversified by suitable figures" (*Institutio oratoria* 6.1.2). He emphasizes that one must touch on large themes and touchstones of the community, appealing to truth, justice, and the community's larger interests (6.1.7). Quintilian also adds that the appeal to fear and the discussion of the danger the audience may be in should come in the peroration rather than in the exordium (6.1.12-13). There can be little doubt that this is an appeal to fear in the face of theophany and also to the deep-seated emotions of piety and reverence and awe that should prompt proper worship, as the close of the peroration suggests. Worship is in some ways the most appropriate topic for epideictic rhetoric, for it involves the praise of God, the chief one who should be praised in epideictic rhetoric. Our author follows closely the conventions for an epideictic peroration as he seeks to convict, convince and galvanize his world-weary audience.

Speakers were urged to use short pithy sentences without a lot of connectives to punctuate the discourse: "I have spoken; you have heard; you know the facts; now give your decision" (Aristotle *Rhetoric* 3.19.6; cf. Cicero *Partitiones oratoriae* 15.53). Our peroration follows these conventions nicely.

This vivid peroration involves a rhetorical synkrisis—a comparison by contrast of two theophanies. Chrysostom understood this quite clearly and remarks on it in *Homilies on Hebrews* 32.3-4, and I will follow his lead here. At the former theophany the people stood far off; at the final one they are said to have drawn near and are beckoned to stay close. At the former theophany they are in the wilderness; at the latter they are at the gates of the new Jerusalem, the ultimate symbol of true human civilization. At the former theophany there was gloom and darkness; at the latter there was a festal celebration complete with partying angels. At the former theophany the people begged God to speak through Moses and not directly; at the latter they are urged to listen directly to God. At the former theophany even Moses the mediator trembled and no one dared to touch the holy mountain; at the latter Jesus the mediator will be present and God's people are beckoned to enter in at his return. At the former theophany sinful Israel is present; at the latter the spirits of just persons made perfect are present. At the former theophany there is blood from violence and judgment on sin; at the latter only the sprinkled blood of Jesus preaches peace and enables mercy. At the former theophany worship amounts to fear and trembling before God; at the latter worship involves awe and wonder and thankfulness and acceptable worship of God. The failure to see the last half of the peroration as a description of the final eschatological theophany destroys the rhetorical comparison and contrast our author has so carefully set up in this tour de force climax of the arguments in this discourse.[61]

> [12:18] *For we do not come up to/approach the tangible/material*[752] *and burning fire and darkness and gloom and whirlwind,* [19]*and trumpet sound and the sound of words, which those hearing begged not to have another word added.* [20]*For they were not even bearing the order "if a wild beast touches the mountain, it must be stoned."* [21]*And so the spectacle was so awesome Moses himself said, "I am terrified," and he was trembling.*
>
> [22]*But we approach/come up to Mount Zion and to the city of the living God, the heavenly Jerusalem, and to the myriad of angels, the festal gathering,* [23]*and to the assembly/church of the firstborn enrolled in heaven, and to the judge of all, God and the spirits of the righteous/just made perfect,* [24]*and to the mediator of the new covenant, Jesus, and to the blood of sprinkling speaking better (things) than that of Abel.*
>
> [25]*See that you do not refuse/disregard the speaking. For if those did not escape who disregarded the warning upon earth, how much less we who turn away from*

---

[61]Craddock, *Hebrews*, p. 156, likens this to Paul's allegory of Sarah and Hagar in Gal 4, but this is no allegory. It is a historical comparison, like the various other historical comparisons in this sermon, with the subtext being that the later revelation, the later mediator, the later theophany is "better." Johnson, *Hebrews*, pp. 328-29, thinks that our author is dealing with Platonic dualism here, contrasting the purely spiritual realm above with the earthly theophany below at Sinai. This is a mistake, since our author has already spoken of the coming of Christ, the final judgment and the resurrection—in short, of the eschatological realities yet to come. Johnson is right that this heavenly city is now above, but the whole point is that what is currently "up there" will be part of the final theophany "out there" when Christ comes with the saints and glory fills our souls.

[752]Some manuscripts add the word *mountain* for clarification, but it is added in several places and is not found in $\mathfrak{P}^{46}$, $\aleph$, A, C and other good witnesses.

the (voice) from heaven; [26] *whose voice shook the whole earth, but now he has promised, saying, "Yet once more I will shake not only the earth but also the heavens."* [27] *But the "yet once more" points to the change/removal of what has been shaken as created, in order that the unshakable remains.* [28] *Therefore receiving an unshakable kingdom let us be grateful, through which we worship acceptably to God with reverence and awe;* [29] *for our God is a consuming fire.*

Hebrews 12:18-24 is one long *ou . . . alla* contrast: we have not come up to Sinai, but to Zion. The main verb that controls the contrast is *proselēlythate* (from *proserchomai*), from which we get the word *proselyte*. The sense of "coming up to" or "approaching" may thus have overtones of conversion—the believers have now converted to the covenant that comes from Zion not Sinai. More probable, however, is the suggestion of Thomas Long that this word should simply be translated "approach" since this is its sense elsewhere (Heb 4:16: 7:25: 10:22). In each of these former examples the reference is to approaching God or the throne of grace or the house of God, which is very similar to the discussion here.[753] Fred Craddock says that the term is cultic in this context and refers to one's approach in worship to the divine.[754] In any case the perfect tense of the verb is significant: it means to approach and remain near, an ongoing state of being.[755] The image is of a pilgrim people of God who after a long trek are now at the edge of the holy mountain awaiting the final worship service, the final divine human encounter, and should not think of going back to Egypt again.[756] Here is the basis of what our author has said frequently about seeing the heavenly reward or the promises from afar. He has this spatial image of the mountain of God in view and with it the final consummate theophany when God will come down and be with his people, once and for all. "This does not mean that listeners have arrived at the heavenly city in any physical sense. . . . The portrayal of a city that transcends experience gives listeners incentive to persevere in the earthly city where they live."[757]

It is quite clear that our author is no Marcionite—the same living God manifested himself on both mountains, as Hebrews 12:29 indicates emphatically: "our" God, who also was and is the God of Israel, is an all-consuming fire. Yet the character of the old and new revelations still differs. The former revelation

---

[753]Long, *Hebrews*, p. 138.

[754]Craddock, *Hebrews*, p. 158.

[755]Koester, *Hebrews*, p. 544, is right to stress that our author does not believe that the audience has yet "arrived" at the eschatological destination. Rather they have just drawn near and still hope for "the city that is to come" (Heb 13:14).

[756]As such then, it is not about "entering" anything, not even heaven. The verb is all about drawing near to God in worship.

[757]Koester, *Hebrews*, p. 550.

on Sinai is said to be awesome and terrifying to God's people, who asked for at least the aural part of it to cease. By contrast the revelation from Zion is more like a giant celebration and party rather than like coming in contact with a tornado or a fifty-thousand-volt electrical wire. Craddock says about the Sinai theophany: "The writer's point is unavoidable: The conditions under which the old covenant was given were dread, fear, distance, and exclusion (Exod 19:23). The old tabernacle, with its curtain, preserved the features of distance, exclusion, and inaccessibility."[758]

Hebrews 12:18-21 is based on several key texts: Deuteronomy 4:11; 5:22-25; Exodus 19:12-19; 20:18-21 (the partial quotation in Heb 12:20 comes from Ex 19:12-13). The word *terrified* is found in a slightly different context at Deuteronomy 9:19, for it is not said there that Moses either was terrified or trembled at Sinai, but later when the people rebelled in the wilderness, Moses feared God's anger.[759] The image here is meant to convey something ear-splitting, eye-popping, mind-blowing—in short, something totally overwhelming. So holy was God that the people dared not directly approach him. If even a wild animal came on his mountain it had to be destroyed. Being a sinner in the presence of a holy God is an unbearable, frightening experience that can be lethal (like contact with nuclear waste or a dreaded and deadly disease that kills on contact), unless an adequate means of the two parties relating is provided. The Israelites asked God to stop speaking to them because it had so terrified them. This contrasts with those gathered at Mount Zion, who are encouraged to listen when the divine voice speaks. "Thus, Sinai is deliberately set forth in an unappealing way in order to sharpen the contrast with what our author calls Zion."[760] The word *pselaphōmenos* refers not merely to the material but to the palpable. It is used in Exodus 10:21 for the "palpable darkness" in Egypt during the plagues.[761] Our author is contrasting the tangible effect of the first theophany with the currently intangible effect of drawing near to the second theophany. He is not making a straightforward material versus spiritual contrast here, because he believes that the better resurrection will be a contrast between temporary and permanent rather than between material and spiritual, which will characterize the final revelation.

---

[758]Craddock, *Hebrews*, p. 158.

[759]There may be here an implicit argument from the lesser to the greater. If even Moses was frightened by the theophany, how much more should the hearers of this discourse be frightened as well. See Quintilian *Institutio oratoria* 5.11.9, on the form of argument; and Koester, *Hebrews*, p. 550, on the point.

[760]Hagner, *Encountering the Book of Hebrews*, p. 162. I am unconvinced that our author is comparing the present experience of salvation by the audience with the past experience at Sinai. The present experience did not involve theophany or voices from heaven.

[761]Koester, *Hebrews*, p. 543.

At **Hebrews 12:22** our author turns to the positive side, having made Sinai and its theophany as ominous, gloomy and frightening as possible. Since the images our author uses are also found in Revelation 21 and Galatians 4:24-31, he appears to be drawing on a common and perhaps well-known stock of Jewish Christian images. Even though he says "we have come up" to or approached Mount Zion, believers have not inhabited it, nor has it come down to them yet. The perfect tense refers to a past coming that has lasting impact on the present. Donald Hagner wrongly holds that this is a description of a present enjoyment of a glorious status.[762] Rather, the joy has been set right before them, but they have not yet enjoyed or taken possession of it. The angels are already celebrating, but then they are in heaven with God. The point our author is making is that believers are on the verge or edge of the consummate reality that God has in mind for them, and so it is much too late to talk about turning back now. They must remain forward looking and act like the church expectant, having neither entered the final rest yet nor received final salvation with all its benefits and rewards yet.

Zion does not stand for the new covenant and its already realized benefits. It stands for the final reconciliation of God with his people when God in Christ comes down to earth. Our author paints a vivid picture of that final theophany so the audience can almost see it. But they have not yet partaken of it or participated in it.

The imagery is developing: our author first speaks generally of Mount Zion, then of the city set on that hill (the city was already mentioned in Heb 11:10, 16 as Abraham's true goal), then of the city as the heavenly Jerusalem. He makes clear that he is not speaking about some already extant material destination like the material Mount Sinai when he adds that we have come to myriads of angels in festal gathering. Festivals were a normal part of Israel's worship (Hos 9:5; Amos 5:21). Even more to the point, references to myriads of angels clearly recall descriptions of divine theophanies, not merely life in heaven (Deut 33:2 and Ps 68:16-17, both of the Sinai theophany). When one knows this tradition, it becomes even clearer that two theophanies are being compared here.[763]

The word *panēgyris*, found in only this verse in the New Testament, though present in the Septuagint, Josephus and Philo, refers to a celebratory gathering at which a "panegyric" would be appropriate—an epideictic speech of praise, celebrating the occasion (Cassius Dio *Roman History* 53.1.4).[764] Here is another

---

[762]Hagner, *Encountering the Book of Hebrews*, p. 162.
[763]Attridge, *Hebrews*, p. 374.
[764]Spicq, "La panegyrie de Heb 12,22."

small clue of how our author views his discourse: it has been leading toward the goal of doxology and worship and has been leading the audience forward into a reembracing of the values, virtues, worship experience and God they had already embraced. The term is a rhetorical signal about the character of this rhetoric. Craig Koester stresses that "in the Greco-Roman world the term *panēgyris* was used for civic festivals and athletic competitions, which drew people from all parts of the empire and from all social classes. Peace was declared during festivals (Isocrates [*Orations* 4.43]), which were times of joy, when one would see people 'in white robes and crowned with garlands' (Philo [*On the Embassy to*] *Gaius* 12)."[765]

There is considerable debate about how to interpret Hebrews 12:22b-23. First of all, does the word *panēgyrei* go with what precedes or follows it? In view of *kai* preceding "myriads" and *kai* following *panēgyrei,* it is most natural to take this word grammatically with what precedes; thus it refers to a festal gathering of myriads of angels who are prepared to celebrate. This is one of the groups of inhabitants of the heavenly city. **Hebrews 12:23** refers to the "*ekklēsia* of the firstborn" enrolled in heaven. In view of both the term *enrolled,* which is never predicated of angels (Lk 10:20; cf. Rev 13:8; Dan 12:1), and the *kai* that separates this group from what precedes and from the reference to God that follows (regardless of which of two possible readings one adopts: "God who is judge over all" or "to the judge, who is God over all"), *ekklēsia* is likely seen as a separate group from the angels. But who are these people? Are they the Old Testament saints? The church? Both? Saints in heaven? Christian martyrs? Whoever they are, they are not the audience of Hebrews, who has only come to see this assembly. They are not yet a part of it. I suspect that this refers to all the deceased Old Testament saints, such as those just listed in Hebrews 11. This suggests that the spirits referred to in Hebrews 12:23 are a more specific group, namely the martyrs, perhaps particularly the Christian martyrs (Rev 6:9-11).

In Hebrews 11 our author said that the one group would not be perfected without the other, but he did not thereby amalgamate the two groups. The word *ekklēsia* could point to the church, except for several factors: (1) this is the normal Septuagint term for the Old Testament assembly or congregation of God's people; (2) in the term's only other use in this homily it refers to God's Old Testament people (Heb 2:12, quoting Ps 22:23) and (3) "firstborn" might well refer to the precedence that Old Testament saints have over Christians in the city. Donald Hagner admits that if *ekklēsia* refers to Christians this is the only place

---

[765]Koester, *Hebrews,* p. 544.

it does so in Hebrews.[766] Hebrews 11:40 might count against this idea, since there it seems that the Old Testament saints' perfecting is held up till Christians come along and get theirs as well. But being firstborn and being first perfected are two different concepts, and this is two different groups. In addition, this is a human group (Old Testament saints) followed by reference to an individual (God the judge), then another and likely different partial group ("the spirits of just persons made perfect") and another individual (Christ). As Christians would more naturally be associated with the latter, the Old Testament saints might more naturally be associated with the former, though I do not rule out a more specific reference to Christian martyrs whose spirits have been perfected.

Many see "the spirits of just persons made perfect" as the Old Testament saints (*1 Enoch* 22.9) or possibly the martyrs among them. The word *spirits* calls attention to those who have been made spiritually perfect/complete (i.e., complete in spirit). Our author is thus envisioning what has happened already above in heaven, not what will happen at the end of history after the last resurrection. That these spirits have been made complete suggests that they are in heaven. And in view of strong emphasis in this document on the connection of completion through suffering (or the completion of Christians by and after death), we are led to think of these persons being Christians, perhaps particularly Jewish Christians, who are the exemplars for the present audience. Hebrews 13:7 may even suggest this is a reference to the leaders of the Roman church who have been martyred.

Since Revelation 6:9 also speaks of the spirits of the martyrs, this group probably is the church triumphant, in particular the martyrs who are in the heavenly Jerusalem, and perhaps even more specifically the Jewish Christian leaders who have given their life for the faith (Heb 13:7), particularly those connected with the Roman church—such as Peter and Paul.[767] Early Judaism had a robust theology of the afterlife and had several opinions on what happened to the spirits of the righteous at death: they entered heaven at once (Wisdom of Solomon 3.1) or were preserved until the final judgment (*1 Enoch* 22.3-7; 2 Esdras [4 Ezra] 7.99). Both Craig Koester and David Peterson stress: "Hebrews provides no clarity about a person's state between death and final judgment."[768] There is certainly no emphasis here or elsewhere in this discourse on believers dying and following Jesus directly to heaven. On the one hand, the language about all being perfected together suggests that all believers will reach the final state of af-

---

[766]Hagner, *Encountering the Book of Hebrews*, p. 163.
[767]But see Dumbrell, "Spirits of Just Men Made Perfect."
[768]Koester, *Hebrews*, p. 546; cf. Peterson, *Hebrews and Perfection*, pp. 163-65.

fairs at the same time. On the other hand, the images of the community of the firstborn and the spirits of the righteous being with the angels suggest that they are coming from heaven to the theophany. Whatever else one can say, it becomes clear that our author, like Paul and the author of Revelation, sees heaven as at most an interim stopping off place on the way to the kingdom of God coming fully on earth.

Fred Craddock rightly points out that calling God the judge of all does not necessarily convey the sense of condemnation, one who will judge in a negative sense, because in biblical tradition God vindicates and exonerates as well as condemns, and for believers God as judge pronounces the final "no condemnation." They can expect from God fairness and impartiality and a keeping of his promises.[769] Judgment in the biblical sense implies moral examination and discrimination that can lead to either commendation or condemnation.

Our author is saying that he, his audience and by extension all Christians on earth have come up to this Mount Zion, but they are not yet on it, as are the angels, the assembly, the spirits, God and Christ. They have drawn near this great assembly and theophany, but they are not yet part of it—hence the exhortation to not draw back but to go on and join the myriad who praise him in his presence.

Hebrews 12:24 speaks of Jesus (again the human name is stressed and put emphatically last) as the mediator of the "new" (meaning "recent") covenant. Only our author uses *neas* of covenant, which refers to new in time as opposed to new in character, but the two adjectives seem to have overlapped in meaning by this point in their development.[770] It is only appropriate that he mentions Christ as mediator of the new covenant in his description of the final theophany event, the final covenant-making event, which because of Jesus' earthly work believers may take part in. Hebrews 12:24 makes a contrast between Christ's blood (seen here as the blood that is sprinkled on the mercy seat, thus making atonement and pleading for forgiveness for us; Heb 10:22; 9:13-21; 1 Pet 1:2) and Abel's blood, which cried out for vengeance from the dust of the ground (Gen 4:10). Here, as throughout Hebrews, our author maintains that the chief difference between the old and new orders is that the new order promises and delivers something better (*kreittōn*). This is the last time he will use this term,

---

[769] Craddock, *Hebrews*, p. 158.
[770] *Kainos* is used at Heb 8:8, 13; 9:13. This way of referring to the new covenant is unique in all Christian literature. I agree with Attridge, *Hebrews*, p. 376, that we are merely dealing with stylistic variation, as is typical in epideictic rhetoric, particularly in the summary peroration, where changing the terms but not the meaning shows one's skills in "invention" and amplification.

which is so key in this homily, for it indicates our author's hermeneutic, his view of the relative merits of the Mosaic versus the new covenant.

Hebrews 12:25 picks up on the note of the blood speaking in Hebrews 12:24, and he warns his audience to not disregard that speaking. Rhetorically speaking, Hebrews 12:25-29 serves as the recapitulation of the peroration while continuing the emotional appeal in Hebrews 12:18-24.[771] Our author then develops another of his a fortiori arguments: for if those who were part of the old covenant could not escape when they ignored the covenant warnings, warnings that were given upon earth, how much more trouble will believers be in if they ignore the warnings that come forth from the heavenly Jerusalem and turn away from its revelation. This is like some of the previous warnings at Hebrews 2:1-3; 6:6-8; 10:28-29 about apostasy, which is what we should expect in a peroration where there is reiteration and amplification of earlier major themes.

Hebrews 12:26 continues the metaphor of speaking and hearing and mentions God's voice shaking the earth, likely alluding to the earthquakes connected with the Sinai events. Then Haggai 2:6 is quoted from the Septuagint quite closely and followed by the usual midrashic running commentary on certain keywords. This quotation has nothing to do with the disappearance of the material universe. The key hermeneutical move is that in **Hebrews 12:27** our author takes the words *eti hapax* to refer to a future and final eschatological shaking of the earth and heaven, after which the only things that will be left are the unshakable things. Only once more will there be an earth-shaking theophany where God sorts out things with his people.[772] All the rest of the created order will be removed. Clearly our author does not believe in the eternality of this earth or even of the heavens. He sees it as all part of the created order that will be "changed" *(metathesis),* not disappear altogether, which matches what he said about the final conflagration in Hebrews 1:10-12. The whole passage from Haggai was surely in our author's mind: "The LORD Almighty says: 'In a little while I will once more shake the heavens and the earth, the sea and the dry land. I will shake all nations, and the desired of all nations will come, and I will fill this house with glory. . . . The glory of this present house will be greater than the glory of the former house,' says the LORD Almighty. And in this place I will grant peace." There could hardly be a more appropriate quotation. First, it could be seen by a Christian writer as alluding to the second coming of Jesus. Second, it refers to a replacement of former glory with greater glory, part of the message of Hebrews throughout the dis-

---

[771]DeSilva, *Perseverance in Gratitude*, p. 468.
[772]See ibid., p. 471, on this phrase and its meaning.

course. Also, the "shake-up" does not have to do with the complete dissolution of the material realm but rather of the sorting of all things and putting them right. Finally, the new and glorious dwelling place of God will be where God grants shalom, final wholeness for his people, hence the language in our passage about all—Old Testament and New Testament saints—being joined together and all being perfected together. To be sure our author envisions the replacement of the temporal and the temporary by the permanent and eternal, which comes down from heaven, but he is not envisioning the replacement of the material realm with a nonmaterial realm simply called heaven, any more than Paul was when he used similar language (1 Cor 7:31; cf. 1 Jn 2:8, 17; Rev 21:1). The heavenly city involves persons like Jesus who have a resurrection body and those who have received at his coming a better resurrection. What our author envisions is not less solid or material, it is more so, more permanent—an unshakable kingdom on earth, as it once was in heaven but has come down and is in the process of being received but has not yet reached its consummate state. Shaking of the earth (i.e., earthquakes) was regularly associated with theophanies and especially with the coming Yom Yahweh, the Day of the Lord (Is 13; 34; Ezek 7; 30:1-9; Joel 2:1-11), and more generally with the end times (2 Baruch 32.1; 2 Esdras [4 Ezra] 6.16; 10.26; Sibylline Oracles 3.675). "The text does not suggest that God destroys a lower realm and preserves a higher one . . .—both heaven and earth are shaken."[773]

Thus, our author finally must end in **Hebrews 12:28** with the warning that the audience be careful to receive (using a present participle). They are in the process of receiving this kingdom, but have not fully done so, and if they pull out before the end there will be hell to pay—literally. This is our author's only mention of receiving a kingdom, but it is an unshakable one that comes as a gift, which should prompt the believer's gratitude, worshiping with reverence in a fashion acceptable to God. There are probably echoes here of Daniel 7:18-22, which is significant because there the kingdom is given to the saints when the Ancient of Days comes down in a theophany for final judgment in favor of the saints and against the beastly nations and they finally possess this kingdom—on earth, not in heaven.[774] Here the theophany involves believers worshiping with a sense of awe about all this, and our author attempts to reinculcate that sense of awe by the imagaic discussion that just preceded. The term *latreuō* is a technical term for the priestly service used elsewhere in Hebrews 8:5; 9:9, 14; 10:2; 13:10, which suggests that this Christian worship is the fulfillment of

---

[773]Koester, *Hebrews*, p. 547.
[774]See Attridge, *Hebrews*, p. 382, on this allusion.

the previous Levitical service (Heb 9:14).[775] The word *deos* ("awe"), which occurs only here in the New Testament, shows up in the Septuagint in scenes of terror, holy or otherwise (2 Maccabees 3.17, 30; 12.22; 13.16; 15.23). Our author on the one hand wishes to say God will be more accessible, but he does not wish to suggest that God ceases to be God or ceases to deserve worship and absolute awe and respect at the eschaton. This is why he adds **Hebrews 12:29**.

Finally our author ends the discussion, as Andrew Lincoln points out in lectures on Hebrews delivered at Gordon-Conwell Theological Seminary, with an inclusio: he began at Hebrews 12:18 with a discussion of fire on the mountain and closes with a reference to God being a consuming fire (drawing on Deut 9:3). This is the same God that the Old Testament people encountered, but now operating through a more gracious mode and covenant. Thomas Long stresses: "This statement is ambiguous. Should we sing the doxology or hide under the pew? The Preacher wants to leave the image undefined, since God's fire both refines and devours, purifies and incinerates. God's word is a two-edged sword (4:12), both severing and saving, and it all depends on whether or not we enter the sanctuary 'by the new and living way that Jesus opened for us.'"[776] Our author sees this final salvo as a panacea "for a church plagued by neglect, apathy, absenteeism, retreat, and near the point of apostasy."[777] It is well to add, however, that the allusion to the consuming fire is a reminder of coming final judgment (Is 33:14; Wisdom of Solomon 16.16; *Psalms of Solomon* 15.4) when Christ returns. It thus nicely rounds out the treatment of the final theophany.

A CLOSER LOOK
Realized Eschatology in Hebrews?

It has long been realized that there a good deal of what may be called realized eschatology in the book of Hebrews. This is perhaps especially clear in the peroration in Hebrews 12:18-29, but even here our author has not completely exchanged all future eschatology for realized eschatology. In the first place, epideictic rhetoric is the rhetoric of what is true in the present. It is not by nature past or future oriented by and large. In keeping with this, we should not expect much discussion of future eschatology in this sermon. That there is some at regular intervals in the homily is telling and reveals that our author very much affirms such future eschatology, though it is not the focus of his present rhetorical piece.

---

[775] Hagner, *Encountering the Book of Hebrews*, p. 167.
[776] Long, *Hebrews*, p. 141.
[777] Craddock, *Hebrews*, p. 160.

The following still-outstanding events need to be kept in mind in evaluating the eschatology of Hebrews:

1. The new Jerusalem, the heavenly city, is clearly described as "the city that is yet to come" (Heb 13:14). It does not say "the heavenly city to which we will go when we die," though our author probably believes that to be true as well.

2. The finally shaking of heaven and earth has yet to transpire (Heb 12:26 says it is promised, but not yet delivered).

3. Believers in the present are in the process of receiving a kingdom (present participle in Heb 12:28), but they have not yet received the consummation of this kingdom.

4. The believers have come "to" Mount Zion, but they have not yet entered it. It is spatially near, but not yet here, so that it could be entered by those still on earth (Heb 12:22).

5. Hebrews 12:15 refers to a grace of God yet to come and a seeing of God yet to come, which the audience, were they to commit apostasy, could miss out on (Heb 12:14-15).

6. Hebrews 11:35 reminds that forward-looking believers still have rewards and promises yet to be received, including "a better resurrection."

7. Hebrews 11:39 reminds us that none of the Old Testament saints received what was promised, but God had planned things so that they would be made perfect "together with us." But when is that to transpire? If Hebrews 12:18-29 is a proleptic portrayal of the final theophany when God the judge and Jesus the mediator descend with the heavenly city, it is only then when the angels, the spirits of the deceased and the living believers will reach such a consummation.

8. The author says in Hebrews 11:16 that God has prepared a better and heavenly place for the Old Testament saints. The word *prepared* implies that they have not yet received it, not least because they will do so in tandem with New Testament saints.

9. The unshakable kingdom comes down from heaven and replaces the present shakable created order after the last judgment falls on that order (Heb 12:27-28). It does not follow from this that we are to see this city or kingdom as immaterial in character.

10. The current material possessions will not be replaced by no possessions but by better and lasting ones (Heb 10:34).

11. The warning about future judgment that will befall those who fall into

the hands of the living God if they have rejected the gospel (Heb 10:26-31) is reinforced by the closing image of the peroration, which warns that "our God is a consuming fire" (Heb 12:29; cf. Heb 10:27).

12. In both Hebrews 10:22 and Hebrews 12:22 the descriptor of the present position of the believers is that they can draw "near" to God and the holy city. They are not said to enter it, and there is not even any discussion of deceased believers entering it when they die, though this is surely implied in several places in the sermon. The emphasis is never on following Jesus into heaven in this sermon.

13. Jesus is seated at the right hand of God, as is often stressed in this discourse using Psalm 110:1, but Hebrews 10:13 stresses that in that posture he is still awaiting for his enemies to be made his footstool.

14. Hebrews 9:28 stresses that Jesus will come a second time to finish the salvific work appointed to him—not to bear sin as he did the first time he came, but to bring salvation to those who are awaiting him. This verse is especially crucial because it makes clear that, however realized some of the eschatology of our author may be, he still sees the consummation of human salvation as awaiting the parousia of Christ.

15. Our author stresses that resurrection from out of the realm of the dead and eternal judgment is the first thing that Christians were taught (Heb 6:2), and they ought not need to be reminded of such teaching. This explains in part why our author feels no need to stress future eschatology, though he certainly affirms it.

16. The great promise of entering the divine rest is still outstanding and remains a promise (Heb 4:1), which is why the author stresses that the audience must strive to enter this rest (Heb 4:11). He draws an analogy with those who failed to enter the promised land and its rest (Heb 3:18-19).

17. The fine balance of our author's eschatology, with its still outstanding future features, is seen in Hebrews 3:14: "We have come to share in Christ *if we hold firmly to the end the confidence we had at first.*"

18. When our author speaks of the future, he does not speak of entering heaven as the end of the eschatological process. To the contrary he speaks in much the same way as other early Jews did about "the world to come" (Heb 2:5). This world to come, country to come, city to come, Savior to come, kingdom that is coming, final judgment to come—all transpires outside of heaven and within a transformed or entirely new and permanent material realm where resurrection is possible and serves as a prelude to final judgment on earth.

19. The coming cataclysm is described in the language of Psalm 102:25-27 in Hebrews 1:11-12. The present order will wear out like a garment and be rolled up like a robe. But the text does not suggest that the material realm/garment will be replaced by something immaterial. To the contrary, it will "like a garment . . . be changed" (Heb 1:12), and Hebrews 12:27 speaks of the shakable things being removed. That final sifting process is not said to leave us only with heaven. It is said to leave us with that which will be permanent—a better garment, an eternal kingdom that the resurrected can enter and a Mount Zion city that believers may approach now but will enter only when Jesus the mediator returns. Jesus is said in the christological hymn that begins this discourse to be the "heir of all things" (Heb 1:2), and this requires that there be some "things" left for him to inherit, and not just "the spirits of righteous persons made perfect." Those spirits are said to await the real consummation until "we" can all partake of it together. This implies that they do not yet experience that full consummation even though apparently they are in heaven now.

I have deliberately worked through the eschatological material in this document from back to front, from peroration to exordium to make clear that the future eschatology becomes more abundant and more evident the further one goes in the discourse, especially in Hebrews 10—12. The peroration emphasizing the final eschatological theophany involving God and Christ thus is crucial in revealing our author's hand so very clearly. In light of this and the restraints that the author was under as he was offering an epideictic discourse that must focus on present truths, there is no reason in the end to read his use of heavenly Zion language any differently than what one finds in Galatians 4 or Revelation 21—22.

Early Jews who had a fully formed eschatology (such as the Pharisees, Qumranites, John the Baptist or Jesus) expected a consummation "down here," not merely "out there," and it is wrong to see our author as an exponent of purely or primarily otherworldly afterlife thinking. To the contrary, he emphasizes the present role of Christ in the heavenly sanctuary and its benefits for those on earth. Otherworldly Christology—not otherworldly soteriology—is his focus.

It is no accident that in the one place that Christ is clearly presented as the example that Christians should follow, in Hebrews 12:1-3, the analogy is drawn between the race Jesus (emphasizing his human name) ran faithfully and truly while on earth, even unto the finish line of death, and the same race the audience should run faithfully to the end of life. The author does not say what happens when the spiritual athlete crosses the finish line. He does not draw an analogy between Christ experiencing heavenly life as the reward and believers doing so. Whenever he speaks of the reward for believers, he talks about what will yet happen at the consummation, when Jesus returns and the dead are raised. This is so very clear in Hebrews 11—12. Perhaps then, it is time to stop suggesting that our author has "overrealized" or mostly "other-worldly" eschatology. He like other early Jewish Christians believed that what is now "up there" will one day be "out there" when Jesus returns. And then there will be no more need to speak of drawing near the heavenly city. Then it will be a matter of entering it once and for all and enjoying the eternal kingdom "on earth as it is in heaven."

FINAL EXHORTATIONS AND EPISTOLARY CLOSING (HEB 13:1-25)

My child, day and night "you should remember him who preaches God's word to you," and honor him as you would the Lord. For where the Lord's nature is discussed, there the Lord is. Every day you should seek the company of saints to enjoy their refreshing conversation. You must not start a schism but rather reconcile those in strife. (*Didache* 4.1-3)

Here he gently hints at those who introduce the observance of "foods." For by faith all things are pure. There is then need of faith, not of "foods." (Chrysostom *Homilies on Hebrews* 33.3)

While some rhetorical discourses ended with the peroration, not all did. Sometimes the peroration served as the climax but not the conclusion of the discourse. In this highly parenetic discourse it is not surprising that the author would want to offer up one final and summary group of exhortations to apply the discourse practically to the audience's immediate situation and needs. But there is another factor at work as well. Our author had the disadvantage of not being able to deliver this discourse in person. He had to have it written down and he had to send it, since he was at some distance from his audience. This being the case, the document ends with an epistolary closing not unlike those in Paul's letters, which in itself is no surprise since our author was part of the larger Pauline circle, as the mention of Timothy shows.

Several decades ago Floyd Filson provided decisive arguments for seeing Hebrews 13 as an integral part of this document,[778] arguments that were strengthened by Harold Attridge and others.[779] Besides there being no textual basis for seeing Hebrews 13 as a later addition to this discourse, Hebrews 13:7-19 reprises

---

[778]Filson, *"Yesterday."*
[779]Attridge, *Hebrews*, p. 384.

one of the main arguments found the document.[780] The grammar, vocabulary, style and content of the chapter comport with the assumption that it is by the same author who penned Hebrews 1—12, though there is a shift in tone and style from the peroration to Hebrews 13.[781] R. V. G. Tasker further demonstrates the integrity of the entire discourse, including Hebrews 13, which he sees as an important part of this document, not a mere addendum.[782] Thomas Long likens this chapter to the concluding "news and notes," "joys and concerns" or "minute for mission" that often follow a modern sermon.[783] The essential exhortations here involve a call to remain and to remember, and such exhortations are clearly epideictic in character, appealing to values already embraced and practiced. This conclusion is reinforced by the repeated stress on doing that which praises or is well pleasing to God (the *euareston* word group in Heb 12:28; 13:16, 21; cf. Heb 11:5-6).[784]

> **13:1** *Let brotherly love continue.* **2** *Do not neglect the love of strangers/hospitality, for through this some entertained angels unawares.* **3** *Bear in mind the prisoners as (if) you were fellow prisoners and also those who are ill treated as being also yourselves in (the) body.* **4** *Honor marriage in every way and (keep) the marriage bed undefiled, for God judges the immoral and adulterers.* **5** *(Be) free from avarice, (as) the way of life, being contented with what there is; for he himself has said, "I shall neither fail you nor forsake you,"* **6** *so that undaunted we may say, "The Lord is a helper to me, I shall not fear. What can human beings do to me?"* **7** *Remember your leaders as those who spoke the word of God to you. Having considered closely the outcome of their way of life, imitate their faith.* **8** *Jesus Christ yesterday and today the same and forever.*
>
> **9** *Do not be carried away by diverse and strange teachings; for it is good for grace to strengthen the heart, not foods, by which those following (such practices) are not benefited.* **10** *We have an altar from which they do not have authority/power to eat who minister at the tent.* **11** *For the blood of animals being brought in for sins in the*

---

[780]Ibid.

[781]Ibid. The individual, apparently unconnected, staccato imperatives are certainly different from what we saw in the peroration.

[782]Tasker, "Integrity of the Epistle to the Hebrews." Rhetorically speaking, as seen from various examples in Paul's letters, when one is sending a speech in the mail to an audience the conclusion of the document becomes more like a letter for obvious reasons. There was news to share, people to greet, travel plans to announce and the like.

[783]Long, *Hebrews*, p. 142. I disagree with Koester, *Hebrews*, pp. 554-56, for Heb 13 is not a peroration or part of a peroration, though it does recapitulate a few of the themes of the discourse. It does not meet the emotive criteria to be a peroration. It is more like final reminders. For example, the end of Ephesians, another epideictic discourse, has a peroration that ends at Eph 6:18 but is followed in Eph 6:19-24 by final instructions and epistolary elements like greetings.

[784]DeSilva, *Perseverance in Gratitude*, p. 484.

holy place by the high priest, the carcasses of these animals are burned outside the camp. [12] *Therefore also Jesus, in order to sanctify through his blood the people, suffered outside the gate.* [13] *So then come out to him outside the camp, bearing his reproach.* [14] *For we do not have here an abiding city, but we search for/look to the one who is to come.* [15] *Through him (then) we offer up sacrifices of praise for everything to God, that is the fruit of lips confessing to his name.* [16] *But do not neglect well-doing and sharing in common, for with such sacrifices God is pleased.*

[17] *Obey and submit to your leaders, as they keep watch over your lives as they must render a word/account, in order that with joy you do this and not with groaning, for this will be advantageous for you.* [18] *Pray for us, for we are persuaded that we have a good conscience, wishing to conduct ourselves well in all things.* [19] *But more than ever I exhort/urge you to do this in order that I may be restored to you quickly.*

[20] *But the God of peace, the one bringing up from the dead the great shepherd of the sheep in the blood of the eternal covenant, the Lord Jesus,* [21] *may he fit together/put you into the proper order in/with all good things unto the doing of his will, doing in us what is pleasing before him through Jesus Christ, to whom be glory forever, amen.* [22] *I exhort you, brothers, endure the word of exhortation and because I have written to you briefly.* [23] *Know that our brother Timothy has been released, in whose company if he comes quickly I will see you.* [24] *Greet all your leaders and all the saints. Those from Italy greet you.* [25] *Grace be with all of you.*

Hebrews 13:1 picks up a theme we have already seen in Hebrews 10:24: the author urges that they continue in brotherly love and not neglect hospitality. The form of the exhortation here suggests that our author wants the audience to continue an activity that they have been doing.[790] The term *philadelphia* is rather rare outside of Christian literature, and its few uses in Jewish literature refer to love between natural siblings (4 Maccabees 13.23—14.1; Philo, *On the Embassy to Gaius* 87; Josephus, *Jewish Antiquities* 4.26). The spiritualized or religious use of the term seems to be something distinctive or at least character-

[785] Although most manuscripts add *oun*, it is notably absent in 𝔓[46], ℵ*, D*, P and others. It may have been accidentally omitted, but this is very uncertain.
[786] Many later manuscripts add "works" to "all good"; this is surely not original.
[787] The addition of *auto* with "doing" (in A, C and ℵ*) is probably just a case of dittography. Some manuscripts change "we" to "you" to conform to the previous "you."
[788] It is uncertain whether the addition of "of eons" was original, but no other final doxology in the New Testament has the shorter form. The longer form is well attested with ℵ, A, C* and others.
[789] Numerous subscripts attempt to indicate where this document came from: Rome (A); Italy (P, 1908); through Timothy (K and others); by Paul (404); Athens (1911); through Timothy but with Paul's blessing (431). In short, guesses were made in view of the closing references to Timothy and Italy.
[790] Hagner, *Encountering the Book of Hebrews*, p. 170.

istic of early Christian discourse (Rom 12:10; 1 Thess 4:9; 1 Pet 1:22; 2 Pet 1:7; cf. *1 Clement* 1.2 and *Shepherd* of Hermas, *Mandates* 8.10, which use *philoxenos*). What is especially telling about this exhortation is that in the Greco-Roman world sibling relationships were seen as the closest and strongest relationships, even closer than parents and children, so our author is drawing on what would be seen as a natural bond, only applying the idea in a religious or spiritual way.[791] Urging the audience to "continue" something is what one would expect in an epideictic speech, and it reminds us that even here in the final exhortations our author is not urging any changes, but is rather reaffirming values and virtues the audience has already been practicing. Our author will extend his application of the analogy with first-century assumptions about ordinary brotherly love when he talks about sharing all things and even suffering abuse for or with one another.

The word *philoxenia* (literally "love of strangers") in **Hebrews 13:2** may refer to traveling Christians who would need hospitality and a place to stay since the inns of the day were notorious as dens of iniquity. In view of the following reference to entertaining angels unawares, the word *stranger* may mean any unknown person. Edwin Hatch stresses: "Every one of those strangers who bore the Christian name had therein a claim to hospitality. For Christianity was, and grew because it was, a great fraternity. The name 'brother' . . . vividly expressed a real fact. . . . A Christian found, wherever he went, in the community of his fellow-Christians a welcome and hospitality."[792] This section of the discourse reminds Christians that they must practice love of both fellow believers and strangers, while at the same time not "practicing" inappropriate kinds of love that violate the marital bed and bond. Hebrews 13:2 probably alludes to the story in Genesis 18:1-8 about Abraham entertaining angels, though it could also be an allusion to stories in Judges 6:11-13 or Judges 13:3-21 (cf. Tobit 5.4-9; 12). This audience was probably familiar with numerous stories about entertaining gods unawares (e.g., the story of Philemon and Baucis or Acts 14:8-13). Zeus in particular was said to be the friend of strangers.

Hospitality was one of the core social practices of the early church for several reasons (Rom 12:13; 1 Tim 3:2; 5:10; Tit 1:8; 1 Pet 4:9). Guests were housed and the church met in homes. Homes were the lifeline of the early church, the medium through which the message spread and sometimes the places where the messengers were lodged. Some might take unfair advantage of Christian hospitality, which is why *Didache* 11—12 provides guidelines in regard to this prac-

---

[791]DeSilva, *Perseverance in Gratitude*, p. 486.
[792]Hatch, *Organization of Early Christian Churches*, p. 44.

tice. Rhetorically, Hebrews 13:1-2 was carefully shaped to please the hearer (e.g., *philadelphia* and *philoxenia*, *epilanthanomai* and *lanthanō*).[793] There is, however, a tension between being hospitable to strangers, which both Jewish and Greek tradition supported (Gen 18:1-8; 19:1-3; Judg 19:19-21; Job 31:32; *Testament of Zebulun* 6.4-5; Homer *Odyssey* 6.207-8; Plutarch *Moralia* 766C; 2 Maccabees 6.2), and accepting strange teaching, which our author says is inappropriate.[794]

Hebrews 13:3 repeats a previous reference to prisoners (Heb 10:33-34), who are to be treated as if one was in their shoes.[795] Christians gained something of a reputation for taking care of their own in prison, even staying with them in prison, as the satire of Lucian's *Death of Peregrinus* 11-12 from the mid-second century shows. While it is possible to interpret the last clause of this verse to mean "as you also are in the body [of Christ]," in view of the first half of the verse it probably means "since you too still have a human body and are fragile, you may be subject to such ill treatment." Thus, "as though you were in their bodies" is the better translation.[796] This is a perfectly natural extension of the exhortation to brotherly love; as Plutarch writes, siblings could be said to be "a single soul [that] makes use of the hands and feet and eyes of two bodies" (*Moralia* 487C-D). Support for this thought can also be found in Philo, who refers to sensitive witnesses of torture inflicted by a sadistic tax collector "whose souls saw facts more vividly than did their eyes, feeling themselves mistreated in the bodies of others" (*On the Special Laws* 3.161).

In the Roman system, prisoners were not provided with anything other than a little bread and water by the jailer, and even that could be withheld. Incarceration was not a form of punishment: it was a holding pattern until a judgment was rendered, and it could go on for a long period of time. This meant that outside help would be needed if the prisoner was not to languish, become ill or even die. Philo reminds us that jailers were "pitiless by nature and case-hardened by practice . . . brutalized day by day . . . by violence and cruelty" (*On the Life of Joseph* 81). Under these circumstances, Christians taking care of imprisoned Christians and even staying with them to prevent abuse was a must, and this included being prepared to take maltreatment or abuse for others, as Moses did (Heb 11:25-26).[797]

---

[793] Craddock, *Hebrews*, p. 163.

[794] Koester, *Hebrews*, p. 558.

[795] There is an epideictic flavor here: they are called to "remember" and so continue to practice what they have already been doing.

[796] Craddock, *Hebrews*, p. 163; Koester, *Hebrews*, p. 558.

[797] Rightly Koester, *Hebrews*, p. 564. On Roman prison conditions see Rapske, *Paul in Roman Custody*, pp. 195-225.

Hebrews 13:4 begins a different sort of exhortation about marriage. The first phrase should be taken as a whole, and there are several grammatical points on which the interpretation hinges. First, there is no verb here, so it may read either "marriage is honorable" or "marriage is to be honored"; probably the latter view is correct since this verse is in a group of exhortations. Second, *en pasin* could be either masculine or neuter; if masculine we may translate "for/in the case of everyone" (i.e., marriage should be honored by all); if neuter it means "in every way" (i.e., marriage should be honored/is honorable in every way). Probably the former is meant since these are all-encompassing exhortations for all the audience.

The second part of the first clause adds "and the marriage bed undefiled." This might be taken as an exhortation to asceticism (i.e., do not have intercourse, which is defiling), but in view of what follows in the *gar* clause, which gives the reason for this exhortation, such an interpretation is surely incorrect. Defiling the marriage bed happens when one is involved with a third party. *Moicheia* refers to adultery, but *porneia,* as F. F. Bruce points out, is not a technical term for a fornicator but rather has a broader meaning of all sorts of sexual aberrations (frequenting a prostitute, bestiality, incest, fornication, etc.); when it is used in a specific sense it often means incestuous sex.[798] The translation "fornicator" is not correct because in a modern context a married person does not commit that sin but rather the sin of adultery. Thus, Hebrews 13:4 is a call to fidelity in marriage, not to asceticism. Keeping the marriage bed undefiled is part of honoring one's marriage, and intercourse outside marriage was widely regarded as defiling by Jews (Gen 49:4; Wisdom of Solomon 14.24; *Testament of Reuben* 1.6; Josephus *Jewish Antiquities* 2.55). There is then no implication that the audience was ascetical. If anything, this is a warning against profligacy, which is a form of dishonoring marriage as much as asceticism (in marriage) would be.[799] Proof that we are on the right track here is Horace's complaint about the sexual immorality in Italy in general and Rome in particular: "Full of

---

[798] Bruce, *Hebrews,* p. 392.

[799] Our author writes to an audience that is part of a world of arranged marriages, not all of which involved love at the outset; and in the Greco-Roman world it was not at all unusual for a husband to frequent prostitutes as a normal means of birth control for the wife. (Seneca *Letters* 94.26 addresses the double standard in regard to men.) Having children in antiquity was a dangerous matter, which also contributed to wives—who did not want their husbands to stray—nonetheless encouraging them to occasionally have one-night stands with prostitutes. Thus, the Jewish ethical stress on marital fidelity and no extramarital sexual activity was seen as a constriction of male privilege. Many Roman husbands would have seen themselves as faithful husbands even though they occasionally frequented a *pornē*. See Witherington, *Women in the Earliest Churches.*

sin, our age has defiled the marriage bed, then our children and our homes"
(*Odes* 3.6.17-32; cf. Juvenal *Satires* 2.29). Horace is referring to the defilement
of the marriage bed by having casual sex outside the context of marriage.[800] Our
author adds that God will judge both the immoral (which includes any sort of
sexual behavior outside marriage) and adulterers (the specific sin of sexual intercourse by a married person with a third party).

Hebrews 13:5 enunciates a familiar theology of "enough." Christians are not
to be avaricious, not to exhibit a love of money (Jas 5:4; *Didache* 15.1; *Shepherd*
of Hermas, *Visions* 3.9.6). This could be the opposite of showing a love for
strangers.[801] Our author does not merely say that believers should not have occasional feelings of avarice, but rather that they must not pursue an avaricious
way of life. The same word is used in 1 Timothy 6:6-10 and 2 Timothy 3:2 to
express similar thoughts, which suggests that our author is probably familiar
with this Pauline teaching.[802] Instead of trying to secure one's own future by
possessions, believers are to trust in the Lord. Whereas Deuteronomy 31:6
seems to be alluded to in the first part of this couplet (in a form found not in
the Septuagint but in Philo *On the Confusion of Tongues* 166), the second quotation is taken from Psalm 118:6, but our author makes one significant change
in the Septuagint, changing "he will" to "I will" and thus making it more personal so that God directly addresses our author's audience. Perhaps this change
was prompted because the same basic promise in the first person is found in
Joshua 1:5. Our author is saying that, in view of the support that believers have
from God and security in him, they may make the words of the psalmist their
own and have no need to hoard money in fear of the future.

In **Hebrews 13:6** Psalm 118:6 is quoted verbatim from the Septuagint. Since
the Lord is their helper, believers should not fear anything from mere mortals.
This may well speak directly to the audiences' fears. Our author refers to the
audience's leaders with the word *hēgoumenoi* three times: in Hebrews 13:17 and
Hebrews 13:24 he is certainly speaking of living leaders, but is he in **Hebrews
13:7** speaking of living leaders or those now dead? It may be a clue about the
earliness of this document that these people are called by only the general
phrase *those who lead*. Two reasons are usually given for thinking that the leaders mentioned in Hebrews 13:7 are dead: (1) the aorist verb mentions those who
"spoke the word," and (2) the second half of the verse could be interpreted to

---

[800]Koester, *Hebrews*, p. 558.
[801]Ibid., p. 559.
[802]Attridge, *Hebrews*, p. 388, is surely right that our author is not trying to correct a problem of
avarice, but reinforce the earlier generous inclinations of the audience as witnessed in Heb
10:34.

mean how their lives ended. Since our author just said that believers have nothing to fear from humans, it would be strange if he immediately contradicted that by referring to those who died at the hands of persecutors.

Our author has already said that none of the living audience now addressed had suffered to the point of blood. If these leaders died from natural causes, this might suggest a later date for this document. To the contrary, that leaders spoke the word of God in the past is likely a reference to the first missionaries who converted the audience and to their definitive first speaking to this audience, which converted them. Furthermore, our author's perspective would be that even martyrdom is nothing to be feared, since God would use it to perfect a believer. The argument for martyrdom on the basis of the second half of the verse has more weight. However, the phrase *the end of the outcome* may mean the successful outcome of their conduct or behavior, not the end of their lives, for if the author had wanted to speak of martyrdom he would have used some other word than *anastrophē*. The successful outcome of their behavior or way of life is to be imitated—that is, their faithfulness, not their way of death. One could argue that faithfulness unto death is included, but even if one takes *anastrophē* to mean "way of life" rather than "outcome" the word *ekbasin* must be given its due. This word does not mean "goal/aim" (like *telos*); it means "end," even end of life (Wisdom of Solomon 2.17-20) or "outcome" (Wisdom of Solomon 11.14). When coupled with *anastrophē* it is naturally seen to mean the "outcome of a life or the end of a way of life."[803] Their faithfulness to the end is what the audience is being encouraged to imitate, and this comports with what was said in Hebrews 11. What may finally decide this issue is Fred Craddock's view that our author is contrasting the leaders whose faithfulness was exemplary but have passed on and Jesus who endures and is faithful and an exemplar forever.[804] In addition, use of the generic term *those who lead* (Lk 22:26; Acts 15:22; Sirach 17.17; 1 Maccabees 9.30) points toward the earliness of this document in that we see nothing of a second-century episcopal structure here, as in the later letters of Ignatius, but equally we hear nothing of apostles either. The compound form *proēgoumenoi* is used later for leaders (*1 Clement* 1.3; 21.6; *Shepherd* of Hermas, *Visions* 2.2.6; 3.9.7). Our author is writing "between the times," say in the later 60s.[805] What is important is that our author assumes and asserts that leaders did and should speak the word of God to converts and po-

---

[803]Koester, *Hebrews*, p. 567, concludes not only that this phrase implies that these leaders have died, but that they died as they lived—their death reflected their faithful pattern of life.
[804]Craddock, *Hebrews*, p. 165.
[805]Laub, "Verkündigung und Gemeindeamt."

tential converts. This is the only activity mentioned here as part of their leadership tasks.

Hebrews 13:8 is familiar to all, and Floyd Filson makes much of the word *yesterday*, which most certainly can mean the recent past. Filson argues that what is meant here is not Christ's preexistent state, but his more recent past on earth when he was faithful, is now faithful and always will be.[806] The statement is not so much an ontological one as a statement about character. Following as it does hard on the heels of the exhortation to "imitate your leaders' faith," the author naturally thinks of the supreme model for Christian faith, Jesus himself, who is the model of constancy. David deSilva writes: "Here, as in 1:12, 'sameness' means 'constancy' and is opposed to 'changeableness' and 'unreliability.'"[807]

Echthes can certainly mean the past as a whole, so I would not rule out the implication of preexistence, and in light of Revelation 1:4, 8; 4:8 it seems likely to at least imply the divinity of Jesus (cf. Plato *Timaeus* 37E; Plutarch *Moralia* 354C).[808] The emphasis of the sentence is on Jesus' constancy yesterday and today and forever, with the words *the same* separating the first two words from "forever." Surely the words translated "forever" mean "forever more," for otherwise there would be no point of mentioning yesterday and today (literally "unto the eons"). Donald Hagner reminds us that the term *yesterday* was applied to Christ's atoning work in Hebrews 9—10 and *today* to Christ's present intercessory work in heaven (Heb 4:14-16; 7:25).[809] When we couple this with references to his faithfulness forever (Heb 1:12; 7:24), the point is that always and from henceforth Jesus can be counted on to be reliable, to be there for the believer.

Beginning at **Hebrews 13:9** and continuing on to Hebrews 13:16 we have one final attempt by our author to compare and contrast the Levitical system and the Christian system of sacrifice. Hebrews 13:9 begins with what seems to be a general remark: do not get carried away by diverse and strange or foreign teachings. Craig Koester says that the reference to "various" teachings indicates that our author does not have in view one specific sort of false teaching.[810] Much has been made of the word *xenos* ("strange"), which occurred earlier in this chapter in the compound word "love of strangers" (Heb 13:2). In view of what follows, our author is not referring to just any sort of ideas that might distract the believer but to certain religious teachings.

---

[806]Filson, *"Yesterday."*
[807]DeSilva, *Perseverance in Gratitude*, p. 495.
[808]Koester, *Hebrews*, p. 560.
[809]Hagner, *Encountering the Book of Hebrews*, p. 172.
[810]Koester, *Hebrews*, p. 560.

It is often suggested that our author would never call Jewish teachings strange, since they were familiar not only to the author but also to the audience. This view overlooks, however, one important point: *xenos* refers to foreign religion (or teachings that come from other religions) in *Shepherd* of Hermas, *Similitudes* 8.6.5 (a document likely influenced by Hebrews) and Josephus *Jewish War* 2.414. Our author might mean teachings that are alien to Christian practice, teachings from another religion—not necessarily "unknown" or peculiar teachings that were obscure or unfamiliar to the audience. In short the English word *strange* may mislead us here. Use of this term proves neither that our author and audience was not Jewish nor that he is dealing with some peculiarly sectarian form of Judaism in his audience, perhaps like that at Colossae.[811] Nothing here suggests that our author is correcting an interpretation of the Lord's Supper as a sacrificial meal.[812]

Our author is likely dealing with early Judaism in general, as he has throughout this document, and is urging the readers not to be diverted or carried away by various Jewish practices.[813] The word *diverse* must militate against the idea that our author is combating some specific Jewish sectarian ideology. In view of Hebrews 13:9b, food laws in particular seem to be in view, something our author has addressed before in Hebrews 9:10, where he said that such rules or teachings were valid only until the coming of Christ and the time of his reformation. Here again he strikes a note that sounds Pauline (1 Cor 8:8; Rom 14:17; Col 2:16, 21-23; 1 Tim 4:3).

Grace strengthening our hearts—not food nourishing our bodies—is what ultimately benefits believers in the spiritual sphere. Craig Koester puts it this way:

> The author has spoken of two possible directions for the human heart. On the negative side, he used Ps 95 to warn about the heart becoming hardened by sin and unbelief (Heb 3:8, 12, 15; 4:7, 12) so that it strays from God (3:10). On the positive side, he reiterated the promise made in Jer 31, which said that God would make a new covenant by writing his laws upon human hearts (Heb 8:10; 10:16) so that people could draw near to him with a true heart (10:22). The grace that makes the heart firm in relation to God comes through Christ (2:9; 4:16) and the Spirit (10:29). Christ's death cleanses the conscience and heart, inaugurating the new covenant (10:22). This message is the food that nurtures and benefits listeners (5:11-14); and any teaching that impedes this message is, by definition, not beneficial.[814]

---

[811]Witherington, *Philemon, Colossians and Ephesians*, ad loc.
[812]Craddock, *Hebrews*, p. 166, thinks it possible in view of the following reference to Christ's sacrifice. The mention of Christ's death does not, however, necessarily refer to a meal that remembers that death.
[813]See the detailed discussion in Attridge, *Hebrews*, pp. 394-96.
[814]Koester, *Hebrews*, p. 568.

Early Christianity spiritualized the meaning of various ideas such as sacrifice, as is evident here in this passage. Mentioning Jewish food laws leads to the point that those involved in such things are not able to eat from the altar that we have. "We" here is surely Christians, "they" are those who rule their lives by the diverse teachings involving food laws. In particular, our author has in mind those ministering in the tent (i.e., priests), but by extension he means all who use such practices. Is our author referring to the eucharist in **Hebrews 13:10**? It seems unlikely in view of his having not done so previously in this discourse. In addition, he has just said that grace, not food, strengthens believers' hearts, and so it is unlikely that he would then turn around and say "except for the eucharistic bread." Our author is contrasting the benefits of grace from Christ's sacrifice with the benefits of the sacrifices under the old covenant. In his view the "altar" that believers have is in the same place as the priest is—in heaven—and so one should no longer look to those who serve in the tent (Heb 8:5; 9:1-10). In telling fashion, this Pauline approach to being Jewish is now applied to Jewish Christians in Rome. Those who, like James, thought that Jewish Christians ought to remain Torah Jews would not likely have been fully pleased with this discourse, especially since it is directed toward Jewish Christians.[815]

In **Hebrews 13:11** our author correctly describes the procedure on the Day of Atonement when sacrifice for sin was made and the blood was taken into the holy of holies but the body was taken outside the camp and completely burned; it was not eaten (Lev 16:27). Those who participate in that sort of sacrifice cannot participate in the benefits of Christ, for he is the antitype—the reality that the foreshadowing rite pointed to. He was crucified outside the city walls (Jn 19:20; cf. Mt 21:39), as was the Roman custom with such executions (Plautus *Braggart Warrior* 2.4.6-7). To participate in the old way presumes that the new way either has not come or is not fully efficacious. Either way, it is a repudiation of the sufficiency of Christ's death and disqualifies one from partaking (eating) of its benefits.

Thus in **Hebrews 13:12** our author draws his conclusions by analogy. The analogy is not perfect, since Christ—unlike the Levitical sacrifice—was not sacrificed within the city walls and then taken out and burned. There is an analogous principle though: Jesus was crucified outside the sacred zone, outside the gate of the holy city.[816] If one wants to get the benefit of Christ's death, one must come forth out of Judaism, out of the camp, out of the Levitical system. Jesus died to sanctify his people by his blood. By so doing he changed the very nature

---

[815]Witherington, *What Have They Done with Jesus?*
[816]Koester, "Outside the Camp"; and Thompson, "Outside the Camp."

of how believers are sanctified, who may be sanctified, and what the word *sanctified* means. It means morally, not physically or ritually, clean—a clean conscience, as our author has already put it.

There are no more unclean places or unclean animals after Christ's death, and human uncleanness is limited to moral not ritual uncleanness. There is a sense then in which Jesus desacralized the earth and its creatures and re-stressed the sanctity of human and divine life together, in fellowship with one another. Our author may be suggesting that Jesus resacralized everything so that nothing is unclean anymore and so we may dwell in a world that is God's world—no longer secular at all, but claimed by and for him by Christ's death. Only that which comes from the human heart may henceforth be called unclean, and Christ has died so that even that may be effectively cleansed. Our author is sometimes said to simply have a switch in mind, whereby the formerly sacred Jewish way is now unclean, but he never says this. Rather, he says that it is obsolete, not profane. Furthermore, his major stress is that Christians come out into the open, be prepared to own their faith in public and be prepared to suffer abuse for Jesus.[817] The main point is not just to prevent them from slipping back into their old ways, though that is part of the issue, but urging them to continue to practice their Christian faith even in public, even by spending time with those who have been shamed—namely prisoners.[818] Thus as a secondary sense of this exhortation our author may mean coming out of the "earthly city," out of Roman culture and its ways, since Christians are resident aliens on the earth, coming out to where one is renounced or abused as Jesus was.[819]

Hebrews 13:13 thus takes the argument a further step. The audience is to come forth from the safety of Judaism and their past, come out of the closet unto where Christ was, and be ready to be fellow sharers in his public reproach. The reason for this is clear: even if one hides in the confines of Judaism it provides no lasting answer to the dilemma, it provides no eternal city of refuge. Christians have no such home base here on earth. Rather, in **Hebrews 13:14** believers look for and diligently search for the city that is to come, as is stressed throughout the argument, especially in Hebrews 9—12.

Some scholars argue that the reference to coming outside the camp should be taken literally to refer to coming outside Jerusalem, envisioning that this homily is written to Jewish Christians during the Jewish war in the 60s, who are

---

[817]Long, *Hebrews*, p. 145.
[818]Lane, *Hebrews*, 2.544-46.
[819]So Koester, *Hebrews*, pp. 571, 577.

still stuck in that city.[820] There are a variety of problems with this view. The first is that, as Loveday Alexander points out, the call in Hebrews 13:12-13 is a call to identify with Christ and with the victim, not a call to get out of Dodge before one suffers![821] The second problem is that our author has been using language in metaphorical ways in this very context (e.g., the sacrifices of Christians), and there is no reason to think he is now using the term *camp* literally. Third, if this is written to Jewish Christians in Rome it could both allude to Old Testament texts and conjure up the image of what went on during the reign of Nero with the execution of Christians in Rome. They were first housed in the Campus Martius, where the soldiers would normally be stationed just outside of Rome; then they were taken outside the camp to a place of execution, as was likely the case with Peter and Paul. If this book is written in the late 60s, the memories of those martyrdoms might well be fresh in the audience's memory, and they would see them as paralleling what happened with Jesus outside the walls of Jerusalem itself. In any event, Andrew Lincoln is surely right to stress that the analogy with what was done with Christ "outside the camp" serves the purpose of "an appeal to the readers to go to Jesus outside the camp, outside the Jewish religious system, in order there to bear the shame he endured."[822] Luke Timothy Johnson adds that we surely have a call here to emulate Christ by bearing suffering, not escaping it.[823] Believers, too, are to "despise the shame" and, like Moses (Heb 11:26), to bear the reproach of the Christ, as opposed to shrinking back into the protective custody of their former Jewish existence.

It may well have been asked, and our author anticipates such a question: have Christians then no sacrifices? Ancient pagans saw Christians as strange since their religion had no altars, no priests and no sacrifices. Yet our author has already mentioned Christ's sacrifice, and he will add in **Hebrews 13:15** the sort that believers can add: the sacrifice of praise "for everything" to God. This is described as offering the fruit of one's lips, confessing to his name. Our author is recontextualizing Psalm 50:14.[824] The highest form of praise is not simply praising God but owning him with one's life, standing up as one of his followers even in public, confessing in public that one acknowledges him as Lord, called here the fruit of lips (perhaps drawing on Hos 14:3). But our author offers his audience another form of sacrificing: the sacrifices entailed in doing good and sharing with one another in need. Both of these things are a form of worship,

---

[820]Mosser, "Exemplars of Faith," drawing on his doctoral work with Richard Bauckham.
[821]Alexander, "Exemplars of Faith."
[822]Lincoln, *Hebrews*, p. 33.
[823]Johnson, *Hebrews*, p. 349.
[824]DeSilva, *Perseverance in Gratitude*, p. 504.

an offering pleasing to the Lord: "For what does the LORD demand of you, but to do justice, love kindness and walk humbly with him" (Mic 6:8). Our author believes that these ultimately are the sacrifices that please God, these ultimately are what praising him is all about, not just verbally offering praise.

The concluding verses of Hebrews 13 are a mixed bag of personal remarks, exhortations about leaders and two separate benedictions, which is not unusual in a letter ending. There are numerous small textual problems in these closing verses, especially as benedictions and greetings tended to be modified over the course of time. The benediction in Hebrews 13:20-21 is one of the more beautiful and familiar in the New Testament and has a specific form.

Hebrews 13:16 calls upon Christians to practice "random acts of kindness" using a rare word: *eupoiia*. These acts are sacrifices that are pleasing to God.[825] In **Hebrews 13:17** the author exhorts the audience to submit to their leaders, using the word *hypeikō*, which is not found elsewhere in the New Testament. He also exhorts obedience, which may suggest that some were insubordinate. Fred Craddock makes the interesting point that our author never exhorts the leaders, always only the congregation.[826] This suggests that he had no issues with the leaders and may even have been one of them. One also gets the feeling from Hebrews 13:24 that there may have been several house churches involved since the audience is told to greet "all" the leaders, which seems to assume that this discourse would not be heard by at least some. This fits the Roman situation well, for we see a variety of separate house churches operating independently in Romans 16.

Our author says that these leaders are responsible to keep watch over his audience's *psyche*, which here means "lives," and will have to render account for it (a similar exhortation occurs in Acts 20:28-31). Our author wants them to render this obedience without groaning but rather with joy, and he is convinced it will prove advantageous to them. All of this suggests sluggishness to obey, or foot-dragging, as does the homily as a whole. The reference "to keeping watch over" may trigger the later image of Jesus as the believers' ultimate shepherd. In any case, the strong word *alysitelēs,* found only here in the New Testament, is used to conclude this portion of the exhortation, telling the audience that causing leaders grief is "harmful" to the congregation as whole. This may be a veiled threat of future judgment.[827] *Shepherd* of Hermas, *Visions* 3.9.10 uses this same language in an address to the Roman church, which among other things pro-

---

[825]Koester, *Hebrews*, p. 572.
[826]Craddock, *Hebrews*, p. 168.
[827]Attridge, *Hebrews*, p. 402.

vides another hint that Hebrews is written to Rome and that the author of the *Shepherd* of Hermas knows Hebrews.

Hebrews 13:18 requests prayer for the author, who is clearly in some sort of difficulty. He wants them to pray to the end that he might be restored to them quickly. Clearly he was at some distance from them, but what was detaining him? Was he in jail, which might make the earlier references to considering those in prison all the more poignant? We cannot be sure. But if he was in prison this would explain why he adds, "We are persuaded that we have a good conscience, wishing to conduct ourselves well in all things," which sounds a good deal like 2 Corinthians 1:12. Does "we" indicate that he was with Timothy in jail? Likely not, since Timothy is said to be coming to the author quickly (Heb 13:23). Alternately, one might interpret Hebrews 13:18 to refer to the author's clear conscience about what he has said and done for his audience, perhaps because some were accusing him of something false in either his words or deeds, presumably at the locale where he is writing.[828] We cannot be sure.[829]

What seems certain is that our author has been involved with the audience in the past as a leader and is hoping and planning to come see them soon.[830] The alteration between "we" leaders in Hebrews 13:18 and "I" in Hebrews 13:19 seems to imply that our author is part of a team of leaders, both where he is and where the audience is.[831] Our author is humble: he does not claim to be perfect but only that he is desiring to act rightly in all things.[832] The verb *restored* can have the connotation of released and allowed to return to the community or home (Papyrus Oxyrhynchus 38.12). **Hebrews 13:19** expends great care on the oral and aural dimensions of the rhetoric, with alliteration of the *p* sound and assonance and rhyme on the end of the words with the *o* sound.[833] William Lane is surely right that this discourse would have been far from anonymous to the audience, though posterity has not preserved his name.[834]

Hebrews 13:20-21 is one of the most beautiful benedictions in the entire Bible, which sums up several of the major christological motifs of this discourse.[835] F. F. Bruce calls this first benediction a "collect," with the following parts:[836]

---

[828]There is no hint that he is considered in any negative light by the audience.
[829]Craddock, *Hebrews*, p. 169.
[830]Hagner, *Encountering the Book of Hebrews*, p. 173.
[831]DeSilva, *Perseverance in Gratitude*, p. 510.
[832]Koester, *Hebrews*, p. 573.
[833]Attridge, *Hebrews*, p. 403.
[834]Lane, *Hebrews*, 2.558.
[835]Hagner, *Encountering the Book of Hebrews*, p. 174.
[836]Bruce, *Hebrews*, p. 410.

1. invocation: "may the God of peace" (a Pauline benedictory phrase in Rom 15:33; 16:20; 2 Cor 13:11; Phil 4:9; 1 Thess 5:23)

2. adjective clause setting forth the ground of the petition: "who brought up/led up from the dead"

3. main petition: "make you completely fitted to do his will"

4. subsidiary remark: "working in us every good thing to do his will" (Phil 2:12-13)

5. appeal or pleading of Christ's death's merit

6. doxology

7. amen

There is no question but that the benediction as a whole is directed to God the Father, who is both acting and petitioned here, for Jesus is only acted upon. There is, however, a question as to whether "to whom be the glory" goes with Jesus or with God. Christ is the nearest antecedent, and this would likely imply here Christ's divinity, an idea already seen in this discourse as early as Hebrews 1. Bruce may be right that the final clause, like the rest, should be applied to God,[837] but a doxology to Christ is not unprecedented (Rev 1:6; 2 Pet 3:18), and on the whole this seems more likely here.[838] In view of Hebrews 1, it is not hard to believe that this last remark might be about Christ, who is said to be seated in the glory seat in heaven.

Hebrews 13:20 provides the only real reference in the whole document to Christ's resurrection, using the interesting verb *anagagōn* ("led up") (cf. Rom 10:7). This usage is probably prompted in the mind of the author by the Greek text of Isaiah 63:11: "Where is he [Moses] that brought up from the earth the shepherd of the sheep?" In the final benediction, Jesus is then seen once more as the greater than Moses. Jesus is not said to have raised himself; rather, he was "led up" from the dead so that he might lead God's people.[839] This is the only reference in this document to Jesus as shepherd, though the comparison would have been natural when our author talked about Moses. This image occurs elsewhere in the New Testament (Mk 14:27; Jn 10:11; 1 Pet 2:25; 5:4; cf. *Psalms of Solomon* 17.40). It is not a major christological image, but it is a tender and important one found in diverse sources. Jesus is said to be brought up from the dead "in the blood of the eternal covenant." This seems to be drawing on Zechariah 9:11, which speaks of God freeing the exiles/prisoners

---

[837]Ibid., p. 412; but see Cranfield, "Hebrews 13:20-21."

[838]Attridge, *Hebrews*, pp. 407-8.

[839]Long, *Hebrews*, p. 146.

by the blood of the covenant.[840] Jeremiah 32:40 speaks of the new covenant as an eternal one, and we should compare the many earlier references to the "better covenant" (Heb 7:22; 8:6, 8-12; 9:15; 12:24). Here *en* surely has the force of "by," which suggests that God vindicated Jesus precisely because he died the perfect death, fully obeying God's will for him. He had completed or perfected his work, he had been perfected for his coming role of high priest in heaven, and so God vindicated him. The covenant established by his blood is said to be an eternal one.

Hebrews 13:21 then changes the subject to the result of that death and resurrection: believers are fully equipped so that they too may follow Jesus' example and do God's will in all good things, while at the same time God is working in believers what is pleasing to him through Jesus. This seems very similar to Paul's remark about working out our salvation with fear and trembling, for it is God who is working in believers to will and to do (Phil 2:12-13). Before believers are enabled to do God's will, God must first work his will and have his way in them.[841] Craig Koester says that, far from God's work making human work unnecessary, God is working in such a way to make fruitful godly human work possible.[842] God is able to work his will in believers because of what Christ accomplished on the cross, because of the blood of the eternal covenant. There is real reason to believe our author was heavily influenced by Paul or some of his letters—especially Romans, 1-2 Corinthians, Galatians and possibly some of the Pastorals, if they were already written and the influence does not go the other way.[843] That our author was in the Pauline circle is likely also shown by his reference to Timothy. What is equally clear from this benediction, with its reiteration of various themes from earlier in the discourse, is that the conclusion of this document in Hebrews 13 is neither haphazard nor accidental. It is a part of the overall plan of the author, tying things together in the end.[844]

Hebrews 13:22 may seem a bit humorous when the author says he has written to the audience briefly! This may be a bit of rhetorical tongue in cheek, but it may also be part of convention (1 Pet 5:12). Quintilian says that brevity is a relative term in a rhetorical discourse; it means "not saying less, but not saying more than the occasion demands" (*Institutio oratoria* 4.2.43). That gives the

---

[840]DeSilva, *Perseverance in Gratitude*, p. 512.

[841]Hagner, *Encountering the Book of Hebrews*, p. 175.

[842]Koester, *Hebrews*, p. 579.

[843]DeSilva, *Perseverance in Gratitude*, p. 511.

[844]So rightly Attridge, *Hebrews*, p. 405, who shows the similarities to Pauline endings and the ending of 1 Peter, as well as a trail of influence that I surmise goes like this—from Paul to the author of Hebrews to the author of 1 Peter (though it may be that the author of 1 Peter is influence by both Paul's works and Hebrews).

speaker wide latitude, but a writer faces the constraints of the length of a roll of papyrus, and Hebrews could certainly have fit on one roll of papyrus (the longest Gospel, Luke's, shows the maximum one could include on a roll of papyrus). In light of Hebrews 9:5, where he says he cannot speak in detail, and Hebrews 11:32, where he does not have time, apparently our author believes he has written a short homily! But if one evaluates this document on the epistolary scale, it is a long letter. Only Romans and 1 Corinthians in the New Testament are longer in the canon, but both 2 Maccabees and *Barnabas* are considered brief even though both are longer than Hebrews (2 Maccabees 2.31-32; *Barnabas* 1.5). As a homily to be read dramatically, even with Hebrews 13 included, it could be done in less than an hour. It is unlikely that Hebrews 13:22 refers only to Hebrews 13.[845] Perhaps we should think of this as the juncture where the author takes the stylus from the scribe and adds a personal conclusion. The audience is exhorted to bear with or put up with this "word of exhortation," a phrase that characterizes the entire document and is used elsewhere of a sermon in epideictic form (Acts 13:15; the verb is used in 1 Pet 5:12).[846] The verb "put up with" (2 Cor 11:1-4, 19-20; Mt 17:17) means to tolerate for a while and suggests that the author suspects the audience's patience is wearing thin.[847]

According to **Hebrews 13:23** our author hopes to soon be joined by Timothy and come to the audience. Whatever else one can say, this probably proves that Timothy is not the author of this document.[848] It also strongly suggests that the audience knows this Timothy, for he requires no further moniker or descriptor than just Timothy.

The social networks in the small religious sect called Christianity were considerable, and likely only a very small pool of leaders had authority beyond local congregations in the 60s.[849] And so a little speculation here may not be amiss. If two Pastoral Letters were written to Timothy in Ephesus in the mid-60s right at the end of Paul's life; if Timothy never made it to Rome to see Paul before his demise; if Timothy was arrested in Troas, as Paul himself seems to have been on a later occasion (2 Tim 4:13);[850] if Timothy was likely incarcerated previously

---

[845] I agree with Koester, *Hebrews*, p. 582, that this conclusion was not likely simply tacked on to the document by another hand. As he says, if someone wanted to turn this into a letter, they would surely have tacked on an epistolary prescript as well.

[846] See the discussion in the introduction and Attridge's "Paraenesis in a Homily."

[847] Craddock, *Hebrews*, p. 173.

[848] Hagner, *Encountering the Book of Hebrews*, p. 176.

[849] On this point see Lampe, *From Paul to Valentinus*, pp. 77-79. The one lacuna in this fine study is that it gives short shrift to Hebrews and its implications for understanding the Roman church. On the social networks issues see Thompson, "Holy Internet."

[850] Witherington, *Letters and Homilies*, 1.378-79.

in Rome for being a Pauline Christian (Philem 1);[851] if instead of reaching Rome Timothy was arrested as he tried to retrieve Paul's things in Troas;[852] and if Apollos, who had spent time in Ephesus (Acts 18), had returned to the city and was writing from there to the Jewish Christians in Rome—perhaps these events would explain several features of Hebrews.

A sequence of events like this would explain why there are echoes in this letter of earlier Pauline Letters (e.g., Galatians, 1 Corinthians, Romans) and also 1-2 Timothy. No one was more likely to have copies of these documents than Timothy and those in the Ephesian church, since Timothy was Paul's right-hand man, especially toward the end of Paul's journeys and ministry. Thus, Apollos is trusting that Timothy will soon be released from jail and may even accompany him to Rome in the spring of 66 or 67 (depending on the precise date when this document was penned). In the meantime, Apollos has been reading some of Paul's letters in preparation for writing this homily. In addition, we know that there was a considerable group of Italians in Ephesus. It was one of the favorite destinations for Romans and a very likely jumping off point for Jewish Christians who had left Rome, perhaps as early as the A.D. 49 purge.

Whatever else we say, the author of this document is known to the audience—and not merely known but considered a leader. So much does the author see himself this way that he does not even defend his credentials with this audience of Roman Jewish Christians. He is too well known and accepted for that. This leaves us with a very limited number of persons within the Pauline circle who could have written this document, especially since the author must have had a preexisting relationship with Roman Jewish Christians.

We have already eliminated Paul and Timothy. This leaves the following short list: (1) Aquila and/or Priscilla, (2) Titus, (3) Luke or (4) Apollos. Despite the opinion of Clement of Alexandria, who thought that Luke had translated this discourse into Greek for Paul, we may eliminate Luke from our list on stylistic grounds and also because of the way our author handles the Septuagint and the general content of the discourse. We also have no evidence that Luke ever had such authority in Rome. We can also eliminate the Gentile Titus. Having been commissioned to deal with the fledgling Gentile church on Crete, he was unlikely to have assumed authority over a group of Jewish Christians in Rome.

This leaves either Apollos or the early Christian power couple: Priscilla and

---

[851]On the provenance of Philemon, see Witherington, *Philemon, Colossians and Ephesians*, ad loc.

[852]The verb *released* commonly refers to release from some kind of incarceration (Mt 27:15; Jn 18:39; Acts 3:13; 16:35-36).

Aquila. Since in a few places our author reveals his hand, it appears that a "he" penned this document. This narrows things down to Aquila and Apollos. In Aquila's favor is that he lived in Rome, whereas this is not clear in the case of Apollos. However, while we are certain that Apollos was an important peripatetic leader in early Christianity who had authority in a variety of churches (1 Cor 3:5-9), we do not know this about Aquila. Since he is almost without exception mentioned after his wife when they are mentioned in Paul's letters and Acts, which is unusual in a patriarchal setting, it is not idle speculation to suggest that Priscilla was the most involved in ministry.[853] We have clear evidence of Apollos being an early Christian leader in a variety of churches, but the evidence is somewhat less demonstrative about Aquila. For me, the clincher is the very character of Hebrews: this discourse was written by a highly educated, Scripture-saturated, rhetorically adept mind who seems to know a bit of Philo. Absolutely no one fits this description better than Apollos of Alexandria, as described in Acts 18. Perhaps, this document is not only *not* intentionally anonymous, perhaps its very character unveils the mystery as to its authorship.[854]

The word *greet (aspasasthe)* in **Hebrews 13:24** was used in antiquity to indicate more intimacy than is common in the West today: it means an "embrace." Our author did not write directly to the leaders, but to the audience, and he separates them into two groups. This suggests a clear leadership structure in the congregation to which the author is writing, but rhetorically this mention also serves as a reminder of the previous exhortations about obeying and respecting leaders in this discourse.[855] Mention of the others with our author from Italy suggests that all of them are currently outside of Italy, not merely outside of Rome. Such third-party greetings were not a normal part of official letters but were common in letters written to friends or family. This reflects the family ethos of the early church.[856]

The letter portion of this document concludes in **Hebrews 13:25** with the standard benediction. *Charis* was the standard word for "greetings" but in the Christian context it took on the larger sense of "grace," which it surely means here. The highest prayer is to wish God's grace for someone. Thomas Long concludes his commentary: "Of course, this is in some ways a standard farewell, but in other ways it sums up the message the Preacher has proclaimed to his congregation. . . . [Grace] is the ultimate message of Hebrews, the ultimate message of the gos-

---

[853]On this point see Witherington, *Women in the Earliest Churches*, pp. 104-27.
[854]On homilies not having epistolary elements at their beginnings, see Witherington, *Letters and Homilies*, 1.38-43.
[855]DeSilva, *Perseverance in Gratitude*, p. 515.
[856]Koester, *Hebrews*, p. 583.

pel. Because of the ministry of the great high priest, the great shepherd of the sheep, grace is with all of you . . . everywhere."[857] Fred Craddock reminds us that, though the word *grace* is used only eight times in Hebrews, it is used as a descriptor of the Father, Son and the Spirit among those eight references.[858]

BRIDGING THE HORIZONS

The book of Hebrews raises a host of questions and possibilities for preaching and teaching, but to a considerable degree, one cannot simply do the same things in both of those arenas. For instance, if I were teaching the book of Hebrews in a church I would deliberately want to raise the larger issue of what is the Christian's relationship to both the Old Testament in general and the Mosaic covenant in particular. How is the Old Testament the word of God for us as Christians? A lot can be done and discussed in a teaching setting that does not simply amount to proclamation.

A lengthy discussion of what the relationship is and ought to be between Jews who live as though the old covenant were still in force and Christians would be fair game in a teaching session. Or again one could profitably discuss various theories of the atonement and sacrifice, or go into some depth explaining the Levitical system and especially the sacrificial rites and the tabernacle, but this is not something one can simply proclaim from the pulpit. One may want to address the Sunday versus the sabbath controversy, but there are only a limited amount of things one can do from the pulpit along those lines.

One may want to tackle in a teaching session the larger issue of eschatology and what our future is as Christians on the basis of Hebrews. Or one may want to give several sessions to the human and divine Christ, as priest and as Son, and explain his actions and roles in the past and present. Some of this will preach, but to the extent it requires extended discussion over the course of more than one session, only portions of it could be proclaimed, due to the very nature and limitations of modern preaching. We must not mistake the giving of mere information, however interesting, for proclamation: "thus says the Lord" is not the same as "thus say the commentators."

In preaching I would certainly want to address the ethical situations addressed in the homily—the dangers of backsliding and apostasy, especially under internal and/or external pressure. The appeal to go on and the motif of the wandering people of God looking up to the bright heavenly Jerusalem as a goal would preach well. One could also address the problems of those who have

---

[857]Long, *Hebrews*, p. 149.
[858]Craddock, *Hebrews*, p. 173.

been Christians for a while and the luster of the first surge of faith has worn off. How does one renew one's faith years down the road?

Though in North America it is mostly a theoretical matter, one could certainly preach on persecution and the need for sticking to one's guns regardless of the reception. There is also some good material in this homily about the theology of enough, or living simply and traveling lightly since this world is not our home. Much could be done with the concepts of worship that this homily presents to us. What is a sacrifice of praise? What amounts to worshiping God—is it ritual acts or doing good deeds or some of both? What arc the value and the liabilities of ritual and ceremony? I think that our author raises these issues well, and they could be addressed. One may also want to address some deeper theological issues: What is the nature of sin and forgiveness? How does grace work subjectively in us? What is grace anyway, besides a proclamation of forgiveness or God's undeserved favor?

This homily is certainly rich in material if the preacher is dealing with a complacent congregation that needs a cattle prod—or perhaps a two-edged sword to prod them. This homily is truly inspiring in its view of both Christ and the communion of saints, and it certainly can be used for a call to higher vision in one's discipleship, a call to setting one's sights higher than before—higher up and further in. One can also teach or preach to good effect on the character and modus operandi of the word of God from this book. Thus there are a multitude of both theological and ethical themes and ideas that one could use to make some good lessons or sermons.

The book also raises questions about the proper nature of our *koinōnia* with another. Can one be a solitary Christian? Not according to our author. We need one another, we need to meet together, we need to exhort one another to love and good deeds, we need to learn to live on the basis of our faith, not on the basis of our fears. Thus we must see this document as meant for us—as both a word of exhortation and a word of comfort (*paraklēsis* entails both). On the basis of what Christ has done and is doing, we also must do what we are called to do, always mindful that he intercedes for us as we journey on toward the new Jerusalem. It would be useful to read this book in tandem with John Bunyan's *Pilgrim's Progress* and discuss both together, as they present rather similar views of the Christian's pilgrimage toward the kingdom of God.

Andrew Lincoln suggests that this pilgrimage motif (which does not mean mere wandering) corresponds nicely with modern enthusiasm for pilgrimages to the Holy Land and elsewhere.[859] He is also right that Hebrews 11 provides a

---

[859]Lincoln, *Hebrews*, p. 107.

countercultural group of heroes who triumph by suffering and dying, not by being warriors, as our author inverts existing notions of what is honorable and what is shameful, particularly what is a shameful way to die.

In a truly profound way, the book of Hebrews raises and provides at least some indirect answers to this question: in what sense and in what ways is the Old Testament applicable to Christian faith and life? In terms of hermeneutics there is, of course, a dialectic involved in which our author reads the Christ event and subsequent Christian life in light of the Old Testament, but the converse is also true, particularly in terms of reading the Old Testament in light of the Christ event in the context of a theology of progressive revelation. The word *better* keeps coming into play. On the one hand, our author does not in any way wish to deny that the Old Testament is sacred Scripture. He stresses that through it God/Christ/Spirit speaks directly to the audience. At the same time, his covenantal theology is such that he does think that various things have been "made old" and eclipsed by the coming of Christ, particularly the sacrificial system as described in Leviticus. "For the writer of Hebrews this entailed critical discernment, as he wrestled with the questions of where the continuity between the two stages of revelation lies, and where the discontinuity between them is such that parts of the former have to be critiqued and pronounced no longer directly applicable."[860]

Inevitably, one of the major issues that Hebrews raises for the average person is the image of God that it conveys. Does God really demand that his Son offer the sacrifice of his life to atone for sin? Does God and his wrath really need to be placated or propitiated? Lincoln correctly points out that it is wrong to find in Hebrews the notion of God imposing some sort of punishment on an unwilling Son who becomes a victim of some sort of divine child abuse: "There is no sense in which Christ's death as sacrifice is to be seen either as the attempt of the Son to placate or change the mind of a Father who is unwilling to be merciful, or as an imposition of a cruel death by a tyrannical Father on an unwilling Son."[861] Christ's sacrifice was completely voluntary, and the Father was very willing to be merciful, but sin had to be dealt with if God was to be reconciled to his creatures. Justice had to be served while paradoxically in the same act mercy was being offered. An atoning sacrifice would not have been necessary if this had not been the case, and this speaks volumes about both the holiness and the love of God.

While not denying for a minute that our author affirms the idea of individual

---

[860]Ibid., p. 109.
[861]Ibid., p. 112.

responsibility for personal sin, Lincoln stresses that

> Hebrews has a conceptual world in which blame for the human plight cannot sim-
> ply be parcelled out precisely to individuals, because humans have unleashed an
> alienation and disorder that goes beyond the individual, involves others in its taint,
> has a collective and corporate dimension, and extends even to the non-human cre-
> ation. If humans were morally isolated individuals, if they were not caught up in
> histories of oppression and victimization, and if there were no pervasive and sys-
> temic evil, then, to be sure, it would make no sense to think of a connection be-
> tween the life of Jesus and the lives of other humans or to consider his death as a
> vicarious sacrifice. Hebrews, however, stresses the solidarity between Jesus as the
> incarnate Son and other humans that counteracts the solidarity of humans in sla-
> very to sin and the fear of death, and enables him as humanity's representative to
> bring about a new situation that no other human acting as an autonomous moral
> agent could accomplish (cf. esp. 2.10-18).[862]

Jesus' death then is seen as the sacrifice that literally ends all such literal sacrifices. It is once for all time and for all persons as well, leaving believers to simply offer the sacrifices of praise and loving-kindness (Heb 13:15-16). "Just as the
necessity for sacrifices that destroy other life has been removed, so has the need
for any self-annihilating sacrifices, such as the sort of self-abnegation that is simply willing to accept habitual physical or mental abuse without non-violent confrontation of its evil. It is not all suffering or suffering per se that is redemptive
but rather the once-for-all suffering of Christ."[863]

This discussion leads us to the question once more of whether and in what
sense Hebrews should be seen as a supercessionist document. On the one
hand, it is apt to point out that there were a variety of forms of early Judaism,
and various of them were highly sectarian. For example, the Qumran community did not think that the form of Jewish religion practiced in the temple of
Jerusalem was just as legitimate as its own practices and beliefs. It thought that
Herod's temple was hopelessly corrupt and would be destroyed, just as Jesus
himself appears to have thought. The Christian form of early Judaism was not
the only one that could and did make a case for the obsolescence of the existing
cultus in Jerusalem. Though a highly eschatological group, the Qumran community did not, however, take the more radical step of suggesting that the Mosaic
covenant and its practices in general were outmoded. This more revolutionary
notion is found only in the Christian form of early Judaism, in particular in both
Hebrews and Paul's letters, and in some respects seems to go back to Jesus him-

---

[862]Ibid.
[863]Ibid., p. 113.

self. In short, it is not possible to avoid the scandal of particularity when it comes to the Christian form of Judaism. There was an inevitability to the parting of the ways between Christian and non-Christian Jews, however long it took in different places, and the parting was only accelerated by the Pauline Gentile mission and its success.

Lincoln sums up well what is going on in Hebrews:

> Its writer holds that, while the Scripture is still the authoritative vehicle of God's self-disclosure, the sacrificial system, the law and the Sinaitic covenant, of which Scripture speaks, have been surpassed by God's new and decisive word in Christ, and so in terms of present Christian experience are no longer appropriate. The law, its symbols and institutions remain crucial for interpreting the fulfillment of God's purposes in Christ but do not determine Christian practice. Christ's once-for-all sacrifice does away with the need for the sacrificial system (cf. 10.4-18) and indeed the covenant with Moses can be described as obsolete (8.13). It is in this sense that Hebrews can be appropriately called a "supersessionist" document.[864]

To this I add the caution that the author no doubt would have argued that he was talking about the completion of the Jewish heritage in Jesus. He would have stressed, had he lived until today, that it is totally anachronistic to talk about the replacement of Judaism as a religion with Christianity as a religion. Our author is not talking about Christianity as some separate religion from Judaism. He is talking about what he sees as the true completion of all the Jewish religion—what it was meant to point to and prepare for and be the basis of. Of course, what he says in Hebrews would inevitably be viewed as supercessionist by those Jews who had not and did not see Jesus as the completion of God's plans for them or the fulfillment of earlier covenants.

In order to escape the notion of supercessionist theology, both conservative and liberal Christians sometime try to cut the Gordian knot of this problem by suggesting that two covenants are in operation at once—one for Jews and one for Gentiles/Christians. Surprisingly enough this approach is found in both ultraconservative dispensationalism and liberal approaches to Paul and Hebrews. There is a problem, a very serious problem, with both of these two-track models: both of them renounce the claims of the New Testament authors about Jesus as the Savior of the world and about the true people of God being "Jew and Gentile united in Christ," and both apply a very different hermeneutic to the Old Testament than we see being applied in Hebrews. Here again Lincoln helps us:

---

[864]Ibid., p. 114.

Without the conviction that Christ was the surpassing fulfilment of the Mosaic covenant, there would have been no reason in the first place for Jews to have become Christians or to remain Christians under pressure (the issue for Hebrews) or for Gentiles to have become Christians rather than proselytes or God-fearers. Without the conviction that Jesus Christ is the decisive revelation of God for all human beings, however the implications of that conviction are spelled out, Christianity is no longer recognizably in continuity with its Scriptural foundation. The suggestion, sometimes made today, that Christians should think in terms of two covenants, one for Jews, based on Moses, and one for Gentiles, based on Jesus, does not allow Jesus *to be the decisive revelation for the people to whom this revelation was given in the first place.*"[865]

We must resist the temptation to whittle off the hard edges of this and other New Testament texts just to make life easier for ourselves. The scandal of particularity cannot be escaped by exegetical gymnastics or hermeneutical legerdemain.

This does not mean, however, that Jews today are guilty of practicing a false religion, a false faith. This is not how either the author of Hebrews or Paul would have viewed the matter. Even when he painfully discusses that many Jews have rejected Jesus (Rom 11) and so says that they have been temporarily broken off from the tree that makes up the people of God, Paul still envisions a time when they can and in some cases will be grafted back into that people. This is a completionist—not a replacement—theology, and Christians today must be always reminded that the New Testament is a Jewish book written almost entirely by Jews and—in the case of Hebrews—for Jews. We must be very mindful and wary of how this book has been misused by later Gentile believers to justify all sorts of anti-Semitic acts.

And this brings us to the most important point: both Paul and our author see salvation as a work in progress that will not be completed until Christ returns and the dead are raised. Only then will there be full conformity of anyone to the image of Christ, and only then will we finally and fully know who is saved and who is not. Between now and then the lost can be saved, and the saved can commit apostasy, and even when Jesus returns some saving is apparently yet to be done.

This means that Christians must live with the eschatological tension of already and not yet, must live with being in the midst of salvation history not at its end and must live with the tension that they themselves are not eternally secure until they are securely in eternity. This being the case, humility and not

---

[865]Ibid., p. 118 (emphasis added).

triumphalism is in order. As Jesus warned, many will come from the east and west and replace many of those we expect to sit at the messianic banqueting table. This in turn means that "the church" has not replaced "the synagogue." God is not finished with any of us yet, and God certainly finds reprehensible anti-Semitism in any form, much less in the form it took in Nazi Germany during World War II. If Jesus died for the sins of the world, then he died not just for the sins of his present followers but even for those who rejected and do reject him, at least in his role as world savior.

My suggestion is that we follow the author of Hebrews: we are called to pursue peace with everyone and the holiness without which none of us will see the Lord (Heb 12:14). We should view every human being as someone whom God loves and for whom Jesus died. We should do our best to love everyone and be more concerned about our own Christlikeness than the perceived lack of it in others. We should get our own house in order. This does not mean that we should neglect a prophetic critique of ungodly behavior, whether by Christians or anyone else. For example, Christians have no business blindly supporting Zionistic Israeli policies that lead to the killing of hundreds of innocent men, women and children, any more than we should support the hate-filled practices of Hamas or Hezbollah or Iraqi Sunni and Shiite suicide bombers. Such support violates the very heart or essence of what Jesus himself called his followers to believe and to be.

Perhaps the best way for me to articulate one way to use Hebrews for preaching and teaching today is to provide a sample. The following sermon was preached at St. Salvator's Church in St. Andrews, Scotland, as part of the July 2006 conference on Hebrews and Theology.

THE CONQUEST OF FAITH AND THE CLIMAX OF HISTORY (HEB 12:1-4, 18-29)

In 1993 I managed to run the Boston Marathon—all twenty-six miles of it. I had trained for it, but nothing could ever prepare me for that sort of life experience. I knew that the only way I would ever see the *archēgos*—the trailblazer out in front of the pack—was if I went up to the starting line before the race began and looked at the Kenyans and Nigerians with their huge upper legs and otherwise lanky and diminutive frames. They would run the race in just over two hours. It would take me about five.

But there were many things I learned along the way. For one thing I learned that I needed to follow the leader and go exactly the same path he had trod. Going off the course would disqualify me. Nor was I to follow pseudorunners like the man wearing a rainbow afro wig who zigzagged across the course for a few miles with a T-shirt that read "Kiss Me, I'm Jesus." No, he was not my trailblazer either. For another thing, while I could take encouragement from the cheering of the great cloud of witnesses lining the race course, which wound through numerous small Massachusetts villages before arriving in town, I would still have to run the race myself. They could not do it for me. I took inspiration from a man pushing his quadriplegic son the whole twenty-six miles of the course and from a 74-year-old lady who urged me to run with her up Heartbreak Hill. When I entered the city exhausted, on a very hot April Patriot's Day, I was roused to new life by the cheering Harvard and BU students riding the aboveground tram as I headed for the Prudential Center. And when I turned the final bend and saw the finish mile, I kept repeating to myself the title of one of my favorite old books: "Are you running with me Jesus?" Finally I fell into the arms of one of my best friends, who took my picture crossing the finish line. Suddenly I was wrapped in a NASA foil blanket and given fruit juices, and I collapsed in a happy heap. I had finished the course.

The great encomium of faith in Hebrews 11 begins with the following stirring phrase: "Now faith is the substance/assurance of things hoped for, the proof/conviction of things not seen. About these things the ancients bore witness." On this showing, faith is not about looking back in longing or in dread or in belief, it is about looking forward toward our hope with conviction and assurance, for the very existence of the miracle of forward-looking faith is called a proof of things not seen. But this stirring beginning to the "hall of faith" chapter in Hebrews has an equally stirring climax—not in Hebrews 11 but in Hebrews 12:1-4.

Unfortunately Stephen Langton (1150-1228), the one-time archbishop of Canterbury, did not serve us well when he provided the still-current division of the Bible into chapters and verses, which divisions I keep reminding my students are not inspired—and sometimes are not even very inspiring. Especially unfortunate is the separation of Hebrews 12:1-4 from the material in Hebrews 11, for Christ is the climactic exemplum of faith, the paradigm and paragon of true forward-looking faith and faithfulness in this sermon called Hebrews.

Famously Jesus is said to be the pioneer and perfector, the trailblazer and finisher of faith. I did not say "of our faith." No word our is either hinted at or explicit in the Greek text. Our author is telling us that while in the marathon race to the finish line of life we are surrounded by many forward-looking folk, a great cloud of witnesses who have gone before us, nevertheless, we are meant to cast off our leg irons and arm weights and focus entirely on Jesus, the leader of the pack, the trailblazer of our path into the heavenly sanctuary, the pioneer of true forward-looking faith and faithfulness. Our author goes on to make very clear that Christ is our ultimate example of faith and faithfulness, for he goes on to add: "Consider him who endured such opposition from sinners so that you will not grow weary and lose heart."

Hebrews 11—12 brings to mind the words of naturalist John Muir: "We look at life from the backside of the tapestry. What we normally see is loose ends, tangled threads, frayed chords. But occasionally light shines through the tapestry and we get a glimpse of the larger design." Hebrews 11—12 is giving us that big-picture glimpse.

Our author is worried about the level of morale among the Jewish Christians in Rome in the 60s, who have already seen Peter and Paul go down for the count, and while they themselves have not yet suffered to the point of bloodshed, they have had property confiscated and they have seen their leaders martyred. The temptation to go native, or to turn back to a safer and more licit form of religion, must have been great. Our author, who provides stern warnings against apostasy throughout his epideictic discourse (e.g., Heb 6), is certainly one of those who believes that Christian believers are not eternally secure until they are securely in eternity.

Thus he exhorts the audience, with real concern about their breaking or abandoning faith, to follow the example of and keep their eyes on the trailblazer Jesus, to endure the same sort of shame he did, to die if need be and to sit down with him in glory. Thus far our author sounds rather like an ancient version of those who promise pie in the sky by and by, and we must seriously ask whether our author has exchanged eschatological afterlife thinking for ethereal otherworld thinking. Many think so, and draw analogies with Philo or the Neoplatonists. I am unconvinced, however, for our author is not at the end of the day a Platonist who sees this world as but a pale shadow of eternity; he is an early and thoroughly eschatological Jewish Christian, as my old mentor C. K. Barrett long ago pointed out, commenting on the eschatological character of Hebrews. Our author is much like the author of Revelation in affirming both a vibrant afterlife and a glorious otherworld lying in the future of true believers. In different places in his discourse he places different stresses on one or the other, but at no point has he simply exchanged his eschatological birthright for pie in the sky.

This becomes especially clear when we hear our author quoting Habakkuk 2:3-4 ("he who is coming will come and will not delay"; Heb 10:37) or when we hear about "the day" of judgment and redemption that is coming (Heb 10:25) or that Christ will appear a second time not to bear sin but to bring salvation (Heb 9:28) or that the heavenly city "to come" is to be entered not merely by dying but by resurrection from the dead (Heb 13:14)—and I could go on. What is surprising in this epideictic discourse is not the focus on what is true now in heaven, for the focus of such rhetoric is the present time; what is surprising is that the future references we do have are not deliberative in character and are not arguing for adoption of some new course of behavior or action in the near future. Instead, our author is arguing for persevering in the beliefs and behaviors the audience had already embraced long ago. And this brings us to the remarkable theophanic language used in the peroration in Hebrews 12:18-29, the truly stirring and emotive climax meant at once to thrill and send a chill down the spine of the audience as final judgment and final salvation is vividly depicted.

Here we have a tale not so much of two cities as of two theophanies. God comes down on Mount Sinai and the people cannot bear the numinous presence and the trumpet blast and the final words of doom and gloom on a sinful people who had been building golden calves while Moses was visiting with God up the hill. No, says our author, if you will persevere in true faith, a better fate awaits the present audience. Rather, he says, you have come to the very edges of a very different mountain—Mount Zion rather than Mount Sinai. Our author has perhaps learned this contrast from Paul (in Galatians). It is the heavenly city, the better country that Abraham saw from a far, that they have now drawn near to. Is our author envisioning his audience being raptured into heaven, into the presence of the angels and the living God, or simply dying and going to heaven?

Like the author of Revelation he envisions a corporate merger of heaven and earth, a replacement of this current world, both heaven and earth, that is wasting away, with an eternal form of heaven and earth, which when Jesus returns and the dead are raised will become heaven on earth. Our author says that we who are still earthbound are receiving a kingdom (Heb 12:28), the very one devoutly to be wished and long prayed for: "Your kingdom come, on earth as it is in heaven." And so our author envisions the second coming as a second theophany, a coming down of the heavenly city to earth, a final judgment and redemption in space and time, not an escape into the bodiless existence of a purely spiritual heaven without a final resolution of the matters of justice and redemption. Chrysostom ably summed up things in his homily on this very text, and I paraphrase him here: At the former theophany the people stood far off; at the final theophany they are said to have drawn near and are beckoned to stay close. At the former theophany they are in the wilderness; at the latter theophany they are at the gates of the new Jerusalem, the ultimate symbol of true human civilization. At the former theophany there was gloom and darkness; at the latter theophany a festal celebration complete with partying angels. At the former theophany the people begged God to speak through Moses and not directly; at the latter theophany they are urged to listen directly to God. At the former theophany even Moses the mediator trembled and no one dared to touch the holy mountain; at the latter theophany Jesus the mediator will be present and God's people are beckoned to enter in at his return. At the former theophany sinful Israel is present; at the latter theophany the spirits of just persons are made perfect. At the former theophany there is blood from violence and judgment on sin; at the latter theophany there is only the sprinkled blood of Jesus, which preaches peace and enables mercy. At the former theophany worship amounts to fear and trembling before God; at the latter theophany worship involves awe and wonder and thankfulness and acceptable worship of God.

This brings us back to the opening definition of faith. It is not just about faith in things in heaven not currently seen. It is also about things hoped for in space and time that are "coming to a theater near us" when Jesus comes back. In his scintillating Freitas Lectures at Asbury Theological Seminary, Mark Allan Powell spoke about the difference between Christian faith's great expectations and the resort to calculations or prognostications. The early church earnestly expected Christ to return, but that expectation was not trivialized into calculation. Expectations, even great expectations, are not dogma or doctrine, they are things devoutly to be wished and earnestly desired. They are based on the promises of God, but they do not try to resolve the tension between the already and the not yet by giving way to predictions.

The earliest Christians, including the author of Hebrews, knew that God has revealed enough of the future to give us hope, but not so much that we do not need to live by faith. Our author insists that we must live by faith just as all those who have come before us, including Jesus, the ultimate model of faith and faithfulness, have done. We have assurance of what is hoped for, but this is in no way the same as having knowledge of when faith will become sight and when hope will be realized. When faith degenerates into speculation or, even worse, into pretended knowledge that "the end is at hand," then it ceases to be the hopeful, forward-looking trusting of God about which our author speaks.

It is ironic to me that both Albert Schweitzer and modern dispensationalists are wrong about the eschatology of Jesus, Paul and other New Testament writers in the same way. Schweitzer thought that Jesus and his followers believed and predicted that the end was definitely at hand and acted accordingly, though, bless their hearts, they were wrong. Modern dispensationalists think the end is now at hand and think they can prove it with multicolored charts, Left Behind novels and escapist theology. Bad theology came out of that revival in Glasgow in the 1820s, which John Nelson Darby attended and which got the rapture theology rolling for the Plymouth Brethren, then for D. L. Moody, then for C. I. Scofield and on and on.

And this comparison of two bad misreadings of the early Christian hope is not just a misreading of the New Testament evidence, but in both cases expectation was wrongly assumed to equal prognostication or prediction, which is not the case. To predict the timing of Christ's return with accuracy would make unnecessary the very sort of trust in God and assurance about the future hope that our author says we should embrace and insists is essential for Christians as they look forward into the future. Great expectations, when coupled with true faith and trust, should never degenerate into paltry prognostications of whatever sort. That is just human beings getting an itchy trigger finger and not being able to leave matters in God's hands.

Two stories of forward-looking faith illustrate this point. Adoniram Judson was a remarkable missionary to Burma, remarkable not least because he seemed to have no success, no converts for well over a decade, yet he stuck to it. The tribes he was ministering to had become impatient and hostile toward him. There came a day of confrontation when the chief of one tribe was ready to throw Judson to the flames and had him tied up. He came and eyeballed Judson and said, "What do you think now of your God, now that you are about to die?" Judson stared right back at him and said in memorable words, "The future is as bright as the promises of God." Famously, it was the tribal chief who blinked, untied Judson and said he would hear more of this God. This was the day Christianity took root in Burma. Judson did not say, "The future is as bright as the predictions of human beings." He knew the difference between trusting in God's promises and reducing expectations to calculations.

I was privileged enough to study in seminary with Elizabeth Elliot, the wife of Jim Elliot, the subject of the recent movie *The End of the Spear*. It is a stirring and true tale of young Christian couples working with the violent Waodani Indians in South America. On furlough shortly before he was martyred, Jim Elliot was asked by a reporter why he was so hopeful in his work with such resistant and violent people. He replied, "He is no fool, who gives up what he cannot keep, to gain what he cannot lose." Shortly thereafter, Jim was killed by one of the Waodani. Only a couple of years ago at a Franklin Graham crusade in Florida, the man who killed Jim Elliot came and gave his testimony. He said: "Formerly, I lived badly badly. But when Jim Elliot came and helped me to see Jesus and then gave up his life for me, I knew I must respond in faith." Indeed so. The great cloud of witnesses referred to in Hebrews did not cease to march the trail into glory in the first century. It has continued on into the present.

The question for us is this: will we embrace this faith in God's promises, will we live as the church expectant, not the church triumphalistic? Will we fix our eyes on Jesus and follow his model of trust in God and faithfulness unto death? If we will, then we have assurance of things hoped for—and even internal proof of things not seen.

Part Two

JAMES THE HOMILY

Introduction to James

TEXT HISTORY AND INTERPRETATION OF JAMES

Though fresh winds have been blowing now for a couple of decades in the scholarly discussion of James and there is renewed interest in the document, ever since the Protestant Reformation the letter of James has existed under a cloud of suspicion as to its authorship, authenticity and thus rightful place in the canon. Luther's proclamation in the New Testament preface in his 1522 German Bible that this letter was "a right strawy epistle, since it has in it no quality of the gospel" was not the only negative voice. Many were willing to see it as a subcanonical or noncanonical text.[2] John H. Elliott even says that it has even been ranked among the "junk mail" of the New Testament in the modern era![3] This is more than a little unfortunate, as James is a rich source of material when it comes to helping us understand the ethical ethos of early Jewish Christianity.

Early church historian Eusebius declares that James is among the "antilegomena," that is, a letter of disputed origin and canonical authority. Yet Eusebius still opines that the document is by James the brother of Jesus and that James is the first of Catholic Letters and "we know that these letters have been used publicly with the rest in most churches" (*Commentary on the Psalms* 2.23, 25). Ori-

---

[1] One example of the fresh approaches can be seen in Bauckham's *James*, which compares James and Søren Kierkegaard to good effect.

[2] On the history of interpretation see the lengthy treatment in Johnson, *James*, pp. 124-61. A dissertation by David Nienhuis (to be published by Baylor Press) wants to revive the suggestion that James is a late-second-century document that draws on the *Shepherd* of Hermas and Clement and is meant as a canonical counterbalance to Paul. Unfortunately for this thesis, we now have extensive evidence of the indebtedness of James to the same form of Jesus' sayings as found in Matthew, a form that antedates Luke and goes back to the Aramaic original. On top of this, James reflects the sapiential milieu of pre-70 Judaism, not the later ecclesial milieu, which was far less sympathetic to Jewish wisdom literature. Lastly, the vast majority of scholars think the influence goes in the other direction—i.e., James influenced Clement and the *Shepherd* of Hermas. Some entertain the idea that 1 Peter reflects knowledge of James. More certain is a connection between James and Jude.

[3] Elliott, "Epistle of James," p. 71.

gen cites it as *hē pheromonē iakōbon epistolē,* seeming to imply that it is disputed or only "apparently" by James, but he himself champions the letter as Scripture and by the brother of the Lord (*Commentary on the Epistle to the Romans* 4.8). It is possible, but not certain, that Theodore of Mopsuestia simply rejected it as Scripture, but the book was very popular among the Eastern fathers, particularly in Alexandria, with the first commentary on James being written by Didymus the Blind (313-98) in Alexandria. In all probability it was the affirmation of Augustine and Hilary, and perhaps Jerome, that led to it finally being accepted as canonical at the Synods of Rome (382) and Carthage (397) in the West, while the inclusion of James in the list of canonical books in Athanasius's paschal letter of 367 seems to have settled matters in the East. It becomes clear that suspicions about James largely originate in a much later era of church history, specifically with Luther and continuing after him.

What were the reasons for these suspicions and problems? There was thought to be an apparent contradiction between this document and those of the dominant theologian of the early Christian church—Paul. James 2 was thought to proclaim something other than justification by faith alone (Gal 3), and this is the main reason for Luther's problems with this letter.

In addition, this document on the surface seems to have little or no specifically Christian content, with the exception of James 1:1 and James 2:1, which are often seen as Christian interpolations into a non-Christian document of Jewish origins.

There is also the problem that this document hardly seems like a letter at all. It mentions no one specifically to whom it is written, makes no personal remarks, sends no greetings or directions to or from anyone, appears to have little continuity from one verse to another, and gives no indication that the author is interacting with specific church problems in any specific place. These complaints have some merit if one insists on reading this document as a letter—which it is not. It is a homily.

Finally, the document is said to give no appearance of being by the Lord's brother, James, as it makes no reference to this at all and reflects no personal knowledge of the earthly Jesus.

All of this leads scholars to argue the following:

- The letter was not written by James the brother of the Lord.

- It is a late-first-century letter at the earliest.

- It is not a letter at all but a collection of paraenetic remarks strung together by catchwords or possibly an adaptation of the Hellenistic diatribe form or even a theological catechetical tract. Especially in the German form-critical tradition as characterized by Martin Dibelius, this document has not been treated as a coherent or even a very Christian document. These views have had influence out of all proportion to their merits and will have to be dealt with before we can exegete the document.

But perhaps some good news would not be amiss at this juncture—the text of James is quite stable, and we do not have to deal with two distinct textual traditions or the Alexandrian versus Western text issue (as in Acts) when it comes to James, not least because Codex Bezae (D) does not include James at all.[a]

Our earliest witnesses to the Greek text of James are $\mathfrak{P}^{20}$ (third century), which includes James 2:19—3:9, and $\mathfrak{P}^{23}$ (third century), which includes James 1:10-12, 15-18. All of the major uncials ($\aleph$, B, A) of the fourth and fifth centuries include the whole text of James, and to this we may add Greek manuscripts 048, 0166, 0173 (all fifth century) and 0246 (sixth century), not to mention $\mathfrak{P}^{74}$ (seventh century), which includes some seventy verses from throughout the document of James.

There is remarkable homogeneity or, put the other way, lack of major textual problems due to variants in these manuscripts. Only 44 of the 108 verses in James have textual variants of note, and perhaps only 14 verses have textual difficulties that require exegetical decisions affecting interpretation (e.g., Jas 1:3, 12, 17, 19, 27; 2:3, 20; 3:3, 6, 8, 9; 4:2; 5:7, 11).[5] We may perhaps attribute this to the neglect of this document in the church, to its not being copied as much as the Gospels or some of Paul's letters, or to its being accepted into the canon of the New Testament only relatively late in the game.[6] Whatever the reason for the lack of textual problems, we are the beneficiaries. It can be added to all of this that the meaning of the text is reasonably perspicuous. The Greek is clear and occasionally eloquent. What causes difficulties is (a) adhering to its advice and (b) comparing it to the Pauline corpus or to Jesus' sayings, which raises intertextual and canonical difficulties.

LANGUAGE OF JAMES

The Greek of James has perhaps been underappreciated. Luke Timothy Johnson says that it rivals the polish and occasionally the eloquence of Hebrews.[7] I

---

[a]There seems to be some rather weak medieval evidence of a Western tradition of James with readings that are consistently different from those found in the Alexandrian tradition; see Amphoux, "La parenté textuelle"; idem, "Quelques temoins grecs"; and Amphoux and Outtier, "Les leçons des versions géorgiennes."

[5]Metzger, *Textual Commentary*, pp. 679-86; and Johnson, *James*, p. 5.

[6]Johnson, *James*, p. 5.

[7]Ibid., p. 7.

388 LETTERS AND HOMILIES FOR JEWISH CHRISTIANS

would stress that the language is very Septuagintal: only thirteen words in James are not found in the Septuagint. This gives the Greek a Semitic feel in places. For example, the phrase commonly translated "doer of the word" *(poiētēs logou)* in James 1:22 would mean "poet" in secular Greek, while "doer of the law" *(poiētēs nomou)* in James 4:11 would have the sense of "lawmaker." This verbiage then has a rather different sense if one knows the Septuagint, which suggests that our author presupposes that his audience of Diaspora Jewish Christians does know that document and its linguistic usages. "Clearly dependent on the LXX are terms like *prosōpolēmpsia* (2:1) and *prosōpolēmptein* (2:9) ['impartiality'/'show partiality'], which cannot be understood except as constructions derived from *prosōpon labein,* the LXX translation of *naśa panim* (see Lev 19:15)."[8] The detailed examination of the Greek of James in Joseph Mayor still stands up to close scrutiny, and his conclusion that our author wrote this document originally in Greek and that it shows familiarity with the Septuagint and seems especially indebted to Sirach, Wisdom of Solomon and Proverbs is important for discerning the voice and character of this document.[9]

VOICE AND RHETORICAL CHARACTER OF JAMES

The enthymeme was a frequent rhetorical form of argumentation used by early Christians, a form that involves an incomplete syllogism. This form of argumentation was frequently used in exhortations of hortatory speeches, and this style of argumentation appears in James with some frequency. In James's 108 verses, there are some 59 imperatives, most of them in the second person (46), and 10 in James 4:7-10 alone, where the tone becomes strident.[10] What is notable about these imperatives is that they usually do not stand in isolation but are accompanied by explanations (using *hoti* in Jas 1:12, 23; 3:1; 4:3; 5:8, 11), warrants (using *gar* in Jas 1:6, 7, 11, 13, 20, 24; 2:11, 13, 26; 3:2, 16; 4:14) or purpose clauses (Jas 1:3; 5:8). There are clear signals that these imperatives do not stand alone but are part of a larger argument, as is shown by the use of *oun* ("so then") (Jas 4:4, 7; 5:7, 16), *dio* ("therefore") (Jas 1:21; 4:6) or even *houtōs* ("and thus") (Jas 1:11; 2:12, 17, 26; 3:5). Thus, while we have relatively few longer sentences (but see Jas 2:2-4; 3:15-16; 4:13-15), it is important to realize that by and large this document does not have isolated exhortations. Instead, it has the sort of enthymematic argumentation, or ethical arguments in shorthand, seen in the Pastoral Letters. While our author is prepared to persuade, he is also not afraid to command,

---

[8]Ibid.
[9]Mayor, *James,* pp. cclxiv-cclxv.
[10]Polhill, "Life Situation of the Book of James."

and he does so regularly as a part of the persuasion.

The question then becomes how proverbs, maxims and various sorts of wisdom speech function in this discourse. Generally speaking we can say that they function to make a point that is then supported by a brief argument, purpose clause, explanation or analogy. At times James even breaks into what could be called diatribe style or speech in character, for example, when our author allows those Christians who practice discrimination in the Christian community (Jas 2:3), those who refuse to help the needy (Jas 2:16), those who have faith but no deeds (Jas 2:18) or those who boast of future plans (Jas 4:13) to speak briefly for themselves. This is not surprising in deliberative rhetoric such as James.

Not only do we have the imaginary interlocutor in the diatribe style in James, but we have the typical posing of pithy direct questions that are instantly answered (Jas 3:13; 4:14; 5:13-14) as well as the posing of numerous rhetorical questions to draw the audience into thinking like the author does, and often these occur in clusters, served up one right after the other for maximum effect (Jas 2:4, 5, 6, 7, 14, 16, 20; 3:11, 12; 4:1, 4, 5). The voice of the author begins to emerge in such material, and it is clearly the voice of an authority figure who is pushing the audience to change its behavior. Sometimes he even becomes rather impatient with the audience. Thus we have short warnings or chiding remarks like "do not be mistaken" (Jas 1:16), "you know this" (Jas 1:19), "do you know?" (Jas 2:20), "do you see?" (Jas 2:22), "this ought not to be so" (Jas 3:10) or even "come now!" (Jas 4:13; 5:1).

Equally clearly this hortatory discourse is one that was meant to be heard, drawing on a full range of oral and aural rhetorical devices. For example, rhythm (Jas 3:6-7) and rhyme (Jas 1:6, 14; 2:12; 3:17; 4:8) are readily used, and James clearly has a strong penchant for alliteration, particularly the *p* sound (Jas 1:2, 3, 11, 17, 22; 3:2), *d* sound (Jas 1:1, 6, 21; 2:16; 3:8) or *k* sound (Jas 2:3; 4:8). Especially telling is the alliteration in James 3:5: *mikron melos . . . megala.* There is also effective wordplay: *apeirastos/peirazō* (Jas 1:13) and *adiakritos/anypokritos* (Jas 3:17).

This document is meant to be read aloud to good rhetorical effect; or better, it is meant to be delivered or performed in a rhetorically effective manner. Of the some 560 words in this discourse, 60 are not found elsewhere in the New Testament. Our author is certainly not just repeating what he has heard before or simply passing on early Christian tradition. He is a master of his source material, and when one notices how much of the document reflects these sorts of rhetorical devices in Greek it becomes nearly impossible to imagine this homily as a translation from Aramaic, rather than something composed originally in Greek. The microrhetoric in this discourse is enough to confirm that our author has had some training in rhetoric, though he is not as adept as the author of Hebrews and tends to stick with simpler forms of rhetoric such as enthymeme, rhetorical questions and diatribe.

Much has been made of the use of "catchword connection" in James, in which separate statements are linked on the basis of catchwords. This sometimes leads to the conclusion that these statements are linked only because they involve similar catchwords or phrases or similar sounding words. Martin Dibelius, for example, concludes from this phenomenon that there is no "continuity of thought" in such material.[11] For the most part this conclusion is false as applied to James.

In the majority of cases there is a connection of sense as well as sound and keywords in such linked materials, but the audience is sometimes expected to supply the missing premise in the enthymeme. There are a few cases where the connection seems to be merely a matter of wordplay (the connection of thought is not clear in Jas 1:12-13, for example), but these are rare. While on the surface James appears beguilingly simple, it expects a lot of the audience in order to achieve full understanding. For example, this text presupposes the ability to pick up allusions to earlier sapiential material (some of it in the Septuagint, some of it from the teaching of Jesus), the ability to understand how such sapiential material functions in deliberative rhetoric as part of argumentation by exhortation and the ability to make logical connections between remarks when one or another premise of an enthymeme is left out.

Our author is known for his vivid language, especially his vivid comparisons, using the rhetorical device known as synkrisis, which we found in such abundance in the sermon of Hebrews. Here, however, the comparison serves the purpose of urging the audience to change their behavior, and so not surprisingly our author is not satisfied with comparing and contrasting what is good and what is better. His use of analogies is most frequently brought forth to show what behavior is bad or forbidden or even evil—whether the comparison is with a wave whipped up by the wind (Jas 1:6), foliage that withers in the sun (Jas 1:10-11), a raging fire in a forest (Jas 3:5-6), fresh or brackish water (Jas 3:11) and the like. But our author uses sapiential examples not only from nature but also from human behavior as well: taming of wild animals (Jas 3:7), reining in a horse (Jas 3:3) or steering a ship (Jas 3:4).

Sometimes in his comparisons or implied comparisons James also draws on exemplary figures from hoary antiquity—such as Abraham (Jas 2:21-24), Rahab (Jas 2:25), Job (Jas 5:10-11) and Elijah (Jas 5:17-18)—but they function differ-

---

[11]Dibelius, *James*, pp. 5-6.

ently than the examples cited in Hebrews 11. The use of vivid language in James sometimes serves as a sort of rhetorical wake-up call to the audience warning them about misbehavior, and sometimes it is clearly used for its shock value, for example, when our author speaks of the tongue being a world of wickedness. One needs to know how such sapiential language works in order to understand its intended effect. Sapiential rhetoric is often compressed into pithy or even paradoxical maxims with brief support in order that they be both memorable and memorizable. The implications require a certain unpacking, and the density of the ideas deliberately forces meditation and reflection. The analogies, of course, cannot be taken literally, but the bite should not be taken out of them by modern warnings about "not overpressing figurative language." James is more than a clever wordsmith or pundit, he is an authoritative teacher wanting a change of behavior among the Jewish Christian communities in the Diaspora.

We are now well served in regard to the rhetoric of James, though there is still much to do and explore. The current advanced state of discussion owes much to the early exploration of this subject by W. H. Wuellner in 1978.[12] As is usual in such study, the beginnings involved analysis of the rhetorical devices or microrhetoric used in James, progressing forward to the question of the macrorhetoric of the document as a whole.

For instance, J. D. N. van der Westhuizen argued at length in 1991 that James 2:14-26 must be seen as an example of a deliberative argument meant to change the conduct of the audience.[13] More compelling is the argument of Duane Watson that the whole of James 2:1—3:12 must be seen as deliberative rhetoric meant to dissuade the audience from certain kinds of behavior and persuade them about others.[14] Watson argues that the three arguments in miniature in James 2:1-13; 2:14-26; 3:1-12 follow the rhetorical conventions in regard to elaboration of a theme. Watson demonstrates that the author is following a rhetorical pattern for elaboration in detail in each case:

James 2:1-13
propositio (Jas 2:1)
ratio (proof from exemplum) (Jas 2:2-4)
confirmatio (Jas 2:5-7)
exornatio (Jas 2:8-11)
   iudicatio (Jas 2:8)
   further confirmation (Jas 2:9-11)

---

[12]Wuellner, "Jakobusbrief im Licht der Rhetorik." A helpful survey of the rhetorical study of James is Watson, "Reassessment of the Rhetoric."
[13]Van der Westhuizen, "Stylistic Techniques and Their Functions."
[14]Watson, "James 2"; idem, "Rhetoric of James 3.1-12."

enthymeme (Jas 2:9-10), incorporating an iudicatio
      enthymeme (Jas 2:11)
conplexio (as epicheireme) (Jas 2:12-13)

James 2:14-26
propositio (Jas 2:14)
ratio (proof from exemplum) (Jas 2:15-16)
confirmatio (Jas 2:17-19)
   anticipation and personification (Jas 2:18a)
   dilemma (Jas 2:18b)
   anticipation and irony (Jas 2:19)
exornatio (Jas 2:20-25)
   amplificatio (repetition, exclamatio and epiphonema) (Jas 2:20)
   proof from exemplum (Jas 2:21-22)
   iudicatio (supernatural oracle) (Jas 2:23)
   amplificatio (repetition of the propositio) (Jas 2:24)
   proof from exemplum (Jas 2:25)
conplexio (similitude) (Jas 2:26)

James 3:1-12
propositio (Jas 3:1a)
ratio (Jas 3:1b)
confirmatio (Jas 3:2)
exornatio (Jas 3:3-10a)
   simile (Jas 3:3-5a)
   amplificatio (Jas 3:5b-6)
      exclamatio (Jas 3:5b)
      definitio and amplification by accumulation and repetition (Jas 3:6)
   proof from exemplum using amplification by accumulation (Jas 3:7-8)
   antithesis (Jas 3:9)
   refining (Jas 3:10a)
conplexio (Jas 3:10b-12a)
   proof from ethos (Jas 3:10b)
   two rhetorical questions (Jas 3:11-12a)
refining (Jas 3:12b)

Ernst Baasland classifies the whole of this homily as deliberative rhetoric, a protreptic wisdom speech in letter form, and outlines it like this:[15]

exordium (Jas 1:2-18), with transitus (Jas 1:16-18)
propositio (Jas 1:19-27)
confirmatio (Jas 2:1—3:12)

---

[15]Baasland, "Literarische Form."

confutatio (Jas 3:13—5:6)

peroratio (Jas 5:7-20)

This is not unlike the conclusions of Lauri Thurén, who also was challenging Martin Dibelius's idea that we have a loosely connected group of maxims or parenesis in James. The document conforms to overall rhetorical structures:[16]

exordium (Jas 1:1-18) introduces the two central themes: perseverance in trials in the practical areas of wisdom/speech and money/action

propositio (Jas 1:19-27) to accept and live by the word

argumentatio (Jas 2:1—5:6) develops the two themes of the exordium in three parts:

money/action (Jas 2:1-26)

wisdom/speech (Jas 3:1—4:12)

a climax dealing with both themes, focusing on the rich man (Jas 4:13—5:6)

peroratio (Jas 5:7-20) consists of recapitulatio/reiteration of themes (perseverance, speech) (Jas 5:7-11) and conquestio/final exhortation (Jas 5:12-20)

Thurén explains that the reason this was not apparent to Dibelius and others is because the author was using the rhetorical technique of insinuatio, taking a subtle approach. But James is anything but subtle or indirect in his rhetoric, nor is he using epideictic rhetoric here, as Thurén suggests. Thurén's analysis of the rhetorical structure of James has much to commend in it, particularly the recognition that we have something like an exordium in James 1:1-18, which gives a preview of certain themes, and a peroration in James 5:7-20, which recapitulates the major themes and then offers a final emotive climax. Thurén is able to show that wise speech and money/action are two hot-button issues that James is especially exercised to deal with in this sermon. The guidance for both speech and action is seen to be the word, as the proposition in James 1:19-27 makes clear, both the word as enshrined in the Septuagint and the word as offered by Jesus, James's brother, and reformulated for the audience by James himself, and even fresh wisdom that comes down from above. In James we are dealing with rhetoric of a less complex sort than that found in Hebrews, and in this case it appears to be deliberative rhetoric—rhetoric to change some aspects of the audience's behavior in the near future.

JESUS' SAYINGS IN JAMES

In an earlier study I concluded that James was mostly conventional wisdom of a generic sort, perhaps written to an audience in Antioch in the form of a circu-

---

[16]Thurén, "Risky Rhetoric in James?"

lar letter.[17] I have since rethought and revised these conclusions. For one thing, the use of Jesus' sayings in this document is anything but just a reiteration of conventional Jewish sapiential material. It rather reflects a combination of conventional and counterorder wisdom for a particular subset of the Christian community, namely, for Jewish Christians. As such it is addressed to Jewish Christians throughout the empire but outside of Israel, rather than just in Antioch or Asia Minor. Traditional Jewish wisdom material about the taming of the tongue is found here—juxtaposed with Jesus' own critique of wealth and the wealthy— but that is what makes this document so remarkable: like the teaching of Jesus it offers something old and new drawn forth from the resource of Jewish wisdom material. It will be helpful to set out a brief list of comparative texts from the Septuagint that have echoes in James:

Sirach 15.11-20	James 1:12-18[a]
Sirach 19.6-12; 20.4-7, 17-19; 35.5-10; 38.13-26	James 3
Proverbs 11:30	James 3:18
Proverbs 3:34	James 4:6
Proverbs 10:12	James 5:20

[a]Betrand, "Le fond de l'epreuve."

More extensive are the parallels between James and the Matthean form of the Q sayings of Jesus found in the Sermon on the Mount/Plain:[18]

Matthew 5:11-12/Luke 6:22-23	James 1:2
Matthew 5:48	James 1:4
Matthew 7:7	James 1:5
Matthew 7:11	James 1:17
Matthew 7:24/Luke 6:46-47	James 1:22
Matthew 7:26/Luke 6:49	James 1:23
Matthew 5:3, 5/Luke 6:20	James 2:5
Matthew 5:18-19 (cf. Lk 3:9)	James 2:10
Matthew 5:21-22	James 2:11
Matthew 5:7/Luke 6:36	James 2:13
Matthew 7:16-18/Luke 6:43-44	James 3:12

---

[17]Witherington, *Jesus the Sage*, pp. 236-47.
[18]This is laid out convincingly by Hartin, *James and the Q Sayings of Jesus*, pp. 144-45.

Matthew 5:9	James 3:18
Matthew 7:7-8	James 4:2-3
Matthew 6:24/Luke 16:13	James 4:4
Matthew 5:8	James 4:8
Matthew 5:4/Luke 6:25	James 4:9
Matthew 7:1-2/Luke 6:37-38	James 4:11
Matthew 6:19-21/Luke 12:33	James 5:2-3
Matthew 7:1/Luke 6:37	James 5:6
Matthew 5:11-12/Luke 6:23	James 5:10
Matthew 5:34-37	James 5:12

Peter Davids rightly concludes on the basis of this evidence that "while James ultimately has wisdom material as his background, this is refracted . . . through the pre-gospel Jesus tradition."[19] These parallels rule out the earlier suggestions that this was not originally a Christian document or was not very Christian in character. To the contrary, as Wesley Hiram Wachob argues in detail, James seems to have come out of the same or an allied community that produced the pre-Matthean Sermon on the Mount.[20] When analyzing these parallels more closely, we notice several things: (1) James rarely cites the saying of Jesus directly; rather he weaves various ideas, themes, phrases into his own discourse; (2) this material is then presented as the teaching of James, not the sayings of Jesus, though one may suspect that the audience would recognize the echoes; (3) it does not appear that Matthew is drawing on James or vice versa, but rather both are drawing on common source material; (4) this in turn suggests, though it does not prove, that the Matthean form of the sayings of Jesus is closer to the original than is the Lukan form.[21]

AUTHORSHIP OF JAMES

When it comes to the issue of authorship one needs to say at the outset that there is no textual support for the view that James 1:1 is a later addition, though the superscription "The Letter of James" is noncanonical and was added later. Nonetheless, James 1:1 mentions a man called James. One may well ask—which James? There are numerous possibilities:

1. James the brother of the Lord

---

[19]Davids, "Epistle of James in Modern Debate," p. 3638.
[20]Wachob, *Voice of Jesus.*
[21]Witherington, *Gospel of Matthew.*

2. James the Less

3. James the son of Zebedee

4. James the son of Alphaeus

5. some otherwise unknown early Christian named James

We may dismiss James the son of Zebedee since he died in 44 before he would likely have been involved in any literary activity (Acts 12:2). The problem with arguing that it is by James the Less, James the son of Alphaeus or an unknown James is precisely that they were not sufficiently well or widely known to have identified themselves in a general letter simply as James, nor could they have assumed the authority that this document assumes without further identification, because of their lack of widespread recognition. As Werner Georg Kümmel rightly states: "In fact in primitive Christianity there was only one James who was well known and who occupied so significant a position that he is designated by the simple names James the Lord's brother. Without doubt James claims to be written by him, and even if the letter is not authentic, it appeals to this famous James and the weight of his person as authority for its content."[22] This James died in 62, a martyr.

The only real question then is whether this designation is accurate or whether this is a pseudonymous document, that is, a document written by someone using the name of Jesus' brother to give weight and authority to this exhortation. We cannot a priori rule out the possibility of a pseudonymous document in the canon since it was a known practice in antiquity—even in Jewish and Christian contexts—but there are good reasons to doubt that such a practice would be seen as simply an accepted literary device that raised no moral issues in regard to plagiarism.[23] The arguments for or against this document being pseudonymous must come from the document itself and its external attestation. There are, however, several general problems that any theory of pseudonymity must face squarely when we are dealing with Christian theological and ethical writings.

It is necessary to suppose that the author was intending to deceive his audience as to who wrote this letter because if the audience knew that the letter was not by James the Just, then nothing was gained by ascribing the letter to him. One must decide whether such a deception comports with the idea of conveying Christian truth.

It is sometimes argued that the early Christian community did not critically

[22]Kümmel, *Introduction to the New Testament*, p. 412.
[23]Witherington, *Letters and Homilies*, 1.23-37.

scrutinize these letters to validate their authenticity. This claim simply makes no sense in the case of James, and the suspicion about James's authenticity even into the fourth century and beyond shows that early Christians were *very* concerned about such matters. This is why so many documents like James underwent a probation period of sorts before they were universally accepted and why the material found in the New Testament Apocrypha was not canonized.

An imitator of a great figure or his writings must necessarily have made an attempt to carefully follow his mentor's words, oral or written, so the imitation would not be detected. In the case of James there were no such earlier writings as far as we know (cf. Acts 15, his brief letter to Gentile Christians),[24] and thus there was all the more reason to make clear that this document is by the *famous* James the Just. This the document does not do. It simply says, without further ado, that the author is James.

It is sometimes argued (e.g., by Kurt Aland)[25] that pseudonymity is the logical conclusion of the presupposition that the Spirit himself was the author. But if the Spirit was inspiring this document, why then attach a name of a human authority? It can only be assumed that on this view inspiration was not enough. It was felt that human authority had to be added for the writing to be accepted and carry weight in the early Christian community. Hebrews gives clear evidence that an anonymous document was perfectly acceptable in the early community and certainly in the latter part of the first century. Thus the motive for producing a pseudonymous document in first-century Christian circles seems lacking. It certainly was not necessary to insure its acceptability if Hebrews is any evidence, unless the document was *known* by the author to lack all inspiration or inherent authority. But James does not appear this way. It assumes an inherent authority and does not bother to argue for it, as even Paul does on occasion.[27]

Joseph Mayor shows convincing evidence that at least two other New Testament documents—1 John and 1 Peter—knew James or the traditions used in it. In the case of 1 Peter a very strong case can be made for literary dependence.[28] As Mayor shows, both 1 Peter and 1 John seem to be expanding on the material found in James, so that dependence in the other direction seems unlikely. This means that James cannot date from the second century. Equally telling is the

[24] Mayor, *James*, pp. iii-iv.
[25] Aland, "Problem of Anonymity and Pseudonymity."
[26] Ellis, "Pseudonymity and Canonicity."
[27] Guthrie, *New Testament Introduction*, pp. 671-84.
[28] Mayor, *James*, pp. lxxxviii-xci.

detailed evidence that Clement knows and uses James:[29]

1 Clement 10.1	James 2:23
1 Clement 11.2	James 1:8; 4:8
1 Clement 12.1	James 2:25
1 Clement 17.6	James 4:14
1 Clement 30.2	James 4:6
1 Clement 46.5	James 4:1
1 Clement 49.5	James 5:20

Clement's use of James rules out James being a second-century document, indeed it cannot date after 90, and if 1 Peter uses James, it must be even earlier. Clement's use also makes abundantly clear that the homily of James had shown up in Rome sometime before Clement wrote his letter—as do the echoes of James in the *Shepherd* of Hermas.[30] Thus, while we must admit that the citing of James by early church fathers prior to Origen is slender, we do have evidence of its very early use in *1 Clement* and the *Shepherd* of Hermas. This is not much different than the evidence for some of Paul's less famous letters.

Many features of this letter suggest a pre-70 date:

- its obvious Jewish sapiential flavor, being of the same ilk as some of Jesus' teachings

- reference to conditions of weather typical of Palestine but not elsewhere, except in southeastern Asia Minor (Jas 5:7)

- use of the phrase "into your *synagōgē*" (Jas 2:2) and reference to elders (Jas 5:14), suggesting an early date before a clear separation from the synagogue and before there were bishops

- simple Christology and preliterary (i.e., before Gospels were likely written) allusions to the Sermon on the Mount[31]

- no sign of the later Gnostic controversies

Perhaps the most serious objection to the authenticity of this letter is the supposed contradiction of James 2:14-26 with Pauline teaching. Several important considerations stand against this view:

---

[29]Plummer, *General Epistles*, p. 20.
[30]See the evidence for echoes of James in the *Shepherd* of Hermas in Johnson, *James*, pp. 75-79.
[31]Davids, *James*, pp. 13-16, shows beyond reasonable doubt that this letter was written by a Christian, in particular by a Jewish Christian.

- Too often James the Just is portrayed as an extreme Pharisaical legalist on the basis of Hegesippus. However, as J. B. Lightfoot and Peter Davids indicate,[32] Hegesippus is not to be trusted on many points, and this document suggests a James that was mediating in his views apart from the passage in question. This view is supported by the portrayal of James in Acts 15.

- Acts 15:19-21 suggests that James was especially sensitive about not offending Jews and strict Jewish Christians and wishing that Moses' teaching on certain works be upheld to prevent strife in the Christian community. If we look closely, James 2:14-26 is not a teaching that denies justification by faith, but one that insists that real faith will produce real work, that is, good works. Paul himself argued against antinomians on various occasions.

The real question is, does knowledge of Paul's teaching necessitate a dating after James the Just? The answer to this need not be yes, because Paul says he met with James early in his Christian ministry (Gal 1:19), and we may be sure they did not discuss the weather. Further, Acts 9 and Acts 15 support the idea that there were various opportunities for James to hear (about) Paul's gospel and perhaps even to have read some of his letters if James the Just died as late as 62. One wonders if Galatians 2:9 does not make explicit that Paul had been thoroughly checked out by James and perhaps was monitored on an ongoing basis if a bad report came to James (Jas 2:22). Thus, conditions exist for the letter of James to reflect knowledge of Paul and correct a misunderstanding of Paul and his doctrine as early as the 50s. This he does in James 2:14-26. Kümmel is right in seeing James as correcting a misunderstanding, not asserting any new anti-Pauline doctrine:

> If the distinctions in the terminology and the divergent polemical aims of Paul and James are taken into account appropriately, and if accordingly, between the two forms of theological statement a considerably larger area of commonality can be established than Luther saw, even then it is unjustifiable to say that, in contrast to Paul, James presents an "additive understanding of faith and works," just as it is unjustified to say that for James "the imperative does appear without an indicative on which it is grounded."[33]

Some, however, object to James being written by Jesus' brother because of the quality of the Greek. This problem is answered in several ways. The Greek in James is good Greek, even literary Greek; however, it is also *simple* Greek and does not rise to the heights of eloquence of various Greek masters. In short, it is the kind of Greek that someone who has learned it well and is pro-

---

[32]Ibid., pp. 19-21.
[33]Kümmel, *Introduction to the New Testament*, p. 415.

ficient, though not usually eloquent in it, would produce. The Semitic tinges suggest an author whose native tongue is another language or at least knows such a language. James would have had access in Jerusalem to Jewish or Jewish-Christian converts who were likely very proficient in Greek and whose aid James could have enlisted in writing his letter. It is not necessary to assume, as Peter Davids does, a later redaction of this letter.[34] There is plenty of evidence for the saturation of Palestine with Greek and Greek culture by the first century, and we may well ask why such a letter would be put out after 70 when the situation had changed so drastically that this letter would hardly address any pressing or non-Jewish Christian concerns. The language factor, then, cannot be decisive against the authenticity of the letter, and the content is consistent with such a view.[35]

The question then becomes, what sort of document is this? Davids shows that Martin Dibelius was wrong that this is simply a group of loosely connected parenetic material.[36] It shows a structure in parts like 1 John, and in some ways it has a cyclical or rondo effect with a repeated returning to certain themes (speech, works, prayer). It cannot be called a theological tract since it has little theology per se, but a lot of ethical remarks. It is clearly a general document, not addressing any one overriding or specific concern of a *particular* church, and thus calling it a Catholic Letter is right, if by *universal* one means all Jewish Christians everywhere. It is, as James 1:1-12 suggests, written from a Jewish Christian context and for one.

It must be allowed that it does not have many of the usual features of an ordinary first-century personal letter. Rather, it is mainly a series of moral exhortations, as no one doubts. It includes both brief sayings (proverbs) and more extended discourses. Diatribe as a genre is applicable to only a part of the letter (Jas 2).[37] If James is attempting to refute at least in part a misunderstood Paulinism, offering a corrective, then it can be called polemic against such misunderstandings. Davids adds:

> In Acts James the Just is portrayed as a mediator, a moderator. . . . The book fits this picture. Against the rich, James levels stinging eschatological denunciation in line with the strongest words of Jesus (Lk. 6:24-26). His church is the church of the poor . . . [who have] fervent eschatological expectation. Yet for all his sympathy for the poor, James refuses to join the Zealots. He demands that Christians give up the world.

---

[34]Davids, *James*, pp. 13-20.
[35]Turner, "Style of the Epistle of James," p. 114, says the style is simple and could have come early and from the apostle.
[36]Davids, *James*, pp. 13-20.
[37]Some Jewish sermons have the same form and elements of the diatribe.

The desire to find financial security is in fact demonic, a test. Furthermore, he calls for the rejection of hatred and strife (4:1-3), abusive words (3:5b-12), and anger (1:19-20). No oaths are to be taken (5:12), including those to the Zealot cause.[38]

I thus conclude that this document was written at least by the 50s by someone we know as James brother of the Lord, as a hortatory sermon. As such it may be seen as in some respects like Matthew's Sermon on the Mount, but only to the extent that both draw on the sayings of Jesus. Thus, the reference to the twelve tribes in James 1:1 may be to Jewish Christians already in the Diaspora, though a wider audience may also be implied and included.

In regard to the personality of James the Just, Acts tells us little, Paul even less, and Josephus mentions only his death. In coordination with 1 Corinthians 15:7, John 7:5 indicates that James likely became a Christian only when Jesus appeared to him. He rose to the preeminent position in the Jerusalem community by at least the 50s because Peter was in prison or off evangelizing, and James appears to have been the one major figure who stayed in Jerusalem (1 Cor 9:5). An ardent but practical Jewish Christian, he tried a via media to keep the church from splitting over the Gentile controversy—and he was killed for his faith in Christ when a high priest acted without authority, taking advantage of an absent Roman ruler.[39]

SOCIAL ETHOS OF JAMES'S AUDIENCE AND HOME CONGREGATION

Assuming then that James wrote this document at a juncture after the Pauline gospel had had some impact not only on Gentile Christians, but also on those few Jewish Christians whom Paul had managed to convert through his preaching in the Diaspora synagogues (2 Cor 11:24), and assuming that it was written after the Jerusalem Council of 50 so that it is no longer necessary to debate the issue of circumcision for Gentiles or table regulations for Christian meals (and in any case the issue of circumcision or sabbath observance for devout Jewish Christians would not likely have been under debate), are there other clues about the social situation out of which and into which our author is writing?

First, we need to keep in mind the likely marginalized status of Jewish Christians in Jerusalem. Some of its members (James Zebedee and Peter) had already been jailed in the 40s, with at least one of them executed: James Zebedee during the reign of Herod Agrippa I in the early 40s. Second, regular food shortages

---

[38]Davids, *James*, p. 34.
[39]Bruce, *Peter, Stephen, James and John*, pp. 86-119.

were created sometimes by a famine in Egypt, sometimes by other factors,[40] which led to a real food shortage crisis in Israel and elsewhere in the eastern part of the empire. This in turn led to James's plea with Paul to remember the poor—those hardest hit by such crises (Gal 2:10)—something he was eager to do to alleviate a difficult social situation in the Jerusalem church. This is why Paul took up the collections he did in his predominantly Gentile churches in various locales, collections that were not brought to Jerusalem until 58. In other words, there was still need to address this issue as late as 58, and things may have gotten worse in the 50s since another famine struck Egypt in the mid-50s. Jewish Christians in Jerusalem may have found it difficult to get work, since the temple was the number one employer in town (construction was still ongoing in the 50s) and since the tensions between non-Christian Jews and Jewish Christians continued to surface. We must also take seriously what Acts 2:42-47; 4:32—5:11; 6:1-2 suggest about this Christian community—that there had been attempts at communitarianism, not unlike that found at Qumran, to make sure that Christian poor, widows and orphans did not go without the basic necessities of life. Under the social circumstances described in these chapters in Acts, and knowing that various external pressures, including famine and persecution, likely set this community in an even more serious state, it is no surprise that James takes a very strong stance on the issue of wealth and poverty, particularly as these phenomena existed in the community. James had been sensitized to these problems in his own church, and naturally he wanted to make sure that other Jewish congregations of Jesus' followers were likewise doing their duty by the poor and not showing partiality to the rich, which could ruin the ethos and koinonia of those communities.

In addition, William Brosend rightly stresses that

> the letter of James was written at a time and in a place of considerable social and political tumult and of considerable socioeconomic stratification. . . . In Jerusalem and Judea, Samaria and Galilee this general climate was exacerbated by political and religious conflict between ruling parties and classes, and a fairly long list of very undistinguished appointments by Rome. . . . By contemporary standards there was an extreme concentration of wealth among the ruling elite (2%-3% of the population), a small class of retainers, a small merchant class, and the vast majority of the population surviving as peasants, peasant artisans, and slaves. Within Judea, Samaria, and Galilee the latter grouping may have accounted for

---

[40] Winter, "Secular and Christian Responses to Corinthian Famines." Garnsey, *Famine and Food in the Greco-Roman World*, rightly distinguishes between famine and food shortage. The latter could be caused by a variety of factors, the most prevalent of which was famine in the bread basket region of the empire—Egypt.

85% or more of the population, with most of the arable land controlled by only a few.[41]

In an environment of such social stratification and economic distress for the many, it is no surprise to hear such strident remarks being made about the wealthy.

We must take seriously James's addressing Christians at some distance from himself, which is why he chooses typical but known examples of the problems to illustrate the social praxis he wants to instill in these congregations. We should not expect, since this is an encyclical, that James would address some particular problem of a specific region or church.[42] He assumes that he has authority over all these largely Jewish congregations and that the charitable and communal practices of the mother church (as outlined in Acts 2—6) should be emulated by other Jewish Christian congregations in the Diaspora. Partiality to the rich was always a deadly thing, as it created stratification in a congregation, with some having second-class status. This ruined the koinonia of such a small community. Pedrito U. Maynard-Reid is absolutely correct that James is referring to the economically poor and rich in various places in his sermon, not just to the spiritually poor or rich, though actual poverty and wealth has its spiritual effects and consequences to be sure.[43]

Leo G. Perdue rightly stresses that the social function of this document is to reinforce the socializing process for Jews who have recently become Christians and due to pressure or persecution or hardship are wavering in their faith.[44] In order for the group to continue to exist as a distinct entity, separate from Judaism, certain boundaries for the in-group needed to be clearly defined over against the larger culture and to a lesser degree over against the Jewish subculture. The parenesis in James presents a group ethic designed to maintain rather clear boundaries between the in-group and the out-group. What the document implies is that Jews who have converted to Christianity were Hellenized Jews who struggled with conforming to the ethos of the larger culture and needed to be drawn back to a more Jewish and sapiential ethical lifestyle. Our author is deeply concerned with issues of moral purity, and he addresses this concern by indicating ways to control speech, limit behavior and properly relate to others. This is the very sort of minority ethic that other Jews, like the author of Wisdom of Solomon or Jesus ben

---

[41]Brosend, *James and Jude*, p. 31.
[42]Against the suggestion of Martin, *James*, p. lxxviii, that James is combating some sort of Jewish astrological teaching, perhaps only as part of some later editorial agenda (Martin thinks the document was composed in two stages).
[43]Maynard-Reid, *Poverty and Wealth in James*.
[44]Perdue, "Paraenesis and the Epistle of James."

Sira, set out to help Jews to survive in a hostile and foreign environment.[45]

Developing this insight, John H. Elliott shows the considerable concern in James for the wholeness and holiness of the community, which is stressed when there is worry about pollution or infiltration of worldly values or ideas or behavior. It is not surprising in such circumstances that James would use cultic language about purity and pollution to reinforce the boundaries of the community. Here the issue is orthopraxy rather than orthodoxy, which makes this sermon in some respects different from 1 John. The document is

> written at the point when, from the author's sense of the situation, cultural plurality and social-economic disequilibrium among the believers had become the seed-bed for discrimination of social classes and the currying of favor from wealthy and powerful patrons (2:1-4 . . .); litigation and dishonoring of the poor (2:6-7) and their neglect (2:13, 14-16), exploitation, and oppression by the wealthy who defraud their laborers, stockpile harvests, and kill the righteous (4:13—5:6); members pursuing their own selfish interests at the cost of their fellows and social cohesion (1:14-15; 4:1-10); brothers speaking evil of and passing judgment upon brothers (4:11-12; 5:9); personal doubt and instability of commitment (1:6-8; 4:8); duplicity in speech (3:1-12); inconsistency between words and action (1:22-24; 2:1-26; 5:12); suffering leading to a loss of patience and hope (1:2, 12-15; 5:7-11); and even apostasy and defection from the community (5:19-20).
> . . . The community and its members were undergoing an erosion of integrity and cohesion at both the personal and the social levels of life.[46]

While we may suspect that the situation was not that drastic in every instance, since this is an encyclical document, clearly enough James wants to nip in the bud tendencies that lead to the disintegration of Jewish Christian communities. He does this, as we shall see, not simply by criticizing various sins but, on the positive side, by attempting to inculcate an ethic that he had seen exhibited in the Jerusalem community (as described in Acts 2—6).

There is one further implication of the social analysis of James. Luke Timothy Johnson puts it this way: "James reflects the social realities and outlooks appropriate to a sect in the early stages of its life."[47] When one couples this with the total lack of any telltale signs of pseudonymity or lateness (e.g., there is no attempt to elaborate on the image, authority or apostolicity of the author) one should conclude that the actual social character of this discourse favors an early date, and its strong assertion of authority over all Jewish Christians

[45]Witherington, *Jesus the Sage*, p. 246.
[46]Elliott, "Epistle of James," p. 75.
[47]Johnson, *James*, p. 119.

favors it having been written by James the Just, the leader of the community of Jewish Christians in Jerusalem.[48]

STRUCTURE OF JAMES

There are many analyses of the structure of James. Here is one of the more detailed ones, indebted to Fred O. Francis's suggestions:[49]

Introduction of Themes in Standard Twofold Opening (Jas 1:1-25)

Epistolary Prescript (Jas 1:1)

    A   testing/steadfastness (Jas 1:2-4)

    B   wisdom/words/reproaching (prayer) (Jas 1:5-8)

    C   rich/poor and doers (Jas 1:9-11)

    A^i testing/steadfastness (Jas 1:12-18)

    B^i wisdom/words/reproaching (Jas 1:19-21)

    C^i rich/poor and doers (Jas 1:22-25)

Linking Passage Summarizing and Previewing Body of Letter (Jas 1:26-27)

Main Exposition (Jas 2:1—5:6)

    A^{ii}underlying concern of testing

    C^{ii} main exposition: faith and action vis-à-vis rich and poor (Jas 2:1-26)

    B^{ii} main exposition: anger over wisdom/words/position (Jas 3:1—5:6)

Closing Remarks in Standard Form (Jas 5:7-18)

    A^{iii}steadfastness/patience until second coming (Jas 5:7-8)

    B^{iii} no strife (reproaching) eschatological judgment (Jas 5:9)

    A^{iv}steadfastness/God's purpose (Jas 5:10-11)

    B^{iv} words: no swearing (Jas 5:12)

    A^{v}prayer and suffering (Jas 5:13-18)

Conclusion (Jas 5:19-20)

---

[48]The only other figures that presumably could have exerted this influence and authority without elaborating on credentials would have been Peter and John, the other Jerusalem pillars, particularly Peter. The evidence of Acts suggests, however, that James was the last man standing in Jerusalem in the 40s and 50s, as these other two apostles itinerated within and outside the Holy Land. Furthermore, the character of the homily of James is very different from 1 Peter, and the latter seems to be dependent on the homily of James in places. Thus, the author of 1 Peter is not likely to be the same person as the author of James. This points to James the Just being the figure in question behind this document.

[49]Francis, "Form and Function."

In this rondo effect the letter opens with steadfastness then prayer and closes with prayer then steadfastness. What this analysis does not recognize is that the rondo effect is created by the deliberate use of deliberative rhetorical patterns to structure the homily. The reader will not be surprised to hear that I conclude that the essential structuring principles of this discourse or sermon are rhetorical in character. Accordingly, I offer the following simple outline:

epistolary prescript (Jas 1:1)
exordium (Jas 1:2-18): the wisdom/word from above
propositio (Jas 1:19-27)
rhetorical arguments and elaborations of various sorts using comparisons and
    enthymemes (Jas 2:1—5:6)[50]
peroratio: recapitulation of major themes (Jas 5:7-12) and final exhortation/
    emotional appeal (Jas 5:13-20)

There are no epistolary elements of any sort at the conclusion of the discourse—which is just the opposite of that found in the homily to the Hebrews. There we have some epistolary closing elements, but not an epistolary prescript; here we have the epistolary prescript but otherwise the document conforms to rhetorical structures. These sermons contain a concerted effort to keep epistolary elements to a minimum so that the discourse as a whole could be proclaimed—and proclaimed all on one occasion. It would take about twenty-five minutes, depending on the pace of the orator, to proclaim the sermon we know as James.

BIBLIOGRAPHY ON JAMES

Unfortunately, not enough small primers serve as introductions to the fascinating homily of James, but of those available the best is Richard Bauckham's intriguing and helpful *James*. Peter Davids's detailed *ANRW* survey of scholarly discussion on James up to the later 1980s is somewhat supplemented by his "James's Message: The Literary Record," but this is mainly a summary of the major themes and ideas in the homily. On the historical and traditional discussion of treatment of James in antiquity, no treatment is better than John Painter's *Just James: The Brother of Jesus in History and Tradition*. On the still controversial but, in my view, genuine ossuary of James, see Herschel Shanks and Ben Witherington III's *Brother of Jesus*. For a general discussion of the importance of James and his work as part of the original inner circle of Jesus, see my *What*

---

[50]Bauckham, *James*, demonstrates at length that a good deal of the elaboration is done in a sapiential manner—that is, it follows patterns already exhibited in earlier Jewish wisdom literature.

Have "They" Done with Jesus? On the history of scholarly discussion of James, a good place to start is Todd Penner's "Epistle of James in Current Research."

Commentaries

The plethora of commentaries on James exhibits quite a few excellent ones, both more and less technical. The classic study that all recent commentators refer to is Martin Dibelius's *James*, which was a translation of his 1964 German commentary and manifests the results of form criticism most commonly associated with Rudolf Bultmann. All subsequent commentaries react, in one way or another, to Dibelius. The German tradition is understandably heavily indebted to Luther and his successors and the way he read James; see Hans Windisch's *Katholischen Briefe*, Franz Mussner's *Jakobusbrief* and Adolf Schlatter's *Brief des Jackobus*. More recent and more helpful is François Vouga's *Épître de saint Jacques*, which shows signs of coming out of the shadow of Dibelius and the Reformed reading of James; J. Cantinat's *Épîtres de saint Jacques et de saint Jude*, H. Frankemolle's *Brief des Jackobus* and Wiard Popkes's *Brief des Jakobus*, which is even more helpful.

Of the small recent commentaries in English two can be especially commended: William Brosend's *James and Jude* and Luke Timothy Johnson's contribution to the New Interpreter's Bible, which is a simplified form of his much more useful *Letter of James* in the Anchor Bible series. Both of these commentaries are cognizant of the social and rhetorical analysis of James and interact with it to one degree or another. Brosend structures his commentary using the rubric of V. Robbins about innertexture and intertexture, sociocultural and ideological textures and sacred and homiletical textures. Also very helpful at the semipopular level is Douglas Moo's 2000 *Letter of James*; although it does not draw on or interact with the rhetorical discussion much, it is to be preferred over his earlier *James*. More dated and less helpful are J. B. Adamson's *Epistle of James* and Sophie Laws's *Commentary on the Epistle of James*. Pheme Perkins is a fine scholar but unfortunately her *First and Second Peter, James and Jude* is too slender to do justice to the Catholic Letters, even though it has some very fine comments on James.

Of the more technical commentaries by evangelicals two stand out: Ralph Martin's *James* and Peter David's more readable *James*. The older technical commentaries are still very helpful and do a better job with grammatical and textual matters of various sorts. Especially to be commended is Joseph Mayor's classic *Epistle of St. James* and James Hardy Ropes's *St. James*, which accomplishes a lot in a short span. Equally interesting for its perspective is Alfred Plummer's *General Epistles of St. James and St. Jude*. The Ancient Christian

Commentary volume that contains James, edited by Gerald Bray, is excellent, but one could have wished for more pages to be devoted to the comments of the church fathers on James.

Adamson, J. B. *The Epistle of James.* Grand Rapids: Eerdmans, 1976.

Bray, Gerald, ed. *James, 1-2 Peter, 1-3 John, Jude.* Ancient Christian Commentary on Scripture: New Testament 11. Downers Grove, Ill.: InterVarsity Press, 2000.

Brosend, William, II. *James and Jude.* New Cambridge Bible Commentary. Cambridge: Cambridge University Press, 2004.

Cantinat, J. *Les épîtres de saint Jacques et de saint Jude.* Paris: Gabalda, 1973.

Davids, Peter H. *The Epistle of James: A Commentary on the Greek Text.* New International Greek Testament Commentary. Grand Rapids: Eerdmans, 1982.

Dibelius, Martin. *James: A Commentary on the Epistle of James.* Revised by Heinrich Greeven. Translated by Michael A. Williams. Edited by Helmut Koester. Hermeneia. Philadelphia: Fortress, 1976.

Frankemolle, H. *Der Brief des Jackobus.* Gutersloh: Gutersloher Verlag, 1994.

Johnson, Luke Timothy. *The Letter of James.* Anchor Bible 37A. New York: Doubleday, 1995.[51]

———. *The Letter of James.* New Interpreter's Bible 12. Nashville: Abingdon, 1998.

Laws, Sophie. *A Commentary on the Epistle of James.* New York: Harper & Row, 1980.

Martin, Ralph P. *James.* Word Biblical Commentary 48. Waco: Word, 1988.

Mayor, Joseph B. *The Epistle of St. James.* 3rd edition. London: Macmillan, 1910.

Moffatt, James. *The General Epistles: James, Peter and Judas.* Moffatt New Testament Commentary. London: Hodder & Stoughton, 1928.

Moo, Douglas. *James.* Pillar New Testament Commentary. Grand Rapids: Eerdmans, 1986.[52]

———. *The Letter of James.* Grand Rapids: Eerdmans, 2000.

Mussner, Franz. *Der Jakobusbrief.* Freiburg: Herder, 1981.

Perkins, Pheme. *First and Second Peter, James and Jude.* Louisville: John Knox, 1995.

Plummer, Alfred. *The General Epistles of St. James and St. Jude.* Expositors' Bible. London: Hodder & Stoughton, 1891.

Popkes, Wiard. *Der Brief des Jakobus.* Leipzig: Evangelische Verlagsanstalt, 2001.

Ropes, James Hardy. *A Critical and Exegetical Commentary on the Epistle of St. James.* International Critical Commentary. Edinburgh: Clark, 1916.

[51]All references to Johnson's *James* refer to his Anchor Bible commentary.
[52]All references to Moo's *James* refer to his Pillar commentary.

Schlatter, Adolf. *Der Brief des Jackobus.* Stuttgart: Calwer, 1956.

Vouga, François. *La épître de Saint Jacques.* Commentaire du Nouveau Testament 2.13a. Geneva: Labor & Fides, 1984.

Windisch, Hans. *Die katholischen Briefe.* Tübingen: Mohr, 1951.

Monographs and Articles

Several monographs on James can be especially commended. Helpful, though tendentious at points (in a liberation theology kind of way—for example, it stresses that God has a preferential option for the poor, even though one of the major messages of this sermon is God's impartiality), is Pedrito U. Maynard-Reid's *Poverty and Wealth in James.* This approach is taken even further in Elsa Tamez's *Scandalous Message of James.* On famine as a cause of poverty in James's world, see Peter Garnsey's *Famine and Food in the Greco-Roman World.* On the issue of travel and traveling merchants, see Lionel Casson's *Travel in the Ancient World.* On the treatment of illness in the first century and in the New Testament, see John Wilkinson's *Health and Healing.*

On James's reliance on earlier wisdom materials, including sayings of Jesus, one can consult Patrick J. Hartin's *James and the Q Sayings of Jesus* and my *Jesus the Sage* at the relevant junctures. This same subject is treated in a more rhetorical and specialized way by Wesley Hiram Wachob's *Voice of Jesus in the Social Rhetoric of James.* Dean Deppe's *Sayings of Jesus in the Epistle of James* is also quite helpful on analyzing the use of the Jesus tradition in James.

In terms of the development of sapiential literature before James, a body of literature that left a deep impression on our author, see John Collins's *Jewish Wisdom in the Hellenistic Age* and *Seers, Sibyls and Sages in Hellenistic-Roman Judaism*, pp. 349-50. Also helpful in sorting out whether James is a sage or a scribe are David Orton's *Understanding Scribe* and H. Gregory Snyder's *Teachers and Texts in the Ancient World*, pp. 181-214.

Patrick J. Hartin provides a detailed analysis of James's use of perfection language in *A Spirituality of Perfection.* Helpful on James's use of the love commandment is Victor Paul Furnish's *Love Command in the New Testament.* A. Chester and Ralph Martin's *The Theology of the Letters of James, Peter and Jude* (with Chester doing James) is helpful in a general way in dealing with the theology of James, but does a poor job of dealing with James's Christology, devoting only two pages to the subject. See instead my *Many Faces of the Christ* and Richard N. Longenecker's *Christology of Early Jewish Christianity.* Still helpful though dated is F. F. Bruce's *Peter, Stephen, James and John.* An influential study that unfortunately continues to perpetuate the idea that James and Paul were likely at loggerheads on faith and works is J. D. G. Dunn's *Unity and Diversity in the New Testament.*

Aland, Kurt. "The Problem of Anonymity and Pseudonymity in Christian Literature of the First Two Centuries." *JTS* 12 (1961): 39-49.

Albl, Martin C. "'Are Any Among You Sick?' The Health Care System in the Letter of James." *JBL* 121 (2002): 121-43.

Alonso-Schökel, Luis. "James 5:2 and 4:6" *Biblica* 54 (1973): 73-76.

Amphoux, Christian-Bernard. "La parenté textuelle du Syr h et du groupe 2138 dans l'épître de Jacques." *Biblica* 62 (1981): 259-71.

———. "Quelques temoins grecs des formes textuelles les plus anciennes de l'épître de Jacques: le groupe 2138 (ou 614)." *NTS* 28 (1982): 91-115.

Amphoux, Christian-Bernard, and Dom B. Outtier. "Les leçons des versions géorgiennes de l'épître de Jacques." *Biblica* 65 (1984): 365-76.

Baker, William R. "'Above All Else': Contexts of the Call for Verbal Integrity in James 5.12." *Journal for the Study of the New Testament* 54 (1994): 57-71.

Bauckham, Richard. *James*. London: Routledge, 1999.

Bertrand, D. "Le fond de l'epreuve épître de Jacques 1,12-18." *Christus* 30 (1983): 212-18.

Betz, Hans-Dieter. *The Sermon on the Mount*. Hermeneia. Minneapolis: Fortress, 1995.

Bruce, F. F. *Peter, Stephen, James and John*. Grand Rapids: Eerdmans, 1979.

Burge, Gary M. "'And Threw Them Thus on Paper': Recovering the Poetic Form of James 2.14-26." *Studia biblica et theologica* 7 (1977): 31-45.

Casson, Lionel. *Travel in the Ancient World*. London: Allen & Unwin, 1974.

Chester, A., and Ralph P. Martin. *The Theology of the Letters of James, Peter and Jude*. Cambridge: Cambridge University Press, 1994.

Collins, John J. *Jewish Wisdom in the Hellenistic Age*. Old Testament Library. Louisville: Westminster/John Knox, 1997.

———. *Seers, Sibyls and Sages in Hellenistic-Roman Judaism*. Leiden: Brill, 1997.

Craigie, Peter C. *The Book of Deuteronomy*. New International Commentary on the Old Testament. Grand Rapids: Eerdmans, 1976.

Davids, Peter H. "The Epistle of James in Modern Debate." *ANRW* 25.5 (1988), pp. 3622-84.

———. "James's Message: The Literary Record," pp. 66-87 in *The Brother of Jesus: James the Just and his Mission*. Edited by Bruce Chilton and Jacob Neusner. Louisville: Westminster/John Knox, 2001.

———. "The Meaning of apeirastos in James 1.13." *NTS* 24 (1977-78): 386-92.

Deppe, Dean B. *The Sayings of Jesus in the Epistle of James*. Chelsea, Mich.: Bookcrafters, 1989.

Dowd, Sharyn. "Faith That Works: James 2:14-26." *Review and Expositor* 97 (2000): 195-205.

Dunn, J. D. G. *Unity and Diversity in the New Testament.* Philadelphia: Westminster Press, 1984.

Elliott-Binns, Leonard Elliott. "James 1.18: Creation or Redemption?" *NTS* 3 (1956-57): 146-61.

———. "The Meaning of ΥΛΗ in Jas. iii.5." *NTS* 2 (1955-56): 48-50.

Ellis, E. Earle. "Pseudonymity and Canonicity of New Testament Documents." Pp. 212-24 in *Worship, Theology and Ministry in the Early Church.* Edited by Michael J. Wilkins and Terence Paige, Sheffield: Sheffield Academic Press, 1992.

Feuillet, André. "Le sens du mot parousie dans l'evangile de Matthieu: Comparaison entre Matth. xxiv et Jac. v, 1-11," pp. 261-80 in *The Background of the New Testament and Its Eschatology: In Honour of Charles Harold Dodd.* Edited by W. D. Davies and D. Daube. Cambridge: Cambridge University Press, 1956.

Forbes, P. R. B. "The Structure of the Epistle of James." *EvQ* 44 (1972): 147-53.

Francis, Fred O. "The Form and Function of the Opening and Closing Paragraphs of James and I John." *ZNW* 61 (1970): 110-26.

Fry, Euan M. "The Testing of Faith: A Study of the Structure of the Book of James." *Bible Translator* 29 (1978): 427-35.

Furnish, Victor Paul. *The Love Command in the New Testament.* Nashville: Abingdon, 1972.

Garnsey, Peter. *Famine and Food in the Greco-Roman World.* Cambridge: Cambridge University Press, 1988.

Guthrie, Donald. *New Testament Introduction.* Downers Grove, Ill.: InterVarsity Press, 1990.

Hadidian, Dikran Y. "Palestinian Pictures in the Epistle of James." *ET* 63 (1952): 227-28.

Hanson, A. T. "Rahab the Harlot in Early Christian Tradition." *JSNT* 1 (1978): 53-60.

Hartin, Patrick J. *James and the Q Sayings of Jesus.* Sheffield: JSOT Press, 1991.

———. *A Spirituality of Perfection: Faith in Action in the Letter of James.* Collegeville, Minn.: Liturgical Press, 1999.

Hayden, Daniel R. "Calling the Elders to Pray." *Bibliotheca sacra* 138 (1981): 258-86.

Horsley, G. H. R., ed. *New Documents Illustrating Early Christianity.* Sydney: Macquarie University Press, 1981-.

Jeremias, Joachim. "Paul and James." *ET* 66 (1954-55): 368-71.

Johnson, Luke Timothy. "Friendship with the World/Friendship with God: A Study of Discipleship in James," pp. 166-83 in *Discipleship in the New Testament.* Edited by F. Segovia. Philadelphia: Fortress, 1985.

————. "The Mirror of Remembrance (James 1:22-25)." *CBQ* 50 (1988): 632-45.

————. "The Use of Leviticus 19 in the Letter of James." *JBL* 101 (1982): 391-401.

Kennedy, George A. *Progymnasmata: Greek Textbooks of Prose Composition and Rhetoric.* Writings from the Greco-Roman World 10. Atlanta: Scholars Press, 2003.

Kirk, J. A. "The Meaning of Wisdom in James." *NTS* 16 (1969-70): 24-38.

Kümmel, Werner Georg. *Introduction to the New Testament.* Translated by Howard Clark Kee. London: SCM, 1979.

Laws, Sophie S. "Does Scripture Speak in Vain? A Reconsideration of James iv.5." *NTS* 30 (1974): 210-15.

Llewelyn, Susan R., ed. *New Documents Illustrating Early Christianity,* vol. 6. Sydney: Macquarie Press, 1992.

Longenecker, Richard N. *The Christology of Early Jewish Christianity.* Vancouver, B.C.: Regent College Press, 2001.

Luther, Martin. *Luther's Works.* Edited by Jaroslav Pelikan et al. Philadelphia: Fortress, 1955-86.

Marcus, Joel. "The Evil Inclination in the Epistle of James." *CBQ* 44 (1982): 607-21.

Maynard-Reid, Pedrito U. *Poverty and Wealth in James.* Maryknoll, N.Y.: Orbis, 1987.

McKnight, Scot. "James 2.18a: The Unidentifiable Interlocutor." *Westminster Theological Journal* 52 (1990): 355-64.

Moo, Douglas J. "Divine Healing in the Health and Wealth Gospel." *Trinity Journal* 9 (1988): 191-209.

Orton, David E. *The Understanding Scribe.* Sheffield: Sheffield Academic Press, 1989.

Painter, John. *Just James: The Brother of Jesus in History and Tradition.* Minneapolis: Fortress, 1999.

Penner, Todd C. "The Epistle of James in Current Research." *Currents in Research: Biblical Studies* 7 (1999): 257-308.

Perdue, Leo G. "Paraenesis and the Epistle of James." *ZNW* 72 (1981): 241-56.

Pickar, Charles H. "Is Anyone Sick among You?" *CBQ* 7 (1945): 165-74.

Polhill, John B. "The Life Situation of the Book of James." *Review and Expositor* 66 (1969): 369-78.

Pritchard, James B., ed. *Ancient Near Eastern Texts Relating to the Old Testament.* 3d ed. Princeton: Princeton University Press, 1969.

Reese, James M. "The Exegete as Sage: Hearing the Message of James." *Biblical Theology Bulletin* 12 (1982): 83-84.

Schmitt, John J. "You Adulteresses: The Image in James 4:4." *NovT* 28 (1986): 327-37.

Seitz, O. F. J. "Afterthoughts on the Term dipsychos." *NTS* 4 (1957-58): 327-34.

———. "Antecedents and Significance of the Term dipsychos." *JBL* 66 (1947): 211-19.

Shanks, Herschel, and Ben Witherington III. *The Brother of Jesus.* San Francisco: Harper, 2001.

Shogren, Gary S. "Will God Heal Us? A Re-examination of James 5.14-16a." *EvQ* 61 (1989): 99-108.

Snyder, H. Gregory. *Teachers and Texts in the Ancient World.* London: Routledge, 2000.

Stulac, George M. "Who Are the Rich in James?" *Presbyterion* 16 (1990): 89-102.

Tamez, Elsa. *The Scandalous Message of James: Faith without Works Is Dead.* Translated by John Eagleson. New York: Crossroad, 1990.

Townsend, Michael J. "James 4.1-4: A Warning against Zealotry?" *ET* 87 (1976): 211-13.

Turner, Nigel. "The Style of the Epistle of James," pp. 114-20 in James Hope Moulton's *A Grammar of New Testament Greek*, vol. 4: *Style*, by Nigel Turner. Edinburgh: Clark, 1976.

Vermes, Geza. *Jesus the Jew: A Historian's Reading of the Gospel.* Philadelphia: Fortress, 1973.

Verseput, Donald. "James 1.17 and the Jewish Morning Prayers." *NovT* 38 (1996): 1-15.

———. "Reworking the Puzzle of Faith and Deeds in James 2.14-26." *NTS* 43 (1997): 101-4.

Wall, Robert W. *The Community of the Wise.* Valley Forge, Penn.: Trinity, 1997.

Ward, Roy Bowen. "Partiality in the Assembly: James 2:2-4." *HTR* 62 (1969): 87-97.

Wilkinson, John. *Health and Healing: Studies in New Testament Principles and Practices.* Edinburgh: Handsel, 1980.

Winter, Bruce W. "Secular and Christian Responses to Corinthian Famines." *Tyndale Bulletin* 40 (1989): 86-106.

Witherington, Ben, III. *The Acts of the Apostles.* Grand Rapids: Eerdmans, 1998.

———. *Conflict and Community in Corinth: A Socio-Rhetorical Commentary on 1 and 2 Corinthians.* Grand Rapids: Eerdmans 1995.

———. *The Gospel of Matthew.* Macon, Ga.: Smyth & Helwys, 2006.

———. *Grace in Galatia.* Grand Rapids: Eerdmans, 1998.

———. *Incandescence: Light Shed through the Word.* Grand Rapids: Eerdmans, 2006.

———. *Jesus, Paul and the End of the World.* Downers Grove: InterVarsity Press, 1992.

———. *Jesus the Sage: The Pilgrimage of Wisdom.* Minneapolis: Fortress, 1998.

LETTERS AND HOMILIES FOR JEWISH CHRISTIANS

———. *Letters and Homilies for Hellenized Christians, Volume 1: A Socio-Rhetorical Commentary on Titus, 1-2 Timothy and 1-3 John.* Downers Grove, Ill.: IVP Academic, 2006.

———. *Letters and Homilies for Hellenized Christians, Volume 2: A Socio-Rhetorical Commentary on 1-2 Peter.* Downers Grove, Ill.: IVP Academic, forthcoming.

———. *The Many Faces of the Christ.* New York: Continuum, 1998.

———. *Paul's Letters to the Thessalonians: A Socio-Rhetorical Commentary.* Grand Rapids: Eerdmans, 2006.

———. *What Have "They" Done with Jesus?* San Francisco: Harper, 2006.

Witherington, Ben, III, and Darlene Hyatt. *The Letter to the Romans.* Grand Rapids: Eerdmans, 2004.

Studies Involving Rhetorical Criticism

Baasland, Ernst. "Der Jakobusbrief als Neutestamentliche Weisheitsschrift." *Studia theologica* 36 (1982): 119-39.

———. "Literarische Form, Thematik und geschichtliche Einordnung des Jakobusbriefes." *ANRW* 2.25.5 (1988): 3646-84.

Church, Christopher Lee. "'Forschungsgeschichte' on the Literary Character of the Epistle of James." Ph.D. diss., Southern Baptist Theological Seminary, 1990.

Cladder, Hermann Johann. "Die Anlage des Jakobusbriefes." *Zeitschrift für katholische Theologie* 28 (1904): 37-57.

Elliott, John H. "The Epistle of James in Rhetorical and Social Scientific Perspective: Holiness-Wholeness and Patterns of Replication." *Biblical Theology Bulletin* 23 (1993): 71-81.

Gieger, Loren G. "Figures of Speech in the Epistle of James: A Rhetorical and Exegetical Analysis." Ph.D. diss., Southwestern Baptist Theological Seminary, 1981.

Johnson, Luke Timothy. "James 3:13—4:10 and the *Topos* περὶ φθόνου." *NovT* 25 (1983): 327-47.

Kuchler, C. G. *Commentatio de rhetorica epistolae Jacobi indole.* Leipzig: Leipziger Verlag, 1818.

Lodge, J. G. "James and Paul at Cross Purposes? James 2,22." *Biblica* 62 (1981): 195-213.

Moore, Bruce R. "Rhetorical Questions in Second Corinthians and in Ephesians through Revelation." *Notes* 97 (1983): 3-33.

Ong, S. H. *A Strategy for a Metaphorical Reading of the Epistle of James.* Lanham, Md.: University Press of America, 1996.

Thurén, Lauri. "Risky Rhetoric in James?" *NovT* 37 (1995): 262-84.

Van der Westhuizen, J. D. N. "Stylistic Techniques and Their Functions in James 2:14-26." *Neotestamentica* 25 (1991): 89-107.

Van Rensburg, Fika, and J. L. P. Wolmarans. "Die argumentatiewe funksie van Jakobus 1:9-11." *In die Skriflig* 31 (1997): 283-90.

Wachob, Wesley Hiram. "Apocalyptic Intertexture in the Epistle of James," pp. 165-85 in *The Intertexture of Apocalyptic Discourse in the New Testament*. Edited by Duane F. Watson. Society of Biblical Literature Symposium Series 14. Atlanta: Scholars Press, 2002.

————. *The Voice of Jesus in the Social Rhetoric of James*. Cambridge: Cambridge University Press, 2000.

Watson, Duane F. "James 2 in Light of Greco-Roman Schemes of Argumentation." *NTS* 39 (1993): 94-121.

————. "A Reassessment of the Rhetoric of the Epistle of James and Its Implications for Christian Origins." Forthcoming.

————. "The Rhetoric of James 3.1-12 and a Classical Pattern of Argumentation." *NovT* 35 (1993): 48-64.

————. "Rhetorical Criticism of Hebrews and the Catholic Epistles Since 1978." *Currents in Research: Biblical Studies* 5 (1997): 175-207.

Wuellner, W. H. "Der Jakobusbrief im Licht der Rhetorik und Textpragmatik." *Linguistica biblica* 43 (1978): 5-66.

James

Epistolary Prescript (Jas 1:1)

> *1:1 Jacob (i.e., James), of God and the Lord Jesus Christ a servant, to the Twelve Tribes, those that are in the Dispersion, greetings.*

Our document begins in **James 1:1** like letters normally began—with the three standard parts: (1) addresser, (2) addressee, (3) greeting. The greeting *chairein* ("greetings, joy") is the typical first-century epistolary greeting in a Greek letter. Paul expanded and modified the form, and Joseph Mayor argues that had James known Paul's letters or later letters like 1 Peter or of 1 John he likely would have used a more elaborate form of greeting.[53] If anything, 1 Peter is dependent on James, which uses simpler forms of expression.

The author makes a wordplay (paronomasia) in the first two verses, yielding in quick succession *chairein, charan*. Thus, as even Martin Dibelius notes, our author is capable of using "literary" devices, and as we shall see he has a whole rhetorical arsenal of them.[54] In the New Testament only James 1:1 and Acts 15:23 have the typical Hellenistic greeting, and both cases deal with documents involving James, one sent to Gentile Christians outside the Holy Land, one sent to Jewish Christians outside the Holy Land.

The name James is Jacob, and the first sentence reads, "James, of God and of the Lord Jesus Christ, a servant." "Christ" is not used as a title ("the Christ") but as a last name here. Peter Davids takes it to be a sign of a Hellenistic editor.[55] This is quite unnecessary since Paul, among others, could use "Christ" as a last name at an early date, and, as Mayor notes, the combination "God and the Lord Jesus Christ" is found in almost every New Testament letter.[56] Cer-

---

[53]Mayor, *James*, p. 32.
[54]Dibelius, *James*, p. 68.
[55]Davids, *James*, p. 63.
[56]Mayor, *James*, p. 29.

tainly the combination "Lord Jesus Christ"—a personal name surrounded by
two titles—is common enough in the Pauline Letters (Rom 1:7; 1 Cor 1:3;
2 Cor 1:2; Gal 1:3; Eph 1:2; Phil 1:2). It is not unlike the famous triple phrase
applied to the emperor—Imperator Caesar Augustus—where the personal
name is in the middle. There is perhaps an implicit rebuttal in the predication
of this phrase of Jesus.

It is conceivable that James here refers to Jesus as *theos,* but he does not say
"God the Father and" or "God the Father of."[57] At the very least, divine authority
is implied and Christ's lordship is explicit. Only James and Jude use the designation *doulos* as a solitary self-description, and it is interesting to speculate what
led Jesus' brothers to call themselves his servants/slaves. Obviously, the word
is suggested by *kyrios* ("master, Lord"). Paul calls himself a *doulos* "of Christ,"
but he regularly adds the designation "apostle." James and Jude were not among
the Twelve, which is why they do not call themselves apostles. There may also
be a sense of humility here, since neither recognized Jesus as Christ until after
Easter. *Doulos* was sometimes used of prophets and could be a title: "a servant
of God" was a special agent and spokesperson for God. It is doubtful, but possible, that it means that here and in Jude 1. William Brosend rightly stresses: "To
claim the status of servant . . . was to choose to be identified not by parentage,
birthplace, or occupation but by the one(s) in whose service one stood. But to
claim the status of slave is to point beyond oneself to one's 'master' in the truest
sense."[58] Douglas Moo's suggestion as to why James did not mention that he
was the brother of Jesus is plausible: his physical relationship with Jesus gave
him no status or authority over the audience he addressed—it was rather his
spiritual relationship with the risen Lord that gave him that authority, hence the
reference to his being Christ's servant.

The difficult part of the verse is the second half: "to the Twelve Tribes, the
(ones) in the Dispersion *[diaspora]*." Here we are told in an indirect way who
the audience is. Unfortunately, there are a host of possibilities:

1. Jews in the Dispersion, that is, those outside Palestine (Joseph Mayor)

2. Jewish Christians outside Palestine (Peter Davids)

3. the church as the true Israel, which is scattered over the earth (including
   in the Holy Land)

---

[57]Moo, *James,* p. 49, is right that if this was James's intent we might have expected the order
of terms to be Lord and God rather than the reverse.
[58]Brosend, *James and Jude,* pp. 32-33.
[59]Moo, *James,* p. 48.

4. the church outside Palestine both Jews and Gentiles

That Jews are the audience is not impossible, in which case this letter would be some sort of first-step apologia for Christianity. Several factors are strongly against this view:

1. The author seems to assume some sort of authority over his audience, which was not the case if Jews are in view.

2. James Moffatt notes that "Twelve Tribes" was a synonym for Israel as a whole, not for Diaspora Jews alone,[60] and even after the destruction of 70 the Twelve Tribes could never be said to be all in the Dispersion since some stayed in Palestine. The second phrase, however, qualifies the first: "the Twelve tribes, that is, the ones dispersed."

If this is an apologia for Christianity of any sort, we would expect more Christology. This letter reads as if it is written to people who are already believers (e.g., Jas 2:1). Thus, no purely Jewish view is satisfactory, nor is any view that says James is writing *to* people in Palestine. The idea that a Jewish Christian in Palestine was in the Dispersion would make very little sense, as Joseph Mayor implies,[61] and goes against the Jewish background of the term. Further, as James Hardy Ropes points out, limiting the Diaspora to some particular region is not supported in the text, since it makes no such qualification and does not hint at conditions in a particular district.[62] The author writes *out* of his experience and may presuppose knowledge of certain conditions in Palestine by his audience, but that is the most that such texts as James 3:7 imply. In contrast to Martin Dibelius's later view, Ropes is quite right to argue:

No kind of early, or of ingenious, dating can bring us to a time when a writer addressing Jewish *Christians* in distinction from unbelieving Jews would have addressed them as "the twelve tribes," if by the *term* he simply meant "the Jews"; and if the term is here used for "the People of God," then the limitation to *Jewish* Christians is not contained in it.[63]

The only problem with this logic is that if James saw Jewish Christians as the true Jews (as in, e.g., Rom 9), then this phrase could certainly mean the true

---

[60]Moffatt, *General Epistles*, p. 7.
[61]Mayor, *James*, pp. 30-31.
[62]Ropes, *James*, pp. 120-27.
[63]Ibid., p. 127 (emphasis original).

Jews in the Diaspora (i.e., Jewish Christians dwelling there).[64] This view is in part supported by 1 Peter 1:1 and 1 Peter 2:11, where "those scattered" are said to be specifically outside Palestine and in Asia Minor. This evidence is especially important if 1 Peter is dependent on James, as it may well be, and it shows that the word *dispersion* actually meant being dispersed—not, as Dibelius thought, Christians all over the world, including in Israel.

EXORDIUM: OF TRIALS AND TEMPTATIONS AND STANDING THE TEST (JAS 1:2-18)

The exordium in deliberative rhetoric establishes rapport with the audience, in part by setting forth the ethos and authority of the speaker, but it also serves as a preview of coming attractions, hinting at some of the themes that will subsequently be dealt with. The goal is to make the audience favorably disposed toward what is yet to come. An exordium in a deliberative speech should be brief and directly to the point, serving as a prelude for what follows (Quintilian *Institutio oratoria* 3.8.10).

Quintilian stresses that deliberative rhetoric requires a certain boldness or impetuosity of speech (*Institutio oratoria* 8.3.14), involving among other things a strong appeal to deeper emotions such as anger, fear, love or hate (3.8.12). We certainly find such direct and pointed speech in James. It is also not a surprise that the subject of doubt comes up immediately in this exordium, for Quintilian says that deliberative discourses serve the purpose of addressing issues where some doubt exists in the audience as to what is the proper behavior or course of action to take (3.8.25). This unit concludes with James 1:18 in view of the way James 1:19 begins, not only with the phrase that signals a new subunit or the end of a unit throughout James ("my brother" or "my beloved brothers"),[65] but with a direct exhortation: "take note."[66] James 1:2-4 establishes the authority and ethos of the speaker and his rapport with the audience (they are "brothers" in the same faith), while James 1:5-18 serves to introduce in brief some of the matter of this discourse.

> [1:2]*Consider it all joy, my brothers, when you fall into various trials,* [3]*knowing that*

---

[64]Rightly Moo, *James*, p. 50. Moo stresses that James is writing to Jewish Christians who have been recently dispersed due to persecution (Acts 11:19). But if this were his meaning we would not have expected the phrase *in the Dispersion* referring to a place rather than a recent process or event.

[65]The phrase appears some ten times in James, but only once in the middle of a unit (at Jas 3:10).

[66]Thurén, "Risky Rhetoric in James?" p. 272.

the proving/testing[67] of your faith works out/results in fortitude. [4]But fortitude has work to complete, in order that you be complete/perfect and whole, in nothing lacking. [5]But if any one of you lacks wisdom, you should ask of God, who gives to all without discrimination and not reproaching it will be given to you. [6]But ask in faith, not doubting, for the one doubting is like a wave on the sea, wind blown and tossed about, [7]for that person must not go on thinking he will receive anything from the Lord, [8]he is a double-minded man, unstable in all of his ways.

[9]But the humble brother should take pride in his high position, [10]but the rich in his humiliation, because as a wildflower withers away, [11]for the sun rises with the scorching heat and dries up the flowers, and its wildflower fades and the beauty of its appearance perishes. So also the rich in his journey (through life) wastes away.

[12]Blessed is the man who stands up to the trial, because being approved, he will receive the crown of life that he[68] promised to his beloved. [13]Let no one who is tempted say, "I was tempted by God," for God is not subject to evil and he himself tempts no one. [14]But each one is tempted by his own desire, being lured and enticed. [15]Then desire conceiving gives birth to sin. But sin maturing engenders death.

[16]Do not be misled, my beloved brothers. [17]Every good favor and every perfect/ complete gift is from above, coming down from the Father of lights, in whom there is no variation or shadow of changing.[69] [18]He deliberately gives birth to us through the word of truth, in order that we might be a kind of firstfruits of his creation.

It is a mistake to see the material in this discourse as just parenesis or hortatory in character. It would be better to call it theological ethics, as it is grounded in a certain view of God and divine activity, as this paragraph makes so apparent. God is the one who sends wisdom, gives every good gift (including perseverance) and is the model of rectitude—not a shadow of a doubt or of any behavior that could be called questionable. James is not serving up commonsense wisdom by and large, but rather revelatory wisdom—wisdom that comes by revelation and presupposes a particular view of God and the

[67]There is a textual problem in regard to the original reading: *dokimon* (supported by only three witnesses: 110, 431, 1241) or the much rarer word *dokimion* (better supported by ℵ, A, B and a host of other witnesses and so should be accepted). See Metzger, *Textual Commentary*, p. 679.

[68]Some manuscripts (C, K, L, P, 1829) make clear that the person in question here is the Lord, but these witnesses are later attempts to clarify the matter. See Metzger, *Textual Commentary*, p. 679.

[69]Because of the obscurity of this phrase, there are several textual variants here. Several minuscules (876, 1518, 1610, 1765, 2138), in an attempt to amplify the point, add "there is not even the least suspicion of a shadow." The least objectionable reading is that found in ℵ, A, C, K and others, which sees only two things referred to here: the variation and the changing shadow. See Metzger, *Textual Commentary*, pp. 679-80.

divine activity that enables human beings to be their best.

The discourse proper opens in **James 1:2** with the astounding command to "consider it all joy," including all the trials and suffering. The phrase should be taken adverbially and might be better rendered "consider it entirely as joy" or "consider it pure joy." But what is meant by "joy" here? Clearly enough it cannot be seen as synonymous with pleasure *(hēdonē)* or even happiness *(eudaimonia)* since this joy exists even in the midst of trials, temptations, suffering. Joy is repeatedly said to characterize the experience of early Christians (Acts 13:52; Rom 14:17; 15:13; 2 Cor 1:15; 2:3; Gal 5:22; Phil 1:4; Col 1:11; 1 Pet 1:8; 1 Jn 1:4; 2 Jn 12).[70] Here in this verse it involves mental calculation or reckoning, as the verb *hēgeomai* indicates. But how does one reckon even suffering as joy? Texts like John 16:20-22; 2 Corinthians 7:4; 1 Thessalonians 1:6 and Hebrews 10:34 make clear that suffering and joy are compatible from a Christian viewpoint. James is talking about the joy of the Lord here, which in the Pauline Letters is said to be part of the fruit of the work of the Spirit within the believer. This seems to refer to the sense of contentment that comes from the assurance of and delight in God's eschatological presence in one's life regardless of circumstance, a presence that is often most evident to the believer precisely when one is in the most duress.

If a more generic sort of religious joy is in mind, which I doubt, one could point to Psalm 28:7 and Nehemiah 8:10: "The joy of the LORD is my strength." This is a joy that only the presence of the Lord can give. The world or circumstances can neither give nor take away this joy; this joy cannot be purchased or stolen; it cannot be bargained for or earned. It is simply a gift from God that is a residual effect of the abiding presence of God in a person's life. This is not, of course, the same thing as feeling happy or cheerful. We must avoid the temptation to reduce this joy to a mere emotion. If one can reckon something all joy then it primarily involves a mental exercise, not a passing emotion.

A CLOSER LOOK
Being Frank with Francis

One of the more influential treatments of James as a letter in the last forty years is that of Fred O. Francis.[71] He believed that he found an epistolary structure in both 1 John and James that disproved Martin Dibelius's contention that

---

[70]Johnson, *James*, p. 177.
[71]Francis, "Form and Function."

there was no real pattern or structure to the exhortations in these documents and that they did not conform to epistolary structures in general. The problem with Francis's analysis is not, however, his refutation of Dibelius's thesis, but rather what he believed the pattern proved—the use of epistolary conventions. While a pattern of repetition is found at the beginning and end of these two homilies, this is because they follow, not epistolary conventions, but rhetorical conventions that dictated that the peroration should recapitulate the themes announced at the outset of the discourse.

We know from Paul to anticipate from his opening prayers the key themes that will be addressed in his letters.[72] James also uses the form of anticipation to announce his themes. The anticipation of key thematic material is twice stated, the second time amplifying or adding to the first. These twofold statements—bless/thank God and call for rejoicing (1 Maccabees 10.25-45)—follow the standard format:

1. testing/steadfastness (Jas 1:2-4 and Jas 1:12-18)

2. wisdom/word/reproaching (Jas 1:5-8 and Jas 1:19-21)

3. rich-poor/doers (Jas 1:9-11 and Jas 1:22-25)

The rest of the letter will draw upon and draw out these themes.

In James 1:26-27 Francis finds a recapitulation of the main themes and also an anticipation of what is to follow, so that these hinge verses look two ways—both summing up and preparing. Clearly one main issue in this discourse is testing of various sorts. Certainly it underlies the development of the two main sections of the discourse (Jas 2:1-26 [faith and action vis-à-vis the rich and poor] and Jas 3:1—5:6 [passion over wisdom, words and position]). James 2:21, on the testing of Abraham, shows that testing is certainly on James's mind.

James 2 is a two-part diatribe functioning not unlike the twofold function of James 1:9-11 and James 1:22-25. Francis sees a chiastic structure in James 1:2-25 (abc/abc/cb, with testing [a] underlying the whole). Francis goes on to argue that James 5:7-20 has closing warnings and a form of epistolary closing not unlike that found elsewhere inside and outside the New Testament. For instance both James and 1 John have (1) eschatological remarks, (2) prayer and (3) thematic reprise. True, a whole group of Hellenistic letters close abruptly with no final benediction or farewell, and some use *pro panton* ("for all") with a health wish formula or an oath formula. Oath formulas and expressions of concern for the addressee's health ("hope all are well") are characteristic of the genre. Francis states:

---

[72]Witherington, *Conflict and Community in Corinth*, pp. 82-90.

Thus the epistolary close of both James and I John combines (1) eschatological instruction, (2) thematic reprise, and (3) reference to prayer. The strictly epistolary function of these elements is borne out by comparison with other early Christian letters and general Hellenistic epistolography.

In summary, Francis urges that scholarship must reassess the literary character of the epistles James and I John in the light of what would appear to be carefully styled opening thematic statements, a recognizable epistolary close, and the rather substantial literary-thematic coherence of the epistles as a whole. James and I John may be understood as epistles from start to finish—secondary epistles in form and in literary treatment of their subject matter.[73]

To these observations we could add how all three major themes are touched on and combined as the letter closes—doing helps produce steadfastness, and praying (i.e., words) is related to enduring testing or suffering. It is not accidental that testing/steadfastness comes in for more stress at the end than do other themes, since that is the underlying and overriding concern here.

Francis is clearly onto something, as the patterns here involve the repetition of key themes. But I John bears none of the standard elements of the closing of a normal letter, much less a Christian one. There are no mentions of travel plans, no mentions of greetings, no final blessing, health wish, benediction.[74] It is possible that the author of 1 John knew and was influenced by the homily called James (as Joseph Mayor thinks),[75] in which case the pattern in the two documents does not represent a common epistolary pattern but rather the influence of one Christian writer on another in regard to closing themes or exhortations. This is a very different matter.

There is a much better explanation of the pattern: both documents conclude with a peroration following the rules of rhetoric in regard to the recapitulation of themes announced at the outset of the discourse. In other words, it is not a matter of following epistolary conventions, but rather rhetorical conventions, applied here to speeches. James is a document meant to be heard, not read, and as such it follows the conventions set up for persuasive speech.

These verses have close parallels to at least two other New Testament passages: Romans 5:2b-5 and 1 Peter 1:6-7. First Peter is verbally closer to James than is Paul, though the thought of Paul is closer to James and corresponds at several points, as Paul speaks of suffering producing endurance and endurance producing character. While Peter may have read James and is attempting to say

---

[73]Francis, "Form and Function," p. 126.
[74]Witherington, *Letters and Homilies*, 1.409-14.
[75]Mayor, *James*, pp. lxxxviii-lxxxix.

something similar, Paul is likely independent. All three may be drawing on common early Christian material, possibly even from Jesus (Mt 5:11-12). William Brosend points out that this is an example of rhetorical gradatio—a stairstep building to a climax by the use of repetition and interlinking of phrases by key-words.[76] We should read these verses as follows: "Count it as utter (*or* supreme cause) for rejoicing, my brothers, when you fall into various trials, knowing that the means of testing your faith results in steadfastness (*or* staying power). But let steadfastness come to its culmination—a perfect work (*or* let it have its complete effect)—so that you will be perfect and wholly complete, not lacking anything." The "it" in James 1:2 that one is to count as utter joy is the trials, mentioned in the subordinate clause. James's perspective is that these trials (here afflictions)[77] are clearly external in origin and are tests of character that one falls into *without* (even against) one's will. In James 1:13-15, he will talk about temptations that arise mainly from *within* and cannot be seen as an occasion for joy. "Trials without and temptations within"—these are the plight of the believer who must remain steadfast.

The word translated "steadfastness" in **James 1:3**, *hypomonē,* can refer to either the act of endurance or the temperament of endurance. In the New Testament it usually refers to unswerving constancy in the faith in spite of trials and temptations (Lk 8:15; 21:19; Rom 15:4). James is not talking about passive patience during trials, but the temperament by which one endures and prevails. The idea is of the refined and tempered and strengthened faith that results from going through the trials, not around them. Our author is not saying the trial or suffering is in itself good, but that we are to look at it from the positive side as an opportunity for strengthening our faith, improving our character. He is not advocating masochism or seeking suffering, but rather knowing how to deal with afflictions when one falls into them. The future tense in James 1:3 indicates that he sees such trials coming, not necessarily that they are already upon his audience—though some may be struggling. Faith is as crucial to James as it is to Paul. His is no mere works gospel (Jas 1:6; 2:1; 5:15). Faith here means one's basic belief in and trust in God. Trials can make one trust God more. The rare word *dokimion* refers to testing or its result (Ps 12:6; Prov 27:21; 1 Pet 1:7).

What is the end product of this testing if one passes the test? **James 1:4** indicates that this testing and the resulting strengthening of one's steadfastness is a process that one must allow to complete its perfect(ing) work. This is not testing to see if a person has faith, but the testing of existing faith so as to strengthen

---

[76]Brosend, *James and Jude*, p. 34.
[77]Ropes, *James*, p. 133.

it.[78] The terms *perfect* and *complete* here are eschatological, and we see here what the end product will be by the time Christ returns—we shall be perfected. The idea of becoming perfect and complete implies a process of adding to that completeness, so that in the end one lacks nothing necessary to stand before the judge (Jas 5:8-9). Thus, the Christian life is to be seen not merely as having faith, but persevering and improving in character so that a "full-formed upright-ness" results—or progressive sanctification, to use the theological term. This is not an experience of instantaneous perfection, but a perfecting process. Equally, it is not just growing up in the faith, but single-minded loyalty and unmixed motives. This is the work that God is doing as believers work out their salvation with fear and trembling. "Endurance, the growing capacity to experience disappointment and challenge with grace, courage, and resolve, is an outgrowth of faith, and itself yields maturity and completion, *telos* (perfection). Part of the subversive wisdom at the heart of James's ideology is the conviction that perfection is the goal, and trials are a part of the journey toward it."[79] How very different this is from the notion that suffering or even bad health is always a telltale indication of lack of faith. To the contrary, James seems to see such trials as part and parcel of all Christians' journeys.

The use of the words *teleios* and *holoklēros* indicates perfection and completion, which are related but not identical concepts. God will not stop working until God has a finished product—a perfect character in each believer. When one reaches that point of having a perfect character the process is complete. We are not told when this result will finally appear—presumably at Christ's appearing. The term *holoklēros* refers in the primary sense to being in good health, physically whole, complete or being of "sound body" (Acts 3:16).[80] It suggests an eschatological nuance here—moral perfection and bodily wholeness comes at the resurrection. James is not merely saying that believers should count it all as joy since God uses trials to strengthen our faith, but he also says that believers must allow endurance to have its full effect: endurance is not the goal, it is just a means to the end, and the believer must fully participate in the process for the end—wholeness and perfection—to be achieved.[81] It is possible to render *teleios* as "mature" here, but doing so loses the eschatological dimension that the text appears to be alluding to. Even maturity is not an end in itself, especially when full conformity to the image of Christ goes well beyond being a mature

---

[78]Moo, *James*, p. 55.
[79]Brosend, *James and Jude*, p. 38.
[80]Johnson, *James*, p. 178.
[81]Moo, *James*, p. 55.

Christian. In any case this kind of thinking would have been familiar to those who had read Wisdom of Solomon, where we hear that perfection without the wisdom from God amounts to nothing (Wisdom of Solomon 9.6) and that wisdom preserved Abraham "blameless before God" through trials (Wisdom of Solomon 10.5). James is clearly dealing with the same constellation of ideas. Wisdom is necessary both to discern and to carry out God's will, both to grow up and to go on toward perfection.

Connecting unrelated verses via an elaborate scheme of catchwords or wordplays is common in parenesis. For example, the wordplay between *chairein* and *charan* connects James 1:1 and James 1:2. Here, James 1:3 ends with *hypomonē* and James 1:4 begins with the same word. James 1:4 ends with *leipomenoi* and James 1:5 has *leipetai*. James 1:5 has *aiteitō* and James 1:6 begins with *aiteitō*. This means that (1) James may be citing catechetical material set in a form so it will be easily memorized and that (2) this is a Greek composition, not translation Greek, for these connections and wordplays are possible only in Greek; this document did not likely have a Semitic original.

James 1:5-8 tells us something about both God and humans: what God willingly gives and what humans can receive if they do so in faith. Several general features of the text call for notice. *Kyrios* in James 1:7 surely refers to God, not Christ, as James 1:5 makes clear. James alternates between using *kyrios* of Christ (Jas 1:1) and of God (Jas 4:15; 5:10, 11). Peter Davids points out that *sophia* ("wisdom") functions for James like *pneuma* ("spirit") does in Paul's letters.[82] Wisdom gives the illumination and strength necessary to stand the test. Wisdom is the special gift of God to believers. As we know from the Old Testament, wisdom could sometimes be personified, and here in James wisdom, which is a gift of the Spirit, is treated and spoken of almost as if it were the Spirit doing the Spirit's job. Wisdom is also viewed by James as the fundamental thing that is lacking—that one should ask of God[83]—and in a sense this homily seeks to remedy that problem by providing godly wisdom to the hearers. To see trials and afflictions in the light that James does—and wants his audience to see—requires wisdom from above. Wisdom of Solomon 7.7 is apt here: "Therefore I [the king] prayed, and understanding was given to me; I called upon God and the spirit of wisdom came to me."

In James 1:5-8 we also gain a clearer sense of what perfection amounts to in James's view. It means being fully equipped with the wisdom (not just knowledge but know-how, steadfastness) to withstand whatever trials or tribulations

[82]Davids, *James*, pp. 71-72.
[83]Johnson, *James*, p. 179.

one may have. It is not unlike Paul's image of the Christian who puts on the full armor of Christ. It is a person lacking nothing in what is needed to deal with life's slings and arrows. Thus, the focus is not on moral purity, per se, but on having an equipped and complete character, which involves moral uprightness and integrity. God here is contrasted to the waverer. God is single-minded and impartial and gives without making the receiver feel belittled. He gives without reservation—unconditionally. To receive it requires an unconditional, totally trusting response.

The person here described as the doubter is not the atheist or the person who has intellectual problems, but the person who knows to ask God for needed wisdom, but is always in two minds (*dipsychos* literally means "double-souled") about everything—"Mr. Facing Both Ways," to use John Bunyan's image. The doubter is like a wave on the ocean now moving toward shore, now moving away. The image is not of a storm-tossed sea, but of the regular ocean movement with sea breeze. The doubter's vacillating prayer bespeaks an underlying lack of full trust in God and manifests itself in an unstable and vacillating lifestyle. The term *dipsychos* is not attested before its use in James 1:8, and it may well have been coined by James himself.[84]

As we shall see, James is a firm believer that as a person's heart is so will be their life and actions. Ralph Martin is right to see in these verses an echo of Wisdom of Solomon 9.6: "For even if one is *teleios* ['perfect/mature'] among the sons of humanity, yet without wisdom that comes from God he will be regarded as nothing."[85] The theme of testing and enduring testing on the basis of divinely given wisdom is shared by these texts. James certainly stands in this tradition, but he freely modifies it to suit the new circumstances after the Christ event. James, in general, should be seen as a person who has drunk deeply from the well of sapiential material—from the Old Testament, from Sirach and Wisdom of Solomon and from his brother—and has formulated his own teaching while being indebted to these sources.

William Brosend points out the likely echo of Matthew 7:7 in James 1:5.[86] In both verses the subject is prayer, and the same verb for asking is in both. Brosend is also right, however, that James takes this idea in a particular direction—asking God for something specific, namely wisdom. James also portrays the character

---

[84]Seitz ("Antecedents and Significance"; "Afterthoughts on the Term *dipsychos*") and others fail to find any precedents or parallels for the term *dipsychos,* and the places where the term turns up in later literature are all dependent on James (including its use in *Shepherd* of Hermas, *Mandates* 9.6).

[85]Martin, *James*, p. 18.

[86]Brosend, *James and Jude*, p. 36.

of God more vividly: God is *haplōs,* which can be rendered a variety of ways: "without hesitation," "singly" or "simply."[87] The word is found only here in the New Testament, and in Classical Greek it certainly means "simply" or "plainly."[88] It is probably right to see here a contrast between God and the double-minded person. God is singled-minded by contrast—God does not hesitate to give, and God does so without reproach and with generosity, giving to "all" (in this case probably all believers).[89] Likewise James 1:6-7 likely echoes Mark 11:23 about how the one who doubts in the heart will not receive what is prayed for. It appears that the believer asking for help must be single-minded and pure—analogous to God's single-minded desire to help and give wisdom. "Arguably the most important theme in James is his concern that Christians display spiritual integrity: singleness of intent combined with blamelessness in actions."[90]

Here I part company with Brosend, who seems to think that because Jesus' sayings are used without attribution James does not view the material as sacred texts or as Scripture.[91] Yet James treats the Old Testament materials and the materials from intertestamental Judaism in the same way. While Brosend is certainly right that James's use of such traditions is fluid and paraphrastic and that James does not use citation formulas, this implies nothing about his view of the authority or inspiration of such texts. His use of them implies that he thinks they offer truth and wisdom. One could even argue that, because James assumes that at least some in the audience will recognize the echoes and their sources, he therefore felt no need to give indications of attribution. In addition, while James is prepared to say that God gives to all without reproach, he then turns around and qualifies this remark by saying that he gives to those who have faith and do not doubt. God's giving of wisdom is in response to prayer that believes that God can and will give. The interactive model of prayer and receiving what one has petitioned for based on real trust in God is noteworthy.

The underlying sayings of Jesus are being drawn on (Mk 11:23/Mt 21:21), which Peter Davids sums up this way:

The author, then, concludes his description of this doubter with a strong condem-

---

[87]These translations, respectively, from Dibelius, *James,* pp. 77-79; Moo, *James,* pp. 58-59; and Johnson, *James,* p. 179.
[88]Martin, *James,* p. 18.
[89]Bauckham, *James,* p. 86, notes that James's way of handling or reexpressing the Jesus tradition is very similar to the modus operandi of Jesus ben Sira in the way he handles the wisdom of Proverbs. This is not a surprise since James knows Sirach and draws on his material at various points, just as he draws on the Jesus tradition.
[90]Moo, *James,* p. 59.
[91]Brosend, *James and Jude,* pp. 36-38.

nation: his divided mind, when it comes to trusting God, indicates a basic disloyalty toward God. Rather than being a single-minded lover of God, he is one whose character and conduct is unstable, even hypocritical. No wonder he should expect nothing from God! He is not in the posture of the trusting child at all. For James there is no middle ground between faith and no faith; such a one, he will later argue (4:8), needs to repent.[92]

The warning of Luke Timothy Johnson about not trivializing what James is saying here is useful: "The content of James' first exhortation . . . is scarcely reducible to a moral truism [i.e., cheer up, trials and suffering are good for you]. The testing of the community's *faith*, after all, cannot simply be equated with the perfection of an individual's *virtue*. Nor is prayer in faith to God for the wisdom to have a faithful perception of trials the same as the self-sufficiency of a sage's wisdom."[93] It is no accident that the beginning and end of this discourse involve a discussion of prayer and its importance and efficacy if one asks in faith. Prayer is the clear talisman that one is living by faith and depending on God for not only the answers, but also the practical help to get through the trials of life.[94] Lack of prayer is a sign of doubting and spiritual instability, a lack of dependence on God.[95]

In James 1:9-11 James introduces another main topic—the poor and the rich. James 1:9 plays on the contrast between pride *(kauchasthō)* and the humble *ho tapeinos*. It is quite clear from the contrast with *plousios* in James 1:10 that the humble are the "humble poor" and the proud are the rich, whereas in Proverbs 3:34 the contrast of the humble is simply with the arrogant, who may or may not be rich. James's concern is with inappropriate sorts of boasting (Jas 3:14; 4:16), but not all boasting is ruled out. This is not surprising since in the wisdom tradition boasting in the Lord is seen as a good thing. In the New Testament outside of James and one reference in Hebrews 3:6, only Paul has anything to say directly about boasting, and Paul also suggests that there are things to boast about, in particular that which comes from the Lord and is done by the Lord, not that which comes from oneself. Behind all such discussions stands Jeremiah 9:23-24: "Let not the wise man boast of his wisdom, or the strong man boast of his strength, or the rich man boast of his riches, but let him who boasts, boast about this: that he understands and knows me . . . declares the LORD."

---

[92]Davids, *James*, p. 75.

[93]Johnson, *James*, p. 183 (emphasis original); cf. p. 182.

[94]Moo, *James*, p. 62, rightly notes that *anēr* in Jas 1:8, unlike *anthrōpos* Jas 1:7, is used in a generic way referring to human beings, not to men or husbands in particular.

[95]*Akatastatos* ("unstable") is found in the New Testament only at Jas 1:8 and Jas 3:8 and in the Septuagint only at Is 54:11.

What is not so clear is whether both the poor and the rich here are envisioned as Christians, or whether we should see a hard contrast here between "the believer" and "the rich." In either case, James is not talking solely about a person's character with his use of *tapeinos* but rather one's economic and social position. Nonetheless, paradoxically, the poor person has something to boast about in this humble condition.

Various problems arise in this passage. First, who are those rich people—rich Christians or rich people in general?[96] Much will depend on the interpretation of James 2:1-7 and James 5:1-6. It is difficult to imagine James 5:1-6 being said of a person who is truly a Christian; however, there is the rub. Quite clearly James 2:2 is talking about wealthy people who come to a Christian meeting. It seems unlikely that James would be speaking about the rich in general because, as James 1:1 indicates, he is addressing those who are part of the believing community, whom James can address directly (Jas 5:1). James refrains from explicitly calling them brothers (Jas 1:9-11), though it may be implied by the parallel with James 1:9a. On the whole it thus appears that James is calling to account both wealthy Christians and the community as a whole, which will be criticized for giving wealthy Christians special treatment or benefits. The parallel structure here favors the conclusion that the rich are envisioned as within the community. This in turn means that the "lowly position" of rich Christians is a reference to their social stigma for identifying themselves with Christ and his people.[97]

Nonetheless, James is profoundly dissatisfied with the behavior of these persons toward poor Christians and warns that if they do not shape up they will face God's final judgment. In this, James sounds much like an Old Testament prophet, excoriating the "fatted calves" who are among and associate with and claim allegiance to Israel and its God. The contrast in the letter between confession and lifestyle as the mark of someone not truly Christian draws specifically on the example of the rich (Jas 2:14-17). James is thus mainly speaking about and to those wealthy ones who claim faith but do not live out its implications (Jas 2 may, however, refer to rich visitors in the congregation).

James 1:10 is somewhat difficult to decipher. Should we supply the word *boast* and make it parallel to James 1:9? Is the verse about the rich Christians being robbed or disenfranchised by persecutors when or after they converted, or is it about, as Joseph Mayor argues, the rich having an attitude of self-abasement

---

[96]Stulac, "Who Are the Rich in James?" The more nuanced approach of Johnson and others suggests that the persons in question are ostensibly and self-identified as Christians but James is calling that into question because of their behavior. This may be correct.
[97]Moo, *James*, p. 66.

and engaging in self-effacing living because they know they must pass away someday and cannot take it with them?[98] Clearly, the rich are not to "glory" in their riches because they are not of lasting value. Riches can pass away in an instant; while the rich are on the move to make more money, they are seen as wasting away. The phrase *en tē tapeinōsei* must be parallel to *en tō hypsei,* so it is a reference to a humble position not a humble attitude, despite Mayor. It is doubtful that James is being sarcastic: "lest the rich boast about his degrada-tion" (i.e., filthy riches). Rather, the rich person should boast in voluntarily as-suming a lower position and more humble circumstances by giving wealth and helping the poor, whereas the poor are relatively better off not facing the temp-tation of riches—they know they are not self-sufficient and must rely on God for everything.

In his description of the transitoriness and ephemeral value of wealth, James is sounding a traditional sapiential note (Job 24:24; 27:21; Ps 49:16-20). The word *kausōni* in **James 1:11** could refer to the scorching east wind, but can equally well mean burning heat. The wind does not rise up at dawn in Palestine; it blows day and night during a several week period.[99] Almost every one of James's analogies drawn from nature is also found in the teaching of Jesus: surg-ing of the sea (Lk 21:25), flowers of the field (Mt 6:28), burning of wood (Jn 15:6), birds of the air (Mt 6:26; 8:20), fountain of sweet water (Jn 4:10-14), fig tree (Mt 7:16), vine (Jn 15:1-5), moth and rust (Mt 6:19), rain (Mt 5:45). Like ear-lier sages, Jesus and James believed that wisdom could be gained from close examination of nature, including human nature as well. Not only do these anal-ogies suit a resident of Israel very well, they also show the intellectual tradition that Jesus and James stand in.[100]

Finally, at the end of James 1:11 *en tais poreiais* may mean "in his travels" or "as he goes through life" or "as he goes about his business," and the second translation might parallel the end of James 1:8. James Hardy Ropes may be right that the point is, however, that the rich person is wasting away even while trying to get more wealth.[101] Both poverty and wealth are tests of character—they are trials to be endured and properly responded to. James 1:9-11's illustration using flowers or grass about transitoriness echoes Jesus' remarks (Lk 14:11; 18:14; Mt 6:30), Psalm 103:15-16 and Isaiah 40:6-8.[102] Not only is wealth fleeting, so is life, and so they both came be compared to grass or wildflowers. It is not clear

---

[98]Mayor, *James,* pp. 45-46.
[99]Davids, *James,* p. 78.
[100]Plummer, *General Epistles,* p. 87.
[101]Ropes, *James,* pp. 148-49.
[102]Brosend, *James and Jude,* p. 40.

whether we should read what is said here in light of James 4:13—5:9, with its clearly eschatological reference to the judgment coming when the Lord returns. In view of the exordium previewing coming attractions, I think that the eschatological overtones must be given their due here, all the more so when the very next verse offers a very Jesuslike eschatological beatitude promising the crown of eternal life. This passage then functions much like Jesus' use of reversal language—counterorder wisdom and ethics are what is appropriate in an eschatological situation. The point of the lengthy analogy between the rich and their money and the beautiful flower that wilts and is destroyed is that judgment is coming upon such persons who boast in that sort of status.[103]

James 1:12-18, while a new subsection, bears a rather clear relationship to the material in James 1:2-11, offering some correlative ideas, with James 1:12 serving as something of a hinge between what has come before and what comes afterward. William Brosend puts it this way: "The blessing on the one who endures temptations recalls the 'consider it nothing but joy' in the face of 'trials of any kind' in v. 2. The 'doubter' of vv. 6-8 anticipates the wrong understanding of temptation in vv. 13-15. The 'perfecting of faith' climax in vv. 3-4 is mirrored in reverse by the elaborate climax, from temptation to death, in vv. 14-15. The giving of wisdom from the God 'who gives to all generously and ungrudgingly' anticipates the giving 'of every perfect gift' in v. 17."[104] To this one can add that God's giving of wisdom anticipates the statement about God giving birth to humans through the word of truth. "The basic dynamic of the passage is clear: (1) the experience of testing naturally calls one to ask about its source; (2) do not think it comes from God, for God is not tempted and tempts not; (3) instead we are tempted by our desires, which if followed lead to death; (4) the unchanging God, on the contrary, gives good things, above all, gives us birth. The interplay of question and answer, temptation and blessing, human desire and divine purpose, birth and death make this a lively and complex passage."[105] This reasoning reflects the long-standing Jewish sapiential tradition in which the real wisdom that matters is a gift from God (Prov 2:6; Sirach 51.17; Wisdom of Solomon 8.21; 9.17; 4Q185 [an unnamed sapiential text]) and God is seen as being generous for lavishing such wisdom on fallen human beings (Sirach 1.9-10).

Makarios, which begins **James 1:12**, immediately reminds us of the beatitudes in the Sermon on the Mount. Some translate the term "happy," but this term is not simply a synonym for *eudaimonia* (on the distinction see Aristotle

---

[103]Johnson, *James,* pp. 190-91.
[104]Brosend, *James and Jude,* p. 44.
[105]Ibid., pp. 46-47.

Nichomachean Ethics 1101A). In the biblical tradition the term is applied to a person in right relationship with God (Deut 33:29; Ps 1:1; 2:12; 32:1), and so the translation "blessed" is the best one.[106] James says, "Blessed is the man who stands up to the test, because when he has been approved he will receive a crown (i.e., [eternal] life), which God has promised to his beloved." Previously we were told that one could fall into a trial or test, and here we see the converse—standing up under it. The author's focus is on eschatological, not temporal, rewards here, that is, the one who persevered and is approved receives eternal life, the ultimate blessing, which God himself promised to his beloved children. The use of *stephanos* may be drawing on the image of the crown of victory bestowed on the winner of a race, which was a laurel wreath not a metal crown (Herodotus 8.26; Rev 2:9-10). An interesting epitaph from Cyprus for a deceased comedian says that he was defeated for (or possibly denied) "the crown of life" *(ton biotou stephanon).*[107]

If James 1:12 was about those who pass the test, James 1:13 is about those about to fail it and in need of a stern warning. Here we see James using a diatribe form, as found at length in James 2. James 1:13 seems to contain an echo of Sirach 15.11-12: "Do not say, 'It was the Lord's doing that I fell away'; for God does not do what he hates. Do not say, 'It was he who led me astray'; for he has no need of the sinful." Alfred Plummer notes that there is perhaps an especially good reason why James would draw on Sirach and the Wisdom of Solomon in his address to Jewish Christians in the Diaspora: those books, at least in their Greek form, came from the Diaspora and were the popular literature of such Jewish persons.[108]

There is much debate as to whether we should take *peirazomenos* to mean "tested," as its original, here in James 1:13, or "tempted." The context probably suggests that we should translate "being tempted" here to go along with the shift from an external to an internal source of difficulty.[109] If so, this provides another catchword linkage: *peirazomenos* and *peirasmon.* Basically, a temptation is viewed as something internal, an inner enticement, while a trial is something external to the person.[110] The verse then reads: "When you are tempted, do not say 'I was tempted by God,' for God is untemptable (i.e., not subject to

---

[106]Johnson, *James,* p. 187.

[107]*Inscriptiones graecae* 14.441. See Horsley, *New Documents Illustrating Early Christianity,* 2.50.

[108]Plummer, *General Epistles,* p. 75.

[109]Ropes, *James,* pp. 153-54.

[110]Rightly Moo, *James,* p. 53. In 1 Tim 6:9 *peirasmon* means "temptation"; see the discussion in Witherington, *Letters and Homilies,* 1.286-87.

evil)[111] nor does he tempt anyone. Rather each person is tempted by his own desire, being lured and enticed (by it). Then desire conceiving gives birth to sin, and sin when full grown engenders death." We see here in these two parallel sentences the two opposite ways a person can go—either trial, approval and life or desire, sin and death, with no middle ground. James wishes to establish that it is quite inexcusable to make God the source of one's temptations. Not only is God immune to temptation and thus he will never conceive or do evil, but also being perfectly good he will not tempt anyone. One might naturally expect the writer to go on and talk about Satan the tempter, but instead he places the responsibility for sin and its source on fallen human nature. James is not trying to tell us what the ultimate source of evil is, though he denies that it is God. Peter Davids says:

> It would be wrong to consider this a theodicy: James is not explaining how a good God can permit evil, but whether God is the efficient cause of the impulse to abandon the faith. His focus is practical rather than theoretical. . . . What makes a given situation a test is not that God has put one there—James will later argue that God gives good gifts (1:17), so presumably he wills good in any given situation—but that the person is willing to disobey him.[112]

James 1:14 applies metaphors of hunting and fishing to temptation. One is lured or drawn in by the bait on the hook or enticed and entrapped by the bait in the net. Philo makes a similar use of this metaphor: "There is no single thing that does not yield to the enticement of pleasure, and get caught and dragged along in her entangling nets" (*On Husbandry* 103). Obviously, temptation can appear very appealing, or else it would not be very tempting. When desire conceives of evil it gives birth to sin, but it is sin that leads to death.[143] Thus in James 1:15 we have the gradatio in reverse—spiraling down to a negative climax—tempted by desire, desire once conceived gives birth to sin, which when fully grown gives birth to death. Put in linear fashion, conception leads to birth, which leads to growth, which leads to death. Some behavior gives birth to life, other behavior gives birth to death. James offers up a sapiential paradox by

---

[111] Davids, "Meaning of *apeirastos*," however, suggests that this rare word might mean "ought not to tempt" rather than "untemptable." Moo, *James*, pp. 73-74, shows the flaws in Davids's evidence and arguments.

[112] Davids, *James*, p. 81.

[113] Various scholars think that James reflects the early Jewish notion of the *yēṣer hāraʿ* and the *yēṣer ṭôb* in each person—the inclination toward evil or good. But James says nothing about an inherent inclination to do good, and evil desire (not inclinations) is at issue here. See Marcus, "Evil Inclination in the Epistle of James." Clearly enough some strains of Jewish tradition saw some sorts of desire as a good thing (e.g., Song of Songs and portions of Ecclesiastes).

drawing on the birth imagery here to describe the process that leads to death and in James 1:18 by contrasting the process that God initiates by which believers become firstfruits of the (new) creation to this process that leads to death. Desire in itself is not sin, but if it is wrongly directed sin is not only conceivable but conceived. Douglas Moo is right: "Christian maturity is not indicated by the infrequency of temptation but by the infrequency of succumbing to temptation."[114] He is also right that this verse probably echoes the discussion of the "loose woman" in Proverbs 5—9.

Matthew 5 is also possibly in the background here. Joseph Mayor says: "The undoubted references to the Sermon on the Mount which occur in this epistle are in all probability actual reminiscences of spoken words."[115] But since James was not a follower of Jesus during his ministry we may assume that he got this secondhand, hearing it from Peter, from another eyewitness or even from a brief written collection of Jesus' sayings.

James 1:16-18 continues on a more positive note. If God does not tempt us or send temptations, what does he send? The answer is good gifts. The imagery here draws on Genesis and the first creation. The word *lights* is plural here, and in the Genesis narrative only the sun and the moon are called lights in this fashion. Calling God the Father of lights is a distinctive way of referring to God, and all the more so when, having called God Father, in the next verse James turns around and says God gives birth to people through the word.[116] With this background, we can make sense out of James 1:17b. Sunlight varies in its amount or intensity depending on the time of year. Unlike this, God and his light do not change or vary. The moon is continually going through various phases that change the amount of light it reflects. God, however, is not like this. Nothing overshadows or changes God, and when God wills to do something it happens.

In this case, what God wills is the new creation that takes place through the word of truth, that is, the gospel of redemption. The result is that believers are already a sort of firstfruits of God's new creation.[117] Rather than being dead, they are already reborn and part of a new world. Obviously, various Pauline texts have similar ideas (1 Cor 15:20-28; 2 Cor 5:17-18). Perhaps James knew Paul's teaching on these matters and varied the imagery to suit his purposes. In any case, this exordium nicely makes emotional contact with the audience, sets up

[114]Moo, *James*, p. 76.
[115]Mayor, *James*, p. 50.
[116]Brosend, *James and Jude*, p. 46.
[117]James may be thinking about a redemptive birth, rather than physical birth, and may be echoing Jewish morning prayers where God is praised as Father of creation and redemption; see Elliott-Binns, "James 1.18"; and Verseput, "James 1.17 and the Jewish Morning Prayers."

and introduces most of the main themes that follow, and as such follows the rhetorical dictums about such introductions.

PROPOSITIO: QUICK LISTENING, SLOWING SPEAKING, INSISTENT DOING OF THE WORD (JAS 1:19-27)

A propositio in a deliberative discourse can serve a variety of functions, but above all it must provide a clue as to the real substance and urgency and theme of the following discourse and its various arguments. It is the main advice the audience must heed and hear, and the arguments that follow are meant to support or spin out the implications and applications of this advice.

What then is the exigence that caused this sermon to be written? The short answer is that James is concerned about a lack of living out the faith in accord with God's word and even with God's law. For James, gospel and law are certainly not antithetical or incompatible at all; obedience to God's perfect law is seen as the natural fruit and expression of genuine faith. What James means by law and what he means by God's word requires close scrutiny. This particular propositio serves also to advise the audience about the proper approach to life so that one does not make mistakes in one's Christian living. Listening, reflecting before speaking, and doing what God commands is the order of the day.

This propositio is not an attempt to produce concord or unity in the audience, which is, since this is an encyclical, in a variety of places widely divided by space. Rather, James wants consistency between speech and action and also a better listening to what the word requires. Appeal to honorable behavior is a higher order or form of deliberative discourse than appeal to expediency or personal benefit or even unity/concord. There can be little doubt that James is addressing the issue of character and honor, and so the appropriate topics are, as Quintilian says, what is "right, justice, piety, equity and mercy" (*Institutio oratoria* 3.8.25-29). Each of these topics will be addressed in what follows, since proper religious behavior is especially the provenance of deliberative rhetoric. Our discourse is about a God who is impartial, faithful, righteous, just, merciful—and who requires of his followers the same sort of behavior. It is no accident that in due course James will trot out the paradigmatic examples of righteous and faithful Old Testament saints—figures like Abraham and Job. In other words, James has chosen the highest form of deliberative rhetoric.

Quintilian adds that it is an easy thing to commend an honorable course of action to honorable persons (*Institutio oratoria* 3.8.38), and clearly enough James, while exhorting the audience strongly, believes that they are capable of being their best selves. The stridency and pungent nature of the rhetoric at various points shows that James is doing his best to shame the audience into the sort of behavior that will be consistent with their self-estimate of being honorable persons. There is no problem with being direct in a deliberative discourse, and Quintilian says that pragmatic topics appropriate to such a discourse are money (even taxes), public service to others and peace (3.8.14). Again, this suits admirably that found in James's discourse following the proposition. In various ways James is doing the same sort of thing and drawing on the same sort of material found in Paul's magnum opus in Romans 12—15.[118] That James has a different slant on some of the same material is clear, and this is in part due to his addressing Jewish Christians in this discourse, those who already revere the law and the sapiential teachings of their tradition, including Jesus' additions to that tradition.

A proposition should be brief, concise, to the point and relatively self-contained, leaving the elaboration on the themes previewed to the discourse that follows (Cicero *De inventione rhetorica* 1.22.32; Quintilian *Institutio oratoria* 4.5.26-28). It is appropriate that the end of the proposition serve as a transition to the first argument, and James 1:26-27 serves this function. Ralph Martin, without realizing it, demonstrates that we are dealing with a rhetorically formed proposition that sets up the following discourse:

> This section (1:19b-27) opens with a survey of five themes in swift succession, all of them due to be expanded in later parts of the letter. The first is the wisdom teaching that places restraint on a hasty and impetuous desire to promote God's cause, seen here as "divine righteousness." The parallel is in 3:14-18. Two major interests then motivate James' counsel: the advocacy of practical obedience to God's message, which must be not only received with humility (v 21) but also acted upon. Fourth, there is the concern for the defenseless members of the community, linked with, fifth, a deliberate turning aside from "the ways of the world" (v 27). This last topic, which is enlarged in 4:1—5:20, is already in the author's mind at vv 19b-20.[119]

The reason for this particular kind of organization of the material is because James is following rhetorical conventions in regard to creating a propositio rather carefully here.

In various ways this discourse should be compared to what Paul says in Galatians to his largely Gentile audience. In the end, both will affirm a form of what can be called the law of Christ as something that Christians need to be obedient to, and that law includes some things from the Mosaic law reformed and reaffirmed, some things from the teaching of Jesus, and some new Christian

---

[118]See discussion in Witherington and Hyatt, *Romans*, pp. 49-51.
[119]Martin, *James*, p. 47.

teachings as well. The difference is that James is fine with Jewish Christians keeping portions of the Mosaic covenant (he thinks it is required), while Paul thinks this unnecessary for his largely Gentile audience and even for himself. James talks about the perfect law of God, while Paul speaks about the new covenant and its requirements.

Unlike with forensic rhetoric, a narration of facts relevant to the discourse was not required in deliberative rhetoric—and we do not have one here. Rather the discourse ensues directly after the proposition. This is not surprising in an encyclical, since the fact and conditions will have differed from Jewish Christian group to Jewish Christian group, and so James is hoping to address the common needs and difficulties that such Christians faced throughout the empire. The rather generic quality of this sermon is intentional because of the broad audience. James is not dealing with one specific set of problems in one specific congregation, and this makes it very different from a deliberative discourse like 1 Corinthians.

> [1:19] *Know this my beloved brothers, all persons should be quick to listen, slow to speak and slow to become angry,* [20] *for the anger of men does not produce the righteousness of God.*[120] [21] *Therefore, having cleaned out all your earwax and your abundant/ overflowing malice with meekness/good will, receive the implanted word that is able to save you.*
>
> [22] *When I say receive the word I mean do it, not just listen to it.* [23] *For if anyone hears the word but does not do it, that person is like one who studies his natural-born face in the mirror,* [24] *and having looked at himself closely is off and immediately forgets what he is like.* [25] *But one who even glances into the perfect law of freedom and continues in it, not being a forgetful hearer but a doer of works, that one shall be blessed for what he does.*
>
> [26] *If anyone thinks he is religious, but is not bridling his tongue, he is deceiving himself in his heart, and his religious observance is in vain.* [27] *Pure and unblemished religion in the eyes of our God and Father is—visiting orphans and widows in their time of affliction (and) keeping oneself spotless from the world.*[121]

In several places in James 1, the author quotes a fragment of material derived from another source. **James 1:19** seems to be a Jewish proverb echoing Sirach

---

[120]The Textus Receptus appears secondary. Instead of the abrupt *iste* the Textus Receptus connected Jas 1:19 to Jas 1:18 by adding *hōste* and letting the following *estō* do the verbal work for what now becomes a clause. The reading adopted in the Greek New Testament is clearly superior and is supported by both Western and Alexandrian witnesses: א, B, C. See Metzger, *Textual Commentary*, p. 680.

[121]The unique reading in 𝔓[74] ("to protect themselves" instead of "to keep themselves") perhaps reflects later stronger concerns about pollution from the world. See Metzger, *Textual Commentary*, p. 680.

5.11-12 ("be quick to hear, but deliberate in answering; if you have understanding, answer your neighbor; but if not put your hand over your mouth)" and Proverbs 29:11 ("a fool gives full vent to anger, but the wise quietly holds it back"). Our author is skillful at incorporating such material and making it part of a whole. This letter is not a patchwork quilt with sloppy seams, and a natural shift appears between James 1:18 and James 1:19. The former talks about God's word, the latter about human words. The imperative *iste* introduces what follows and could be translated either "this you (already) know" or "be sure of this." There might be room for debate on other subjects but not when it comes to listening to and heeding God's word. Robert Wall sees this verse as the thesis statement or proposition of the entire discourse and then proceeds to divide the discourse accordingly: James 1:22—2:26 is about being "quick to hear"; James 3:1-18 is about being "slow to speak"; and James 4:1—5:6 is about being "slow to anger."[122] William Brosend says, however, that this "suggestion is interesting but flawed, for any reading of James that does not emphasize the persistent call to faithful practice, or doing, is inadequate."[123] Brosend then opts for James 1:22 as the thesis statement of the discourse. Both writers are partially correct, since James 1:19-27 is a self-contained rhetorical unit that makes up the proposition or thesis statement of the discourse.

Orgē in **James 1:20** may mean the eschatological justice or retribution of God that will fall on the world at the end. A reference to God's eschatological anger would comport with James 5:9 and the idea of being saved from the wrath by the word in James 1:21. This is unlikely here, however, since the subject of James 1:20 is human conduct, not God's. Human anger does not produce the type of righteous action that reflects God's standard.[124] The Sermon on the Mount likely lies in the background here, where Jesus condemns angry and malicious words and tells those who speak such that they are liable to Gehenna (Mt 5:22). This verse is important also because the language of righteous/righteousness *(dikaios/dikaiosynē)* is introduced into the discourse here and will become a major theme (Jas 2:23-24; 3:18; 5:6, 16).

Joseph Mayor notes that the use of *andros* makes it possible that James is specifically exhorting *men* who were mouthing off, perhaps thinking that their anger was godly or righteous.[125] That men were the typical speakers in synagogues and other Jewish public meetings supports this conclusion. Some ancient texts

---

[122]Wall, *Community of the Wise*, p. 71.
[123]Brosend, *James and Jude*, p. 49.
[124]Davids, *James*, p. 93.
[125]Mayor, *James*, p. 65.

suggest that anger was more associated with men than with women (Longinus *On the Sublime* 32). James is not speaking against righteous indignation, however, but against ordinary anger or malice toward another. Perhaps James the sage realized that men especially have a problem with properly expressing their anger, or maybe we should see *andros* as equivalent to *anthrōpos,* as seems to be the case elsewhere in James (Jas 1:8, 12, 23).[126] In any case, this is probably an echo of Proverbs 17:27, which connects speaking with anger: "A man of knowledge uses words with restraint, and a man of understanding is even-tempered" (cf. Sirach 1.22-24). The connection is the propensity of the quick-tempered person to speak too quickly and in an ill-advised manner.[127] Douglas Moo reminds us that James is likely reflecting on sayings of Jesus like Matthew 5:20, which speaks of his followers' righteousness exceeding that of the Pharisees and scribes, and that James is probably not prohibiting righteous anger, for "wisdom sayings are notorious for the use of apparently absolute assertions in order to make a general, 'proverbial' point. . . . So we can assume that James intends us to read his warning as a general truth that applies in most cases: human anger is not usually pleasing to God, leading as it does to all kinds of sins. That it can never be pleasing to God would be an interpretation that is insensitive to the [sapiential] style in which James writes."[128]

Here we may sense a contrast between anger/wrath and righteousness. But what does the phrase *righteousness of God* refer to? Is it a descriptor of God's character like that found in James 1:17? Does this phrase build on James 1:19 and refer to what God expects of Christians—that they manifest in their behavior the righteousness of God? Or is this a reference to God's righteous verdict that he proclaims or a right standing that God gives, as in justification?[129] The problem with this last suggestion is that James is addressing those who are already Jewish Christians, and he is not discussing what happened to them at the point of their conversions. William Brosend is right, however, that the verb *ergazomai* here refers to something humans "produce" or "work."[130] The context indicates that James is talking about human behavior, and so we should see an objective genitive here—the righteousness that God requires believers to work out instead of manifesting their own all-too-human anger, just as God is working his own righteous character into them. This interpretation comports completely

---

[126]Brosend, *James and Jude,* p. 49, makes the wry comment that "as far as I know the only evidence that males are more likely to forget what they see in the mirror is anecdotal."
[127]Moo, *James,* p. 82.
[128]Ibid., p. 84.
[129]Laws, *James,* p. 81.
[130]Brosend, *James and Jude,* p. 50.

with what follows, which speaks of the word of God implanted in the inner self (and within the community), which saves the person.

James 1:21 draws a conclusion on the basis of James 1:19-20. A deliberate alliteration on the *p* sound characterizes this verse in the Greek, thereby punctuating the exhortation and making it memorable to the listener.[131] Because anger (including condemning, cursing, even cursing one's oppression) will not bring about God's final judgment, one should be slow to vent or express one's anger. Instead of such speaking, Christians are to clean out their ears and listen. *Rhyparia* in a metaphorical sense can mean moral filth or avarice (Jas 2:2; 1 Pet 3:21), but Joseph Mayor notes that it literally refers to earwax.[132] The context does not favor the purely metaphorical sense, for the context is hearing and receiving the word. There may be a connection between what is said here and the discussion in 1 Peter 1:23—2:2 since both passages refer to new birth through the word, followed by an exhortation to get rid of evil behavior and embrace the word.[133] The word is to be received with either meekness or good will. *Emphyton* must surely mean "implanted" because one cannot receive something that is "innate," and "ingrafting" does not quite fit here (Herodotus 9.94; *Barnabas* 1.2; 9.9). The word gets so deeply rooted that it becomes a part of one's very being and is able to save the person (compare Jesus' metaphor of the seed sown in Mk 4:1-20; Mt 13:3-23). Salvation here is seen as future, that is, salvation on the day of judgment—a future sense of salvation also seen at James 2:12; 4:12; 5:15, 20.

Psychē does not mean "soul" here, but "self" or "life." The New Testament authors show no interest in saving only part of a person, but rather wish to save the whole person, and that is what the word means here—yourself, your being; your No radical dualism is in evidence. Meekness is said to be the means of cleaning out one's malice. *Praytēti* may echo the reference to lowliness in James 1:9 but in any case it is an important descriptor of both Christ's (Mt 11:28-30) and a Christian's (Gal 5:22-23) character. It is not an accident that many of the character traits listed in the New Testament include virtues that were not seen as virtues in the Greco-Roman world, and "meekness," which was seen as weakness by most non-Jewish persons in that world, is one of them. This is one of the examples where Christian character and conduct

---

[131] Johnson, *James*, p. 201.

[132] Mayor, *James*, p. 66, cites an example from Clement of Alexandria, who in turn quotes Hippocrates on this word. It is also found in Artimedorus (second century A.D.); Martin, *James*, p. 48.

[133] It is possible that Peter knows James's letter since 1 Peter was likely written considerably after James. But see Moo, *James*, p. 85.

is meant to model itself on the distinctive character traits of Jesus.

It is entirely possible that **James 1:22-25** is simply a further development of what precedes, that is, "When I say receive the word I mean do it, not just listen to it." In any event, the section begins with a charitable assumption that they *are* doing the word: "But *continue to be doers* of the word and not just listeners deceiving yourselves."[134] James 1:21 implies that this probably means deceiving oneself about salvation or at least about the authenticity of one's Christian life. Orthodoxy that is not coupled with orthopraxy and real fruit in God does not impress James. James 2:19 says that even the demons believe all the right doctrines but it does them little good. Here is a salutary lesson against those who pride themselves on their orthodoxy, but who have so spiritualized and allegorized the gospel's demands that they do not take seriously the cost of discipleship and the demand for deeds of compassion and righteousness. William Brosend aptly puts it: "When all is said, all is not done."[135] Paul says something similar in Romans 2:13: "It is not those who hear the law who are righteous in God's sight, but it is those who obey the law who will be declared righteous."[136]

James 1:23-25 raises a host of questions. Obviously, we are dealing with a metaphorical sapiential comparison, so we must not press the text too far. The point of the comparison seems to be the transitoriness of the mirror image's effect and the transitoriness of the effect of hearing *only* without doing. Joseph Mayor thinks of a comparison between looking at one's earthly appearance[137] and looking into God's word and seeing one's eternal character.[138] This misses the point that the contrast is between seeing/forgetting to heed what one has seen and seeing/doing, not between the two forms of looking and what can be seen in each mirror.[139] Peter Davids says: "The momentariness and lack of real effect is the point of the parable, not a comparison with a different type of mirror or a different way of seeing."[140] There is thus no need to see any devel-

---

[134]On the durative force of the verb *do*, see Davids, *James*, pp. 96-102.

[135]Brosend, *James and Jude*, p. 51.

[136]Plummer, *General Epistles*, p. 102, suggests that perhaps James had read Paul or vice versa. It would have to be the latter if the homily of James was written in the early 50s and Romans in the late 50s, but both can be said to be under the influence of Jesus' teaching.

[137]That the key phrase means something like "natural or birth face" seems clear from the parallels: Gen 31:13; Ruth 2:11; Wisdom of Solomon 3.12; 12.10. See Johnson, *James*, p. 207.

[138]Mayor, *James*, p. 71.

[139]Mirrors and what one could see in them were often the subject of metaphorical use in Classical Greek literature and commonly symbolized one of three things: (1) purity (based on the clean surface of the mirror), (2) self-knowledge and (3) indirect knowledge. James is clearly using the image in the second sense. See Horsley, *New Documents Illustrating Early Christianity*, 4.150.

[140]Davids, *James*, p. 98.

oped contrast between fallible human mirrors, made of copper and bronze and giving a mediocre likeness even when polished, and God's law as the mirror of the soul. The interesting word *epilēsmonē* means "forgetfulness" occurs nowhere else in the New Testament, but Sirach 11.27 says that the afflictions of an hour cause forgetfulness of pleasure. Alfred Plummer says that a "hearer of forgetfulness" is the antithesis of a "doer of the word."[141] Another possible echo of Sirach is found in the use of *poiēsei* in James 1:25, referring to "doing" the law. Sirach 19.20 uses the same term to say that in all wisdom there is a "doing" of the law.

Luke Timothy Johnson does an excellent job of showing both how the image of looking into a mirror as a metaphor of moral improvement (with the mirror sometimes signifying the distance between image and reality) was common in the Greco-Roman world and how the image of looking into the law as into a mirror was found in earlier Jewish wisdom literature (especially Wisdom of Solomon 7.26).[142] One of the keys to understanding the use of the metaphor here is that the verb "look" differs in the two phrases. Here we have *parakyptō*, which seems to mean to lean over or stoop down in order to peer in or gaze intently, to ponder hard at what one is looking at (Lk 24:12; Jn 20:5; especially 1 Pet 1:12).[143] The transitory glance—however clearly it may have taken in the image—is contrasted with deep reflection.

The real crux of the matter is what "law" means in James 1:25—the Mosaic law, Christian teaching, a combination of both? We should probably not see the mirror analogy or parable as a full-blown allegory as if "the word is represented by a looking-glass that faithfully portrays a person's God-designed 'image.'"[144] Looking into the mirror and seeing one's own image and forgetting is one thing; looking into the law and seeing God's character and remembering and doing is another. It may be well to remind ourselves that mirrors were far from perfect in antiquity (1 Cor 13:12), and James is hardly going to say that the law, which he calls perfect, is like an inexact mirror image in a bronze mirror. The analogy is between a person looking into two different things and then either not acting on what is seen or acting on it appropriately. The law is not called a mirror here. An analogy is, after all, a comparison between two largely unlike things that in some specific way are alike. Duane Watson rightly says: "Argumentation from example is a standard feature of deliberative rhetoric. Examples used in proof

[141]Plummer, *General Epistles*, p. 109.
[142]Johnson, "Mirror of Remembrance."
[143]Johnson, *James*, p. 209.
[144]Martin, *James*, p. 46, citing Ropes, Dibelius, Davids and others.

usually incorporate a comparison of likes, unlikes, or contraries; *those from un-likes being most suitable to exhortation in deliberative rhetoric* (Quint. 5.11.10)."[145] James is choosing the most suitable sort of examples for his deliberative discourse, and we will see another such example in James 2:2-4.

A CLOSER LOOK
The Word or the Law? James's View

William Brosend rightly notes that there are only five uses of the term *logos* in James, and with the exception of the incidental use of the term in James 3:2, where it refers to speaking, they are all clustered in James 1 (Jas 1:18, 21, 22, 23).[146] The term helps link the exordium and the proposition of this discourse. If "be ye doers of the word" is so essential to James's discourse, why does he cease talking about the *logos* after James 1? Brosend suggests that "it appears that as James's argument unfolds, *logos* is replaced by *nomos* (law), which is first found at 1:25, and that for James the two terms are in many ways synonymous."[147] Let us see if this suggestion makes sense.

First, James 1:22 speaks of "the word." Whatever *nomos* means in James 1:25, it is likely to be the same thing as the "word" of James 1:22 in view of both the content and context of these verses, since even Martin Dibelius recognizes that they are interconnected.[148] Second, since Jesus' teaching underlies so much of this letter surely that background cannot be excluded from this saying about word or law. Third, this law is not said to be a yoke, but rather a law that gives liberty. Fourth, James 2:8-11 defines this law in part as a law from God, a royal law. It must involve at least the Old Testament love commandment and parts of the Decalogue. Just as obviously, however, it must include that Christian parenesis and teaching of Jesus that James has already used to exhort his audience. Thus, I agree with Peter Davids that for James law means all three—Old Testament law, Jesus' teaching and Christian ethics.[149] This comports with the use of *logos* in a broad sense in James 1. Augustine said long ago: "James does not say 'of the words' but 'of the word' despite the fact that there are so many words from the Holy Scriptures that are venerated in the church" (*Sermons* 77.22). Moreover, James sees Jesus' law as a "new law" that gives freedom, unlike the old law by itself. James 1:25 may contrast this perfect law and what had been given before.

---

[145]Watson, "James 2," p. 103 (emphasis added).
[146]Brosend, *James and Jude*, p. 53.
[147]Ibid.
[148]Dibelius, *James*, p. 108.
[149]Davids, *James*, pp. 99-100.

This law is *new* in part because it is implanted in the believer—it does not just exhort a person from outside, and it becomes so deeply rooted in the believer that the doing of it is freedom and a freely chosen act, not a mere duty or compulsion. Jeremiah 31:33's "write the law on their hearts" may be compared at this point. This law, if it is divine, gives freedom. God's word, if implanted, is able to save not to kill. However, James is not saying that obedience saves a person. God's word and grace do that.

James is addressing those who are already Christians and giving them kingdom ethics, what God requires of them after the new birth and on the way to final salvation. James is thus not at variance with Paul, who also talks about Christian ethics as the "law of Christ" and relates freedom and obedience to God's word or law (Gal 5:13-14). In short, James's perspective is like that of his brother Jesus and not to be radically contrasted with Paul's view. The Old Testament law must be *reinterpreted* in light of what God has done in Jesus. This means that some of it is fulfilled and no longer applicable; some of it is retained and reaffirmed; some of it is expanded on or radicalized; and some new commandments are offered as well.

Some of the old law's central teaching is reemphasized and stressed and made central, such as the law of love or the love commandment. Some of it has added to it various new things, including the law's new role in a believer's life so that it all could be called a new law or a perfect law of liberty. Eschatological, not temporal, blessing appears to be in view in James 1:25. A doer of God's word will be blessed instead of cursed on that day that is coming. Douglas Moo's conclusions are worth quoting:

> The "law" of v. 25 must be substantially equivalent to the "word" of vv. 22-23. Yet that "word" must be closely related to, if not identical to, the "word of truth" through which men and women are regenerated to salvation (v. 18). Taken together, these points suggest that James's "law" does not refer to the law of Moses as such, but to the law of Moses as interpreted and supplemented by Christ. Perhaps then, the addition of the word "perfect" connotes the law in its eschatological, "perfected" form, while the qualification "that gives freedom" refers to the new covenant promise of the law written on the heart (Jer. 31:31-34 . . .), accompanied by a work of the Spirit enabling obedience to that law for the first time.[150]

Whenever a new covenant is created—and not just an old one renewed— it will have to have at least some new provisions and stipulations; while it may reiterate some of the old ones as well. The eschatological covenant is neither a mere renewal nor a mere fulfillment of any previous ones. It and its

---

[150]Moo, *James*, p. 94.

"law" have no built-in obsolescence, it is perfect, as James says (Ps 19:7). This law gives freedom, which is the very opposite of what Paul says about the Mosaic law's effect on fallen human beings. Is it too much to think that James, like Paul, believed that the eschatological law had been given by Christ with the new covenant, that which Paul calls "the law of Christ" in Galatians James calls the royal or "perfect law"? Perhaps not, but in any case Luther's contrast between Paul's James's views of the law was clearly mistaken. Both James and Paul argued for obedience to this new law, whether one calls it the perfect law or the law of Christ. Both were indebted to Jesus, who associated blessedness with hearing the word of God/his own words and keeping or doing them (Lk 11:28; Mt 7:24). Thus, while commentators like Alfred Plummer go too far when they say to read *gospel* whenever one see the word *law* in James, they are on the right track, for James is talking about the law or commandment portion of the new covenant.[151] Ralph Martin stresses that both *gospel* and *law* are interchangeable with the term *word* in this sapiential discussion.[152] In other words, James's use of the term *law* is flexible, as William Brosend stresses.[153]

In his concern for himself and his own audience, Plummer shares James's own concern for his audience:

> But it is much to be feared that with many of us the interest in the sacred writings which is thus roused and fostered remains to a very large extent a literary interest. We are much more eager to know all *about* God's Word than from it to learn His will respecting ourselves, that we may do it; to prove that a book is genuine than to practice what it enjoins. We study Lives of Christ, but we do not follow the life of Christ. We pay Him the empty homage of an intellectual interest in His words and works, but we do not the things which He says. We throng and press Him in our curiosity, but we obtain no blessing, because in all our hearing and learning there is no true wisdom, no fear of the Lord, and no doing of His Word.[154]

---

[151]Plummer, *General Epistles*, p. 102.

[152]Martin, *James*, p. 45.

[153]Brosend, *James and Jude*, pp. 66-68. It is possible to add that perhaps James believed that Jewish Christians especially in Jerusalem needed to continue to keep the whole Mosaic law in addition to the teachings of Jesus and James (and other Christian teachers). Yet clearly he is not in favor of the multiplication of teachers, all of whom might have something more to add to the moral code of Christianity. There is also the possibility that he expected less of Jewish Christians in the Diaspora than he did of Jewish Christians in Jerusalem, simply because the former could not keep all the festivals by coming to Jerusalem. Perhaps this is why this homily mentions nothing about keeping festivals or sabbath or kosher or the like.

[154]Plummer, *General Epistles*, p. 110 (emphasis original).

The transitional verses James 1:26-27 lead to the first major exposition of a theme. Peter Davids says:

> The final section of this introductory chapter sums up what has preceded and bridges between it and chap. 2. The subject has been true Christianity, and three marks stand out: (a) a true Christian must control his tongue (1:19-21, but also chap. 3 and with it the wisdom sayings, 1:5-8), (b) he must engage in charity, which was certainly the teaching of Jesus (1:22-25, 9-11; chap. 2), and (c) such a one must resist temptation, i.e., the world (1:2-4, 12-15; chap. 4). The summary first states (a) negatively, then (b) and (c) positively.[155]

The term *thrēskos* likely refers to religious observance—rites and rituals, prayer and fasting, the elements of worship and devotional practice—while *thrēskeia* refers more generically to religion in its cultic aspects (Wisdom of Solomon 14.18, 27; 4 Maccabees 5.7, 13; Acts 26:5),[156] something that is reinforced by the further use of the term *aspilos* ("undefiled, spotless") (1 Tim 6:14). James says that all these religious practices are futile if not accompanied by (1) a bridled tongue, (2) helping orphans and widows when they are bereaved and in need and (3) keeping away from the evil aspects of the world that can taint one's faith and life. Religious observance without ethical practice is a matter of deceiving oneself in one's own heart—it is an exercise in futility. Here, of course, James is simply reiterating a repeated refrain in the Old Testament about taking care of the marginalized in one's community (Ex 22:22; Deut 26:12; Is 1:17; Jer 22:3; Zech 7:10; Tobit 1.8; Sirach 35.16; 2 Esdras [4 Ezra] 2.20). The warning against self-deception is apt, especially for Jews in a Greco-Roman environment like the Diaspora, where religion was regularly associated with correct and exacting performance of religious ritual and not necessarily with various codes of ethical conduct. Of course, both Jews and pagans insisted that proper cultic worship must be accompanied by proper behavior, but this connection was not always made or obvious in pagan religion.[157]

The tongue is depicted as a runaway horse needing to be reined in lest it do damage. James 1:26 picks up on what is said in James 1:19. "Pure and undefiled" in James 1:27 says the same thing from positive and negative viewpoints. The phrase *God and Father* as applied to God is typical of Paul and early Christian usage, not just of James. God is a father to the fatherless, and so should the audience be. Here surely James has in mind Psalm 68:5, where

[155]Davids, *James*, pp. 100-101.
[156]Johnson, *James*, p. 211.
[157]But see Verseput, "Reworking the Puzzle."

God is said to be a father to the fatherless and a defender of widows.[158] These concerns would be especially urgent in a highly patriarchal world where property was largely controlled by and passed from male to male and where a person without a father or husband was in severe jeopardy of poverty and destitution. Chrysostom reminds: "We can become more like God if we are merciful and compassionate. If we do not do these things, we have nothing at all to our credit. God does not say if we fast we shall be like God. Rather he wants us to be merciful, as God himself is. 'I desire mercy' he says, 'and not sacrifice'" (Catena 9). With this background, James now develops this practical Christianity in James 2.

ELABORATION OF THEMES, PART ONE: RICH AND POOR, WORD AND DEED (JAS 2:1-26)

> [James] throws together things so chaotically that it seems to me he must have been some good, pious man who took a few sayings from the disciples of the apostles and tossed them off onto the paper.[159]

> The entire document lacks continuity in thought.[160]

> Mercy is the highest art and the shield of those who practice it. It is the friend of God, standing always next to him and freely blessing whatever he wishes. It must not be despised by us. For in its purity it grants great liberty to those who respond to it in kind. It must be shown to those who have quarreled with us, as well as to those who have sinned against us, so great is its power. It breaks chains, dispels darkness, extinguishes fire, kills the worm and takes away the gnashing of teeth. By it the gates of heaven open with the greatest of ease. In short mercy is a queen that makes humans like God. (Chrysostom Catena 13)

Sometimes the heritage of the Reformation is more of a burden than a blessing, for it has prevented whole generations of commentators, especially German ones, from recognizing the rhetorical skill and art and structure of James's homily. Commentaries written in the last twenty years or so have begun to show some repentance from this travesty, but the various attempts to find structure and coherence in James's discourse have seldom paid attention to rhetorical signals, preferring to use epistolary or literary analysis (e.g., searching for chiasms, inclusios and the like).[161] With varying degrees of per-

---

[158]Moo, *James*, p. 97.

[159]Luther, *Luther's Works*, 35.397.

[160]Dibelius, *James*, p. 2.

[161]As with Hebrews, since James is an oral document, meant to be proclaimed, not primarily pored over as a text, the audience hearing such an oral performance would be oblivious to all but the most compact and obvious chiasms, not ones that went on for pages.

suasiveness, these studies have shown the thematic logic and coherence of James's composition.[162] With the exception of W. H. Wuellner[163] and a few others, there has been no attempt to analyze James from a rhetorical standpoint. Fortunately we now have the detailed work of Duane Watson on James 2—3 to partially remedy this problem. What emerges from his convincing work is the degree to which James is relying on rhetorical conventions to help him organize and present his themes.[164]

James 2:1—5:6 provides the supporting arguments for the theses already alluded to or enunciated in James 1. Since James can presuppose a Jewish Christian audience whose world of discourse and thought already includes many of the themes, ideas and imperatives he will use, what was needed was not apologetical arguments that start from ground zero with formal proofs and presume no commonality with the audience or polemics that assume an adversarial situation, but rather elaboration of common themes, ideas, stories, wisdom sayings, analogies, Scriptures and the like.

Watson shows how both sections of James 2 follow the same pattern to elaborate their propositions into complete arguments.[165] Parenesis and diatribe are incorporated into this pattern as major components of the amplification of the argument. I see no need to quibble with Watson's analysis of James 2 (see introduction above) and rely on it in what follows, but a few points deserve comment. First, however, this pattern of elaboration was not conjured out of thin air by James. Rather he follows the rhetorical literature of the period (*Rhetorica ad Herennium* 4.43-44.58; 2.18.28-29.46; 3.9.16; *Rhetoric to Alexander* 1.1422a25-27; Hermogenes, "Elaboration of Arguments" and *Progymnasmata* [discussion of the elaboration exercise for the chreia]).[166] This well-known rhetorical pattern was used before, during and after the time of James.

Second, throughout this material James uses deliberative rhetoric to persuade his readers to change their behavior or, better, to dissuade them from showing partiality, from omitting acts of charity and from ignoring the dangers

---

[162]See, e.g., Francis, "Form and Function"; Fry, "Testing of Faith"; Vouga, *Jacques*, pp. 18-23; Burge, "And Threw Them Thus on Paper"; and Forbes, "Structure of the Epistle of James."

[163]Wuellner, "Jakobusbrief im Licht der Rhetorik."

[164]Watson's "James 2" needs to be consulted in detail. Johnson, *James*, pp. 218-19, while recognizing the deliberative nature of the rhetoric here, prefers to see in Jas 2 one continuous argument about faith and deeds. While it is right to see Jas 2:14-26 as a further development of some ideas already enunciated, in terms of rhetorical structure it stands apart from Jas 2:1-13 and should be treated as a separate rhetorical subunit.

[165]Watson, "Reassessment of the Rhetoric." I am grateful to the author for letting me read and make use of a working draft of his paper before it was published.

[166]For more details, see Watson, "Reassessment of the Rhetoric"; and idem, "James 2," p. 96.

of becoming official speakers, namely, teachers. It is not surprising that argumentation (by example and precept, by personification and appeal to authoritative traditions, by rhetorical question and imperative) is the primary modus operandi. Nor are references to what is advantageous, expedient, honorable, profitable and necessary at all surprising, as all of this is characteristic of deliberative rhetoric. While some features of diatribe are found in James 2, these features are worked into James's rhetoric and do not constitute the major structuring principle of the material. James 2:14-26 especially shows diatribe elements, but they are made to fit within the rhetorical elaboration in play in that unit. Diatribe was, after all, a very flexible literary form, involving dialogue with an imaginary interlocutor. Use of an imaginary interlocutor had been common in Greek literature since the time of Plato. The term *diatribe* had even been used as a title for Stoic works by Zenon and Cleanthes in the third century B.C. and by the time of James had become so widely used as a literary device that it was adopted and adapted for many different purposes. James uses it within the confines of his rhetorical elaboration of themes to reinforce the persuasive power of the discourse.[167]

Third and perhaps most important, while the examples that James draws on are not purely hypothetical, we must beware of thinking that James has in mind specific situations in specific congregations, for two good reasons: (1) this is an encyclical, and (2) the parallel between example and reality can be partial or complete according to the rules of deliberative rhetoric (Quintilian *Institutio oratoria* 5.11.5-7). They were often not historical examples at all, but things the rhetor thought might be happening or were in danger of coming to pass, and so such examples were chosen to forestall such problems (Aristotle *Rhetoric* 20.1393a2-1393b4; *Rhetoric to Alexander* 8.1429a28).

In deliberative rhetoric it was not uncommon to take an extreme (and largely fictional) example of a tendency that might only just be beginning to rear its head, in order to stop the tendency developing in the wrong direction. Thus "we have to question continuously whether or not the objections of the interlocutor and the examples actually reflect the situation of the church or are components in the argumentative scheme which itself is addressing a related situation."[168]

If we accept that the use of the diatribe here is pedagogical and hortatory in character rather than polemical, we should not imagine that James is envisioning real opponents already arguing such views against him, much less that he is arguing with Paul here! What we can say for sure is that James is

---

[167]See the discussion in Horsley, *New Documents Illustrating Early Christianity*, 4.43.
[168]Watson, "James 2," p. 121.

concerned that partiality, dead orthodoxy and too many attempts at authoritative teaching without first listening to the word may and probably do exist in some of the Jewish Christian congregations he is addressing, and he aims to nip the problems in the bud with these sorts of patterns of persuasion and dissuasion.

²:¹*My brothers, do not keep the faith of our glorious Lord Jesus Christ in partiality.* ²*For if a man with a gold ring and luxurious clothes enters the meeting, but also a poor man in filthy rags (comes in),* ³*but you look at the luxurious clothes he is wearing and you say (to the former), "Be seated here in a good place," and to the poor man you say, "You stand here or sit at my feet,"*[169] ⁴*do you not make a distinction among yourselves and are judges (using) false standards of judgment?*

⁵*Listen, my beloved brothers, has not God chosen the poor in the eyes of this world to be rich in faith and inheritors of the kingdom that he promised those who love him?* ⁶*But you slight/dishonor the poor. Is it not the rich who oppress you and with their own hand drag you into court?* ⁷*Are they blaspheming the good name, the name called over/given to you?* ⁸*If, however/indeed, you observe the supreme/sovereign law according to Scripture, "love your neighbor as yourself," you do well.*

⁹*But if you show partiality you commit sin, being convicted by the law as a transgressor.* ¹⁰*For whoever keeps the whole law, but stumbles at one point, is answerable for (the breaking) of all of it.* ¹¹*For he who said, "Do not commit adultery," also said, "Do not murder.' But if you do not commit adultery, but murder, you have become a transgressor of the law.* ¹²*So speak and so act as those who will be judged by the law of freedom.* ¹³*For judgment without mercy will be shown to those not having mercy. Mercy overrides/triumphs over judgment!*

¹⁴*Of what use is it, my brothers, if someone says they have faith, but cannot have works? Is that (sort of) faith able to save him?* ¹⁵*If a brother or sister exists with little/ no clothes and lacking food for the day,* ¹⁶*but one of you says, "Go in peace/goodbye, warm and food yourself" and does not give them the bodily necessities, of what use is it?* ¹⁷*So even faith, if it has not works, is totally useless/dead by itself.* ¹⁸*But if someone says, "You have faith and I have works." Show me your faith without works, and I will show you faith by my works.* ¹⁹*You believe God is one?*[170] *You do well/good for you. Even the demons believe (that) and shudder.* ²⁰*But you wish to know (for cer-*

---

[169]Some excellent manuscripts ($\mathfrak{P}^{74}$, ℵ, C², K and most minuscules) add the word *here* to make the contrast with *stand there* clearer. See Metzger, *Textual Commentary*, p. 680.

[170]Several textual variants involve either the definite article before the word *theos* or the placement of the noun *theos*. $\mathfrak{P}^{74}$, ℵ, A and numerous others favor the traditional Jewish way of rendering the formula: "one is God' *(heis estin ho theos)*. Probably those texts that either moved "God" to the middle of the phrase and/or deleted the article were following the style of Christian expressions like 1 Cor 8:6; Eph 4:6; 1 Tim 2:5. The reading of the Textus Receptus, which places the word *theos* with the definite article first to give it the emphatic place in the phrase, is obviously later and secondary. See Metzger, *Textual Commentary*, p. 681.

tain), O empty-headed person, that faith without works is useless?[171] [21]*Abraham, our father, was he not vindicated by works, offering Isaac his son upon the altar?*[22]*You see that faith cooperates with his works, and by his works faith was perfected,*[23]*and the Scripture was fulfilled, saying, "But Abraham believed and it was reckoned to him as righteousness, and he was called God's friend."*[24]*You see then that a person's vindication is from works and not from faith alone.*[25]*Similarly, even Rahab the whore, was she not justified by works, entertaining the messengers and sending them out another way?*[26]*For as the body without (the) Spirit is dead, so also faith without works is dead.*

The first of two major subsections of James 2 deals with the matter of showing partiality especially vis-à-vis the rich and the poor. In the background is the idea that God is no respecter of persons, with the implication that neither should his people be. Our author is picking up earlier discussions in sapiential literature against favoritism (Sirach 7.6-7) that stress God's impartiality (Sirach 35.10-18). James addresses his audience as "my brothers" once more, so we may be sure he considered them Christians. However, they are Christians under construction and requiring instruction from James's viewpoint.

It is a cardinal error to impose modern images of church visitors when we read of the rich man in James 2. With Christianity not yet a public or licit religion in the Roman Empire, it was very unlikely that someone would be allowed to wander in off the street into a Christian service. While the meetings would not necessarily be highly secretive, one gets the impression that they were by invitation only. A household owner might well invite a number of friends to attend, some of whom were likely not Christians. But the household setting left this up to the host or at least required consultation with the host if one was bringing in strangers. Thus the scene envisioned here is not of a rich person who is a total stranger simply wandering into the service. Whether Christian or not, he would be known by one or more persons at this service and would likely have been invited to it.

Using a typical structure, James's direct address ("my brothers") in **James 2:1** is followed by an imperative, illustrations and explanations.[172] He begins with his proposition for this rhetorical subunit: the issue is showing favoritism or partiality, and what he intends to prove is that partiality and faith in the glorious Lord Jesus are incompatible.[173] That some Christians would exhibit both to-

---

[171]The Textus Receptus has the word *nekra* probably because of Jas 2:17 or Jas 2:26. But this destroys the nice wordplay in the Greek between *argē* and *ergē*. This reading is adequately supported by B, C* and various others. See Metzger, *Textual Commentary*, p. 681.

[172]Mayor, *James*, p. 79.

[173]Watson, "James 2," p. 102.

gether is unacceptable and reprehensible, for it amounts to a violation of the love commandment. *Doxa* must be seen as qualifying the whole list of Jesus' names. The awkward phrasing of Jesus' name literally reads "of the Lord, our Jesus Christ, of the glory." But it is unlikely to be a later Christian insertion precisely because of its awkwardness.[174] This person is thinking in Aramaic but composing (or having someone compose) in Greek.[175] Christians have faith in an exalted Lord who will one day return and judge. Peter Davids says: "Thus those who hold 'the faith of our glorious Lord' with partiality are not debasing just any belief, but rather a faith-commitment in the one exalted Lord Jesus whose glory will be fully revealed in eschatological judgment. As the tone implies, this is no matter for casualness or trifling; final judgment is at stake."[176] The word *doxa* probably has eschatological overtones.[177]

In addition, the key phrase in this crucial thesis statement literally reads "keep/hold the faith of the Lord." Though this is regularly rendered "faith in the Lord," this is not exactly what James says, and if that was what he meant he could have used the preposition *en*. This in turn may well suggest that Jesus is seen as the exemplar here of impartiality and that believers are to keep the "faith of the Lord" (i.e., his trustworthy and faithful ways) by modeling themselves on his behavior. In a stratified world of showing or giving face to one person or another who was thought to be of higher status or more honorable, both James and Jesus deconstructed this practice of "sucking up" to the well heeled.

The phrase *en prosōpolēmpsiais* (literally "to receive face"), which William Brosend translates "with your acts of favoritism," is significantly found at Leviticus 19:15: "You shall not render an unjust judgment; you shall not receive/give face to the poor or defer to the great: with justice you shall judge your neighbor."[178] This suggests that one must be impartial to all and not show any favoritism to the poor or the rich. The phrase suggests making judgments on the basis of "face," that is, the outward appearance of someone, just as we

---

[174] Dibelius, *James*, p. 127. As Moo, *James*, p. 100, points out, there is no textual basis whatsoever for an insertion here.

[175] If James is having someone compose this document, then some of the rhetorical skill may not reflect his own training but that of his scribe, whether in the synagogue or in a more general school of rhetoric in Jerusalem.

[176] Davids, *James*, p. 107.

[177] Moo, *James*, p. 101.

[178] Brosend, *James and Jude*, pp. 57-58, has a helpful discussion. Since Lev 19:18 on love of neighbor is nearby, one could argue that James is doing an exposition of this whole portion of Leviticus, at least at the outset of his discourse here. See Moo, *James*, p. 102; and Johnson, "Use of Leviticus 19."

might talk about the "face value" of something.[179]

But is James suggesting, contra Leviticus, that one should show partiality to or a "preferential option for" the poor? No; rather, he is saying that one should *not* show favoritism to the rich, which is then unfair to the poor, nor should one slight the poor and so dishonor them. All persons should be treated fairly regardless of their socioeconomic status. Since there is imbalance in a fallen world full of self-centered acquisitive persons, one can argue that God is concerned about balancing the scales, about justice for all, and in a fallen world this may appear to be partiality for the poor. Divine and human advocacy for the poor is necessary just to overcome the inequities experienced by the poor. This is what James has in mind, and it is in accord with what Leviticus says about impartiality.

James 2:2 is more difficult and moves into a hypothetical or possible example of showing partiality. The hypothetical nature of the example is seen in the conditional clause (*ean* plus the subjunctive), which indicates a "more probable future condition." A definite possibility, to be avoided, is in mind, but not something already plaguing the audience. Duane Watson says that James 2:2-4 provides the ratio, the reason or causal basis for the exhortation that will establish its truth.[180] Here we have a proof from example, with the punch line coming in James 2:4 to prove the point—partiality and faith in or faithfulness to the example of Christ are inconsistent because it makes a person a partial judge of other persons, indeed of other Christians.

What sort of gathering then is implied here—the Jewish synagogue, the Christian church or some sort of Christian law court? Against the first option, even though the word *synagōgē* is used, James implies that his Christian audience has some control over what is happening when visitors enter this meeting, and he says "your assembly," which surely implies a Christian one. *Synagōgē* is found elsewhere in early Christian literature of the church (Heb 10:25; *Didache* 16.2; Ignatius *To Polycarp* 4.2).[181] Yet James 5:14 shows that James is perfectly capable of using the term *ekklēsia* of the Christian gathering.

Against the third option, not only does James 2:6 use a different word for law court (*kritērion*), but we have evidence of visitors (1 Cor 14:23) and well-to-do people becoming members of the Christian community, including the Jewish Christian community in Jerusalem (Acts 4:32—5:11). First Corinthians 6:1-8 is not an entirely apt parallel since Paul says they are going to pagan

---

[179]Moo, *James*, p. 102.
[180]Watson, "James 2," p. 102.
[181]Mayor, *James*, p. 82.

law courts, but argues for them to settle it among themselves in the community. This implies that there were no church law courts when Paul was writing in the 50s. That James says *your synagōgē* rules out pagan courts here. It is a mistake to read later Jewish traditions back into our text (e.g., Babylonian Talmud, tractate *Shevu'ot* 31a: "How do we know that, if two come to court, one clothed in rags and the other in fine raiment worth a hundred manehs, they should say to him, 'Either dress like him, or dress him like you'"). Finally, *synagōgē* is not used elsewhere in the New Testament to refer to a law court.

James then is likely speaking of a Christian worship assembly. If it was like Jewish worship in a small building or home, some might have to stand and others sit. Later sources give evidence that visitors were allowed in and ushered to a spot, a duty that deacons later had.[182] Jewish custom gave honored places in the synagogue to special people and benefactors (Mt 23:6; Mk 12:39; Lk 11:43; 20:46), and it would not be surprising if Jewish Christians carried this custom over. William Brosend says that both poor and wealthy examples in James are likely viewed as visitors since both are directed where to sit.[183] I am in full agreement with Brosend that we are dealing with a hypothetical, but possible, situation and not one involving a law court. Nothing is said in the telling of this tale about why the rich or poor man came into the assembly, and the partiality issue is raised not in regard to their behavior but rather that of the one seating them, which implies a judgment on the Christian usher's part. *Ean gar* makes it entirely unlikely that James is alluding to a notorious event that has already happened in the community. Finally, recognizing that we are dealing with deliberative rhetoric here simply punctuates the likelihood that this is a hypothetical story constructed by James, a parable, if you will, to teach a lesson.[184]

James finds this behavior unacceptable. The contrast between the rich and poor man may be played up a bit, but wearing gold rings and fine clothes was widely practiced among well-to-do Jews and Gentiles in first-century culture, and the description of the poor man as both in bad clothes and being dirty may suggest that he is a beggar.[185] The gold ring may possibly refer to a person of

---

[182]Ropes, *James*, pp. 188-89.
[183]Brosend, *James and Jude*, p. 58.
[184]Contrast Brosend, *James and Jude*, pp. 61-62, with Walls, *Community of the Wise*, pp. 102-3; Maynard-Reid, *Poverty and Wealth*, pp. 48-67; and the ultimate source of this mistaken line of thinking: Ward, "Partiality in the Assembly."
[185]This is not necessarily the case. Having spent a fair bit of time in mosques and churches in the Middle East, I know that the majority of the people are poorly clad and smell, but this does not mean they are beggars. It has as much to do with the climate as anything else.

equestrian rank and so a potential benefactor to the congregation, the rank signaled by the wearing of this gold ring. **James 2:3** makes quite clear that the
believer seating these visitors is judging them purely by appearances—which
often leads to partiality. "The rich person is invited to sit rather than to stand, to
proximity rather than to distance, to comfort or prestige rather than to discom-
fort and dishonor."[187] The verb *epiblepo* can have the sense of "look upon with
favor" as is clearly the case in Luke 1:48 and Luke 9:38, the other two uses of
the term in the New Testament (cf. Ps 13:3; 25:16; 33:13; 69:16). In addition, the
verb is in the plural, which suggests that this favoritism involved more than one
Christian usher or leader.[188] The phrase *sit at my feet* is sometimes a technical
phrase for "be my disciple" (Lk 10:39), but that is not likely meant here.

Various commentators take *en heautois* in **James 2:4** to imply that the visitors
are Christians. This is not a necessary inference because the focus is on the one
showing partiality and what is going on from the angle of the one seating these
persons. Obviously issues among the brothers and sisters could involve visitors
and various non-Christians. The problem is that the Christians welcoming the
visitors are showing partiality, which is unacceptable regardless of what status
these visitors have so far as believing or honor is concerned. When the visitors
are with the believers they are considered part of the worshiping group. The
partiality is happening in Christian worship, which is the last place it should
happen, since worship is supposed to be where God is perfectly glorified and
people are treated as God treats them. Judging by appearances (Jas 2:3a) is judging by a false and all too human standard of judgment (Jas 2:4). It is probably
right to hear echoes here of the teaching of Jesus in parables like those found
in Luke 14:7-14 or Luke 16:19-31, which demonstrate the dynamics of the rich-
poor contrast, how they are treated in this life and different places of honor at
a gathering.

James 2:5 begins another thought, with a statement about the poor followed
by two about the rich. The major arguments in James contain little *Stitchwort*
connection and more flow of thought and logical structure. James 2:5-7 contains
brief arguments corroborating the reason already given and thus serves as a confirmatio.[189] This confirmation asks three rhetorical questions, all of which expect

---

This is the suggestion of E. A. Judge in Horsley, *New Documents Illustrating Early Christian-ity*, 1.111, which also translates *Supplementum epigraphicum graecum* 1683: "The synagogue of the Jews honored Tation, daughter of Straton, . . . with a gold crown and a seat of honor." This was because she paid for the provision of certain parts of the synagogue. It is possible that a similar sort of scene is described here by James.
[187]Johnson, *James*, pp. 222-23.
[188]Moo, *James*, p. 104.
[189]Watson, "James 2," p. 104.

the answer yes from the audience. The function of such questions is to force the audience to answer the questions for themselves, but in a way that coheres with the conclusion James wants them to draw. Quintilian says that the point is not so much to elicit information as to firm up or emphasize the right conclusion, the main point in the mind of the audience (*Institutio oratoria* 9.2.7). Partiality to the rich is bad for the poor and makes no sense because the rich are oppressors of Christians. The three questions serve as a way of amplifying the point that partiality is inconsistent with Christian faith, with the most disturbing question left for last as a climax (Quintilian *Institutio oratoria* 8.4.9-14). "Not only does the audience oppress those God has chosen as heirs, but it upholds those who blaspheme his name!"[190]

The idea of God showing special concern for the poor is well known from the Old Testament (Deut 16:3; 26:7). Jesus too picks up the idea of the election of the poor (Lk 6:20), and we have similar thoughts in Paul (in 1 Cor 1:27-28 God chose the lowly things of this earth).[191] James 2:5 speaks of the poor from the world's viewpoint, but rich in what really matters (faith) and what comes through faith (the status of being inheritors of the kingdom). It does not follow from this that James romanticizes poverty or really means economically poor, not merely "poor in spirit." He will suggest that spiritually these folks are far from poor—indeed they are rich (*plousious* refers to being rich in the realm of faith).[192] It is not implied that they had more faith or more abundant faith in comparison to others—no comparison is made. It is quite clear that the kingdom mentioned here is viewed as future—it is what God has promised to those who love him, a promise not yet fulfilled.

It is thus wrong to suggest that poverty here has simply become a religious

---

[190]Ibid., p. 105.

[191]Moo, *James*, pp. 107-8, with others assumes that "election" here means chosen for eternal salvation. This may not, however, be the case. God chooses people for a variety of purposes, and even if one argues that God especially favored the poor with opportunities to be converted, James does not think that only the poor are saved or even that the poor who have been converted are in no danger of future judgment, particularly if they do not "do the works of the royal law." The matter of God's election is complex, and one should not simply assume that election language refers to eternal salvation, when it can refer to being chosen for particular historical purposes, such as Cyrus was in Old Testament times. For example, the poor can be chosen by God to shame the rich into being impartial and merciful without these particular poor persons automatically being saved in this process. They need to be rich in faith and persist in belief and behavior that comports with the gospel to receive final salvation. First Cor 1:27-28 is a close parallel, but again it is not about election unto eternal salvation.

[192]The term *wealthy* has a similar metaphorical use for "wealthy in regard to children" in *Corpus inscriptionum graecarum* 4, cited in Horsley, *New Documents Illustrating Early Christianity*, 4.30-31.

concept.[193] The social dimensions of the poverty must not be overlooked, even if James does share some ideas about "the pious poor." The poverty spoken of is both physical and spiritual, as is the wealth, but no one person in the contrasting example embodies both kinds of wealth or poverty. The poor in question are believers; they may be rich in faith, but this does not give permission for other Christians to treat their physical poverty as if it did not matter. Elsa Tamez helpfully puts it this way:

> I do not mean that the poor are not pious, but only that if we make the poor and the pious synonymous then real economic oppression and God's concern for this very class of people are lost. The rich become the pious poor and the poor [become] rich in piety, and the economic order and the unjust power stay as they are. Thus the rich always come out ahead; they are rich in real life and piously poor before God and thus heirs of God's reign.[194]

Equally true are the remarks of Alfred Plummer:

> He does not say or imply that the poor man is promised salvation on account of his poverty, or that his poverty is in any way meritorious. . . . He is spared the peril of trusting in riches, which is so terrible a snare to the wealthy. He has greater opportunities of the virtues which make man Christlike, and fewer occasions of falling into those sins which separate him most fatally from Christ. *But opportunities are not virtues, and poverty is not salvation.*[195]

While this quotation romanticizes the poor to some degree (do the poor really have less temptations and more opportunities for virtue?—it seems more likely that they are mostly too busy trying to survive by whatever means necessary), Plummer nevertheless makes a good point. James is not saying that poverty is the way of salvation or even salvation itself. He is rather warning about the dangers of the other extreme. The poor as described here are heirs of the kingdom, which is the only use of *basileia* in James, who seems to use the term in its eschatological sense of something that one inherits or enters in the future, not the present.

In **James 2:6** *ētimasate* means "to dishonor or show disrespect" to those whom God has especially showered favor upon. Paul shares a similar view about shaming those who have nothing, and the social context that presupposes disunity and favoritism in the assembly is also similar (1 Cor 11:22).[196] This is a very unwise course of action, and James 2:12 indicates that the perpetrators are

---

[193]Dibelius, *James*, pp. 126-27.
[194]Tamez, *Scandalous Message of James*, pp. 44-45.
[195]Plummer, *General Epistles*, p. 125 (emphasis added).
[196]Johnson, *James*, p. 229.

accountable for such actions on judgment day. The standard of judgment is the "law of liberty," that is, the new law of Christ that combines something old and something new. Playing up to the rich does not make sense on another score either, since generally speaking it is the rich who were oppressing believers and having them hauled off to court. James may have some particular incident in mind, but the remarks seem to be generalizations. Thus, we have irony here—the church is oppressing that one poor fellow who came in, while the rich oppress "you," that is, the church as a collective whole. What sense then does this behavior make, considering God's word and standards, says James? In **James 2:7**, the rich are labeled blasphemers—blaspheming Jesus' good name, perhaps because they profess to be pious but their deeds are impious. And if we did not get the point from James 2:1 that James believes that Jesus embodies the glorious presence and nature of God, this verse makes it clear, as Alfred Plummer says: "If it [Christ's name] can be blasphemed it is a Divine Name."[197] James 2:7b may refer to the name of Jesus being called over believers as they are baptized, but James's interests lie in their current behavior.[198]

James 2:8 presents a problem: should we translate "royal/sovereign law" or "supreme law" and thus see James labeling the love command as *the* essence of the law? Victor P. Furnish is likely right when he indicates the drift of James's thought:

> Even if you keep all the (other) commandments of the law, but by showing partiality to the rich, neglect the one commandment to love your neighbor (the poor brother), then you are in fact guilty under the whole law. Thus, if we take into consideration this continuation of the argument, it would appear that the commandment of Lev. 19:18 is regarded as one among many which are to be kept by the faithful Christian.[199]

If this is right, we should probably translate this phrase "royal law." What may be decisive here is that *nomos* is used for a collective body of law, not just an individual commandment, and so selections from it are found in James 2:8, 11.[200] Thus, even if we translate "supreme law" (cf. "perfect law" in Jas 1:25) it refers to the law as a whole, the law of Christ. Joseph Mayor notes how James

---

[197] Plummer, *General Epistles*, p. 116. This is another case where it is a mistake to judge a person's Christology on the basis of silence or a different subject matter. Simply because this sermon does not say a lot about Christ does not mean that James had a low or no Christology. I would hate to have one of my ethically focused sermons analyzed for the trace elements of Christology in it! See Witherington, *Incandescence*.
[198] Moo, *James*, p. 109.
[199] Furnish, *Love Command*, p. 179.
[200] Against Mayor, *James*, p. 90.

2:8b-11 is reminiscent of the decree that James issued in Acts 15, which favors the latter's authenticity.[201] One should also compare Galatians 5:14, where Paul says that this particular commandment sums up the law.

Careful scrutiny of what Paul and James say about the law as it applies to Christians shows that they have similar views on this subject.[202] Rhetorically speaking this verse deals with the beginning of the exornatio in the form of an adjudication—a judgment made by God that is nonnegotiable (*Rhetoric to Alexander* 1.1422a25). In this case the judgment involves the citation of Leviticus 19:18, and this will be followed in James 2:9-11 by two enthymemes. James 2:8 makes evident that perhaps the most serious problem with showing favoritism is that it is a blatant violation of the great love commandment to love neighbor as self. But why is the law here called "royal" (cf. *basilikos* in Jn 4:46, 49; Acts 12:20, 21)? Douglas Moo suggests a connection with the use of the kingdom language in James 2:5 *(basileia)*.[203] This might mean the law pertaining to the eschatological kingdom of God. But Jesus identified the dual love commandments as the first and greatest commandment (Mt 22:37-40). This suggests that the word *royal* might mean the commandment of King Jesus, the one he particularly emphasized became the norm for the way that all other commandments should be interpreted and applied.[204]

James 2:9 makes the point in as drastic a fashion as possible: playing favorites is not only unacceptable to James, it is a sin against God, one that will lead to conviction under the law as a transgressor. To show partiality is to fail to love the poor neighbor, and to fail to do this is to violate the whole law. One does not have to violate all the commandments to be a lawbreaker, but the conceptual idea in **James 2:10** is this: the law is one because God, who is one, gave it to believers. It is his word. James here is offering a short form of a syllogism, an enthymeme that requires supplying the missing premise, in this case the minor premise. In full form it would look something like the following:

> major premise: whoever keeps the whole law but fails in one point has broken the law

---

[201]Ibid., p. 91.
[202]Here we must make a distinction between what Paul says about the outmoded and obsolescent Mosaic covenant and what he says about the law of Christ, which is not simply a reiteration of the Mosaic law, but includes some commandments from it. If James includes within the royal and perfect law his own and Jesus' teachings, then he too is not simply talking about a reiteration or reinterpretation of the Mosaic law. On Paul's view, see Witherington, *Grace in Galatia*, pp. 341-56.
[203]Moo, *James*, pp. 111-12.
[204]Johnson, *James*, p. 230.

minor premise: showing partiality is a failure to keep a part of the law

conclusion (Jas 2:9): if you show partiality you are a transgressor of the whole law[205]

James 2:11 provides a second enthymeme, which makes the same point a slightly different way, as follows:

major premise: God who said "do not commit adultery" also said "do not kill"

minor premise: if you break any individual command you break the law since they are all from one source

conclusion: if you do not commit adultery but do kill, you have still become a transgressor of the whole law[206]

The phrase *he who said* in James 2:11 indicates that the author saw the law as God's very words—God spoke it. There is no higher endorsement for the law. Paul (Gal 5:3) and Jesus (Mt 5:18-19; 23:23) also express the unity of the law. Being under the law obligates one to obey the whole law (Rom 2:13). The point of stressing the wholeness of the law is, according to Peter Davids, as follows: "James uses the idea skillfully to point to the underlying attitude and cut away any grounds the person may have for a flippant disposition toward the commands against partiality ('After all, I'm keeping the decalogue very well')."[207] To draw an analogy: it is like putting a single drop of food coloring in a glass of water—all the water is affected. One sin taints the whole character and one sin means *the* law, not just *a* law, has been broken. The remedy is not stated here, but it is obviously not to ignore the law.

James mentions adultery first and then murder from the Ten Commandments, which may suggest that he is following the Septuagint (ℵ, B), which has them in this order (Ex 20:13-14; Deut 5:17-18). Paul also chooses these same two prohibitions to highlight as representative examples in Romans 13:9 (cf. Lk 18:20). Was there perhaps a common Christian ethical code grounded in the Old Testament, the teaching of Jesus and some Christian instructions from the apostles that both knew and were adhering to? If this code existed, it did not just involve the Mosaic law as reinterpreted by Jesus, not least because Jesus added his own imperatives, some of which were at variance with what the Mosaic covenant demanded.[208]

---

[205]Similarly Watson, "James 2," p. 106.
[206]On the use of enthymemes in moral arguments see Witherington, *Letters and Homilies*, 1.68-71.
[207]Davids, *James*, p. 117.

James 2:12-13 draws to a conclusion the first elaboration of an argument, using a device called a *conplexio* or *conclusio*, which ties up the loose ends in the form of an *epicheireme*, which in turn is a completely stated argument where the audience need not supply the minor premise:

> major premise: for judgment without mercy is shown to one who has not mercy
>
> minor premise: yet mercy triumphs over judgment
>
> conclusion: therefore speak and act as though you will be judged under the law of liberty[209]

"The role of vv. 12-13 as a conclusion is underscored by the use of the emphatic construction *houtōs . . . houtōs* in v. 12 which brings the *topoi* of saying and doing together."[210] The ultimate sanction for behavior was that it was what God had explicitly stated was the divine will, and this comports with the advice about such an argument in the rhetorical handbooks, which says that one must "call to mind what great concern the matter under discussion has been to the immortal gods . . . and again how sanction has been provided in these matters by laws" (*Rhetorica ad Herennium* 2.30.48).

James 2:13 may draw on the teaching of Jesus in the Sermon on the Mount again, in particular Matthew 5:7: "Blessed are the merciful for they will be shown mercy," and Matthew 6:12: "Forgive us our trespasses as we forgive." James, however, turns the beatitude into its converse to make his point. The theme of mercy is common in wisdom literature (Sirach 27.30—28.7).

The believer's status before God at the last judgment is affected by the life lived after conversion. Paul too knows the idea of salvation by faith, coupled with a judgment of the believer's deeds (2 Cor 5:10). There also comes a point, apparently, where the disjunction of profession and practice is such that one's salvation is in jeopardy: the good tree will produce good fruit and, if it does not, it may be judged to be not a good tree after all, no matter what label is put on it. Judgment without mercy means severe, unrestrained judgment—the full wrath of God. James 2:13b may quote a proverb meant to give hope: "Mercy triumphs over/overrides judgment." God looks on human hearts and lives, which would allow us to render the maxim this way: "Mercy boasts over judgment," or "Mercy has the bragging rights over judgment" in God's way of view-

[208]Johnson, *James*, p. 231, finds a bevy of allusions to Lev 19 in James. Besides Lev 19:15 and Lev 19:18, there is Lev 19:16 in Jas 4:11; Lev 19:13 in Jas 5:4; Lev 19:18b in Jas 5:9; Lev 19:12 in Jas 5:12; Lev 19:17b in Jas 5:20.
[209]Watson, "James 2," p. 107.
[210]Ibid.

ing things.[211] He expects complete loyalty and obedience. Obviously, there are times when humans are unable to do what they intend to do, whether something internal or external prevents it in a fallen world and dealing with fallen people. Those who strive to do God's will and still fall short have both repentance and the mercy of God to fall back on, or otherwise no one will stand on the judgment day (1 Cor 3:13-14). But more than this, James would have us know that if believers are merciful instead of judgmental they are mirroring the character of God and fulfilling an essential requirement of the royal law.

A CLOSER LOOK
The Voice of Jesus in the Rhetoric of James

In his detailed rhetorical study of James 2:5 and its various contexts and intertextual echoes, Wesley Hiram Wachob draws our attention to the various sociorhetorical questions that this material raises. One of his important social conclusions, which is absolutely right, is that "the cultural rhetoric in James is subcultural to Jewish culture. And there is no evidence that the religious community of James is in competition with another religious group, as, for example, there is [in] Matthew's rhetoric. Rather, it appears that the people whom James addresses are surrounded by people within a Greco-Roman value structure, and they are trying to find their way in an environment that is dominated by those values."[212] This in turn means that we should not expect to learn a great deal about James's own community in Jerusalem, where the author was certainly surrounded by Jewish culture and values. Some of James's concerns reflect the difficulties he has seen in his own community in regard to partiality, wealth and poverty, and various teachers and teachings, but by and large this document tells us more about James's audience in the Diaspora than about the community out of which James writes.

Wachob's second important conclusion, with which I concur, is that James's rhetoric will certainly be seen as countercultural by the dominant culture that surrounds the various Jewish Christian communities being addressed. This means that one of the social functions of the rhetoric of this homily is to help the audience establish proper boundaries with the world. To put it a different way, this homily is not mainly about rebutting Paul or establishing different boundaries than the Pauline communities had. It does not reflect internecine warfare between dueling Christian communities. I do think, however, that James may have attempted to clear up mistaken notions about Paul's gospel

---

[211]On the translation see Dowd, "Faith That Works," p. 196.
[212]Wachob, *Voice of Jesus*, p. 195.

that could have existed in some Jewish Christian communities. If, for example, some of these communities had been visited by "Judaizers" (to use an old term), as Galatians, Colossians and Philippians suggest, then this clarification may have been needed.

Wachob goes on to suggest that James's rhetoric is subcultural to the Jewish culture, by which he means that it is largely consonant with earlier Jewish values and rhetoric. In my view this is a yes-and-no proposition. To the extent that James emphasizes some of the distinctive counterorder wisdom of Jesus (and his own teaching) he is not simply reflecting the larger Jewish subculture. For example, James's take on the issues of wealth certainly reflects the views of Jesus more than that in conventional Jewish sapiential sources like Proverbs or Sirach.[213] And Wachob rightly notes that James also takes on conventional honor-shame notions by suggesting that all persons should be treated the same—impartially and justly (Jas 2:4, 9; 4:6-12). This deconstructs the usual pecking order in which the courts were heavily biased in favor of the well-to-do who had time, money and opportunity to bring suits against their social inferiors, while those inferiors had no such resources and were likely to be shamed if they tried to take on a higher status person in a matter of justice or equity.

In addition, Wachob suggests that the reaudiencing of the love commandment in James 2:5 functions to stress not only how loving neighbor is a fulfilling of the law but how loving neighbor is a means of loving God, indeed the main means of doing so. Practically speaking, this then implies a special responsibility for the few more well-to-do members of the audience, such that they must undertake deeds of mercy to alleviate the poverty, hunger, indigence of the majority of the audience who are poor economically even if they are rich in faith.[214] Rich outsiders who may visit the community are not to receive special treatment, thus intentionally deconstructing the stratification of the larger society within this specific community. James seems to be suggesting that the more well-to-do could obtain honor by being patrons of the congregation's less well off. This comports with texts like Acts 4:32—5:11, which suggests that sharing in such fashion had been successfully attempted in James's own community (Peter's complaint is not that Ananias and Sapphira kept some of their liquid assets but that they lied about it).[215] It also suggests that obligatory patronage is a very different social model than the collection and central distribution of all goods. The homily of James, like Acts, seems to suggest a social system other than what could be called communism, though one could call it communalism, for the ethic particularly binds the wealthy to

---

[213]See the discussion in Maynard-Reid, *Poverty and Wealth in James*, pp. 48-67, on Jas 2:1-13.
[214]Wachob, *Voice of Jesus*, pp. 196-97.
[215]See the discussion in Witherington, *Acts of the Apostles*, pp. 204-20.

certain behaviors in relationship to the poor Jewish believers. These are the neighbors that James is particularly concerned about. There may also be an implicit critique in James of the culture of acquisition, but if so it is a subdominant theme in the discourse, not the dominant note sounded.[216] James 4:11-12 makes clear, however, that no Christian should judge another one on the basis of economic status or resources.

Wachob states succinctly one of his stronger and more compelling conclusions—that Martin Dibelius was wrong about the existence of the literary genre parenesis: "We found that there is no such thing: paraenesis is not a literary genre but [rather] the positive mode of deliberative rhetoric. So, we decided to cast our lot not with Dibelius but with the ancients: that is, with Aristotle, Quintilian, and Cicero, and the teachers of elementary rhetorics, Theon and Hermogenes."[217] This is decidedly a step in the right direction and, if it is followed, will lead to many fruitful studies of James.

It is unfortunate that Wachob persists in his unlikely view that James is pseudonymous, when his own research pushes him in another direction. In a series of rhetorical questions near the end of his study, he concludes:

> Is it not rather interesting that the very first and primary argumentative unit in the whole discourse, James 2.1-13, uses the first and primary saying (Q[Matt] 5.3) in a Jewish *epitome* of the teachings of Jesus (Q[Matt] 5—7) as its first and primary proof that acts of partiality are incompatible with Jesus' faith? Is it only coincidence that the first and primary argument in a letter that wishes to be heard [as being] from James the Just is about "justice"? Is it only coincidence that Jesus' faith and the whole law are shown to be, in quite good rhetorical fashion, interrelated and inseparable; that holding Jesus' faith and fulfilling the whole law mean fulfilling the love-commandment? Is it only coincidence that James the Just is made to speak the same wisdom that Jesus spoke?[218]

Frankly these are far too many coincidences for there not to be a more direct connection between the author of James and the speaker of the Sermon on the Mount. Clearly enough, James had correctly absorbed Jesus' insistence on the central love commandment being the hermeneutic that one should apply to the law in general. It is right to conclude that James comes out of the same sort of sapiential Jewish ethos as does the Sermon of the Mount. The reason is much more straightforward than the suggestion that someone cleverly made James a stellar example of rhetorical "speech in character." It is that the homily of James is written by James the brother of Jesus who does not

[216]Wachob, *Voice of Jesus*, p. 197.
[217]Ibid., p. 199. Wachob provides the necessary detailed history of research on James and parenesis on pp. 25-58.
[218]Ibid., pp. 200-201.

have to establish his authority with his Jewish Christian audience; he merely has to exercise it, as he does in this discourse. In doing so he is aptly and appropriately following in the footsteps of Jesus the sage and his teachings.

James 2:14-26 may be called the storm center of the letter or certainly the portion that has drawn the most attention and most fire, and not just from Luther. It has been more troublesome in Protestant circles than in Catholic because of the vital aspect of justification by faith alone in Protestant thinking. But long before Luther and Calvin there was much discussion about the relationship of James to the theology of "justification by faith" found in Galatians and Romans.

A CLOSER LOOK

Dueling Apostles? The Discussion Ancient and Modern

The church fathers before the Reformation saw at least an apparent tension between Paul and James, but resolved it in a way that did not dismiss or ignore the insights of James and without relegating James to the noncanonical dustbin. For example, Chrysostom says, "Even if someone believes rightly in the Father and the Son, as well as the Holy Spirit, if he does not lead the right kind of life, his faith will not benefit him at all as far as his salvation is concerned. . . . We must not think that merely uttering the words is enough to save us. For our life and behavior must be pure as well" (*Catena* 15). Bede clarified that Paul was talking about initial justification, which is by grace and through faith: "What Paul meant was that no one obtains the gift of justification on the basis of merit derived from works performed beforehand, because the gift of justification comes only from faith. . . . James here [Jas 2:14-26] expounds how Paul's words ought to be understood" (*On James* 93.22).

Augustine got a little tired of critics who simply thought James and Paul were contradicting one another: "Holy Scripture should be interpreted in a way that is in complete agreement with those who understood it and not in a way that seems to be inconsistent to those who are least familiar with it! Paul said that a man is justified through faith without the works of the law, but not without those works of which James speaks" (*On the Christian Life* 13). The distinction was made between prebaptismal faith, which was by grace and through faith alone, and postbaptismal faith, which is combined with works.[29]

---

[29] This same opinion was expressed in almost the same way in the modern discussion by Martin, *James*, p. 81: "Paul denies the need for 'pre-conversion works' and James emphasizes the 'absolute necessity of post-conversion works'" (quoting and following Moo). The assessment is correct, but commentators were saying this well before the Reformation. In other words, this insight is not unique to the Protestant tradition.

Andreas adds: "For the same Abraham is at different times an example of both kinds of faith" (*Catena* 16; Oecumenius makes the same point and distinction in his *Commentary on James* [*Patrologia graeca* 119.481])—ignoring that Abraham was never baptized! Finally, Chrysostom, seeking to balance the ledger, stresses that "faith without works is dead, and works without faith are dead as well. For if we have sound doctrine but fail in living, the doctrine is of no use to us. Likewise if we take pains with life but are careless about doctrine, that will not be any good to us either. It is therefore necessary to shore up the spiritual edifice in both directions" (*Homilies on Genesis* 2.14).

The gist of this discussion, especially as perceived by Chrysostom and Augustine, was on the right track. James is not talking about how one comes to Christ or receives initial justification or salvation at all. Even when he uses "righteousness" language, he is referring to final vindication or justification at the eschaton. He is addressing those who are already Christians about how they should live. At the same time, Paul is equally clear that postconversion behavior can affect whether one is vindicated in the end, at the final judgment. Both James and Paul are quite sure that moral apostasy is possible and a real danger for the Christian. They are also in agreement that obedience and working out one's salvation after initial salvation is not optional for the Christian. The modern discussion, not surprisingly, surpasses the preoccupation of the ancient one in trying to sort out the differences between James and Paul on these matters. For example, Peter Davids writes:

> These data mean that neither the works which James cites nor the justification which results are related to Paul. Rather, the works are deeds of mercy (which therefore fit with the opening verses of this section) and the ἐδικαιώθη refers not to a forensic act in which a sinner is declared acquitted (as in Paul), but to a declaration by God that a person is righteous, *ṣaddîq* (which is the implication of the "Now I know" formula of Gn. 22:12; cf. Is. 5:23 . . .). Adamson is correct in seeing that a moral rather than a primarily judicial emphasis is intended (although of course there is some judicial tone in any declaration of standing by "the judge of all the earth" . . .).[220]

Or consider the remarks of James Hardy Ropes:

> In the discussions of the Apostle Paul the contrast is the same in terms, but its real meaning is different and peculiar. Paul's lofty repudiation of "works" has nothing but the name in common with the attitude of those who shelter their deficiencies of conduct under the excuse of having faith. Paul's contrast was a novel one, *viz.* between the works of an old and abandoned system and the faith of a newly adopted one. His teaching was really intended to convey a doctrine of forgiveness.

---

[220]Davids, *James*, p. 127.

Our author, on the other hand, . . . is led to draw the more usual contrast between the faith and works which are *both* deemed necessary under the *same* system. Hence, while faith is the same thing with both—an objective fact of the Christian life, the works of which they speak are different—in one case the conduct required by the Jewish law, in the other that demanded by Christian ethics. That the two in part coincided does not make them the same. One was an old and abandoned failure, impotent to secure the salvation which it was believed to promise, the other was the system of conduct springing from and accompanying a new life.[221]

I agree with Alfred Plummer that we also must not see James 2:14-26 as a direct response to that found in Galatians (or Romans for that matter):

> Had St. James been intending to give the true meaning of either or both of these statements by St. Paul [i.e., Rom 3:28; Gal 2:15-16], in order to correct or obviate misunderstanding, he would not have worded his exposition in such a way that it would be possible for a hasty reader to suppose that he was contradicting the Apostle of the Gentiles instead of merely explaining him. He takes no pains to show that while St. Paul speaks of *works of the law*, i.e., ceremonial observances, he himself is speaking of good works generally, which St. Paul no less than himself regarded as a necessary accompaniment and outcome of living faith. . . .
>
> It is most improbable that, if he had been alluding to the teaching of St. Paul, St. James would have selected the Unity of the Godhead as the article of faith held by the barren Christian. He would have taken faith in Christ as his example.[222]

This last point, about James's stress on the oneness of God, is right and shows among other things that James is surely speaking to Jews in this homily, in this case to Jews who follow Jesus, who took monotheism for granted, who professed Jesus—the great earmark distinguishing them from all others in the Diaspora.

It is equally right to point out, as Plummer does,[223] that both Abraham and Rahab were favorite topics of discussion when it came to the matter of faith and works in early Judaism (e.g., Wisdom of Solomon 10.5; Sirach 44.20; 1 Maccabees 2.52. cf. Heb 11:17; Mt 1:5). James's discussion of Abraham is closer to the earlier Jewish one than to the later Pauline one, for the good reason that not only does James focus on the binding of Isaac story, but he

---

[221]Ropes, *James*, pp. 204-5.

[222]Plummer, *General Epistles*, pp. 142, 152 (emphasis original). See Plummer's telling exposition of Luther's own comments on pp. 147-48, where he shows that if Luther himself were consistent he would have seen that Paul equally with James believes that faith without works is dead.

[223]Ibid., pp. 156-58.

also stresses that Abraham is an example of faith that manifests itself in action, in obedience to God. James is pursuing the same line of discourse found in Matthew 12:37: a person is vindicated (i.e., justified or accounted righteous) as a result of what they have done or said.[224] This is a different matter than the discussion of the basis of initial justification or salvation. And once and for all I must stress that when Paul speaks of works of the Mosaic law, in fulfillment of the Mosaic covenant, he is talking about something very different than James's discussion of works that come forth from and express Christian faith: "James and Paul simply do not mean the same thing when they write of 'works,' and interpreters who write as if they did distort the thought of both."[225]

All of this does not, however, rule out the possibility that James is dealing with some issues raised by Jewish Christians from what they have heard—and perhaps misunderstood—about the teaching of Paul in its early stages in the early 50s when Judaizers from Jerusalem went behind Paul in Antioch, Galatia and perhaps elsewhere, trying to add observance of the Mosaic covenant to the Pauline gospel even for Gentile Christians.[226]

Both James and Paul were concerned about what later came to be called "dead orthodoxy"—faith without its living expression in good works. While it may be true that "'faith without works' spares individuals the embarrassment of radical disruptions in their lives or relationships,"[227] the truth is that both Paul and James were all about radical disruptions in the lifestyles that people had previously been accustomed to. James is busy deconstructing various prevailing social customs and habits and offering up in sacrifice various sacred cows, but Paul did the same thing in his own way.

Sharyn Dowd suggests that "James is using Paul's vocabulary, but not his dictionary,"[228] which is clever but not quite right. They are both drawing on previous Jewish usages of this vocabulary, and even consideration of only the Abraham stories in Genesis 12—22 exposes a range of meaning of the term *faith*, the importance of obedient deeds and the range of meaning of the *ṣaddiq* language. Yet there is some force in the point Dowd makes:

> Paul never uses *pistis/pisteuō* to mean a mental agreement with a theological construct that has no implications for behavior. In fact, he never uses a *hoti* clause after the noun. . . . But even more important is the fact that Paul would have been incapable of constructing a sentence analogous with James

---

[224]See the helpful discussion in Moo, *James*, pp. 133-36.
[225]Brosend, *James and Jude*, p. 81.
[226]Rightly Moo, *James*, p. 121; and Martin, *James*, pp. 95-96.
[227]Perkins, *Peter, James and Jude*, p. 113.
[228]Dowd, "Faith That Works," p. 202.

2:19 in which correct faith is attributed to demons. In Paul's writings the subject of *pisteuein/echein pistin* is always one for whom "Jesus is Lord" (Rom 10:9), a confession possible only under the influence of the Holy Spirit (1 Cor 12:3). The fact that James can speak of the "faith" of demons shows he knows a use of the term that is foreign to Paul's thinking.[229]

The problem with this is twofold: (1) the person speaking may be the interlocutor not James—that is, James is perhaps being accused of believing that God is one, just as the demons do—and (2) James also thinks that purely mental or even verbal faith is dead faith or useless faith, not real living Christian faith. Dowd's argument provides further support for the contention that James does not know Paul's letters and the common way he expresses such matters.[230]

I agree with William Brosend that we may assume that Paul and James knew something of each other's gospel both from personal conversation and hearsay, but not from reading each others letters. And with him I think it is right to conclude that "it is probably true that Paul and James did not think or worry about each other nearly as much as interpreters of James think and worry about Paul but about as much as interpreters of Paul worry and think about James. . . . The history of interpreting James using Paul as the measuring rod always inhibits appreciation of James."[231]

It is a sad irony that, when Luther discusses faith in his preface to his Romans commentary, he unwittingly provides an apt summary for much of what James is trying to say about faith and works in James 2:

> O it is a living, busy active mighty thing, this faith. It is impossible for it not to be doing good things incessantly. It does not ask whether good works are to be done, but before the question is asked, it has already done this, and is constantly doing them. Whoever does not do such works, however, is an unbeliever. He gropes and looks around for faith and good works, but knows neither what faith is nor what good works are. Yet he talks and talks, with many words about faith and good works.[232]

---

[229]Ibid.

[230]Here I bring up a further point: when Paul met with James and Peter in Jerusalem after his conversion, what language did they speak? It could have been Greek, but it surely is more likely to have been Aramaic, the primary language of discourse for Jews in Jerusalem and a language that Paul will have learned since he moved to Jerusalem many years before as a youth (Acts 22:3; 26:4-5). This in turn would mean that James had never heard Paul express his views on faith in Greek.

[231]Brosend, *James and Jude*, pp. 79-80.

[232]I follow the translation of Moo, *James*, p. 144.

Ralph Martin is correct that both sections of James 2 are connected: (1) both
James 2:1-13 and James 2:14-26 use the diatribe style; (2) both choose polemical
examples to punctuate the points being made; (3) the underlying problem of
mistreatment of poor believers surfaces in both sections; (4) in both sections
faith and works are seen as inevitably and intimately connected and (5) in both
sections impartiality is seen as a hallmark of real faith.[233]

James 2:14-26 uses the diatribe form, including debate with a straw man *(tis)*
that James sets up and refutes, but in the form of a deliberative Jewish homily
with careful parallelism in two stanzas, each with two parts: James 2:14-17, 18-
20 and James 2:21-24, 25-26. This section also has an inclusio formula: (1) opening catchphrase in James 2:14a: *ti to ophelos* ("what use is it?"); (2) statement repeated as example; (3) catchphrase repeated in James 2:16c. James uses little
parables or examples to get his point across, not unlike his brother and Lord.
The elements that indicate a diatribe or homiletical style are as follows:

1. *ō anthrōpe kene* ("o, empty[-headed] person") in James 2:20 (cf. 1 Cor
   15:36; Mt 23:17)

2. possible wordplay in James 2:20: *ergon arge* ("useless works")

3. an imaginary opponent: *tis* ("someone") in James 2:18, which meshes
   with the use of *ean* in James 2:14 (a future more probable condition:
   James is worried that someone *might* say such a thing)

4. *all' erei tis* in James 2:18: a forestalled objection that is enunciated then
   refuted

5. *deixō* and *deixon* ("show me, demonstrate to me") in James 2:18, asking
   for proof; and the address to an individual *(sou/sy* and *tis),* who is seen
   as in the Christian community, not a pagan or Jew

6. *tis . . . ex hymōn* ("one from among you") in James 2:16, indicating an internal Christian squabble—not a diatribe against godless pagans and their
   lack of charity

All of these diatribal elements are incorporated into a deliberative elaboration
of key themes, as Duane Watson shows:[234]

- proposition (Jas 2:14)

- reason as the causal basis of the proposition that undergirds it (Jas 2:15-16)

- confirmation, which restates the thesis (Jas 2:17)

- an imaginary opponent speaking only once (using personification)—"you

---

[233]Martin, *James*, p. 79.
[234]See the convincing detailed discussion of Watson, "James 2," pp. 108-16.

have faith, but I have works"—and James anticipating what an opponent would say and forestalling it by answering in advance (Jas 2:18-19)

- exornatio (Jas 2:20-25), where additional proof is offered that faith without works is dead by drawing on two famous examples from the Old Testament—Abraham and Rahab

- proposition restated (Jas 2:24, 26), showing just how crucial it is to this argument

- conclusion stated by way of an analogy (Jas 2:26)

William Brosend makes the same point about the structure this way: "The structure of 2:14-26 is similar to that of 2:1-13. James states his theme in the first verse (v. 14), offers a vivid and compelling example concluding with an emphatic restatement of his theme (vv. 15-17), and develops his argument with logic (presented through an interlocutory dialogue, vv. 18-19) and proofs from Scripture, restating his theme at the beginning and end of the proofs (vv. 20-26)."[235]

Several aspects of this discourse reinforce the point that our author is a Jewish Christian talking to Jewish Christians:

1. reference to Abraham as "*our* father" (Jas 2:21)

2. midrashic treatment of the Old Testament stories of Abraham and Rahab

3. emphasis on works and the sort of righteousness that results from doing good deeds, especially deeds of charity

4. reference to Abraham as the friend of God—a popular Jewish designation of Abraham (2 Chron 20:7; Is 41:8; Philo *On Sobriety* 56, which renders Gen 18:17 with the phrase "Abraham my friend")[236]

5. anthropology: the human being is body and breath, or body and Spirit—not soul (*psychē*) and body and not a trichotomy

All of this likely implies that James thinks that at least some of his Jewish Christian audience knew well these Old Testament stories and their context, if not also the way they were interpreted in Jewish circles. Joseph Mayor has a fascinating rabbinic quotation that embraces the very sort of so-called faith James is inveighing against: "As soon as a man has mastered the thirteen heads of the faith, firmly believing therein . . . though he may have sinned in every possible way . . . still he inherits eternal life."[237]

It would be hard to overestimate how strongly the issue of faith and works

---

[235]Brosend, *James and Jude*, p. 71.
[236]Mayor, *James*, p. 96.
[237]Ibid., p. 96.

and salvation is stressed here. This passage contains 14 of the 19 uses of the terms *pistis* and *pisteuō* in James, 12 of the 15 uses of the term *ergon*, and 1 of the 5 uses of the verb *sōzō*. In other words, 27 words in this brief passage (216 total Greek words) are these four terms or some 12.5% of the passage.[238]

James 2:14 begins by asking the Christian audience whether a faith without works is useful or useless. To ask about the profit, use or benefit of something is a common question in deliberative rhetoric. The nature of the conditional sentence here shows that James thinks this question might well arise. The second remark is also a rhetorical question—"is your faith able to save you?"—to which the implied answer is no, if "faith" means the type of faith that James is attacking. James here broadens the previous discussion to the more expansive topic of faith and works. Recognizing the use of the anaphoric definite article before the second use of the word *faith* is crucial to understanding this verse: the question should be translated, "Can that [sort of] faith save him?"[239]

James is following the rhetorical advice that suggests that one should stick with, and reiterate, one's strongest point the longest (*Rhetorica ad Herennium* 4.45.58), precisely because all of the rest of the argument rests on this crucial point about the necessary connection between living faith and good works.[240] The discussion here has moved on from talking about visitors to the assembly of faith to "brothers and sisters" (one of the many occasions of the use of the term *adelphoi* in the New Testament in a nonphysical sense).[241] Christian treatment of fellow Christians is at issue here.

A little parable in **James 2:15-16** begins with *ean,* indicating a condition that is future but probable. As was the case in the first half of this chapter, the ratio takes the form of an example. It differs from the earlier example in that here the rhetorical question expects a negative answer. The deliberative topic of "what profits a person" is being raised here (*Rhetoric to Alexander* 7.1428b10).

There were plenty of destitute Christians in the first century needing aid from the community. A scantily clad and hungry brother or sister—*gymnoi* need not imply naked, but rather underclothed or poorly clothed, rather than unclothed[242]—is so indigent they do not even have enough food for today.[243] The

---

[238]Brosend, *James and Jude*, pp. 72-73.

[239]Rightly Moo, *James*, p. 123.

[240]Watson, "James 2," p. 108.

[241]Brosend, *James and Jude*, p. 73.

[242]Papyrus Wisconsin 73 (a letter) contains a lament in lines 19-20 by a woman that "she has nothing to wear" (*gymnē estin);* see Horsley, *New Documents Illustrating Early Christianity*, 2.79; and Moo, *James*, p. 124.

[243]On *tēs ephēmerou trophēs* as daily sustenance, see Mt 6:11; Lk 11:3. The phrase is probably an echo of the Lord's prayer; see Martin, *James*, p. 84.

response in James 2:16 is meant to seem shaky and shallow. It sounds pleasant enough, even concerned in a superficial way: "Hope you are well fed and clothed." But this is an anti-Christian and unloving response that is unacceptable. Beneath the surface is the idea that deeds of mercy are not an option but an obligation for those who profess and have real faith.

"Go in peace" is what the person says to the indigent person. It could mean, as Joseph Mayor suggests, "have no anxiety,"[244] but it was a stereotyped parting formula and often meant no more than "goodbye," although here it more likely has the fuller sense of "blessings" (Gen 15:15; Ex 4:18; Judg 18:6; 1 Sam 20:42; Mk 5:34; Lk 7:50).[245] The phrase *thermainesthe kai chortazesthe* should be translated as middles ("warm yourself and feed yourself"), not passives ("be warmed and be filled"). If so, then the person in question is being very callous, juxtaposing warm words with cold deeds.[246] Like so many others since, this person is saying, "Pull yourself up by your bootstraps," or "Do it yourself." Quite clearly, what was being asked for was not some luxury item, but the necessities of the body, clothing and daily bread, but the person in question did not even give these. Luke Timothy Johnson says: "It is not the form of the statement [depart in peace] that is reprehensible, but its functioning as a religious cover for the failure to act."[247]

To this behavior James rejoins: "If you say you have faith and fail to help—of what use is it? What good does it do you or anyone else?" Possibly, we should translate *kai* in **James 2:17** as "even" and read "so [or in the same way] *even* faith, if it does not have works, is dead by itself." James has thus made two key points: (1) living faith necessarily entails good deeds, and (2) faith and works are so integrally related that faith by itself is useless or dead, unless coupled with works. Joseph Mayor writes that the sort of "faith" James is critiquing is "not merely outwardly inoperative but inwardly dead."[248] Peter Davids summarizes well:

> For James, then, there is no such thing as a true and living faith which does not produce works, for the only true faith is a "faith working through love" (Gal. 5:6; . . .). Works are not an "added extra" any more than breath is an "added extra" to a living body. The so-called faith which fails to produce works (the works to be produced are charity, not the "works of the law" such as circumcision against which Paul inveighs) is simply not "saving faith."[249]

---

[244]Mayor, *James*, p. 97.
[245]Ropes, *James*, p. 207.
[246]Mayor, *James*, p. 98.
[247]Johnson, *James*, p. 239.
[248]Mayor, *James*, p. 99.
[249]Davids, *James*, p. 122.

James 2:17 should also be seen as an example of amplification, since it reiterates the initial proposition about faith and works (Cicero *Partitiones oratoriae* 15.54).[250]

Thus far we have no problems understanding James's meaning, but the rest of the chapter has many difficulties. First of all, who is *tis* in **James 2:18**—someone who agrees with James or James's imaginary interlocutor? Who is this "someone who says"? Where do the words of "someone" cease and James's start again? One clue to answering the last question may be the adversative (but) in James 2:20, and certainly we must take seriously the adversative that begins James 2:18: "But someone will say." James Hardy Ropes points out, however, that the writer does not return to the more natural plural, instead of the singular "you," until James 2:24.[251]

Rhetorical analysis and recognition of the use of the diatribe form helps solve this problem. It is not sufficient to suggest that the discussion is meant to be seen as some sort of truly abstract nonadversarial statement ("one chooses faith, another action"; or even worse, "there is faith on the one hand; there is works on the other").[252] Throughout James 2:18-20 the opponent starts the debate, and "you" is James or his ally. James has his imaginary opponent accuse him of being a "faith without works" person, whereas the speaker takes the supposedly higher ground of touting his works.[253]

The proper rhetorical protocol is that whoever speaks first in such a debate should first state their own proofs and only then rebut the arguments of the opponent (Aristotle *Rhetoric* 3.17.1418b14). This is what happens here, and rebuttal comes only after the opponent has stated his view in James 2:18a. But the opponent takes a reactionary and defensive posture here—"I have works, while you have faith"—thereby apparently placing himself in the positive category as a person of Jewish orthopraxy, while James has only orthodoxy—mere faith—on his side. James's position is that the two things cannot and must not be divorced, while the opponent suggests that they can be. Thus, he accuses James of mere faith and hypocrisy. The examples James cites prove the point that real faith works—the two go together.[254]

The evidence of the diatribal form, along with "O man" in James 2:20, suggests strongly that when James says "but someone will say" in James 2:18a he is turning to the argument of his opponent. The problem is not the grammatical

---

[250]See the discussion in Watson, "James 2," p. 109.
[251]Ropes, *James*, p. 216.
[252]But see McKnight, "James 2:18a."
[253]See the discussion in Brosend, *James and Jude*, p. 74.
[254]Moo, *James*, p. 120.

structure but the train of thought. Perhaps James envisions two believers hypo-thetically debating each other, and then he interjects a rebuttal at James 2:18b. The problem is very clear. This "person" is still dichotomizing faith and works, as if they could be separate gifts of different Christians. The argument would be, "Works are alright, but that's not my gift" (or vice versa). To this dichotomizing James responds, "Show me a person with faith but without works, and I'll show you my faith by my works."

To believers who pride themselves on right belief—and in James 2:18-19 faith clearly means something other than what it usually means for James, not trust in or active dependence on God, but rather mere belief that God exists—James says: "So you say you believe God is one. Good for you; however, so do de-mons, and they are shuddering in their belief—fearing the wrath of God to come. A lot of good that faith did them." The sarcasm in **James 2:19** is hard to miss.[255] The demons are the ultimate example of faith divorced from praxis, of right confession divorced from right living. "A wonderful choice of words: *phris-sen* is the involuntary reaction of the body in shaking, as in a fever, and is fre-quently used for reactions of fear (Plato *Phaedrus* 251A; Philo *The Worse Attacks the Better* 140)."[256]

The phrase *God is one* has its background in the basic Jewish confession, the Shema: "Hear, O Israel, the LORD our God is one" (Deut 6:4). The point of the Shema is the unity of God's being, his uniqueness and his being the one true God:

> But there were also theological implications and the context of this verse indicates its source as a direct revelation from God (v. 1). The word expresses not only the *uniqueness* but also the *unity* of God. As one God (or the "Unique"), when he spoke there was no other to contradict; when he promised, there was no other to revoke that promise; when he warned, there was no other to provide refuge from that warning. He was not merely first among the gods, as Baal in the Canaanite pan-theon, Amon-Re in Egypt or Marduk in Babylon; he was the one and only God and as such he was omnipotent. It was this all-powerful Unique God who imposed on Israel the charge to love him, thereby revealing another aspect of his character.[257]

James is stressing essential matters and probably implying that "you believe in the unity of God, you ought also to believe and practice the unity of faith and works." The reference to the demons existing and believing is characteristic of the Gospels (Mk 1:24; 5:7). The demons were perfectly orthodox and perfectly lost.

In **James 2:20** James becomes even more sarcastic: "So you want evidence,

---

[255]Brosend, *James and Jude*, p. 75.

[256]Johnson, *James*, p. 241.

[257]Craigie, *Deuteronomy*, p. 169 (emphasis original).

O empty-headed one [cf. Rom 2:1; 9:20], that faith without works is useless/ without profit *[argos]*—let's turn to the Scriptures." Again the deliberative theme is stressed. *Argos* could be translated "workless"—faith without works is workless or faith without works will not work![258] The two examples from Scripture that James cites were standard examples of true faith among the Jews. He chooses the most stellar example (Abraham) and in some ways the most scandalous example (Rahab the harlot). James probably knows how much Abraham was idolized in the Jewish tradition: *Jubilees* 23.10 ("Abraham was perfect in all his deeds with the Lord, and well pleasing in righteousness all the days of his life"); Sirach 44.19 ("no one has been found like him in glory") and 1 Maccabees 2.51-52 (Abraham was reckoned righteous not on the basis of his faith but as result of passing the test and remaining faithful and obedient when he was asked to sacrifice his son). Clearly James does not push his use of the exemplary Abraham to these extremes, but he stands in the tradition of seeing Abraham as the *exemplum par excellence*. It is of more than passing interest that the use made of Genesis 22 here is similar to its use in Hebrews 11:17-19, which says that when tested Abraham by faith brought forth Isaac and offered his son. This may suggest that some standard interpretations of the key Old Testament figures circulated in Jewish Christian circles.[259]

James refers to two events in Genesis: the promise to Abraham (Gen 15) and the story about the offering of Isaac (Gen 22). As was frequently done in midrashic exegesis, James combines two texts here to stress in **James 2:21** that it was on the basis of his obedient offering of Isaac (i.e., his deed of obedience) that Abraham was *edikaiōthē* ("justified or vindicated"). Robert Wall may be right that this one climactic example of obedient faith may be a shorthand reference to all ten of the tests that Abraham passed, which led to this conclusion of vindication.[260] In any event the verb *synergei* in **James 2:22** should be seen as an iterative imperfect that implies that faith was working along with works at the same time side by side; it implies that these two things coexisted in Abraham's life over a period of time.[261] Peter Davids ably shows the Jewish train of James's thought here.[262]

But there is a larger issue here because even in Genesis 15 Abraham's believing entailed ensuing obedience—he did what the Lord told him in going to Canaan, in bringing his son for sacrifice and in so many other ways. His was not a faith separated from works of obedience. James's point is that, *even* in the case

[258]Dowd, "Faith That Works," p. 199.
[259]Johnson, *James*, p. 243.
[260]Wall, *Community of the Wise*, p. 136.
[261]Dowd, "Faith That Works," p. 201.
[262]Davids, *James*, p. 127.

of believing Abraham, his works were essential as an expression of faith. In what sense was he vindicated? His trust in God was vindicated, for he dared to offer his son, trusting God to provide or take care of the situation. If this is what James takes *edikaiōthē* to mean, it is very different from Paul's notions. Abraham trusts in God that he already had been or was vindicated when he offered Isaac—and there was divine intervention. In a real sense, faith was made perfect by his trusting obedience.

James can thus go on to say: "You see that faith cooperates with his works, and by works his faith was perfected. The two go together hand in hand, works perfecting faith, which is by implication imperfect without it." The concept of righteousness at least in **James 2:23** seems to be Jewish—not "counted/considered righteous" but "declared to *be* righteous," that is, righteous by means of deeds. Abraham's belief was belief in action.[263]

The point of James's argument, then, has nothing to do with a forensic declaration of justification; the argument is simply that Abraham did have faith, which here unlike other places in James means monotheistic belief. Abraham was famous for this in Jewish tradition—but he also had deeds flowing from that faith. Thus, James is not dealing with works of the law as a means to become saved or as an entrance requirement (he never speaks of "works of the law"); rather, he is dealing with the conduct of those who already believe. He is talking about the perfection of faith in its working out through good works. Paul put it this way: "Work out your salvation with fear and trembling" (Phil 2:12) or "faith working itself out through love" (Gal 5:6), while James speaks of faith coming to mature expression—to its perfect end or goal—in works. These two ideas are similar, as the church fathers noted.[264]

This still leaves the difficulty of **James 2:24**—a statement that Paul would never have made. If, however, we take—and we should—the vindication in James 2:24 as referring to that final verdict of God on one's deeds and life work, then even Paul can be said to have agreed. Even he speaks of a final justification/vindication that is dependent on what believers do in the interim (Gal 5:5-6).[265] This final vindication or acquittal is in view here. Paul would agree that one cannot be righteous on that last day without having done some good deeds between the new birth and that last day in the spiritual pilgrimage. Thus James

---

[263]Ibid., pp. 127-28.
[264]Johnson, *James*, p. 243.
[265]It is a mistake to think that "final justification" means declared innocent or acquittal here. Rather it has to do with God's recognition that someone has behaved in a way that can be called right or righteous, and at the last judgment those acts are vindicated to be righteous. Against, Moo, *James*, pp. 138-41, who is following Jeremias, "Paul and James."

2:24b only apparently contradicts Paul, not least because not even Paul thought faith alone kept one in the kingdom, though it did get one into it.

A secondary and more daring example in **James 2:25** is intended to illustrate the same ideas (*homoiōs* ["similarly"] makes this clear): Rahab, who entertained the Hebrew spies and chucked them out (*ekbalousa* is literally "cast out") the back window when the enemy approached. Jewish traditions suggested that Rahab converted, married Joshua, become a good Jewish mother of priests and even became the ancestor of Jeremiah and Ezekiel.[266] She was mainly celebrated for her hospitality to the Jewish spies, but even in later Christian texts she is an example of faith (*1 Clement* 12.7). James's point is that if everyone from Abraham to Rahab received final vindication because of faith *and* works, so shall the followers of Jesus. Rahab's faith is not mentioned, but it was widely held to by Jews.[267] The rhetorical strategy here involves forestalling the objection: "But I am not a towering figure of faith like Abraham"—to which the proper reply is, "At least you could follow the example set by Rahab!"[268] The last example then removes all excuse for doing nothing and shames the audience into action. Since both Abraham and Rahab are examples of those who exercised faith and hospitality (which contrasts nicely with the first example in this section, where no hospitality is shown to the poor), this may in part explain why these two historical examples are cited here.[269]

After these illustrations it is well to ask once more if James necessarily shows knowledge of Paul's letters here. I think not, and Peter Davids shows how even the common words are not found in the same context and do not have the same content.[270] The point, rhetorically speaking, of using these historical examples from the sacred text is that they provide inartificial proofs from a source that neither the author nor audience can challenge. In other words, James is arguing from strength here. It is also rhetorically effective to make the opponent look dimwitted by the initial exclamation, followed by the implication—do you not even know some of the most famous stories in the Bible about faith and works going together?

James is not dealing with the basis on which Gentiles enter the community of faith, but rather the nature of the faith, of true Christianity. Does it necessarily entail deeds of mercy? It is possible that James got wind of some sort of perverted or garbled Pauline summary that had been heard by his audience, but

---

[266]The later rabbinic discussion is fascinating. See Johnson, *James*, pp. 244-45.

[267]See the discussion in Hanson, "Rahab the Harlot."

[268]Plummer, *General Epistles*, p. 163.

[269]Johnson, *James*, p. 249; and Moo, *James*, p. 143. *First Clement* 12.7 may support this suggestion.

[270]Davids, *James*, p. 131.

this is not a necessary assumption. Jews were fascinated with Genesis 22 and the story of Abraham, and much of the common terminology is to be explained by both James and Paul drawing on the same Old Testament text, possibly both relying on the Septuagint version. Thus I reject J. D. G. Dunn's conclusion:

> The most striking passage in James is 2.14-26, his polemic against the doctrine of faith without works. This seems to be directed against the Pauline expression of the gospel, or more precisely, against those who have seized on Paul's slogan, "justification by *faith* (*alone*)." It was Paul who first expressed the gospel in this way (particularly Rom. 3.28); so the view which James attacks certainly goes back to Paul. That Paul's argument *is* in view is also indicated by the fact that James in effect refutes the Pauline exegesis of Gen. 15.6: "Abraham believed God and it was reckoned to him as righteousness." This, affirms James, was "fulfilled" in Abraham's *work*, not in his faith—that is, not in "faith alone" (contrast Rom. 4.3-22, particularly vv. 3-8; Gal. 3.2-7).[271]

Finally, in **James 2:26** James sees human beings as dichotomous or unified— an animated body or possibly spirit and body (although *pneuma* may mean "breath" or, most likely, "life principle," it does not mean "Holy Spirit" here). The point of analogy, or "figure of thought" as it would be called in rhetoric (*Rhetorica ad Herennium* 4.45.59), is this: just as a body is not alive without its animating or life-giving principle, so no faith is alive or useful that does not necessarily entail works. Such a similitude provides a vivid punctuation to the final reiteration of the main proposition of this whole part of the argument. We may have expected James to compare spirit and faith and body and works, but the reverse is done here in an attempt to say something striking, and the meaning is still clear. If it is a mere shell of a confession, faith is like a stinking corpse. Works are the animating and animated side of faith—what gives it life. Peter Davids puts it this way: "Neither soul nor body is desirable alone; a body without its life-force is simply a rotting corpse. Likewise, says James, faith is useful when joined to works, but alone it is just dead, totally useless. Dead orthodoxy has absolutely no power to save and may in fact even hinder the person from coming to living faith, a faith enlivened by works of charity (i.e., acts of love and goodness)."[272]

Elaboration of Themes, Part Two: Teachers Taming the Tongue (Jas 3:1-18)

Teaching without setting an example is not only worthless but also brings great

---

[271]Dunn, *Unity and Diversity*, p. 251 (emphasis original).
[272]Davids, *James*, p. 134.

punishment and judgment on the one who leads his life with such heedlessness . . . who does not want to practice what he preaches. (Chrysostom *Catena* 18)

James reminds us here that even good people are not perfect and that we all need to be led by the grace of the Holy Spirit, for there is no one who can go through life without ever sinning at all. Nevertheless, there are different kinds of sins, and James singles out one area of our lives where perfection is attainable, namely control of the tongue. We may be imperfect, but we can still learn to avoid deception, abuse, cursing, pride, boasting, envy, quarreling, lying, perjury and so on. (Bede *On James* [Patrologia latina 93.27-28])

The wisdom that is from above is pure because it thinks only pure thoughts, and it is peaceable because it does not dissociate itself from others on account of its pride. The other virtues mentioned here are the common possession of any wise person, and they will manifest themselves in a life full of mercy and other good works. (Bede *On James* [Patrologia latina 93.31])

The second major section of the elaboration portion of the discourse begins at James 3:1. The argument focuses principally on the role of teachers in the community, but the overarching theme of pure speech involves all the community members. This chapter is characterized by difficult Greek grammar, and many words that are either uncommon or unknown elsewhere in the Greek New Testament (*hapax legomena*). This phenomenon arises not from the theme of wisdom in James 3:13-18 but from the use of analogies in James 3:2-12, which are drawn from stock illustrations that were often clustered together—bridle and rudder, charioteer and helmsman.[273] Peter Davids points out that much material in this chapter has numerous parallels in Greek and Jewish literature and that James apparently adopted and adapted various proverbs, stock phrases and typical illustrations here.[274] In other words, James was wise enough to use familiar maxims and illustrations, thereby increasing the likelihood of acceptance for what he is saying and the teaching's inherent authority, as his audience will likely be familiar with such sapiential ideas.[275] Nevertheless, he made them his own and used them for his purposes, and he shaped

---

[273]Dibelius, *James*, pp. 185-90.
[274]Davids, *James*, p. 135.
[275]That many of these ideas and illustrations are stock items in Greco-Roman wisdom shows not only the scope of James's knowledge, but his effort to speak a wisdom to his Diaspora audience with which they will be familiar. While it is probably right that James is adapting earlier adoptions of Greco-Roman wisdom into Hellenistic Jewish ways of discoursing, nonetheless he is creative in the way he handles the material. It was the task of the sage to reformulate things in a way that was coherent and congenial with the author's own manner of teaching and the audience's capacity for learning. In other words, he has made the material his own, whatever its source.

them into a powerful deliberative elaboration of another key theme.

While James 3:1-12 involves some grammatical and lexical difficulties, its rhetorical structure matches that found in both halves of James 2. I follow Duane Watson's outline of James 3:1-12 (see the introduction).[276]

There is a debate whether James 3:13-18 continues the line of argumentation found in James 3:1-12 or begins another topic of discussion. Luke Timothy Johnson argues that James 3:13—4:10 is a rhetorical unit developing the topic of envy.[277] I recognize the merits of this view, but there are close connections between James 3:1-12 and James 3:13-18. For example, key terms like *pikron* (Jas 3:11, 14) and *akatastaton/akatastasia* (Jas 3:8, 16) are by no means ordinary or incidental. Furthermore, since this is a wisdom discourse offered up by a sage, it is perfectly natural to see "those who are wise" (Jas 3:13) as those who are called teachers (Jas 3:1); Franz Mussner says that the link between the two verses is unmistakable as these are two ways of speaking of the same person—the teacher.[278] Most commentators recognize that James 3:13-18 continues various themes of the first section of James 3:1-12, while beginning to develop the new theme of envy as well.[279] James 3:13-18 is a transitional section that goes with both what has come before and what comes after it. François Vouga sees James 3:13 as the conclusion of the first rhetorical unit in this chapter, with James 3:14-18 forming a reprise of James 3:1-13.[280] I agree with Duane Watson that James 3:13 goes with the following unit, but it is a hinge verse linking that unit to James 3:1-12. It also looks back to James 1:5, where the theme of wisdom that comes down from heaven was announced.

Robert Wall argues that James 3 is an elaboration of the original imperative in James 1:19 that the audience be "slow to speak."[281] There is definitely something to this suggestion, but the focus here is not on just anybody curbing the tongue, but specifically teachers or sages. James will later say that elders in the community have various leadership functions (Jas 5:14), which is unsurprising since elders were part of James's own Jerusalem Jewish Christian congregation (Acts 15) and a part of synagogue life before the Jewish Christian movement even began. The social structure of leadership in the congregations James is addressing involves elders who are teachers or perhaps elders and sages. James M. Reese suggests that in James 3 we reach the heart of the discourse, what

---

[276]Watson, "Rhetoric of James 3.1-12."
[277]Johnson, "James 3:13—4:10."
[278]Mussner, *Jakobusbrief,* pp. 168-69.
[279]Reese, "Exegete as Sage," pp. 83-84.
[280]Vouga, *Jacques,* pp. 93-104.
[281]Wall, *Community of the Wise,* p. 75.

James is really driving at—the instruction of teachers and the wisdom they should convey.[282]

I outline the second half of this chapter as follows:

rhetorical question for the "wise" and "learned" with criteria for demonstrating their wisdom (Jas 3:13)

topic of envy and ambition introduced in a rhetorical synkrisis—the antithesis of godly wisdom (Jas 3:14-15)

social consequences of antiwisdom (Jas 3:16)

nature and effects of godly wisdom (Jas 3:17)

social consequences of godly wisdom (Jas 3:18)

The structure of this subunit is determined by two rhetorical devices—a rhetorical question opens the section, and the rhetorical comparison of antiwisdom with true heavenly wisdom and the social consequences of each fills out the rest of the unit. Here again we do not have a formal proof structure but a form of a rhetorical elaboration pattern to deal with an important standing topic of discussion. The chapter as a whole deals with sages and their wisdom and the need for them to practice what they preach, living a wise and godly life, which especially includes having full control over their tongues and over the selfish desires they may harbor in their hearts.

That we should see a division after James 3:18 can be deduced from the topic of quarreling not being introduced until James 4:1, but James 4:1 is asyndetic, and no particle or conjunction suggests a connection with James 3:18. The discussion of the two kinds of wisdom is not carried forward into James 4, and furthermore the key and repeated vocabulary changes, beginning at James 4:1.[283] While the topics of jealousy and envy are introduced in James 3:13-18, these topics are not dealt with in full before James 4, and in any case it is James's manner of operation to introduce themes in one rhetorical unit before he fully develops them in the next. I thus conclude that Johnson and those who follow him are wrong about James 3:13—4:10 being a single unit. Johnson shows that these verses broach the subject of envy, but he does not show that this block of material is a *rhetorical unit*, which it is not. The rhetorical signals suggest that the unit stops with the inclusio about heavenly wisdom in James 3:18, which reiterates some of what is said at James 3:13-14. Finally, the intertextual echoes of *Testament of Gad* and *Testament of Simeon* do not come to the fore until we

---

[282]Reese, "Exegete as Sage," pp. 82-85.
[283]Moo, *James*, p. 167.

get to James 4, which is another clue that we should see James 4:1 as beginning another unit.

> [3:1] *Let not many of you become teachers, my brothers, knowing that we will receive more severe condemnation.* [2] *For many times/ways we all stumble. But if one does not stumble in what he says, that man/person is perfect, able to bridle even his whole body.* [3] *But if we put the bridle of horses in their mouths in order for us to make them obey us, even their whole bodies can be turned.* [4] *Or take ships being so big and driven by stiff breezes (yet) they are led by the smallest rudder wherever the impulse of the steerer wishes.* [5] *So also the tongue is a small member and a great boaster. Behold what a small fire sets alight what a great forest!* [6] *And the tongue, a fire, constitutes the world of wickedness in our members, staining the whole body and setting aflame the cycle of life and being set aflame by hell/Gehenna.* [7] *For all kinds of animals, birds, reptiles and sea creatures are subdued and have been subdued by humankind.* [8] *But no one is able to control the tongue of human beings, a restless evil, full of deadly poison.* [9] *By it we bless our Lord and God, and by it we curse human beings who are made in the likeness of God.* [10] *From the same mouth comes blessing and curse. My brothers, this ought not to be.* [11] *Can both sweet and bitter water gush forth from the same opening?* [12] *Is a fig tree able to produce olives or a vine of figs? Neither can saltwater produce sweet.*
>
> [13] *Is anyone wise and understanding among you? Let him show it by his way of life, his words in unpretentious wisdom.* [14] *But if you have bitter zeal and party spirit in your heart, do not boast and give the lie to the truth.* [15] *That sort of "wisdom" does not come down from above, but is earthbound, "natural," diabolical.* [16] *For where there is zeal and party spirit, there is restlessness and every evil practice.* [17] *But the wisdom that is from above is first pure, then peace-loving, considerate, obedient, full of mercy and good fruit, without being divided, without hypocrisy.* [18] *But the fruit of righteousness is sown in peace, by those who make peace.*

James 3:1 begins with a warning: "Let not many of you become teachers." *Didaskalos* was used of Jesus in the Gospels and of rabbis in early Judaism, but we should not read later Jewish customs of ordination into this Greek equivalent of rabbi. Teachers in Jewish and Christian contexts were highly esteemed and

---

[284] The proper reading here is surely *ei de* rather than *ide,* which James uses nowhere else, since it is both the more difficult reading and scribes would have tended to conform the text here to something like Jas 3:4-5. See Metzger, *Textual Commentary,* p. 682.

[285] The question here is whether *houtōs,* which is found in many witnesses (ℵ, C², K, L, P and many minuscules), is a later addition to enhance the comparison or whether the omission of this word in A, B, C* and several other important manuscripts should be preferred. In this case, the shorter reading seems more likely, and it is even possible that the scribe's eye dropped down to the next word *oute* and added *houtos* not only to enhance the comparison but to provide some rhetorical flare by assonance here. See Metzger, *Textual Commentary,* p. 682.

revered (Mt 13:52). It was thus both natural and normal for many Jews and Christians to desire to exercise this highly coveted function. "Clearly, it was an office of some social rank. . . . Thus there was quite an impulse for those fit and unfit to press into this office."[286]

It appears clear in our text that James is warning about ethically, not doctrinally, subversive teachers—those who say one thing and do or live another. The reason why many should not desire such a job was "knowing that we will receive more severe judgment." This principle is made explicit in Jesus' words (Mt 12:36; Lk 20:47; Mk 12:40). In James 3:1 then we already have the rationale or reason why not many should become teachers. The word *knowing* implies that James's audience had already been taught on this matter, perhaps from the Jesus tradition. The reference is to accountability at the last judgment.

The word *krima* should likely be translated "condemnation" not "judgment," for in the New Testament it normally refers to the outcome of judgment rather than the judgment itself (Mk 12:40; Lk 23:40; Rom 2.2, 3.8; 5:16).[287] This suggests that James has in mind the eschatological review of deeds, rather than current human criticism, and there may be an echo of Mark 12:38-40 here. James includes himself among the ranks of teachers: "*we* shall receive." And he would certainly agree with Alfred Plummer: "There is something seriously wrong when the majority in the community, or even a large number, are pressing forward to teach the rest."[288] This exhortation presupposes a social situation much like that in the synagogue, where almost anyone who was able to speak in public could come forward and do so (1 Cor 14:26, 31), but we are a long way from ordained rabbis or teachers in this imperative.

A CLOSER LOOK
James: Sapiential Scribe or Creative Sage?

Early Judaism during the time of Jesus and James had long since seen a cross-fertilization of wisdom, prophetic and apocalyptic traditions.[289] This is hardly a surprise since there was such biblical precedent. Daniel, for example, was a sage and court counselor who also had apocalyptic visions and foresaw eschatological scenarios. While there were differences between scribes and sages and prophetic figures in early Judaism,[290] any of these figures could be

---

[286]Davids, *James*, p. 136.
[287]See the discussion in Moo, *James*, p. 149.
[288]Plummer, *General Epistles*, p. 166.
[289]See the helpful study of Collins, *Jewish Wisdom in the Hellenistic Age*.
[290]Witherington, *Jesus the Sage*, pp. 122-42.

teachers, including teachers of the law. Luke 5:17-21 equates scribes and teachers of the law, a combination also seen in Gamaliel (Acts 5:34), while Matthew 23:34 provides a clear distinction between scribes, sages/wise men and prophets. This is not surprising because the First Evangelist is himself a sapiential scribe, carefully recording and editing his source material in a sapiential and eschatological manner.[291]

Our discussion of what James was can be honed and refined by thinking about how the First Evangelist, another Jewish Christian writer deeply influenced by the wisdom tradition, should be characterized. What especially prompts this discussion is that first-person verbs are quite rare in James and, apart from hypothetical questions (Jas 1:13; 2:18; 4:13, 15), occur in this homily only at James 3:1-3 and James 5:11. The latter reference stands out because it involves a beatitude—one of the most familiar forms of sapiential speech that Jesus used. But here James self-identifies as a teacher, and since he does not refer to himself as an apostle or prophet this seems quite significant. Apostles are missionaries, and James stayed put in Jerusalem. Prophets are oracles, quoting God, but James does not do this. But sages are another matter altogether, and they seem to have made up the bulk of teachers in Jesus' and James's era (Acts 13:1; Eph 4:11). William Brosend helpfully reminds us "teachers are known by the content of their teaching. This may be exactly what James intended, claiming a significant role that nonetheless turned attention away from himself to his message while accepting the responsibility that comes with presuming to instruct others."[292] But some distinctions are necessary to understand James's role and the ethos and nature of his teaching.

The term *grammateus* itself has a range of meanings, but all of them presuppose a person who is literate, who can read and write and who, educationally, is in the upper echelons of society, since only 10% of all ancients could read and write. There was considerable power in being a scribe in those sorts of social circumstances. But was a Jewish scribe simply a copier of documents? Was James a sapiential scribe like the First Evangelist, or would it be better to call him a creative sage in his own right?

James's homily was written in Greek, not in Hebrew or Aramaic, and it reflects the traditions of Jewish writers who wrote in Greek and Jewish writers who knew rhetoric. James reflects the Jewish sapiential tradition in his era, and so we need to look more closely at sapiential scribes and sages such as Qoheleth (Ecclesiastes), Ben Sira and the author of Wisdom of Solomon. Fortu-

---

[291]Witherington, *Gospel of Matthew*, introduction.
[292]Brosend, *James and Jude*, p. 95.

nately, Sirach provides clear evidence about the way Jewish scribes worked in the intertestamental period and continuing on into the New Testament era. Sirach 39.1-10 speaks of the ideal Jewish sapiential scribe:

> He who devotes himself to the study of the law of the Most High
> will seek out the wisdom of all the ancients,
> and will be concerned with prophecies,
> he will preserve the discourses of notable men
> and penetrate the subtleties of parables;
> he will seek out the hidden meanings of proverbs,
> and be at home with the obscurities of parables.
> He will serve among great men and appear before rulers. . . .
> If the great Lord is willing, he will be filled with the spirit of understanding;
> he will pour forth words of wisdom
> and give thanks to the Lord in prayer.
> He will direct his counsel and knowledge aright,
> and meditate on his secrets,
> he will reveal instruction in his teaching,
> and will glory in the law of the Lord's covenant;
> many will praise his understanding,
> and it will never be blotted out;
> his memory will not disappear,
> and his name will live through all generations;
> nations will declare his wisdom,
> and the congregation will proclaim his praise.

Many things could be remarked on in this passage but most importantly the law is talked about in a context in which law, prophecy, parable, proverbs and the like are all viewed from a sapiential viewpoint, as divine wisdom meant to give guidance to God's people. Ben Sira first clearly identifies Torah with wisdom and suggests that wisdom became incarnate, so to speak, in Torah.[293] The First Evangelist sees himself in the light of this description of a Jewish scribe and so sees his task as interpreting and presenting the life and teachings of Jesus as revelatory wisdom from God. He will argue that Jesus himself, rather than Torah, is the incarnation of God's wisdom and that therefore Jesus' own wise teaching provides the hermeneutical key to understanding law, proverb, prophecy, parable and other things. But is this the agenda and modus operandi of James? The answer must be no. He is more like the person whom the First Evangelist writes about—Jesus, who was a sage and creator of parables, aphorisms, riddles and the like.

The First Evangelist, who ought more appropriately to be called the first

---

[293]Witherington, *Jesus the Sage*, pp. 335-80.

Christian scribe, saw Jesus as an eschatological and royal sage, not just another wise man. The issue here is not the content of Jesus' teaching but its form. In form, Jesus' teaching is overwhelmingly sapiential in character, even when the content may involve eschatology. Furthermore, literature that reflected the cross-fertilization of wisdom, prophecy and apocalyptic had become enormously popular and influential and may even have helped spawn or at least spur on a whole series of wise men or sages in the era just prior to and contemporaneous with Jesus (e.g., Hanina ben Dosa, Honi the circle drawer),[294] including that unique figure—the visionary sage—a mold that both Jesus and James fit.

In his study on sages in Hellenistic-Roman Judaism, John Collins makes these telling remarks:

> Comparison of Enoch and Daniel, on the one hand, and *4 Ezra* and *2 Baruch*, on the other, shows there are significant variations in the ideal of the visionary sage in the apocalyptic literature. . . . There however are some consistent features of apocalyptic wisdom that distinguish it from traditional Hebrew wisdom. Most fundamental of these is the claim to have, and reliance upon, a supernatural revelation. Even a sage like Ezra who disavows heavenly ascents, still relies on dreams and visions. . . . The apocalyptic sage is not at a loss, as Qoheleth was, to know what God had done from beginning to end (Qoh 3:11), because he claims to have access to the recesses of wisdom in the heavens. . . . One finds, then, in the sages of the apocalypses a denial of earthly wisdom, but also a claim to a higher, superior wisdom.[295]

Several things about this quotation are interesting for our purposes. While James does not at all renounce wisdom derived from the analysis of nature and human nature, nevertheless he attributes his most crucial insights about life to the wisdom that comes down from above—that is, revelatory wisdom.[296] In this respect he is very much like Jesus, who as an apocalyptic sage drew on both sorts of wisdom traditions.

I differ with David Orton's characterization of the First Evangelist as an apocalyptic scribe more in the line of the authors of some of the Enochian literature than in line with Ben Sira. To the contrary, the description found in Matthew 13:52, which most scholars think provides a clue to help us under-

---

[294]Vermes, *Jesus the Jew*.

[295]Collins, *Seers, Sibyls and Sages*, pp. 349-50.

[296]One could argue that James believed that even his insights into life based on nature or human nature came from God and not merely from human observation or tradition.

[297]Orton, *Understanding Scribe*. The analogy with Qumran does not work well since the Qumran documents do not speak about scribes and their tasks, and it is a mistake to confuse a sage, or teacher such as the Teacher of Righteousness, with a scribe. A sage is an originator of wisdom; a scribe, by and large, is an interpreter and explainer of previous wisdom.

stand the First Evangelist, points us in the direction of Ben Sira, not Enoch: "Therefore every teacher of the Torah who has been instructed about the kingdom of heaven is like the owner of a house who brings out of his storeroom new treasures as well as old." This person (1) is a teacher, (2) knows the law and teaches it and (3) has been instructed about the kingdom of heaven (a— if not the—major subject of Jesus' parables and other teachings). "New" has to do with what the teacher has recently been instructed about (the kingdom), whereas "old" refers to Torah. In other words, this teacher does not limit himself to the Torah, but also deals in new treasures, namely, the various teachings of Jesus. In this regard it is understandable why the author of this gospel is such a strong critic of Pharisees and their scribes. It is not the noble task of a scribe that he objects to; he is, after all, one. Rather, our author has issues with the Pharisaic scribes who dwell on Torah and its amplification and refuse to recognize the teaching of Jesus and his perspectives on earlier Jewish wisdom, including the law. Our author is operating in a profoundly Jewish milieu where the teachings of the Pharisees rival the teachings that the First Evangelist seeks to offer.

Another helpful clue to the modus operandi of the First Evangelist is found in Ecclesiastes 12:9-10. The sapiential scribe is one who is to weigh/ assess, study and arrange/set in order the *mĕšalîm*—the parables, proverbs, aphorisms, riddles of the wisdom tradition. This description reflects the three stages of literary composition: experimenting with, refining/shaping and then arranging in a collection. The scribe is not merely to record but to enhance the wisdom examined by arrangement and elegance of expression, though always expressing himself with care. Wisdom is meant to be both a guide and goad in life, both a handhold and something that helps one get a grip on life (Eccles 12:11).[298] The scribe is an inspired interpreter and editor of his sources, but he is self-effacing and points to others as the sages or teachers whose material he is refining, restoring and presenting. If we were to characterize the First Evangelist we would have to say that he is remarkably like the description of the sapiential scribe in Sirach. And James is very indebted to the same sort of Jewish wisdom sources—Wisdom of Solomon and Sirach. But James operates quite differently than the First Evangelist in various respects.

In the first place James is offering his own wisdom, not merely redacting the wisdom of the past. Nowhere is this clearer than in the way he handles the Jesus tradition as opposed to the way the First Evangelist handles it. The latter quotes Jesus and attributes the material to Jesus. James on the other

---

[298]Witherington, *Jesus the Sage*, pp. 72-73.

hand draws on the Jesus tradition without attribution and modifies it to suit his own purposes, melding it together with his own wisdom—sometimes revelatory and counterorder wisdom, sometimes conventional wisdom. There is a reason that James, like Paul, calls himself a servant *(doulos)* of Jesus Christ and not his secretary or scribe *(grammateus)*. He too has received revelation, and he too has insights to share and new perspectives on previous wisdom teaching, including that of his brother. James does not feel it necessary to quote Torah often to give authority to his discourse, and unlike what his brother manifested he is perfectly at home using Greco-Roman rhetorical techniques to address with maximum possible impact Jewish Christians in the Diaspora—that is, in a rhetoric saturated Greco-Roman environment.[299]

We will never know whether Jesus was capable of wielding rhetoric in the way James does, and since he never addresses foreigners in any lengthy Greek discourse we cannot guess. But whatever else we may say, James proves to be a multifaceted and multitalented sage in his own right, able to address audiences outside his own setting in persuasive ways, while still manifesting the same Jewish *Gestalt* with that mixture of wisdom and eschatological fervor and content found in the teachings of Jesus. Like his brother he is a creative generator of new traditions/wisdom as well as a reframer of old wisdom, and so he certainly does not merely fall into the category of creative scribe like the First Evangelist (i.e., a person whose skill is editing and assembling data whether old or new). If we call the First Evangelist the first Christian scribe in the Christian era, we may call James the first Jewish Christian sage in that era. And like his brother, James is prepared to offer a new law, a royal and eschatological and perfect law that combines elements from the Mosaic covenant (like "love your neighbor") with other things. Law is seen as but one form of wise teaching, and it is handled in a sapiential way. It is truly unfortunate that James was caricatured as someone who had not captured Jesus' vision of things, but rather merely rehearsed older Jewish wisdom teachings.

But there is a problem seldom noticed here. In Matthew 23:8-10 Jesus warned his disciples that they were not to be called rabbis or teachers, because they had one teacher—Jesus himself. James's caution about not many becoming teachers may fall in line with Jesus' warning, and Jesus' warning may be said to be against the honorific side of things as it involved early Jewish teachers—in other words, whoever was a teacher was not to seek the status and praise for doing so. Rather they were to follow Jesus' own more humble example. This is

---

[299]Consult Snyder, *Teachers and Texts*, pp. 181-214.

probably how James would have understood this saying of Jesus.[300]

Furthermore, while James follows the Jewish practice of identifying the proper teacher with the sage,[301] he models for these teachers something that goes well beyond scribal activities or job descriptions. In other words, while he does not want many to follow in his footsteps and become teachers/ sages (cf. Heb 5:12), he certainly assumes and hopes that a few will do so to guide the Jewish Christians in the Diaspora, some who are perhaps already the elders in those places. The criteria for being such a teacher includes character (emphasized in Jas 3), knowing earlier wisdom, being open to new revelatory wisdom and having the ability to articulate it persuasively. One need not be a scribe to be a sage or need not become a scribe in preparation for being a sage. Good character, knowledge of the word and openness to new insight from God would suffice. One need not necessarily even be literate to do this, though James certainly was. Richard Bauckham stresses that James was such a creative sage that he even felt free to rephrase his brother's own teaching as well as that of the Old Testament. In commenting on James 3:11-12 Bauckham notes that "James is not *quoting* or *alluding* to the saying of Jesus [Mt 7:16], but, in the manner of a wisdom sage, he is *re-expressing* the insight he has learned from Jesus' teaching (Luke 6:43-45; Matt. 12:33-35; 7:16-18). . . . Just as Ben Sira, even when he repeats the thought of Proverbs, deliberately refrains from repeating the words, so James creates an aphorism of his own, indebted to but no mere reproduction of the words of Jesus."[302]

To judge from the subsequent history of Christianity after the apostolic age, both prophetic and sapiential figures who claimed independent authority and revelation gradually came under an increasing cloud of suspicion, as we see in *Didache* 11—13. The church tended to marginalize such figures and has continued to do so throughout church history. We may thus be thankful that the writing of a figure like James the sage became enshrined in the canon of the New Testament, despite the bumpy ride it took to get there. It reminds us that our roots look rather different than most of the current limbs now growing from the tree. It reminds us that early Christianity was a movement not just of the faithful reiteration of older traditions but of fresh revelation, fresh wisdom from and about Christ, who came to be called the very wisdom of God, the ultimate revelation of the mind and character of God.

[300]Brosend, *James and Jude*, p. 94.
[301]Reese, "Exegete as Sage," p. 83.
[302]Bauckham, *James*, p. 91 (emphasis original).

James 3:2 is very important because it makes clear that whatever James meant by the word *perfect* in James 1—2 it was *not* complete sinlessness. Everyone stumbles (sins) many times (or in many ways), he adds. "All" refers to all believers, not just all teachers, and James again includes himself in this category. This verse provides the confirmation of the proposition, which begins with *gar*. This confirmation relies on a maxim of sorts, which would be widely recognized and accepted since it was a form of a proverb known all over the Greco-Roman world (Thucydides *History* 3.45.3; Epictetus *Discourses* 1.11.7; Seneca *De clementia* 1.6.3; Philo *That God Is Unchangeable* 75; Sirach 19.16; Rom 3:23). The audience thinks it is hearing an indisputable proof from everyday life.[303] Alfred Plummer suggests something of an enthymeme here, with the logical flow as follows: Some of us must teach. All of us frequently fall, particularly in the area of speech. Teachers who fall are more severely judged than others. Therefore do not many of you become teachers.[304]

Ptaiō in the New Testament refers to sin, not just moral mistakes (Jas 2:10; 2 Pet 1:10; Rom 11:11), or the act of falling or stumbling into sin. Again, it contains echoes of earlier Jewish wisdom thinking: "Who has not sinned with his tongue?" (Sirach 19.6; cf. Prov 12:13; 13:3; 21:23; Sirach 14.1; 20.18; 22.27). But what does *teleios* mean? As in James 1:4, it means completeness in virtue, operating from unmixed motives, living a life consistent with one's conversion— not sinlessness. In other words, it is a description of a truly mature Christian.[305] James's comment on sin is reinforced later in James 3:8: "But no one is able to control the tongue (completely)." Teachers, however, must be able to have more control of the tongue than others, and that is the issue here. In an ancient story from our period, King Amasis of Egypt sent a sacrifice to Bias the sage, asking him to send back the best and worst part. Bias sent back the tongue![306]

James 3:2 continues: "But if someone does not sin in what he says." This conditional statement with *ei* does not imply anything about its necessary fulfillment or its impossibility. It is not a future more probable condition, however, and so one may take it in its immediate context to imply that it is not likely to happen at present, but it is expected to happen. Clearly, James wants believers to bridle their tongues, though presumably he does not expect them to do it perfectly or without relapse. James sees one's tongue or speech as crucial because of the

---

[303]Watson, "Rhetoric of James 3.1-12," pp. 55-56.
[304]Plummer, *General Epistles*, p. 169.
[305]Ibid., p. 170.
[306]Ibid., p. 173.

potential harm or good it can do to the body of Christ.[307]

In **James 3:3-5** three examples are trotted out—using the rhetorical logic that if something is true of the lesser thing, then it is also true of the greater thing[308]— to provide the *exornatio* in the form of simile, example, amplification and even judgment. This is meant to confirm the proposition and solidify the argument by use of wisdom speech.[309] James thinks that sapiential examples are especially persuasive with his audience, as he uses an abundance of them in this sermon. The first reiterates an idea already heard in the discourse—namely, that bridling the tongue leads to directing the whole body (Jas 1:26). *Sōma* probably does not mean person here, since almost always the term focuses on the outer and material part of the person, as in the example of how a bridle controls the mouth and thereby turns the whole horse.

It may be asked why this metaphor is chosen. Perhaps a teacher is seen as the mouth of the body of believers, and the teacher is being warned to control his tongue. Duane Watson shows that all three examples are stock illustrations used in various ways all over the Greco-Roman world.[310] One reason why so many unique words appear in this section is precisely because James is borrowing from other sages' discourse rather than simply creating examples in his own style. For example, Plutarch combines ship and tongue (*De garrulitate* 10) and horse, ship rudder and tongue (*Quomodo adulator ad amico internoscatur* 12.33F), while Philo combines horse, ship and fire (*Allegorical Interpretation* 3.223-24).[311] The fire analogy amplifies the force of these analogies by stressing the damage that can be done (*Rhetorica ad Herennium* 2.29.46).

The second analogy is different because it focuses on how a small tongue/ rudder can guide a huge boat under the firm control of the pilot. This leads to the slightly different conclusion that, though the tongue is small, it has a huge effect, indeed a hugely negative effect if it is given to boast greatly (Jas 3:5). Peter Davids suggests: "This is not so much a pessimistic change in usage . . . but a slow shift in thought from the power of the tongue to the evil of the tongue to the need for proper control. It is not that the tongue steers the ship, but that the proper helmsman is often not in control."[312] More helpful is Luke Timothy

---

[307] For a possible reference to the body of Christ here and the teacher's effect on it, see Martin, *James*, p. 110.

[308] Brosend, *James and Jude*, p. 88.

[309] Watson, "Rhetoric of James 3:1-12," p. 57.

[310] Ibid., p. 58.

[311] See the helpful discussion in Dibelius, *James*, pp. 185-90, where a plethora of examples are set out.

[312] Davids, *James*, p. 140.

Johnson's insight that James sets up the application he wants by putting three illustrative components in place first: "James makes all three components explicit: the guiding desire (the steersman), the means of control (the rudder), and that which is controlled (the ship), corresponding in turn to human desire, the tongue, and the body."[313]

The rudder analogy could also be directed at congregational leaders who were in charge of *kybernēsis*—of giving direction to the congregation. This metaphorical term for leading or giving leadership in the New Testament (1 Cor 12:28) is a naval term, and the *euthynōn* ("pilot") in James 3:4 can be linked to the ship's *kybernētēs* ("navigator") in Acts 27:11.[314] It is easy to see why the rudder analogy might come to James's mind, since similar analogies were common in ancient sources of wisdom. For example, the Egyptian "Instruction of Amenem-Opet" reads: "If the tongue of a man [is] the rudder of the boat, the All-Lord is its pilot."[315] The analogies are understandably imperfect. James is seeking control of the tongue, but if the tongue needs to be controlled then it is not like the bridle bit or the rudder that does the controlling.[316]

Rhetorical flourishes are evident in this passage: the catchwords *ptaiō* and *chalinos* linking several thoughts in James 3:2-3; alliteration of *mikron, melos, megala* in James 3:5; and *hēlikon* balancing *hēlikēn* in James 3:5 in the highly rhetorical phrase *hēlikon pyr hēlikēn hylēn anaptei* and providing a nice contrast: "how small a flame ignites so great a forest." The word used here, *hylēn*, indicates "wood" not "forest," and so it is possible that the Palestinian brush is in view, since forests were not plentiful in James's locale.[317] There is a strange combination of awkwardness and gracefulness here. The tongue as not merely powerful, but evil and destructive; it is said to be fire, which has Old Testament parallels (Prov 16:27; Is 9:18).[318] "Whereas vv. 2-3 presented the positive side that bridling the tongue indicated mastery of the body, v. 6 presents the negative side that in fact the tongue stains the whole body."[319]

James 3:6 is exceedingly difficult to make sense of in terms of words and syntax. What do we do with the phrase *the wicked world*—is it a predicate for the convoluted sentence that begins "the tongue constitutes," is it a gloss, or is it the title for what follows? What does *kosmos* mean here? Surely it means what

[313]Johnson, *James*, p. 258.
[314]Martin, *James*, p. 105.
[315]Pritchard, *Ancient Near Eastern Texts*, pp. 423-34.
[316]Brosend, *James and Jude*, p. 89.
[317]Elliott-Binns, "Meaning of ΥΛΗ."
[318]Mayor, *James*, p. 113.
[319]Watson, "Rhetoric of James 3.1-12," p. 60.

it did in James 1:27 and James 2:5—"the world"—not a metaphorical reference like "a world of difference."

Peter Davids is right that the tongue reveals our relationship to or embodiment of the principles of the world of wickedness.[320] In the background we may hear the dominical saying, "It is what comes out of a person that defiles him" (Mk 7:15). The tongue is our means of communicating with the wicked world, and this is our point of contact with it. With parallels in Orphic categories,[321] *trochon tēs geneseōs* may mean the wheel of birth or existence or the cycle of life (Virgil's *Aeneid* 6.748: "When time's wheel has rolled a thousand years"). It seems not to imply fatalism here or some cyclical view of history, but the course of life (womb to tomb). Thus James is saying that the tongue sets on fire the whole course of life. I agree with William Brosend that we should not see here some profound allusion to deeply philosophical concepts, but an example of James's rhetorical flourish: "What it does accomplish is to push the limits of the tongue's capacity to the beginning (the 'cycle of nature') and end ('on fire by hell') of creation. . . . The cumulative rhetorical effect of 3:2-8 is an emphatic, if confusing, warning and denouncement of the tongue—human speech. The presumption . . . seems to be that more harm than good comes from speech."[322] If Brosend is right, then in a sense this is a capsule summary of the whole human story as found in the Bible and a reminder of how the tongue always keeps getting human beings in trouble throughout history.

More certainly, in James 3:6 we press behind the individual human responsibility for evil in James 1—2 to the ultimate source of evil—*geennēs,* which may be another way of saying the devil.[323] Used by Jesus to refer to hell, the term *gehenna* originally referred to the Valley of Hinnom where garbage was dumped and burned outside Jerusalem and where in an earlier era there had been child sacrifice (Jer 32:35; *Greek Apocalypse of Ezra* 1.9; Mt 5:22-30; cf. *2 Clement* 5.4). The original analogy was that "hell is like a stinking, burning, garbage dump." "'Fire,' it is sometimes truly said, 'is a good servant, but a bad master,' and precisely the same may with equal truth be said of the tongue."[324] Jesus ben Sira offers a variant on this point: "If you blow the spark, it shall burn; if you spit on it will be quenched; and both of these come out of your mouth" (Sirach 28.12).

See Tongue Thule

---

[320]Davids, *James*, p. 142.

[321]Ropes, *James*, pp. 235-39.

[322]Brosend, *James and Jude*, p. 91.

[323]The connection between Gehenna and the devil in early Jewish Christianity can be seen in the description in Rev 20:10, where the devil is thrown into the eternal lake of fire—the image of Gehenna.

[324]Plummer, *General Epistles*, p. 174.

James 3:7 in a sense shows the frustration of human existence—persons seem to be able to control and subdue every other sort of creature, except themselves, and especially the tongue. "Particularly noteworthy is the use of different tenses of δαμάζω showing that the animals are (present tense) and have been (perfect tense) tamed, but the tongue is not able to be (aorist infinitive). There is assonance or alliteration in πετεινων ἑρπετων (v. 7) and δαμάσαι δύναται . . . ἀκατάστατον κακόν . . . ἰουΘανατηφόρου (v. 8)."[325] Since James 3:7-8 is a virtual summary of Philo's argument in *On the Creation of the World* 83—88, it is not completely out of the question that James may have known some of the works of his contemporary and is drawing on them in his homily, which was written in the 50s.[326]

James 3:8 then takes us a step further when we are told that the tongue is poisonous and bears death. We should likely see here in the background the story of creation and fall, where the serpent is poisonous and his words ultimately bring death to humanity, or Psalm 140:3, which tells us that evil people "make their tongues as sharp as a serpent's; the poison of vipers is on their lips." The description of the tongue as a restless evil probably also envisions an agitated snake. That James is thinking of the Genesis story is confirmed by what he goes on to say about blessings and curses and people in the image of God (Jas 3:9). In short, the tongue is like the snake, goaded on by the evil one, a restless evil itself looking to stalk a person and defile. It taints the whole body (Jas 3:6). The reference in James 3:7 to subduing animals also comes ultimately from the creation story (especially Gen 1:26). And the reference to the cycle of generation harkens back to the genealogies in Genesis as well. From the mouth of the snake came honeyed words ("you shall be") but also a bitter pill to swallow, once sin was heeded.

James 3:9 may indicate a Jewish reference to blessing God's name, as a good Jew would do whenever God's name was mentioned: "Yahweh, blessed be his name." With the first-person plural here James again identifies himself with his worshiping audience.[327] The duplicity of the tongue is a commonplace in early Jewish literature, particularly wisdom literature (Prov 10:11; 18:21; Sirach 5.9—6:1; 22.27; 28.13-26; *Testament of Benjamin* 6.5-6). Is James still thinking here of a snake—with a forked tongue perhaps? The idea of blessings and curses coming out of the same mouth is shown in two ways. (1) To bless God and

---

[325] Watson, "Rhetoric of James 3.1-12," p. 61.

[326] Moo, *James*, p. 161 and n18, on the close parallels.

[327] Johnson, *James*, p. 261. It does not follow from this that James is simply addressing problems in worship (contra Martin, *James*, p. 118), as he is speaking more broadly and generically.

curse someone in God's image makes no sense since human beings are God's children (hence the reference to Father) and are his representatives. James seems to be saying that cursing the representative is the same as cursing the one whom he represents, so such cursing is inappropriate for Christians. Perhaps he is referring to a serious cursing or damning of another person.[328] (2) It is unnatural, for even in nature a stream does not produce both bitter/brackish and sweet/freshwater from the same source. This imagery may imply that James is thinking of the Dead Sea and its saltwater *(halykon)* and the various places where water gushes out of an opening in the cliffs. Fig trees, olive trees and vines were the big three producers of fruit in Palestine and that vicinity. James says that fruit-producing trees do not produce a fruit that is foreign to its nature. The reference to "Lord and Father" is unique in the Bible, and both terms refer to God the Father, not to the Son and the Father (Ps 41:13). Here again James may be calling to mind Sirach: "Praise is not seasonable in the mouth of a sinner" (Sirach 15.9). Douglas Moo reminds us that curses and blessings in antiquity were seen as words with inherent power that could effect what they spoke. They were seen as more than the mere audible pronunciation of certain words. These notions are likely in play here.[329]

In **James 3:10** James asserts his authority, chiding the audience: "Brothers, this ought not to be." We may hear echoes from Luke 6:28 here (cf. Rom 12:14). James must now reiterate the initial proposition and so round off this segment of the argument. Beginning with this verse and continuing through the rest of this chapter, James reflects knowledge of material in the *Testament of the Twelve Patriarchs*, for example, *Testament of Benjamin* 6.5: "The good set of mind does not talk from both sides of its mouth: praises and curses, abuse and honor, calm and strife, hypocrisy and truth, poverty and wealth, but it has one disposition, uncontaminated and pure toward all persons." Our author has already spoken of double-mindedness (Jas 1:8; cf. Heb 4:8), but here he seems to suggest that this condition issues in duplicity of speech.[330]

The two rhetorical questions in **James 3:11-12** summarize the immediately preceding discussion in James 3:9-10. Both questions expect a negative response—no—to reinforce that only good things should come out of a Christian teacher's mouth. It is possible that the word pictures painted here come from James's own memory of seeing the freshwater and saltwater springs at the Dead Sea, but if so it seems to undercut his point since the two different sort of springs

---

[328]Mayor, *James*, pp. 121-22.
[329]Moo, *James*, p. 163.
[330]Johnson, *James*, p. 264.

issue out of the same cliffs; perhaps emphasizing that the same spring—rather than the same general locale—cannot produce two kinds of water.[331] More likely the apocalyptic reversal scenario is in view, where upheaval in the earth allows this phenomenon to happen (2 Esdras [4 Ezra] 5.9). There may also be an allusion to Jesus' teaching about trees and the fruit they bear (Mt 7:16-18; 12:33-36; Lk 6:43-44).

James 3:13-18 shifts gears a bit to a discussion of having and speaking and showing wisdom rather than its converse—speaking evil or antiwisdom. James intends to end this part of the discourse on a more positive note and implies here that there is wisdom and there is what passes for wisdom. Those who claim to be wise and understanding should show outwardly their wisdom by their deeds and good way of life. Such a wisdom that lets actions speak for it is unpretentious—unlike those who pride themselves on their wise words, which are not confirmed by a wise lifestyle. The "movement in 3:13-18 is from the 'wisdom' shown through the 'good life' to the 'earthly . . . wisdom' to 'wisdom from above.'"[332] James has an inclusio here, since heavenly wisdom is discussed at both the beginning and end of this section.[333]

James 3:13 begins with a rhetorical question that refers once more to the teachers. The sentence itself has a nice inclusio, beginning and ending with *sophos/sophia*. When he asks where is the sage or person of understanding, James may be echoing Job's questioning in Job 28:12. Job is in the process of denying that real wisdom can be found "below" by searching the earth or that it can be bought: "It is hidden from the eyes of every living thing, concealed even from the birds of the air. . . . God understands the way to it and he alone knows where it dwells. . . . And he said to the people, 'The fear of the Lord—that is wisdom'" (Job 28:21, 23, 28). James echoes this text here and takes the same view as Job—real wisdom must be revealed from above, and it requires reverence for God and a humble spirit to receive it. James has already said that the implanted word must be received with meekness (Jas 1:21). James is the only sage in the New Testament who mentions or alludes to Job (Jas 5:11), which strengthens the likelihood of the allusion to Job here.

James goes on to say that the real sage will demonstrate wisdom through works and a good way of life, which involves submission to the wisdom and will of God and gentleness with others—that is, unpretentious wisdom or "wisdom in humility/meekness." Douglas Moo suggests a genitive of source here: in

---

[331]Hadidian, "Palestinian Pictures in the Epistle of James"; cf. Laws, *James*, p. 157.
[332]Brosend, *James and Jude*, p. 101.
[333]Martin, *James*, p. 125.

the humility that comes from true wisdom, and this is probably right.[334] Richard Bauckham points out that *prautēs* is often associated with "fear" or revering the Lord (Sirach 1.27; cf. Prov 15:33; 22:4), so that James is talking about the same godly wisdom—or wisdom that has come down from God—that he has referred to before, and those who humble themselves and receive and believe it can have it.[335] The phrase *good life* or *the good lifestyle/way of life (kalēs anastrophēs)* is a theme picked up and developed in 1 Peter 2:12 (also 1 Pet 1:15; 3:1-2, 16; 2 Pet 3:11).[336] James may be echoing here a list of virtues frequently associated with wisdom in earlier sapiential literature. Wisdom of Solomon 7.21-28 teaches these virtues, and the result is that the person in question becomes a friend of God, like Abraham. James 3:13 should be compared to James 3:17, which lists more virtues associated with wisdom, including peacemaking.[337] By contrast, antiwisdom involves ambition and envy, and James will go on to speak about it as well. But true wisdom leads to humility and peacemaking.

In the Greco-Roman world meekness or humility was usually not seen as a virtue of free persons, much less persons of social status. It was a quality expected of slaves. Jesus, however, proclaimed an ethic of servanthood that included humility, and he even went so far as to say that he came to be such a servant (Mk 10:45; Mt 11:29; 21:5). It is no surprise then that he pronounced a blessing on the meek as the dominion of God was breaking in (Mt 5:5) or that James, who sought to emulate him, spoke not only of meekness, working against the flow of the agonistic culture, but called himself the servant of his brother Jesus (Jas 1:1). James correctly absorbed the character of Jesus' ethic. The Greek idea of wisdom prized intellectual ability and accomplishment and even the knowledge of the esoteric or highly abstract. This is why the term *philosophia* ("love of wisdom") was applied to things by Socrates, Plato and Aristotle. James's sapiential focus is very different from this tradition.

Alfred Plummer does a good job of plumbing the depths of James's attitude about and approach to wisdom, which is through the heart (and will) to the head, and not the reverse. He reminds us that James did not think wisdom and intelligence or even wisdom and knowledge are one and the same, especially

---

[334]Moo, *James*, p. 170.

[335]Bauckham, *James*, p. 84.

[336]Moo, *James*, p. 169. This raises the possibility that the apostle to the Jews (Gal 2:7), namely Peter, had read James's letter or at least knew its contents, which is entirely likely if he worked with congregations to which it was sent. I date 1 Peter at least a decade after the homily of James was sent. In Gal 2:9 Paul indicates that James, Peter and John were going to focus on the mission to the Jews. This supports the contention that this letter, if it is by James—as I have argued—was sent only to Jewish Christians.

[337]Perkins, *Peter, James and Jude*, p. 122.

when we are dealing with fallen human beings. According to Plummer, himself a great mind and scholar, James believed that

> to develop a man's intellectual powers is not always the best way to make him "humble himself as a little child." . . . First purify the heart and regenerate the will, and then the recovery of the intellect will follow in due course. It is easy to reach the intellect through the heart, and this is what the wisdom that is from above aims at doing. If we begin with the intellect, we shall very likely end there; and in that case the man is not raised from his degradation, but equipped with additional powers of mischief. . .
>
> It is evident that the heavenly wisdom is preeminently a *practical* wisdom. It is not purely or mainly intellectual; it is not speculative; it is not lost in contemplation. Its object is to increase holiness rather than knowledge, and happiness rather than information. Its atmosphere is not controversy and debate, but gentleness and peace. It is full, not of sublime theories or daring hypotheses, but of mercy and good fruits. It can be confident without wrangling, and reserved without hypocrisy. It is the twin sister of that heavenly love which "envieth not, vaunteth not itself, seeketh not its own, is not provoked, taketh no account of evil."[338]

Thus, it is no accident that James implores here: "Show me your way of life, that you have learned the lessons of biblical wisdom, which involves walking humbly with one's God and one's neighbor."

James 3:14 suggests that one should stifle any zealous, fanatical or envious ideas one has in one's heart. The word *zelos* can refer to a person who is zealous in a positive sense or jealous in a negative sense, but the modifier *pikron* ("bitter")—a word already used in James 3:11 to refer to brackish waters that are of no use—makes perfectly clear what the sense is here: "bitter jealousy" refers to envy. Boasting about such things gives the lie to the truth, that is, it denies the truth by words and actions. Apparently James is countering the party spirit that existed in any agonistic culture where various teachers and philosophers and others were vying for prominence and a following among the same believers. The term *eritheia* occurs only once in earlier Greek literature: in Aristotle it refers to the "narrow partisan zeal of factional, greedy politicians in his own day" (*Politics* 5.3.1302b4; 1303a14).[339] The word is probably related to the more familiar term *eris* ("strife"), which Paul uses about the effects of jealousy (Gal 5:20; 1 Cor 3:3; 2 Cor 12:20). Preening, boasting, vaunting oneself and one's wisdom over another's betrays the very quality one is boasting about and shows that the person in question does not understand or at least does not model biblical wisdom.

---

[338]Plummer, *General Epistles*, pp. 210-11, 213 (emphasis original).
[339]Moo, *James*, p. 171.

James warns about boasting about it and in that way denying the truth about wisdom or, better, giving the lie to the truth. Probably he has in mind the warning from Jeremiah 9:23-24: "Let not the wise man boast in his wisdom . . . but let him who boasts boast about this: that he understands and knows me." It is understandable why James would say this, since in his view this wisdom does not come chiefly or only from study or intellectual efforts of various sorts—it comes from being open to what God gives.

James 3:15 says that the nonbiblical wisdom that consists in boasting and speaking divides the community; it did not come down from heaven, it came up from hell. It is earthly, it is unspiritual or natural, it is diabolical. This antithetical parallelism shows what constitutes true and false wisdom. The first of the three descriptors, *epigeios,* means the opposite of heavenly (Jn 3:12; 1 Cor 15:40; 2 Cor 5:1; Phil 2:10) and so "earthly" is an appropriate translation, but as Luke Timothy Johnson suggests, on the basis of Philippians 3:19, "earthbound" would be better because we are talking about a perspective that refuses to consider God's realm or the character of God's wisdom.[340] The second term, *psychikos,* does not mean "soulish"; rather, every New Testament use of it has a negative connotation and is placed in opposition to what is viewed as spiritual, hence the translation "unspiritual," though it literally means "natural" (1 Cor 2:14; 15:44, 46; Jude 19). The climactic term is clearly the most pejorative: *daimoniōdes* (literally "pertaining to demons") is found only here in the entire Bible. This false wisdom is demonic or comes from demons or demonic influence as opposed to the wisdom that is from above.[341]

James is then denying that any supposed wise persons or teachers are spiritual or spiritually mature if they are carving up Christ's body and puffing up themselves. That sort of proud and divisive speech leads in **James 3:16** to a restlessness among believers, disunity and all sorts of evil practices (again with alliteration: *pan phaulon pragma*). Alfred Plummer puts thing aptly: "It may have a right to the name of wisdom. . . . But an inspiration which prompts men to envy and intrigue, because, when many are rushing to occupy the post of teacher, others find a hearing more readily than themselves, is the inspiration of Cain and of Korah, rather than of Moses or of Daniel. The professed desire to offer service to God is really only a craving to obtain advancement for self."[342] The term *akatastasia* is a cognate of the term used in James 1:8 and James 3:8

---

[340]Johnson, *James*, p. 272.

[341]Moo, *James*, p. 173, who relates this to the Johannine triad "the world, the flesh, the devil." Here may be another small hint that the author of the Johannine Letters knew this homily of James and was influenced by it. Cf. also Jn 8:44 on the language here.

[342]Plummer, *General Epistles*, p. 202.

a cyclical

to refer to the double-minded person or the duplicitous tongue. It refers to a restlessness that creates disorder. These warnings especially make sense if James has in mind particular leaders or teachers of the community.[343] His deepest desire is that they model a countercultural wisdom and ethic.

Words, James implies, are powerful inciters and revealers of human character. By contrast the kind of wisdom that God sends can be recognized by the various fruit that accompanies it: it is pure, not tainted, not arising from mixed motives or attempts at self-glorification; it is considerate of others; it is teachable and obedient; it is full of merciful deeds, sincere, not a front, impartial. The list that begins in **James 3:17** can rightly be compared to Paul's list of the fruit of the Spirit in Galatians 5:22-23. Although Douglas Moo points out that the verbal overlap is minimal,[344] at the level of ideas they enunciate the same sort of character—one that is humble, peace-loving, upright and directed at others. While it is understandable why some see wisdom in James as equivalent to the Spirit in Paul,[345] this goes too far. What we can say is that wisdom in James is seen as producing some of the same effects as the Spirit does in Paul's writings, and this is all the more understandable if the Spirit conveys the heavenly wisdom to the believer.

James 3:17 may be a rhetorical gradatio or ladder that descends from the most important to the least. This is suggested by the use of the term *first* in reference to the purity of this wisdom. *Hagnos* refers not to ritual purity but to moral purity and even innocence. The second quality, peace-loving, leads to the final comment in this section about peacemakers in the next verse. Thus while purity seems to be preeminent among the qualities, the rest—except for the second-place peace-loving—seem to be on a level plain and flow out of purity.[346] It may be better to say that this is a list of the effects of godly wisdom on a human being.

The rhetorical form of this list is totally lost in translation: one word at the beginning of the list and four at the end begin with the *a* sound, and in the middle all the words begin with the *e* sound, so that assonance carries the list for-

---

[343]Martin, *James*, p. 132. While I do not agree with Martin's overly specific reading of James, as though James had a particular problem and a particular set of adversaries in mind, I think that James's focus here is on leaders in all these various Jewish Christian congregations. The problems referred to here—boasting, self-promotion, envy—were endemic to an agonistic society like the Greco-Roman world. James wants the audience to manifest a countercultural wisdom and ethic.

[344]Moo, *James*, p. 175.

[345]See the discussion in Kirk, "Meaning of Wisdom in James." Davids, *James*, p 56, takes a similar line.

[346]So Plummer, *General Epistles*, p. 207.

ward: *eirēnikē, epieikēs, eupeithēs, eleous*. This rhetorical device is called epiphora.[347] Furthermore, the second, third and fourth words all rhyme by ending with a similar sound: *eirēnikē, epieikēs, eupeithēs*. The last of these terms requires further comment: it occurs only here in the New Testament and literally means "easily persuaded," not "submissive," as it is sometimes rendered. Thus the triad is peace-loving, considerate, yielding to persuasion.[348] These are the virtues one should bring to a hearing of true wisdom, and in a dialogue one should not seek to vaunt oneself over others but rather listen and be willing to be persuaded if they manifest godly wisdom. James is not, however, talking about being gullible or naïve.[349] He is talking about graciousness in one's approach to a dialogue with another person, not an approach that is unloving and self-centered and creates divisions and rivalries. The end of the list is especially composed for rhetorical effect: the last two qualities are *adiakritos* ("without wavering") and *anypokritos* ("without hypocrisy"). In composing this list of wisdom's fruit James may be thinking of the ode to wisdom and her marvelous qualities in Wisdom of Solomon 7.22-30.

Part of what makes this homily persuasive is its sound, for it shows that the sermon writer is wise enough to make the sound of the discourse comport with the content of the discourse. If one is offering heavenly wisdom, it ought to sound heavenly in the ancient rhetorical way of thinking. This list contrasts nicely with the threefold list about the antiwisdom being earthly, worldly, devilish, which not incidentally sounds abrupt—the three words are very different in form and do not manifest the harmony of alliteration or assonance or rhythm or rhyme, which is only appropriate since James is arguing that this antiwisdom creates chaos and disorder and a lack of harmony. The rhetorical form reinforces the content and is intended to make the discourse more compelling and persuasive. We totally lose this sense when we reduce this to a nonoral text, whereas the text is intended to be a surrogate for or a transcript of actual oral communication.

Righteousness, a way of life pleasing to God, is the fruit of peacefulness working in the community, and it is sown in peace, not in strife as **James 3:18** suggests. This implies that the proper context, the proper milieu, a peaceful and harmonious one, must be established before growth in righteousness and wisdom can take place (since righteousness here means growing in sanctification

---

[347]Martin, *James*, p. 126.

[348]Ibid., p. 134. One would expect persuasion to be highlighted in a deliberative rhetorical discourse that seeks to persuade in regard to conduct.

[349]Moo, *James*, p. 176.

and character, a moral improvement is in view here and not the objective right standing with God). Wisdom does not arise out of turmoil and pride but out of humility and teachableness, out of an atmosphere that allows one to learn and revere and be sincere and not put on a show for personal advancement. This wisdom takes time to help others, instead of taking advantage of others and helping oneself. Restlessness is the product or byproduct of fake wisdom, and righteousness is the fruit of working in peace as a peacemaker.

Thus, James insists that both unity *and* purity must be maintained among God's people and insisted on. To stress one over the other is to either ignore sin or fracture the whole body of Christ. The wise person will steer the middle course, insisting on righteousness but also on mercy and peace, for the body of Christ must grow as a body, not simply as individual members of it. James 3:18 stresses that righteousness does not come from anger or fighting or envy or party spirit or divisions or rivalry; it comes from peacemakers sowing in peace. Finally, James is not here calling persons to conversion.[350] He addresses his audience as brothers and sisters in Christ, and his concern is that they get on with progressive sanctification, processing out of their lives the wisdom of this world and manifesting increasingly godly wisdom and its qualities and traits. He is addressing partially socialized Christians who are prone to follow the ways of the larger agonistic culture and even, when wisdom is the professed goal, tend to manifest patterns of jealousy, rivalry, factionalism and other forms of selfish behavior. In short, he is seeking to forestall or head off Jewish Christians behaving badly and not manifesting the countercultural wisdom and ethic of the gospel. This corrective critique will be taken further in James 4.

ELABORATION OF THEMES, PART THREE: COMBATING THE DESIRES AND ANTIWISDOM OF THE MERCENARY AND MILITARY MENTALITY (JAS 4:1—5:6)

> Wars, and factions, and fightings have no other source than the body and its lusts. For it is for the getting of wealth that all our wars arise, and we are compelled to get wealth because of our body, to whose service we are slaves; and in consequence we have no leisure for philosophy, because of all these things. And the worst of all is that if we get any leisure from it, and turn to some question, in the midst of our inquiries, the body is everywhere coming in, introducing turmoil and confusion, and bewildering us, so we are prevented from seeing the truth. (Plato *Phaedo* 66-67)

James is not trying to take away our freedom to decide, but he is showing us that

---

[350]Against Johnson, "James 3:13—4:10," p. 332.

it is not just what we want that matters. We need God's grace to complement our efforts and ought to rely not on them but on God's love for us. As it says in Proverbs, "Do not boast about tomorrow, for you do not know what a day may bring forth." . . . James does not remove the power to do good, but he shows that it is not just a matter of one's own will. To do good as we ought, we need the grace of God. (Chrysostom *Catena* 32)

What then? Has luxury been condemned? It certainly has—so why do you continue to strive for it? A man has bread, but the excess has been trimmed away. A man has wine, but the excess has been cut off there also. God desires that we should pray not for impure food but for souls set free from excess. For everything that God has created is good, and nothing that has been received with thanks is to be despised. (Chrysostom *Catena* 34)

There is considerable debate, and no agreement, among commentators about how to divide the material in James 4. Some connect it (or at least James 4:1-10) with what precedes on the basis of the recurring notion of envy.[351] Not just envy or jealousy is in play here, but covetousness of various sorts that longs to satisfy the desires of the heart for sex, money, power and the like. While the theme of acquisition of wealth is not at the forefront of the argument in James 4:1-10, it is announced there, further developed in James 4:11-17, and then brought to a rousing climax at the end of the argument in James 5:1-6, where the rich are taken to task. The theme of the rich and their sins has already been addressed earlier in James 1—2, but here James takes the gloves off and the rhetoric becomes a good deal more polemical, especially in the concluding section in James 5:1-6.

This rhetorical unit has several subsections: James 4:1-10; 4:11-12; 4:13-17; 5:1-6. The phrase *age nyn* in the parallel opening of James 4:13-17 and James 5:1-6 makes clear that these are new subunits, but it also suggests that these are two paragraphs, one general and one particular, dealing with the same subject. The traveling merchant seeks to make money, and the result of such efforts is that some do become rich, so James must show them the outcome of that lifestyle.

In terms of rhetorical strategy, James followed the protocol that one might expect when dealing with a difficult subject: one saves for last the most difficult and troubling of the subjects one must persuade the audience about. This rhetorical tactic is called *insinuatio*, and it is a regular practice when addressing an audience that one does not know personally or that the author does not already have a close personal relationship with. We see this approach in Romans, where Paul leaves the ticklish subject of Jews and their future in God's plans until Romans 9—11, not least because Paul is addressing an audience he did not convert

---

[351]Ibid., pp. 332-35.

and had not personally visited with. The lines of authority in such situations are less clear, and when one attempts deliberative rhetoric, trying to persuade the audience to behave or believe differently than they have in the past, insinuatio is an appropriate way to proceed, especially since one must establish rapport with the audience at the outset of the discourse and work one's way up to the more difficult subjects to be addressed.[352] The stronger emotions—love and hate, fear and faith, joy and grief—are appealed to near the end of the discourse. This argument takes the audience into that territory with its hair-raising polemics and vituperation and thus prepares for the emotional last hurrah, the peroration that begins at James 5:7.

But another rhetorical convention is also in play here. The proper order for a rhetorical discourse is that by and large one puts forward positive arguments first and then turns in the latter stages of the discourse to refutatio, in this case refutation of alternative views about the wise way to live: the culture's conventional wisdom about the "good life" is taken on with vehemence. It is not an accident that more of James's rebuttal is saved for the end of the argumentative section of this homily.

Is this a call to the unconverted? No, it is a rebuttal of those in the community (Jas 4:1: "among you") who are largely pursuing the world's vision of the good life. There is a call to repentance, but the call is going out to members of these congregations who fit these descriptions. Quintilian calls this prolepsis, the anticipatory forestalling of a rebuttal one might expect to hear of what has already been advocated in this discourse (*Institutio oratoria* 4.1.49-50).

In a rebuttal in advance, done in diatribal style here, a premium is not put on invention or the introduction of new topics. Rather one uses the same sort of topics, tropes, figures, rhetorical devices used earlier in the discourse, only now with more direct, in-your-face rhetorical tactics. Along the way, this final elaboration of themes already broached earlier in the discourse will use the by-now-familiar dose of rhetorical questions, diatribal style with direct address to the offenders, enthymematic forms of argumentation, alliteration, assonance, colorful sapiential images and wordplay. James has not run out of energy or rhetorical imagination. His discourse comes to a stirring climax here, which has left many generations of Christians scrambling for cover lest these strong words be targeted at them!

[4:1] *From whence come quarrels and whence fights among you? Do they not come from this, from your pleasures warring in your bodily members?* [2] *You desire and*

---

[352]Witherington and Hyatt, *Romans*, pp. 236-38.

you have not—(so you) kill. And you covet and are unable to obtain (so) you fight and quarrel. You have not because you do not pray. ³You pray and do not receive because you pray wrongly, so that you might spend (it) on your pleasures. ⁴Adulteresses!⁽³⁵³⁾ Do you not know that friendship toward the world is enmity toward God? Whoever then wishes to be a friend to the world constitutes himself an enemy of God. ⁵Or do you suppose it is without reason the Scripture says: "God jealously longs for the spirit that he has caused to dwell⁽³⁵⁴⁾ in us" ⁶but he gives more grace. Therefore he/it says: "God opposes the proud, but gives grace to the humble." ⁷Submit then to God, but resist the devil and he will flee from you. ⁸Draw near to God and he will come near to you. Cleanse your hands, sinners, and purify your hearts, you double-minded/waverer. ⁹Be wretched/sorrowful and mourn and weep. Let your laughter be turned into mourning—and your joy into gloom. ¹⁰Humble yourself before the Lord and he will lift you up.

¹¹Do not speak against one another, brothers. The one speaking against his brother or judging his brother speaks against the law and judges the law. But if you judge the law, you are not a keeper of the law, but sitting in judgment of it. ¹²There is (only) one lawgiver and judge, who is able to save and destroy. But who are you to judge your neighbor?

¹³Come now, you who say, "Today or tomorrow we will go to their city, and we will spend a year there and do business and make money." ¹⁴You are such that you do not know what will happen tomorrow, what your life will be like. For you are a mist that is seen for a while, then also disappears. ¹⁵Instead you should say, "If the Lord wills we will live and do this or that." ¹⁶But now you boast in your airs of arrogance. All such boasting is evil. ¹⁷So then, the one who knows the good he should do) and does not do it, it is sin for him.

⁵:¹Come now, you rich, weep, howling at the wretchedness that is coming upon you. ²Your wealth has rotted and your cloak is moth-eaten, ³your gold and silver is covered with rust and its poison will be (for) evidence/testimony against you, and it will consume your flesh like fire. You hoarded (it) in the last days! ⁴Behold the wages of the worker who mowed your fields/estate that has been withheld⁽³⁵⁵⁾ by you cry

---

⁽³⁵³⁾Some manuscripts, perhaps those written by scribes who took this direct address as literally referring to adulteresses, added a reference to adulterers as well. The shorter reading that uses only the feminine form of the word is well supported by ℵ*, A, B and numerous others and is to be preferred. See Metzger, *Textual Commentary*, pp. 682-83.

⁽³⁵⁴⁾Some manuscripts (K, L, P and others) have *katōkēsen* ("dwells") here, from the more common verb *katoikeō*. The causative form *katōkisen*, however, is much better supported (𝔓⁷⁴, ℵ, A, B and numerous others), and since it is the rarer form it is likely to be original. See Metzger, *Textual Commentary*, p. 683.

⁽³⁵⁵⁾Two possibilities here have about equal weight in terms of manuscript support: A, B², P and some minuscules read *apesterēmenos* ("defraud") (Mal 3:5 may be echoed here if the Septuagint reading is the original one), while the rare word *aphysterēmenos* is attested by two strong witnesses (ℵ and B*). Metzger, *Textual Commentary*, p. 685, prefers the more common reading because the stronger term *defraud* occurs in a passage full of emotive language.

aloud, and the cries of those who reaped has come into the ears of the Lord Almighty.
⁵You lived in luxury upon the earth and you were pleasure loving/self-indulgent.
You have fattened yourselves/your hearts in the day of (your) slaughter!⁶ You con-
demned, you murdered the righteous (one)! Does he not actively resist/oppose you
(now)?

James 4 includes material that again likely draws on the Sermon on the Mount and other Jesus traditions. It has sufficient parallels with 1 Peter (esp. 1 Pet 4—5) to lead one to suspect either that 1 Peter is dependent on James or that both are using parenesis that was used widely in the early church. Either conclusion is possible, but since James is likely the earlier of these two documents, it is possible to envision a scenario in which Peter read this homily, since he was working in some of the Diaspora congregations to which James likely wrote (1 Pet 1:1).

Beginning in **James 4:1** James tells us the source of quarrels and fights in the Christian community. One can only suppose that he is speaking generally here, not of the world's struggles but of those within the church *(en hymin)*. The source of the problem is pleasures that are fighting within the "members" of a believer's body. *Hēdonōn* is better translated "pleasures" here because James elsewhere uses another word for "desires" (Jas 4:2). The relationship of the two is close, and James may have in mind desire for pleasures or perhaps pleasurable feelings that conflict with one another—the passion for gold and glory conflicts with the passion for God, for example.

One of the ways that James is ramping up the rhetoric is by resorting to the language of war and violence, and the contrast with the discussion immediately preceding about peace and peacemaking could hardly be starker.[356] *Polemos* (and related terms) normally refers to armed conflict (Rev 12:7, 17; 13:7; 16:14; 17:14; 19:11, 19; 20:8). James even speaks of their cravings being at war *(strateuomai)* within their bodily members *(melesin)*. It is perfectly clear from this last phrase that the terminology is being used in a metaphorical way, and the attempt to see here a reference to Christians being the victims of Jewish zealots or fighting in some conflict with Jews before or during the Jewish wars in the 60s is simply ignoring all of the rhetorical signals here, including the plain use of the phrase *within you*.[357] This language no more literally refers to something that has already happened than does the exclamation "adulteresses" in this context. It is thus a mistake to think that James is referring to a literal case of murder that has *already* transpired in James 4:2. Conjectured emendations of the word

---

[356]Plummer, *General Epistles*, p. 214.
[357]Against Martin, *James*, p. 144.

phoneuete ("kill") to *phthoneite* ("jealous") in **James 4:2**—first proposed by Erasmus—have no textual basis whatsoever and are completely unnecessary. The reference to murdering is natural in combination with the reference to coveting, as alluding to two of the Ten Commandments. The real sense of James 4:1-2b is given by William Brosend, who shows the structure of the sentences:[358]

A where comes war and where comes fighting among you?

B from your desires warring in your bodily members

C you long for something and have not

C' you murder and covet

B' but you are unable to obtain

A' you fight and make war

The war within the individual leads to envy and strife with others in the Christian community. This could lead to real violence, but James wisely shows where all this could lead. The internal source of community friction and factions and un-Christian and unwise behavior could lead to blows and worse if these sinful desires are allowed to play themselves out in human melodramas and tragedies.

The structure of James 4:2 is controversial, and Joseph Mayor provides the best understanding of the verse:

> In the present case it may be safely said that no sane writer, no one who had the slightest feeling for rhetorical effect (and St. James is both eminently sane and eminently rhetorical) could have used φονεύετε in the sense of μισεῖτε before ζηλοῦτε. There is no reason here to lay an exaggerated stress on the idea of hate, if nothing more than hate is intended: not only does it make a mere bathos of ζηλοῦτε, but it weakens the force of the following μάχεσθε καὶ πολεμεῖτε. . . .
>
> Can anyone doubt that the abrupt collocations of φονεύετε and μάχεσθε are employed to express results of what precedes, and that in the second series ζηλοῦτε καὶ οὐ δύνασθε ἐπιτυχεῖν correspond to ἐπιθυμεῖτε καὶ οὐκ ἔχετε in the first series? Unsatisfied desire leads to murder (as in the case of Naboth); disappointed ambition leads to quarreling and fighting.[359]

Desire can, of course, end in murder, as in the case of Naboth. It cannot be objected that this is too abrupt for James, since he is often abrupt, or that he could not mean literal murder, because he may mean that, even if indirectly, at

---

[358]Brosend, *James and Jude*, p. 108.
[359]Mayor, *James*, pp. 135-36.

James 5:6 (murder by starvation), and clearly at James 2:11 he was not speaking of a mere metaphorical use of hate. But James is talking about what *could* happen if things are allowed to run their course unchecked. He is not dealing with actual cases of murder in the congregation, which would have called for a much less anecdotal and much more direct and extended response than this[360] and, certainly as Mayor says, would not have led to putting the word *murder* before the word *jealous* in the complaint list! James appears to fear a catastrophe among Christians (cf. 1 Pet 4:15) who were vying for what they wanted. It is possible that this discussion harkens back to the rivalry and struggle mentioned in James 3 in regard to teaching positions and gathering a following. All three of the other New Testament occurrences of the term *machē* (which is related to the Greek word for sword, *machaira* [Mt 26:52]) refer to verbal quarrels or even inward anxiety (2 Cor 7:5; 2 Tim 2:23; Tit 3:9).[361] You covet, says James, but you cannot get what you want so you fight and quarrel for it. The more important points are these: (1) James is focusing on the starting point of all such quarrels and struggles, namely, what is going on in the heart of one or more persons and the desires, lusts and the like that are at war within the bodily members of such persons and (2) James is trying to nip potential disasters in the bud by unmasking their internal sources. First Peter 2:11, which may be indebted to this very passage and even be the earliest exegesis of it, says, "Dear friends, I urge you, as aliens and strangers in the world, to abstain from sinful desires, which war against your inner self/soul."

Luke Timothy Johnson fruitfully suggests that James may be indebted to passages in the *Testament of the Twelve Patriarchs* that deal with the same themes. For example, Simeon confesses after attempting to seize and kill his brother Joseph that "envy dominates the whole of a man's mind [and] keeps prodding him to destroy the one whom he envies" (*Testament of Simeon* 3.2-3). Johnson sums up helpfully:

> In addition to the coherent thematic framework provided James 3:13—4:10 by the Testaments as a whole, then, the *Testament of Simeon* offers eight separate points of similarity: (1) the explicit call to conversion [better: repentance]; (2) the synonymous use of ζῆλος and φθόνος; (3) the attribution of envy to a πνεῦμα which is a deceiver; (4) the tendency of envy toward murder; (5) the role of envy in generating societal unrest and war; (6) the turning from the evil spirit to God by prayer

---

Rightly Moo, *James*, p. 180 ("we still must wonder whether James would have been content with the little that he says here had the believers to whom he is writing actually been killing one another"); and p. 184 ("the best alternative is to take 'you kill' in its normal, literal sense, but as a hypothetical eventuality rather than an actual occurrence").

[361]Moo, *James*, p. 180; and Townsend, "James 4:1-4."

and mourning; (7) the giving of grace by God to those who turn from envy (or Beliar) and turn to the Lord; (8) the portrayal of envy's opposite as simplicity of soul and goodness of heart.[362]

Not all of these parallels are equally compelling but the general atmosphere or *Gestalt* of the two documents and the discussion of the internal struggle is much the same. James reflects a deep indebtedness to the literature of early Judaism or at least to its substance.

To some these verses will sound like the typical struggle between the haves and the have-nots, but James lives in a world of "limited good," that is, possessions are viewed as a zero-sum game—if you have it, I do not, and the only way for me to get it is to win it, take it, steal it or the like. In this behavior, Christians are acting just like the world (Jas 4:4), which does not recognize God. Furthermore, it is not the have-nots who are praying for more, but the haves, whose thirst for acquisition has not been slacked. The predators are the higher status persons with the power and muscle to take what they want. It is not the humble that need humbling here, it is the proud, the well-off, the rich, the covetous.[363] Why such bad behavior? "It derives from the premise that being depends on having, that identity and worth derive from what is possessed. In such a view, to have less is to be less: less worthy, real, or important. To have more is to be more. Fundamental to envy also is the conviction that humans exist in a closed system, a finite world of limited resources. There is only so much to go around. The world is a zero sum game. . . . The logic of envy moves towards competition for scarce resources."[364] These sorts of assumptions are fundamentally at odds with a belief in an all-powerful, omnibenevolent God who answers prayers, particularly when his creatures are in genuine need!

One other consideration of importance turns the interpretation of this first paragraph in the direction of the last paragraph in James 5:1-6. Throughout this discourse, James echoed things he has heard from previous wisdom literature, including from Sirach. And Sirach 34.21-22 may have some bearing on the interpretation here: "The bread of the needy is the life of the poor; he that defrauds him of it is a man of a blood [i.e., a murderer]. He that takes away his neighbor's living slays him *[phoneuōn]*; and he that defrauds the laborer of his hire is a blood-shedder." James 5:1-6 is certainly echoing some of this, but perhaps James 4:1-2 is already thinking along these lines.

[362]Johnson, "James 3:13—4:10," p. 345.
[363]Alonso-Schökel, "James 5:2 and 4:6," finds in Jas 4:6—5:6 a homily on Prov 3:34 warning the rich, through a series of images against exploiting the poor.
[364]Johnson, *James*, p. 288.

Aiteisthai in James 4:2 and *aiteite* in **James 4:3** appear to have the more specialized sense of "pray," not just "ask," and we should likely see Matthew 7:7-10 in the background here. James argues that receiving does not automatically or magically follow praying, if you do not pray rightly. His readers are asking for the wrong things, that is, money or other items that they can spend on their pleasures. James is apparently condemning a certain kind of hedonism here, that is, one who lives for and by pleasures or desires and is so egocentric that he or she asks only for what gratifies desires. It is no wonder, suggests James, that the answer to these prayers is no! Luke Timothy Johnson says that the ultimate perversion produced by envy is that it prompts a person to turn to God to satisfy his or her lusts or wicked desires: "The gift-giving God is here manipulated as a kind of vending machine precisely for purposes of self-gratification. . . . In this case, 'prayer' is a form of idolatry!"[365] If you ask for bread God will not give you a stone or a snake, but if you ask for a snake, the answer will be no (Mt 7:7-10). The phrase *dioti kakōs aiteisthe* explains why one does not receive: "Because you pray/ask wickedly/wrongly." Alfred Plummer makes the provocative comment: "The fulfilment of an unrighteous prayer is sometimes its most fitting punishment."[366]

James 4:4 begins abruptly and sharply: "Adulteresses!" This catches one's attention since up to now the form of direct address has been "brothers" or "dear brothers" or "brothers and sisters."[367] Used metaphorically of believers who are prostituting themselves to the world, the flesh and the devil (or to their pleasures), the term has an Old Testament background when Israel was called an adulteress (Is 1:21; 50:1; Jer 3:7-10; 13:27; Ezek 16:23-26; 23:45; Hos 2:5-7). In the New Testament the church is seen as feminine in relationship to God (Eph 5:22-23; Rev 21),[368] so infidelity could be called adultery as well. James, however, uses the plural to indicate that *individuals* within the church were selling out to the world and its pleasures. *Kosmos* cannot mean what it sometimes means in James (i.e., the world as God created it), but rather the fallen world that sinful humans and their institutions and practices have transformed. Peter Davids stresses: "Two diametrically opposed pairs are presented: friendship and enmity are used to underline the polar opposition between God and the world. Here is a radical *ethical* dualism of the type found in 1 Jn. 2:15-17 and elsewhere in the Johannine corpus. The world is not the created order or the earth, but the

---

[365]Ibid., p. 278.
[366]Plummer, *General Epistles*, p. 224.
[367]Moo, *James*, p. 186.
[368]Schmitt, "You Adulteresses."

whole system of humanity (its institutions, structures, values, and more) as organized without God."[369] We might say that *kosmos* is viewed here, as in John's Gospel (Jn 8:23; 12:31; cf. Jas 1:27), as the fallen world organized against God. There is no middle ground here. One is either friend of the world or friend of God. The first illustration that follows conveys the idea that God is requiring of believers their single-minded and wholehearted devotion. God yearns for them and for the spirit he caused to dwell in them. Accordingly, having divided loyalties, serving two masters, is unacceptable to God.

Something must be said about *hē philia* with the world. The ancient concept of friendship meant far more than just a feeling of being well disposed toward someone or something. Luke Timothy Johnson reminds us that the ancient ideal of friendship was close to what we today would say about a genuine marriage. Friendship involved sharing all things in a unity that involved both the spiritual and the physical.[370] True friends are *mia psychē* ("one soul") with each other (Euripides *Orestes* 1046; Aristotle *Nichomachean Ethics* 1168B). Doubtless some of this may be seen as attempted compensation for living in a world of arranged marriages, many of which seem to have been rather loveless in character, to judge from what little we know. But still, the ideal of true friendship in antiquity (David and Jonathan, Abraham and God—already mentioned by James) goes far beyond modern superficial concepts of friendship. Here James contrasts friendship with the wholehearted embracing of the fallen world and its values and predilections. This love is said to be "enmity with God," a deliberate rejecting of God and God's will. James puts things in black and white, to force decisions on those Christians who are too much in love with the world and its lifestyle.[371] Henry Parry Liddon's comments are on target:

> The world is human nature, sacrificing the spiritual to the material, the future to the present, the unseen and the eternal to that which touches the senses and perishes with time. The world is a mighty flood of thoughts, feelings, principles of action, conventional prejudices, dislikes, attachments, which have been gathering around human life for ages, impregnating it, impelling it, moulding it, degrading it. . . . According to his circumstances the same man acts upon the world, or in turn is acted on by it. And the world at different times wears different forms. Sometimes it is a solid compact mass, an organization of pronounced ungodliness. Sometimes it is a subtle, thin, hardly suspected influence, a power altogether airy and impalpable, which yet does most powerfully penetrate, inform, and shape human life.[372]

---

[369]Davids, *James*, p. 161 (emphasis added).
[370]Johnson, *James*, p. 279.
[371]For a fuller study, see Johnson, "Friendship with the World."
[372]Cited in Plummer, *General Epistles*, p. 230.

James 4:5 is notoriously difficult to decipher, indeed it may be the most difficult verse in the New Testament, and we may ask a bevy of questions about it:

1. Where does the quotation begin and end?

2. Where does this quotation come from?

3. Is *pneuma* the Holy Spirit, "breath/spirit" (i.e., the human animating principle God gave a person at birth; Jas 2:26) or an evil spirit or influence?

4. What is the subject of *epipothei*?

5. Is *pros phthonon* part of the title? And is it likely that it goes with what follows, since *hē graphē legei* usually introduces a quotation?

Taking these questions one at a time, let us first ask if the subject of *epipothei* is the Holy Spirit (i.e., "the Spirit he caused to live in us longs jealously"), then James fails to tell us what the Spirit yearns jealously *for*. While plenty of Old Testament texts describe a jealous God (Ex 20:5; 34:14), none use these precise words. We simply do not know where this quotation comes from, and happily it is the only example in the New Testament of a citation whose source is completely unknown.[373]

James does not elsewhere refer to the Holy Spirit in this letter, and if we take *pneuma* as human spirit then *epipothei* and *katōkisen* have the same subject—God. Since James has Genesis 1—2 in view in James 3, this may also be the case here. If so, then it refers to God's creating humanity in his image—causing his breath (spirit) or animating principle to dwell in the body he formed.

Peter Davids and James Hardy Ropes insist that this must be a verbatim quotation, but as 1 Corinthians 2:9 shows this need not be the case—it could be a more general allusion to Genesis 6:3-7 and Ex 20:5 used in a midrashic way.[374]

De after *meizona* in **James 4:6** likely indicates a contrast with the quotation and shows where James picks back up: God requires single-minded loyalty of all believers and longs for them to return to him, but God gives them more grace so believers may properly respond. Elsewhere in the New Testament the verb *epipotheō* and its cognates are used in a positive sense to refer to a longing or yearning, not a lusting (Rom 1:11; 2 Cor 5:2; 9:14; Phil 1:8; 2:26;

---

[373]One of the more popular extracanonical conjectures is that this refers to *Apocalypse of Moses* (= Greek version of the *Life of Adam and Eve*) 31; Moo, *James*, p. 190, says that the introductory phrase that identifies the quotation as coming from Scripture is always applied elsewhere in the New Testament to the canonical Old Testament books. Even less convincing is the suggestion of Laws, "Does Scripture Speak in Vain?," who renders this verse: "Is pious longing the proper manner of the soul's desire?" and sees an allusion to verses like Ps 42:1 and Ps 84:2.

[374]Davids, *James*, p. 162; Ropes, *James*, pp. 263-64; and Mayor, *James*, p. 140.

1 Thess 3:6; 2 Tim 1:4; 1 Pet 2:2).[375] The sense then is that, like a parent, God jealously and protectively longs for our human heart, for the very spirit that God put in us to be loyal to God. "God is a jealous God, and the Divine love is a jealous love; it brooks no rival. And when His Spirit takes up its abode in us it cannot rest until it possesses us wholly, to the exclusion of all alien affections."[376]

A second quotation, in James 4:6, is from Proverbs 3:34 and is also found in 1 Peter 5:5-6. Those who humble themselves and submit totally to God receive grace, indeed "more grace." Those who exalt themselves are opposed by God and may be called God's enemy, because they strive to take God's place in their own lives.

James 4:7 seems to begin a series of stock exhortations.[377] James is no fatalist; he believes that Satan can be resisted and will flee in the face of such resistance (cf. 1 Pet 5:8-9). This is the only place in the Bible where Satan is said to flee if resisted. He does *not* have dominion over the believer unless the believer submits to him willingly. Here again, James suggests that the ultimate source of personal evil is suprapersonal and supernatural—that is, the devil (so also Mt 4:1-11; Lk 22:31; Jn 13:2, 27). "Every Christian is endowed with sufficient power to withstand Satan. . . . There is a manifest and telling antithesis between the devil who yields to opposition, and the God who responds to invitation."[378] William Brosend is right that these verses echo Psalm 24:3-4: "Who shall ascend the hill of the Lord? And who shall stand in his holy place? Those who have clean hands and pure hearts, who do not lift up their hearts to what is false, and do not swear deceitfully."[379]

James 4:8 is dealing with the process of repentance, and we may perhaps see here a sermonic fragment of an exhortation to proselytes. Washing of hands was a symbolic ritual indicating the cleansing out of the old leaven. When James says draw near to God, he is addressing Christians and is not suggesting that acceptance by God or initial salvation for the nonbeliever can be achieved by following these steps. James speaks too often of God's grace given and received to suggest a quid pro quo here. Rather, he is talking about rapprochements between a wayward believer and the Lord. *Dipsychos* was seen in James 1:8 as referring to the double-minded or wavering person, Mr. Facing Both Ways—the Janus figure. James knows perfectly well that "the results of intimacy with the

---

[375]Plummer, *General Epistles*, p. 234.
[376]Ibid., p. 235.
[377]Davids, *James*, pp. 165-66.
[378]Plummer, *General Epistles*, p. 240.
[379]Brosend, *James and Jude*, p. 112.

world cannot be undone in a day,"[380] but progress can be made only if someone repeatedly calls the young Christian to account. Once again James seems to be familiar with material in the *Testament of the Twelve Patriarchs*, for fleeing the devil and drawing near to God are juxtaposed in *Testament of Dan* 6.2. While I quite agree that the subject here is God drawing near to repentant believers, it is saying too much to conclude that this material could not also apply to God's approach to the lost.[381]

James 4:9 is not a description of how Christians must always be solemn or puritanical; it refers to the conduct that befits repentance and acknowledgement of sin. Pheme Perkins puts it this way: "The turn from laughter to weeping (v. 9) must be understood in the context of wisdom literature. Fools delight in doing wrong (Prov. 10:23; Sir. 21:18-20; 27:13). James is not suggesting that the righteous should go about in a state of morbid depression over their sins. . . . If such people turn to God, they discover that the things that previously gave them joy are evidence of the distance that separated them from God."[382]

James 4:10 clearly indicates that self-humbling leads to God lifting up, but the converse follows if someone exalts themselves. It is right to see here echoes of Luke 6:25 (laughter turning to weeping) and Luke 14:11 (humble being exalted). The author of 1 Peter may again be indebted to what is said here because the same quotation of Proverbs 3:34 occurs in 1 Peter 5:5, followed by the exhortation: "Humble yourselves therefore, under God's mighty hand, that he may lift you up in due time."[383]

James 4:11, which begins the second subsection in the third elaboration of themes, provides the corollary subject of speech: slander. The discussion begins with an imperative and the term *brothers*, which is surprising after having just called them "adulteresses"! Yet, as Pheme Perkins points out, a line of thinking probably links this section with what immediately precedes it.[384] *Testament of Simeon* 4.4-7 makes love of others the result of driving out the spirit of envy/jealousy. That James is not likely speaking here about just any kind of criticism should be obvious since he is plenty critical at various points in this discourse and presumably saw no inconsistency. The key verb here, *katalaleō,* and its cognates are relatively rare in the New Testament (Rom 1:30; 2 Cor 12:20; 1 Pet 2:1, 12; 3:16; cf. Ps 50:20; 101:5). The literal meaning of this verb is "to speak against"

---

[380]Plummer, *General Epistles*, p. 239.

[381]Against Moo, *James*, p. 193.

[382]Perkins, *Peter, James and Jude*, p. 126.

[383]I will deal more thoroughly with the intertextual echoes between James and 1 Peter in *Letters and Homilies for Hellenized Christians, Volume 2*.

[384]Perkins, *Peter, James and Jude*, p. 128; and Johnson, "James 3:13—4:10," pp. 344-45.

(Prov 20:13; Wisdom of Solomon 1.11), but the translation "to speak evil" likely goes too far.[385] James simply prohibits this behavior on several grounds. (1) To speak against a brother is to speak against the law, to judge a brother is to judge the law. The law of loving neighbor (he likely has in mind the royal or supreme law of Lev 19:18 mentioned in Jas 2—3) implicitly rules out such a judgmental attitude and such judgmental or slanderous speech.[386] (2) To sit in judgment of the law is ipso facto not to keep or obey it, for one must submit to it to do the latter, and in James 2:8-11 there is an obligation to keep the whole law. (3) There is but one lawgiver, God, not two; thus to judge brother and law is to usurp God's function and place—God alone is able to fulfill the task of law: giving and carrying out its blessings and curses, saving or destroying.

James 4:12 makes likely that James was referring to the law about the neighbor: "Who are you to judge your neighbor *[plēsion]*?" This passage draws a connection between God as lawgiver (the word *nomothetēs* occurs only here in the New Testament; cf. Ps 9:20) and God as judge. The person who laid down and knows the law intimately is in the best position to judge whether someone has violated it. Believers are not in such a position. William Brosend points out that the phrase *lawgiver and judge*, like the phrase *to save and to destroy*, encapsulates the roles of God from the beginning of salvation history in the exodus-Sinai event (when the law was first given) to its end at the last judgment.[387] For James, as for Jesus, the heart of that law at the human level was the command to love neighbor as self—and how much more one's fellow believer. The ethic that undergirds this entire discourse—and indeed the Sermon on the Mount—is that central command to love God and neighbor.[388] This ethic most shapes James's vision of what the Christian community ought to be like. The reason that judging one's fellow believer is a matter of judging the law itself is presumably because it is a violation of Leviticus 19:18 as well as a matter of setting oneself over rather than under the law's scrutiny. If one is slandering a brother one is not loving them. We should probably see Leviticus 19:16, which speaks against slander, behind the beginning of this subunit, which immediately precedes the passage (Lev 19:18) alluded to at the end of this subunit.[389] There is a delicate balance here, for if what one says about a brother is true, Jesus requires that one say it in person—not to others. This is speaking the truth in love, rather than "speak-

[385]Brosend, *James and Jude*, pp. 117-18.
[386]For an interesting application of this advice, see John Wesley's sermon "The Cure of Evil Speaking."
[387]Brosend, *James and Jude*, pp. 120-22.
[388]Johnson, "Use of Leviticus 19," ably demonstrates this point.
[389]Moo, *James*, p. 197; and Martin, *James*, p. 163.

ing against" the brother, and so is not a violation of Leviticus 19:18. These points are often missed because the rhetorical structure here is overlooked. Here is a brief outline of the way this complex enthymeme works:

imperative: do not speak against one another (i.e., brothers and sisters)

reason: the one speaking against/judging the brother or sister is judging the law

suppressed premise: only the lawgiver can evaluate and use the law to judge persons

result of judging/speaking against others: you are not a doer but a judge of the law

suppressed premise: you have usurped the role of God!

affirmation: there is one lawgiver and judge, who is able to save or destroy

rhetorical question as conclusion: who are you to judge your neighbor?[390]

Furthermore, James has already made the point at James 2:13 that mercy triumphs over judgment when God is the judge. The implication is that even if one is dealing with another believer's sin and is not guilty of slander, one still needs to remember that the heart of the law, as seen by Jesus, is love and mercy. James would not have us rank ourselves with the one called "the accuser of the brothers" in Revelation 12:10, and he does not require that the audience have no uncharitable thoughts about their brothers or sisters, though that would be a good thing as well. He is concerned here, as before, with speech. Even if one cannot control one's thoughts about others, one need not speak slander.[391] "As always in James, the theological statement serves as warrant for moral exhortation: it is because God alone has power of life and death that God alone has the right to reveal the law and judge by the law. Any human seizure of that right—especially in secret—is revealed as pitiful pretension."[392]

James 4:13-17 turns to the realm of business and business planning, which James describes adequately enough. Traveling merchants were plentiful during the imperial age, and since the Pax Romana was generally in place they could go to most places throughout the empire and sell their wares. In an elaborate shrinelike tomb near the city gate of Hierapolis, a deceased person (Flavius Zeugsus) brags on his tombstone that he made over forty sailing journeys to Rome and back successfully on business. James has precisely these kinds of persons in mind: people with relative high status, business capital and a business

---

[390]Brosend, *James and Jude*, p. 120, rightly sees some of this but does not state the suppressed minor premises, which are what make the logic work here.

[391]Plummer, *General Epistles*, pp. 259-60.

[392]Johnson, *James*, p. 307.

plan. The problem is, they did not factor God or mortality into the equation—two not inconsequential factors.[393]

Neither James nor Jesus is opposed to necessary planning or honest business, but they are opposed to leaving God and his will out of such plans and calculations. This criticism is leveled at the attitude and orientation of the person who is heedless of his or her vulnerability and status before God, coupled with an arrogance about being able to accomplish his or her purposes unhindered by anything and without aide.

Age nyn ("come now") in **James 4:13** indicates a new subject for discussion and debate. While the same construction appears again at James 5:1, which may imply that we should see similarities between these two paragraphs, the very fact that the construction is used twice implies that we are dealing with two different, though perhaps related, subjects and that the phrase serves to mark off what came before from what follows. This phrase is found in the diatribe (Epictetus *Discourses* 3.24, 40) and elsewhere in Greek literature, going all the way back to Homer (cf. Judg 19:6; Is 43:6).

In the New Testament era, one frequently had to become a traveling merchant to make money before hoping to settle down in Palestine or elsewhere. James imagines a merchant pointing to a map and saying to his partner, "Let us go to such and such a city." The phrase *eis tēnde tēn polin* makes quite clear that James is not targeting some specific notorious well-known example, but on the other hand this is not a purely hypothetical discussion. James knows that these sorts of plans go on, even by Christian merchants. The problem is the same as the problem in the parable of the rich fool in Luke 12:16-21, which may well be in the background here. The merchant does not consider that today and tomorrow are in God's hands. He is oblivious to what God's will might be in regard to his going or not going, doing or not doing. He operates on the assumption that he can accomplish what he intends, without God, and he does not expect death to intervene or any other obstacles to stop him. His confidence level is not low: the speech of the businessman concludes with, "We will be making money" (literally "we will gain"), which could be better rendered, "We will be making a profit."

The brief metaphor in **James 4:14** indicates how transient and ephemeral is

[393] On ancient traveling merchants and their comings and goings from Israel, see Maynard-Reid, *Poverty and Wealth in James*, pp. 68-80. I differ with his equation of those addressed here with those spoken of in Jas 5:1-6, who seem more likely to be non-Christians. This is an important point, as it suggests that James is not simply condemning the making of money by Christians; the issue is the arrogant and self-sufficient rather than godly attitude, coupled with the failure to do good (Jas 3:17).

human life: it is like smoke or mist—here today, gone tomorrow; seen now, disappearing soon thereafter. This is a common observation in wisdom and prophetic literature (Prov 27:1; Eccles 1; Sirach 11.18-19; Wisdom of Solomon 2.4; 5.14). Hosea 13:3 says that idolaters "shall be like the morning mist, or like the dew that goes away early." This probably echoes what James already said of the rich in James 1:10-11, in which case we are probably meant to see this paragraph as preparation for the final salvo in James 5:1-6, where the rich take their lumps.[394] Those who would build something more lasting must build within the divine architect's plans and will. The godly attitude is always prefaced with "if the Lord wills." The idea of God's will and a believer's conformity to it is well known in Judaism and Christianity, but also in Greek thought: "if the gods will or are propitious" was a common phrase in the Greco-Roman world. The context here gives it more biblical content, as does its monotheism.

This paragraph surely indicates that at least some merchants among the Jewish Christian communities in the Diaspora needed an exhortation like this. It is not purely hypothetical, but addresses a possible problem, based on James's knowledge of the members of these churches. This is in no way surprising. For example, the remains of an elaborate and ornate synagogue in Sardis date to near the biblical period and reveal the considerable wealth of a good deal of the Jewish community in that city. There were well-to-do Jews in many cities of the empire, as seen in both texts and inscriptions from the period. In addition, even some synagogue leaders converted to Christianity (Acts 18; 1 Cor 1). It is no surprise, then, that some rich Jewish Christian merchants are in the congregations that James is addressing.

I am in full agreement with those who reject the idea that James is talking about non-Christians here. Douglas Moo says: "James chastises these merchants for failing to look at life from a Christian perspective. . . . James would hardly address non-Christians in this way."[395] James could not address non-Christians in these letters unless they were visitors in one or another of these congregations. We also need to avoid thinking of these persons as traveling salesmen who work for others and are not usually rich. James is thinking of a person who runs his own business, sets his own agenda and salary and travels to many different places throughout the Roman Empire.[396] Those who could afford it could travel with some speed on land by horse or horsedrawn carriage or in the Mediterranean by boat. Between the 10% of the population that were rich and the

---

[394]Brosend, *James and Jude*, p. 123.
[395]Moo, *James*, p. 201.
[396]On travel in the empire, see Casson, *Travel in the Ancient World*.

10% that were absolutely poor lay everyone else, including most of the merchant class, though some of them became rich.[397]

Seneca, a famous Roman Stoic philosopher and advisor to Nero, provides the interesting tale of Cornelius Senecio, a Roman knight (and so not a patrician or an ordinary pleb):

> He who was venturing investment by land and sea, who had also entered public life and left no type of business untried, during the very realization of financial success and during the very onrush of the money that flowed into his coffers, was snatched from the world! . . .
>
> How foolish it is to set out one's life, when one is not even owner of the morrow! O what madness it is to plot out far-reaching hopes! To say: "I will buy and build, loan and call in money, win titles of honor, and then, old and full of years, I will surrender myself to a life of ease." . . .
>
> We plan distant voyages and long-postponed home-comings after roaming over foreign shores . . . and all the while death stands by our side. (*Letters* 101)

Obviously these tales were common and James was drawing on a familiar scenario.

James is not asking the audience in **James 4:15** to simply recognize that they are mortal and that life is transitory and vulnerable. He is asking that they realize that God is in control and that therefore the proviso for any plan must always be "if it is God's will," an expression even used by pagans (Plato *Alcibiades* 1.135D). This means that things that are clearly not God's will as revealed in God's word should never be attempted or put into the plan. Even the lives of the well-to-do merchants are still in the hands of God. This proviso has come to be called "the Jacobean condition," but "your will be done" is already present in the Lord's Prayer and elsewhere (Mt 6:10; 26:42; Acts 18:21; Rom 1:10; 15:32; 1 Pet 3:17).[398] God's will encompasses various things. The phrase in question reads, "If it is the Lord's [probably God rather than Christ] will, *we will live* and will do this or that." In God's hands are not merely the issues of life, but life itself. The phrase *will of God* or *will of the Lord* is not found in the Septuagint, but this expression is not uncommon in the New Testament ("will of God" in Mk 3:35; Rom 12:2; 1 Cor 1:1; Heb 10:36; "will of the Father" in Mt 7:21; 12:50; 18:14; 21:31; "will of the one who sent me" in Jn 4:34; 5:30). It appears that Jesus may have brought this phrase to the forefront of discussion among early Jews, and James is following his lead.

James 4:16 rules out all arrogant boasting by believers because it is not

---

[397]On these estimates, see Maynard-Reid, *Poverty and Wealth in James*, p. 74.
[398]Moo, *James*, p. 204.

merely obnoxious but also evil—exalting the creature as if humans were the creators of their own destiny. While those who boasted about their profits or wealth made in business are possibly in view,[399] we must see the very business plan itself as something of a boast: it assumes that travel to the city in question will be safe; it assumes that circumstances and health will allow them to stay in that city for a year; it assumes that profits will be made—and all these assumptions are made without so much as a "if God permits." It is easy to see the connection between this verse and what comes before it.[400] The term *alazoneia* indicates airs of arrogance or insolent self-confidence and self-assurance that manifests itself in arrogant speech. The *alazōn* was the braggart and a stock character in Greco-Roman literature.[401] What James objects to is neither the travel nor the business nor even the making of a profit, but rather the arrogance of planning such activities without even taking into consideration God and mortality and, we might add, without consulting God in prayer about such things (as James has already said in this chapter).[402] To assume that one can control the events of the future and so work out this business plan is presumptuous, to say the least.

James 4:17 should be seen as a summary statement not unlike those in James 1:18; 2:13; 3:18. While it may be an isolated proverb or maxim, using the third-person singular verb, since James added *oun* ("therefore"), he sees this sentence as a proper conclusion to this entire paragraph.[403] This is a very clear reference to sins of omission: failing to do the good that one knows one can do when a situation presents itself is seen as a serious moral issue—as a sin (*Testament of Simeon* 6.1). While this reminds us of the earlier example of the rich person who says to the poor man "be warm" but does nothing to help, here James may be alluding to the failure to pray and place one's plans into God's hands.

James 4:13-17 then should be seen as a bridge passage paving the way for what comes in James 5:1-6. Knowledge of God's will is not enough to avoid sin. One must also act upon that knowledge. If this is seen by James as a summary of what immediately precedes (as *oun* suggests), then Peter Davids may be right to say: "Thus it may well be that while on one level James is warning merchants about forgetting God in their business, on a deeper level he is reflecting on ideas such as those in Lk. 12:13-21 and viewing the whole motive of gathering wealth rather than doing good with it (i.e. sharing it with the poor) as a failure to follow

---

[399]Perkins, *Peter, James and Jude*, p. 130.
[400]Plummer, *General Epistles*, pp. 263-66.
[401]See the discussion in Johnson, *James*, p. 297.
[402]Moo, *James*, p. 202.
[403]Davids, *James*, p. 174.

known standards of Christian guidance, i.e. the total tradition about sharing with others."[404] Luke Timothy Johnson puts it this way:

> James' critique cuts deeper than that, however, for he challenges the very view of
> reality assumed by such "friends of the world." Their speech betrays a perception
> of the world as a closed system of limited resources, available to their control and
> manipulation, yielding to their market analysis and sales campaign. When James
> recommends that they say "If the Lord wills it, we will both live and do this thing,
> or that thing," he is not recommending an empty piety, but a profoundly different
> understanding of reality. He challenges their construal with the perception given
> by faith and friendship with God: that the world is an open system, created by God
> at every moment, and infinitely rich in the resources provided by God for humans
> to exist and prosper in cooperation, rather than in competition. And within *this* un-
> derstanding, their pretension and boasting is not the symptom simply of foolish
> heedlessness. It is the symptom of something evil (*ponēra;* 4.16).[405]

James 5:1-6 deals with a somewhat different group of people than those in James 4:13-17, though we may note the similar opening address: "Come now." While James 5:1-6 may be dealing with a subset of those in James 4:13-17—trav-eling merchants who managed to become rich—James 5:1-6 apparently deals with the wealthy landed class who have *choras* ("fields or estates"), and they are not likely Christians or entrepreneurs/business persons.[406] Joseph Mayor says: "The terms chosen have reference to the different kinds of wealth, σέσηπεν to corn and other products of the earth, σητόβρωτα to rich fabrics, κατίωται to metals; giving examples of corruption arising from an external cause (the moth), or internal, whether deep-seated rottenness or superficial rust."[407] These rich people are apparently sedentary, not traveling merchants, and they are known for their agricultural estates, rich clothes and accumulation of goods and silver coins. James stresses that such people are already on the way to eschatological judgment and certainly should not be admired or emulated or served. Further-more, a key rhetorical device signals that we are not dealing with the same group of people in James 4:13-17 and James 5:1-6. The former paragraph man-ifests the diatribal style, while the latter is more like a woe oracle. What this sug-gests, rhetorically, is that the former group are those whom James thinks he has and can still have a dialogue with, while the latter are not.[408]

From a rhetorical standpoint, an orator knew quite well that what one said near

---

[404]Ibid.
[405]Johnson, *James*, pp. 307-8 (emphasis original).
[406]Ropes, *James*, p. 288.
[407]Mayor, *James*, p. 154.
[408]Moo, *James*, p. 210.

or at the end of a discourse would be what was left ringing in the audience's ears, since this document was meant to be read aloud to these congregations and prob- ably few of them would be able to read and peruse this material later, treating it as a written text. This in turn puts a premium on a discourse's final argumentation and the peroration that follows it. James's addressing the rich and the issue of riches at several points throughout the discourse and now returning to it in a major and polemical way indicates that this was his most important concern for the Jewish Christians he was addressing, susceptible as they were to persuasion, persecution, manipulation by those in their cities and towns more powerful and influential than most of their members. The temptation by Christian merchants and others to become clients of such people or emulate them must have been considerable. Commentators understandably have a hard time seeing how James 5:1-6 comports with the gentler tone of James 4:13-17, but the answer is not that difficult: James is speaking about a different group of people here, the non-Christian rich who in some cases seem to have been oppressing some of the audience.

One must also note the connection to the original sequence in the book. Discussion of the rich in James 1:9-11 is followed by a blessing *(makarios)* in James 1:12 on those who persevere through the test. Similarly the subject of the rich in James 5:1-6 is followed in James 5:7 by an exhortation to patience *(makrothymēsate)* until the Lord returns. The question once again becomes, who are these rich people: Christians, pagans or Jews? Whoever they are, James has saved his most stinging critique for the very end of the discourse, where he concludes the elaboration of major themes and prepares to offer a final summary peroration.

James 5:1 starts out in rousing fashion as James summons the rich to view in advance their coming demise. This beginning is not unlike the woe oracles found in Hosea 5:1; Amos 4:1; 5:1 (cf. Mt 23; Rev 18). The knowledgeable in the audience will know that they are in for some heavy rhetorical weather. The rich are invited to view their funeral in advance. They should begin to weep *(klausate*—aorist) and wail *(ololyzontes*—participle with the force of the imperative) because of the miseries that are heading right their way. These two Greek words are onomatopoetic—they sound like what they connote, reminding us again of the oral and rhetorical character of the document. Isaiah 13:6 speaks of wailing because the Day of the Lord is near, and this is certainly what James has in view. *Ololyzontes* is used exclusively in the Septuagint when the subject is God's judgment on those who have committed apostasy (Ezek 21:17; Hos 7:14; Amos 8:3; Zech 11:2; Is 10—24 passim).[409] The word *talaipōria* ("misery") occurs in the

---

[409]Johnson, *James*, pp. 298-99; and Moo, *James*, p. 211.

New Testament only here and at Romans 3:16.

James 5:2-3 expands on the plight of the rich: rot and rust and ruin have already attacked their assets and they do not even know it! William Brosend notes the perfect tense verses here ("has rotted," "has become mildewed," "has rusted").[410] Since James goes on to speak of the same things using future tenses ("their rust will witness against you"), these perfect tenses indicate that it is a done deal—the judgment is so certain that one can say that it has already begun.[411] All that the rich put store in and put up in store has only stored up wrath and fire for them. Brosend is probably right that the sense of the phrase *will eat your flesh like fire* is to draw an analogy with the rust: just as the rust will destroy their coins, so the fire of judgment will eat their flesh—will eat the rich (Judith 16.17)![412] James knows that gold and silver do not rust, but they do tarnish and require polish (Sirach 29.10), which is likely what he has in mind. If coins were made with impure silver or gold, they were subject to corrosion of a sort. James also talks about money standing as "evidence against you" in the last days, and Luke 12:23 may well be in the background here.

James 5:3b is very vivid: "You have laid up treasure in the last days." If this means "you have stored up wealth in the last days," then James is accusing them of hoarding in the eschatological age, which is precisely when such means of security will be of no use at all. They may have thought they were laying funds aside for their golden years, their own last days, but they were hoarding things that would end up testifying against them in the last days![413] The teaching of James's brother contrasted laying up treasures in heaven with laying up treasures on earth where moth and rust do destroy (Mt 6:19-20; cf. Sirach 29.10-12 on laying up treasures according to the commandments—that is, almsgiving is a laying up of treasure).[414] But James takes the image a step further by talking about laying up treasure for the judgment. The image is of a heavenly accounting of deeds, and the negative columns in ledgers are full. "Here he condemns the rich for living in 'the last days' . . . but nevertheless living as if they had all the time in the world and their judgment was not near."[415] They were living as though there was no tomorrow, to borrow another colloquial phrase.

---

[410]Brosend, *James and Jude*, p. 132.

[411]Martin, *James*, p. 177.

[412]Brosend, *James and Jude*, pp. 132-33.

[413]Johnson, *James*, p. 301. The remark becomes highly sarcastic or ironic in this case.

[414]Perkins, *Peter, James and Jude*, p. 131.

[415]Brosend, *James and Jude*, p. 134.

A CLOSER LOOK
The Social Setting of James Once More

As the possible *Sitz im Leben* out of which this material could have been written, let us suppose that James is writing at a time when Jewish persecution of Christians had or was increasing. James will have known the expulsion of Jewish Christians from Rome in 49 and the confiscation of their property as they were expelled. Paul speaks of "the churches of Judea who suffered from the Jews who killed the Lord Jesus and the prophets and drove us out" (1 Thess 2:14-15), and Paul's own letters suggest that persecution is happening to the audience. This happened early on, for Paul wrote this passage in 1 Thessalonians around 51-52 in reference to previous events. It is quite clear that Christians were still visiting synagogues and proselytizing during this period and before, and it is also clearly likely that Jews were reciprocating—if for no other reason than to check and see if heresy was on the loose among Jewish followers of Jesus.

The imprisonment of Peter and the stoning of Stephen provide evidence of problems brewing in the house churches in Jerusalem. We are told clearly of how Paul went into church meetings and dragged off Christians. Thus, everything converges on the possibility if not the likelihood that the "rich" visiting the church were Jews, perhaps even Jewish spies (which would make the reference to Rahab in James 2:25-26 all the more pointed), possibly some who were sent by the temple priests or Sadducees to check out these Christian troublemakers.

This might suggest that James 2:5-7 is talking about rich (Jews) dragging Christians off to (religious) court, though pagan court would also do if the point was to get Christians into hot water. It would also explain the uncertainty expressed by James as to whether these visitors were to be seen as believers, for the synagogue and the church had not yet irrevocably split (but Jas 2:7 suggests that they were coming into the church meeting and blaspheming Jesus' name either in words or by their treatment of poor Christians). Famine and food were serious problems for these early Jewish Christians, and Paul was anxious to take up a collection for them (cf. Josephus *Jewish War* 5.424-28 on the fate of the rich Jews around 70).

If James is writing out of, rather than to, such a situation (although he sends the letter to those outside Palestine because he wants them to know about it), this helps to explain the generalness of the letter. The "poor" is simply a designation for poor Christians—who apparently constituted about 99% of the church in Judea and Jerusalem. We must also reckon with a few rich Jewish converts, which no doubt upset the Jewish hierarchy and hurt their pocketbooks. If then this is a clash between rich Jews (comparatively speaking) and poor Jewish Christians, we can understand the reason and nature of the apocalyptic and eschatological denunciation in James 5:1-6.

James, perhaps excerpting some of his sermons preached against such rich persecutors, includes this material in his letter to warn those outside Jerusalem of similar possibilities and problems (in Acts 5:17-42; 8:1-3; 13:49-51 Jews incite the well-to-do to persecute Christians in the Diaspora; cf. Acts 19:23-41). Perhaps James 5:1-6 is juxtaposed with James 4:13-17 because James does not want Christian merchants to end up like these wealthy Jews. The eschatological flavor here comports with having moved from parenetic exhortation to eschatological and prophetic denunciation.

The strident tone of this section exceeds, for the most part, what we saw before in this letter. This is rather like the curse sanctions in Luke 6:24-26, and that passage is probably in the background here. The tone is of impending doom for the rich. It is so near that the author can stress the irony of these rich having stored up for a future that will never be because they did it in the last days. But what rhetorical and social function did this woe oracle serve if it is addressed to Jewish Christians, most of whom were not rich?

Most commentators think that the warnings about coming eschatological judgment serve to comfort the poor and oppressed in the audience, and there may be some truth to this. The warning may also have been meant to warn off Christian merchants and other well-to-do Christians from following the examples of such rich persons. But there is a further function in this section: a sanction has been placed on the entire Jewish Christian community not to emulate or encourage or enter into reciprocity relationships with people whose lifestyles are self-destructive spiritually now and physically later at the judgment. James reminds that these are the people who defraud the poor day laborers (and perhaps even defrauded some in the audience), so why would one want to be like or live like them? James 5:6 adds a further point: these are the kind of people who murder righteous people, indeed who murdered "the righteous one," which may well refer to Jesus. In short, they embody the antiwisdom that James has been preaching against throughout the sermon, having made quite clear that "friendship with the world" amounts to renouncing one's Christianity and going to war with God. Lastly, why would the audience want to live in a fashion that will lead to them being judged and sent straight to Hades? There is nothing here to envy. James wants the audience to see the eternal consequences of such a behavior more than he wants to comfort or console those who do not live like this, indeed are the victims of such lifestyles of the rich.[416]

---

[416]Moo, *James*, p. 210.

James 5:4 begins with *idou* ("listen up"), as once again James demands the complete attention of the audience. James 5:4-6 contains at least four indictments of the rich: (1) they are holding back wages from farm workers and harvesters; (2) they are living in luxury and pleasure; (3) they are fattening themselves (their hearts) up for slaughter and (4) they are condemning and murdering "the righteous one."[417] The first and the fourth of these are wrongs done to others, but notably the other two are in essence wrongs done to themselves by living a luxurious lifestyle while defrauding their own workers.

That the rich withheld the wages of poor day laborers working for them and hoarded an accumulation for themselves speaks of their own corruption. This may echo Leviticus again: "You shall not keep for yourselves the wages of a laborer until morning" (Lev 19:13). James can call rich non-Christian Jews to account with some force, since Leviticus 19 has moral authority over them and they know that they must obey it. James is not concerned about only the transitory nature of earthly goods or life, but the power of hoarded earthly goods to destroy human kindness and duty and character and to corrupt the whole person. The rich have lived in luxury, in self-indulgence upon the earth, and what they spent on themselves they took from those to whom they owed it.

The rich are said in **James 5:5** to have fattened themselves up, but woe will come to them since they did it in the very day of slaughter and will not be able to enjoy it. The image is of an animal, like a cow, fattened for slaughter. Quite clearly the eschatological tone comes in James 5:4, where we are told that the cries of the sowers and reapers have come into the ears of the Almighty Lord, with the implication that he has heard them and is about to come and act on this knowledge. The day of slaughter here is yet another image for the coming day of judgment, and unwittingly the rich have fattened themselves up for that day and they will be the victim. This may echo *1 Enoch* 94.6—99.16, which also serves up woes on the rich: "Woe to you, you rich ones, for you have trusted in your riches, and from your riches you shall depart. . . . You have become ready for the day of slaughter."

In **James 5:6**, however, the poor workers are the victims and the rich have condemned and murdered them—if "the righteous" refers to "them"—the victims. This may echo Sirach 34.25-27: "The bread of the needy is the life of the poor; whoever deprives them of it is a man of blood. To take away a neighbor's living is to murder him; to deprive an employee of his wages is to shed blood."[418] *Katedikasate* may refer back to James 2:6 and the dragging of Chris-

---

[417]Brosend, *James and Jude*, p. 134.

[418]See the discussion in Maynard-Reid, *Poverty and Wealth in James*, pp. 93-94.

tians into court, and "murdering" may refer to the sin of failing to love and feed their own workers—never mind their neighbors—and thus indirectly killing them by a deliberate act of selfishness and withholding of wages due, withholding it from those who are not opposing them, but helping them. All this makes good sense of the passage; however, since we have an eschatological context, something more may also be in view. Does *ton dikaion* refer to "the righteous poor" as a collective noun? If so, it would fall in line with texts like Psalm 37:32 ("the wicked watch for the righteous and seek to kill them") and Amos 2:6 ("they sell the righteous for silver, and the needy for a pair of sandals"). Or could it refer to a particular individual—namely Jesus?[419]

A CLOSER LOOK

The Use of the Terms "Lord" and "Righteous One" in James 5

A frequent lament in regard to the homily of James is that there is no Christology in it. Even if we had only James 1:1 and James 2:1, this would be false, since James 2:1 has considerable substance to it. In addition, there is submerged Christology throughout, as James draws on the teaching of Jesus as authoritative for his communities.[420] Furthermore, few scholars doubt a reference to the parousia in James 5. But is there more? Richard Longenecker certainly thinks so, and I must interact with him at this juncture and with the work of Andrew Chester on the theology of James and conjectures from several others.

It is possible that *ton dikaion* in James 5:6 is not a collective singular term for "the righteous" but rather a reference to Jesus, the righteous one. Longenecker argues for this identification of Jesus here.[421] He points to Acts 22:13-16 (cf. Acts 3:14-15; 7:52; 9:17), which may indicate that the term *righteous one* was used in the earliest days of primitive Christianity of Jesus (1 Jn 2:1, 29; 3:7;[422] 1 Pet 3:18). He concludes: "As such, it was most appropriate in the Christian mission to Jews; and, to judge, by the New Testament distribution of the title, was distinctive to early Jewish Christianity."[423] We know the Jewish tendency to avoid the direct divine name, and Jewish Christians probably used such circumlocutions of Jesus as well. Longenecker suggests that James 2:7 re-

---

[419]Commentators (e.g., Martin, *James*, p. 182) who think that James was written or at least redacted by disciples of James after his death see here a reference to James himself, who was known as James the Just/Righteous. The problem with this suggestion is that nothing in the document itself prepares us for such an allusion here, whereas Christ is mentioned again in this very chapter. See Moo, *James*, pp. 218-19.

[420]Witherington, *Many Faces of the Christ*.

[421]Longenecker, *Christology of Early Jewish Christianity*, pp. 46-47.

[422]Witherington, *Letters and Homilies*, 1.499-500.

[423]Longenecker, *Christology of Early Jewish Christianity*, p. 47.

fers to blaspheming the name of Jesus.[424] *Kyriou sabaōth* in James 5:4 possibly refers to Jesus as Lord of the hosts (angels) or Almighty Lord, with the implication that he has heard and will answer the cry for vindication when he returns (cf. Luke 18:6-8).

The word *sabaōth* implies a mighty Lord with a vast army who in this case is on the side of the poor. If the wretchedness of the rich is coming (impending), then we can perhaps read James 5:6b as a question about Jesus: "Is he not resisting you?" The answer is yes, the eschatological day of judgment is at hand—he has heard the cries and is coming to respond. He is already resisting the rich. But perhaps a better translation is, "He did not resist you." The reference to murder then would be to Jesus' literal murder through the machinations of a few well-to-do and influential Jews, a notion that comports with 1 Thessalonians 2:14-15, which was written at about the same time as this homily.[425] Jesus then becomes the model for the pious, righteous poor suffering at the hands of the rich.

Support for the contention that James 5:6 refers to Jesus comes from Wisdom of Solomon 2.12-20, where the wicked plot against the righteous one to have him killed. In that text Solomon—the epitome of wisdom—is the righteous one in question, and in other early Jewish Christian texts written to Jewish Christians, in particular the First Gospel, Jesus is portrayed as "the Son of David"—one like but greater than Solomon. In Matthew's Gospel he is portrayed as wisdom come in the flesh.[427] It is thus quite believable that James may have seen Jesus as Solomon and thus read the Wisdom of Solomon as yet another text with significance for understanding Christ and the lives of his followers. James 5:6b does not say, "*They* were not opposing/resisting you"; it says, "He [the righteous one] was not opposing you." James undoubtedly knew the story of the end of Jesus' life, and he may well have known the application of Isaiah 53 to Jesus' death at an early date (Mk 10:45). Acts 8:32-35 and 1 Peter 2:21-25 provide evidence of a tradition about Jesus' nonretaliation. All in all, then, a reference to Jesus is quite possible in James 5:6.[428]

This leads to a further question: What does James mean by "parousia of Jesus" in James 5:7? I will discuss this in detail below, but here I note André

[424]Ibid., p. 45.
[425]Witherington, *Paul's Letters to the Thessalonians*, ad loc.
[426]The view that Christ was referred to in Jas 5:6 was common with the church fathers, including Bede, Cassiodorus, Theophylact and others. Theophylact says: "It cannot be denied that this verse refers to Christ, especially since James adds that there was not resistance. Nevertheless it also includes others who suffered   and he may even have been speaking prophetically of his own approaching death" (*On James* [Patrologia graeca 125.1184]).
[427]Witherington, *Gospel of Matthew*, ad loc.
[428]Johnson, *James*, p. 305.

Feuillet's conclusion to his fascinating article on the parousia:

> The conclusion that we are able to reach in this study is that Matthew 24 and James 5:1-11 refer the parousia of Christ to the historic judgment on the Jewish people [in A.D. 70], a different view from other writings of the New Testament that apply the parousia to the supreme manifestation of Christ at the end of world history. This particular position of Matthew and James explains in the two cases the same thing: we are in the presence of the hands of an ancient way of speaking anterior to the epoch of Pauline preaching, which imposed on the parousia motif the technical sense it has retained ever since.[429]

This means that in James the parousia of Jesus refers to the judgment on the Jews culminating in the destruction of Jerusalem in 70. Being a Jewish Christian, James would be especially sensitive to such a prospect in any case, and he may well have known Jesus' pronouncement of judgment on the temple and the center of Jewish life (Mk 13:1-2, 14-23; Lk 21:20-24). God's judgment on his own chosen people as the first installment of his general judgment on humanity would be the end of the then-known world of Jewish and Jewish Christian concern and would easily be described as we have it here. Like other prophets, Jesus juxtaposed various eschatological events in Mark 13 without telling us the time of them or the time between such events; rather, he sees these events like mountains in a range, which from a distance appear to be bunched together but are actually separated by various valleys. For James and the Jews and the Jewish Christians writing in the years that began the crescendo up to the year of obliteration around 67-70, indeed the coming of the Lord as judge was near. The Christians in Judea needed to be patient and steadfast and be prepared; but for the Jews the axe was about to be laid to the tree—they needed to make sure they were not rotten wood about to be chopped down and burned.

The year 70 spelled the effective end of Jewish Christianity as the dominant influence in the church, and Judaism also would never be the same. The Jerusalem-centered world had expired, to be replaced by Diaspora Christianity. Perhaps James wished to make Christians in the Diaspora aware of what

---

[429]Feuillet, "Le sens du mot parousie dans l'evangile de Matthieu," pp. 278-79. The French original reads: "La conclusion que nous croyons pouvoir dégager de cette étude, c'est que Matth. xxiv et Jac. v.1-11 entendent la Parousie du Seigneur au sens du jugement historique du peuple juif, à la différence des autres écrits du Nouveau Testament qui appellent Parousie la manifestation suprême du Christ à la fin de l'histoire du monde. Cette particularité propre à Matthieu et à Jacques s'explique dans les deux cas de la même façon: nous sommes là en présence d'une manière de parler archaïque antérieure à l'époque où la prédication paulinienne devait imposer au mot Parousie le sens technique qu'il gardera par la suite." See the critique in Martin, *James*, pp. 180-81.

was on the horizon for him and his fellows in Jerusalem. If so, this is a prophetic document and maybe of a very early date.

As interesting as this is, some of these suggestions are more probable than others. First, not many find Feuillet's suggestion compelling in regard to the reference to the coming destruction on Jerusalem in 70. One of the reasons for this is precisely because the other early witnesses that James had relationships with did not identify the return of Christ as the coming destruction of Jerusalem. They conceived the possibility that the two might be associated, but the tradition was for a cosmic event at the second coming, with messianic birth pangs like wars and the destruction of the temple *preceding* the parousia. This is clear enough in Paul, 1 Peter, Mark and Matthew, some of which material or tradition James would likely have known.

Longenecker's conjecture that Christ is referred to in James 5:6 may well be correct. And since Christ's return will be spoken of in James 5:7-9, where he is portrayed as the coming judge, it is perfectly feasible to see a reference to Christ in James 5:4 as well. If this is correct, James 5 proves to be a highly christological chapter.

Unfortunately, in his study of the theology of James, Andrew Chester devotes exactly two pages to Christology and says absolutely nothing about the Christology of even the conventional references to the parousia in James 5![430] James 5 does not appear on his radar screen under the heading of Christology, but nor do all the allusions to Jesus' sayings either. Chester mentions that *kyrios* refers to God and to Christ in this homily, but makes very little of it, even though it suggests that Christ was seen as a divine figure, to whom is applied the Yom Yahweh traditions about the coming judge in James 5. As with the general neglect of James, his high Christology has been overlooked or dismissed as well. In the general rehabilitation of the importance of the homily of James, we can hope that future studies will do a better job of appreciating and taking seriously the Christology found in this document.

PERORATION: WAIT, PRAY, RESCUE THE WANDERING FOR THE LORD IS COMING (JAS 5:7-20)

The word of the prophet went forth and suddenly the air was changed, and the sky became bronze, not because its nature was altered but because of the electric effect that was produced. Suddenly the elements were transformed, as the prophet's words fell like a fiery bolt on the hollow parts of the earth, and immediately everything dried up, became a desert and disappeared. (Chrysostom *Catena* 38)

---

[430]Chester and Martin, *Theology,* pp. 43-44.

εναγγελ..

A man who converts others will have his own sins forgiven. (Origen *Homilies on Leviticus* 2.5)

The final section of James's discourse begins with the connective particle *oun* ("so then"), which indicates that we have reached a conclusion to what has been said before and indeed the conclusion of the whole discourse, otherwise known as the peroration or final harangue. This peroration has several subsections, and most divide it as follows: James 5:7-11; 5:12; 5:13-18; 5:19-20. Nothing is very epistolary about this conclusion. Entirely missing are any final greetings, mention of travel plans, doxologies, benedictions, final farewells, amens and the like. Rather this discourse ends like 1 John does, with exhortations right to the end of the document, including a crucial final one that ends the document rather abruptly (1 Jn 5:21). This is certainly not how ancient letters normally ended, and the attempts by Fred O. Francis and others to see the ending of James or 1 John as following some sort of epistolary pattern are exercises in futility.[431] This discourse is a sermon, and it ends as sermon—with some stirring words left in the hearers' ears—and it follows rhetorical conventions in doing so. It is intended as a surrogate or transcript for an oral proclamation.

Quintilian informs us that a peroration ought to be brief and to the point, with short pithy phrases and sentences preferred. In a deliberative discourse it can either rehearse some of the facts or themes previously presented or give an emotional appeal or both (*Institutio oratoria* 6.1.1). A final elaboration of themes spoken of before, such as prayer, is to be expected. *Rhetoric to Alexander* 33.1439b12-14 reminds us that a deliberative recapitulation can take five different forms: (1) enumeration of previous topics, (2) argumentation on some previous topic, (3) proposal of policy, (4) interrogation and (5) irony. The expected final emotional appeal can come either with these forms or separately. Aristotle says that the three main functions of a deliberative peroration are recapitulation, emotional appeal and amplification (*Rhetoric* 3.19.1).

All three of these things are going on in James 5:7-20. For example, under the heading of amplification comes a proposal of specific new policy or behavior based on what has been previously said in the discourse. Thus the exhortation against grumbling against one another in James 5:9 builds on the earlier "judge not lest you be judged" theme; the exhortation about oaths in James 5:12 builds on the previous discussion about the taming of the tongue; and the exhortation in James 5:19-20 to rescue believers who have wandered off builds on the warnings against friendship with the world in James 4. James offers two ex-

---

[431]Francis, "Form and Function."

amples to flesh out and reinforce these appeals: Job in James 5:10-11 and Elijah in James 5:17-18, with the former reinforcing the exhortation to patience and the latter reinforcing the exhortation to effective prayer.

The peroration has an emotional appeal in two forms: anger management (Jas 5:12) and a call to be compassionate (Jas 5:13-16)—to pray and praise and anoint and confess—thus giving a glimpse at the inner life of a healing congregation. Pity or compassion is one of the major emotions one should arouse in a peroration (Quintilian *Institutio oratoria* 3.8.12), and James does this by appealing for help in the healing of the sick and the dying and in rescuing the wandering from becoming lost. This advice helps overcome the divisions and acts of partiality that existed in these congregations and the self-seeking behavior that divides and stratifies the assemblies.

James 5:12 may perhaps be seen as a transitional verse to the emotional appeal. James Hardy Ropes notes how James 5:12-18 relates to the religious expression of strong emotion.[432] The swearing may relate to what goes before: those who are suffering might be led to swear or curse their situation instead of persevering without the urge to take revenge on their foes.[433] In any case, James 5:7-20 nicely fulfills all three rhetorical functions that Aristotle says should be in a good peroration: recapitulation, emotional appeal, amplification. Rhetorical conventions, not epistolary ones, explain the multifaceted nature of the conclusion here.

> [5:7]*Be patient then, brothers, until the parousia of the Lord. Look! The farmer waits for the precious fruit of the earth, waiting patiently upon it until it receives the early and late (rains.[434] [8]You also wait patiently. Make your heart resolute because the parousia of the Lord is near. [9]Do not groan, brothers, about one another, lest you be judged. Behold, the judge is standing at the door.*
>
> [10]*Take for example, brothers, the endurance of hardship and long-suffering of the prophets, who spoke in the name of the Lord. [11]Behold, we call blessed those who endured. You have heard of the endurance of Job, and you have seen the end of the Lord that the Lord is full of pity and compassionate.*
>
> [12]*But above all, my brothers, swear neither by heaven nor by earth nor with any other oath. Rather let your yes be yes and your no no, lest you fall under judgment.*
>
> [13]*Does anyone suffer hardship? He should pray. Is anyone in good spirits? He should play the harp/sing praises with the harp. [14]Is anyone ill? He should call the*

---

[432]Ropes, *James*, p. 300.
[433]But see Davids, *James*, pp. 188-89.
[434]The original text, supported by $\mathfrak{P}^{74}$, B, 048, 1739 and others, does not have a noun here, and thus the noun *hyeton* is added in A, K, L, P and most minuscules, in accord with the regular phraseology in the Septuagint. See Metzger, *Textual Commentary*, p. 685.

elders of the church to him and they will pray near him, anointing him with oil in the name of the Lord. [15]*And the prayer arising out of/offered in faith, will cure the sick one, and the Lord will raise him up. Even if he has committed sin, it will be forgiven him.* [16]*Confess then to one another your sins and pray for each other in order that you be cured. The petition of the righteous person is able to accomplish much in its earnestness.* [17]*Elijah was a person like us, and he prayed earnestly that it not rain, and it did not rain upon the earth for three and a half years.* [18]*And again he prayed. And the heavens gave rain and the earth produced its fruit.* [19]*My brothers, if one of you has wandered from the truth, someone should turn him (back/ around).* [20]*Remember that the one turning a sinner from his wandering way saves him/his life[435] from death and this will overshadow/over many sins.*

The division with what precedes James 5:7-11 is signaled by "so then" (*oun*), which indicates that the final conclusions will now be brought to light.[436] A smooth transition is made from the end of the last elaboration of a theme in James 5:1-6 to the peroration: "since the former is true about the rich (and especially their impending doom) . . . so then you must act as follows."[437] Luke Timothy Johnson says that the clear return to addressing the Christian audience is signaled by the threefold reference to "brothers" in this subsection (Jas 5:7, 9, 10).[438]

Two themes are interwoven in the first subsection of the peroration: (1) patience/patient waiting/long-suffering *(makrothymia/makrothymeō* and *hypomonē)* (Jas 5:7, 8, 10, 11) and (2) the coming of the Lord and his judgment (Jas 5:7, 8, 9, 12). The believer is to have patience until the coming and judgment transpire. The combination of patience and parousia is well known in the Gospels (Lk 18:6-8; Mt 25). James dealt with (rich non-Christian) persecutors in James 5:1-6, and he deals with (poor Christian) sufferers in James 5:7-12. The stress here is on patience with other people (and oneself), while in James 1:2-12 the emphasis was on endurance of difficult situations, which is also stressed in the Job illustration in James 5:11.[439] *Makrothymia* and *hypomonē* differ: "The first is the long-suffering which does not retaliate upon oppressive persons, the second the. endurance which does not succumb under oppressive things."[440] But Douglas Moo

---

[435]Some scribes, confused by the ambiguity of the phrase *save his life from death* (whose life— the converter or the one being converted?), either move the word *autou* ("his") to follow "from death" (so $\mathfrak{P}^{74}$, B and some minuscules) or omit the word altogether (K, L and most minuscules). The word should be retained and not moved, as this is the more difficult reading that explains the others. See Metzger, *Textual Commentary*, p. 686.

[436]Wall, *Community of the Wise*, p. 251 (on *oun* signaling the conclusion to the entire discourse).

[437]Plummer, *General Epistles*, p. 291.

[438]Johnson, *James*, p. 312.

[439]Brosend, *James and Jude*, p. 142.

says that the two terms are often used together and overlap in sense (cf. *Testament of Joseph* 2.7).[441] I agree with Johnson that the audience needed more than endurance: they needed patience under long-suffering as well.[442]

James 5:7 gives the illustration of a farmer who is a small landowner desperate for a crop—his very life and livelihood hang in the balance. He is anxious for the precious fruit, but must exercise patience—until the fall and spring rains come and make the crop possible. It is out of the farmer's hands, he must wait on the one who sends the rains. The person who wrote this knew about the regular fall and spring rains in Palestine-Syria, and this is further evidence that a Jewish Christian who is or has resided in Palestine is writing this homily.[443] With other evidence this supports the traditional view of James writing in Palestine. The believers are to remain resolute until Jesus returns and remedies the situation soon. Three times in this section James uses *idou* ("look") (Jas 5:7, 9, 11) to demand the audience's attention to what he is saying. This gives an urgent tone to this part of the discourse, but it may reflect only that the author knows the audience's attention may need to be regalvanized near the end of his discourse.

This section is very eschatologically oriented: patience is invoked until the parousia, which is said in **James 5:8** to be near. Patience is not the only requirement: the author also wants the audience to "strengthen their hearts" (cf. Ps 111:8; Sirach 6.37; 22.16) or, as we would say, "steel their nerves" by remembering that Christ is coming to resolve the situation. The term *parousia*, which refers to a royal arrival (in the generic sense it means "presence"), had become something of a technical term in earliest Christianity for the return of Christ (Mt 24:37, 39; 1 Thess 2:19; 3:13; 4:15; 5:23; 2 Thess 2:1, 8; 2 Pet 1:16; 3:4; 1 Jn 2:28). On the usual interpretation of *parousia*, James either (1) thought that the end of all history was at hand but was wrong or (2) does not mean exactly what he says but rather means something like, "The end could come at any time (sooner or later)." The image in James 5:9b of the judge standing at the door, which implies nearness—the judge is about to come into their space—stands against this latter suggestion. But talking about an event being near can also mean (3) near in space or time or both.

In the Gospels the verb *ēngiken* is used most often of the kingdom being near or here ("has arrived"). It cannot refer to something that is two thousand years distant in history, unless James was simply wrong. It is hard to believe that Jesus'

---

[440]Plummer, *General Epistles*, p. 292.
[441]Moo, *James*, p. 222.
[442]Johnson, *James*, p. 313.
[443]Martin, *James*, pp. 190-91.

brother, who is so saturated in Jesus' words that he uses them as if they were his own, never bothering to quote directly or indicate their source in this homily, would not have known Jesus' famous saying (Mk 13:32) about no one—not even Jesus—knowing the day or the hour of the parousia. This means that James 5:8 is dramatic rhetorical hyperbole (#2 above), or that the term *parousia* has a different meaning here (à la André Feuillet), or that James is referring to the spatial nearness of the Lord—standing right at the door (in Acts 9:3 this verb means spatial nearness).

James has an intertextual echo of Philippians 4:4-6, where Paul exhorts his readers to rejoice and pray for the Lord is near. Paul is not talking about the temporal nearness of the return of Christ at all. He is reflecting on texts like Psalm 145:18-19 ("the LORD is near to those who call upon him") and Psalm 34:17-18 ("the LORD is near to the brokenhearted"), which goes on to speak of the righteous calling on the name of the Lord (cf. Ps 119:151) in a juxtaposition of the themes of perseverance, prayer and the nearness of God. Exactly the same thing occurs in James 5: James believes the Lord is spatially near the righteous in his audience, and he also believes that Christ could return at any time and so could be also temporally near. Some combination of #2 and #3 above thus best explains James's meaning here (cf. Mk 13:28-29).[444]

This conclusion in no way suggests that James did not live with the possibility that Jesus' return could be imminent. William Brosend shows in detail just how much James's eschatology is future oriented, even to the point that salvation (Jas 1:21; 2:5; 5:11, 15, 19-20) and the coming judgment (Jas 2:12-13; 3:1; 4:12; 5:4, 9) are also viewed in a future-oriented way.[445] In this regard this homily of James sounds very much like the early eschatological material in 1-2 Thessalonians, without however any apocalyptic features or visionary material. Brosend concludes: "The thoroughgoing nature of the eschatological expectations in the letter of James argues for similar expectations in the community for and to which he wrote."[446] Thus, writing to a community eager for the return of Christ, James does something remarkable: "St. James makes the unconscious impatience of primitive Christianity a basis for his exhortation to conscious patience"![447]

In a pressure situation, it would not be surprising if some were complaining or literally groaning—as **James 5:9** puts it, referring to strong emotion—about other believers. Such complaining or blaming of one another is not only fruit-

---

[444]Witherington, *Jesus, Paul and the End of the World*; and Johnson, *James*, p. 316 (on the spatial nearness concept conveyed here).

[445]Brosend, *James and Jude*, pp. 146-47.

[446]Ibid., p. 147.

[447]Plummer, *General Epistles*, p. 290.

less and uncharitable, it was also liable to incur God's anger and judgment and, as with the subject of James 5:12, is another example of the misuse of speech.[448] James is reminding his readers that judgment includes, even starts, with the house of God. Yes, God's true people will be vindicated and liberated from their oppressors, but they also will be held accountable for their own conduct (Jas 1—2), and so they need to stop the blame game or venting with and upon each other.

The appeal to Job in **James 5:10-11** provides an example of steadfastness and endurance *(hypomonē)*, not patience per se. Job was rather impatient at various points, but later Jewish tradition emphasized his patient endurance *(Testament of Job* 1.5; 27.6-7). He persevered despite great suffering *(kakopathia)* (cf. Jas 5:13; 2 Tim 2:9; 4:5), thus implying "so can you." Job is surprisingly placed in the company of the prophets known for their endurance of suffering and, in some cases, martyrdom (Lk 13:34). Perhaps on further review James 5:10 encourages us to distinguish the two groups, for the prophets[449] are said to manifest "long-suffering" under torment while Job exhibited patient endurance or steadfastness in difficult situations or trials (Sirach 44.16—50.21; Hcb 11:32-38). The two qualities go together but are not identical.

The term *hypodeigma* has the sense of "pattern" or "model" for imitating, not just "example" (Sirach 44.16; 2 Maccabees 6.28).[450] The use of historical examples to secure an argumentative point is typical of deliberative rhetoric. Since these examples are scriptural, the assumption is that they have authority and cannot be gainsaid. Thus Job and Elijah provide inartificial proofs for the points James is making, raising the persuasive level of the discourse. James reckons those blessed who stand fast under pressure and persecution, and so **James 5:11** may allude to the Beatitudes in Matthew 5:10-12 (cf. Lk 11:49). It is not clear whether the beatitude in view here is dying and going into God's presence or the experience of eschatological beatitude when Jesus returns.

It is possible that James 5:11b is part of the illustration of Job and should read, "You have seen the result/end the Lord brought about, that is, how (in the end) the Lord was full of pity." If this is right, then *kyrios* here means God and not Jesus. However, James 5:11a and James 5:11b are clearly but passing reminders of well-known stories, and if James is going to appeal to the endurance of the prophets why not appeal to the end of Jesus' life as well, the example

---

[448]Martin, *James*, p. 192.

[449]Presumably Old Testament prophets like Elijah or Jeremiah who suffered are meant here. See Mt 5:11-12; 24:37; Acts 7:52.

[450]Johnson, *James*, p. 317.

par excellence? If so, then the reference is to how compassionate Jesus was, for he too suffered and even on the cross had pity on others (Lk 23:43). On the whole, however, *kyrios* probably means God, in which case James is probably thinking of the end of the story of Job when God appeared to him (Job 42:7-12), with perhaps an allusion to the audience being patient like Job until Christ appears.[451] Or, since *telos* can refer to the goal or purpose, the point may be to remind the audience of the goal or purpose of Job's suffering and endurance.[452] In any event, this is the only direct mention of Job in the New Testament, though the book that bears his name is likely quoted at 1 Corinthians 3:19. James expects his audience to have heard Job's story, though this may mean that they knew the early Jewish traditions about Job rather than the book of Job itself.[453] James expects the eschatological outcome to involve not just judgment of all, but also blessing for some who are faithful to the end. This beatitude should be read in light of the similar one in James 1:12.

James 5:12 may strike us as an abrupt change of subject, but this may be dictated by the way a writer in telegraphic fashion enumerates the previous topics in a peroration. Here we return to the themes in the opening exordium (Jas 1:2-18), with the themes now listed in reverse order: oaths, prayer, health wish, steadfastness. Thus, after James 5:11 the major themes are summoned up and rounded off in a disjointed nature, but this is precisely what one expects in a peroration where various topics are reviewed and in some cases amplified.

It is quite evident that James is in James 5:12 closely dependent upon the material in Matthew 5:33-37,[454] though James's grammar is less Semitic and more Classical than Matthew's. Oaths are forbidden and no obvious exceptions are indicated. James is possibly referring only to casual swearing here, however, he does not say so (nor does Jesus).[455] The point of oaths is to swear the truth to some remark, which implies the general unreliableness of all remarks without oaths. James, like his brother, indicates that Christians should be without need of such devices and should mean what they say and say what they mean all the time without duplicity or deception or outright falsehood. This is part of being a sincere and honest Christian. Someone who abuses or even uses such oaths is in danger of accountability at the judgment. Better to not involve God in this way than call down judgment on oneself.

[451]Plummer, *General Epistles*, p. 297.
[452]Moo, *James*, p. 230.
[453]Clement of Rome, however, seems to know the book in the latter part of the first century (*1 Clement* 17, 20, 26, 39, 56).
[454]Davids, *James*, p. 189.
[455]Ibid., pp. 188-91; and Ropes, *James*, pp. 300-303.

The importance of this point is punctuated by the phrase *pro pantōn,* which literally means "before all" (or "before everything else") but has the sense here of "above all" or even "most of all" (1 Pet 4:8; *Didache* 10.4).[456] In this verse James is aligning himself with some of the most radical and counterorder wisdom of Jesus, for the Old Testament certainly did not prohibit oaths.[457] This is taking truthfulness in speaking to what Richard Bauckham calls "a novel extreme." Bauckham adds: "By making unusually transparent reference to this particular saying of Jesus, James aligns himself with the most distinctive of his master's instructions, claims the latter as the source of the extremity of his own teaching on speech ethics, and brings his whole treatment of the topic of speech to a conclusion which sums it up as comprehended in Jesus' uncompromising demand for total truthfulness in speech."[458]

The compact enthymematic construction in James 5:12 can be unpacked as follows:

admonition: do not swear by heaven or earth or use any oath

suppressed premise: a follower of Jesus should always simply speak the truth

positive counterwisdom in a maxim: instead "let your yes be yes and your no be no"

rationale: so that you may not fall under condemnation

It is not adequate to see either Jesus or James simply recontextualizing Leviticus 19:12, which forbids false swearing, not all swearing or oath-taking. The antithetical structure in Matthew 5:33-37 must be given its due, and James insists just as strongly as Jesus does on simply telling the truth without adding any validating oath formulas. Since there are no Old Testament or early Jewish prohibitions on all oaths outside of the Jesus tradition, Hans-Dieter Betz is quite right to conclude: "On the whole, the Old Testament evidence shows that oaths as such were viewed positively and that misuse was to be avoided as contrary to the Torah."[459]

This verse provides clear, if indirect, evidence of just how radical Jesus' teaching was at some points. Oaths were fundamental to ancient covenant/treaty making, and Jesus is suggesting that, as the eschatological saving reign of

---

[456] Baker, "Above All Else," wants to see this as a mark indicating that this is the single most important point in the whole discourse, but this ignores the rhetorical signals. We are in the peroration, and this is the central point of the peroration—nothing more and nothing less.
[457] Some fine Christian commentators cannot imagine that Jesus or James would actually say something that indicates that the Mosaic law is no longer valid and that a new set of rules applies in the eschatological age. See Plummer, *General Epistles*, pp. 305-6.
[458] Bauckham, *James*, p. 93.
[459] Betz, *Sermon on the Mount*, p. 262.

God is breaking in, a new covenant completely different from earlier covenants in that it is written on hearts will require no oaths to attest to its truth. This comports with Jesus' handling of his own teaching in which he speaks in the first person and without footnotes or citation of other human authorities. Jesus' "I say" is all that accompanies the statement of some truth. James says "above all avoid oaths," but he just as easily could have said "above all tell the truth"—that is, mean what you say and vice versa. From a rhetorical viewpoint the *nai nai . . . ou ou* formula in the maxim is an example of epanadiplosis or repetition of key terms for the sake of emphasis.[460] It is precisely this part of the maxim that the Matthean and Jamesian forms of the saying share verbatim, and Paul writing in the early 50s knows it as well (2 Cor 1:16-19).

Why all this emphasis on no oaths? The answer, we may surmise, has to do with early Judaism placing a high premium on truth-telling but the larger Greco-Roman culture not sharing this concern for precision and exactitude in regard to the truth. Many believed that only one's own inner circle deserved and required truth-telling. One was not obligated to tell the truth to strangers, foreigners or enemies. Jesus and James will have none of this. Duplicity must be replaced by simplicity in the kingdom. Swearing about or to the truth must be replaced by straightforward bearing witness with the truth or by the truth in the name of the one who said, "I am the way, the truth and the life." This truly countercultural approach to truth-telling reminds us that oath-taking is for those with a credibility gap that no Christian should have. This countercultural wisdom is especially striking in a largely oral culture where there were not reams of written documents to call persons to account. But the Jesus movement was to be so strongly grounded in trust and truth that oath-taking would become otiose and obsolete, even in an oral culture. The prohibition of swearing altogether is what the text actually says, and Douglas Moo's attempt to limit this to voluntary swearing as opposed to official swearing is not convincing.[461] No such distinction is indicated here.

James 5:12 has a definite article before the first occurrence of both *nai* ("yes") and *ou* ("no"), and this form of the saying recurs in Justin's *First Apology* 16.5 and Clement of Alexandria's *Stromateis* 5.99.1; 6.67.5. That these later Christian writers follow the form of the saying in James rather than in either Matthew or Paul suggests perhaps that James preserved the earliest form of the saying or

---

[460]Brosend, *James and Jude*, pp. 152.

[461]Moo, *James*, pp. 233-34. He is right that the verse is not focusing on the modern problem of "cursing"; but insofar as such swearing involves God's name it would be included in this ban.

that the homily of James had more widespread influence in the early church than is sometimes thought.[462] The church continued to debate whether oath-taking was allowed by Jesus. Besides Christians' refusal to swear by *genii* of the emperors (Tertullian's *Apology* 32 says that they were prepared to swear by the safety of the emperors; cf. Origen *Against Celsus* 8, 65; *Martyrdom of Polycarp* 9—10), we have the vigorous debate between Pelagius and Augustine in which Pelagius takes the position that all swearing of oaths is prohibited in the New Testament while Augustine is prepared to allow some kinds of oaths (Augustine *Letter* 157; cf. 125, 126).

James 5:13 returns to the theme of testing and the means of persevering: *kakopathei* is not a reference to illness but rather suffering produced by hardship (cf. Jas 5:10).[463] It is a general term for some sort of physical problem or personal circumstance causing distress. It should probably not be translated "is anyone of you in trouble?" because that would imply that the person had done something wrong, whereas that need not be the case here. James's response to such a situation is not to (1) grin and bear it or (2) lash out against the persecutor or source of the problem—but rather talk to the one who is in control of all of this: God. Alfred Plummer sees a clear connection between these two verses: James 5:12 prohibits one form of expressing one's strong feelings, and James 5:13 suggests an appropriate way and place to vent one's strong feelings—namely in religious devotion of various sorts.[464] There may be something to this, but James is not suggesting that one should vent one's anger in church rather than by oaths.

James 5:13b is the opposite of James 5:13a: is anyone feeling good, in good spirits? Again, the response is not to do something by yourself, but rather to do something that connects you to God. *Psalleto* originally meant "to pluck/play the harp" (Herodotus 1.155; Lucian *Parasite* 17) or "to sing praises with harp accompaniment." Here it probably means simply "to sing praises" (as in Eph 5:19). The noun *psalmos* means "song" (1 Sam 16:18; Job 21:12; various psalm titles). In any case, this verse advises a form of celebrating involving God and giving him glory and thanks. Thus far, then, we have learned that when one is suffering one should pray, and when one is in good spirits one should praise.[465] This is how James sees the appropriate response to the extremes of life, and the response in both cases is directed toward God.

---

[462] Perkins, *Peter, James and Jude*, p. 134.
[463] Martin, *James*, p. 205.
[464] Plummer, *General Epistles*, pp. 315-16.
[465] Perkins, *Peter, James and Jude*, p. 137.

James 5:14 refers to someone who is sick,[466] at least sick enough that they cannot go to the *presbyteroi* of the church but must have them come to their house.[467] The word *presbyteros* by itself could mean simply the older (and wiser?) people in town; however, here it is qualified by "of the church" (*ekklēsia*), a phrase that occurs later in Acts 20:17 to indicate an office or function of the church (cf. Acts 11:30; 14:23; 15:2, 23; 1 Pet 5:1). Since the term is not used in the Gospels of Jesus' followers but rather of the elders of the synagogues (e.g., Mt 15:2; 26:3; Lk 22:52), it appears likely that *presbyteros* refers to an office or function of synagogue life that Christians took over and used in their community. These are officials of the local assembly, which implies that they are not traveling missionaries or apostles. They appear to be those left in charge of a local church by the apostles, though an apostle could also be an elder (1 Pet 5:1).[468]

We are not told here what the elders' relationship is to other functionaries in the church, but part of their duty was to pray over the sick person. The phrasing likely indicates that hands were laid on or over the sick person. Alfred Plummer is surely right that this passage makes clear that even at an early date there was already some sort of leadership structure in place in all the churches. It was never, and was never intended to be, a leaderless meeting or movement of the like-minded. Plummer puts it this way: "In the present case the sick person is not to send for any members of the congregation, but for certain [ones] who hold a definite, and apparently an official position. If *any* Christians could discharge the function in question, St. James would not have given the sick person the trouble of summoning the elders rather than those people [i.e., Christians] who chanced to be near at hand."[469]

Apparently simultaneous with this praying is anointing the person with oil, a practice that was used by the Twelve when they went out on a mission venture (Mk 6:13). This practice was common, and anointing with oil could be used for a ritual anointing, soothing cracked skin and as part of the burial process. Anointing as part of a medicinal procedure was common in antiquity (Is 1:6; Lk 10:34; Cassius Dio *Roman History* 53.29; Strabo *Geography* 16; Pliny the Elder *Natural History* 23.39-40; Josephus *Jewish Antiquities* 17.172 [bathing in oil when one is near death]; Celsus *De medicina* 2.14, 17; 3.6, 9, 19 [rubbing oil on those with fevers or aches]; Galen *De simplicitate medicamentum temperatum* 2

---

[466]Since the term *astheneō* is not qualified by an added phrase like "in mind," it is unlikely that spiritual illness is in view here. With Moo, *James*, pp. 236-37; and against Pickar, "Is Anyone Sick Among You?"; and Hayden, "Calling the Elders to Pray."

[467]Brosend, *James and Jude*, p. 153.

[468]Mayor, *James*, pp. 169-70.

[469]Plummer, *General Epistles*, p. 324 (emphasis original).

["the best remedy for paralysis"]; *Gospel of Nicodemus* 19).[470] James does not suggest that the oil has any magical properties—his focus is on prayer as the main activity, and the reference to anointing with oil is in a subordinate clause.[471] Mark 6:13 may suggest that oil was a vehicle used by believers through which God might act to heal, but in any case it is clearly not an *ex opere operato* concept—God is the actor and in control. This is to be done in the Lord's name, which is probably Jesus' name here, not God's as elsewhere in this chapter. The one who said "I am the resurrection" will raise up the sick person from a sickbed, with the verb *raise up* probably referring to restoration to health of someone quite ill (Mk 5:41).

What is said here differs from 1 Corinthians 12:9, 28-30. James does not suggest that some particular person with a particular spiritual gift of healing will be doing this, but simply the elders of the church. This brings up a further point: perhaps James's Jewish Christians were not the charismatic wing of the early church, to use an anachronistic term. The contrast could hardly be stronger between 1 Corinthians and James in regard to the reference to the Holy Spirit. James says nothing or next to nothing about the Holy Spirit, whereas Paul cannot say enough about the work of the Spirit. And whatever else we say about Hebrews, it also spends precious little time discoursing on the Holy Spirit. This indicates that the more pneumatic side of the early Christian movement was primarily the Gentile side of the movement.

James 5:15 indicates that a prayer, in order to be useful, has to be offered out of a person's faith posture, trusting God.[472] The cry of desperation of an unbeliever will not avail, according to James. What James means by "prayer of faith" is probably revealed in James 1:5-6: praying without wavering or doubting. This is probably not a prayer that believes something *specific* about what God will do, although that is not excluded, but a prayer that is offered out of a

---

[470] On ancient medicine and the use of olive oil in its practice, see Wilkinson, *Health and Healing*; and Albl, "Are Any Among You Sick?" One of my favorite examples from the papyri is a prescription to cure hair loss in Hermopolis Magna, which includes "soaking resin in bitter wine[,] smooth it on, alternately pouring oil of myrtle and wine so that it has the thickness of honey and smear it on the head before a bath and after a bath" (Llewelyn, *New Documents Illustrating Early Christianity*, 6.191).

[471] It is possible that the use of the oil is symbolic, signifying the setting apart of this person for prayer and divine concern, but without some indication in the text the reference should be taken as a medicinal act (but see Shogren, "Will God Heal Us?"). One might have expected the verb *chriō* ("to anoint") here if a symbolic act was meant.

[472] The unusual word for prayer here, *euchē*, can mean "oath" in some contexts, particularly in the Septuagint (Gen 28:20; 31:13; Num 6:2; Deut 12:6; Ps 50:14; cf. Acts 18:18; 21:23), but in light of Jas 5:13, it surely must have its other normal sense of "prayer" here. See Johnson, *James*, p. 332.

basic unconditional trust that God knows what is best and can handle the situation. *Sōzei* does not likely refer to a person's spiritual salvation, but to curing the sick person. James 5:15b is simply another way of saying James 5:15a: if the person is cured, he or she has been raised up from the sick bed. This is not a reference to resurrection at the last day as a consolation prize; this is a prayer of faith by others for the sick person, who have come to pray over him or her. In other words, this verse cannot be used to suggest that healing depends on the faith quotient of the ill person, who must pray for himself or herself.[473]

It should also go without saying that this text is not a basis for the Catholic rite of extreme unction. This is not anointing a person and cleansing his or her soul or performing last rites in preparation for death, but rather making a person well, restoring health in this life.[474] While prayer can be powerful and effective, it has provisos: (1) it must be a prayer of faith, and (2) it must be the prayer of a righteous person, which can be a vehicle through which miracles can happen, but it is not the pray-er or the prayer that raises the person, rather, "the Lord will raise him up."

James 5:15c has the *ean* plus subjunctive mood conditional clause: "And if he has committed sin." Considering this a possibility, James perhaps links sickness to sin, as in Mark 2:1-12, which implies a link between forgiveness and healing.[475] Since the Greek is *kan* (Jn 8:14; 10:38; 11:25) and not *kai ean* or *ean de,* Alfred Plummer helpfully suggests the translation "even if he has committed sins."[476] In the New Testament there is no one-to-one correspondence between suffering and sinning—the latter is not always the cause of the former, sin does not always result in physical illness or suffering, suffering cannot always be explained as a result of someone's sin. This is a fallen and evil world—sometimes people suffer undeservedly (Lk 13:1-5; Jn 9:1-3). Sometimes, however, the wages of sin is sickness, suffering, even death, and James considers this probable in this case. If a person has sinned, he or she will be forgiven. This sentence is not qualified by "if he repents." But "so then" *(oun)* in the next sentence indicates that because James 5:14 is true, one should do what James 5:15 exhorts. The gist of the verse then seems to be that "even if sickness is due to sin, the sin can be forgiven and the sickness cured."

The present imperative verb in **James 5:16**—"confess your sins to one another in order that you be cured"—suggests that James expects this to be a re-

---

[473]Rightly Moo, *James*, pp. 243-45. See especially Moo, "Divine Healing."
[474]Rightly Plummer, *General Epistles*, pp. 326-27.
[475]Perkins, *Peter, James and Jude*, p. 137.
[476]Plummer, *General Epistles*, p. 334.

peated activity in the church.[477] We cannot be sure if he is referring to sin sickness or physical sickness linked to sin or both. "To one another" clearly urges open confession to other Christians (but not necessarily to the elders); it does not mean confess to a priest or to God in private.[478] It is also not clear whether James means in church and in public.[479] The lesson here is "confession is good for your soul" and necessary. James does not suggest it, he commands it. Confessing and praying go together, for admission of sin is both to God and to God's people, but we must pray for others lest they wander into sin (Jas 5:19-20). Luke Timothy Johnson rightly stresses the communal and spiritual nature and effect of healing in such cases: "Certainly, James has something more than physical well-being of the members in mind. A community is healed as *ekklēsia* when, in trust and vulnerability, it is able to pray and confess sins together. Such speech establishes the community as based in 'the word of truth' and restores it from whatever alienation has affected it from the sickness and sin."[480]

Clearly, James's main subject is prayer in general, not specific confession, because he gives the illustration in **James 5:17-18** of Elijah as one who prayed and things happened. Elijah was a person of *homoiopathēs,* which literally means of "like passions/feelings" but can have the simpler sense of "of like nature" (Acts 14:15; Plato *Republic* 409B; Wisdom of Solomon 7.3; 4 Maccabees 12.13).[481] This seems to be a "from greater to lesser" sort of argument: if Elijah can pray with such stupendous results, then surely we can pray and someone can be healed. Lest one become discouraged by the "righteous person" requirement for such a prayer to be efficacious, our author reminds us that Elijah was a person "of like nature."[482] I am not sure that this would persuade all in James's audience, considering the exalted view of Elijah in early Judaism. He was not viewed as "just like us."

The reference to Elijah contains several difficulties. First Kings 17—19 does not say that the drought was for 3.5 years (compare 1 Kings 18:1 and Lk 4:25). Nor does it suggest that Elijah's prayer brought the drought upon the land (1 Kings 17:1 says that "rain will come only at my word," not that "drought will come because I prayed"; cf. 1 Kings 18:41; Sirach 48.3 [drought is attributed to

---

[477]Martin, *James,* p. 210.

[478]See the helpful and detailed discussion in Plummer, *General Epistles,* pp. 336-40, on the origin and history of oracular confession to a priest. It appears that we owe it to Pope Leo the Great, who in 459 wrote to some bishops sanctioning the practice of such private confession to a priest.

[479]Davids, *James,* pp. 195-96.

[480]Johnson, *James,* pp. 343-44.

[481]Ibid., p. 336, on the Classical uses of the term.

[482]Perkins, *Peter, James and Jude,* p. 139.

Elijah's prophecy rather than to his prayer]). First Kings 18 may suggest that Elijah prayed but it does not explicitly say so: we are not told that he prayed earnestly, nor is he depicted in 1 Kings as a great man of prayer (1 Kings 17:20-22).

Accordingly, as Peter Davids indicates, this may possibly be a midrash, or perhaps James is drawing on rabbinic midrashes that depict Elijah as a great man of prayer and one to call on in a time of need (2 Esdras [4 Ezra] 7.109; cf. Mishnah, tractate *Ta'anit* 2.4; Babylonian Talmud, tractate *Sanhedrin* 113a; Mk 15:35).[483] There is, however, perhaps enough allusion to Elijah as a man of prayer and enough connection to the drought to warrant the conclusion that James and Luke 4:25-26 draw, though one may not exclude the possibility that James is drawing to some extent on popular ideas and literature of the day about Elijah and is once more showing familiarity with the Jesus tradition.

Energoumenē in James 5:16 might serve the same function as the reduplication in James 5:17 ("he prayed a prayer," implying that he prayed earnestly), that is, to intensify and indicate fervent/earnest prayer, but more likely it means "when it is effective."[484] The point is not that someone will get what they want if only they pray hard enough and are righteous enough, but rather if one lives according to God's will (i.e., is righteous, not perfect) one will know how and what to pray. The prayer of such a person is able to accomplish much when it is in accord with God's plan. There is no idea here of God's arm being twisted. No one can persuade God to do something that is against God's will. Nor does prayer inform God of something God is ignorant about. Rather, it is our way of showing concern about something and gives us an opportunity to be a vessel through which God acts to heal and help, just as he used Elijah.

James 5:19 deals with steadfastness in reverse, using a future or probable conditional statement: *ean* plus subjunctive verb. James anticipates that this could or may well happen. "Wandering" does not seem to be doctrinal error so much as ethical wandering from the truth, that is, one's way of life becomes entangled in sin. Perhaps we are meant to think of a person like the one described in James 1:8, about whom compassion and concern is now shown. James is clearly talking about a believer *(en hymin)* doing this, and so it is equally clear that James did not believe that some sort of immunity from backsliding or apostasy was given to the Christian. Rather, Christians must be on their guard against such a real possibility, and believers must be ready to help turn someone around who is heading down that road.

Peter Davids states quite plainly: "To wander (πλανηθῇ) is to apostatize, i.e.

[483]Davids, *James*, pp. 197.
[484]Ibid., pp. 196-97; Ropes, *James*, pp. 309-10; and Mayor, *James*, pp. 177-79.

to reject the revealed will of God and to act contrary to it, either through will-fulness or the deceit of others (including demonic powers)."[485] This is probably an echo of Wisdom of Solomon 5.6 ("we wandered away from the truth"). James did not believe in "once saved, always saved." The result of turning someone back from the error of their ways (i.e., sinful actions and lifestyle) is stated in **James 5:20**: to save their life *(psychē)* or save them from death. *Thanatos* likely refers to eternal death, not just mortal death.

The last phrase of the letter baffles many: "And this will overshadow/cover many sins." James 2:13 ("mercy triumphs over/overrides judgment") exhibits a similar concept. The phrase does not likely mean atone for (i.e., cover by blood) but rather to overshadow, overcome or outweigh. In the background here is Proverbs 10:12: "Love covers a multitude of sins"—a saying that also stands in the background of 1 Peter 4:8, providing yet another possible connection between the homily of James and 1 Peter.

The soul being saved must be that of the erring party, but whose sins are covered? Most suggest that the Proverbs background indicates the sins and errors of the believer who rescues the fallen one. James is exhorting them and suggesting that they also will benefit from such a deed of love. Their mercy will not go unrewarded. God will weigh this deed more heavily than many of their sins. Once again then we have the concept that what we do in this life as a believer affects our standing in heaven or the way our life and deeds will be judged on the last day. Pheme Perkins puts it this way: "The conclusion encourages readers to recognize that 'mercy triumphs over judgment' (2:13b . . .). The perfect wisdom that James encourages Christians to seek from God does not mean perfectionism. Though members of the Christian community should seek out wisdom, single-hearted obedience to God, and love of others, failure to achieve that goal should not cause discouragement,"[486] because of the truth that mercy in the end is God's last word for his children.

On the other hand, Alfred Plummer insists that the sins of the convert are in view, on the premise that a person burdened with their own sins would not be that concerned or prepared to be rescuing others. This view yields two parallel clauses at the end of the sentence: "He saves his life/soul from death and covers a multitude of (his own) sins."[487] The problems with this reading are severalfold. First, there are certainly known cases of flawed ministers who set aside their own difficulties and become agents of the conversion of others. Furthermore,

[485]Davids, *James*, p 198
[486]Perkins, *Peter, James and Jude*, pp. 139-40.
[487]Plummer, *General Epistles*, pp. 352-53.

the person described as acting throughout James 5:20 seems to be the one turning the sinner from error, saving him (the verb *kalypsei* has as it subject either "this" or "the one turning around"). Our verb does not mean "forgive," but "overshadow" or perhaps "cover." Is James saying that the agent of conversion has the power to cover or overshadow that other person's sins? Surely not, for God covers sins (Ps 32:1-2; 85:2) and has mercy and grace. In the saying "love covers a multitude of sins" the beneficiary of the covering is the one who is doing the loving. If we take seriously the intertextual echo, it seems likely that the one whose sins are covered by such an act is the one who is the agent of conversion. Thus the final clause means something like "this act covers a multitude of sins," and James probably has in mind the eschatological tribunal when such mercy will be shown. While there is an outside chance that Luke Timothy Johnson may be right in taking a future tense view of this covering, so that the convert by his or her conversion has suppressed or prevented future sins,[488] this ignores the intertextual echo and there are no clear examples where the verb *kalyptō* has such a sense. Finally, the Bible provides more than sufficient evidence that bringing others to repentance can have spiritual benefits for oneself: Ezekiel 3:21 promises that if Ezekiel will warn God's people he will save his own life as well, and in 1 Timothy 4:16 Paul tells Timothy that he will save both himself and his audience if he will heed Paul's teaching.

We have now come to the end of a very rich and challenging and much neglected discourse. What may we conclude from it? It was written by someone who knew Jesus' words well, by someone who knew Palestine and its conditions. In view of the lack of mention of the fall of Jerusalem in 70, it was likely written early in the 50s but no later than the 60s. Its main themes—steadfastness, impartiality, wisdom, good deeds, charity—are fundamental things that Christians need to be exhorted about on an ongoing basis. The strong condemnation about rich oppressors should cause us all to examine our actions and lifestyle in how we relate to the poor. Nothing here suggests a late Catholic theology or church situation, and much suggests its earliness. The author is saturated in the Old Testament and loves to tell stories and parables to illustrate or make his points. The letter is elaborately and carefully constructed in a rhetorical way and is not just a random parenesis (which is not, in any case, a literary genre). This is a circular homily written in anticipation of a parousia that might come at any time. It contains a stern warning that God holds Christians accountable for their behavior. Finally, James exhorts us to not be two-minded, not to waver. A person who is able to withstand tests and temptations and be faithful to God in

[488]Johnson, *James*, p. 339.

spite of circumstances—that person is *teleios,* a complete or mature or perfected person (but not sinless). That person is strong and does what is right in intention and action as best he or she can with God's help in a fallen world. As a general homily, this document offers much of value to a church that is always undergoing trials and temptations. James would have heartily agreed with the words of "What a Friend We Have in Jesus":

> Have we trials and temptations? Is there trouble anywhere?
> We should never be discouraged. Take it to the Lord in prayer.
> Can we find a friend so faithful, who will all our sorrows share?
> Jesus knows our every weakness, take it to the Lord in prayer.

But what in the end can we say about James? James stands at the epicenter of early Jewish Christianity—fixed like a rock in Jerusalem, no traveling evangelist he. If the measure of a man is seen in those he influenced, then James is clearly a giant. The intertextual echoes in 1 John and 1 Peter suggest that Peter and the Beloved Disciple—the major figures responsible for early Jewish Christians in the Greco-Roman world—were deeply indebted to the teaching and orientation of James toward the fledgling communities being birthed from Jerusalem to Rome. In this remarkable homily called "the Letter of James," James is steering the ship of Jewish Christianity.

And what do we learn of the man himself from this remarkable polemical salvo? James did not have a problem assuming authority over those he had not personally converted or discipled. His sense of authority in relationship to the Jewish Christians in the Diaspora is clear in the document, yet his homily is also an act of persuasion or deliberative rhetoric meant to change the audience's mind and behavior, meant to help them renounce "friendship with the world" and do a better job of embracing "friendship with God." At the heart of the homily is the attempt to remove the inequities that existed in these congregations between rich and poor, between have and have-nots.

Equally clearly, James believes that that sort of social program requires a higher vision, the embracing of a more heavenly countercultural wisdom, to be enacted even in part. He dispenses some of this wisdom in this homily and hopes that it becomes implanted in the hearts of many in the audience. He pleads for a living faith that works, that does good deeds of piety and charity. He insists on impartiality and generosity of spirit toward all, even including the lowest of the low. Like Jesus he insists on the ethic of the Sermon on the Mount, not as an ideal, but as something that by grace becomes the Magna Carta of freedom and possibilities for a truly Christian community. Like Paul he believes that salvation is by grace through faith, but this does not settle the matter of how

Christians should behave thereafter. Faith that is not perfected in godly works is no living faith at all, and for both James and Paul, in differing ways, Abraham is the benchmark of both faith and obedience.

James, wary of the cult of personality, prefers to call himself only the servant of Jesus and warns strongly against too many desiring to become teachers in the community. Few could have matched his knowledge of the Scriptures, the teaching of Jesus and early Jewish wisdom literature (e.g., Sirach, Wisdom of Solomon), and even fewer had his aptitude for and skill with rhetoric. He was the orator par excellence. It is a shame that he has been viewed as a mere appeaser or compromiser in early Christianity or, even worse, as someone who opposed the bold missionary work of Paul with the Gentiles and his message of salvation by grace through faith. James was neither of these persons, but he was a skillful diplomat, as Acts 15 shows, working out a necessary compromise.

And to judge from both Acts and this homily, James was no hard-line Judaizer either. Although he probably believed that all Jewish Christians should continue to keep the Mosaic covenant, especially in the Jerusalem community, he says nary a word in his homily about circumcision, sabbath keeping or food laws. Were these the subject of discussion in Jewish Christian churches in the Diaspora? It is hard to tell, but neither 1 John nor 1 Peter suggest that they were, and Paul's fulminations in Galatians and elsewhere pertain almost entirely to Gentile Christians and others who are part of his congregations. So much more could be said about James, but one remark must suffice: he is the one person who held together the teachings of Jesus and early Judaism and the Jewish Christian churches and at the same time extended the right hand of fellowship to Paul and his mission of salvation by faith. For this he deserves our eternal praise and admiration.

JAMES AND THE AUTHOR OF HEBREWS—TWIN SONS OF DIFFERENT MOTHERS?

Without question, the books we call Hebrews and James are very different from one another, even though they both address a common audience, at least in part, for they are both written to Jewish Christians in the Roman Empire. Hebrews is written more specifically to one group of Jewish Christians in Rome under duress, while James is written as an encyclical that certainly would have included Jewish Christians in Rome but was not limited to them. In all likelihood, these two documents were written at least ten or more years apart, with Hebrews being written when a great deal more water had passed under the bridge and Jewish Christians in Rome were in an even more compromised position than they had been when James wrote. An emperor in the mid-60s was actively looking for scapegoats in Rome to blame the fire on, and one gets the sense from Hebrews that the major apostolic figures had given the last full measure of their lives and were gone. This is not the case, and not the problem, when the homily of James was written.

But apart from a somewhat common audience (in the superficial sense of lumping together all Jewish Christians of that period), these two documents are very different. One is written by a creative exegete who relies on the authoritative texts of the past and quotes them regularly, the other is written by a creative sage who makes all his source material his own. While the author of Hebrews certainly is influenced by the wisdom tradition, especially in his Christology, James is not merely a borrower of wisdom literature, ideas and images but a creator of such materials. While the author of Hebrews drinks from the sapiential font, the author of James is immersed in it, swimming in it (but not swimming upstream). It is his natural element. Furthermore, these two authors show no evidence of knowing each other's materials, whereas, a good case can be made that the authors of 1 Peter and 1 John know James's homily or at least some of his source material. Having said this, both James and Hebrews manifest the futurist eschatology of the earliest Christians and a primitive vision of the leadership structure of the Jewish Christian community. James speaks of teachers and elders and of himself simply as a servant, whereas the author of Hebrews speaks of teachers and preachers and sees himself as both of these. In neither case do we hear anything remotely like early Catholic notions of ecclesiology that seem to have begun to develop in the second century. No monarchial bishops are to be found in these sermons, and no apostles are referred to in either document.

The authors of these two documents reflect the results of the Hellenization of Judaism long before these documents were ever written. They reflect a good knowledge of Greek and a better than average knowledge of rhetoric, with the author of Hebrews using epideictic rhetoric to speak to his audience and James using deliberative rhetoric. The author of Hebrews is clearly the more skilled rhetorician, but James is quite capable of forming maxims, examples, enthymemes and welding them together into careful elaboration patterns on key themes. Neither of these writers shows a bit of hesitancy in using rhetoric in order to persuade their audiences about a variety of things, and both show a real concern with praxis and the possibilities of Christians' committing apostasy. The warnings about this specific danger are equally strong in both documents. While the author of Hebrews is indebted to Paul and/or his letters and comes out of the Pauline circle, James is not dialoguing with Paul but is prepared to correct misreadings of the Pauline gospel in regard to faith and works. Both share a love for the Old Testament saints and their stories and were quite prepared to draw on those stories to inspire other Jewish Christians to emulate their fore-bears' faith, prayer life, perseverance and the like.

Spiritually speaking, both persons have a great reverence for Christ and a high Christology, though we could have wished that James had said more about that subject, and both are devout men of prayer and profound students of the Scriptures. Both manifest a clear sense of spiritual authority over their audience. Both look forward to the day when Christ returns and justice is done and things are rectified through resurrection. The eschatological forward motion of these homilies is clear, as Hebrews climaxes with the great final theophany (Heb 12) and James with a connection of praxis and patience and parousia (Jas 5). Both were certain that they lived in the eschatological age, and both urged their audiences to be the church expectant, standing on tiptoe and scanning the horizon for Jesus. These two apples did not fall far from the Jesus tree, and James may be called a direct offshoot from that tree, manifesting the same kind of interesting and wise foliage.

We may be grateful that the writings of these two profoundly converted persons made it into the canon, giving us a glance at the vibrant life of early Jewish Christianity as it gestated in the middle of the first century. These documents give the lie to the notion that it was all about Paul and his Gentile converts after the apostle to the Gentiles had gotten his missionary work into high gear. Nothing could be further from the truth. There were two important streams of Christianity flowing forth from Jerusalem and Antioch heading west across the empire: a mostly Jewish one and a mostly Gentile one. They crossed paths, cross-fertilized and occasionally crossed swords, though they always saw each other as fellow Christians, while still maintaining somewhat distinctive and independent existences even into the waning decades of the first century. It remains to be seen what more light can be shed on these things by the homily of Jude, who presents yet another form of early Jewish Christian literature—one grounded in apocalyptic and prophetic traditions.

BRIDGING THE HORIZONS

One of the great difficulties in preaching James is that when one strips it of its original spiritual, social and rhetorical ethos it comes off sounding like a prophetic rant of sorts, guaranteed to turn more people off than it motivates, at least in Western society. William Brosend says that the difficulty with this material is not so much cognitive, knowing what it says or means, but experiential, figuring out how to live it out.[489] This difficulty is only exacerbated by James's telling us that faith without these kinds of works is dead.

---

[489]Brosend, *James and Jude*, pp. 164-66.

Preaching this material has both impediments and impetuses. The impediment is that James makes us very uncomfortable. We have to start asking questions: How have I shown favoritism when I should not in the Christian community? When will I take responsibility for my own actions and stop blaming God, the devil or other outside forces when I give in to temptation of some sort? Am I actually a rich person who has been so corrupted by the society I live in that I have rationalized away my moral responsibility to help the poor? When is the last time I confessed my sins to other Christians and allowed myself to be held accountable? But precisely because we fall short in these and other areas that James mentions, there is impetus to be brave enough to preach and teach about these things, not in a censorious manor, but in a way that will hopefully be convicting and convincing to all.

James's ethic has an undergirding and overriding divine sanction. A compassionate and merciful God is also just and righteous and holds us accountable for our behavior. These are not random ethical remarks without theological grounding by a man perpetually angry with the world's fallen ways. And when we realize that Paul would have pronounced the amen to much of what James says in this discourse, especially when it comes to the issue of Christian behavior, we cannot allow ourselves to fall back into the default mode of thinking that says, "I am, after all, saved by grace through faith regardless of my behavior." This thinking leads many to give themselves permission to do all sorts of things that are sinful and a violation of one's relationship with God. This whole way of thinking about salvation and faith is faulty. Genuine faith works itself out in godly, good, helpful behavior. Such behavior is the natural fruit and manifestation of such faith. No faith mentioned in the New Testament involves bare belief without implications for behavior.

And even with the current heightened awareness of the importance of spiritual formation, we need to be reminded that James would have nothing to do with a spiritual formation that is so otherworldly that it is no earthly good and has no practical social outworkings. The behavior of the rich man in James 2 has a vestige of that sort of spirituality. The spirituality that James has in mind always has social consequences, because one is a part of a body of believers, with whom one is to worship, sing, pray, confess, serve, witness, work and so build up the body of Christ.

One of the ways of preventing a person from misusing James by strip-mining it for spiritual McNuggets is to teach this material in the context of ancient Jewish wisdom literature. The audience needs to study this material in the light of earlier Jewish wisdom literature. There needs to be an awareness of how aphorisms, parables, riddles, enthymemes and allegories work. There needs to be

awareness not only of how figurative this language is but also how ethically serious it is. James should be seen in part as a reapplication of the Sermon on the
Mount to a wider audience, a reapplication of what Jesus taught his original disciples. James thinks that this material is directly applicable to a wide variety of
persons in a wide variety of places who are in a wide variety of stages in their
spiritual pilgrimages and who lived at various times and in various conditions
in the first century.

The issue of taming the tongue in the internet and soap opera age takes on
a whole new life. People would benefit from reading John Wesley's famous sermon on this subject, "The Cure of Evil Speaking," in which he insists that a
Christian should never speak ill of any absent person, of anyone not there to
defend themselves. Teachers and preachers especially need to hear James's
warnings about loose tongues and about becoming teachers. This comports
nicely with James's exhortations about humility.

Clearly enough as well, James believes that the Christian should be prepared
to suffer wrong rather than inflict it. We have the author's encouragement that
trials can purify and prove the mettle of one's faith and that they should be
counted as joy. There is reassurance that if we ask for divine assistance in such
situations God will provide it. There is a call for patient endurance, not seeking
revenge or retaliation, leaving judgment in the hands of God.

No doubt, James saw his brother act out much of the behavior that James
describes in this homily. Jesus cared for the poor; Jesus did not show partiality;
Jesus taught his followers to pray as a way of relying constantly on God; Jesus
taught his disciples to prepare for and expect suffering and persecution; Jesus
taught his disciples to have strong faith, to heal the sick, to confess their sins;
Jesus taught his disciples to measure their words and not swear oaths. James
was saying what he admired in his brother, and he urged his audience to do so as
well. This is still a clarion call worth hearing, worth striving to live up to, worth
repeating. The homily of James will not be tamed, domesticated, and should not
be truncated, trivialized or dismissed as an inculcation of minor virtues. Holiness, mercy, love, righteousness, compassion, generosity of soul and spirit are
no minor virtues. We still have much wisdom to learn from James and even
more to learn about how to live it out. Hearing and rehearing this discourse is
a good place to start such greater fidelity, greater conformity to the image of
Christ.

Part Three

JUDE—ANOTHER BROTHER'S SERMON

Introduction to Jude

on a letters speed
see 665

I broached the subject of early Jewish sermons in the first volume in this series[1] and addressed the matter further while discussing the homilies of Hebrews and James above. Here, however, something more needs to be said about the relationship between letters and speeches, including sermonizing ones. The speech was a far more widespread and influential phenomenon than the letter in the Mediterranean world in which our authors wrote. This is so not just because only 10%-15% of the populace was literate, but also because Greco-Roman rhetoric and its various forms and modifications (Attic, Asiatic, Jewish) had a much longer and more influential history than letter writing. When letter writing came into its own in the first century B.C., letter writers were constantly trying to figure out how to put discourse into written form, and letters were constantly shaped by the rudiments, rules and structures of rhetoric.

This is very clear in the comments that leading exponents of letter writing make about what they are doing. Cicero is very blunt about the matter: a letter is a speech in written medium (*Ad Atticum* 8.14.1), and Pseudo-Demetrius says that a letter is half of a dialogue or a surrogate for a dialogue (*De elocutione* 223). Epistolary elements would be added to the beginning and end of the speech since the document had to be sent, but otherwise a letter is most often the transcript of a speech, mentally composed following long-ingrained rules of rhetoric.

It is thus quite the wrong way around to talk about figuring out how rhetoric could be used in an epistolary mode. The issue was how, in a predominantly oral and rhetorical culture, letters could be written to faithfully reflect the rhetorical nature of discourse and especially the various forms of public discourse. It is extraordinarily difficult in a text-based and computer-screen culture like ours to think of oral communication as primary and of a text as a secondary thing reflecting the patterns of oral speech, but that is how we must conceive

---

[1]Witherington, *Letters and Homilies*, 1.38-46.

of the world of the New Testament writers. One other point is germane: epistolary theorists came long after, and on the coattails of, rhetorical theorists, who
went all the way back to Aristotle and continued through the New Testament
era with figures like Quintilian. It is thus a mistake to turn to figures like Pseudo-
Libanius and others, who come after our period and who are consolidating epistolary theory at a later date, as guides for how to read the New Testament and
its rhetoric.

Jude offers us a sermon in rhetorical form that has only an epistolary opening
to indicate that it came to the audience in a written form, though it was likely
delivered orally at the point of destination. We must think constantly in terms
of the oral majority of the culture and how literate persons like Jude were trying
to speak into their situations.

JUDE THE MAN

The brother of Jesus we know as Jude was named Judas. This particular name
occurs in various forms some forty-five times in the New Testament, of which
twenty-three are references to Judas Iscariot and so are of no relevance to this
study. Ancient commentators occasionally thought that Judas in Luke's list of the
Twelve (Lk 6:16) might be Jesus' brother, but two things count against this: (1)
the normal meaning of the phrase *Judas of James* is Judas son of James, not
brother of James, unless the context specifies otherwise and (2) John 7:5 clearly
states and Mark 3:21, 31-35 implies that Jesus' brothers did not believe in him
during his ministry and that his physical family is clearly distinguished from the
family of faith. Presumably Judas not Iscariot in John 14:22 is this same member
of the inner circle of the disciples, not Jesus' brother. Judas the Galilean (Acts
5:37) was a famous Zealot and clearly not Jesus' brother. Judas who had a house
in Damascus and hosted Paul (Acts 9:11) is surely not our Judas either, since we
have no reason to expect that Jesus' brother would be living in Damascus so
soon after the crucifixion. Judas called Barsabbas (Acts 15:22) was a companion
of Silas, and his second name distinguishes him from others mentioned in Luke-
Acts, including the person we are concerned with.

Our Judas/Jude is clearly mentioned as Jesus' brother in Mark 6:3/Matthew
13:55, but he is mentioned third in the earlier Markan listing and fourth in the
Matthean listing. This may mean that he was not the next brother in line after
James to be the head of Jesus' family (this was determined by age). This may in
turn explain why he did not succeed James as head of the Jerusalem church. In
the New Testament, the only brothers named James and Jude are the brothers of
Jesus, the same ones said to be present in the upper room at Pentecost (Acts 1:14),
after having not been followers of or believers in Jesus during his ministry (Jn 7:5).

Jude is also referred to by name in Eusebius's *Ecclesiastical History* 3.19.1-20.6, following the account of Hegesippus. That the canonical document bearing the name Jude begins with the identification "brother of James" (Jude 1) establishes the connection with the holy family beyond reasonable doubt. That the author calls himself a servant of Jesus, as does James in James 1:1, does not count against his blood kinship with Jesus but simply reflects his humility and his use of a common title that Christian leaders used in that era to establish or make a claim to authority in a church setting (Phil 1:1). Richard Bauckham stresses that the connection of this Judas and this document to the holy family is secure because "the only man in the early Church who could be called simply James without risk of ambiguity was James the Lord's brother."[2]

We have no evidence that James was an itinerant, so 1 Corinthians 9:5 likely means that Jesus' brother Jude was an itinerant Jewish Christian missionary who was married and traveled with his wife. Since Paul does not suggest that these brothers were missionaries to Gentiles (like himself) and since Jude's discourse is likely addressing a Jewish Christian audience using various Jewish traditions, even extracanonical ones, it is very likely that he was a missionary to Jews (like Peter).

Julius Africanus writes: "From the Jewish villages of Nazareth and Kokhba [about ten miles northwest of Nazareth] they [i.e., the relatives of Jesus] traveled around the rest of the land [i.e., Israel] and interpreted the genealogy they had and from the Book of Days as far as they went on their travels" (quoted in Eusebius *Ecclesiastical History* 1.7.14).[3] This likely confirms that, apart from James, the family of Jesus was based in Galilee after Easter, which is perhaps another reason that Jude did not succeed James as leader of the Jerusalem church. A second-century Coptic fragment of the *Acts of Paul* suggests that Judas who hosted Paul in Damascus immediately after his conversion experience (Acts 9:11) was the brother of Jesus. But would our Jude be residing in Damascus only a couple of years after Jesus' crucifixion? This seems unlikely and goes against the tradition that Julius Africanus knows. I agree with Bauckham that this idea likely arose because early Christians, like early Jews, "loved to identify figures who bore the same name."[4]

Julius Africanus's reference to the genealogy of Jesus probably means that,

---

[2]Bauckham, "Jude, Epistle of," p. 1101.
[3]That Jude refers to others (but not himself) as "apostles" might reflect that this term was reserved for those who were evangelizing non-Jews, such as Paul and his coworkers. But Jude 17 seems to suggest that the audiences addressed in this discourse were parts of congregations founded by apostles.
[4]Bauckham, *Jude and the Relatives of Jesus*, p. 68.

in light of the genealogies in Matthew and Luke, Jesus's origin required some explaining, especially the genealogical irregularities and the virginal conception of Jesus.[5] Such explanations were the very sort of thing that Jewish Christians would especially want and need elucidation on, especially if Jesus' origins were already being challenged by other Jews, as the Gospel of Matthew, likely written in Galilee in the last couple of decades of the first century, probably suggests.

The book of Acts says very little about missionary work in Galilee after the Pentecost events. Only after persecution and in the wake of the scattering of the Greek-speaking Jews is the Jerusalem church said to truly begin mission work outside of Jerusalem and its environs (Acts 8:14-25; 9:32—10:48). Even then the missionary activity seems to be confined to Judea and Samaria, though Acts 11:19 suggests travel further afield. Acts 9:31, however, plainly indicates a well-established church in Galilee at that juncture, presumably in the mid- to late 30s. This is probably another example of Luke not wanting to go beyond his source material. He had contacts with the Jerusalem church and its vicinity and learned about the mission work that radiated out from that locale. He simply had no knowledge about Jude and his activities, about what happened to the relatives of Jesus other than James, or about missionary activity in Galilee and its immediate vicinity.

In his landmark study on early Christian mission, Eckhard Schnabel concludes that a mission based in Galilee could easily have reached southern Syria, Damascus, Phoenicia, various places in the Decapolis and other places east of the Jordan (Pella?). Both he and Richard Bauckham conclude that likely extensive missionary activity in Galilee and its surrounding areas did not result from missionaries sent out from Jerusalem. That Symeon (a cousin of Jesus) and not Jude (the brother of Jesus) takes over the leadership of the Jerusalem church upon the death of James in 62 suggests that Jude was not long based in Jerusalem and that his missionary work took him elsewhere.[6] Bauckham concludes: "From the beginning the Jewish Christian mission was not only to pilgrims in Jerusalem, but also extended throughout Palestine through the travels of missionaries among whom the younger brothers of Jesus and other members of the family were prominent. It is as missionaries engaged in preaching Jesus the Messiah to their fellow-Jews that the relatives of Jesus are primarily to be envisaged."[7] Jude's discourse suggests controversy and competition on this mission field, particularly from some more libertine Jewish teachers of some sort. But

---

[5]Witherington, *Gospel of Matthew*, introduction.
[6]Schnabel, *Early Christian Mission*, 1.749-50.
[7]Bauckham, *Jude and the Relatives of Jesus*, p. 375.

again I stress that 1 Corinthians 9:5, written in the early 50s, shows that Paul takes it for granted that his audience knows that Jude and others of Jesus' brothers are both married and traveling evangelists. This raises important questions about the provenance and date and character of the canonical document that bears Jude's name.

Jude 17 is sometimes thought to exclude Jude from the apostolic era, for he seems to refer to apostles as part of a previous generation. But this misreads the verse, which actually says that our author was not among the apostles who founded the churches he is currently addressing in this discourse.[8]

According to Eusebius, quoting the earlier material of Hegesippus, the two grandsons of Jude were brought before Emperor Domitian (which if true would have transpired in the late 80s or early 90s) on the basis of the accusations of some Jews that they were relatives of the condemned Jesus and descendants of the Davidic line.[9] The accusations failed, however, to produce a guilty verdict, and these descendants of Jude were set free. Two things are important about this tradition: (1) in the account quoted by Eusebius, Hegesippus says that Jude was "the Savior's brother after the flesh" and that this was the ground of the accusation of Jude's grandsons and (2) mention of grandsons confirms what 1 Corinthians 9:5 already suggested, namely that Jude and other brothers of Jesus were both actual brothers of Jesus and were married. Eusebius also says that Jude had children and grandchildren (*Ecclesiastical History* 3.19.1-20.7). If this tradition is based in fact, it suggests that by this juncture Jude, along with the other brothers, was already deceased, or else the accusations would have been made against him personally, not against his grandsons. This in turn suggests that we look for a date for Jude somewhere in the early or middle part of the first century.

GALILEE AND THE HELLENIZING OF THE HOLY LAND

What do we know about the history of Jude's Galilee, particularly in the first sixty years of the New Testament era? Is it plausible that a manual worker from Nazareth could have received enough education to write a document like Jude? What would the social situation of his audience be like?

Jude's adult lifetime was a era of rising tensions in the Holy Land. Pilate was sent into exile in disgrace in 36-37, and he was followed by one bad procurator after another. This only fueled the Zealot movement, which had strong Galilean

---

[8] Watson, *Jude*, p. 474.

[9] Bauckham, *Jude and the Relatives of Jesus*, pp. 94-95. This account is confirmed by an independent source in Epiphanius Monachus's *Life of the Blessed Virgin* 14 (Patrologia graeca 120.204) and should not be lightly dismissed.

connections. Since Jude does not mention the death of his brother James in 62, we may take it that his document was written sometime in the 40s or 50s during this wave of rising tension and rebellion leading to the Jewish war in the 60s. We know from Paul's letters written in the 50s (e.g., Galatians, 1-2 Thessalonians, 1-2 Corinthians and Romans) that the Jerusalem church was suffering from famine in the late 40s and required a collection for famine relief (Acts 11:27-29).[10] To this mix we must add the following: (1) the expulsion of some Jewish Christians from Jerusalem synagogues; (2) the persecution of Jewish Christians by Saul and presumably others (1 Thess 2:13-16);[11] (3) the multicultural milieu of Galilee with its various Hellenistic cities and (4) rhetoric as a staple of early Jewish education for literate males. J. Daryl Charles puts it this way: "If Josephus the historian, Theodorus the rhetorician, Meleager the poet, and Philodemus the philosopher hailed from Galilee, perhaps it is indeed time to dispel the myth of 'Galilean illiteracy.'"[12]

Martin Hengel was right when he stressed that "there was no stopping the penetration of the Greek language even in Jewish Palestine, and the young Jew who wanted to rise a stage above the mass of the simple people had to learn it."[13] This was all the more the case in lower Galilee, since it contained the Greek city of Scythopolis (part of the Decapolis), bordered on various other Greek cities and witnessed the building of a Hellenistic style city in Sepphoris only a short walk from Nazareth. If Jude was a craftsman left to run the family business in Nazareth, he may well have needed the skills of a salesman in a city that had major construction during the reign of Herod Antipas and Herod Agrippa after him (i.e., well into the 40s and beyond) with a need for woodworking of various sorts. To this end he needed both Greek and rhetoric—the art of persuasion.

Many scholars are still skeptical about how Hellenized the Holy Land may have been at this time. Hellenization has to do mainly with the languages spoken in a particular region, and the evidence is now clear for Judea, Galilee and Samaria. Hengel puts the matter this way: "Judaea, Samaria and Galilee were bilingual (or better, trilingual) areas. While Aramaic was the vernacular of ordinary people, and Hebrew the sacred language of religious worship and of scribal discussion, Greek had largely become established as the linguistic medium for trade, commerce and administration."[14] There are telltale signs that the

---

[10]Witherington, *Acts of the Apostles*, pp. 371-73.

[11]On the importance and genuineness of this text, see Witherington, *Paul's Letters to the Thessalonians*, ad loc.

[12]Charles, "Literary Artifice in the Epistle of Jude," p. 118.

[13]Hengel, *Judaism and Hellenism*, 1.60.

[14]Hengel, *"Hellenization" of Judaea*, p. 8.

spread of both the Greek language and Greek culture accelerated in the Holy
Land during the century before and the century after the turn of the era. For
example, Herod the Great changed over to purely Greek inscriptions on Jewish
coins and weights, a drastic change from the Maccabean period. For the Greek
cities of the Decapolis, including Scythopolis, coins had been minted in Greek
since the third century B.C. Even a sectarian and retro environment like Qumran
used Greek loanwords (e.g., in the Copper Scroll). In addition, various bilingual
inscriptions are found in the Holy Land from our period, with the second language always being Greek.

Hengel points to the degree of Hellenization of the cities of the coastal
plain (e.g., Gaza, Dor, Caesarea, Acco), which were on the Via Maris, the sea
road along the coast. Grave and synagogue inscriptions from these cities from
our period are mostly in Greek. If Philip the Evangelist was, as Acts 6 suggests, a Greek-speaking Jew, then we may envision him and others (including
Peter) evangelizing in Greek in these very cities (e.g., the Cornelius story in
Acts 10).

Was then the lower Galilee of Jesus' family some Aramaic backwater, removed from the influence of Hellenism? Hengel answers this with an emphatic
no: "Galilee, completely encircled by the territories of the Hellenized cities of
Ptolemais, Tyre and Sidon in the west and north-west, by Panias-Caesarea Philippi, Hippos and Gadara in the north-east, east and south-east, and finally by
Scythopolis and Gaba, a military settlement founded by Herod, in the south, will
similarly have been largely bilingual."[15] Thus, while Mark Chancey is quite right
that Galilee was not predominantly inhabited by Gentiles, it was inhabited by
Jews, almost all of whom had long since adapted to the influence of Greek language and culture to one degree or another.[16]

As Hengel points out, the Gospels themselves indicate that Jesus spoke with
centurions, Syrophoenicians, Pontius Pilate and others, which would have
surely required conversation in Greek from time to time. In addition, Jesus and
his family were not peasants, despite the recent assertion of some scholars
overly influenced by modern social-scientific and cultural anthropological theories.[17] Peasants are bound to the land, but do not own it, and what we know
about Jesus' family is that they were craftsmen—woodworkers and builders.
Hengel stresses: "We may assume that Jesus himself, who as a building craftsman *belonged to the middle class,* and to an even greater degree his brother

---

[15] Ibid., pp. 14-15.
[16] Chancey, *Myth of a Gentile Galilee.*
[17] Hanson and Oakman, *Palestine in the Time of Jesus.*

James, was capable of carrying on a conversation in Greek."[18] While the term *middle class* is anachronistic, his point is well taken. There is no evidence that Jesus or his family were day laborers or peasants, whereas the evidence suggests that Jesus and presumably other members of his family had some education (e.g., he could read scrolls; see Lk 4) and knew some Greek. Since Greek was the language of commerce and trade and since Jesus' family members were craftsmen who had to do business in places in Galilee like Sepphoris or with people who came to them from such Hellenized cities, this immediately suggests that they needed to know enough Greek to deal with such day-to-day conversational situations.

Though it may seem counterintuitive to some of us, Jerusalem was the epicenter of Greek culture and Greek language in Judea from which the culture disseminated outward. Numerous Greek inscriptions have been found in Jerusalem, including the famous Theodotus inscription and the Jerusalem temple warning inscription (*Corpus inscriptionum judaicarum* 2.1400 and 2.1404). What is more telling is that a good third of the epitaphs on ossuaries and grave steles in Jerusalem from our period are in Greek. This is in part because various Diaspora Jews came to Jerusalem to die and be buried, but this does not explain all of the evidence by any means. This is what makes the Aramaic rather than Greek inscription on James's ossuary all the more interesting.[19]

L. Y. Rahmani concludes from the detailed study of all the extant Jerusalem ossuaries that even the lower-class population of Judea had a speaking knowledge of Greek, which was probably in everyday use, though this does not imply that they knew Greek literature or would have been able to write Greek in a refined manner.[20] But the evidence is everywhere that Herod and upper-class Jews in Jerusalem were furthering the influence of Hellenic culture in their building projects—including a Greek theater in the shadow of the Temple Mount and many homes that architecturally owed much to Hellenistic style.

Acts 1:14 then becomes important because it mentions that the brothers of Jesus are living in Jerusalem—that is, they were located where they could further their knowledge of both Greek and rhetoric as their evangelistic movement began to gather steam, when the obvious need for being able to write fluidly and convincingly in Greek became important. The Greek-speaking (Diaspora) synagogue communities in Jerusalem (Acts 6:9), where the Septuagint was read,

---

[18]Hengel, *"Hellenization" of Judaea*, p. 17 (emphasis added).
[19]Shanks and Witherington, *Brother of Jesus*.
[20]Personal communication from L. Y. Rahmani, cited in Hengel, *"Hellenization" of Judaea*, p. 10.

could have provided further impetus for this development of knowledge of Greek when people like Stephen began to convert to this new Jewish messianic movement. The need to have more such converts would have provided further impetus for James and Jude to improve their Greek language and rhetorical skills. Evidence suggests that the family of Jesus had some education, knew the Torah, including some of the Septuagint translation, and, at least in the case of James and Jude, could have had some training in rhetoric in Jerusalem after Easter.

As Hengel points out, the rhetorician Tertullus (Acts 24:1) is brought by the Jewish authorities to Caesarea from Jerusalem to argue their case, and his brief speech certainly reflects his knowledge of rhetoric. He did not likely make a living by offering forensic speeches in Greek in Judea, and so he likely earned his living teaching rhetoric in Jerusalem.[21] The book of Tobit, which is in excellent Greek, uses rhetoric and shows that already in the time of Ben Sira in Jerusalem there was a market and a taste for such Greek and rhetorical literature in Jerusalem. This in turn means that there had to have been education in these subjects in Jerusalem for almost two centuries before the time James and Jude wrote their sermons.[22]

As David Daube pointed out long ago, half of Gamaliel's pupils in Jerusalem are said to have been trained in the "wisdom" of the Greeks, which would include both philosophy and rhetoric. These pupils could have included Saul of Tarsus, James and Jude, or they could have gotten it from a similar school in Jerusalem or from those who had been taught in such a school.[23] In short, the historical conditions were both right and ripe for Jude, as well as James, to have learned Greek and the art of persuasion in Greek for the sake of advancing the messianic Jewish movement focusing on Jesus, even if initially they were only thinking of sharing it with more Hellenized and Diaspora Jews.

JUDE—THE DISCOURSE: ITS RHETORIC AND RELATIONSHIPS

Jude, like most of the so-called General Letters, has suffered from a distinct if not intentional neglect in the Christian world. Tucked away behind 3 John and before Revelation, most people do not even know where the book is, never mind what it is about. As it fills only one page of text, it hardly deserves to be called a book; it is rather a brief sermon following the conventions of deliberative rhetoric, with an epistolary opening and a doxological conclusion.

If this document is written by the brother of James, it is then no surprise that

---

[21]Ibid., p. 26.

[22]Ibid., p. 27.

[23]Daube, "Rabbinic Methods of Interpretation"; and Judge, "St. Paul and Classical Society."

there is some reason to think that our author knows not only James but perhaps also his writings. J. Daryl Charles points out the elements that these two homilies share:[24]

1. a general address (Jas 1:1; Jude 1-2)

2. a hortatory conclusion (Jas 5:20; Jude 22-23)

3. a sizable presentation of demonstrative (i.e., deliberative) proofs (Jas 2:1—4:12; Jude 5-11)

4. a series of admonitions (Jas 4:13—5:18; Jude 12-23) grouped into two pairs, the first aimed at opponents (Jas 4:13—5:6; Jude 12-15), the second at believers (Jas 5:7-18; Jude 17-23)

5. an exordium or introduction that hints at the problems (Jas 1:2-8; Jude 3-4)

6. inversion of order, which addresses an issue twice (Jas 2:1—3:14 and Jas 3:15—4:8a; Jude 5-6 and Jude 7-10)

7. concatenation (Jas 3:6; 4:7-11a; Jude 12-13, 22-23) and inclusio (Jas 1:2/1:12; 2:14/2:16; 2:17/2:26; 4:13/5:1; 5:9/5:12; Jude 6/13, 22/23)

8. catchwords, especially at strategic junctures

9. hymnic or doxological material (Jas 3:13-18; Jude 24-25)

10. a concluding exhortation to turn the sinner from the errant way (Jas 5:20; Jude 23)

Charles reminds us that the verbal correspondence between James and Jude is quite striking, with a higher degree of correspondence between these two documents than any other two documents in the New Testament (with the exceptions of Colossians and Ephesians and of Jude and 2 Peter): "All told there are ninety-three cases of verbal agreement which occur in the two letters, with twenty-seven terms occurring two or more times in both. Astonishingly, *each* of the twenty-five verses of Jude averages approximately four words found in the letter of James—an extraordinary rate of verbal correspondence."[25] In addition, Charles remarks that there are thematic overlaps between these documents: "While both James and Jude are strongly motivated by ethical concerns each assumes a doctrinal foundation already laid with the readers."[26] The most important theological correspondence is that both writers refer to Jesus as Lord who performs the functions at the second coming previously predicated of Yahweh, including execution of judgment on the ungodly (Jas 5:7-11; Jude 3-5): "Thus

---

[24]Charles, *Literary Strategy in the Epistle of Jude*, pp. 75-76.
[25]Ibid., p. 77.
[26]Ibid., p. 79.

OT theophany and NT Christology merge in the view of the writer."[27]

While this is perhaps not enough to suggest direct literary dependency of the homily of Jude on that of James, it is enough to suggest that both have drunk from the same Jewish well and that Jude is aware of and is writing in the wake of, though not directly borrowing from, the homily of James. Both writers show some real skill in using Koine Greek, and we may assume that both gained this skill in Jerusalem after Easter, though it may have been gained earlier in Galilee.

Jude bears not only a "family" resemblance to James, but this little document almost certainly bears some sort of literary relationship to 2 Peter. In the first place, nineteen of Jude's twenty-five verses appear in some form in 2 Peter. Nigel Turner stresses:

> Stylistic relationship with 2 Pet is shown as follows: Jude 2 optative (2 Pet 1:2), Jude 3 *all zeal* (2 Pet 1:5), *beloved* (2 Pet 3:1, 8, 14, 17), Jude 5 *put you in remembrance . . . though you knew* (2 Pet 1:12), Jude 17f *but beloved, remember the words which were spoken before of the apostles of the Lord. . . . "There shall be mockers in the last time who shall walk after their own lusts"* ([2 Pet] 3:1, 2, 3).
>
> Two of the words which Jude and 2 Peter share are not found elsewhere in the NT: *empaiktēs* and *huperogka.* Another word is not found elsewhere in Biblical Greek: *suneuocheisthai,* and the following are very rare in Biblical Greek: *zophos, spilas/os.* Both authors use Biblical words, but neither quotes the OT directly, unlike 1 Peter. The proportion of NT hapax in Jude and 2 Peter is the highest in the NT.
>
> 2 Peter has a more vibrant, excited style than Jude's and he is also more pretentious and artificial than either Jude or 1 Peter. He is probably more consciously stylistic. Both authors have a rhythmical and rhetorical style, but more of the underlying Jewish Greek appears in 2 Peter than in Jude.[28]

Jude is a manifestly more concise and more primitive document than either James or 1 Peter, and Jude 4-18 is very detailed and careful writing in midrashic form, whereas 2 Peter is more diffuse, without midrashic structure, and its eschatological outlook seems to be of a later period. Richard Bauckham says:

> It is reasonably easy to see how, e.g., Jude 6-8 could have been rewritten in a new literary form, with a slightly different purpose, in 2 Pet 2:3b-10a, and how an author who failed to perceive or was not interested in the midrashic structure and allusions of Jude 8c-16 could have revised the material in writing a straightforward passage of denunciation in 2 Pet 2:10b-18. It is much more difficult to imagine Jude constructing his elaborate midrash with 2 Pet 2 before him. It is easy to see how the author of 2 Peter could have seen Jude 8c-16 as useful material for composing a

---

[27]Ibid.
[28]Turner, "Style of Jude and 2 Peter," p. 144.

denunciation of the false teachers' sins, but it is difficult to see why it should have occurred to Jude to find in 2 Pet 2:10b-18 a quarry for material to use in constructing a midrash designed to show that the false teachers and their doom have been predicted in Scripture. There are cases where a more complex literary work is based on a simpler one, and *a priori* that might even seem a more likely procedure, but consideration of this particular case seems to indicate that it must be one in which the more complex work is prior.[29]

To this J. N. D. Kelly rightly adds:

> In a general way Jude is a more spontaneous and vigorous piece of writing, and also harsher in tone. Again, both catalogue examples (mostly the same ones) from Biblical history, but while Jude is careless of their correct chronological order, 2 Peter observes it scrupulously. Both appeal to these incidents in order to emphasize God's severity in dealing with sinners, but 2 Peter softens the denunciatory tone by introducing reminders of His graciousness towards righteous men like Noah and Lot. Finally their attitudes to scripture suggest that 2 Peter is the later document. On the one hand, while Jude freely draws illustrations from *1 Enoch* and the *Assumption of Moses,* even quoting (14f.) the former, 2 Peter condenses or cuts out these features with a consequent loss of picturesque detail and even, on occasion (see on ii.11), intelligibility; plainly he has stricter views on the OT and is reluctant to employ apocryphal books. On the other hand, his manner of speaking about Paul's letters (iii.16) betrays his awareness that an embryonic NT canon is beginning to be recognized. His at first sight curious failure to reproduce the exact wording of Jude is to be explained, in part at any rate, by the fact that he is a self-conscious stylist with a passion for opulent diction; but it is also possible that he did not have the earlier tract on his desk before him as he wrote, but preferred to trust his memory.[30]

This raises questions about the authorship of 2 Peter (which will be addressed in the third volume in this series). Besides 2 Peter, no other reasonable contemporary document manifests traces of Jude. However, Jude was popular in the second and third centuries and widely accepted as Scripture in Rome (Muratorian Canon, ca. 200), Atria (Tertullian, 160-225) and Alexandria (Clement, 150-215).

Only later did the book fall into disfavor because of its use of apocryphal material from the books of *1 Enoch* and the *Assumption of Moses*. This caused Origen, Eusebius, Chrysostom and Jerome to have doubts about the book's appropriateness as a canonical book, and the church in Syria generally rejected

---

[29]Bauckham, *Jude, 2 Peter,* p. 142.
[30]Kelly, *Peter and Jude,* p. 227.

the book until the sixth century. On the other hand, such notable figures as Athanasius (367) included it in his famous canon. Luther regarded Jude as dependent on 2 Peter and as postapostolic and did not include it among his group of "true, certain, chief books of the New Testament." Jude had some difficulties being accepted in the church between the mid-second and sixth centuries and later by Luther, but early on it was accepted and popular and this judgment is important.

There are two possible reasons why Jude was placed where it is in the canon: (1) perhaps a canonical collection of General Letters had James first and Jude last, thus framed by sermons from the brothers of Jesus (Robert Wall, personal conversation). There may be something to this, but why would the Petrine and Johannine letters be placed between these two sermons? (2) Or perhaps Jude comes just before Revelation because it has the same early Jewish apocalyptic and eschatological character as Revelation.

Who wrote this book? Jude brother of James could be one of only two people: (1) Jesus' younger (perhaps youngest) brother or (2) Jude the prophet who was a fellow worker with James in Acts 15. The arguments for this being a pseudonymous document are weak on numerous grounds:

1. It would be very difficult to successfully pull off a pseudepigraphical letter in early Christianity, which had a concern about intellectual property and pseudepigraphical documents in the first century. No literary convention in that era allowed one to think that pseudepigraphical letters were an acceptable literary device.[31]

2. The ethical, theological and especially the Jewish eschatological content in this letter bespeaks a Jewish Christian atmosphere, not a late Catholic atmosphere. William Brosend puts it this way: "The letter pulses throughout with anticipation of the Lord's return, cares nothing for office or position, and deals with a dispute easily understood as possible in earliest Jewish Christianity."[32]

3. Jude was too obscure a person for someone to use his name to add authority to a document, and if the point was to add authority to the document surely Jude's being Jesus' brother would have been mentioned. If one counters that perhaps this document was pseudonymously written to a Jewish-Christian community that knew and revered Jude and the family of Jesus in general,[33] it may be insisted that if they knew Jude and

---

[31]Witherington, *Letters and Homilies*, 1.23-27.
[32]Brosend, *James and Jude*, p. 4.
[33]Bauckham, *Jude and the Relatives of Jesus*, pp. 171-78.

if this comes from a Palestinian Jewish community would they not also have known that he did not write this document or at least what sort of document and style he was likely to write? Palestinian Jewish Christianity and its successors in the Diaspora would surely be the least likely to be fooled or accept such a document if it was inauthentic.

The Greek and the rhetoric of this document are rather good but not beyond the scope of a literate person living in Galilee, especially if a scribe was used to compose the document itself (cf. 2 Thess 3:17). Duane Watson puts it this way: "Having an elementary education (which included some rhetorical training), hearing weekly exposition of the Old Testament in the synagogue, living in Galilee (an area dotted with Greek-speaking cities), and needing to increase proficiency in Greek to effectively preach to Greek audiences would have gone a long way toward explaining how Jesus' brother could come to possess competency in these skills. Thus there is really no strong reason to argue that the author could be anyone other than Jude, the brother of Jesus and James."[34]

Against E. Earle Ellis's thesis that Jude the prophet wrote this book[35] are two salient points: (1) he equates the terms *brother* and *coworker*, but "James and the brothers" in Acts 15:18 is not the same expression as "brother of James" and (2) he conceives that Jude's opponents are the same as those causing Paul trouble in Galatia, that is, Judaizers, but Judaizers were legalists, which seems inconsistent with their being libertines, as depicted in Jude.

The letter of Jude, like the letter of James, has an air of assumed authority over its audience, not an authority that had to be proved or indicated by saying "brother of Jesus." On the other hand, to say "brother of James" is significant (1) if Jude was written when James was head of the church or (2) if Jude is written to a group that had high respect for James. Jesus was in heaven and could not be visited if one wanted to check out Jude's credentials, besides which Jude had come to view Jesus as so much more than his physical brother but rather as his Lord. That he—like James—begins his letters with "a *doulos* of Jesus" indicates the position he takes in relationship to Jesus. He does not try to infer equality or near equality with Jesus by insisting, "I am Jesus' brother," perhaps because he had long since learned that physical relationships availed not in Jesus' kingdom (Mk 3:31-35).

Other interesting parallels between James and Jude suggest that they came out of the same milieu:[36]

---

[34]Watson, *Jude*, p. 474.

[35]Ellis, *Prophecy and Hermeneutics in Early Christianity*, pp. 221-36.

[36]Mayor lists a host of other similarities in *James*, pp. i-lxvii.

1. Both share a love for colorful illustrations and metaphorical speech.

2. Both are saturated in the Old Testament, although unlike James, Jude manifests a use of the Hebrew Old Testament, not the Septuagint.

3. Both insist on moral strictness and use stern language in rebuking sin.

4. Both use *agapētoi* three times.

There are also notable differences:

1. Jude does not manifest a lot of contacts with Jesus' sayings, but then his discourse is much briefer than James.

2. Jude feels free to use the Pseudepigrapha—*1 Enoch, Assumption of Moses*—unlike James, but this was very common among Jews of this era and probably Jewish Christians. This just happens to be the only place where such usage got into the canon.

3. Jude seems more than James to be combating a specific kind of opponent, not just general ills, and he has only one main theme, whereas James has at least three interwoven themes. Basically, Jude is telling his people to fight for the faith (Jude 3, 20-23) because the false teachers are people whose behavior and teaching are condemned and dangerous (Jude 4-19). Jude is almost entirely a specific polemic.

4. Jude has abundant use of Scripture or apostolic citation followed by interpretation and application in a midrash pesher fashion—a technique where ancient texts were applied to current situations and were seen to prophesy to these specific current situations.[37] The pesher formula "this is (like) that" is found in Jude. This hermeneutical technique made clear how these events were foreseen and condemned by God's spokesmen. Jude also manifests a use of typology, whereby something in the Old Testament is an antitype of something today. In this regard Jude is more Jewish than James, and more similar to Hebrews than to James.

The Greek of Jude is in general better and more literate than James's, and just as James had many *hapax legomena*, so also does Jude—fourteen unique words in a short discourse.[38] Jude manifests a wide vocabulary, but his syntax is rather ordinary. There are also protruding Semitisms and parataxis, which are indications of Biblical Greek (*hagios, psychikos, klētos*), as well as rhythm, rhyme and a fondness for triplets (Jude 8, 11; cf. Jude 2, 4, 3-7).[39] Charles Landon puts

---

[37]Ellis, *Prophecy and Hermeneutics in Early Christianity*, pp. 222-23.
[38]Bauckham, *Jude, 2 Peter*, p. 6. Cf. Turner, "Style of Jude and 2 Peter," pp. 139-40.
[39]Mayor, *Jude*, p. lix.

it this way: "There are at least 11 groups of catchwords in Jude, 19 occurrences of triadic illustration, 24 instances of synonymous parallelism, and 18 instances of contrast or antithesis. The predominance of such stylistic features and of a carefully designed midrashic rhetorical structure make Jude one of the most stylistically distinctive books of the New Testament."[40] Richard Bauckham bests sums up the linguistic evidence:

> [Jude] was probably still a very young man when he became a Christian missionary, and if his missionary travels took him among strongly Hellenized Jews there is no reason why he should not have deliberately improved his command of Greek to increase his effectiveness as a preacher. A wide vocabulary, which Jude has, is easier to acquire than a skill in literary style, where Jude's competence is less remarkable. The kinds of skills he shows are the rhetorical skills which a Jewish preacher in Greek would need.[41]

Nothing in the language would prohibit Jude, Jesus' brother, from having written this, and various things positively suggest it.

It is sometimes alleged that Jude must be late because it exhibits later concerns for passing on the fixed Christian tradition and uses *pistis* to mean a deposit of teaching. Against this, as Ellis shows, Paul manifests both of these phenomena in his undisputed letters (e.g., Gal 1:23; 1 Cor 11).[42] Further, mention of the false teachers being written of long ago (Jude 4) is a reference to the Old Testament, not to the teaching of the apostles being ancient, as we see from Ellis's structural analysis of the book.[43] Whatever flaws there are in his analysis, this much is certain: Jude 4 does not refer to apostolic teaching. Further, Jude 17 clearly indicates that Jude's audience had heard the apostles personally. This is no postapostolic document! The following outline takes into account the toggling back and forth between citations and commentary:[44]

1. general introduction (Jude 1-4): address and greetings (Jude 1-2) and reason for writing/theme to be addressed (Jude 3-4)

2. introduction to midrashic scriptural citation (Jude 5a)

3. conglomerate citation introduced by *hoti*: Numbers 14:25; Genesis 6:1-4; *1 Enoch* 10.4-6; Genesis 19:4-25; 2 Peter 2:6, 10 (Jude 5b-7)

4. commentary section introduced by *houtos* (Jude 8)

---

[40]Landon, *Text-Critical Study*, p. 142.
[41]Bauckham, *Jude, 2 Peter*, p. 15.
[42]Ellis, *Prophecy and Hermeneutics*, p. 233.
[43]Ibid., pp. 221-23.
[44]Bauckham, *Jude, 2 Peter*, pp. 5-6.

5. conglomerate citation introduced by *de: Assumption of Moses* (?), Zechariah 3:2 (Jude 9)

6. commentary section introduced by *houtos* (Jude 10)

7. conglomerate citation introduced by *hoti:* targum on Genesis 4:8; Deuteronomy 23:4; Numbers 16 (Jude 11)

8. commentary section introduced by *houtos* (Jude 12-14a)

9. conglomerate citation introduced by *legō* and *idou: 1 Enoch* 1.9; 1QapGen (Genesis Apocryphon) 2.20-22 (Jude 14b-15)

10. commentary section introduced by *houtos* (Jude 16-17)

11. citation of apostolic teaching introduced by *legō* and *hoti* (Jude 18; cf. 2 Peter 3:3; 2 Timothy 3; 4:3; Acts 20:29-30)

12. commentary section/concluding exhortation introduced by *houtos* (Jude 19-23)

13. closing benediction/doxology (Jude 24-25)

The transition from text to commentary is especially obvious because of the shift in verb tense: every commentary section is in the present tense, while the citations can be past tense (Jude 5-7, 9, 11, 15) or future tense (Jude 18). Notably, Jude 18 is the apostolic teaching section and differs from the Scripture citations in this respect also.

In addition, catchword connections link various parts of the letter:

krisis (Jude 6, 9, 15)
kyrios (Jude 4, 5, 9, 14, 17, 21, 25)
laleō (Jude 15, 16)
sōzō (Jude 5, 23)
tēreō (Jude 1, 6 [twice], 13, 21)

A rhetorical outline of the discourse helps us see some of its other prominent features. William Brosend basically outlines the rhetorical structure as follows:[45]

epistolary salutation (Jude 1-2)

exordium, narratio, proposition: intruders marked out for judgment are in your midst (Jude 3-4)

three proofs from sacred tradition: exodus, angels, Sodom (Jude 5-10)

  first summation: dreamers defile and blaspheme (Jude 8)

---

[45]Brosend, *James and Jude*, p. 166; see also Watson, *Invention, Arrangement and Style*, pp. 29-79.

example of judgment: Michael versus the devil over Moses' body (Jude 9)
second summation: blasphemers are destroyed (Jude 10)

three more proofs from sacred tradition: Cain, Balaam, Korah (Jude 11-16)
    third summation: blemishes on love feasts (Jude 12-13)
    example of judgment: Enoch's prophecy (Jude 14-15)
    fourth summation: grumblers and troublemakers (Jude 16)

final peroration: exhorting the faithful (Jude 17-23)
   remember the words of the apostles (Jude 17-19)
   build yourself up and pray (Jude 20)
   keep yourself in the love of God (Jude 21)
   have mercy on some, save others (Jude 22-23)

benediction (Jude 24-25)

This is far more elaborate than J. Daryl Charles's analysis:[46]

prooimion (Jude 1-2)
diegesis (i.e., thesis) (Jude 3-4)
pistis (proofs) (Jude 5-16)
epilogos (Jude 17-23)

Duane Watson's original rhetorical analysis looks like this:[47]

epistolary prescript (Jude 1-2)
exordium (Jude 3)
narratio (Jude 4)
probation, composed of three proofs (Jude 5-16)
peroratio (Jude 17-23)
    repetitio (Jude 17-19)
    adfectus (Jude 20-23)
doxology (Jude 24-25)

What these analyses do not reveal is that our author is engaging in the rhetorical art of synkrisis or comparison. In this case the contemporary false teachers are likened to various ancient prototypes of such folks, both human and angelic, and their fate is likened to the fate of such misbehavers.

None of these outlines looks particularly epistolary in character. They suggest some sort of Jewish rhetorical sermon that has an epistolary prescript only because it was written down and sent to a remote audience. The conclusion of

---

[46]Charles, *Literary Strategy in the Epistle of Jude*, p. 28.
[47]Watson, *Invention, Arrangement and Style*, p. vii. In his more recent *Jude*, p. 480, Watson puts Jude 3-4 together under the heading of a petition to contend for the faith.

this document is not epistolary at all—it involves a doxology. Thus the term *epistolary* is applicable to only the first couple verses of this document and reflects the discourse being written down and sent to the audience rather than directly delivered to them in person. I conclude that this document, like James, is carefully constructed and written by one of the Lord's brothers, presumably his youngest brother. Its Jewish Christian flavor is obvious.

When should we date the book? Joseph Mayor suggests that Jude was born around A.D. 10 and could have lived out the century (ninety years old?).[48] We know nothing of his death. He was probably a traveling missionary, and 1 Corinthians 9:5 likely refers to Jude, since James seems to have stayed in Jerusalem. Jude then was married and his wife traveled with him. He could have written this letter anywhere between 35 and 100, except that it is used in 2 Peter. If we date 2 Peter between 90 and 100, then Jude must be before that. Further, there is no mention of the destruction of Jerusalem in 70, or even its aftershocks, which so shattered the Jews' world and worldview. It is hard to believe that there would be no trace of this event if Jude was written after it.

Jude 1 suggests that James is still alive, and this puts Jude before 62. The reference to the apostles implies that the author was probably contemporary with them, but perhaps not one of them. At the least, the reference to the apostles in Jude suggests that he is addressing communities that other apostolic figures founded. Again, this leads to the period of 62 or before since Peter and probably other apostles died in the 60s. More precise than this, we cannot be, but nothing prevents a date in the early 50s or as late as 60-61.[49] In any event, it breathes the atmosphere of the earliest Jewish Christianity, in a region with false teachers but not enough apostolic figures to police the situation directly. There is nothing approaching the early Catholic structures of monarchial bishops in this document.

JUDE'S AUDIENCE

One thing immediately apparent in Jude is that the boundaries of the community he addresses are porous enough that outside Jewish teachers can enter and stir up the audience. This surely suggests a time prior to the Jewish war in the 60s and well before the major separation of Jews and Jewish Christians after the fall of Jerusalem in 70, a divide probably reflected in Matthew's rhetoric against the Pharisees.[50]

The use of purity language to reinforce porous boundaries provides another

---

[48]Mayor, *Jude*, p. cxlviii.
[49]Bauckham, *Jude, 2 Peter*, p. 13.
[50]See the helpful discussion by Hengel, "Early Christianity."

social dimension for analyzing Jude. While I am rather skeptical of some of the cultural anthropological analyses applied by Jerome Neyrey and others to Jude's purity language (as the concepts often need to be more firmly grounded in the actual social values and behavior of persons in the Greco-Roman world), he is on to something. Neyrey puts it this way:

> Ancient Jews and Greeks alike thought of the universe and all in it as a *kosmos*, an organized and structured whole. This general sense of order and appropriate classification is what is meant by "purity" on a general, abstract level. . . . Something is "pure" or "clean" when it is in accord with the social expectation of order and propriety; conversely, things are "polluted" or "unclean" when they violate the common assumptions of the way the world is structured. . . . All attempts to classify, to hierarchize, to draw boundary lines and the like indicate a strong sense of "purity" or order.[51]

Language about "pollution" occurs in Jude 8, "blemishes" in Jude 12 and "shame" in Jude 13. The false teachers are portrayed as "out of bounds" and violating the order and rules and ethics of the community. Neyrey fails to say that our author's sense of order is not grounded merely in the "way things always have been" or the creation rules of the cosmos. His sense of order is grounded eschatologically in the way that God reoriented things in Christ's first coming and will continue to reorient things in the eschatological judgment. Our author's ethics are grounded in the new world order coming into being and in the way things ought to be, not in the way things always have been since the Fall.

Coupled with use of early sacred Jewish traditions (both canonical and apocryphal), the purity language makes clear that Jude is addressing Jewish Christians in a way that would most effectively persuade them to divest themselves of the influence of the false teachers. Jude becomes a word on target when one recognizes that author and audience share a universe of discourse that is eschatological, esoteric, text-based and early Jewish Christian in various respects.

With regard to the opponents in Jude, Ruth Anne Reese suggests that one of the purposes

> of the book of Jude as a whole is to shame the opponents who are denying Jesus and acting for their own benefit. At the same time, the book recognizes that these opponents have power and have been using that power to look out for themselves at the community's gatherings. Jews and Gentiles lived in both the Greco-Roman community and within the Christian community (another world). In the Christian community they might find themselves acting out of different understandings of

---

[51]Neyrey, *Jude and 2 Peter*, pp. 10-11.

what it meant to have honor (honor belonged to those within the community who affirmed their belief in Jesus Christ and practiced those beliefs in practical ways)— whereas, in the greater culture, affirmation of Jesus Christ would be a reason for ridicule and shame rather than honor. In a culture that values the group over the individual, the implications of following Jesus for one's position within the society and within one's own family were a challenge to the foundations of their way of life. . . . The epistle of Jude is addressed to a group known as the Beloved. In contrast to the beloved, there is another group, the ungodly. They are often referred to throughout the letter as simply *houtoi* ("those people") (Jude 8, 10, 12, 16, 19). They are a group of people who are a secret part of the Beloved. In other words, while the letter makes a strong case for a difference between us, the beloved, and them, the ungodly, it also indicates that this division is happening right within the group of people to whom the letter is addressed, the Beloved. The others are characterized as ungodly people who reject authority, do what they please, and speak in a manner that leads to arguments, division, murmuring, and speaking against God. This is a group who takes advantage of God's grace and forgiveness as well as their position within the Christian community to lead a life that is lacking in godliness, purity, and self-control.[52]

We must take seriously then that the false teachers have some clout, some *auctoritas* as the Romans would call it, within the audience that Jude addresses, and they have been wielding it in self-serving ways, to judge from what Jude says about them.

GREEK TEXT OF JUDE

A telltale sign of the relative neglect of Jude's discourse is that, despite its difficult text-critical problems,[53] prior to Charles Landon's 1996 study there had been no systematic or thorough treatment of this subject.[54] Carl Axel Albin's 1962 study discussed only twenty-one variation units,[55] and Sakae Kubo's very particularistic 1965 study focused on the relationship of $\mathfrak{P}^{72}$ and Codex Vaticanus (B) for what it can tell us about Jude and 2 Peter and their possible interrelationship.[56] The following manuscripts are especially helpful in determining the original text of Jude: $\mathfrak{P}^{72}$, $\aleph$, A, B, K, L, Y and 049. Landon looks at 95 variants and concludes that A and B are most likely to preserve correct readings (69 and 70 readings, respectively), while $\mathfrak{P}^{72}$ interestingly preserves

---

[52]Reese, *Jude* (manuscript). My thanks to Ruth Anne Reese for allowing me to read her commentary in manuscript form.
[53]Bauckham, "Letter of Jude," p. 3792.
[54]Landon, *Text-Critical Study.*
[55]Albin, *Judasbrevet.*
[56]Kubo, $\mathfrak{P}^{72}$ *and the Codex Vaticanus.*

only 57 correct readings and 38 incorrect ones.[57] This serves as a warning that earlier manuscripts do not necessarily preserve original readings. Much depends on the carefulness of the scribe copying the given document, regardless of its age. We must study Jude verse by verse, taking each textual issue as it comes.

Bibliography on Jude

It was possible thirty years ago for Douglas Rowston to dub Jude the most neglected book in the New Testament.[58] He could not have foreseen the large number of commentaries, monographs, doctoral dissertations and seminal articles that would be written on Jude between 1975 and 2006. Few if any other twenty-five-verse segments in the New Testament have been so thoroughly analyzed in this period, using all sorts of new methods: social-scientific commentary (Jerome Neyrey), rhetorical commentary (William Brosend), detailed analysis of early Jewish literature as the proper context for understanding Jude (Richard Bauckham), modern literary theory (Ruth Anne Reese), ancient theory that sees form and content coinhering (J. Daryl Charles) and text criticism (Charles Landon). Jude has even been "debated" by Cicero to determine whether he knew rhetoric (Thomas Wolthuis)! The author surely could never have imagined all this verbiage spent on his little sermon. There is as of yet no introductory primer on Jude, like we have for other New Testament books, but in light of all the above, someone is bound to do one soon.

Of the commentaries old and new on Jude, happily a goodly number can be commended. None is more deserving than Richard Bauckham's *Jude, 2 Peter*, which frankly has been neither equaled nor eclipsed since it came out over twenty years ago. From a cultural anthropological and social-scientific viewpoint, Jerome Neyrey's *2 Peter, Jude* is a helpful supplement to Bauckham's landmark study, as is Duane Watson's *Letter of Jude* and William Brosend's *James and Jude*—two brief commentaries that introduce the reader to the rhetorical dimensions of the text by drawing on the considerable twenty-year discussion of this topic. These analyses require supplementation by Watson's earlier and crucial *Invention, Arrangement and Style*. Of the Continental commentaries, perhaps the most helpful is Anton Vögtle's *Judasbrief*.[59]

---

[57]Landon, *Text-Critical Study*, p. 148.
[58]Rowston, "Most Neglected Book in the New Testament."
[59]A special thanks to an old Gordon-Conwell Theological Seminary friend, Scott Hafemann, for help with the main part of this bibliography.

Commentaries

Bauckham, Richard. *Jude, 2 Peter.* Word Biblical Commentary 50. Waco: Word, 1983.

Beasley-Murray, George R. *The General Epistles: James, 1 Peter, Jude, 2 Peter.* Bible Guides 21. New York: Abingdon, 1965.

Bigg, Charles. *A Critical and Exegetical Commentary on the Epistles of St. Peter and St. Jude.* International Critical Commentary. Edinburgh: Clark, 1901.

Boor, Werner de, and Uwe Holmer. *Die zwei Briefe des Petrus und der Brief des Judas.* Wuppertal: Brockhaus 1976.

Bray, Gerald, ed. *James, 1-2 Peter, 1-3 John, Jude.* Ancient Christian Commentary on Scripture: New Testament 11. Downers Grove, Ill.: InterVarsity Press, 2000.

Brosend, William. *James and Jude.* Cambridge: Cambridge University Press, 2004.

Chaine, Joseph. *Les épîtres catholiques: La seconde épître de saint Pierre, les épîtres de saint Jean, l'épître de saint Jude.* 2nd edition. Études bibliques 27. Paris: Gabalda, 1939.

Craddock, Fred B. *First and Second Peter and Jude.* Louisville: Westminster John Knox, 1995.

Cranfield, C. E. B. *I and II Peter and Jude: Introduction and Commentary.* Torch Bible Commentaries. London: SCM, 1960.

Dalton, W. J. "Jude." In *A New Catholic Commentary on Holy Scripture.* Edited by Reginald C. Fuller, Leonard Johnston and Conleth Kearns. London: Nelson, 1969.

Felten, Joseph. *Die zwei Briefe des heiligen Petrus und der Judasbrief.* Regensburg: Manz, 1929.

Fronmüller, G. F. C. *The Epistle General of Jude.* New York: Scribner, 1867.

Fuchs, Eric, and Pierre Reymond. *La deuxième épître de saint Pierre; l'épître de saint Jude.* Commentaire du Nouveau Testament 13b. Neuchâtel: Delachaux & Néstlé, 1980.

Green, Michael. *The Second Epistle General of Peter and the General Epistle of Jude.* Tyndale New Testament Commentaries. Grand Rapids: Eerdmans, 1968.

Grundmann, Walter. *Der Brief des Judas und der zweite Brief des Petrus.* Theologischer Handkommentar zum Neuen Testament 15. Berlin: Evangelische Verlagsanstalt, 1974.

Hauck, Friedrich. *Die Briefe des Jakobus, Petrus, Judas und Johannes.* 8th edition. Das Neue Testament Deutsch 10. Göttingen: Vandenhoeck & Ruprecht, 1957.

James, M. R. *The Second Epistle General of Peter and the General Epistle of Jude.*

Cambridge Greek Testament for Schools and Colleges. Cambridge: Cambridge University Press, 1912.

Kelly, J. N. D. *A Commentary on the Epistles of Peter and of Jude.* Harper's New Testament Commentaries. New York: Harper, 1969.

Kistemaker, Simon J. *Expositions of the Epistles of Peter and of the Epistle of Jude.* Grand Rapids: Baker, 1987.

Krodel, Gerhard. "The Letter of Jude," pp. 92-98 in *Hebrews, James, 1 and 2 Peter, Jude, Revelation.* Edited by Gerhard Krodel. Proclamation Commentaries. Philadelphia, 1977.

Lawlor, George Lawrence. *Translation and Exposition of the Epistle of Jude.* International Library of Philosophy and Theology Series. Nutley, N.J.: Presbyterian & Reformed, 1972.

Leahy, Thomas W. "The Epistle of Jude." Vol. 2, pp. 378-80 in *The Jerome Biblical Commentary.* Edited by Raymond E. Brown, Joseph A. Fitzmyer and Roland E. Murphy. Englewood Cliffs, N.J.: Prentice-Hall, 1965.

Leaney, A. R. C. *The Letters of Peter and Jude: A Commentary on the First Letter of Peter, a Letter of Jude and Second Letter of Peter.* Cambridge Bible Commentary. Cambridge: Cambridge University Press, 1967.

Leconte, René. *Les épîtres catholiques de saint Jacques, saint Jude et saint Pierre.* Paris: Cerf, 1953.

Lenski, R. C. H. *The Interpretation of the Epistles of St. Peter, St. John and St. Jude.* Columbus: Wartburg, 1945.

Luther, Martin. *Commentary on the Epistles of Peter and Jude.* Translated by J. G. Walch. Reprinted Grand Rapids: Kregel, 1982.

Manton, Thomas. *An Exposition of the Epistle of Jude.* Cambridge Bible Commentary. Reprinted London: Banner of Truth, 1958.

Mayor, Joseph B. *The Epistle of St. Jude and the Second Epistle of St. Peter.* London: Macmillan, 1907.

Michl, Johann. *Die katholischen Briefe.* 2nd edition. Regensburger Neues Testament 8. Regensburg: Pustet, 1968.

Moffatt, James. *The General Epistles: James, Peter and Judas.* Moffatt New Testament Commentary. London: Hodder & Stoughton, 1928.

Neyrey, Jerome H. *2 Peter, Jude.* Anchor Bible 37C. New York: Doubleday, 1993.

Payne, David F. "Jude." In *A New Testament Commentary.* Edited by G. C. D. Howley. London: Pickering & Inglis, 1969.

Perkins, Pheme. *First and Second Peter, James and Jude.* Louisville: John Knox, 1995.

Plummer, Alfred. "The Epistle of St. Jude." In *A New Testament Commentary for English Readers*, vol. 3. Edited by C. J. Ellicott. London: Cassell, 1884.

————. *The General Epistles of St. James and St. Jude*. Expositors' Bible. London: Hodder & Stoughton, 1891.

Plumptre, Edward Hayes. *The General Epistles of St. Peter and St. Jude*. Cambridge Bible for Schools and Colleges. Cambridge: Cambridge University Press, 1910.

Reese, Ruth Anne. *The Letter of Jude*. Two Horizons Commentary. Grand Rapids: Eerdmans, forthcoming.

Reicke, Bo. *The Epistles of James, Peter and Jude*. Anchor Bible 37. New York: Doubleday, 1964.

Reuss, Joseph. *Die katholischen Briefe*. Echter-Bibel 3. Würzburg: Echter, 1952.

Schelkle, Karl Hermann. *Die Petrusbriefe, der Judasbrief*. 5th edition. Herders theologischer Kommentar zum Neuen Testament 13.2. Freiburg: Herder, 1980.

Schlatter, Adolf. *Die Briefe des Petrus, Judas, Jakobus, der Brief an die Hebräer*. Stuttgart: Calwer, 1964.

Schneider, Johannes. *Die Briefe des Jakobs, Petrus, Judas und Johannes: Die katholischen Briefe*. 9th edition. Das Neue Testament Deutsch 10. Göttingen: Vandenhoeck & Ruprecht, 1961.

Schrage, Wolfgang, and Horst Balz. *Die "Katholischen" Briefe: Die Briefe des Jakobus, Petrus, Johannes und Judas*. 11th edition. Das Neue Testament Deutsch 10. Göttingen: Vandenhoeck & Ruprecht, 1973.

Seethaler, Paula-Angelika. *Hoffnung im Leid: Die Petrusbriefe, der Judasbrief*. 3rd edition. Stuttgarter kleiner Kommentar: Neues Testament 16. Stuttgart: Katholisches Bibelwerk, 1972.

Sidebottom, E. M. *James, Jude and 2 Peter*. New Century Bible. London: Nelson, 1967.

Soden, Hermann von. *Hebräerbrief, Briefe des Petrus, Jakobus, Judas*. 3rd edition. Hand-Commentar zum Neuen Testament 3.2. Freiburg im Breisgau: Mohr, 1899.

Spitta, Friedrich. *Die zweite Brief des Petrus und der Brief des Judas*. Halle a. S.: Waisenhauses, 1885.

Staffelbach, Georg. *Die Briefe der Apostel Jakobus, Judas, Petrus und Johannes*. Lucerne: Räber, 1941.

Summers, Ray. "Jude." Vol. 12, pp. 232-39 in *The Broadman Biblical Commentary*. Edited by Clifton J. Allen. Nashville: Broadman, 1972.

Vögtle, Anton. *Der Judasbrief der zeite Petrusbrief*. Benzinger: Neukirchener Verlag, 1994.

Watson, Duane F. *The Letter of Jude*. New Interpreter's Bible 12. Nashville: Abingdon, 1998.

Windisch, Hans, and Herbert Preisker. *Die katholischen Briefe.* 3rd edition. Handbuch zum Neuen Testament 15. Tübingen: Mohr, 1950.

Wohlenberg, Gustav. *Der erste und zweite Petrusbrief und der Judasbrief.* 3rd edition. Kommentar zum Neuen Testament 15. Leipzig-Erlangen: Deichert, 1923.

Wolff, Richard. *A Commentary on the Epistle of Jude.* Grand Rapids: Zondervan, 1960.

Monographs and Articles

Adam, Alfred. "Erwägungen zur Herkunft der Didache." *Zeitschrift für Kirchengeschichte* 68 (1957): 1-47.

Albin, Carl Axel. *Judasbrevet: Traditionen Texten Tolkningen.* Stockholm: Natur och Kultur, 1962.

Barns, Thomas. "The Epistle of St. Jude: A Study in the Marcosian Heresy." *JTS* 6 (1905): 391-411.

Bartlet, James Vernon. *The Apostolic Age: Its Life, Doctrine, Worship and Polity.* Ten Epochs of Church History 1. New York: Scribner, 1899.

Bauckham, Richard. "James, 1 and 2 Peter, Jude," pp. 303-17 in *It Is Written: Scripture Citing Scripture: Essays in Honour of Barnabas Lindars.* Edited by D. A. Carson and H. G. M. Williamson. Cambridge: Cambridge University Press, 1988.

———. "Jude, Epistle of." Vol. 3, pp. 1098-1103 in *The Anchor Bible Dictionary.* Edited by David Noel Freedman et al. New York: Doubleday, 1992.

———. *Jude and the Relatives of Jesus in the Early Church.* Edinburgh: Clark, 1990.

———. "The Letter of Jude: An Account of Research." *ANRW* 2.25.5 (1988): 3791-3826.

———. "A Note on a Problem in the Greek Version of I Enoch i.9." *JTS* 32 (1981): 136-38.

Beckwith, Roger. *The Old Testament Canon of the New Testament Church and Its Background in Early Judaism.* Grand Rapids: Eerdmans, 1985.

Beker, Johan Christiaan. "Jude, Letter of." Vol. 2, pp. 1009-11 in *Interpreter's Dictionary of the Bible.* Edited by G. A. Buttrick. New York: Abingdon, 1962.

Berg, Clayton L., Jr. "The Theology of Jude." Th.M. thesis, Dallas Theological Seminary, 1954.

Berger, Klaus. "Der Streit des guten und des bosen Engels um die Seele: Beobachtungen zu 4QAmr[b] und Judas 9." *Journal for the Study of Judaism* 4 (1973): 1-18.

Birdsall, J. Neville. "The Text of Jude in $\mathfrak{P}^{72}$." *JTS* 14 (1963): 394-99.

Black, Matthew. "The Christological Use of the Old Testament in the New Testament." *NTS* 18 (1971-72): 1-14.

———. "Critical and Exegetical Notes on Three New Testament Texts: Hebrews xi.11, Jude 5, James i.27," pp. 39-45 in *Apophoreta: Festschrift für Ernst Haenchen.* Edited by Walther Eltester and F. H. Kettler. Berlin: Töpelmann, 1964.

———. "The Maranatha Invocation and Jude 14, 15 (I Enoch 1:9)," pp. 189-96 in *Christ and Spirit in the New Testament: In Honour of Charles Francis Digby Moule.* Edited by Barnabas Lindars and Stephen S. Smalley. Cambridge: Cambridge University Press, 1973.

Boobyer, G. H. "The Verbs in Jude 11." *NTS* 5 (1958): 45-47.

Bruce, F. F. "Jude, Epistle of." Vol. 2, pp. 831-32 in *The Illustrated Bible Dictionary.* Edited by J. D. Douglas. Revised edition edited by Norman Hillyer. Leicester: IVP/Tyndale, 1980.

Burkitt, Francis Crawford. "Moses, Assumption of." Vol. 3, pp. 448-50 in *A Dictionary of the Bible.* Edited by James Hastings. Edinburgh: Clark, 1900.

Cantinat, Jean. "The Catholic Epistles." In *Introduction to the New Testament.* Edited by André Robert and André Feuillet. New York: Desclée, 1965.

———. *Les épîtres de saint Jacques et de saint Jude.* Sources bibliques. Paris: Gabalda, 1973.

Cassuto, Umberto. "The Episode of the Sons of God and the Daughters of Man (Genesis vi 1-4)." Vol. 1, pp. 17-28 in Cassuto's *Biblical and Oriental Studies.* Translated by Israel Abrahams. Jerusalem: Magnes, 1973.

Chancey, Mark A. *The Myth of a Gentile Galilee.* Cambridge: Cambridge University Press, 2002.

Charles, J. Daryl. "Jude's Use of Pseudepigraphical Source-Material as Part of a Literary Strategy." *NTS* 37 (1991): 130-45.

———. "'Those' and 'These': The Use of the Old Testament in the Epistle of Jude." *JSNT* 38 (1990): 109-24.

Charles, R. H. *The Assumption of Moses.* London: Black, 1897.

Charlesworth, James H. "The Pseudepigrapha as Biblical Exegesis," pp. 139-52 in *Early Jewish and Christian Exegesis: Studies in Memory of William Hugh Brownlee.* Edited by Craig A. Evans and William F. Stinespring. Atlanta: Scholars Press, 1987.

Chase, F. H. "Jude, Epistle of." Vol. 2, pp. 799-806 in *A Dictionary of the Bible.* Edited by James Hastings. Edinburgh: Clark, 1899.

Childs, Brevard S. "Jude," pp. 488-93 in Childs's *The New Testament as Canon: An Introduction.* Philadelphia: Fortress, 1985.

Cladder, Hermann Johann. "Strophical Structure in St. Jude's Epistle." *JTS* 5 (1903-4): 589-601.

Cone, Orello. "Jude, the General Epistle of." Vol. 2, cols. 2630-32 in *Encyclopaedia Biblica*. Edited by T. K. Cheyne and J. Sutherland Black. London: Clark, 1901.

Cothenet, Édouard. "La tradition selon Jude et 2 Pierre." *NTS* 35 (1989): 407-20.

Daniel, C. "'Faux prophetes': Surnom des esseniens dans le Sermon sur la Montagne." *Revue de Qumran* 7 (1969): 45-79.

————. "La mention des esseniens dans le texts grec de l'épître de S. Jude." *Muséon* 81 (1968): 503-21.

Danker, Frederick W. "Jude, Epistle of." Vol. 2, pp. 1153-55 in *The International Standard Bible Encyclopedia*. Edited by Geoffrey W. Bromiley. Grand Rapids: Eerdmans, 1982.

Daube, David. "Rabbinic Methods of Interpretation and Hellenistic Rhetoric." *Hebrew Union College Annual* 22 (1949): 239-62.

Davidson, Samuel. *An Introduction to the Study of the New Testament.* 3rd edition. London: Kegan Paul, Trench, Trübner, 1894.

Dehandschutter, Boudewijn. "Pseudo-Cyprian, Jude and Enoch: Some Notes on 1 Henoch 1.9," pp. 114-20 in *Tradition and Re-Interpretation in Jewish and Early Christian Literature: Essays in Honour of Jürgen C. H. Lebram.* Edited by Jan Willem van Henten, Henk Jan de Jonge, Peter T. Van Rooden and Jan Wilm Wesselius. Leiden: Brill, 1986.

Deichgraber, Reinhard. *Gotteshymnus und Christushymnus in der frühen Christenheit.* Studien zur Umwelt des Neuen Testament 5. Göttingen: Vandenhoeck & Ruprecht, 1967.

Denis, Albert-Marie. "Fragmenta Pseudepigraphorum quae supersunt Graeca." In *Pseudepigrapha veteris testamenti graece*, vol. 3. Edited by Albert-Marie Denis and Marinus de Jonge. Leiden: Brill, 1970.

Desjardins, Michel. "The Portrayal of the Dissidents in 2 Peter and Jude: Does It Tell Us More about the 'Godly' Than the 'Ungodly'?" *JSNT* 30 (1987): 89-102.

Dubarle, André-Marie. "Le peche des anges dans l'épître de Jude." Pp. 145-48 in *Memorial J. Chaine.* Bibliothèque de la faculté catholique de théologie de Lyon 5. Lyon: Facultés catholiques, 1950.

Dunn, J. D. G. *Unity and Diversity in the New Testament.* Philadelphia: Westminster Press, 1984.

Dunnett, Walter M. "The Hermeneutics of Jude and 2 Peter: The Use of Ancient Jewish Traditions." *JETS* 31 (1988): 287-92.

du Plessis, P. J. "The Authorship of the Epistle of Jude," pp. 191-99 in *Biblical Essays 1966.* Potchefstroom: South African Society for the Study of the Old Testament, University of Stellenbosch, 1966.

Ellis, E. Earle. "Prophecy and Hermeneutic in Jude," pp. 221-36 in Ellis's *Proph-*

ecy and Hermeneutic in Early Christianity: New Testament Essays. Wissenschaftliche Untersuchungen zum Neuen Testament 18. Tübingen: Mohr, 1978.

———. *Prophecy and Hermeneutics in Early Christianity.* Grand Rapids: Eerdmans, 1978.

Ermoni, Vincent. "Jude, épître de saint." In *Dictionnaire de la bible,* vol. 3. Edited by Fulcran Vigouroux. Paris: Vigouroux, 1910.

Eybers, I. H. "Aspects of the Background of the Letter of Jude." *Neot* 9 (1975): 113-23.

Farrar, Frederic W. *The Early Days of Christianity,* vol. 1. New York: Burt, 1882.

Feuillet, André. "Le premier cavalier de l'Apocalypse." *ZNW* 57 (1966): 229-59.

Flanders, Henry Jackson. "The Relation of Jude to II Peter." Ph.D. diss., Southern Baptist Seminary, 1951.

Fossum, Jarl. "Kyrios Jesus as the Angel of the Lord in Jude 5-7." *NTS* 33 (1987): 226-43.

Frost, Stanley B. "Apocalyptic and History," pp. 134-47 in *The Bible in Its Literary Milieu.* Edited by John Maier and Vincent Tollers. Grand Rapids: Eerdmans, 1979.

Fuller, Reginald H. *A Critical Introduction to the New Testament.* London: Duckworth, 1966.

———. "Early Catholicism: An Anglican Reaction to a German Debate," pp. 34-41 in *Die Mitte des Neuen Testaments: Einheit and Vielfalt neutestamentlicher Theologie: Festschrift für Eduard Schweizer.* Edited by Ulrich Luz und Hans Weder. Göttingen: Vandenhoeck & Ruprecht, 1983.

Gardiner, Frederic. "The Similarity between the Epistle of Jude and the Second Epistle of Peter." *BSac* 11 (1854): 114-39.

Gillming, Kenneth E. "An Expositional Study of Jude." Th.M. thesis, Dallas Theological Seminary, 1954.

Glasson, T. Francis. *Greek Influence in Jewish Eschatology.* Biblical Monographs 1. London: SPCK, 1961.

Gloag, Paton J. *Introduction to the Catholic Epistles.* Edinburgh: Clark, 1887.

Goodspeed, Edgar J. *An Introduction to the New Testament.* Chicago: University of Chicago Press, 1937.

Grundmann, Walter. "Stehen und Fallen im qumranischen und neutestamentlichen Schrifttum," pp. 147-66 in *Qumran-Probleme.* Edited by H. Bardtke. Schriften der Sektion für Altertumswissenschaft 42. Berlin: Akademie Verlag, 1963.

Gunther, John J. "The Alexandrian Epistle of Jude." *NTS* 30 (1984): 549-62.

Hahn, Ferdinand. "Randbemerkungen zum Judasbrief." *Theologische Zeitschrift* 37 (1981): 209-18.

Hanson, K. C., and Douglas E. Oakman. *Palestine in the Time of Jesus*. Minneapolis: Fortress, 1998.

Harm, Harry. "Logic Line in Jude: The Search for Syllogisms in a Hortatory Test." *Occasional Papers in Translation and Textlinguistics* 1 (1987): 147-72.

Harnack, Adolf von. *Geshichte der altchristlichen Litteratur bis Eusebius*, vol. 2: *Die Chronologie der altchristlichen Litteratur bis Eusebius 1*. Leipzig: Hinrichs, 1897.

Harvey, Anthony E. "The Testament of Simeon Peter," pp. 339-54 in *A Tribute to Géza Vermès: Essays on Jewish and Christian Literature and History*. Edited by Philip R. Davies and Richard T. White. Sheffield: JSOT Press, 1990.

Hassold, William J. "Keep Yourselves in the Love of God: An Interpretation of Jude 20, 21." *Concordia Theological Monthly* 23 (1952): 884-94.

Head, Peter M. Review of Charles Landon's *Text-Critical Study of the Epistle of Jude*. *NovT* 41 (1999): 181-85.

Heiligenthal, Roman. "Der Judasbrief: Aspekte der Forschung in den letzten Jahrzehnten." *Theologische Rundschau* 51 (1986): 117-29.

———. "Die Weisheitsschrift aus der Kairoer Geniza und der Judasbrief." *Zeitschrift für Religions- und Geistesgeschichte* 44 (1992): 356-61.

Hengel, Martin. "Anonymität, Pseudepigraphie und 'Literarische Fälschung' in der jüdisch-hellenistischen Literatur." Vol. 1, pp. 231-329 in *Pseudepigrapha*. Edited by Kurt von Fritz. Geneva: Fondation Hardt, 1972.

———. "Early Christianity as a Jewish Messianic Universalistic Movement," pp. 1-41 in *Conflicts and Challenges in Early Christianity*. Edited by Donald Hagner. Harrisburg: Trinity, 1999.

———. *The "Hellenization" of Judaea in the First Century after Christ*. Translated by John Bowden. Philadelphia: Trinity, 1989.

———. *Judaism and Hellenism*. 2 vols. Translated by John Bowden. Philadelphia: Fortress, 1981.

Hiebert, D. Edmond. *An Introduction to the Non-Pauline Epistles*. Chicago: Moody, 1962.

———. "Selected Studies from Jude, Part 1: An Exposition of Jude 3-4." *BSac* 142 (1985): 142-51.

———. "Selected Studies from Jude, Part 2: An Exposition of Jude 12-16." *BSac* 142 (1985): 238-49.

———. "Selected Studies from Jude, Part 3: An Exposition of Jude 17-23." *BSac* 142 (1985): 355-66.

Hofmann, Johann Christian K. von. *Die Heilige Schrift Neuen Testaments zusammenhangend Untersucht*. Nördlingen: Beck, 1875.

Howard, George. "The Tetragram and the New Testament." *JBL* 96 (1977): 63-83.

Jost, W. "Poimen: Das Bild vom Hirten in der biblischen Überlieferung und seine christologische Bedeutung." Ph.D. diss., Giessen University, 1939.

Joubert, Stephan J. "Facing the Past: Transtextual Relationships and Historical Understanding in the Letter of Jude." *Biblische Zeitschrift* 42 (1998): 56-70.

———. "Language, Ideology and the Social Context of the Letter of Jude." *Neot* 24 (1990): 335-49.

Judge, E. A. "St. Paul and Classical Society." *Journal of Ancient Christianity* 15 (1972): 19-36.

Kahmann, Johannes. "The Second Letter of Peter and the Letter of Jude: Their Mutual Relationship," pp. 105-21 in *The New Testament in Early Christianity.* Edited by Jean-Marie Sevrin. Louvain: Louvain University Press, 1989.

Keil, Carl Friedrich. "The Fall of the Angels: An Exegetical Examination of Jude 6 and 2 Pet. ii.4." *EvQ* 8 (1856-57): 171-86.

Kennedy, George A. *The Art of Persuasion in Greece.* Princeton: Princeton University Press, 1963.

King, Marchant A. "Jude and 1 and 2 Peter: Notes on the Bodmer Manuscript." *BSac* 121 (1964): 54-57.

Klijn, A. F. J. "Jude 5 to 7." Vol. 1, pp. 237-44 in *The New Testament Age: Essays in Honor of Bo Reicke.* Edited by William C. Weinrich. Macon, Ga.: Mercer University Press, 1984.

Knoch, Otto. "Der zweite Petrusbrief; der Judasbrief." Welt der Bibel: Klein Kommentare zur Heiligen Schrift 8. Düsseldorf: Patmos, 1967.

Knox, A. D. *"Spilades." JTS* 14 (1913): 547-49.

Kruger, M. A. *"Toutois* in Jude: 7." *Neot* 27 (1993): 119-32.

Kubo, Sakae. "Jude 22-23: Two-Division Form or Three?" pp. 239-53 in *New Testament Textual Criticism: Its Significance for Exegesis: Essays in Honour of Bruce M. Metzger.* Edited by Eldon Jay Epp and Gordon D. Fee. Oxford: Clarendon, 1981.

———. $\mathfrak{P}^{72}$ *and the Codex Vaticanus.* Salt Lake City: Utah University Press, 1965.

———. "Textual Relationships in Jude," pp. 276-82 in *Studies in New Testament Language and Text.* Edited by J. K. Elliott. Leiden: Brill, 1976.

Kugelman, Richard. *James and Jude.* New Testament Message 19. Dublin: Veritas, 1980.

Landon, Charles. *A Text-Critical Study of the Epistle of Jude.* Sheffield: Sheffield Academic Press, 1996.

Laperrousaz, Ernest-Marie. "Le Testament de Moise (generalement appele 'Assomption de Moise'): Traduction avec introduction et notes." *Semeia* 19 (1970): 1-140.

Leahy, Thomas W. "Jude, Epistle of St." In *The New Catholic Encyclopedia*, vol. 8. Edited by W. J. McDonald et al. New York: McGraw-Hill, 1967.

Leconte, René. "Épître de Jude." In *Dictionnaire de la bible: Supplément*, vol. 4. Edited by Louis Pirot and André Robert. Paris: Letouzey & Ané, 1949.

Litfin, A. Duane. "A Biblical Strategy for Confronting the Cults." *BSac* 135 (1978): 232-40.

Luther, Martin. "Sermons on the Epistle of St. Jude." In *The Catholic Epistles*. Luther's Works 30. Translated by Martin H. Bertram. Edited by Jaroslav Pelikan and Walter A. Hansen. St. Louis: Concordia Publishing House, 1967.

Lyle, Kenneth R. *Ethical Admonition in the Epistle of Jude*. New York: Lang, 1998.

Magass, Walter. "Semiotik einer Ketzerpolemik am Beispiel von Judas 12f." *Linguistica biblica* 19 (1972): 36-47.

Maier, Friedrich. "Der Judasbrief: Seine Echtheit, Abfassungszeit und Leser: Ein Beitrag sur Einleitung in die katholischen Briefe." Biblische Studien 11.1-2. Edited by Otto Bardenhewer. Freiburg im Breisgau: Herder, 1906.

Marshall, I. Howard. *Kept by the Power of God*. London: Epworth, 1969.

Massaux, Édouard "Le texte de l'épître de Jude du Papyrus Bodmer VII ($\mathfrak{P}^{72}$)," pp. 108 25 in *Scrinium lovaniense: Mélanges historiques, historische opstellen Étienne van Cauwenbergh*. Edited by J. Duculot and S. A. Gembloux. Gembloux: Duculot, 1961.

Mayor, Joseph B. "The Epistle of St. Jude and the Marcosian Heresy." *JTS* 6 (1905): 569-77.

————. "Notes on the Text of the Epistle of Jude." *ET* 6 (1904): 450-60.

Mees, Michael. "Papyrus Bodmer VII ($\mathfrak{P}^{72}$) und die Zitate aus dem Judasbrief bei Clemens von Alexandrien," pp. 133-41 in *Homenaje al p. Angel C. Vega: Miscelanea patristica*. Edited by Andrés Manrique. El Escorial, Spain: La ciudad de Dios, 1968.

Merkelbach, Reinhold. "Zwei Beiträge zum Neuen Testament." *Rheinisches Museum für Philologie* 134 (1991): 346-51.

Milik, J. T. *The Books of Enoch: Aramaic Fragments of Qumrân Cave 4*. Oxford: Clarendon, 1976.

Mitchell, Margaret M. *Paul and the Rhetoric of Reconciliation: An Exegetical Investigation of the Language and Composition of 1 Corinthians*. Tübingen: Mohr, 1991.

Moffatt, James. *An Introduction to the Literature of the New Testament*. New York: Scribner, 1925.

Mulholland, John Field. "Apocalyptic Truth according to Jude." *Religion in Life* 12 (1943): 248-55.

Mullins, Terence Y. "Petition as a Literary Form." *NovT* 5 (1962): 46-54.

Nickelsburg, George W. E. *1 Enoch: A Commentary on the Book of 1 Enoch 1—36, 81—108*. Hermeneia. Minneapolis: Fortress, 2001.

O'Banion, John D. "Narration and Argumentation: Quintilian on 'Narratio' as the Heart of Rhetorical Thinking." *Rhetorica* 5.4 (1987): 325-51.

Oleson, John Peter. "An Echo of Hesiod's Theogony vv. 190-2 in Jude 13." *NTS* 25 (1979): 492-503.

Osburn, Carroll D. "The Christological Use of I Enoch i.9 in Jude 14, 15." *NTS* 23 (1977): 334-41.

———. "I Enoch 80.2-8 (67.5-7) and Jude 12-13." *CBQ* 47 (1985): 296-303.

———. "The Text of Jude 5." *Biblica* 62 (1981): 107-15.

———. "The Text of Jude 22-23." *ZNW* 63 (1972): 139-44.

Pearson, Birger A. "James, 1-2 Peter, Jude," pp. 382-406 in *The New Testament and Its Modern Interpreters*. Edited by Eldon Jay Epp and George W. MacRae. Philadelphia: Fortress, 1989.

Perrin, Norman. *The New Testament: An Introduction*. New York: Harcourt Brace Jovanovich, 1974.

Philippi, Ferdinand. *Das Buch Henoch, sein Zeitalter und sein Verhältniss zum Judasbriefe*. Stuttgart: Liesching, 1868.

Pieper, Karl. "Zur Frage nach der Irrlehre des Judasbriefes," pp. 66-71 in *Vorlesungsverzeichnis Paderborn 1939-40*. Paderborn: Die Gesamthochschul Paderborn, 1940.

Prado, J. "Judasbrief." *Sacramentum mundi* 2 (1968): 976-78.

Reed, Jeffery T., and Ruth Anne Reese. "Verbal Aspect, Discourse Prominence and the Letter of Jude." *Neot* 9 (1996): 181-89.

Reese, Ruth Anne. *Writing Jude: The Reader, the Text and the Author in Constructs of Power and Desire*. Biblical Interpretation 51. Leiden: Brill, 2000.

Richards, W. Larry. "Textual Criticism on the Greek Text of the Catholic Epistles: A Bibliography." *Andrews University Seminary Studies* 12 (1974): 103-11.

Ross, John M. "Church Discipline in Jude 22-23." *ET* 100 (1989): 297-98.

Rowston, Douglas J. "The Most Neglected Book in the New Testament." *NTS* 21 (1975): 554-63.

———. "The Setting of the Letter of Jude." Ph.D. diss., Southern Baptist Theological Seminary, 1971.

Rubinkiewicz, Ryszard. *Die Eschatologie von Hen 9—11 und das Neue Testament*. Österreichische biblische Studien 6. Klosterneuburg: Österreichisches Katholisches Bibelwerk, 1984.

Sahlin, Harald. "Emendationsvorschlage zum griechischen Text des Neuen Testaments." *NovT* 25 (1983): 73-88.

Sasson, Jack M. "A 'Genealogical Convention' in Biblical Chronology." *Zeit-*

schrift für die alttestamentliche Wissenschaft 90 (1978): 171-85.

Schelkle, Karl Hermann. "Der Judasbrief bei den Kirchenvätern," pp. 405-16 in *Abraham unser Vater: Festschrift Otto Michel.* Edited by Otto Betz, Martin Hengel and Peter Schmidt. Arbeiten zur Geschichte des antiken Judentums und des Urchristentums 5. Leiden: Brill, 1963.

Schnabel, Eckhard J. *Early Christian Mission,* vol. 1: *Jesus and the Twelve.* Downers Grove, Ill.: InterVarsity Press, 2004.

Schulman, Grace. "Jude, Not Obscure," pp. 331-45 in *Incarnation: Contemporary Writers on the New Testament.* Edited by Alfred Corn. New York: Viking, 1990.

Schweizer, Eduard. "Die hellenistische Komponente im neutestamentlichen sarx-Begriff." *ZNW* 48 (1957): 237-53.

Seethaler, Paula-Angelika. "Kleine Bemerkungen zum Judasbrief." *Biblische Zeitschrift* 31 (1987): 261-64.

Sellin, Gerhard. "Die Haretiker des Judasbriefes." *ZNW* 77 (1986): 206-25.

Shanks, Herschel, and Ben Witherington III. *The Brother of Jesus.* San Francisco: Harper, 2001.

Soards, Marion L. "1 Peter, 2 Peter and Jude as Evidence for a Petrine School." *ANRW* 2.25.5 (1988): 3826-49.

Staab, Karl. "Die griechischen Katenenkommentare zu den katholischen Briefen." *Biblica* 5 (1924): 296-353.

Streeter, Burnett Hillman. *The Primitive Church.* London: Macmillan, 1929.

Symes, John Elliotson. *The Evolution of the New Testament.* London: Murray, 1921.

Szewc, Eugeniusz. "'Chwaty' w listach Judy i 2 Piotra ('Les gloires' dans les épîtres de St. Jude et deuxieme de St. Pierre')." *Collectanea theologica* 46 (1976): 51-60.

———. "'Doxai' in den katholischen Briefen und die qumranische Literatur." *Folia orientalia* 21 (1980): 129-40.

Taylor, Vincent. "The Message of the Epistles: Second Peter and Jude." *ET* 45 (1933-34): 437-41.

Testuz, Michel. *Papyrus Bodmer VII-IX: L'épître de Jude; les épîtres de Pierre; les Psaumes 33 et 34.* Cologne/Geneva: Bibliotheca Bodmeria, 1959.

Turner, Nigel. "The Style of Jude and 2 Peter," pp. 139-44 in James Hope Moulton's *A Grammar of New Testament Greek,* vol. 4: *Style,* by Nigel Turner. Edinburgh: Clark, 1976.

Van Gemeren, Willem A. "The Sons of God in Genesis 6:1-4." *Westminster Theological Journal* 43 (1981): 320-48.

Vielhauer, Philipp. *Geschichte der urchristlichen Literatur: Einleitung in das*

Neue Testament, die Apokryphen und die apostolischen Väter. Berlin/New York: de Gruyter, 1975.

Weissengruber, Franz. "Zum Problem der Pseudepigraphie und des Kanons." *Studien zum Neuen Testament und seiner Umwelt* 13 (1988): 179-91.

Werdermann, Hermann. *Die Irrlehrer des Judas und 2. Petrusbriefes.* Beiträge zur Förderung christlicher Theologie 17.6. Gütersloh: Bertelsmann, 1913.

Whallon, William. "Should We Keep, Omit or Alter the οἰ in Jude 12?" *NTS* 34 (1988): 156-59.

Wikgren, Allen. "Some Problems in Jude 5," pp. 147-52 in *Studies in the History and Text of the New Testament in Honor of Kenneth Willis Clark.* Edited by Boyd L. Daniels and M. Jack Suggs. Salt Lake City: University of Utah Press, 1967.

Winter, Sara C. "Jude 22-23: A Note on the Text and Translation." *Harvard Theological Review* 87 (1994): 215-22.

Wisse, Frederik. "The Epistle of Jude in the History of Heresiology," pp. 133-43 in *Essays on the Nag Hammadi Texts in Honour of Alexander Böhlig.* Edited by Martin Krause. Nag Hammadi Studies 3. Leiden: Brill, 1972.

Witherington, Ben, III. *The Acts of the Apostles.* Grand Rapids: Eerdmans, 1998.

———. *The Gospel of Matthew.* Macon, Ga.: Smyth & Helwys, 2006.

———. *Jesus the Seer.* Peabody, Mass.: Hendrickson, 1999.

———. *Letters and Homilies for Hellenized Christians, Volume 1: A Socio-Rhetorical Commentary on Titus, 1-2 Timothy and 1-3 John.* Downers Grove, Ill.: IVP Academic, 2006.

———. *Letters and Homilies for Hellenized Christians, Volume 2: A Socio-Rhetorical Commentary on 1-2 Peter.* Downers Grove, Ill.: IVP Academic, forthcoming.

———. *New Testament History.* Grand Rapids: Baker, 2001.

———. *Paul's Letters to the Thessalonians: A Socio-Rhetorical Commentary.* Grand Rapids: Eerdmans, 2006.

Wolter, Michael. "Die anonymen Schriften des Neuen Testaments Annaherungsversuch an ein literarisches Phaenomen." *ZNW* 79 (1988): 1-16.

Wolthuis, Thomas R. "Jude and Jewish Traditions." *Calvin Theological Journal* 22 (1987): 21-41.

Wordsworth, Christopher. *The New Testament of Our Lord and Saviour Jesus Christ,* vol. 2. 2nd edition. London: Longman, Green, 1882.

Wright, John Stafford. "The Canon of Scripture." *EvQ* 19 (1947): 93-109.

Zwaan, Johannes de. "Minuskelgruppen in 2 Petri und Judas." *ZNW* 12 (1911): 76-82.

Studies Involving Rhetorical Criticism

It is disappointing that of the resources listed below, the only ones that meaningfully interact in detail with Greco-Roman rhetoric are those of Duane Watson and J. Daryl Charles. Lauri Thurén's "Hey Jude!" is actually an exercise in applying the hermeneutics of suspicion to Jude and suggesting that the author was not merely hyperbolic on occasion but that his polemics should be taken with a grain of salt, as Thurén thinks they considerably and deliberately distort the truth about the false teachers. There is no independent way to verify this criticism, since we do not also have a document from these other teachers, and so this is entirely an argument from silence. I see no justification for accusing Jude of bad faith or for suggesting that he is resorting to mere sophistry and ad hominem attacks. Jude is a pastor genuinely concerned about both the truth and the influence of false teaching on his audience. It would ill suit his purpose of persuading about the truth if he was by means of his rhetoric playing fast and loose with the truth. I suspect that this all-too-modern and cynical view aligns with George Kennedy's definition of a rhetorician as "an unscrupulous trickster with words."[60]

While entertaining, not much more helpful is Thomas Wolthuis's imaginative dialogue between Cicero and Jude in "Jude and the Rhetorician," where Jude has his consciousness raised about his using rhetoric—something he is assumed to be oblivious about. This reflects the all-too-common attitude that Galileans like Jude were too bucolic or rustic to have known rhetoric. To the contrary, one can counter that the person who wrote this document in some of the New Testament's best Greek shows that he has a level of Greek education that would have included training in at least the rudiments of rhetoric, particular from the handbooks.

Stephan Joubert's "Persuasion in the Letter of Jude" applies insights from the new rhetoric with some helpful results, but methodologically his essay mixes new and old rhetorical theory in a prpoblematic way, for the very good reason that the author Jude could have used only Greco-Roman rhetoric. Margaret Mitchell rightly points out that "the audience-based perspectives of the New Rhetoric tend to misconstrue the method's basic orientation and objectives, and hence they have confused the rhetorical analysis of NT literature through the application of terminology that has been subtly 'redefined.'" In particular, C. Perleman and company are interested in their own revision and reappropriation of ancient rhetoric to address modern philosophical (particularly epistemological) questions, and they operate with a theory of meaning (i.e., that it is in the eye of

---

[60]Kennedy, *Art of Persuasion in Greece*, p. 23.

the beholder) that ancient rhetoricians would never agree with. The new rhetoricians seek to expand the use and lexicon of rhetoric and are not all that interested in analyzing and classifying ancient texts.[61] In other words, their work should be seen as an exercise in new application, not in exegesis or the interpretation of the meaning of ancient texts. Ernst Wendland is right that Duane Watson's analysis of the rhetoric of Jude is not without some issues, but his own attempt to apply the more general categories of James Muilenburg, which amounts to a sort of literary criticism of a broader sort, is not all that helpful in getting at what is going on in Jude.

Charles, J. Daryl. "Literary Artifice in the Epistle of Jude." *ZNW* 82 (1991): 106-24.

———. *Literary Strategy in the Epistle of Jude.* Scranton, Penn.: University of Scranton Press, 1993.

Cladder, Hermann Johann. "Strophical Structure in St Jude's Epistle." *JTS* 5 (1903-4): 589-601.

Joubert, Stephan J. "Persuasion in the Letter of Jude." *JSNT* 58 (1995): 75-87.

Thurén, Lauri. "Hey Jude! Asking for the Original Situation and Message of a Catholic Epistle." *NTS* 43 (1997): 451-65.

Watson, Duane F. *Invention, Arrangement and Style: Rhetorical Criticism of Jude and 2 Peter.* Society of Biblical Literature Dissertation 104. Atlanta: Scholars Press, 1988.

———. "The Oral-Scribal and Cultural Intertexture of Apocalyptic Discourse in Jude and 2 Peter," pp. 187-213 in *The Intertexture of Apocalyptic Discourse in the New Testament.* Edited by Duane F. Watson. Society of Biblical Literature Symposium Series 14. Atlanta: Scholars Press, 2002.

Webb, Robert L. "The Eschatology of the Epistle of Jude and Its Rhetorical and Social Functions." *BBR* 6 (1996): 139-51.

Wendland, Ernst R. "A Comparative Study of 'Rhetorical Criticism,' Ancient and Modern: With Special Reference to the Larger Structure and Function of the Epistle of Jude." *Neot* 28 (1994): 193-228.

———. "'Dear Children' versus the 'Antichrists': The Rhetoric of Reassurance in First John." *Journal of Translation and Textlinguistics* 11 (1998): 40-84.

Wolthuis, Thomas R. "Jude and the Rhetorician: A Dialogue on the Rhetorical Nature of the Epistle of Jude." *Calvin Theological Journal* 24 (1989): 126-34.

York, Hershael W. "An Analysis and Synthesis of the Exegetical Methods of Rhetorical Criticism and Discourse Analysis as Applied to the Structure of First John." Diss., Mid-America Baptist Theological Seminary, 1993.

---

[61]See the thorough discussion and analysis of Mitchell, *Paul and the Rhetoric of Reconciliation*, pp. 5-9 (quotation on 7-8).

Jude

EPISTOLARY PRESCRIPT AND OPENING DISCOURSE ELEMENTS: "NECESSITY AROSE" (JUDE 1-4)

Jude's discourse is exceedingly brief. It would take no more than a few minutes to deliver orally, and since it ends with a doxology, this sermon may well have been envisioned as the closing element in a worship service—the final salvo that ended the service with a bang and a benediction.

The compact nature of the discourse is shown by the exordium, narratio and proposition or thesis statement all being run together in Jude 3-4. The exordium does not need to establish rapport with the audience because this has already been accomplished in the epistolary prescript with the reference to the audience having been loved by God and kept safe and the author's wishes for mercy, peace and love to multiply among them. The author has a profound concern and love for the audience, and he has already established his authority and ethos by means of his reference to his being a servant of Jesus and brother of James. Still, the beginning of Jude 3 continues the positive feeling of the prescript with reference to Jude's eagerness to write to the audience about the salvation he shares in common with them, which not only places him on a level plain with the audience but implies that he sees them as a group of saved people, despite the dangers of the false teachers he will thereafter enumerate.

The narratio in Jude 3b indicates the rhetorical exigence, the facts that prompted and necessitated the writing of this discourse: some false ones, foreshadowed in Scripture, have crept into their worship and fellowship meetings. The thesis statement that will be proved in what follows is then boldly asserted: these persons are transforming a gracious and grace-filled spiritual environment into a polluted and debauched one that instead of properly honoring Christ disowns him. In other words, a serious problem has arisen and a change in behavior and approach of the audience to these persons is required.

Our author's rhetorical strategy for dealing with this problem is rather simple—by means of inartificial (i.e., midrashic handling of scriptural texts and sa-

cred Jewish traditions) and artificial (creation of colorful similes) proofs he will
show that these false ones are like other such false persons who had had disastrous effects on the people of God. Jude's rhetorical comparison or synkrisis has
a difference here: comparison is not done by contrast, but by finding other similar examples.[62] The intended rhetorical effect is to cast odium on the false ones
and thereby get the audience to distance themselves from these intruders and
so shore up the boundaries of the community.

One of the clearest signs that the audience is a Jewish Christian one is that
our author expects examples from the Old Testament and other intertestamental
Jewish sources to carry considerable weight with the audience and persuade
them of the truth about those who have "crept in." Quintilian reminds us that
the highest sort of authority and persuasive power comes from oracles, words
from the deity: "Supernatural authority . . . is derived from oracles" (*Institutio
oratoria* 5.11.41). Our author begins with proofs from Scripture itself (Jude 5-7)
and then moves on to proofs from other sacred Jewish traditions (Jude 8-10),
following the rules about using the strongest or most compelling proofs first and
then turning to other authoritative sources (*Institutio oratoria* 5.12.14). The
story about Michael and the body of Moses is assumed to have authority; this
presumes not only that the author and audience share a universe of Jewish discourse, but that they value and honor even lesser known Jewish traditions.

Quintilian points out the overlap between epideictic and deliberative rhetoric:
"The same things are usually praised in the former as are advised in the latter" (*Institutio oratoria* 3.7.28). One can conversely say that the same things that are de-
nounced with invective in the former are advised against in the latter. In truth, invective and polemics could be found in any form of rhetoric, and so we need not
conclude that Jude has a mixture of deliberative and epideictic rhetoric just because invective is found here. The question to be asked is this: what rhetorical
function does the invective or pejorative language serve? And the answer is this: to
warn the audience to change behavior and stop associating with and being hospitable to those who have "crept in" to their assemblies. Quintilian goes on to remind
us that deliberative oratory should not be restricted to questions of expediency; he
prefers that it deal primarily with what is honorable and dishonorable, what is
good and evil (3.8.2-5). In his view only what is good and honorable is expedient.
In other words, Quintilian, like Jude, takes the high ethical road when it comes to
the use of rhetoric. Thus we see overlap between the concerns of these two species of rhetoric, and it is sufficient to say that we can see Jude as a deliberative
discourse, with the polemical volume turned up in places, from start to finish.

---

[62]Witherington, *Letters and Homilies*, 1.68-72.

Quintilian specifically enumerates ways to cast odium on certain behaviors or vices through the citing of parallel bad examples. To encourage someone to avoid a bad example, the orator should draw an analogy "as in the story of Paris, it has been predicted that they would be the cause of the destruction to many . . . others have been loathed because their natural advantages were nullified by their vices: the poets for instance tell us that Nireus was a coward and Pleisthenes a debauchee. . . . Some have been branded with infamy after death like Maelius whose house was leveled to the ground, or Marcus Manlius, whose first name was banished from his family for all generations to come" (*Institutio oratoria* 3.7.19-21). These are the same sort of stock negative examples that Jude pulls from the Jewish tradition to make evident that the interlopers are immoral and a bad influence that should be shunned, because if one participates in their debauchery and false teaching it leads to judgment and destruction as at Sodom and Gomorrah.

> [1]*Jude, servant of Jesus Christ, but brother of James, to those called, having been loved*[64] *by God the Father and kept safe for Jesus Christ.* [2]*Mercy to you and peace and love be multiplied.* (use for greeting in early)
>
> [3]*Behold, with all eagerness I was going to write you concerning our common salvation, but necessity arose for me to write urging you to continue to contend for the faith once delivered to the saints.* [4]*For some people crept in whose judgment was long ago written of—for this—godless persons, they are transforming the grace of our God into debauchery and disowning our only Master*[64] *and Lord, Jesus Christ.*

Our letter begins with the usual form of salutation in a Jewish letter with a few additions by Jude. The name given in **Jude 1** is Judas, but we call him Jude. He calls himself a servant of Christ, a designation that also appears in James 1:1. It may derive here from the idea that Christ has freed believers from the bondage of sin and

---

[63]Instead of "being loved," which is well supported by $\mathfrak{P}^{72}$, ℵ, A, B and many minuscules, the Textus Receptus, following K, L, P and the majority of minuscules, has *hēgiasmenois,* probably following 1 Cor 1:2, since the word order and combination with "in God the Father" is a bit unusual. See Metzger, *Textual Commentary,* p. 723; and Landon, *Text-Critical Study,* pp. 52-53. The love language is part of the catchword connection that Jude uses to bind this whole discourse together, beginning with the epistolary prescript.

[64]Elsewhere in the New Testament the term *despotēs* normally refers to God the Father, except at 2 Pet 2:1, which is not an unimportant parallel, since the author of 2 Peter is drawing on Jude, and 2 Pet 2:1 thus suggests that Jude 4 refers to Christ. The Textus Receptus following K, L, P and most minuscules appends the word *theon.* The shorter reading and the allusion to Christ is decisively supported by $\mathfrak{P}^{72}$, ℵ, A, B, C and a host of other witnesses. See Metzger, *Textual Commentary,* p. 723. The Textus Receptus was based on some late Byzantine witnesses, which were the only manuscripts available to Erasmus and Theodore Beza. Landon, *Text-Critical Study,* pp. 65-67, thinks that God is meant here. I find this unlikely both on internal and external grounds: the reading for the omission is stronger textually in terms of earliest and best witnesses, and internally it makes good sense as well, not to mention the probable first exegesis of the phrase in 2 Pet 2:1.

death for serving Christ. Since Jesus has freed believers, they now belong wholly to him. This thought may partially be behind the use of the term *kept* in Jude 6.

William Brosend points out that our author is writing in a context in which he can assume that both Jesus and James are well-known authority figures:

> Identification as "the brother . . . of the Lord" was not necessary. The identification with James . . . tells us that the "James" in question was of sufficient stature to the audience as to need no qualifications, a status that can only be ascribed to James the Just/of Jerusalem, the "brother of the Lord." Second it tells us that the author of Jude was confident enough in the identification of James and Jesus that he need not claim it for himself—identification with James accomplished both.[65]

Jerome Neyrey stresses that "the lesser is identified in relation to the more prominent brother, a cultural phenomenon rooted not just in the Bible (Gen 10:21; Exod 4:14; Josh 15:17; 1 Sam 14:3) but in the general ancient culture. A younger sibling, whose birth ranks him lower than his older brother, claims honor by blood ties with his richer, stronger, or more influential brother."[66] Neyrey also points out that Jude is claiming ascribed or derived authority rather than achieved authority, the higher sort of authority that one has by blood lines of divine bequeathal not from something one has done or accomplished. In our culture the honor hierarchy tends to run in just the opposite direction—exalting the self-made person.[67]

The idea may be that God is keeping believers until their master, Jesus, returns to claim what belongs to him. Richard Bauckham suggests that the term *doulos* may have come to have a rather technical sense meaning "Christian worker" or "leader." In view of Isaiah 40—55 perhaps being in the background of the use of the terms *beloved, called* and *kept* (Is 42:6; 48:15), perhaps Jude is a servant of God's people and of Jesus, just as Jesus the suffering servant was.[68] Jude makes clear to his audience which Jude he is by saying that he is James the Just's brother. This manner of self-identification is what one expects from a young brother who has a more famous older brother still alive and whom he does not and cannot relate to as an equal any longer, if he ever did. This must

---

[65]Brosend, *James and Jude*, p. 168.
[66]Neyrey, *2 Peter, Jude*, p. 47.
[67]I am not, however, sanguine that Neyrey made his case that we should see Jude as a riposte or response to the challenging of Jude's honor. Jude says nothing about the intruders challenging him or his credentials. At most, one could suggest that Jude is providing resources so that the audience can contend with the false teachers. Furthermore, the immoral and greedy and selfish behavior of these teachers, not primarily their teaching, is seen as a denial of the gospel and of Christ's grace.
[68]Bauckham, *Jude, 2 Peter*, pp. 23-24.

have been a daunting experience for Jude to be a relative of these two men and yet still pursue his calling as a Christian evangelist and teacher.

The word *klētois* is important in various regards. First of all, the Christian community is treated as the true development of Israel. The church, or at least the Jewish part of it that Jude is addressing, is now the called, the beloved, the kept of God—terms used of Israel in the Old Testament. This did not mean that Israelites no longer had a place in God's community, but it did mean that allegiance to Christ was necessary for such a place in the community. The idea of election—that God set his love on and singled out certain called individuals—is often implied in the New Testament. Several things may be said about this idea: (1) being called and being chosen are sometimes distinguished in the New Testament (Mt 22:14); (2) Jude mentions "those called"—that is, a group of individuals, not an individual—which aligns with the general notion in both Testaments that election usually involves calling God's people as a corporate group, although individuals (even Christ) are sometimes designated by God for specific tasks, that is, called to a ministry without focus on ultimate or final salvation and (3) the call always requires a human response in faith to the call, and as this letter's very writing makes abundantly clear, God's election and human response must go hand in hand or else there is a danger to the one called out. The reason Jude writes is because he fears that some of the called ones might not listen and follow the false teachers out of the kingdom and down the road to Sodom and Gomorrah. Though he can call them loved and kept by God, he must also urge them to keep themselves. Bauckham puts it superbly:

> Jude knows that the divine action in calling, loving, and keeping safe must be met by a faithful human response, and when he takes up the themes of v 1 in v 21 it is to put the other side of the matter: his readers must *keep themselves* in the love of God and faithfully *await* the salvation which will be theirs at the Parousia. The divine action does not annul this human responsibility.[69]

No more than James did, Jude does not apparently believe once saved always saved regardless of one's conduct subsequent to conversion. The word *planē* (Jude 11) often implies a wandering away from the truth and the kingdom—real apostasy that brings on God's all too real condemnation, as in the case of the fallen angels. We are dealing here with a mystery—divine election and human response—and both must be affirmed. God's grip on believers is firm, and there is security in it (Rev 3:10). But this becomes false security if believers do not persevere and work out their salvation with fear and trembling

---

[69]Ibid., p. 27 (emphasis added).

by the power of God's grace working in them to will and to do.

Thus, Jude must warn the called, yes even the elect, of the clear and present dangers of false teachers. This is one of Jude's favorite themes in this letter: Christians are God's special loved ones: *agapētoi*. The triad in **Jude 2**—mercy, peace and a bundle of love/love multiplied (cf. 1 Pet 1:2 and 2 Pet 1:2 on *plethynoy*[70]—is unique in the New Testament and Old Testament. These three items are derived from God; they are not innate properties. Jews might wish peace or even mercy and peace, but Jude adds love in abundance (cf. Jude 21). The Christian religion, like the Christian God, is chiefly characterized by the term *agapē* in the New Testament. Jude wishes his listeners to get an abundant share of these things from God. He omits the traditional Pauline greeting *charis* ("grace"). In these first few verses Jude has established rapport and ethos and secured the allegiance of his audience by framing his discourse with assurances that the audience is not among the condemned—rather they are being kept for salvation.[71]

The next two verses are critical for understanding this letter, as they introduce both good news (Jude 3) and bad (Jude 4), both faith to be contended for (Jude 3) and opponents to be contended against (Jude 4). Richard Bauckham stresses that Jude 4 introduces the critique and condemnation found in Jude 5-19, while the positive message of Jude 3 is expanded in Jude 20-23 (which is no appendix, but rather the climax of the letter).[72] From a rhetorical viewpoint Jude 3-4 establishes rapport with the audience and narrates the problematic facts in question and the thesis statement to be proved in the examples that follow. Quintilian reminds us that the narratio should be brief and clear, a succinct statement of the facts, as here (*Institutio oratoria* 4.2.4). Rapport is in part established by Jude's third use of the term *agapē* in the first twenty-five words of his document, just as negative emotions toward the false teachers will be generated by the use of colorful language and analogies. Quintilian speaks of the necessity of being "plausible in imagination . . . vehement in censure . . . vivid in description" (4.2.123-24)—all of which aptly describes our discourse.

Agapētoi in **Jude 3** refers to the believers whom Jude is addressing—loved by God and also by Jude (cf. Jude 1). Jude had been eager to write them a positive letter expounding "our common salvation." However, when he heard about their problems with the false teachers, he had to deal first with the crisis they caused. This suggests a real discourse addressing real problems, and Jude 3-4

---

[70]One small pointer to the influence and also the date of Jude is found in this same phrase, including the "love multiplied" clause, occurring in the prologue of the *Martyrdom of Polycarp*. See Moffatt, *General Epistles*, p. 229.

[71]Perkins, *Peter, James and Jude*, p. 141.

[72]Bauckham, *Jude, 2 Peter*, p. 29.

tells the occasion for this discourse (and the rhetorical exigence that provoked its writing). That Jude does not specify whom he wrote to is *not* critical, since undoubtedly his messenger delivering his discourse knew.

"Our common salvation" suggests that Jude sees salvation as something shared in the present, but in Jude 21 we will see that it also has a future dimension for Jude, and thus, as is true for Paul, it is an already-and-not-yet matter. The idea that salvation is shared in common among believers suggests that salvation, like election, is a collective phenomenon: a person is chosen to be part of the body of Christ and with it be saved. Thus, against our modern overemphasis on individuals being saved, we would do well to recognize that no one is saved in or for solitude. A person is saved into the community of faith, which is not just the sum of its individual parts, and saved to serve God. Contending for the faith involves his audience doing what he, Jude, does: engaging (1) in a negative critique of the false teachers and their ideas and (2) in a positive response of what this faith should amount to. Pheme Perkins points out that if salvation is held in common, then the invasion of the community by false teachers threatens this shared salvation not only by denial of God's grace but also by tempting some in the audience to give up that common salvation and follow their own aberrant teachings and so divide the community and cause apostasy of some.[73] No wonder these intruders are seen as a clear and present danger even to those who are in some sense kept by God.

Richard Bauckham shows in detail that nothing in Jude's use of the phrase *pistis* once for all passed down" cannot be paralleled elsewhere in the New Testament, especially in Paul. Use of this idea need not be seen as a sign that this discourse comes from the latter part of the New Testament era. To the contrary, the desire and necessity of passing on in a rather fixed form the truth about the once-for-all-time salvation events was with the church early on. Paul's discourses reveal that sayings of Jesus, narratives, hymns, creedal statements, ethical material, apostolic teaching and Old Testament catena were all being passed down orally and written early on. This process merely accelerated as the eyewitnesses died out, as Bauckham stresses:

> God's purpose in the gospel is to save sinners, not to promote sin.
>
> Like other NT writers, Jude identifies the true gospel as the one which the apostles who founded the churches preached to the first converts. This appeal to the past, and to a form of tradition, is not to be seen as an "early Catholic" fossilization of the faith into fixed formulae or orthodox belief. Rather it was present in early Christianity from the start, bound up with the notion of the apostolate, and necessarily inherent

---

[73]Perkins, *Peter, James and Jude*, p. 148.

in a message about God's saving action in historical events. It excludes neither the living inspiration of the Spirit nor legitimate theological development, but requires that they be tested against the standard of the original gospel.[74]

Technical language for the passing on of sacred tradition is used here ("entrust"). Jude uses the same sort of athletic metaphor found in Paul about contending for the faith (1 Cor 9:24-27; Rom 15:30; Col 1:29—2:1; 1 Tim 6:12; 2 Tim 4:7). The strong verb *epagōnizomai,* found only here in the New Testament, could be translated "struggle for" (Plutarch, *Moralia* 1075D; cf. 593DE).[75] William Brosend rightly points out that Jude's use of the terms *necessity, saints, faith* and *entrust* have precedent or parallels in Paul's letters (respectively in 2 Cor 9:7; Phil 4:22; Gal 1:23; Rom 6:17).[76] This vocabulary does not reflect later postapostolic ecclesiastical terminology. Calling believers saints or holy ones *(hagioi)* was common in the early church, and it may have originally implied something about their moral rectitude. If so, Jude is contrasting his audience (with whom he has basic affinities) to the false teachers who are morally corrupt. It is not clear from this verse whether our author had actually begun drafting a discourse on "our common salvation" and then of necessity put it down to write this discourse due to receiving distressing news or whether, as seems more likely, he had intended to write such a discourse for them, but the more pressing need had to be dealt with first.

Jude 4 indicates that these people were deceptive: they had slipped in and were slowly injecting poison into the body of Christ (cf. Gal 2:4; Jn 10:1; Philo *On the Creation of the World* 150; Polybius *Histories* 1.18.3). Ruth Anne Reese puts it this way: "They slipped in secretly. That is, their entrance was not bold or self-proclaiming; rather, it was unnoticed, gradual, and careful."[77] Rhetorically Jude 4 is the narratio followed by the statement of the major theses of the brief discourse (Quintilian *Institutio oratoria* 4.2.31). *Asebeis* ("godless/without piety") is the chief description of them, primarily for their ethical misbehavior, but also because their conduct is based on aberrant theological principles, that is, antinomianism. Christians are supposed to recognize Jesus as their one master. Julius Africanus, who lived in Emmaus around 200, says that the relatives of Jesus called themselves "the master's folks" *(desposynoi)* (in Eusebius' *Ecclesiastical History* 1.7.14), which suggests that Jesus was called *despotēs* at an earlier point in time, such as here and at 2 Peter 2:1, which is probably based on the usage in Jude.[78] Jesus is their Lord and Master but instead they are busy disowning the one

[74]Bauckham, *Jude, 2 Peter,* p. 41.
[75]Kelly, *Peter and Jude,* pp. 246-47.
[76]Brosend, *James and Jude,* p. 169.
[77]Reese, *Jude* (manuscript).
[78]Mayor, *Jude,* p. 26.

who rightfully owns the believers. Jude 4 contains two parallel phrases, the former dealing with God ("transforming God's grace") and the latter with Christ. God's grace, that is, his gracious offer of salvation through the gospel, should not be seen as an opportunity for moral perversity. Christians are freed from sin, but not free to do as they please. Rather they are freed to do as God pleases. Liberty should not be used for license, but these false teachers were doing precisely this and using grace as an opportunity to sin! This amounted to perverting God's grace into an excuse for debauchery. Because they were doing this, Jude warns that the condemnation of these people was written of long ago—which is surely a reference to the Old Testament and apocryphal texts he will cite to show that these false teachers are in for the most severe sort of judgment on judgment day. The complaint about these false teachers regards both their ethics and their theology: they are antinomian or libertine in behavior and heterodox in their denial of Jesus Christ. They will also be accused of one of the biggest social sins of the era—violating and abusing the community's hospitality. The analogy with wandering stars probably suggests that they were itinerant prophets or teachers, rather like those described in *Didache* 11.3-12; 13.1-3, which also warns Jewish Christians against such persons. While it is possible that the term *master* refers to God here, it more likely means Jesus, especially in view of Jude's reference in the prescript to his being Christ's servant/slave.[79]

The implication is that if anyone follows these false teachers they will be in for a similar condemnation. The examples that follow make it very likely that this audience is Jewish Christian, because Jude assumes that all he has to do is remind them of various Old Testament and other popular Jewish texts that they are already familiar with. William Brosend says that our author followed a very adept rhetorical strategy in his initial characterization of the "intruders."[80] They have not entered the community according to the way an honest Christian teacher would do. They have slipped in under the radar and apparently under false pretenses (literally "stolen in among you"). "When boundaries are threatened, one sounds the alarm, posts guards, and seeks to identify, neutralize, and expel the threatening pollution."[81]

Jude also alerts the audience to their having been condemned long ago for their sinful behavior. "The claim of ancient condemnation was a favorite rhetorical strategy and served two purposes. First, in a culture that valued the well known and antique over the unfamiliar and new, older was always better and oldest best, so by placing his interpretation and treatment of a new and present

---

[79]Rightly Watson, *Jude,* p. 485.
[80]Brosend, *James and Jude,* p. 170.
[81]Neyrey, *2 Peter, Jude,* p. 55.

threat, Jude seeks to gain the advantage and weight of the tradition for his position in what was likely a difficult debate."[82] Our author is not just warning the audience against negative spiritual consequences of following false teaching but also wants them to actively contend for the faith (Jude 3). Galvanizing the audience for such a task is one of the main aims of this discourse.[83] The two propositions announced in Jude 4, which the discourse will demonstrate, are (1) that false teachers are ungodly and subject to judgment and (2) that they are the very ones foretold in Jewish prophecies about the false teachers of the last days.[84]

A CLOSER LOOK
Jude's Use of Sacred Texts and Traditions

Apart from the closing doxology, few aspects of the homily of Jude have attracted more attention and caused more consternation than the author's use of various canonical and pseudepigraphical texts to build his case against the intruders. William Brosend notes that the issue cannot be neatly divided into two categories—the way Scriptures are handled and the way other materials are handled. "None of the examples . . . can be understood simply on the basis of a biblical citation but must be interpreted in light of understandings prevalent in the first century of our era."[85] In other words, Jude exhibits a combination of text and commentary (i.e., sacred text and sacred tradition). This is why Richard Bauckham and others rightly stress that when this book applies ancient materials to contemporary situations it involves a contemporizing or midrashic way of handling the text, such that one can say "this is that" or "this is just like that." Jude is operating out of an apocalyptic and eschatological worldview that is manifested in this case in assuming and asserting that ancient Scriptures are not only relevant to what was happening in his own day but were coming to pass and to fulfillment in his day.

Jude's handling of this material can be mystifying to those not familiar with early Jewish exegesis and apocalyptic and eschatological texts of the era.[86] But even this familiarity can lead to the wrong conclusions. For example, after noting that Jude cites only Jewish, not Christian, sources (which is no surprise if his discourse is the earliest or one of the earliest Christian documents), Pheme Perkins states: "Since the material includes a reference to Enoch and a tale

---

[82]Brosend, *James and Jude*, p. 170.
[83]Watson, *Jude*, p. 477.
[84]Ibid., p. 484.
[85]Brosend, *James and Jude*, p. 171.
[86]A good point of entry for this discussion can be found in Wolthuis, "Jude and Jewish Traditions"; and Charles, "Jude's Use of Pseudepigraphical Source-Material."

known only from apocryphal traditions, Jude is not limited to canonical sources. The only direct quotations in the letter come from the apocryphal traditions (vv. 9, 14b-15) and the prophetic words attributed to the apostles (v. 18). *Therefore, authority does not appear to reside in the canonical text as much as it does in the testimony of ancient traditions about wickedness and divine punishment.*"[87] To the contrary, it is far more likely that Jude assumes that his audience already knows or has access to the Old Testament material and therefore he need only cite the material they are less likely to know or have ready to hand.

The following examples show that our author relies on something other than just the Old Testament here:

1. Genesis 6:1-4, which does refer to the sexual fraternizing of angels with human women, does not refer to the punishment of these angels or to angels leaving their proper place and violating the creation order. These ideas derive from later Jewish traditions found in *1 Enoch* 6.1-2; 7.1; 54.4-5; 64.12; 69.5; *Testament of Reuben* 5.6. The more one studies Jude and *1 Enoch* together the more one becomes impressed with how indebted our author is to this noncanonical source.

2. While Old Testament scholars debate what the sin of Sodom and Gomorrah was, there is no doubt in Jude's mind that it involves sexual improprieties of a severe sort, not only of a heterosexual but also of a homosexual nature. This is very much like that found in Philo, who refers to the residents of Sodom throwing off the yokes of nature and engaging in forbidden forms of intercourse, including men mounting men (*On the Life of Abraham* 135). Clearly Jude knows and accepts these expansions of the tradition that go beyond the text of Genesis. On the destruction of the cities themselves, he seems also to know traditions like those found in Wisdom of Solomon 10.6-7.

3. The story about the battle between the archangel Michael and the devil over the body of Moses is not found in the Old Testament at all, but according to Clement of Alexandria comes from a work entitled the *Assumption of Moses*. There is nothing remotely like this in the account of Moses' death in Deuteronomy 34:5-6, and extant fragments of the *Assumption of Moses* unfortunately do not contain this story.

4. The stories in Numbers 22:15-18; 31:16; Joshua 24:9-19; Nehemiah 13:2 do not directly suggest that Balaam's error refers to greed, but later Jewish tradition (Philo *On the Life of Moses* 1.268, 295-99; cf. Josephus *Jewish Antiquities* 4.126-30) fills out the story along the lines that Jude follows.

---

[87]Perkins, *Peter, James and Jude*, p. 142 (emphasis added).

5. None of what Jude has to say about Enoch is grounded in the Old Testament, and Jude quotes *1 Enoch* 1.9 directly, which is obviously an important text for Jude since it contains his major themes of judgment and ungodliness.

Much more could be said along these lines, and Bauckham's detailed study of this material deserves close scrutiny.[88] The outcome of the study is clear: Jude reads the Old Testament through and in light of the later Jewish traditions, and he supplements the Old Testament with noncanonical traditions from the *Assumption of Moses* and *1 Enoch*. Our author clearly presupposes his audience's familiarity with the wider corpus of early Jewish literature or at least the traditions in them. Not surprisingly, he cites the extracanonical material but basically expects the audience to know the more familiar Old Testament stories.

Jude does not cite this material because he is a lover of arcane lore or interested in esoterica. Rather he is a skilled rhetorician, and he uses it for hortatory or parenetic purposes to warn the audience against listening to the false teachers, who are like these horrible examples. In other words, Jude makes homiletical use of this material to deal with a contemporary situation that is viewed as dangerous and distressing. J. Daryl Charles sums up ably:

> Possessing a striking literary style as well as strategic knowledge of writings associated with sectarian Judaism, Jude weaves a brief yet forceful polemic against his opponents, drawing on literary sources readily recognized by his audience. Into this argument the allusions to *1 Enoch* and the *Assumption of Moses* are posited. As part of his literary strategy, Jude assumes and builds upon several motifs fundamental to intertestamental Jewish literature—the fate of the ungodly, theophany and judgment, rebellion in heaven and fascination with angelic powers.[89]

Today we might say that Jude throws everything at them but the kitchen sink to make the audience divest themselves of these false teachers and their teachings. The upshot is clear—if these opponents are like the worst examples in Jewish tradition, they should be avoided and shunned at all costs. That this was the successful rhetorical effect of the discourse is suggested by its finding its way into the canon, despite its small size and character.

PROBATIO: PROOFS OF THE CHARACTER AND FATE OF THE INTRUDERS (JUDE 5-16)

In order to deal with problematic visiting teachers or prophets and get the au-

[88]Bauckham, *Jude, 2 Peter*, pp. 46-48.
[89]Charles, "Jude's Use of Pseudepigraphical Source Material," pp. 144-45.

dience to repudiate or expel them, it was necessary to use polemic. "The rhetorical success of the letter lies in the author's ability to make his negative characterization of the rival teachers stick in the readers mind."[90] Since this discourse is meant to be delivered aloud, our author will accomplish this rhetorical end by using catchwords, clever and colorful metaphors, dramatic citations and readings of text and several other rhetorical devices. The aural dimension of the text aids in and is a part of the act of persuasion, something too often overlooked by commentators who simply treat Jude as if it were a text meant to be read silently and privately. Jude lived in a culture where such polemics were deemed appropriate and a normal part of discourse, especially when one was warning about something dangerous. We should not evaluate this material on the basis of modern conventions about politeness or civility.

The narration and the proofs were supposed to work together hand in glove. The statement of the facts was meant to flow right into the proofs or logical arguments, such that the proof was meant to be the verification of what was asserted in the facts (Quintilian *Institutio oratoria* 4.2.79). Quintilian is perfectly clear that narration and proofs are two seamless means of instructing the audience (8 preface). Jude 3-4 and Jude 5-16 provide a good example of oratio continua,[91] and three proofs are offered in Jude 5-16 to demonstrate that the characterization of the false teachers in Jude 4 is accurate.

From a rhetorical viewpoint it was perfectly appropriate to draw examples from both history and fiction to make one's points about virtue and vice. The "praise of famous men and the denunciation of the wicked" (Quintilian *Institutio oratoria* 2.4.26) was an important part of any rhetorical discourse, regardless of its species, but this was especially the case if one wanted to change someone's behavior, as in Jude. Quintilian suggests that, after starting with the rhetorical exercise of praising or blaming someone, the next natural step in the process is rhetorical comparison, where one compares or contrasts the merits of two characters or groups of people (2.4.21). In any rhetorical discourse, such as Jude's, it was expected that the speaker would tailor, edit, modify or amplify the facts and examples to suit the message, for "we must state our facts as advocates not witnesses" (4.2.109).

When we realize that Jude is trying to persuade his audience in regard to the false teachers, not just educate or inform his audience, we begin to understand the character and nature of his discourse. Persuasion would happen by story plus comparisons plus logic, and known story summaries would be edited as forms of

---

[90]Neyrey, *2 Peter, Jude*, p. 55.
[91]O'Banion, "Narration and Argumentation," pp. 325-30.

proofs. "The oration was a synthesis of different species of argument, including prose and poetry, artistic and inartistic proof, and especially narration and logic."[92]

[5]*But I wish to remind you, though you know all (this), that the Lord*[93]*once for all saved the people from Egypt (but) the second time he destroyed the unbelievers.* [6]*Angels who did not keep to their own domain but abandoning their own abode—these he has kept until this great day of judgment (in) perpetual bondage under gloomy darkness.* [7]*Just as Sodom and Gomorrah and the surrounding cities committed fornication and went after other flesh in like manner to these (people). They are set before you as evidence/examples of those undergoing the punishment of eternal fire.*

[8]*Likewise, nevertheless, those dreamers defile the flesh but flout the dominion and malign the glorious ones.* [9]*But Michael the archangel, when he argued with the devil disputing concerning Moses' body, did not dare to bring a charge of blasphemy but said, "The Lord rebuke you."* [10]*But these people, whatever they do not understand, they malign/blaspheme. But whatever by instinct like irrational animals they knew from experience has corrupted/destroyed them.* [11]*Alas for them that have followed the way of Cain and have abandoned themselves to the error of Balaam for the sake of a reward and have been destroyed in the controversy of Korah.*

[12]*These are the very ones who are hidden danger/rocks feeding/shepherding with you in your love feasts*[94] *without reverence, looking after (only) themselves. They are waterless clouds carried away by a strong wind; unproductive fruit-bearing trees— doubly dead having been uprooted;* [13]*wild waves of the sea foaming with shameful deeds, wandering stars for whom the gloom of eternal darkness is kept reserved.*

[14]*But even Enoch the seventh from Adam prophesied about these (men) saying: "Behold the Lord came with his ten thousand angels* [15]*to execute judgment on/for all and to convict all persons concerning all their godless works that they impiously committed and concerning all their hard words that they spoke against him, these godless sinners."* [16]*These men are grumblers, malcontents, living/following according to their own desires, and their mouth utters huge/arrogant words showing partiality for the sake of gain.*

---

[92]Ibid., p. 339.

[93]Manuscripts A, B, 33, 81, 322, Origen, Jerome, Bede and other witnesses provide impressive support for the reading "Jesus" (rather than "Lord" or "God"). This may be an example of confusion caused by the use of nomina sacra, the capital letter Greek abbreviations used for the sacred names. KC (i.e., the abbreviation for "Lord") could very readily be mistaken for IC ("Jesus"), especially when copying from a manuscript in a small hand. Jude nowhere else uses just the human name "Jesus," but always the combination "Jesus Christ." See Metzger, *Textual Commentary*, pp. 723-24. Landon, *Text-Critical Study*, pp. 70-77, concludes that "Lord" referring to God the Father is likely original here. It is tempting to read "Jesus" here, since in 1 Pet 3 Jesus is seen as having a role in relationship to the imprisoned fallen angels, which could also be the case here (cf. Jude 6). 𝔓[72] wins the prize for most peculiar reading: "God Christ."

[94]Instead of *agapais*, which is well attested by ℵ, B, K, L and most minuscules, a few manuscripts (82, 378, 460), apparently influenced by 2 Pet 2:13, read *apatais* ("deceptions, enticements"). See Metzger, *Textual Commentary*, p. 725.

In the first major proof of this discourse in Jude 5-10, Jude draws on three negative examples that were often used together in early Jewish and Christian literature (Sirach 16.7-10; Cairo Genizah *Damascus Document* 2.17—3.12; 3 Maccabees 2.4-7; 2 Pet 2:4-10a) to demonstrate that ungodly behavior precipitates God's judgment.[95] In Jude's arrangement, these three examples are not given in chronological order but rather in a rhetorically more effective manner, with the punishment becoming more specific and severe with each example: destruction by natural death, imprisonment in chains in a spiritual place until final judgment, punishment by eternal fire. This rhetorical device uses amplification by augmentation (Cicero *Partitiones oratoriae* 15.54; Quintilian *Institutio oratoria* 8.4.3-9). Jude proves his case by making comparisons between these examples and what he predicts will happen to the false teachers and those who follow them, which is a deliberative form of arguing (Aristotle *Rhetoric* 1.9.1368a40; *Rhetoric to Alexander* 32.1438b29-32).

When Jude uses the term *remind* in **Jude 5**, he does not wish to merely jog the memory of his audience but he means "heed and avoid the example of," not just "bear in mind." He expects his audience to be familiar with these examples. They are called to act on their knowledge of the previous course of action that God took with such sinful people. The term *kyrios* ("Lord") likely refers to God the Father here, but it is ambiguous and in view of 1 Peter 3 our author could be envisioning Jesus' involvement with the fallen angels. In any case, this is an example of how God saved his people, bringing them out of bondage in Egypt but virtually wiping them out when they lapsed into sin in the wilderness. Their sin was "not believing" (*mē pisteusantas*), as evidenced and proved by their conduct. Richard Bauckham suggests that this is applied to the false teachers and any who should choose to follow them: even though God may have saved them once (at conversion), if they act in this fashion they will be destroyed (at the judgment, at the parousia).[96] This is a stern warning clearly directed toward believers—no once saved, always saved idea here. Pheme Perkins puts it this way: "The example of the wilderness generation (v. 5) establishes the principle that Jude wishes readers to draw from all the examples: those who have been saved by God can still be condemned if they are unfaithful.[97] There is some contro-

---

[95] Watson, *Jude*, p. 488.

[96] Bauckham, *Jude, 2 Peter*, p. 50.

[97] Perkins, *Peter, James and Jude*, p. 149. I am also in complete agreement with Perkins that Neyrey's notion that Jude is defending his own honor in this discourse, in the form of an honor riposte, "has no direct support in the text" (p. 150). So far as we can tell, Jude has a good relationship with his audience, and they have not challenged his authority, nor do we have any direct evidence that the false teachers suggested that Jude's authority was not valid. If someone's honor is being challenged by the false teachers, it is that of Jesus and indeed of God.

versy over how to read the term *deuteron*. Ruth Anne Reese suggests: "It usually means 'a second time,' and that meaning is hard to understand in this context. It seems to be referring to either a second salvation or a second instance of disbelief. If one gives it a more chronological sense such as 'after this,' then the reference can be more clearly tied to God's judgment on the wilderness generation whose rebellion was a demonstration of their disbelief."[98]

With **Jude 6** we return to a wordplay using the term *tēreō* ("keep"). In Jude 1 God kept or had a firm grasp on believers; here the angels do not keep to their proper domain but rather abandon their abode and come to earth and have relations with women, a much commented on event in early Judaism (cf. *1 Enoch* 6—19; 86—88; 106; *Jubilees* 4.15, 22; 5.1; 1QapGen [Genesis Apocryphon] 2.1; *Testament of Reuben* 5.6; *2 Baruch* 56.10-14). As a result God must keep them in perpetual bondage until the great and terrible day of judgment. Again the lesson is clear: if believers wish to be kept by God they must keep to their proper sphere and keep God's commandments and keep on relying on him, not the false teachers. Genesis 6:1-4 is quite clearly in the background of Jude 6, and it is interpreted, embellished and added to by various Old Testament apocryphal texts. This story is about angels lusting after humans, but the Sodom story was about humans lusting after angels, and in *1 Enoch* 10.4-6 Michael is instructed to bind these angels in chains until the day of judgment. J. N. D. Kelly and Richard Bauckham make clear that Jude is relying on *1 Enoch* and the *Assumption of Moses*.[99] J. Daryl Charles addresses what these three examples of judgment have in common: "All three paradigms—unbelieving Israel, the dispossessed angels and Sodom and Gomorrah—are for the present purpose of Jude and his audience ongoing examples . . . of divine judgment. The reason is that they *all exhibit an unnatural rebellion*."[100] The second half of Jude 6 may be referred to in 1 Peter 3:19: "Jesus preached to the spirits in prison." This is seen as only an interim condition, lasting only until the last judgment: the chains are eternal only in the sense that they will last until the last day and final judgment. Jude 6 is in essence reiterated and amplified in Jude 13, where the false teachers are compared more directly to the evil angels and likewise will share the "deep darkness."

---

[98]Reese, *Jude* (manuscript).
[99]Kelly, *Peter and Jude*, p. 257; and Bauckham, *Jude, 2 Peter*, pp. 51-52.
[100]Charles, *Literary Strategy in the Epistle of Jude*, p. 118 (emphasis original).

A CLOSER LOOK

Inspiration and Authority and the Citing of Noncanonical Texts

Jude's use of texts like *1 Enoch* and the *Assumption of Moses* is precisely what placed his book in the doubtful category as Scripture in the second century and afterward. We must decide several matters: (1) Is citing apocryphal material unworthy of scriptural authors? The answer must be no, and most scholars with a high view of Scripture will simply point out that God directed or inspired Jude to use the true parts of *1 Enoch*. (2) In what sense is *1 Enoch* true? Does Jude take *1 Enoch* to be a record of real historical events, or could he have used a myth or a legend to drive home a true point? We cannot decide a priori what the biblical authors will do until we see what they actually do.

Our view of inspiration must fit the text, not vice versa. A moment's reflection will suggest that it is perfectly possible for a biblical author or character to convey real truth, even about history, but using the vehicle of a fictitious story. Jesus does precisely that with the parables. Thus, what genre is *1 Enoch*, and how did Jude view it and use it? Did he see it as history or myth or some combination or mythical reflections on history? This becomes even more dramatically important when we are told that the archangel Michael debated Satan over the body of Moses—something the Old Testament gives no inkling of! At least Jude 6 is based on Genesis 6:1-4, but not so Jude 9. At this point we can make only some tentative suggestions as to how to deal with this:

1. There is no question that *1 Enoch* and the *Assumption of Moses* contain a lot of mythical and legendary material. Jude held this material in common with his audience: these stories had a moral for Israel.

2. The example in Jude 6 is sandwiched between two clearly historical examples in Jude 5 and Jude 7. This suggests that Jude saw the story of the fallen angels as historical (he handles Genesis 6:1-4 with restraint, unlike its use in *1 Enoch*). Jude 9, however, is separated from the first three examples by Jude 8, which may suggest that Jude saw this illustration as different and that he was now turning to fictitious or legendary examples to condemn the false teachers (a good debater would use all kinds of examples to make his case). Since, however, Jude 11 contains more biblical and historical examples (Cain, Balaam, Korah), it could be that Jude viewed all of the examples alike.

The story in Jude 9 is by definition suprahistorical, involving two more-than-human figures, possibly in a nonnatural sphere, in which case Jude 9 could not be labeled historical on any normal terms, though it could be real. While Jude 9 may be viewed by Jude as about a real suprahistorical event, we cannot rule out the possibility that Jude used a fictitious example to make his point about the behavior of the false teachers. Whatever the intention of the inspired author here, we must follow where he leads and not insist that he lead only in ways we want him to lead. Jude is dependent on *1 Enoch* 6—19 here, especially *1 Enoch* 10, where these angels, called the watchers (i.e., peeping Toms), are bound by the archangel Michael and temporarily placed in darkness under the earth until the day of judgment, when they will be thrown into Gehenna.

It is no surprise that Jude's use of *1 Enoch* and other apocryphal material confused the church fathers. For example, Bede says, "It is not easy to see what part of Scripture Jude got this tale from, though we do find something like it in Zechariah" (*On Jude* [Patrologia latina 93.126]). He continues:

> The book of Enoch, from which this quotation is taken, belongs to the Apocrypha, not because the sayings of the prophet are of no value or because they are false but because the book which circulates under his name was not really written by him but was put out by someone else who used his name. For if it were genuine it would not contain anything contrary to sound doctrine. But as a matter of fact it includes any number of incredible things about giants, who had angels instead of men as fathers, and which are clearly lies. Indeed, it was precisely because Jude quotes him that for a long time his letter was rejected by many as being uncanonical. Nevertheless it deserves to be included in the canon because of its author, its antiquity and the way in which it has been used, and particularly because this passage which Jude takes from Enoch is not in itself apocryphal or dubious but is rather notable for its clarity with which it testifies to the true light (*On Jude* [Patrologia latina 93.129]).

Well before Bede, Tertullian seems rather willing to accept *1 Enoch* as Scripture, partly because of Jude's use of it: "Since Enoch in the same book tells us of our Lord, we must not reject anything at all which genuinely pertains to us. Do we not read that every word of Scripture useful for edification is divinely inspired? As you very well know, Enoch was later rejected by the Jews for the same reason that prompted them to reject almost everything which prophesied about Christ. It is not at all surprising that they rejected certain Scriptures that spoke of him. . . . But we have a witness to Enoch in the epistle of Jude the apostle" (*On the Dress of Women* 3.3).[101] The debate over whether *1 Enoch* was canonical raged over several centuries, and the final conclusion was negative (Jerome *De viris illustribus* 4; *Apostolic Constitutions* 6.16.3). In general the earlier opinion was more favorable (*Barnabas* 16.5; Tertullian *Idolatry* 15.6; Clement of Alexandria *Extracts from the Prophets* 3).

---

[101]See Bray, *James, 1-2 Peter, 1-3 John, Jude*, pp. 252-55, for easy access to these quotations in translation.

We may take comfort then from not being alone in trying to puzzle these things out. What the use of such traditions shows, surely, is that Jude is writing an ad hoc document to a specific Jewish Christian audience conversant with early Jewish material, even some of the more arcane bits of it. He did not envision his discourse falling into our hands, these many centuries later. The inclusion of this document in the canon of the New Testament however indicates that the church fathers saw it as of some enduring and endearing worth, even though it was never included in the early lectionaries.

Jude 7 refers to the famous example of Sodom and Gomorrah whose sin, in addition to general immorality, was going after "strange flesh," that is, angel visitors. The Greek clearly refers to "different flesh," and so one of their sins was a violation of the creation order. Though the intention of the Sodomites was probably homosexual (i.e., the text does not suggest that the Sodomites knew the visitors were angels, not men), the Sodomites are condemned for the same sin as the angels in Jude 6—they violated the creation order and went after a different kind of being for a sexual partner, only here the initiative is on the part of humans, whereas in Genesis 6:1-4 it is the reverse. J. N. D. Kelly states:

> Many have interpreted *lusted after different flesh* . . . as meaning "indulged in sodomy." The Greek, however, does not tolerate this: it simply states that the *flesh* they desired was *different* (these good angels appeared in human form, but their *flesh* presumably was *different* in kind), whereas in homosexuality, as J. Chaine . . . aptly remarks, "the natures are only too alike." The solution lies in recognizing that, while the writer is singling out the Cities of the Plain as examples of immorality, his attention is focussed not so much on their unnatural conduct (for this, cf. Rom i.24, 27) as on the close parallel between their behaviour and that of the wicked angels. Both had made their sin even more appalling by lusting after *different flesh*—the angels because, spiritual beings though they were, they had coveted mortal women, and the Sodomites because, though only human beings, they had sought intercourse with angels. It is probably legitimate . . . to infer that he is snidely accusing the innovators of homosexual practices.[102]

Jude reminds his readers that the cities of Sodom and Gomorrah are still smoldering, due to underground sulfur (Josephus *Jewish War* 4.483; Philo *On the Life of Moses* 2.56; cf. Wisdom of Solomon 10.7; *1 Enoch* 67.4-13 [smoking valleys connected with fallen angels]).[103] This serves as a reminder to the audience of the awful nature of the eternal fire that the wicked experience as a pun-

---

[102]Kelly, *Peter and Jude*, pp. 258-59 (emphasis original).

[103]Bauckham, *Jude, 2 Peter*, pp. 54-55.

ishment. The audience is called to look into the abyss and turn back. Three or four sins seem to be found in the story of Sodom and Gomorrah: (1) inhospitality, (2) violating creation-order boundaries, (3) behavior and (4) perhaps rape, though that is more apparent in the Genesis story than here in Jude. The term *deigma,* usually "example," probably means "evidence," as it frequently does in deliberative rhetoric. Jude lays the evidence before the audience, and the judgment of the false teachers is left to them.

The verbs in Jude 5-19 toggle back and forth between aorist tense and present tense, which has a quite specific function, as Ruth Anne Reese argues:

> The aorist tense is generally used for examples drawn from other sources while the present tense is used to draw comparisons to the Others or to make general statements about the Others. The allusion or metaphor or quotation almost always comes first and is followed by a linkage to the Others. It becomes easier to see this movement between descriptive material like allusions and denotative material about the Others, when one pays careful attention to the tenses in the material. Jude's emphasis is on the present tense, and the aorist tense is used to support the argument he is making in the present tense. The chart below shows the movement between the examples that Jude recounts using the aorist tense and his application of those examples in the present tense to the group that has secretly slipped into the church.[104]

The author identifies the people set out as examples with the actions of the others and signals this by changing verb tense and the type of language (i.e., shifting from allusion to simile):

Examples Using Aorist Tense	Applications Using Present Tense
Egypt (Jude 5)	
angels (Jude 6)	
Sodom and Gomorrah (Jude 7)	
	they dream (Jude 8)
Michael the archangel (Jude 9)	
	they blaspheme (Jude 10)
Cain, Balaam and Korah (Jude 11)	
	they are spots in the love feasts (Jude 12)
Enoch (Jude 14-15)	
	they are grumblers (Jude 16)

---

[104]Reese, *Jude* (manuscript).

In **Jude 8** Jude begins to compare his examples to the behavior of these people, that is, to the false teachers. Richard Bauckham suggests that the three examples climax with the reference to Sodom and Gomorrah and that we may consequently look for a close connection between the sins of the false teachers and those of the Sodomites.[105] Jude 8 may refer to nocturnal pollutions resulting from erotic dreams, but the participle "dreaming" probably qualifies all that follows. These dreamers (1) defile the flesh, (2) flout the Lord's dominion and (3) malign the angels (i.e., "glorious ones") (cf. the parallel in Jude 4b-c).

Apparently the false teachers do this on the basis of their visionary experiences, which Jude downgrades to mere "dreamings" (cf. Deut 13:1-5; Is 56:10; Jer 23:25). "With the word and its connotations Jude implicitly argues that the sectarians' authority is false, thus effectively decreasing their ethos and that of their doctrine and practice."[106] The main thing we know about these false teachers is that they reject God's law, that is, they are antinomian, recognizing no law and no divine or angelic authority over them if it means a restriction of their ways and experiences. Apparently they saw themselves as so spiritual that they had transcended a necessity to worry about affairs of the body or deeds. Their spirituality was not affected one way or another, they seem to have claimed. Thus, they could indulge in various deviant acts and claim that these were not sin since they were not under law and that it did not adversely affect them since they were spiritual.

In early Judaism the giving of the law was thought to be through angels to Moses and not directly, as the Old Testament seems to imply (Acts 7:38, 53; Heb 2:2; Gal 3:19; cf. *Jubilees* 1.27-29; Josephus *Jewish Antiquities* 15.136; *Shepherd of Hermas, Similitudes* 8.3.3). Thus, the false teachers' slander of angels was probably part of their rejection of the law. Since angels were guardians of the created order (as was the law that they mediated), Jude sees these false teachers as the Sodomite violators of the creation order God made. They reject any authority that conflicts with their own. Like the fallen angels, by these activities they have abandoned their proper place in the created order; like the Israelites they have wandered into apostasy; like the Sodomites they have committed sexual sin and insulted the angelic realm. The conclusion that Jude wishes his audience to draw is that the false teachers malign what they do not really understand—spiritual matters—but since they are so sexually experienced their only real knowledge is in an area they share with mere animals. This carnal knowledge corrupts them or will lead to their destruction.

---

[105]Bauckham, *Jude, 2 Peter*, p. 55.
[106]Watson, *Invention, Arrangement and Style*, p. 55.

Jude 9-10 should be seen as an amplification of Jude 8, drawing on a tradition from the *Assumption of Moses*,[107] which in turn draws on Zechariah 3:2: "May the LORD rebuke you!" In Zechariah Yeshua/Joshua the high priest is standing before the angel of the Lord and before Satan (Zech 3:1), and Satan is accusing Yeshua/Joshua, while the angel of the Lord issues the rebuke. Jude has a similar dispute between a high angel (in this case Michael) and Satan. The intertextual echo suggests that the false teachers pretend they have even more authority, more right to speak for God than God's greatest angels, and even dare to slander angels, something that even Michael refrained from in his dispute with the evil angel Satan, when he merely invoked God to rebuke Satan. In Jude 8-10 Jude demonstrates the two points made in the narration in Jude 4: the false teachers are licentious, and they reject authority.

Jude 10 brings this first proof to a conclusion, for this is the first time we hear about judgment of the sectarians themselves, not just about judgment of the parallel examples.[108] The false teachers have already been stigmatized as "these people," which rhetorically speaking serves to distance both the author and the audience from them. They are clearly the problem that generates this discourse and are the focus of the strong polemic, and repeated use of the term *houtoi* (Jude 8, 10, 11, 12, 16, 19) is an example of anaphora, as our author keeps reminding the audience that he is talking about the same troublemakers.[109]

Jude 11-13 provides the second major proof, and like the first in Jude 5-10, Jude chooses three examples of particular ungodly persons to draw analogies with the false teachers (in Jude 5-10 it was three groups of ungodly persons). **Jude 11** is a woe oracle not unlike that found often in the Old Testament and in the teaching of Jesus (Mt 11:21; Lk 6:24-26). The word *ouai* appears thirty-one times in the teaching of Jesus and fourteen times in Revelation, but only twice elsewhere in the New Testament (here and 1 Cor 9:16). This likely implies that Jude saw himself as a true prophet in distinction from the false teachers, who may have seen themselves as persons receiving revelation as well. The aorist

---

[107]On the reconstruction of this source, which unfortunately is mutilated at the crucial juncture, see Bauckham, *Jude, 2 Peter*, pp. 65-76. There is some debate as to whether the *Testament of Moses* and the *Assumption of Moses* are (a) two works or (b) two parts of the same work or (c) two names for the same work. I think it was a single work, the end of which dealt with the dispute alluded to here and perhaps with the assumption of Moses or at least his death and proper burial, thus giving rise in a later Latin manuscript to the title *Assumption of Moses* and in the Latin version to Clement of Alexandria's comment on this text (Bauckham, *Jude, 2 Peter*, p. 67). On the suggestion of two documents, see Neyrey, *2 Peter, Jude*, pp. 65-66.

[108]Watson, *Invention, Arrangement and Style*, p. 56.

[109]Neyrey, *2 Peter, Jude*, pp. 71-72.

verbs reinforce this conclusion, which in turn reinforce what was said in Jude 4: the condemnation of such false teachers was designated long ago.[110] Furthermore, Jude normally introduces oracles by others with a preface (Jude 14, 17); that he does not do so here further indicates that this is a prophetic utterance of Jude himself.[111]

This section contains three more examples, but in this case they are individuals, and once again the nonbiblical wider Jewish tradition seems to be presupposed. Once again Jude carefully arranged his three examples using the device of amplification by augmentation. Pheme Perkins states: "Jude arranges the series in ascending order from walking on a road, to abandoning oneself to error, to perishing in a rebellion. The suggestion is that the opponents are on a similar course."[112] The way of Cain is the way of murderers, but in the wider Jewish tradition he was seen as one who entices others to sin, and this may especially fit the false teachers. Jude may especially be thinking of Wisdom of Solomon 10.3, which speaks of Cain "falling away from God's wisdom in his anger, perished himself, due to his fratricidal anger."[113] Greed and envy were also associated with Cain (Josephus *Jewish Antiquities* 1.52-66; Philo *On the Sacrifices of Cain and Abel* 38-39; *Testament of Benjamin* 7.5; cf. *1 Clement* 4.7). A Palestinian targum suggests that Cain rejected the idea of divine righteousness and future judgment and demonstrates how Jude is dependent not just on the Old Testament text but on its expansive treatments in later Jewish literature:

And Cain said to Abel his brother: "Come! Let the two of us go out into the open field." And when the two of them had gone out into the open field, Cain answered and said to Abel: "I perceive that the world was not created by mercy and that it is not being conducted according to the fruits of good words, and that there is favoritism in judgment. Why was your offering received favorably, and my offering was not received favorably from me?" Abel answered and said to Cain: "I perceive that the world was created by mercy and that it is being conducted according to the fruits of good works. And because my works were better than yours, my offering was received from me favorably and yours was not received favorably from you." Cain answered and said to Abel: "There is no judgment, and there is no judge and there is no other world. There is no giving of good reward to the just nor is vengeance exacted of the wicked." Abel answered and said to Cain: "There is judgment, and there is a judge, and there is another world. And there is giving of good

---

[110]Watson, *Jude*, p. 491.
[111]Boobyer, "Verbs in Jude 11," suggests that the verbs in this verse refer to punishment, but Neyrey, *2 Peter, Jude*, p. 75, says that these three verbs describe the commission of the crime, not the punishment, for which Jude uses "perish."
[112]Perkins, *Peter, James and Jude*, p. 152.
[113]Moffatt, *General Epistles*, p. 238.

reward to the just and vengeance is exacted of the wicked in the world to come." Concerning this matter the two of them were disputing in the open field. (Targum Neofiti 1 on Genesis 4:8, trans. Bauckham)

Jude uses aorist-tense verbs *(eporeuthēsan, exechythēsan, apōlonto)* to indicate that the future condemnation is certain: it is an accomplished fact. This may be a prophetic use of the aorist, which again may imply that Jude sees himself as a prophet. *Planē* ("error") causes the false teachers "to wander" *(planētai)* (Jude 13). Jude will play on this noun and this verb in what follows: the false teachers are "wandering stars" who have wandered into error. Wandering stars could be planets, but comets and meteors that did not pursue a patterned course were especially terrifying to the ancients, because they appeared to be celestial beings that had rebelled from the order of the heavens and gone off, charting their own course.[114] This becomes an apt metaphor to describe the trajectory of the false teachers.

One might assume from the Old Testament (e.g., Num 22—24) that Balaam could be seen in a relatively positive light.[115] This was not the case in first-century Jewish tradition (Josephus *Jewish Antiquities* 4.126-30; cf. Rev 2:14; Mishnah, tractate *Avot* 5.19), where Balaam's main flaw was encouraging Balak to entice Israel into sin, in particular some sexual sin. In any event Balaam was seen as the ultimate source of Israel's apostasy.[116] Balaam, however, was seen as particularly notorious because he did his prophesying for pay (Philo *On the Life of Moses* 1.266-68). Thus, he was a greedy seducer of Israel. This description fits Jude's view of the false teachers. It was not wrong for early Christian teachers to expect pay for their work, but often there was abuse of Christian generosity (1 Cor 9:4; Rom 16:18; 1 Tim 6:5; Tit 1:11).[117]

The controversy of Korah involves the rejection of Mosaic authority by Korah and company (Num 16; 26:9-10). He was the classic example of one who rejected the law and the authority of Moses. Jewish tradition saw him as one who created schism and, though this may have been in Jude's mind, "it is likely that the real significance of Korah for Jude is as one who denied the divine authority of the Law."[118] The focus is not on Korah's sin, as it was in the case of Cain and

---

[114]Perkins, *Peter, James and Jude*, p. 153.
[115]See the discussion in Witherington, *Jesus the Seer*, pp. 34-37.
[116]Bauckham, *Jude, 2 Peter*, pp. 81-82.
[117]There is no evidence in the New Testament of Christian prophets being paid. Greco-Roman oracles spoke for pay (e.g., the oracle at Delphi), and perhaps the example of Simon Magus in Acts 8 is worth reflecting on. The most pertinent example is perhaps Acts 16:16, where some do divination for pay.
[118]Bauckham, *Jude, 2 Peter*, p. 84.

Balaam, but on his destruction—swallowed up by the earth straight into Sheol (Num 26:10; cf. Num 16:30). Once again Jude has for rhetorical reasons not followed chronological order, which would have had Korah before Balaam, for the fate of Korah provides a more dramatic conclusion demonstrating that sin leads to judgment and punishment. From a rhetorical viewpoint a prophecy is especially powerful as a proof of an argument, as it brings in the divine view of the matter and so serves as the strongest sort of proof—an inartificial one from an unimpeachable external authority.[119] Richard Bauckham aptly sums up the significance of these three examples: Jude "compares the false teachers first to Cain, the great prototype of sinners. . . . Secondly, they are compared to Balaam . . . who, in his greed for financial gain, hurried eagerly to give the advice which led Israel into the disastrous apostasy at Beth-peor. Thirdly, they are compared to Korah, the archetypal schismatic, who contested the authority of Moses and disputed the divine origin of certain laws."[120]

Houtoi eisin in **Jude 12-13** clearly applies the prophecy of Jude 11 to the false teachers.[121] Jude 12, however, presents a number of problems that we must first resolve in order to interpret it. The first problem is the word *spilades*. Its normal meaning is "rock/hidden rock" not "blemishes/stains," and pace Richard Bauckham it seems to mean rocks here.[122] Polybius gives this account of a fleet of ships:

> They had crossed the strait in safety and were off the territory of Camarina when they were overtaken by so fierce a storm and so terrible a disaster that it is difficult adequately to describe it owing to its surpassing magnitude. For of their three hundred and sixty-four ships only eighty were saved; the rest either foundered or were dashed by the waves against the rocks *[spilasi]* and headlands and broken to pieces, covering the shore with corpses and wreckage. (*Histories* 1.37.2)

Ruth Anne Reese comments that

> the rocks in Polybius' account are part of the overall destruction that the Roman fleet suffered. Likewise, the others engage in activities that prove to be destructive to themselves and to the community. In a similar usage, Plutarch says that when people encounter vice their experience is "like a hidden rock *[spilados*—here translated 'hidden rock'] appearing in fair weather, and the soul is overwhelmed and confounded" [Plutarch, *Moralities* 2.101b12 (Loeb translation)]. This usage shows

---

[119]Watson, *Invention, Arrangement and Style*, p. 58.
[120]Bauckham, *Jude, 2 Peter*, p. 91.
[121]Watson, *Invention, Arrangement and Style*, p. 57.
[122]See the discussions in Bauckham, *Jude, 2 Peter*, pp. 85-86; Neyrey, *2 Peter, Jude*, pp. 74-75; Knox, "*Spilades*"; and Whallon, "Should We Keep?"

the element of surprise. The person does not expect to encounter danger, to encounter a rocky shore on which their life could be destroyed when they engage in vice, but the rock takes them by surprise and they are overwhelmed. These examples point to the danger and hidden nature connected to the word *spilas*.[123]

Joseph Mayor agrees that the word refers to reefs or rocks submerged and thus to hidden dangers to a ship.[124] Jude is warning his audience against the hidden dangers of getting too close to these false teachers, who are like sunken rocks and can cause spiritual shipwreck. They are all the more dangerous because they have been accepted into fellowship with the believers at their love feasts and so one's defenses will be down to the dangers of spiritual shipwreck that lie (on couches) right in their midst. Second Peter 2:13 uses a different word: *spilos* ("spot"). This provides a good example of the mistake to read Jude in light of 2 Peter. Rather the order of reading should be the other way around: 2 Peter is the later text and draws on and modifies Jude.

Agapē feasts at this time were part of the celebration of the Lord's Supper and seem to have involved a fellowship meal (1 Cor 11:20-34; Acts 2:46). Apparently, these were evening meals (Acts 20:7, 11) and involved intimate sharing with one another.[125] Obviously having a betrayer in this setting, where everyone is open and trusting, was especially dangerous to the church. Because these men have no scruples (*aphobos* [literally "without fear"] possibly means "without reverence," which may mean that they had no scruples against taking advantage of Christians in such a situation), they are especially dangerous. The word *poimainontes* refers to these people, supposed to be shepherds looking after others, but only looking after (i.e., shepherding) themselves, feeding themselves. They are egocentric to the core. There is perhaps an echo here of Ezekiel 34:2-4, 8 (cf. Is 56:11), which speaks of shepherds who feed themselves instead of their flocks.

Jude 12b-13 provides four examples from nature to indicate the character of these so-called shepherds. Jude chose examples from each of the four areas of nature: (1) air/clouds, (2) earth/trees, (3) water/sea and (4) heavens/stars (cf. *1 Enoch* 2.1—5.4; 80.2-8). Richard Bauckham is perhaps overexegeting here to see an allusion to the irregular behavior of nature in the last days.[126] The first two illustrations show that whatever good the false teachers may appear to offer or say they can do, they do not deliver. These teachers are like clouds that float over the Palestinian coastline, promising rain but never delivering (Prov 25:14).

---

[123]Reese, *Jude* (manuscript).
[124]Mayor, *Jude*, pp. 40-41.
[125]Brosend, *James and Jude*, p. 178.
[126]Bauckham, *Jude, 2 Peter*, pp. 87-91.

False teachers are also like fruit trees at harvest time that are both sterile and uprooted—no fruit and no life, thus doubly dead. This may contain an allusion to Jesus' saying in Matthew 7:16-20, which draws an analogy between a false prophet's teachings and evil fruit. False teachers are also doubly deadly, not benefiting believers and being dead and uprooted in themselves (false teachers face the "second death" in Rev 2:11; 20:6, 14; 21:8).

The third illustration shifts to the bad effects these false teachers have, rather than the good effects they do not have. They are like a wave that brings seaweed and garbage up on the shore (Is 57:20). The metaphor breaks down with *aischynas:* they are foaming with shameful deeds, the overflow of their evil character. They are also like wandering stars (*1 Enoch* 18.13-16; 21.1-6; 88.1-3), which is a likely reference to planets that appear to wander from their course, or to comets or meteors that manifest an apparently erratic course. "Wandering stars" may be an allusion to fallen angels, who are closely associated with the stars in Jewish tradition. In any case, God has reserved for them the gloom of eternal darkness, in contrast to the earlier eternal fire (Tobit 14.10; *1 Enoch* 63.6). Clearly the author intends this as a metaphorical description of life without God forever, not a literal description of what hell is like (it cannot be both utterly dark and utterly light forever). The teachers are thus accused of disorderly, useless and harmful conduct, of acting like irrational and amoral animals. *First Enoch* 80.6 describes all of nature becoming disorderly and lawless just before the eschatological end of things. And the fate of such star beings is utter and outer darkness (*1 Enoch* 18, 20). The rhetorical intent and effect of this colorful language was to create a negative emotional response, to create pathos, in this case appealing to one's sense of fear and horror at betrayal and shameful behavior.[127] "The six metaphors of vv 12-13 provide a powerful series of mental images and associations which seriously diminish the ethos of the sectarians especially with regard to their leadership and teaching roles, and elicit much negative pathos against them."[128]

Jude 14-16 contains the first (and only) example of a direct quotation—not from the Old Testament but from *1 Enoch*. Jude demonstrates or provides the rhetorical proof (i.e., a proof from example; Quintilian *Institutio oratoria* 5.11.36-44; Cicero *De inventione rhetorica* 1.30.48) that the ungodly false teachers were spoken of long ago in prophetic texts, in this case *1 Enoch* 1.9.[129] William Brosend says that the rhetorical strategy of quoting an authoritative source

---

[127]Watson, *Invention, Arrangement and Style*, p. 61.
[128]Ibid., p. 64.
[129]Watson, *Jude*, p. 494.

is a good tactic, as it allows Jude to pronounce judgment without himself having to do it in his own voice.[130] The real clout of this quotation is that citing an inspired oracle means that these words carry the ethos and authority of God, and so God is directly condemning these false teachers. Jude here further works out and demonstrates the charges leveled against the false teachers in the narratio (Jude 4).[131]

It is probable, as Richard Bauckham argues, that Jude knew the Greek version of Enoch, but made his own translation from the Aramaic version (4QEnoch [Book of Watchers] 1.1.15-17) from memory.[132] One of the more important changes from *1 Enoch* 1.9 is Jude's insertion of *kyrios*, so that the prophecy refers to Christ's second coming, not to God's coming in general for judgment. Another salient change is Jude's swapping Enoch's judgment on "all flesh" to judgment on only the ungodly *(asebeis)*.[133] Characteristic of the way that Old Testament and Jewish prophecy or texts are so often handled in the New Testament, Jude tailors the text to fit the application. The term *ungodly* is the key catchword of this section, and it is Jude's chief complaint against these teachers: they are ungodly—rejecting God's word, authority, commandments, required lifestyle and so on. They are impious in both words and deeds. Three verbs of divine action ("coming," "execute judgment," "convict") are paralleled by a threefold repetition of the ungodliness of the false teachers.[134]

It is quite possible that this citation of *1 Enoch* 1.9 was alluded to in Jude 4. This is the written text that speaks of the condemnation *(poiēsai krisin)* of these false teachers. The Enoch quotation does not necessarily mean that Jude thought of the book of Enoch as Scripture, but he did see him as a true prophet. Jude's view of prophecy (Jude 4) involves prophets sometimes saying things about the distant future, not just the near future. Genesis 5:24 says that Enoch walked with God, and most Jewish commentators took this to imply Enoch's especially holy nature or righteous condition. He walked with God in contrast to these false teachers, and thus he can be relied upon. Jude clearly sees Enoch's prophecy as referring to Jude's opponents.

Being the seventh from Adam (by inclusive reckoning; cf. *1 Enoch* 60.8; *Jubilees* 7.39), Enoch was seen as special by Jews and Christians into the second

---

[130]Brosend, *James and Jude*, p. 179.
[131]Watson, *Invention, Arrangement and Style*, p. 64.
[132]Bauckham, "Note on a Problem"; Osburn, "Christological Use of *1 Enoch* i.9." The Greek text of Enoch varies in at least six or seven points from that found in Jude.
[133]Watson, *Invention, Arrangement, Style*, p. 65, says: "Such omission provides better application to the sectarians and avoids the misconception that the audience will be destroyed at the parousia along with the sectarians."
[134]Ibid.

century and beyond. He may even have been seen as a type of Christ. Jack Sasson shows that being placed seventh in a genealogical list indicates special importance.[135] One could hardly cite a more ancient authority, or one more blessed by God, than Enoch, if it was believed that *1 Enoch* was written by the person mentioned in Genesis. It is even possible that early Christian writers (e.g., Tertullian, Clement of Alexandria, the author of *Barnabas*) saw *1 Enoch* as Scripture.[136] Clearly, early Christians highly valued the book.[137]

The verb *ēlthen* in Jude 14b is a prophetic aorist:[138] their doom is so sure (cf. Jude 11) that Jude can speak of it as having already happened. Though Jude 15 could refer to the judgment on all (perhaps in an attempt to put the fear of God into his audience, who might be tempted to follow the teachers' example), nonetheless, Jude says that this prophecy refers to these *(toutois)* false teachers in Jude 14. They are guilty of godless deeds and hard words spoken against God or his will and world. Jude 15 repeats the same terms for rhetorical effect: "all" (four times), "impious" (three times) and "judge/convict" (two times). In all probability, the reference to God coming with the angels in Zechariah 14:5 (and possibly Deut 33:2) is in the background here. In the New Testament the angels are seen as those who not only save (harvest) the redeemed, but also cast the wicked into the fiery furnace (Mk 13:27; 2 Thess 1:7; Mt 13:41, 49-50)—they are the executors of the final verdict pronounced by Jesus the Lord.

This judgment will involve convicting the godless of their sin, that is, not merely condemning them but making it so that they will see the error of their ways. These impious men dared to speak "hard words," that is, words of defiance or resistance to God's law or word or possibly (cf. *1 Enoch* 5.4) slanderous words against God's word. Pheme Perkins rightly reminds us that "speech is much more carefully controlled and monitored in a traditional, hierarchical society than it is in modern democracies. We can hardly recapture the sense of horror at blasphemy that ancient society felt because for us words do not have the same power that they do in traditional societies. Words appear to have considerably less consequences than actions. In traditional societies, the word is a form of action."[139]

The phrase *ungodly sinners* is not merely redundant but indicates that this is not accidental sin, but deliberate ungodliness in word and deed, consistent with

---

[135]Sasson, "Genealogical Convention."
[136]Kelly, *Peter and Jude*, p. 277.
[137]Nickelsburg's *1 Enoch* provides a complete critical and detailed treatment of the relevant portions of *1 Enoch*.
[138]Black, "Christological Use of the Old Testament," pp. 10-11.
[139]Perkins, *Peter, James and Jude*, p. 154.

their character. Like the Israelites in the wilderness these people are "murmurers" (*gongystēs* appears only here in the New Testament; cf. Ex 16—17; Num 14:2; 17:10) against God and God's will. Continually disgruntled, they are never satisfied with God's way, but rather follow their own way and desires.[140] Joseph Mayor puts it this way: "As the fear of God drives out the fear of man, so defiance of God tends to put man in His place, as the chief source of good or evil to his fellows."[141] They were a law unto themselves.

Apparently, part of the false teachers' ways involved "big talk," which flattered their supporters (especially those who could remunerate them for services rendered) and amounted to showing partiality to some of God's people (i.e., those who could help them economically or otherwise). The interesting phrase *thaumazontes prosōpa ōpheleias charin* refers to giving face or showing partiality in order to get on the good side of their potential patrons (cf. Jas 2:1-7). These false teachers may have been willing to overlook the sins of their patrons.

Jerome Neyrey rightly stresses that throughout this discourse Jude has been accusing the false teachers of being out of control, of not controlling their mouths. Their sins seem mainly to be sins of speech: they deny the Lord (Jude 4), they insult the glorious ones/angels (Jude 8), they engage in disputes (Jude 9), offer defiant or hard words against the Lord (Jude 15) and are disgruntled murmurers who also apparently indulge in flattery of patrons (Jude 16). "Jude, then, reflects not only a common polemic against ambitious and destabilizing speech, but also the underlying cultural assumptions about the value of social control and its replication in bodily control."[142]

PERORATION: "TEARING DOWN AND BUILDING UP" (JUDE 17-23)

In a peroration an orator intends to bring the discourse to a climax, summing up some of the main points (the so-called *repetitio*) and making a final emotional appeal (the *adfectus*), trying to reach the audience at the level of their deeper emotions such as love and hate, fear and trust (Quintilian *Institutio oratoria* 6.1.1-9; Aristotle *Rhetoric* 3.19.1419b.1-3; Cicero *De inventione rhetorica* 1.52-56). The structure of this peroration is easy to discern: Jude 17-19 serves as the summary statement, and Jude 20-23 makes the final emotional appeal.[143] Jude's discourse has depended on both emotion and argument, as Jude strove to get the audience to make a sharp break with the false teachers. The use of amplification, repetition and emotion is a measure of how serious Jude viewed

---

[140]Moffatt, *General Epistles*, p. 240.
[141]Mayor, *Jude*, p. 46.
[142]Neyrey, *2 Peter, Jude*, p. 79.
[143]Watson, *Invention, Arrangement and Style*, pp. 67-68.

the situation. For obvious reasons, the final emotional appeal is sometimes called the conquestio, as the end of the discourse is supposed to "conquer" or "win over" the audience. Cicero says that the conquestio ought to refer to the most fundamental values, to clear instances of good and evil (*Partitiones oratoriae* 17.58). Thus, this section references both positive (faith, prayer, God's great love, Christ's mercy, eternal life, salvation) and negative (contamination by sin, punishment by fire) topics.[144] Altruism is also appealed to, as the audience is asked to rescue the perishing. All of this is especially appropriate for a deliberative discourse so the audience will see the results of choosing one course of behavior or another.

William Brosend rightly notes the change in tone in this section, which repeats the term *beloved* concludes the discourse with a positive exhortation. He also notes an implicit synkrisis or rhetorical contrast between the false teachers and the true Christians in the audience:[145]

"these people"	"beloved"
scoff	remember
cause division	build themselves up
bombastic in speech	pray in the Spirit
indulge in their own lusts	keep themselves in God's love
are destroyed and will perish	look forward to mercy
show partiality/flatter for personal gain	have mercy

Jerome Neyrey helpfully reminds us,

> When Jude compares and contrasts the scoffers with loyal disciples, he praises those who are group-oriented and blames those who act individualistically. Group-oriented persons internalize the norms and values of the group and seek to satisfy the expectations of those who are arbiters of honor and shame. Thus Jude exhorts them, and in so doing resocializes them to the expectations of true discipleship. His exhortation, moreover, is but a reminder of the tradition, the group's social conscience (v 17).[146]

> [17]*But you, beloved, remember the things spoken beforehand by the apostles of our Lord Jesus Christ,* [18]*that they said to you, "In the last age/times there will be scoffers following their own ungodly desires."* [19]*These are the ones creating divisions, they are "natural," not having the spirit.*

---

[144]Ibid., p. 73.
[145]Brosend, *James and Jude*, p. 181. See the similar chart in Neyrey, *2 Peter, Jude*, p. 85.
[146]Neyrey, *2 Peter, Jude*, p. 88.

> ²⁰*But you, beloved, build yourselves up in your most holy faith, praying in the Holy Spirit,* ²¹*keep yourselves in the love of God, wait for the mercy of our Lord Jesus Christ unto eternal life.* ²²*And have mercy on some, the waverers/those under condemnation/those disputing;* ²³*on others, save (them) from the flames, snatching them; still others have mercy (mixed) with fear, hating even the garment polluted by the flesh.*[147]

In Jude 17-19 we basically come to the end of Jude's charges against the false teachers, with Jude 20-23 being the positive exposition of what the believers must do and be.

At first glance **Jude 17** appears to start a positive section since it begins "but you beloved," but Jude 17-19 provides the transition for the positive material beginning in Jude 20. Thus Jude 17-19 makes a natural transition from the final proof that preceded it, which dealt with problems caused by the false teachers. The repetition here of some of the things said earlier is rhetorically appropriate, but it also indicates that there is some doubt in the audience, or at least part of it, on how to view the false teachers. Therefore, the teaching is reinforced by appeal to authoritative teaching—that of the apostles, through the quoting of an oracle or prophecy, a strong form of inartificial proof.[148] Cicero advised that one should play the trump card last (*De oratore* 2.77.314); that is, one should use the most outstanding and unimpeachable resource in the peroration, in this case the prophecy of Jesus and the teaching of the apostles based on it is that resource.

In Jude 17-19 Jude reminds the disciples of what they had heard before by giving one more citation—perhaps the climactic citation—this time from the church's own apostles. All that was said in the commentary on Jude 5 about the verb *remind* also applies here, but in this case Jude possibly refers to what these believers were taught when they became Christians or at the founding of their church. Against the usual exegesis that sees here a looking back to a past apostolic age, what is "past" are the words that the apostles prophesied, not the apostles themselves, but clearly Jude sees his audience as the apostles' contem-

---

[147]Metzger, *Textual Commentary*, pp. 725-27, reminds that there are some significant textual problems in Jude 22-23. Is the audience called to have mercy on the waverers or to convince them? Are there two or three parts to this exhortation ("some . . . others . . . still others")? The probability is that Jude, with his preference for triads, had a three-part formula dealing with doubters, apostatizers and false teachers. Probably too certain scribes changed "have mercy" in Jude 22 to "convince" in order to differentiate this clause from the "have mercy" clause at the end of Jude 23. However, 𝔓⁷² has a two-member clause, as does Clement of Alexandria, *Stromateis* 6.8.65. Cf. Bauckham *Jude, 2 Peter*, pp. 108-9, for a defense of the shorter text; see also Landon, *Text-Critical Study*, pp. 131-34. For the threefold division of the phrases, comporting with Jude's love of triads, see Winter, "Jude 22-23"; Kubo, "Jude 22-23"; and Birdsall, "Text of Jude."

[148]Watson, *Invention, Arrangement and Style*, p. 69.

poraries: "This is what they kept saying to you" (Jude 18a). William Brosend puts it this way: "There is nothing in the text itself that requires the words to have been spoken 'long ago,' only before the appearance of the opponents. In other words, the phrase cannot be used as evidence that Jude wrote long after some distinct period known as 'the apostolic age.'"[149]

Apparently Jude does not include himself as one of these founding apostles (nor did James see himself in the apostle category). They are apostles of our Lord, just as Jude is a servant of our Lord.[150] Unlike James, Jude had not seen his brother raised from the dead. First Corinthians 15:7 says that Jesus appeared to James and then to all the apostles. Perhaps Jude is included in this latter group of "all the apostles," but 1 Corinthians 9:5 gives cause for doubt that Jude is in the latter group since Paul distinguishes between the "brothers of the Lord" and the "other apostles" (i.e., other than Paul and Peter). Yet Acts 1:14 tells us that both Mary and the brothers are present in the upper room after Easter. We may assume that they all came up to the Passover festival (in Jn 7:2-8 the brothers are going to the Feast of Tabernacles), and we know that Jesus appeared to James. Perhaps he told the other brothers, and they gathered in the upper room after Easter. In any case, these brothers are clearly seen as married traveling evangelists and church leaders (1 Cor 9:5). Oecumenius remarks that the predictions Jude refers to are those found in 2 Peter and most of Paul's letters. Therefore he concludes that Jude must have been writing toward the end of his life when he was exceedingly old and all the apostolic ministries were coming to an end (*Commentary on Jude* [Patrologia graeca 119.720]).[151]

It is not unlikely that several apostles could be involved in the founding of one church or group of churches (e.g., Acts 8 says that both Peter and John were involved after Philip had done the initial evangelism in Samaria), and if Jude is writing to a group of Jewish Christian churches all the more so. Jude 1 does not rule out an audience larger than one church, though Jude is likely dealing with a problem confined to a specific area, perhaps in Galilee. The original disciples, following Jesus' teaching (Mt 7:15-20; 24:11; Mk 13:22; 1 Tim 4:1-3; 2 Tim 3:1-9; 4:3-4; 2 Pet 3:3), warned of people who were false teachers and who scoffed at true religion. In **Jude 18** *empaiktai* ("scoffers"), an extremely derogatory term in early Judaism, refers to a typical Old Testament type of troublemaker—one who despises or ignores and mocks true religion and/or morality (Ps 1:1; Prov 1:22; 9:7-8; Is

---

[149]Brosend, *James and Jude*, p. 180.
[150]Bauckham, *Jude, 2 Peter*, p. 104.
[151]Bray, *James, 1-2 Peter, 1-3 John, Jude*, p. 256. This assumes that Jude is dependent on 2 Peter, whereas the reverse is likely the case.

28:14; Cairo Genizah *Damascus Document* 1.14; 4QpIsa[b] [Isaiah Commentary]). Scoffers characterize this last age and live according to their desires to do ungodly things, not merely thinking ungodly thoughts. Jude is here again using a catchword—*tōn asebeiōn*[152]—probably a paraphrase of Jude's favorite term of the gist of the apostolic teaching. Joseph Mayor characterizes scoffers this way:

> If they turned the grace of God into licentiousness, they would naturally mock at the narrowness and want of enlightenment of those who took a strict and literal view of the divine commandments: if they made light of authority and treated spiritual things with irreverence, if they foamed out their own shame and uttered proud and impious words, if they denied God and Christ, they would naturally laugh at the idea of a judgment to come.[153]

These scoffers are said to have arisen in the last time or age. It is well known that the early church saw itself as living in the eschatological age, the age when prophecies and promises of God and his messengers were fulfilled. Jude uses the generic phrase *the end time* instead of the technical phrase *the last days.*

Jude 19 is somewhat difficult. *Apodiorizontes* probably means "creating division," though it may mean making distinctions (which could be an allusion to showing partiality in Jude 16c). It is altogether likely that the false teachers were playing up to believers with money, and this was creating divisions in the church. Jude 11 suggested that like Korah they were gathering their own elite group within the church and so splitting it. Perhaps they were claiming to be the spiritual ones in the church and suggesting that those who wanted to be spiritual should follow them. This need not imply incipient Gnosticism, but in any case Jude applies his most dismissive epithet: these men are not spiritual, they are all too "natural"—following their natural instincts and desires and being involved in all sorts of natural not spiritual activity, in immoral activity. *Psychikos* here as elsewhere refers to the natural part that human beings are born with and is contrasted to what they do not have—the Spirit (here clearly the Holy Spirit, which is a gift of God, not a natural endowment). It does not refer to the soul but to the natural animating principle in living beings (1 Cor 2:14). Pheme Perkins suggests that Jude may be alluding to the earlier depiction of the false teachers as being like irrational animals (Jude 10), those that do not have the Holy Spirit.[154] This being the case, Jude states boldly that these teachers are not Christians at all, much less super-Christians. They do not even have the Holy Spirit, as their unholy behavior shows.

---

[152]Bauckham, *Jude, 2 Peter*, p. 105.
[153]Mayor, *Jude*, p. 47.
[154]Perkins, *Peter, James and Jude*, p. 155.

Finally, in **Jude 20-23** Jude is able to get to the positive exhortation that he had hoped to spend a whole letter on (cf. Jude 3) in the form of a final emotional appeal. Here he states what it means to contend for the faith. Rhetorically speaking here, as in the exordium, the stops must be pulled out and the emotions must be appealed to, in this case the appeal to pathos (Quintilian *Institutio oratoria* 4.1.28; 6.1.9-12; Cicero *Partitiones oratoriae* 1.4), only here at the end the appeal to the emotions must be more intense. The first part of the peroration raised the level of indignation against the false teachers, whereas these verses become the conquestio, where the deeper positive emotions of the audience are appealed to, including the fear of losing some friends to the "fire."[155] Thus we hear on the positive side about love, mercy, faith, hope and salvation and on the negative side about contamination, fire and judgment.

The connections of this section with Jude 1-3 are evident. There God is keeping them in his love; here they are to keep themselves in his love. There mercy is wished for the audience; here believers are to wait for the mercy of Jesus (at the judgment day), and mercy is what believers are to have on Christians with problems. There the faith delivered to the saints (holy ones) is alluded to; here allusion is made to the most holy faith. There the theme was "our common salvation"; here Jude stresses how to foster and persevere in that common salvation. Instead of splitting and disputing, Christians are called to build themselves up. Here the image is of building up the community, not individual believers building themselves up.[156] Ruth Anne Reese puts the matter this way: "The pronoun is the reciprocal . . . *heautous,* 'each other.' . . . The command is not for each individual to look after him- or herself, rather the command is for all to look out for the others in the group. This is a direct contrast with the behavior of the Others; after all, they are described as people who 'shepherd themselves or each other' (v. 12)."[157]

The foundation for this construction job of building up is their most holy faith. Jude presumes that they have this faith, but they need to use it as a foundation. Faith here again apparently means the gospel—what they believed when they were converted—and its implications for human conduct. It is thus a faith that entails holy conduct. The ideas of holiness and mercy are reiterated here as the antidote to ungodliness and judging or showing partiality and creating divisions, which are the problems.

The second part of the positive response to problems is that believers are

---

[155]Watson, *Invention, Arrangement, Style,* p. 72.
[156]Watson, *Jude,* p. 497.
[157]Reese, *Jude* (manuscript).

called to pray in the Spirit. This may mean charismatic prayer, including glosso-lalia; it certainly means prayer with the guidance of the Spirit of God and thus praying in accordance with God's holy will for his people, who must be holy. The third and main part of the positive response is to keep themselves (*tērēsate*) in the context where they can experience God's love for them. *Tērēsate* is the main verb, the rest are subordinate participle phrases. Perseverance is thus something that believers must actively engage in, because there is a real danger of apostasy by real Christians. I. Howard Marshall rightly says of Jude's perspective:

> Perseverance accordingly is closely linked with the activity of God in believers. Edification takes place by means of faith, which is a gift of God; prayer is made in the Spirit; the readers are to remain in the love of God and await the mercy of Christ; and ultimately it is God who keeps them from falling. At the same time, perseverance depends upon specific *acts* of Christian discipline and devotion; a person who bestirs himself to do these things will not fall. Here is a paradox which does not admit of closer explanation; to speak of synergism is not to elucidate but simply to express the paradox. We have a situation whose limits may be charted, but whose depths cannot be plumbed.[158]

The antidote to apostasy involves reaffirming the faith that one believed when one was saved, building up the community not tearing it down, praying in the Spirit, keeping oneself in God's love by being obedient to his will and commands (keeping the faith) and waiting for the mercy of Christ our Lord that he will bestow only on those who have persevered to the end. On them will fall the pronouncement, "Neither do I condemn you," and thus they may enter into eternal life—the ultimate blessing. Even for those who persevere, Jesus will grant this gift of eternal life on the basis of mercy, not deserts, since even true believers often fall short of what God desires and requires. Believers are to wait for this mercy, this "no condemnation," at the parousia and not suppose that the way of the false teachers, who may now be encouraging indulgence in and ignoring of sin, is the way to deal with sin. Jude tells believers how to deal with sinners, those doubting and apostatizing.

Richard Bauckham is probably wrong to see only two clauses here.[159] Just as believers are to wait on Jesus' mercy, so now they are to have mercy not only on the waverers, but even on the false teachers. He uses the term *mercy* twice, since he holds out the final prospect and goal as receiving mercy from Christ. If the false teachers were pneumatics and antinomians, Jude here is saying that genuine life in the Spirit leads one toward embracing the teaching of the apos-

---

[158]Marshall, *Kept by the Power of God*, pp. 167-68.
[159]Bauckham, *Jude, 2 Peter*, pp. 108-10.

tles, not away from it.[160] James Moffatt puts things well: "The real experience and possession of the Holy Spirit inspires prayer, not any proud sense of superiority to others or any false independence towards God. Prayer is love in need appealing to Love in power, and the upbuilding of the church depends upon this living intercourse between God and His People."[161]

There is implicit Trinitarian thinking here (keep in God's love, pray in the Spirit, wait for Christ's mercy). Clearly Jude saw all three as deity, for they all perform God's saving work. "This exhortation contrasts the church that is able to pray in the Spirit with the false teachers, who may claim to possess the Spirit but are, in fact, devoid of it (vv. 8, 19)."[162] *Diakrinomenous* here may mean (1) those under judgment, (2) doubters or waverers or (3) disputers. In Jude 9 it referred to the archangel disputing with the devil, and this may be meant here. Perhaps, however, we are to see a progression here from bad to worst (doubters, then those apostatizing, then those apostate).[163] We are not told *how* to have mercy on these people, only to have it, and presumably it involves some activity—whether personal kindness, compassion for their failings, patience, prayers and so on. Tenderheartedness is in order: "You shall hate no one, but some you must reprove, for some you must pray, and some you must love more that your very life" (*Didache* 2.7).

William Brosend is right to note the parallel to the way James ends, where the discussion is also about restoring a wandering sinner, saving them from eternal death and thereby covering a multitude of sins (Jas 5:19-20).[164] This may suggest that Jude knew James's sermon or at least knew James's teaching on such a matter and agreed with it. The same message can be conveyed in two different ways: James's approach is sapiential, he stands in the tradition of the sage; Jude's approach is apocalyptic and prophetic, he stands in the tradition of prophets who speak on matters eschatological. Yet both want to deal with the erring in a compassionate and merciful way when it comes to pastoral practice.

One is to snatch from the flames those who are on the way to apostasy and thus save them. Here the flames are in all probability the flames of hell, not of temptation (cf. Jude 7), and so the implication is that this is where the false teachers are heading. The image of the brand plucked from the burning[165] likely

---

[160]Moffatt, *General Epistles*, p. 243.

[161]Ibid., pp. 243-44.

[162]Watson, *Jude*, p. 497.

[163]Perkins, *Peter, James and Jude*, p. 156.

[164]Brosend, *James and Jude*, p. 182.

[165]This is what John Wesley was called when he was rescued from the parsonage fire in Epworth as a young lad, and it shaped his self-understanding throughout his life. It also shaped his mother, who resolved to train John in earnest, giving him over to the Lord.

comes from Zechariah 3:1-5. The high priest in Zechariah's vision is snatched
from the fire and his filthy garment is exchanged for a pure one. The height of
compassion is reached when Jude exhorts believers to have mercy (pity?) on the
false teachers. They are to have mercy on them, but condemn and hate their sin.
Jude clearly draws a distinction between loving the sinner and hating the sin. The
image of the undergarment, stained by either excrement or semen (probably the
latter in light of Jude 8), is especially graphic here, but such images are appropriate in this emotive rhetoric, which concludes the discourse and seeks to make
sure the audience embraces the right opinion and course of action.

One is to have mercy on this final group cautiously, which probably means,
as Richard Bauckham suggests, praying for them, not associating with them and
thereby contaminating oneself.[166] Having mercy on them while still standing in
fear of the Lord and his coming judgment is the tension that believers are to
preserve. Not tolerance of sin or indulgence in it, but patience with the sinner
is advised. The implication may be that even these false teachers may be
brought back to the true and pure faith. If so, then, as Marshall says: "The earlier
prophecy of their final destruction and doom spoken of even in *1 Enoch* should
be seen as conditional. Their doom is fixed if they persist in this course of action." But while there is life, there is opportunity for repentance. "The fact that
they are said to have been predestined to judgment (Jude 4) simply means that
God's purpose for wicked men is a judgment from which they will not escape."[167] Bauckham adds:

> Nevertheless, there is no question of abandoning such people to their fate. That
> Jude continues to hope for their salvation is suggested not only by ἐλεεῖτε ("have
> mercy"), but also by the source of his picture of the soiled garments in Zech 3:3-4.
> Joshua's "filthy garments" were removed and replaced by clean ones, as a symbol
> of God's forgiveness (3:3-5). Similarly, if Jude's opponents will abandon their sin
> and all that is associated with it, forgiveness is available for them.[168]

The final phrase about the stained undergarment is a symbol of sins involving
the human flesh. It is most unlikely that Jude here sees human flesh as inherently sinful in its physicality—alluding to the sins that the false teachers were
engaging in that involved the flesh. But apparently those sins are not viewed as
unforgivable. Ruth Anne Reese says:

> The Beloved are not to direct their efforts toward condemnation of the Others; rather

---

[166]Bauckham, *Jude, 2 Peter*, p. 116.
[167]Marshall, *Kept by the Power of God*, pp. 167-68.
[168]Bauckham, *Jude, 2 Peter*, p. 117.

their efforts are to be directed toward mercy and salvation tempered by wisdom and humility in the hope that some who have been the Others will once again join the community of the Beloved. The mercy and the salvation that they offer to the Others is not offered from their own ability to save but rather is born out of the community life they share. This is a life that is deeply rooted in the love of God and the mercy of Jesus Christ. This is what empowers them to extend mercy and salvation.[169]

Closing Doxology: The Divine Guardian (Jude 24-25)

Jude's closing doxology is one of the most beautiful in the Bible, and if people know this homily at all they know this part.[170] A doxology was commonly used to close prayers, sermons and even letters (2 Pet 3:18; Rom 16:25-27). Jude's doxology is like that at the end of a sermon and is neither preceded by nor followed by any final greetings. This is one more indicator that we should see this discourse as a homily, a sermonizing letter, which has only an epistolary prescript. Duane Watson helpfully evaluates this conclusion from a rhetorical viewpoint: "The doxology brings his *peroratio* and the entire letter to an emotional climax. By ending his appeal with a focus upon God, Christ, and their future hope, his audience is ever more persuaded to act as Jude advises. It is an effective way to end deliberative rhetoric, and far more effective for emotional appeal than an epistolary postscript. . . . It functions almost as a prayer, and serves to increase Jude's ethos, exhibiting his concern that his audience not fail to see the consummation of their hopes."[171] The background for Jude's doxology lies in Jewish liturgical terms and practices, for early Jewish and Jewish Christian doxologies shared ideas, content and form.[172]

Pheme Perkins rightly points out that this doxology by implication finds Jude recognizing that exhortations alone will not stem the tide of false teaching in the audience. God is thus invoked to take action and guard the audience. She is also right that this doxology places the audience at the final judgment in the courtroom in the presence of God, reminding them that their behavior now affects the garments they will be wearing then![173]

[24] *To the one who is able to guard you from stumbling and make you stand in the presence of his glory without blemish, in jubilation;* [25] *to the only God, our Savior, through Jesus Christ our Lord, belong glory, majesty, might and authority before all time and now and forever more, Amen!*

---

[169]Reese, *Jude* (manuscript).

[170]A benediction is a word of blessing on believers or a recognition of God's blessedness; a doxology is a word of praise and glory to God (from Greek *doxa* ["glory"]).

[171]Watson, *Invention, Arrangement and Style*, p. 76.

[172]Bauckham, *Jude, 2 Peter*, pp. 119-21.

[173]Perkins, *Peter, James and Jude*, pp. 157-58.

This is the third doxology in the New Testament that opens "to him who is able" (Rom 16:25; Eph 3:20). **Jude 24** speaks of God who is able to "keep" or, more likely, "guard" a person so that they do not stumble. The point will be that if believers place their trust in God and themselves in his hands, he is more than able to keep them from stumbling. One could translate the adjective *aptaistos* (a *hapax legomenon*; cf. 3 Maccabees 6.39) "free from slipping."[174] This seems to imply that the author does not see apostasy as inevitable or necessary in any particular case; it also implies that apostasy, not just falling into a particular sin on one occasion, is in view. "The general sense is that God will protect Jude's readers from the dangers of falling into the sinful ways of the false teachers and thereby failing to attain to final salvation" (cf. 2 Thess 3:3).[175]

Here is not the place to discuss whether it is ever inevitable in a particular individual case that a Christian sin. We may simply say that God's grace is sufficient even in our weakness, but in a fallen world we may have to make some lesser-of-two-evils choices, in which case God's grace is sufficient to help us to make the best of a bad situation. The result of being kept is that at the end of the process one stands in God's presence—in the presence of his glory (*doxa* means the "radiance" of his presence). Jude envisions a worship setting when the kingdom finally comes. The believer is depicted as a "perfect" sacrifice, that is, one without blemishes that would lead God to find fault (1 Thess 3:13; Col 1:22; Eph 1:4; 5:27).[176] Believers are offered by God to himself, who has kept and purified them and made them stand in his presence. There are shouts of jubilation when this happens on this great day. Richard Bauckham says:

> Drawing on traditional liturgical material, he [Jude] pictures the last day as the eschatological festival of worship, in which the achievement of God's purposes for his people will take the form of his presentation of them as perfect sacrifices in his heavenly sanctuary, offered up to the glory of God amid the jubilation of the worshipers. All Jude's concerns in the letter, to combat the false teaching for the sake of the health of the church and the Christian obedience of its members, are finally aimed at this goal: that they should in the end be found fit to be a sacrificial offering to God.[177]

Jude 25 is derived from traditional Jewish ascriptions: our God is the only God, he is our Savior (Rom 16:27; 1 Tim 1:17; cf. 1 Tim 1:1; 2:3; 4:6). It is not clear whether "through Jesus Christ" goes with what precedes or with what fol-

---

[174]Moffatt, *General Epistles*, p. 246.
[175]Bauckham, *Jude, 2 Peter*, p. 122.
[176]See the discussion in Neyrey, *2 Peter, Jude*, pp. 99-100.
[177]Bauckham, *Jude, 2 Peter*, p. 124.

LETTERS AND HOMILIES FOR JEWISH CHRISTIANS

lows. The former makes good sense: God is our Savior through (the work and person of) Jesus. However, it may go with what follows: glory belongs to God through Jesus the mediator. This would mean that we recognize these attributes in and through Jesus or praise him for these attributes that we have seen through Jesus. First Chronicles 29:11 is the model for many of these sorts of ascriptions in a doxology. God has glory, but he also has majesty. He is not just majestic, he has might (he is not a lame-duck creator). Not only does God have might, but God has authority to act according to the divine will. This doxology was known and influential in the second century, for it is echoed in the doxology found in *Martyrdom of Polycarp* 20. One thing makes this doxology stands out: God's glory is spoken of in the past, present and future tenses. Normally, God's glory extends infinitively from the present into the future (Rom 11:36; Gal 1:5; Phil 4:20; 2 Tim 4:18; Eph 3:20-21).[178] Jude stresses the eternal and transcendent nature of the biblical God who is the sole Savior, through Jesus.

I suspect that Jude himself has formed or tailored this doxology to provide the rhetorically perfect conclusion to this discourse and the worship service in which it would be dramatically and orally presented. Doxologies such as this could be used to end arguments or portions of a discourse more often than to end the whole discourse (but see Rom 16:25-27 and 2 Pet 3:18, which are likely influenced by Jude).[179]

All these things may at all times be ascribed to God, for God never changes. God was this way before all the past age (singular) of history existed, is now and will be for all the ensuing ages (plural) of time and eternity. This is like "Jesus Christ the same yesterday, today and forever" in Hebrews 13:8. Possibly, though not certainly, the preexistence of Jesus is implied here. In any event the discourse ends with *amen* ("so be it"). This Jewish affirmation affirms the truth of what has been asserted. Probably Jude's audience would be expected to pronounce this amen when the discourse had been completely read to them in the congregational worship service. To all this we simply say, Amen!

CONCLUSION

Having come to the end of our discussion of three fascinating Jewish Christian documents, Hebrews, James and Jude, one is immediately struck by how very different from one another these documents are. Hebrews shows a great exegete and exhorter at work, James a sage who is able to form and reform wise sayings, and Jude the strong voice of an apocalyptic prophetic figure. The

---

[178]See the discussion in Neyrey, *2 Peter, Jude,* pp. 100-101.
[179]Ibid., pp. 94-95.

scribal preacher/teacher, the sage, the prophet were all important roles played by different persons in early Christianity, but these roles were not viewed as the most crucial for the local church. These documents show the remarkable diversity of leadership roles within Jewish Christian contexts and remind us that the later truncating and narrowing down of ministerial roles to just a few types (e.g. apostles, elders, deacons, overseers) led to an impoverishment of leadership offered to the church. Much was lost when the Jewish Christian stream of Christianity went its own way and eventually became a smaller and smaller stream as time went on. For one thing, the profound grounding in the Old Testament and early Jewish literature and lore was mostly lost. Had strong voices like those in these three documents still dominated the Christian landscape it is hard to believe that the Gnostic movement, with its dualism and dislike for creation theology and the Old Testament, could ever have gotten traction in any part of the church. The rise to dominance of the Gentile part of the early church allowed aberrations grounded in pagan thought to become possible. The authors of Hebrews, James and Jude would have all seen documents like the *Gospel of Thomas* and its successors as not sufficiently Christian because they were not sufficiently and positively grounded in Jewish texts and traditions. We need to keep these things in mind when we are regaled with modern claims about Gnostic documents reflecting earliest Christian thought. This is patently false.

The success of the Gentile wing of the early church is in part what led to the difficulties that documents like Hebrews, James and Jude had in getting into the canon. They were too "Jewish" in character, and this did not sit well with the insidious growth of anti-Semitic thought within both the mainstream church and its Gnostic offshoots. Thank goodness reason and historical memory prevailed and these thoroughly Jewish documents were included in the canon, with all their esoterica and early Jewish flair. Hebrews, James and Jude are signal reminders that Christianity was in its origins a form or subset or sect of early Judaism, however uncomfortable that was to make the church of the second through fifth centuries and beyond.[180]

Several things bind these three documents together, and it is not just the love

---

[180] Because there is so much overlap between 2 Peter and Jude, I will reserve my comments about preaching and teaching Jude for the next volume in this series. Here it is sufficient to say that it is not easy to teach or preach from Jude unless the audience has already been taught about (1) the nature of apocalyptic prophecy, (2) the nature and use of Jewish apocryphal material, (3) the nature of ancient polemics and invective in the context of ancient rhetoric, and (4) the issue of how boundaries and discipline were enforced in the apostolic age in comparison to how they are carried out today. If my exegesis is correct, even the false teachers are to be shown mercy by the audience according to this highly polemical discourse.

of the Old Testament and Jewish lore and their creative handling of such material, including the Jesus tradition in James. It is also the strong sense of the eschatological moment. All three authors write as those who are convinced they are living in the eschatological age under eschatological conditions. Their wisdom and advice and exhortations are given accordingly. All three bear witness as well to the boundaries of even the Jewish Christian part of the church being rather porous, rather susceptible to false teachers and false prophets slipping in and doing damage.

This is writ large in the Johannine Letters, but it is equally clear in these documents as well, especially in Jude. Furthermore, these documents share a common concern about the cultural pressures that can lead Christians to conform to worldly values or even contemplate one form or another of apostasy. All three writers caution against such forms of spiritual, theological, ethical and practical defection. It is perfectly clear that they saw their churches in danger from within and without, and they are busily trying to shore up those porous boundaries and do damage control and healing of wounds. Equally clearly, these documents do not look to apostles to do all the heavy lifting in regard to these tasks. The apostles seem to be nowhere in sight in these congregations, or they are figures who were not presently on the scene when Hebrews and Jude were written. Clearly enough, the myth of the pristine and untroubled nature of early church life is quickly dispelled when one reads these sermons. The modern church should be cautious what it longs for when it offers exhortations to "be more like the churches of the New Testament era"!

Oddly enough, the shortest of these documents seems to have cast the longest shadow in its own era, for Jude shows up almost verbatim in 2 Peter at points, but close behind it is the influence of James on 1 Peter. In short, these documents raise all sorts of questions about the degree and intricacy of social networks in earliest Christianity, from both the Gentile side of the church (as the Pauline influence on Hebrews and 1 Peter shows) and the Jewish side of the fence (as the influence of Jude and James on 1-2 Peter shows). Surely not only the literate leaders of the early Christian movement were influenced by each other's work, including their writings; surely we are glimpsing only the tips of the icebergs of early Christian community in the hints and glints of light on this subject that these documents shed. I am left with the impression that, while there were two dominant missions and streams of church life in the first century (one more Gentile and largely Pauline, one more Jewish and largely non-Pauline), the degree of cooperation and cross-fertilization without actual amalgamation must have been considerable.

There were not just two occasionally intermingling streams to early Christianity. There was some intentionality in the intermingling, and both of these streams lay within the larger, broader bed of a river that, both believed, flowed from the throne of God and of Christ. In other words, boundaries separated the whole Christian movement from other early Jewish movements, even though there were streams within those broader boundaries. Christianity was a distinguishable movement in the first century, and within that broader category there were two major streams flowing along from the same source and basically heading in the same eschatological direction.

The reason a large part of the church today finds the documents in this volume heavy going is because the church is both almost entirely un-Jewish at this point and unfamiliar with the literature and lore, the hermeneutics and homiletics, the rhetoric and reasoning of its Jewish heritage, even including the Old Testament. In my mind the only remedy for this is total immersion—immersion in the deep and strong currents of this material in its original rhetorical and social contexts. Then and then only do these Jewish Christian streams, which appear convoluted and muddy on a superficial modern glance, become clear, refreshing, life-giving water to a dry and thirsty contemporary audience.

Index of Ancient Sources

Clegg   July 2nd

289 "The measure of light & measure of depth"

✗ 292 " " on Scripts crisis and Co

                                    Parthenomesa 319

322~3 "The Ascent from Isa" "rhyming ends of words"
                        on his end
✗ " " on pseudo-epigraphs & etc by ET Pot. 515 "has a jealous
         as almost impossible ;   "   "

394 " an unscrupulous traders "   585

    598 Withthough   The Hermeneutics of Suspicion 594
         plane quite P' ET P. drawing from him
                                            going things out
                          puzzle doing things out

76
Exil
Ghelinein 412

141 tour de force   Tour de force 358
172i   116 Peshar   on 1st blush   gordion knot
                    115 Midrash   119 eatena   "recoil
CF   Reb Encomium Panegyric 123   331
    116   232   500"   Panehart 135   68 Heb. 6:11   291
                                                         The on-st ru rub.
442   188"   115 Lk 12   disentagle
      833 165"   162 Lk. 8:11 the   hoi-is-is a O.T.
                                    & barrenness hits   steep to plags. Dongiver pl
GOD "disbelief" in the mind pages "This can be key-verses - as
    "unbelief" in a refusal, a closed mind to what is happening.
                                    So-this is theme..

178 "Rhetorical..."
                                    197 Melchezidek ✗
                                    277 As c 1/117
                                       277

378 / Heart Great Hill
     see Matt.   galilee

                                    289 a Reference to Paul
                                    118 on Rev.
                                    ✗146 cortez a glory in which
13 6/50 27   220 Rev " xerebraveturn
I-88-9. isa 26:20, 11   Jerusalem up him
156: psalms 573
       577 actor 1 Rev 1   368 Lk. tongs pergyn
       577   92-160 AD
       577 603   550 The Deny in but 6 11
                                          The Magna Carta
                                     566 This...sa ready Mis
                                     566 Act, 1:14 Acts 6:9
                                          Jesus tomb & Jerusal
                                     601 #Phil✗
                                     618. Deny Carl Chel